SQL

SECOND EDITION

Sakhr Youness,
Pierre Boutquin et al.

SAMS

A Division of Macmillan USA
201 West 103rd Street
Indianapolis, Indiana 46290

Unleashed

SQL Unleashed, Second Edition

International Standard Book Number: 0-672-31709-5

Library of Congress Catalog Card Number: 99-62964

Printed in the United States of America

First Printing: November 1999

01 00 99 4 3 2 1

Trademarks

All terms mentioned in this book that are known to be trademarks or service marks have been appropriately capitalized. Sams Publishing cannot attest to the accuracy of this information. Use of a term in this book should not be regarded as affecting the validity of any trademark or service mark.

Microsoft is a registered trademark of Microsoft Corporation. SQL Server is a registered trademark of Microsoft Corporation. Oracle is a registered trademark of Oracle Corporation.

"This publication was produced using the Advent 3B2 Publishing System."

Warning and Disclaimer

Every effort has been made to make this book as complete and as accurate as possible, but no warranty or fitness is implied. The information provided is on an "as is" basis. The authors and the publisher shall have neither liability nor responsibility to any person or entity with respect to any loss or damages arising from the information contained in this book or from the use of the CD or programs accompanying it.

Publisher
Michael Stephens

Acquisitions Editor
Shelley Johnston

Development Editor
Matt Larson

Managing Editor
Charlotte Clapp

Project Editor
George E. Nedeff

Copy Editor
Lisa Lord

Indexers
Bruce Clingaman
Kevin Fulcher

Proofreaders
Wendy Ott, Betsy Smith
Mary Ellen Stephenson

Technical Editors
Rich Blum, Pierre Boutquin,
Joe Duer, Ben Forta,
Yujing Gao,
Donna Matthews, Ivan Oss

Team Coordinator
Pamalee Nelson

Media Developer
Craig Atkins

Interior Design
Gary Adair

Cover Design
Aren Howell

Copy Writer
Eric Borgert

3B2 Design
Scott Cook

3B2 Production
Brandon Allen

Contents at a Glance

Table of Contents

About the Authors

Sakhr Youness, PE, MCSD, has been a professional engineer since 1996, and a Microsoft-certified solutions developer since 1997. He is a senior software architect at AppNet Systems Corporation in Southeast Michigan. He co-authored two books, one for SAMS, SQL Server 7.0 Programming Unleashed, and one for Wrox Press about SQL Server 7.0, which is expected to be published in late 1999. Mr. Youness has also conducted many technical reviews for MacMillan and Wrox books, in different areas, such as Microsoft Visual Basic, Visual Basic for Applications, Microsoft Visual Studio, SQL Server 7.0, and Oracle 8.0.

Mr. Youness has extensive experience using Microsoft and Oracle tools to develop client/server and multi-tier applications. As part of his work at AppNet, Mr. Youness provides consultation to and develops solutions for AppNet's clients to help them develop Web-based multi-user applications based on the Microsoft DNA architecture.

Mr. Youness enjoys doing home projects, like growing vegetables in the summer, going out with his wife, Nada, and playing with his 21-month old daughter, Maya. Among his hobbies are swimming, playing basketball, reading, and watching sporting events. He can be reached by email at `syouness@home.com`.

Umachandar Jayachardran holds a bachelor's degree in Electrical and Electronics Engineering from College of Engineering, Guindy, Madras, India. He is working as a database analyst in West Palm Beach, Florida. He is an MCDBA, MCSE+I, MCP+I, and MCSE. He specializes in MS BackOffice and Visual Studio development tools. His primary areas of expertise include Microsoft SQL Server, Oracle 7.3, Visual FoxPro database applications, and ISAPI/ASP applications. He loves working with SQL Server and spends his time hacking the various undocumented statements. His other interests are classic rock, alternative music, and books on math and astronomy. His favorite authors are Carl Sagan, Richard Feynmann, and Alistair Maclean. He is an audiophile who loves collecting CDs, music books, and equipment. He is an SUV enthusiast and owns a Nissan Pathfinder 4x4. He wishes to thank his parents, family, and friends for all the support and inspiration that he has received over the years.

Pierre Boutquin is a senior analyst in the corporate treasury of a major Canadian bank, where he helps develop leading-edge market risk management software. He has over a decade of experience implementing PC-based computer systems with in-depth knowledge of object-oriented analysis and design, Visual Basic, Visual C++, and SQL. He co-authored *Visual Basic 5 SuperBible*, *Visual Basic 6 SuperBible,* and *Visual Basic 6 Interactive*

Course, published by The Waite Group. He has also contributed material on COM and Internet programming for other Visual Basic books. Pierre's spare time is mainly owned by Koshka and Sasha, his two adorable Burmese cats. While petting them, he often thinks how nice it would be to find more time and get back into chess or keep up with news from Belgium, his native country. You can reach him at `boutquin@hotmail.com`.

Matt Larson is a database manager in the J. D. Edwards software development team located in Denver, Colorado. Matt holds a Bachelor of Science in Business Administration (emphasis on Information Systems) from the University of Colorado where he graduated first in his class. He has also written and/or edited for *Microsoft SQL Server 7.0 DBA Survival Guide, Microsoft SQL Server 7.0 in 21 Days, SQL Server 7.0 Unleashed, Oracle8 Server Unleashed, Oracle Development Unleashed, Peter Norton's1 Guide to Linux*, *Peter Norton's* Guide to Windows 98 Premier Edition, and *Oracle Unleashed*, Second Edition. When he's not working, Matt spends most of his time with his best friend, confidante, and better half, Melanie. Matt can be reached at `mattlarson@usa.net`.

Frank Torres is a programmer/analyst for Glendale Community College in Glendale, Arizona, and has been working there for the last 12 years. In addition to working on large database projects with Oracle, Frank also administers several UNIX servers and does Web development with everything from PERL/CGI and HTML to the graphics with Macromedia Flash and Fireworks. However, Frank Torres is probably more well known throughout the United States and internationally as the owner of `www.sqlcourse.com`. This unique site offers a free intro to SQL tutorial that allows visitors to practice what they learn online with the SQL Interpreter. Users can create their own tables and perform selects, inserts, updates, deletes, and drops—all online with immediate feedback.

Mike Schuler was born in Spain. With elementary schooling in Argentina and Swiss and German parents, Mike speaks four languages; he admits his university-learned French could use a refresher course. Mike finished a BASc in Electrical Engineering at UBC in Vancouver, worked as an engineer, and returned to the same halls for an MBA in Finance and Operations Research. He founded IBX datasystems in 1974 with a fresh proprietary operating system and competed locally with IBM, DEC and Wang in the turnkey business systems market. "Those days were fun—we could change the multi-user OS literally overnight. My partner was a whiz in kernel programming—and UNIX was the model." Before tackling his current DBsurfer project (`http://www.dbsurfer.com/`), which was based on the remnants of a multiuser database system that was only locally commercialized, he used to have time to go diving in the Caribbean and Hawaii. "I love diving at 3–5 am; it's quiet and the fish are very approachable," Mike says. Now between DBsurfer and consulting, he barely has time to keep an eye on his networked laptop that serves as a real-time control for a 500 square feet "organic" greenhouse he built.

Jo Norman is a University of Wisconsin-Green Bay graduate with a bachelor's degree in Marketing/Market Research. She learned SQL because it was the only reliable means of retrieving research data from the many relational databases she worked with during a 10-year stint of collecting data for higher education at St. Norbert College, Oregon Graduate Institute of Science & Technology, Reed College, and Portland Community College. She is currently a senior technical trainer for a wireless telecommunications software development company in Bellevue, Washington. She writes for, and tech-edits, computer-related books in her "spare time" to keep her skills fresh, and to keep pace with new technologies. She offers special thanks to her loving husband, Stu, for always being there, and for reminding her to come up for air occasionally.

Contributing Authors:

Joe Duer

Guy van den Berg

Dedication

To my small family: my wife, Nada, and my daughter Maya, and to my parents who helped make me what I am now.

-Sakhr

Acknowledgments

Writing a book is an extremely laborious process. It involves staying up long nights and ruining many weekends reading, writing, and re-writing. It also involves searching through literature and discussing many issues with experts who know the details of certain topics.

This book was the outcome of a great deal of hard work on the part of many people who made it a success. I would like to thank all the co-authors who helped me finish this book. Their input made it possible to meet the challenge of deadlines and finish the book on time while maintaining a good quality. I would also like to thank my family so much, especially my lovely wife, Nada, and beloved daughter, Maya, for their patience and support as I was spending long periods of time away from them working on the book. I would not have been able to make it without their support.

Finally, my thanks to the Sams family for the efforts they spent to ensure the successful release of the book ON TIME.

-Sakhr Youness

Tell Us What You Think!

As the reader of this book, *you* are our most important critic and commentator. We value your opinion and want to know what we're doing right, what we could do better, what areas you'd like to see us publish in, and any other words of wisdom you're willing to pass our way.

You can fax, email, or write me directly to let me know what you did or didn't like about this book—as well as what we can do to make our books stronger.

Please note that I cannot help you with technical problems related to the topic of this book, and that due to the high volume of mail I receive, I might not be able to reply to every message.

When you write, please be sure to include this book's title and author as well as your name and phone or fax number. I will carefully review your comments and share them with the author and editors who worked on the book.

Fax: 317-581-4770

Email: mstephens@mcp.com

Mail: Michael Stephens
Publisher
Sams Publishing
201 West 103rd Street
Indianapolis, IN 46290 USA

Introduction

Relational database products and services are still the leading databases in the world of information technology. These databases are used in client-server, n-tier, and Web-based applications. Businesses and corporations use them to store day-to-day data, as well as mission-critical information. Developers around the world use these databases as the cornerstone for their applications because, without data, there is no meaning for these applications.

The market for such database management systems (DBMSs) is still extremely hot. It is expected to continue to be in demand for years to come. Tens of thousands of consulting companies around the world offer services related to database management systems. Their number is only expected to increase, as these systems are becoming the de facto databases for Web-based applications.

Database publishing is already proving to be the future of the World Wide Web, allowing Web developers to supply up-to-the-minute, detailed content on demand. eCommerce is another field that is growing and is expected to grow by enormous proportions in the next few years. eCommerce is based on relational databases that capture the data passed in the transactions in a timely fashion.

Relational databases offer great flexibility as to the type of data they can store and the speed at which the data can be processed and retrieved. These systems scale from the small desktop, beginning with a small personal database written with a tool like Microsoft Access, to huge corporate data stores that contain hundreds of thousands of daily transactions in their DBMSs. DBMSs can handle enormous amounts of data, such as Oracle Corporation's server and IBM's DB2.

Due to the increasing use of these systems, more and more applications are made to interface with them, allowing for data exchange and analysis. For example, it is currently easy to extract data from a relational database from within Microsoft Excel, using this same program to analyze it and produce appropriate graphs and reports. It is also easy to interface geographical information systems with these databases to produce highly informative and interactive, database-driven applications.

Structured Query Language (SQL) is the standard programming language on the market today used to communicate with an RDBMS (relational DBMS). This language was born as a result of the need to communicate with these databases. All tasks, such as creating database objects or retrieving, inserting, updating, and deleting information, are ultimately done through SQL statements.

The American National Standards Institute (ANSI), the International Standards Organization (ISO), and other consortiums and regulating bodies first created this standard, SQL0, in 1986 to make sure that this language is used in the same way across all implementations by all vendors. It is this standard that has maintained this language as the universal language for database access. Database vendors have to comply with minimum requirements according to the standard in their own implementation of SQL. They can deviate in certain areas, but as for the regular tasks of creating database objects, querying the database, inserting, deleting, or updating its data, most implementations are similar. As a result, this similarity makes it easy to migrate skills from one implementation to another. The original SQL standard was updated in 1989 (and so is also known as SQL-89 or SQL1); this was further updated in 1992 (and so is known as SQL-92 or SQL2). The next standard, SQL3 (old SQL-99), is under development and is estimated to be released in 1999. However, for reasons that will be made clear in Chapter 23, SQL3 and SQL-99 are not identical.

Many good tools are now available to simplify writing SQL statements. These tools are usually referred to as query-by-example (QBE). Microsoft Access was one of the pioneers in this regard. While these tools can really build nice SQL statements, sparing the developer from writing SQL code, they can also create errors leading to erroneous results without warning, especially when the task that needs to be performed is highly complex, or the tool is not used correctly. These tools often fall short when you try to write an embedded SQL statement in a program you are writing in another programming language, with the SQL statement using dynamic SQL. Therefore, it is still imperative for good developers to know SQL and know how to write SQL code when they need to.

Who Should Read This Book?

This book provides in-depth coverage of all of the important SQL-92 standard topics, as well as many of the new SQL3 standard topics. This book is designed for database programmers, administrators, and college students. I assume that the reader is at an intermediate to advanced level with previous programming knowledge of at least one language, and has had some interaction with SQL (maybe a few months of experience). The reason this knowledge is needed is that knowing how to program with at least one programming language gives you some of the skills needed to write code. After you acquire these skills, you can apply them to any language you choose, including SQL, making the learning process easier and more fun.

Also, I assume that you have already read an entry-level book on this subject. Readers do not need any fancy machines and software to run the examples in this book. With some skill, you can use a PC that runs Microsoft Access or MySQL. As for SQL beginners, don't despair yet! This book includes a quick SQL refresher in Appendix A. This refresher will introduce the basics of SQL. If you read the refresher carefully, and apply its examples, you can get to a level where you can read the rest of the book in order, without much difficulty.

Once you are done reading this book, you'll have acquired great knowledge on the SQL standard, how it is applied by different SQL vendors through their implementations, and most importantly, you'll be able to write advanced SQL code in your programs.

Who Should Buy This Book?

If you do or intend to use SQL all the time or occasionally, this book is a fine reference. For all others, SQL is likely somewhere in your future and having this book available should make tasks a lot easier.

Power users, independent and corporate IT professionals, and technical professionals who are seeking a definitive reference book for their migration to Access 2000 programming and development, will benefit from using SQL Unleashed.

College students and SQL beginners will also benefit from owning a copy of this book, if they intend to master the language and to program with it at an advanced level. This book, serving as a learning tool and a reference, will make these goals easier to accomplish.

How This Book Is Organized

This book is structured so that you can pick any chapter and read it. If a chapter relies on information in another chapter, references are added to make it easy to locate the other chapter. For instance, if you are an experienced SQL programmer, but want to know what the new SQL3 brings to the table, you can skip the SQL-92 chapters and head for the chapters that discuss Call Level Interface (Chapter 21), Persistent Stored Modules (Chapter 22), and The Next Standard: SQL-99 (Chapter 23).

On the other hand, if you don't have sufficient experience in SQL, or even if you are a newcomer to the world of database programming and SQL, you can start with the refresher appendix that discusses the basics of SQL with many examples. This refresher is designed to get you up and running as quickly as possible. If you think the Appendix is not enough, you can always pick a Sams book on the subject, such as *Sams Teach Yourself SQL in 21 Days*, Third Edition, and then come back and read the rest of the chapters of this book. If you do so, you'll become an expert on the subject.

The examples can be run on any SQL-compliant database, although slight changes for some scripts will be necessary based on the SQL implementation your server is using.

Contents and Structure of *SQL Unleashed*

The chapters in this book are roughly grouped thematically. In Chapter 1, "The SQL Standards," you'll learn about the different bodies behind the SQL standard as we know it today. You'll even learn how to contact these bodies and contribute to their efforts in fine-tuning the SQL standard.

The following chapters deal with database design and data definition language (DDL). Chapter 2, "Relational Databases," discusses relational databases, including data access methods, relational database management systems, table design, normalization and de-normalization of tables, and the exciting topic of using data modeling tools to design the database. Chapter 3, "Table Creation and Manipulation," discusses table creation and manipulation, including table constraints and indexes. This is followed by Chapter 4, "Data Types," which as the name implies discusses the different data types in SQL, including the numeric, character, and temporal data types. It also discusses the functions provided by SQL to handle these types and convert them from one to another. Chapter 5, "Handling Arrays in SQL," discusses arrays in SQL, and Chapter 6, "Other Schema Objects," discusses other schema objects that can be created in SQL. These objects include temporary tables, assertions, and domains.

The next two chapters discuss data manipulation. Chapters 7, "Inserts, Updates and Deletes," and 8, "Transactions in SQL," focus on inserting data in the database, updating existing records, and deleting some records if needed. These chapters also discuss transactions in SQL and the role they play to keep data consistent for the end user.

The next series of chapters is perhaps the most interesting, because it handles data retrieval. In Chapter 9, "Patterns and Ranges in SQL," you will read about advanced features of the SELECT statement, and the predicates that can be used with it. These predicates make SQL a powerful and flexible language, able to quickly retrieve the needed data from the bottom of the database tables. The predicates include keywords, such as LIKE, BETWEEN, IS NULL, and IN, to mention a few. Chapter 10, "Table Joins," discusses table joins and how they can be used in SQL statements. Chapter 11, "Sorting and Grouping," covers data sorting and grouping with the aggregate functions, which bring the power of summarizing the data in the database and presenting it in a form that makes sense to the user and helping him conduct trend analyses and make decisions based on existing real data. Set operations, such as UNION, INTERSECT, and MINUS, are discussed in Chapter 12, "Sets and Subsets Operations." These operations are another way to partition the existing data to make sense out of it. Subqueries are discussed in Chapter 13, "Subqueries." These structures give the SQL programmer greater capabilities in retrieving data while using it in other queries. Chapter 14, "Creating and Using Views," discusses views, which serve many purposes, including helping maintain security of the data preventing unwanted access and limiting people to certain fields based on their privileges.

The following chapters discuss more advanced SQL implementations. In Chapter 15, "Trees and Hierarchies," such implementations include constructing trees and hierarchies of related data in a report format that is user-friendly and easy to understand. Advanced topics, like dynamic SQL, embedded SQL, and using cursors are discussed in Chapters 16, "Dynamic SQL, "and 17, "Embedded SQL,." Dynamic SQL allows the database developer to write the SQL code without knowing the fields to be retrieved before run-time. Once the table fields to be retrieved are known, the SQL statement is constructed on-the-fly and submitted to the database server for processing. Embedded SQL is a powerful tool that allows developers to write SQL code within their own programs, as opposed to doing so interactively with the database engine. This technology merges the powerful features of full-fledged programming languages, such as C, COBOL, and the like with the powerful features of SQL in retrieving data. Chapter 18, "Implementing Cursors," discusses implementing cursors. Cursors are a great feature brought about by the SQL-92 standard. They allow navigation through records one at a time. They also allow for updating and deleting the records when needed. Chapter 19, "Optimizing Query Performance," adresses optimizing query performance. It discusses techniques such as indexes, transactions, joins and subqueries, and temporary tables. In doing so, the indicated chapter presents the pros and cons of the optimization techniques, and makes recommendations when possible of what to use in which conditions. Security issues are discussed in Chapter 20, "Security Issues." These issues include setting up users, roles, and privileges to control user access to the database. It is extremely important to control such access, because databases host the data on which a business is founded and are considered critical for its existence.

The next three chapters are an exciting series that discuss the new advancements in the SQL standard and the anticipated SQL3 standard to be specific. Chapter 21, "Call Level Interface (CLI)," discusses the call level interface (SQL/CLI), the application programming interface that allows direct neutral access to the database management system regardless of the vendor. SQL/CLI is a powerful tool that also allows you to access the database from your programs, giving you the ability to create data objects, manipulate the data, and retrieve it in an efficient manner. Persistent stored modules are discussed in Chapter 22, "Persistent Stored Modules." A summary of the new features in the SQL3 standard is discussed in Chapter 23, "The Next Standard: SQL-99." This gives you a heads-up on what is coming, and prepares you to handle it smoothly and in a way that benefits you and your programs.

The last chapters discuss the two major SQL implementations: the Oracle SQL implementation through Oracle SQL (Chapter 24, "Oracle SQL") and PL/SQL (Chapter 25, "Oracle PL/SQL"), and the Microsoft SQL Server implementation of SQL through Transact-SQL (Chapter 26, "Microsoft Transact-SQL").

Conventions Used in This Book

The following typographic conventions are used in this book:

- Code lines, commands, statements, variables, and any text you type or see onscreen appears in a `mono` typeface. **`Bold mono`** typeface is used to represent the user's input.
- Placeholders in syntax descriptions appear in an *`italic mono`* typeface. Replace the placeholder with the actual filename, parameter, or whatever element it represents.
- *Italics* highlight technical terms when they're being defined.
- The ➥ icon is used before a line of code that is really a continuation of the preceding line. Sometimes a line of code is too long to fit as a single line on the page. If you see ➥ before a line of code, remember that it's part of the line immediately above it.
- The book also contains Notes, Tips, and Cautions to help you spot important or useful information more quickly. Some of these are helpful shortcuts to help you work more efficiently.

CHAPTER 1

Structured Query Language (SQL) Standards

In This Chapter

Since the publication of the American National Standards Institute and International Standards Organization (ANSI/ISO) official standard in 1986, SQL has been regarded as the premier standard query language for relational databases. Before achieving this status, SQL was simply one of many database query languages working to change the face of data retrieval from relational databases.

Gaining in popularity in the 1980s were UNIX-based computing systems. SQL ascended as the standard for these increasingly popular computing systems. Personal computers (PCs) and local area networks' growth in power and popularity in the early 1990s made them perfect candidates for SQL as well.

SQL standards were perhaps the most important factor in its popularity. Although most people refer to a singular "SQL standard," there are actually many standards defined for SQL other than the official ANSI/ISO standard. Work by IBM's DB2 product group produced another "standard SQL," which became a standard because it was widely used and recognized by the industry as being standard, not because it was approved by a standards organization.

SQL Standards Defined

With the exponential growth of applications dedicated to data, data management, and data retrieval, the need for updated standards has never been more apparent. Each new wave of complexity and diversity emphasizes the importance of a data manipulation language for relational databases that is built around a set of universal standards and addresses the architectures of today's computing environment.

SQL standards have incorporated many extensions over the years to keep up with emerging technologies. In 1991, ANSI updated the standard with a version known as SAG SQL. (*SAG* is the acronym for *SQL Access Group*.) Other groups continue to add to the SQL standard and are currently involved in SQL:1999 (formerly called SQL3), SQLJ, and SQL/MM standard development. SQL4 standard development is also underway by the same standards and validation groups.

In broad terms, the SQL standard is a definition or format that has been approved by recognized standards organizations and validated by the National Institute of Standards and Testing (NIST). Additionally, the SQL standard has been accepted as a de facto standard by the computing industry.

SQL standards not only affect the computing industry as a programming language; they also have a broader, generalized impact on operating systems and data formats.

From a user's standpoint, the SQL standard has made it possible to combine products from different manufacturers, enabling the creation of customized systems. Without SQL standards, only databases and data management software from the same company could be used together. SQL standards also reduce ramp-up time for new-hires joining a new computing environment and make critical skills in data management portable.

One of the hopes for standardization of a database query language was to make databases portable. Large steps in this direction have been achieved through SQL standards, but portability is still not 100% because, as is the case with any language, there are numerous dialects of SQL. Although very similar, the small differences between dialects are enough to deny SQL the claim to absolute portability.

American National Standards Institute (ANSI) and the International Standards Organization (ISO)

The initial issuing of official standards for SQL came from the American National Standards Institute X3H2 committee and the International Standards Organization (ISO). The X3H2 committee is the U.S. group responsible for the SQL standard.

The X3H2 committee began work on the official standard in 1982, after being charged with defining a standard language for relational databases. Many languages were discussed in their early meetings, but their awareness of the commitment of large-scale developers, such as IBM, to SQL helped them decide on SQL as the language to build the standard around.

The International Standards Organization made important contributions to developing, testing, and adopting the SQL standard. ISO, a voluntary, non-treaty organization founded in 1946, is responsible for creating international standards in many areas, including computers and communications.

Several countries around the world participate in the SQL standard development process through ISO. Countries actively engaged in participation with ISO are Australia, Brazil, Canada, France, Germany, Japan, Korea, The Netherlands, United Kingdom, and the United States.

ISO and IEC (the International Electrotechnical Commission) constitute a specialized system for worldwide standardization. National groups that are members of these organizations are involved in the development of international standards through technical committees, which are established by the respective organization to deal with particular fields of technical activity.

In the area of information technology, ISO and IEC established a joint technical committee, known as ISO/IEC JTC 1. Draft International Standards, which are adopted by the JTC, are circulated to national groups to be voted on. If 75% of the national groups vote to adopt the standard, the draft standard is published as an International Standard.

Many of the committee members from ANSI and ISO were representatives from database development companies that were already using a dialect of SQL. They were highly motivated to see SQL become standardized.

Federal Information Processing Standard (FIPS)

Under the Information Technology Management Reform act, the U.S. Secretary of Commerce approves standards and guidelines developed by the National Institute of Standards and Technology (NIST) for federal computer systems' use.

The standards and guidelines issued by NIST appear as Federal Information Processing Standards (FIPS). They govern use of federal computing systems throughout all branches of the government. NIST develops FIPS when the federal government has compelling requirements, such as for interoperability or security, and there are no acceptable industry solutions or standards.

The ANSI/ISO SQL1 standard was adopted by the U.S. Government as a Federal Information Processing Standard. ANSI/ISO SQL1 became the government standard under the name FIPS 127-1-Database Language SQL (ANSI X3.135). FIPS upgraded to the FIPS 127-2-Database Language SQL (ANSI X3.135-1992) on June 2, 1993.

An important objective of FIPS PUB 127-2 is to reduce overall software costs by making it easier and less expensive to maintain database definitions and database application programs. This is done to enable transfer of these definitions and programs among different computers and database management systems, including replacement database management systems. Conformance to FIPS SQL is mandatory for all federal procurement of relational model database management systems.

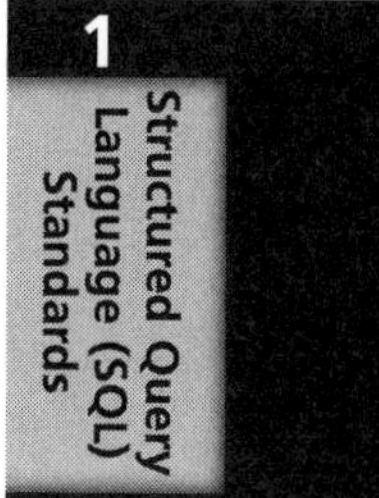

ANSI/ISO SQL1 was minimally expanded and revised in 1989, which is why the first SQL standard is often referred to as SQL89, as well as its original designation as SQL1. SQL89 standard extensions and revisions involved the work of the SQL Access Group (SAG) and others. A more global revision process brought about ANSI X3.135-1992 (SQL92) a few years later.

National Institute of Standards and Technology (NIST)

The National Institute of Standards and Technology (NIST) is a U.S. government organization that provides assistance in developing standards. NIST was formerly the National Bureau of Standards.

NIST's role is to ensure exact and compatible measurements through the generation, certification, and issuance of Standard Reference Materials (SRMs).

SQL-89

ANSI's X3H2 committee published their first standard (ANSI X3.135) in 1986. It was published as an ISO standard in 1987. Because it was developed to encompass many existing dialects of SQL, it addressed a very narrow band of language standards, leaving many issues open to dialectical interpretation. This created a weak standard that was later strengthened by extensions and expansions. Since its initial inception, the SQL standard has remained a work in progress. SQL-89 became known as SQL1, followed a few years later by a full revision and expansion known as both SQL-92 and SQL2.

SQL-92

Many differences in SQL dialects have been eliminated by the greater detail and precision of the ANSI-1992 SQL2 standard (the successor to ANSI-1989 SQL1). Similarities and differences between SQL1 and SQL2 include the following:

- **Error codes:** SQL1 does not specify exact values for certain error codes, leaving vendors free to include their own unique codes. SQL2 specifies exact error codes.
- **Data types:** SQL2 standardizes several data types available in commercial dialects, such as variable length character, date, time, and money. SQL2 does not include graphical and multimedia object data types.
- **System tables:** SQL2 standardizes the structure of the system catalog, which is not even mentioned in SQL1.

- **Embedded programmatic interface:** SQL1 specifies an abstract technique for using SQL from within each host programming language. SQL2 specifies an embedded interface for the most popular programming languages.
- **Dynamic SQL:** SQL1 does not include features necessary for developing database interfaces, such as user-friendly query tools and report generators. Dynamic SQL features are found in commercial dialects and SQL2 includes support for them.
- **Semantic differences:** Both SQL1 and SQL2 designate specific items as implementer-defined, resulting in dialects that can differ on all these details. The result is two ANSI-compliant dialects producing different results for the same query. Implementer-defined items include handling of null values, column functions, and duplicate row elimination.
- **Collating sequences:** Collating sequence is not addressed in SQL1. SQL2 specifies how users can request a certain collating sequence.
- **Database structure:** SQL1 picks up after a specified database is open and active. The details of connecting to a database differ widely and although SQL2 expands SQL1 on this issue, these differences still persist.
- **Portability:** SQL2 addressed the issues of transparent portability of applications across different DBMS products. Microsoft's ODBC was also designed to remediate portability issues. True transparent access to multiple vendor products is still more of a wish than a reality, however. The portability issue is revisited in SQL:1999.

The broad changes in the ANSI/ISO SQL2 standard significantly strengthened it and made it even more controversial. SQL1 easily passed through the various review and validation committees and was less than 100 pages. SQL2, which made sweeping changes, was more contentious in its development process and took many months of discussion to reach approval. The final page count on this revision is well over 500 pages, which include something not considered in SQL1 levels of conformance. This was included to ensure that the extensive updates and enhancements in SQL2 were implemented and adhered to.

Levels of Conformance

The SQL standard addresses three levels of conformance. In SQL2 there is explicit information for each new or expanded feature definition about which aspects must be supported to attain each conformance level. Compliance with SQL standard levels of conformance is required in all federal procurement.

The conformance levels described in SQL2 are Entry SQL, Intermediate SQL, and Full SQL. Entry SQL requires only minimal additional capability over SQL1. Intermediate SQL is a major enhancement over Entry SQL, but does not address the most system-dependent and DBMS brand-dependent issues that are addressed in Full SQL. Full SQL is a major enhancement over Intermediate SQL and requires full implementation of all SQL2 features and revisions.

A fourth level of conformance was later defined by the National Institute of Standards and Technology (NIST). Called Transitional SQL, it can be seen in the FIPS 127-2 document as a temporary specification that falls approximately halfway between Entry SQL and Intermediate SQL. Conformance to Entry SQL is the minimum required in all federal procurements of SQL products.

Despite the detailed definitions and explicit levels of conformance, there are still differences in the implementations of commercial SQL products, and many SQL dialects continue to exist.

SQL X/Open Standard

X/Open is an international consortium of vendors whose purpose is to define the X/Open Common Applications Environment to provide application portability. They also produced the X/Open Portability Guide (XPG). The X/Open SQL standard and RDA 10/94 specification relies on the ISO/IEC Remote Database Access (RDA) SQL standard, which defines a message format for remote communication of SQL database language query and update statements to a remote database. This specification defines use of the message fields and other implementation information, such as sequencing and optional features. This SQL specification shows how SQL statements map to the RDA protocol.

X/Open is responsible for the X/Open Portability Guide, a document that defines the interfaces of the X/Open Common Applications Environment. X/Open System Interface (XSI) is also part of the X/Open Common Applications Environment.

SQL Access Group

Database interoperability, which was not addressed by early SQL standards, was addressed independently by a group of vendors who formed the SQL Access Group (SAG) in 1989. SAG is now part of the X/Open organization.

In 1991, SAG published its specification for Remote Database Access (RDA). Because the RDA specification was closely tied to OSI protocols that had not yet been widely accepted, the RDA specification was not immediately successful in creating a standard for RDA.

SAG's second standard was far more successful. As a result of urging from Microsoft and using Microsoft's draft, SAG defined the standard for a Call-Level Interface (CLI), on which ODBC is based. The CLI Standard was published in 1992; that same year Microsoft released its hugely successful Open Database Connectivity (ODBC) specification to the market. In 1993, SAG submitted the CLI to the ANSI and ISO SQL committees.

CLI Specification

SQL/CLI is a programming interface designed to support SQL access to databases from off-the-shelf application programs. It provides an international standard implementation-independent CLI to access SQL databases. Because of CLI, client-server tools can easily access databases through dynamic link libraries (DLLs). CLI supports and encourages a robust set of client/server tools.

SQL/CLI consists of routines that allocate and deallocate resources, control connections to SQL servers, execute SQL statements using similar mechanisms to Dynamic SQL, get diagnostic information, and control transaction termination. It was added as an addendum to the SQL2 standard after Microsoft and Macintosh adopted CLI and ODBC as the de facto standard for PC access to SQL databases. It was completed as ISO standard ISO/IEC 9075-3:1995 Information technology -Database languages -SQL -Part 3: Call-Level Interface (SQL/CLI). The current SQL/CLI effort is adding support for SQL3.

The ODBC Connection in Standard Setting

Open Database Connectivity (ODBC) is the broadly accepted application programming interface (API) for database access. ODBC uses SQL as its database access language and is based on the CLI specifications from SQL X/Open and ISO/IEC for database APIs. ODBC is a standard for accessing many different database systems, and contains interfaces for Visual Basic, Visual C++, and SQL. The ODBC driver pack has drivers for Access, Paradox, dBASE, Text, Excel, and Btrieve databases.

To enable database access, ODBC allows an application to submit statements by using SQL's ODBC dialect. ODBC then translates these statements to whatever dialect the database understands. For this method to work, both the application and the DBMS must be ODBC-compliant—that is, the application must be capable of issuing ODBC commands, and the DBMS must be capable of responding to them.

ODBC was defined by SAG. Although Microsoft was one member of the group and the first company to release a commercial product based on SAG's work, ODBC is not a Microsoft standard.

ODBC drivers and development tools are available now for Microsoft Windows, UNIX, OS/2, and Macintosh.

SQL Persistent Stored Modules (SQL/PSM)

SQL Persistent Stored Modules specifies the syntax and semantics of a database language for declaring and maintaining persistent procedures and invoking them from programs developed in a standard programming language.

The SQL/PSM standard defines

- The specification of statements to direct the flow of control within a procedure
- The declaration of local cursors
- The declaration of local variables
- The declaration of local temporary tables

It also includes the definition of tables in the Information Schema, which describes the structure and content of persistent SQL modules.

Object-Oriented Databases (OODB)

In an object-oriented database (OODB), each module, or object, combines data and sequences of instructions (procedures) that act on the data. In traditional, or procedural, programming, the data and instructions to the data are separated. A group of objects that have properties, operations, and behaviors in common is called a *class*; classes are united through inheritance and share certain characteristics and relationships.

By reusing classes developed for previous applications, new applications can be developed faster, with improved reliability and consistency of design. Object-oriented data speeds the development of programs and makes maintenance easier by reusing objects that have specific behaviors, characteristics, and relationships associated with them.

Objects inherit characteristics from their class and all higher-level classes to which they belong, and have their characteristics modeled by the attributes assigned to them. Objects work together through a system where they communicate with each other by messages and respond to communication by executing *methods*, which are programs stored within objects that define how to communicate with each other through their interfaces.

Encapsulating an object within a limited set of defined interfaces hides an object's internal structure and data from view as well as hiding the implementation of the interface. Objects have unique identifiers, usually in the form of an abstract pointer called an *object handle*, that distinguish them from each other. The object handle of one object is often stored within another object and used as a reference to point to the first object. Object handles are stored as data item attributes within the object.

The classes are organized into *collections*, or class libraries, which are then accessible for building and maintaining applications.

Object-oriented databases have managed some success in the marketplace in competition with relational databases. However, the replacement of relational databases that was envisioned early on has not occurred, and current efforts have created object-relational hybrids. With abstract data types and encapsulation, you see the use of object-oriented data in a relational model. Object-relational models have also stretched the relational model to include large data objects, structured/abstract data types, sequences, sets, arrays, stored procedures, user-defined data types, handles, object IDs, and tables-within-tables, which are parallel to the relationships between object classes.

The Object Data Management Group (ODMG) is one of many groups working to provide a standard for object-oriented database technology. An international effort for strong object-oriented capabilities in SQL3 is also underway.

Object Data Management Group (ODMG)

For the Open Database Management Group (ODMG), 1998 was a year of major change. ODMG broadened its focus and became the standards organization for persistent object storage. At the same time, it redefined its membership criteria to allow participation by individuals from all sides of object storage, including database and middleware vendors, tool developers, consultants, end users, and academicians.

The ODMG standard is now an Object Storage API standard that can work with any DBMS or tool. The group is in the process of changing all references to "object databases" (ODBMS) to "object data."

In creating the Object Storage API, ODMG worked outside traditional standards bodies to make quick progress. Its motive for working independently was its belief that standards groups are well suited to incremental changes to a proposal after a good starting point has been established. The group felt it was difficult to perform substantial creative work in such organizations because of their lack of continuity, large membership, and infrequent meetings.

ODMG believes it is important to note that relational database standards started with a database model and language implemented by the largest company involved (IBM). For its work on the Object Storage API, the group selected and combined the best features of implementations available to it.

Before ODMG, the lack of a standard for object databases was a major limitation to widespread acceptance and use. The success of relational database systems came from the standardization they could offer. The acceptance of the SQL standard allowed a high degree of portability and interoperability between systems. The SQL standard simplified learning new relational DBMSs and represented broad endorsement for the relational model.

These factors are also significant for object DBMSs. The scope of object DBMSs is more global than that of relational DBMSs because they integrate the programming language and database system and encompass all of an application's operations and data. A standard is critical to make DBMS applications practical.

ODMG's focused efforts have given the object database industry a jump start toward standards that might otherwise have taken several years. ODMG enables vendors to support and endorse a common object database interface that customers can use to write their applications.

ODMG's goal is to establish a set of standards that allow an ODBMS customer to write portable applications. The data schema, programming language binding, and data manipulation and query languages must be portable. ODMG's standards proposal will be instrumental in allowing interoperability between the ODBMS products for heterogeneous distributed databases communicating through the OMG Object Request Broker.

ODMG is working to bring programming languages and database systems to a new level of integration and move the industry forward as a whole through the advancement of real products that conform to a more complete standard than is possible with relational systems. ODMG has progressed further than the least common denominator of initial relational standards with its efforts to provide portability for the entire application, not just the small portion of the semantics encoded in embedded SQL statements.

The ODMG member companies, representing almost the entire ODBMS industry, support the expanded standard. ODMG's proposed specification has become a de facto standard for this industry, and it has used its specification work with standards groups such as the OMG and the ANSI X3H2 (SQL) committee.

ODMG's goal is source code portability instead of producing identical ODBMS products. There will be differences between products in performance, languages supported, functionality unique to particular market segments, accompanying programming environments, application construction tools, small versus large scale, multithreading, networking, platform availability, depth of functionality, suites of predefined type libraries, GUI builders, and design tools.

ODMG has used existing work from standards groups and from the literature as the foundation for its proposals when possible. The greater part of its effort, however, is derived from the heartiest features of the ODBMS products currently available. These products offer proven implementations of ODMG standards components that have been used in the field.

It is important to define the scope of ODMG's efforts because ODBMSs have an architecture that differs substantially from other DBMSs. ODBMS transparently integrates database capability with the application programming language instead of supplying only a high-level language for data manipulation. This transparency makes learning a separate DML unnecessary. It also precludes the need to copy and translate data between database and programming language representations explicitly and supports substantial performance advantages through data caching in applications. The ODBMS includes a more powerful query language model that incorporates lists, arrays, and results of any type.

SQL:1999 and Beyond

The standard specification of SQL is under continual development. Draft documents at various stages of development are available for review from representatives in the ANSI/ISO/IEC standardization process.

American National Standard X3.135-199x was prepared by Technical Committee Group X3H2-Database Languages, working under the auspices of Accredited National Standards Committee X3, Information Processing Systems. SQL3 is compatible with SQL-92 in that, with a few minor exceptions, SQL language that conforms to the SQL-92 standard also conforms to SQL3 and is treated in the same way by an implementation of SQL3 as it is by an implementation of SQL-92. Known incompatibilities between SQL-92 and SQL3 are stated in Informative Annex E, "Incompatibilities with X3.135-1992 and ISO/IEC 9075:1992."

Technical changes between SQL2 and SQL3 include improvements and enhancements to existing features, as well as definition of important new features, including the following:

- Support for active rules (triggers).
- Support for abstract data types.

- Support for multiple NULL states.
- Support for PENDANT referential integrity.
- A recursive union operation for query expressions.
- Support for enumerated and Boolean data types.
- Support for SENSITIVE cursors.

Implementations of the SQL3 ANSI/ISO Standard can exist in environments that also support application programming languages, end-user query languages, report generator systems, program library systems, data dictionary systems, and distributed communication systems, as well as various tools for database design, data administration, and performance optimization.

The latest SQL3 working draft addresses the requirement for objects and object identifiers in SQL. This draft also specifies supporting features such as inheritance, encapsulation, subtypes, and polymorphism.

Data types frequently referred to as "SQL3 types" are the new data types being adopted in the nearly finished version of the ANSI/ISO SQL standard. The JDBC 2.0 API provides interfaces that represent mapping these data types into the Java programming language. With these new interfaces, you can work with SQL3 data types the same way you do other data types.

SQL3 data types give a relational database increased flexibility in what can be used as a type for a table column. For example, a column can now be used to store the new type Binary Large Object (BLOB), which can store very large amounts of data as raw bytes. A column can also be of type Character Large Object (CLOB), which is capable of storing very large amounts of data in character format. The new type ARRAY enables the use of an array as a column value. SQL3 user-defined types (UDTs), structured types, and distinct types can all be stored as column values.

Levels of Conformance in SQL3

SQL2 was defined with three hierarchical levels of conformance (plus a later defined fourth level), but SQL3 has been defined quite differently. Core SQL3 must be implemented for all implementations claiming conformance to SQL3. It is a superset of the features found in Entry SQL2 implementations, with features added from the higher levels of SQL2, as well as a few new SQL3 features.

From levels higher than the Entry SQL 2, Core SQL3 has borrowed the `ALTER TABLE` statement, `WITH HOLD` cursors, `RIGHT` and `LEFT OUTER JOIN` statements, and `CALL` and `RETURN` statements. Also included in Core SQL3 are distinct data types.

There are nine packages of features* beyond the SQL Core3 that an implementation might support, which are described in an annex to the standard:

PKG001	Enhanced datatime facilities
PKG002	Enhanced integrity management
PKG003	OLAP facilities
PKG004	SQL/PSM
PKG005	SQL.CLI (Call Level Interface)
PKG006	Basic object support
PKG007	Enhanced object support
PKG008	Active database
PKG009	SQL/MM (multimedia) support

**Some features appear in more than one package.*

Because nearly every relational database system vendor is represented in the SQL3 development committee (H2), there is good reason to believe SQL3 features will be released in upcoming products from these vendors. Some have even indicated their intentions to begin releasing products with SQL3 features as soon as each feature emerges from the approval process.

In the United States, SQL3 is being processed as both an ANSI Domestic project and as an ISO project. Originally, SQL3 was expected to be completed in 1998, but in mid-1999 it is still a work in progress. With the intention that it will be completed and released in 1999, the name was changed to SQL:1999.

You can find additional reading on the topics covered in this chapter on the home pages of the organizations discussed. Bookmarking their Web sites makes keeping up to date on the status of SQL advancements and enhancements as easy as logging on to the Internet.

- Public FTP Directory of ISO WG3 Database Language Base Documents

  `ftp://jerry.ece.umassd.edu/isowg3/dbl/BASEdocs/public/`

- National Institute of Standards and Technology

  `www.nist.gov`

- FIPS 127-2-Database Language SQL

  `www.itl.nist.gov/fipspubs/fip127-2.htm`

- The Open Group

  www.opengroup.org/
- American National Standards Institute

  www.ansi.org/
- ISO Homepage (English)

  www.iso.ch/welcome.html

Summary

The SQL standard is an evolution rather than a static entity. As technology grows and melds and blends, SQL adapts without compromising its integrity because of the many organizations that govern its development.

Industry leaders in the arena of relational data management continually raise the bar and mark it with a modification to the standard, just to return in a few years or months to raise the bar again. SQL standards function as the road map to fully integrated relational object and data storage and manipulation, and the foundation for future advances. Since the standard is a road map that is being drawn as the road is being built, it is a living document that will, and must, continually change.

CHAPTER 2

Relational Databases

In This Chapter

Data storage has been a major area of research since the early days of computers. Data was first stored in flat files in a table format. Accessing the data was anything but an easy task, especially as these files grew in size to hold tens and hundreds of thousands of rows of data. Therefore, these rudimentary tables evolved into what is now known as *relational database management systems (RDBMSs)*. This chapter describes this evolution with an illustration of how to build an optimum relational database. The chapter also discusses the use of database modeling and design tools to speed the design process and make it more manageable.

Data Storage and Data Access

Data storage and data access have gone through several evolutionary, and sometimes revolutionary, stages since the 1960s. The milestones of this path started with flat file systems, followed by the advent of hierarchical and network database management models, and ended with the relational model. These milestones are explained in some detail in the following sections.

Flat File Systems

The database is an electronic record-keeping system. Early implementations of this system included electronic sequential storage devices, such as tape drives, which keep data in a *flat file* format. The main characteristics of flat file systems include the following:

- Data is laid out in a table format with the *columns* (fields) having fixed length and data types and *rows* (records) having the same length. Figure 2.1 depicts the standard flat file format.
- A new record is started every *x* bytes; *x* is the length of the record.
- New records are appended to the flat file at the end, without having to order the rows in any particular order.

FIGURE 2.1
Flat files had fixed-length records and fixed-length fields with predefined data types.

Emp_Fname	Emp_Lname	Department	Department_Manager	Department Bldg.	Department_Region	Employee_N
John	Doe	Accounting	Jerry L.	BLD2	Midwest	123
John	Doe	Accounting	Jerry L.	BLD2	Midwest	123
Jack	Doe	Accounting	Jerry L.	BLD2	Midwest	125
Jack	Doe	Accounting	Jerry L.	BLD2	Midwest	125
Jack	Doe	Accounting	Jerry L.	BLD2	Midwest	125
Jack	Doe	Accounting	Jerry L.	BLD2	Midwest	125
Jack	Doe	Accounting	Jerry L.	BLD2	Midwest	125
Scott	K	Accounting	Jerry L.	BLD2	Midwest	223
Scott	K	Accounting	Jerry L.	BLD2	Midwest	223
Scott	K	Accounting	Jerry L.	BLD2	Midwest	223
Scott	K	Accounting	Jerry L.	BLD2	Midwest	223
Scott	K	Accounting	Jerry L.	BLD2	Midwest	223

Retrieving one particular record from a flat file system requires a search of the entire file. Records are read one at a time with some processing performed on each.

Flat file systems evolved into *sequential flat file systems*, in which data is ordered based on a key field. This ordering makes retrieving a certain record from the file faster than with flat file systems.

FIGURE 2.2
Sequential flat files are flat files with an ordered key field (Employee_No).

Emp_Fname	Emp_Lname	Department	Department_Manager	Department Bldg.	Department_Region	Employee_N
Jack	Doe	Accounting	Jerry L.	BLD2	Midwest	125
Jack	Doe	Accounting	Jerry L.	BLD2	Midwest	125
Jack	Doe	Accounting	Jerry L.	BLD2	Midwest	125
Jack	Doe	Accounting	Jerry L.	BLD2	Midwest	125
Jack	Doe	Accounting	Jerry L.	BLD2	Midwest	125
John	Doe	Accounting	Jerry L.	BLD2	Midwest	123
John	Doe	Accounting	Jerry L.	BLD2	Midwest	123
Scott	K	Accounting	Jerry L.	BLD2	Midwest	223
Scott	K	Accounting	Jerry L.	BLD2	Midwest	223
Scott	K	Accounting	Jerry L.	BLD2	Midwest	223
Scott	K	Accounting	Jerry L.	BLD2	Midwest	223
Scott	K	Accounting	Jerry L.	BLD2	Midwest	223

Random access storage devices, such as hard disks, brought with them more data storage and access improvements. With these devices, you can directly read a specific block on the disk, without having to spool through the whole device. This feature introduced the concept of data indexing on the disk. Records are indexed to make their retrieval much faster. Indexes are kept in a separate file on disk. An index file includes records with the key of the data file saved sequentially along with the corresponding location of the record on disk. This system is often referred to as an *index sequential flat file system*. Accessing a certain record causes the much smaller sorted index file to be searched for the key value of the record and the location. After the information is found in the index file, the record can be located directly. Figure 2.3 illustrates this process.

The layer between the data and the user is called the database manager, or the *database management system (DBMS)*. The previous data storage paradigms had simple procedural DBMSs. A DBMS was typically written in a procedural language, such as COBOL, PLI, or the more modern C or Pascal. Those programs operate on the data in all the usual ways: retrieving existing records, inserting new records, deleting records, or changing existing records. These programs, however, are not usually end-user friendly. Therefore, another high-level layer was created to allow the user, who is not usually a programmer, to interact with the database. This layer is called the *query language*.

Note

Query language is really a misnomer. The English word *query* suggests retrieval only. However, query languages also involve inserting, updating, and deleting data.

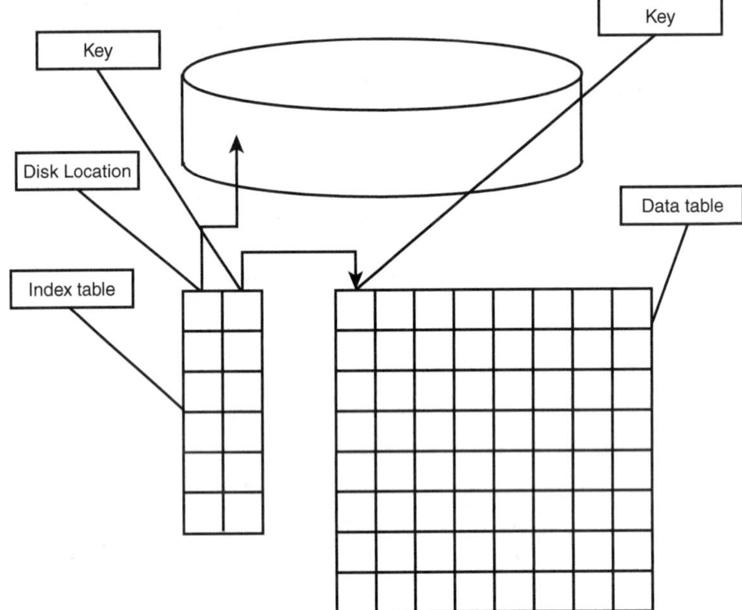

FIGURE 2.3
Random access storage devices introduced the possibility of indexing the data in flat files.

The demand for more complex data manipulation was growing as hardware and operating systems became more sophisticated. Performing set operations, rather than just record operations and transactions, is an example of complex data manipulation. As the amounts of data stored in flat file systems became larger and larger, manipulating the data became more difficult. This growth also revealed inefficiencies in data storage and handling. As an answer to these difficulties, new modes of database systems emerged. The most important of these models are the hierarchical model, the network model, and the relational model.

Hierarchical Database Models

According to this model (see Figure 2.4), data is stored in non-sequential files, and indexes are structured as trees. Records are related to each other in a hierarchical fashion. That means the data is located on "tree" nodes, practically on the leaf level, although it can be stored at higher levels in the hierarchy. The best way to visualize this kind of database is by picturing an upside-down tree, with one table serving as the root and other tables branching out of it. The relationships between the tables are parent-child relationships, with a child having only one parent, and a parent able to have multiple children.

The strictly structured data storage in this model makes it easy to understand and implement the database schema and makes the database structure easy to conceptualize. However, many-to-many relationships, explained later in the chapter, cannot be adequately represented. These relationships have to be represented as two one-to-many relationships, using bidirectional logical relationships with two trees, which leads to unavoidable redundancies. Also, because every index key is associated with every insertion in the tree structure, it becomes difficult to perform data deletions.

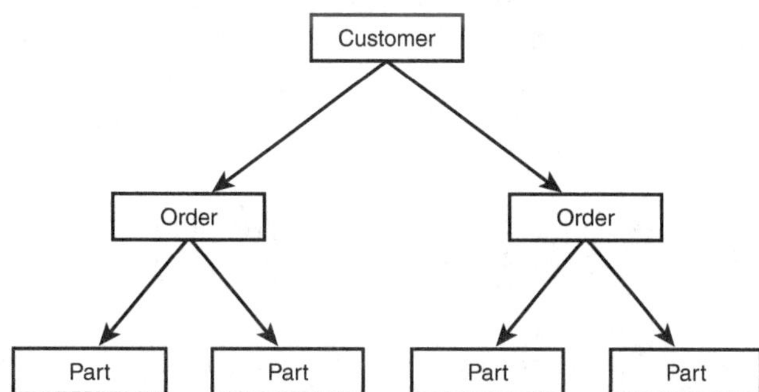

FIGURE 2.4
A representation of hierarchical databases.

Network Database Models

The network model (see Figure 2.5) was introduced to answer some of the drawbacks of the hierarchical model. It specifically addresses the data redundancy problem by representing data as sets, rather than hierarchies. Conceptually, the network model looks pretty much like the hierarchical model, except that a child node can have more than one parent. This allows the network model to support many-to-many relationships.

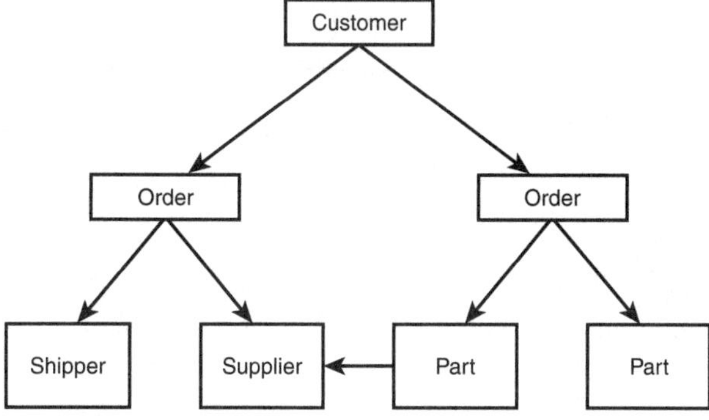

FIGURE 2.5
A representation of network databases.

Although this model was a dramatic improvement over hierarchical databases, it was difficult to implement and maintain and was always associated with higher costs.

Relational Database Management Systems (RDBMSs)

Dr. E. F. Codd first defined the relational model and the normal forms in 1970, and others extended this model after him. In short, a *relational database* is composed of tables related to one another through some of their fields. In this section, I cover the basics of RDBMSs, discussing their history, flexibility, ease of use, administration, and modification. Today, the majority of database management systems are based on the relational model.

Note

Dr. Codd published his famous paper "A Relational Model for Large Shared Databanks" in the *Communications of the ACM* Journal. This paper caused a revolution in the world of data management, and we still see its effects.

RDBMS History

As a mathematician working for IBM, Dr. Codd defined how relational DBMSs can be constructed based on data's relationship to each other in their entities. His work caused a revolution in the way databases were built. Until then, the most common types of database management systems were based on the hierarchical database model or the network database model.

The standard functions available in relational databases include the following:

- Support for client/server as the mainstream architecture
- Support for a database access using a standard language-independent application programmer's interface (API)
- Support for multiprocessing servers, including symmetrical multiprocessing servers, and massively parallel processing servers
- Support for the Structured Query Language (SQL)

Future Direction

The biggest change in relational database technology will be caused by the increased use of the Internet and intranet technologies. It is expected that eventually the Web browser will become both the universal client interface and application-programming interface for RDBMSs.

RDBMS vendors are expected to continue making their database management systems more and more sophisticated. With increasing data storage needs, RDBMSs are expected to handle very large databases, many users, and various data types, such as those for video, picture, and sound. With the improved handling of very large databases, RDBMSs are expected to improve their decision support systems (DSS) capabilities.

Finally, two areas will be addressed by database and other software vendors in the future: integration of heterogeneous platforms, networks, and databases, and integrated management of these components. These two areas will help keep RDBMS the database management system of choice to handle enterprisewide-distributed data needs.

> **Note**
>
> A fairly recent direction in database modeling is the introduction of object-oriented databases. Such databases allow schema objects to have other objects nested within them. For example, you can have nested tables that represent certain data hierarchical structures. These concepts are discussed in more detail later in Chapter 23, "The Next Standard: SQL-99."

RDBMS Model Features

In its simplest form, a relational database is a collection of data tables that relate to each other through at least one common field, such as Social Security number. Some of the inherent advantages of relational databases are flexibility, increased capability, and ease of administration and modification.

Flexibility

RDBMS users are no longer locked into specific hardware requirements, network configurations, or network protocols. With relational databases and modern operating systems, many products are compatible and users have a broader range than ever to choose from to satisfy their data management needs.

Increased Capability

Relational databases allow more data to be available to users. They also make it easier to see the relationships between different groups of data. Data retrieval is done through the RDBMS's "ad hoc" reporting capability, which gives access to all tables and data in a way that's easy to understand.

Relational databases have capabilities that make them the database model of choice for Web-based applications. Many RDBMS vendors are building support for Web applications in their systems to allow data in the relational database to be easily published on the Web or accessed interactively through the Web browser.

Ease of Modification and Administration

One of the greatest advantages of relational databases is the ease of modification. In legacy systems, modifications almost always involved a professional programmer who changed many programs, incurring a big expense. With a properly designed relational database, such changes might mean changing only a single table.

Another benefit of relational databases is the ease of administration. With less duplication of data throughout the database, and with better organization of the file system, relational database administration becomes an easy task compared with older systems.

Note

The current trend in relational database system administration is to automate many of the administration tasks by using wizards and graphical tools. Examples include the newly improved Oracle Enterprise Manager and the highly advanced SQL Server 7.0 Enterprise Manager.

Codd's 12 Rules

In 1985, Dr. Codd designated 12 rules with which relational databases should comply. Although these rules have been unofficially adopted as the definition of relational databases, they actually represented an ideal goal, more than a definition of a relational database. Most commercial DBMSs adapt or bend these rules as needed, and almost none adhere to them fully.

1. All information in a relational database is represented explicitly at the logical level in exactly one way, by values in tables. This rule basically defines what a relational database is.

2. Each piece of data is guaranteed easy access by using a combination of table names, primary key, and field name. This rule stresses the importance of primary keys in accessing data in the relational database.
3. Nulls are supported for expressing missing or non-applicable values in the database regardless of the field's data type. Nulls are distinguished from zeros or empty strings.
4. Database description is represented in a similar way to the data (data catalog). This allows certain users access to this catalog to query it and modify it if needed through the database language (SQL).
5. Database language should support certain items, including data definition, view definition, data manipulation (ad hoc and programmatically), integrity constraints, authorization, and transaction boundaries (`begin transaction` , `commit transaction`, and `rollback transaction`).
6. Theoretically, updatable views should also be updatable by the system.
7. Database language should be able to handle a base relation and a derived relation not only in selecting data, but also in inserts, updates, and deletes. This rule stresses the set-oriented nature of relational databases. It requires that rows be treated as sets in insert, delete, and update operations, not just in select operations.
8. Application programs and terminal activities remain logically unimpaired whenever any changes are made in storage representations or access methods.
9. Application programs and terminal activities remain logically unimpaired whenever information preserving changes of any kind that theoretically permit unimpairment are made to the base table. This rule and rule number 8 help insulate the user or application from the low-level implementation of the database.
10. Integrity constraints in a relational database should be definable in the database language (SQL) and stored in the system catalog, not in the application programs.
11. A relational DBMS has distribution independence. This rule stresses that a relational database should support distributed systems.
12. Integrity rules and constraints should be applied consistently at the row level as well as at the multiple row level.

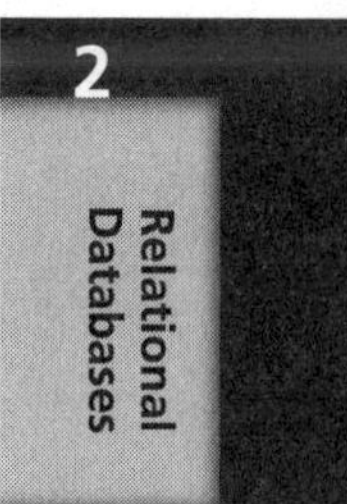
2
Relational Databases

Table Design: Entities and Relationships

Relational databases have schemas that define their objects and the relationships between these objects. The most important object in the schema is the table. This section discusses table and relationship design according to the relational model.

Table Design

The database schema defines the objects in the database and the rules under which they operate. The main object in the database schema is the table. Tables can be permanent (base tables), virtual (views), or temporary (global and shared tables).

A table, referred to as an *entity*, is a set of zero or more rows of data, and a *row* is a set or one or more columns with each column having a specific data type. Table design in relational systems is extremely important, and should take into account that tables are related to each other to minimize redundancy. In this section, I discuss how uniqueness is established in tables and what kinds of relationships can exist among tables in a relational database system.

Primary Key

According to Codd's rule number 2, each record in a table should be uniquely identified. The field or combination of fields that define this uniqueness is called the primary key. For example, in an employee table, the field that stores the employee Social Security number can be used as a primary key because every employee has a unique value for this field. Of course, this would require that ever employee have a valid Social Security number on file as primary keys must all contain actual values (NULL values are not allowed).

Figure 2.6 shows an example of a composite primary key, in which several fields are needed to identify a unique row. In this example, the transaction table in an order entry database has four fields composing the primary key: `customer_id`, `employee_id`, and `order_date_time`.

Note

Even though composite keys are possible in relational databases, you should use them carefully. If the table becomes large, scanning the index on a composite key will not yield much of a performance benefit. It is recommended that an additional field be added that makes the record unique and allows fast scans of the primary key index. This key can be an automatically incrementing number (for example, a sequence in Oracle, or an identity column in Microsoft SQL Server). In the previous example, such a field could be called `order_date_time`.

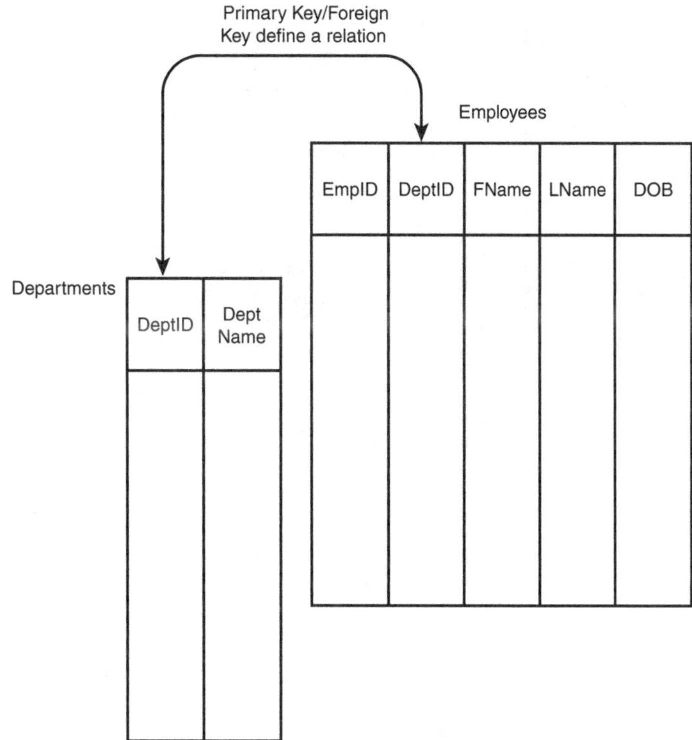

FIGURE 2.6
A primary key can be composed of multiple fields, in which case it is called a composite key.

Foreign Key

A column in one table whose value matches the primary key in another table is called the *foreign key*. Figure 2.7 shows that the `DeptID` field is a foreign key in the `Employees` table in a human resources database. You will notice that the `DeptID` field is the primary key in the `Departments` table. A department with the id `5`, for instance, can be seen in two records in the `Employees` table.

Just as Figure 2.7 implies, a primary key/foreign key combination defines a parent/child relationship, giving the ability to represent hierarchies in the relational database. Figure 2.8 shows that a table can contain more than one foreign key if the table is involved in relations with more than one table. In addition to the `DeptID` field, the `ComputerID` field is also a foreign key in the `Employees` table and is related to the primary key in the `Computers` table.

Table Relations

Table relations describe how the data in the tables are related. A record in a table can be directly related to one record or to multiple records in another table. This defines several possible relationships among tables. These relationships are discussed in the following sections.

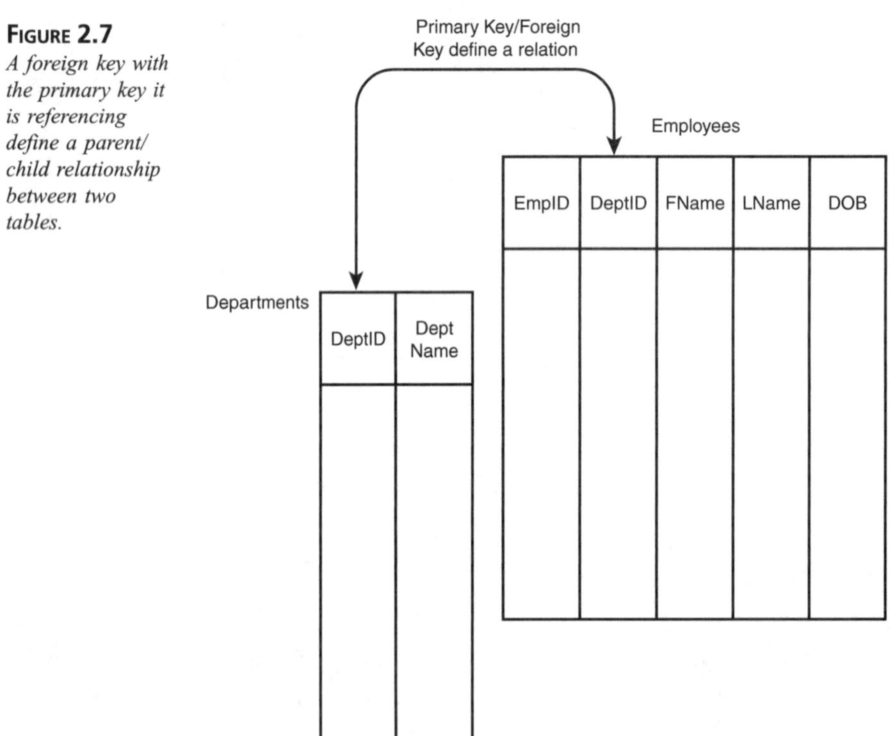

FIGURE 2.7
A foreign key with the primary key it is referencing define a parent/ child relationship between two tables.

One-to-One Relationship

In a one-to-one relationship, the key value of a table can appear only once in a related table. For example, in an office space database, each employee is related to one cubicle. The `cubicle_id` field, which is the primary key in the `cubicles` table, has one value for each employee in the `employees` table (see Figure 2.9).

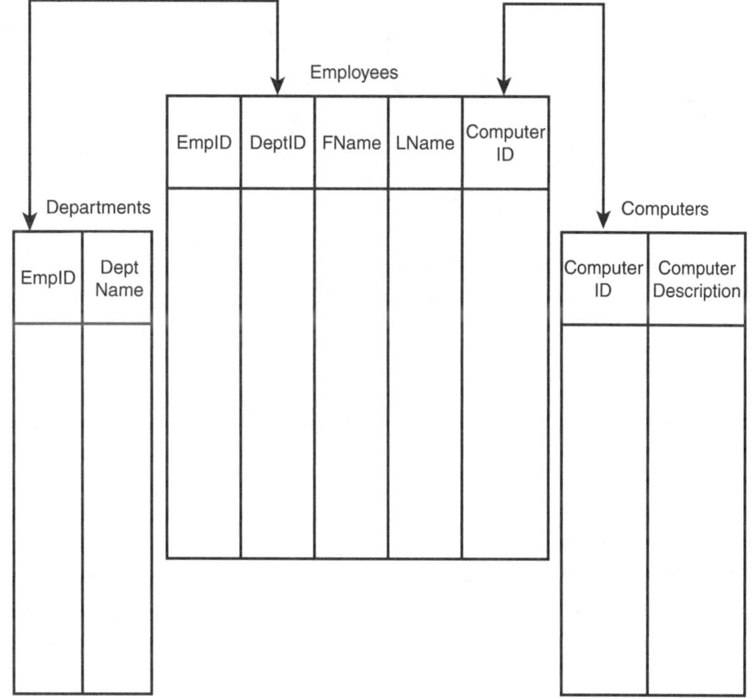

FIGURE 2.8
More than one foreign key can be found in a table that is related to many other tables.

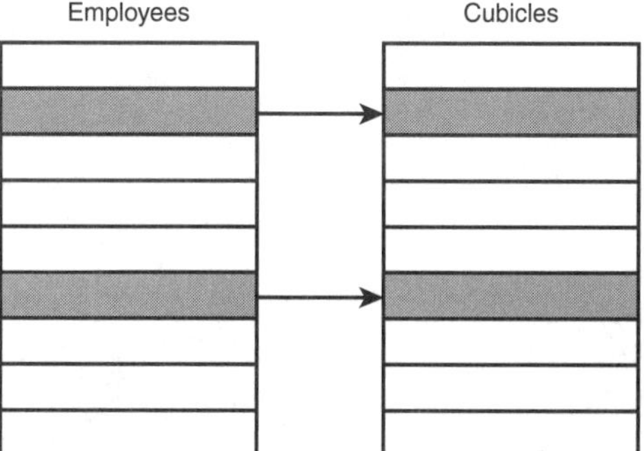

FIGURE 2.9
Example of a one-to-one relationship.

One-to-Many Relationship

In a one-to-many relationship, the key value of a table can appear many times in a related table. For example, each employee in an employee database belongs to one department, but each department can have many employees in it. This is the most commonly used form of relationship, and is depicted in Figure 2.10.

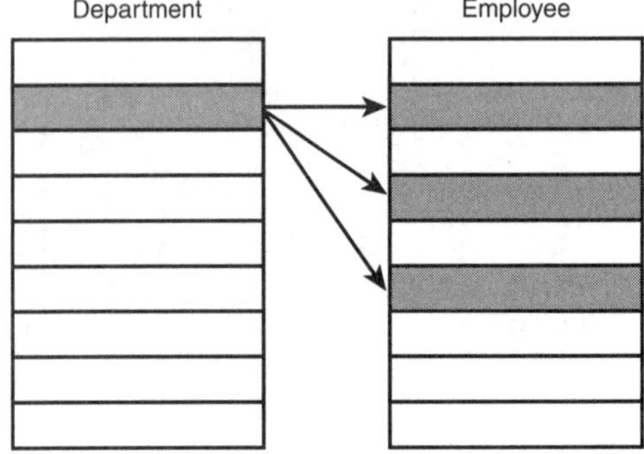

FIGURE 2.10
Example of a one-to-many relationship.

Many-to-Many Relationship

In a many-to-many relationship, the key value of a table (first table) can appear many times in a related table (second table). The opposite is also true: The primary key of the second table can appear many times in the first table. For example, in a classes and students database, you would expect a student to have multiple classes in a department and more than one student to be enrolled in a class. These many-to-many relationships are difficult to deal with, so they are usually broken into two one-to-many relationships. Figure 2.11 illustrates this concept. In the figure, a new table, `Title_Author`, is created as a middle table between the `BookTitle` and `Authors` tables. Each of these tables shares a one-to-many relationship with the new table.

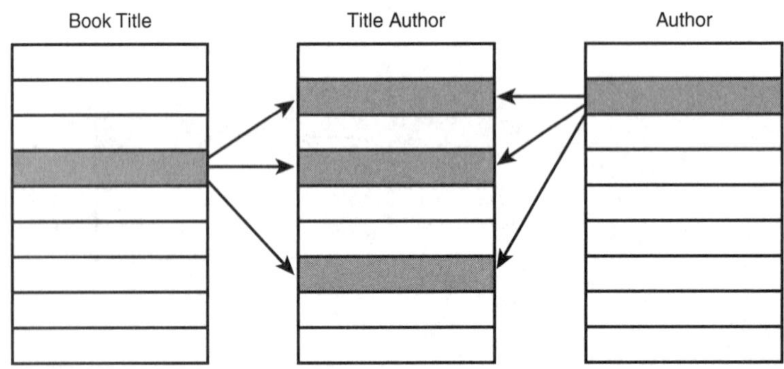

FIGURE 2.11
A many-to-many relationship is split into two one-to-many relationships.

Normalization

Data normalization means getting the tables into at least the third normal form (3NF). This section describes table normalization and the different normal forms. In the process, a sample database is designed, starting with a flat table.

The Flat Table

Imagine that you are storing book information for a company library in a spreadsheet. The spreadsheet includes a huge table with fields such as the following (never mind the data types for now—they are explained in detail in Chapter 4, "Data Types"):

`Author_Name`	Character data
`Author_Notes`	Character data
`Book_Title`	Character data
`Book_Topic`	Character data
`ISBN`	Character data
`Book_Copy_Right_Year`	Date
`Book_Edition`	Numeric, integer
`Publisher_Name`	Character data
`Publisher_Adress`	Character data
`Purchase_Price`	Currency
`Date_Purchased`	Date/Time
`Shelf_Code`	Character data
`Cover_Type`	Character data
`Book_Pages`	Numeric, integer
`Quotes`	Array of character data
`Quote_Page_Number`	Numeric, integer
`Contributing_Authors`	Array of character data

You have 21 fields (including the five keywords array fields) that you need to populate for every book in the company book collection using the spreadsheet. Looking at the fields, you'll notice a big problem with using such a model to represent data. The problem is unnecessary data redundancy. For example, for every book written by John Doe, the John Doe `Notes` field is populated with the same information. Had you added author address and phone number to the table, those pieces of information would also have been repeated for every book written by this gentleman. Another example is the publisher information for each book, which is repeated for every book published by a certain publisher. This data redundancy leads to losing a lot of time entering the data and wasting valuable storage space.

The following sections describe how this problem can be solved to come up with an optimized data model.

Functional Dependency (FD)

One of the key concepts in solving this problem involves finding (and eliminating unneeded) dependencies. By definition, given a relationship (table) `R` that has attributes `X` and `Y`, if attribute `Y` is functionally dependent on attribute `X`, this dependency can be represented symbolically as the following:

```
R.X ----> R.Y
```

This is read as `R.X` functionally *determines* `R.Y`. For example, in an `employee` relationship (table) `E`, the `SSN` (Social Security number) field determines the fields `FirstName` and `LastName`. This means that for a given Social Security number, I can tell what the first name and last name in the table are. To express this symbolically, write:

```
E.SSN ----> E.FirstName
E.SSN ----> E.LastName
```

or

```
E.SSN ----> E.(FirstName, LastName)
```

Note

If attribute `X` is a candidate key in the relationship (table), particularly if it is a primary key, then all other attributes in the relation are determined by `X`. In the `employee` table, if the Social Security number (`SSN`) is the primary key, all the other fields depend on it in their determination.

```
E.SSN ----> E.FirstName

E.SSN ----> E.LastName

E.SSN ----> E.Street

E.SSN ----> E.City

E.SSN ----> E.State

E.SSN ----> E.Zip
```

```
E.SSN ----> E.Phone

E.SSN ----> E.email
```

Multivalued Dependency (MVD)

Similar to functional dependency, multivalued dependency (MVD) means that given a value of attribute X, I can determine a set of values of attribute Y. For example, knowing the department name, I can find a list of employees in that department. Symbolically, this is expressed as:

```
E.Department ---->> E.Employees
```


First Normal Form (1NF)

Let's consider maintaining information in your company library again. The first normal form means that the table does not have any repeating groups, and each field is an atomic (scalar) value. This means that no arrays, tables, or other data structures found in other programming languages are permitted in the table. In this example, you have a field (`contributing_authors`) that is an array of several values. If you flatten this array in one field that includes all the information of all the fields, you will seem to be doing okay. However, this is not quite true yet. Doing so causes what is known as *delete*, *update*, and *insert anomalies*.

Note

The terms *delete, update*, and *insert anomalies* mean that deleting or updating one of the elements of the array in the "array" field, or inserting a new element, will lead to erroneous information in the database. For instance, if one of the contributing authors changes the topic she is writing on, the other contributing authors will seem to have written about both topics—the one first listed for them and the new one.

To put the table in the first normal form, you need to split the data into two tables: one about authors and one about books. A many-to-many relationship exists between the two tables. As you saw earlier in the section on relationships, this can be resolved by creating a "middle" table that shares a one-to-many relationship with both tables. According to that, the database will look like this:

Titles Table	
Book_Title	Character data
Book_Topic	Character data
ISBN	Character data
Book_Copy_Right_Year	Date
Book_Edition	Numeric, integer
Publisher_Name	Character data
Publisher_Adress	Character data
Purchase_Price	Currency
Date_Purchased	Date/Time
Shelf_Code	Character data
Cover_Type	Character data
Book_Pages	Numeric, integer

Authors Table	
Author_Name	Character data
Author_Notes	Character data

Other author fields here, such as address, phone, and so on.

Author_Title Table (the middle table)	
Authors.Author_ID	Numeric, integer
Titles.ISBN	Numeric, Integer
Contribution	Character

Quote_Title Table (another middle table)	
Quotes.Quote_ID	Numeric, integer
Titles.ISBN	Numeric, Integer
Quote	Character
Quote_Page_Number	Numeric, integer

Quotes Table	
Quote_ID	Numeric, integer
Quote	Character data

Notice that in the `Titles` table, I took out the main author's fields too. To compensate for this, I added a field to the `Author_Title` table (`Contribution`) that tells what role the author had on the book (main, contributing, or review). Notice, too, that I did the same thing with the `Quotes` field, which was an array that included quotes taken from the book.

Second Normal Form (2NF)

For a table to be in the second normal form (2NF), it has to be in 1NF and have a key that determines all non-key attributes in the table. For example, given an ISBN, you can determine the book topic (assuming that an ISBN is unique for each book), author, and other information about the title. Therefore, the ISBN can serve as a key field for the `Titles` table, which means the `Titles` table is already in second normal form.

Third Normal Form (3NF)

A table is said to be in third normal form if, and only if, the non-key attributes are mutually independent and fully dependent on the primary key. So for a table to be in 3NF, it has to be in 2NF, and its non-key attributes must be mutually independent. In this example, you saw that the titles table is already in 2NF. If you examine the non-key attributes, you'll notice that by knowing the publisher name, you can tell the publisher address, meaning that the non-key field (`Publisher_Address`) is dependent on the non-key attribute (`Publisher Name`), as shown here:

```
Publisher Name ----> Publisher_Address
```

Therefore, the table is not in 3NF. To make the table compliant with 3NF, create an additional table for the publisher information, and the database schema becomes as follows:

`Publishers` Table	
`Publisher_ID`	Numeric, integer
`Publisher_Name`	Character data
`Publisher_Address`	Character data

`Titles` Table	
`Book_Title`	Character data
`Topic_ID`	Numeric, integer
`ISBN`	Character data
`Book_Copy_Right_Year`	Date
`Book_Edition`	Numeric, integer
`Publisher_ID`	Numeric, integer
`Purchase_Price`	Currency
`Date_Purchased`	Date/Time
`Shelf_Code`	Character data

Cover_Type	Character data
Book_Pages	Numeric, integer

Authors Table

Author_Name	Character data
Author_Notes	Character data

Other author fields here, such as address, phone, and so forth.

Author_Title Table (the middle table)

Authors.Author_ID	Numeric, integer
Titles.ISBN	Numeric, Integer
Contribution	Character

Quote_Title Table (another middle table)

Quotes.Quote_ID	Numeric, integer
Titles.ISBN	Numeric, Integer
Quote	Character
Quote_Page_Number	Numeric, integer

Quotes Table

Quote_ID	Numeric, integer
Quote	Character data

Topics Table

Topic_ID	Numeric, integer
Topic	Character data

Higher Normal Forms

Three more normal forms exist beyond the 3NF level. These forms are Boyd-Codd normal form (BCNF relations), fourth normal form (4NF) relations, and projection join normal form, or 5NF (PJ/NF relations). These normal forms are seldom achieved when normalizing the tables of a relational database because generally the benefits of doing so are not great compared with the cost of doing the normalization. These normalization forms are discussed briefly in the following sections.

Boyd-Codd Normal Form

> **Note**
>
> An attribute in a relation (table) is said to be a candidate key for the relation if and only if it is unique at any given time, and if the attribute is composite (composed of several sub-attributes). Eliminating any of its components results in destroying the attribute's uniqueness. According to this definition, every relation has at least one candidate key. Actually, most relations have just one candidate key, but can have more than one. An example is the `Titles` table, in which there is a primary key (`ISBN`) that is a candidate key, and another composite candidate key composed of the `Book_Title`, `Book_Edition`, and `Publisher_ID`.

As originally conceived, the third normal form still had some deficiencies. This form did not handle certain cases well enough. These cases include relations with the following characteristics:

- Multiple candidate keys
- The candidate keys were composite
- The candidate keys overlapped (had at least one attribute in common)

Therefore, a new normal form (Boyd-Codd normal form) was introduced to handle these deficiencies. According to this normal form, every determinant in the relation has to be a candidate key. In terms of functional dependency, arrows are always going out of the candidate keys—and only candidate keys.

> **Note**
>
> The reason this normal form was not called a fourth normal form is that it only extends the third normal form, making it simpler to define, but stronger by eliminating its deficiencies.

Fourth Normal Form (4NF)

This normal form makes use of the multivalued dependencies (MVD). It actually reduced the number of MVDs in a table. For example, consider a database with departments, employees, and projects, among other items. Each department defines multiple projects and multiple employees. Take the following table:

Department	*Project*	*Employee*
Dept1	Proj1	John D.
Dept1	proj1	Frank D.
Dept1	Proj2	John D.
Dept1	Proj2	Frank D.
Dept2	Proj3	Scott D.
Dept2	Proj3	Jack D.

According to 4NF, the table is split into two tables—`Department/Project` and `Department/Employee`—so that there is only one MVD in each table.

Projection Join Normal Form (5NF)

This normal form handles relations that are three-way or greater. These relationships are not handled properly with popular CASE tools because they allow only binary relationships. (The CASE in CASE tool stands for Computer Assisted System Engineering. These are the tools used for database design.) Using CASE tools to represent such a relation yields more tables than needed, which leads to an anomaly called *join-projection anomaly.* An example is the following table showing car buyers, sellers, and the bank doing the financing:

Buyer	*Seller*	*Bank*
John	Farmington Ford	First National
Scott	Dearborn Mercury	CASE Bank
Mary	Troy Chevrolet	First Federal

Using the CASE tools to represent this three-way relationship yields three tables: `Buyer/Seller`, `Buyer/Bank`, and `Seller/Bank`. If you select data from these tables, you might come up with values such as John, Farmington Ford, CASE Bank, that aren't in the original table. This is what's called a join-projection anomaly.

Denormalization

As you saw in the previous section, normalizing the tables in a database to at least the 3NF offers benefits that are especially evident if the database tables undergo a lot of update, insert, and delete activities. A classic example of such a database is a production database that undergoes many transactions in an online transaction processing (OLTP) system. In this type of system, data is seldom queried, and if it is, only small recordsets are returned.

The opposite of an OLTP system is one that's connected to a data warehouse, or a series of data marts, and performs online analytical processing (OLAP) of the data in the system. This system usually undergoes little, if any, insert, update, and delete activity, but performs long queries against the tables and retrieves huge recordsets for reporting purposes. As you will see later, normalization should be eased up a little to optimize the performance of this type of system.

Chapter 1, "The Structured Query Language (SQL) Standards," described the basics of SQL and how tables can be joined on the primary-foreign key combinations to retrieve the data in a form that serves the purpose of front-end applications. Table joins do improve performance in OLTP systems, but they might impair performance in OLAP systems. This is true if multiple joins are used in a query to retrieve data from several tables. Let's take the database you built in the data normalization section as an example. Assume that this database includes data for 3,000,000 books. If you try to report all quotations on the books published by Sams, you end up writing a query that has four table joins (see Listing 2.1). If the report should include some of the author and publisher information, that information is retrieved through the table joins.

2
Relational Databases

LISTING 2.1 Selecting Data for a Report from the Book Collection Database

```
SELECT   b.Publisher,
t.Topic,
b.Book_Title,
b.ISBN,
q.Quote,
q. Quote_Page_Number,
a.AuthorName,
a.Notes
FROM   Topics t INNER JOIN
(Books b INNER JOIN
(Authors a INNER JOIN Quotations q ON
a.AuthorID = q.AuthorID) ON
b.BookID = q.BookID) ON
t.TopicID = b.TopicID
WHERE  b.Publisher = 'Sams';
```

The query results in multiple scans of the tables involved in the SQL statement. The `quotation` table is scanned first. For each record scanned, the `books` table is scanned to get the author ID. After the author ID is retrieved, the `authors` table is scanned to retrieve other needed author information, such as the first name and last name. Also, scanning the `books` table results in retrieving a topic ID, which is used to scan the `topics` table to retrieve the topic text. As you can see, there is a lot of work for the database engine to do to build this simple report. This amount of work causes the query to be slow and use the database server resources for valuable time.

Eliminating one join improves the database engine performance, and eliminating another join practically makes it fly. So how can you do that? The answer is simply by breaking the normal form rules, denormalizing some of the tables, and allowing for some redundancy. To eliminate the join between the `books` table and the `topics` table, all you need to do is include the topic (text) in the `books` table, instead of the `topic_id`. The previous SQL statement would then look like Listing 2.2.

LISTING 2.2 Selecting Data for a Report from the Book Collection Database in a More Efficient Way

```
SELECT   b.Publisher,
b.Topic,
b.Book_Title,
b.ISBN,
q.Quote,
q. Quote_Page_Number,
a.AuthorName,
a.Notes
FROM    Books b INNER JOIN
(Authors a INNER JOIN Quotations q ON
a.AuthorID = q.AuthorID) ON
b.BookID = q.BookID
WHERE  b.Publisher = 'Sams';
```

Use of Data Modeling and Database Design Tools

There are many computerized tools that help database designers generate schemas normalized to at least the third normal form (3NF). These tools use what is known as *entity-relationship (ER) diagrams* to describe the data. Designed to work with the most popular database management systems in the market, they help designers produce scripts to create the database after it has been designed. They also help designers reverse-engineer existing databases, creating ER diagrams that help analyze their design and modify it if necessary. One of the most popular tools is ERWIN, which is produced by Logic Works. Microsoft Visual Studio allows such data modeling in a simpler, more limited fashion. Microsoft Access allows you to do the same for its databases.

Summary

You have seen how relational databases evolved from earlier kinds of data representations and how such databases can be optimized. You also looked at the different normalization forms available with these databases, their benefits, and how to achieve them. Because the table is the only structure in SQL, I will focus on how it can be created and manipulated in the next chapter.

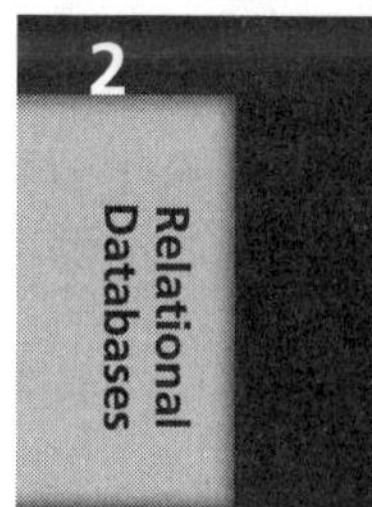
2
Relational
Databases

Table Creation and Manipulation

In This Chapter

It is difficult for programmers to separate the concept of `table` versus `file`. In SQL databases, data is stored in sets (tables), not in files. In other words, data stored in a particular table does not map exactly to one operating system file. Instead, several tables can be stored in the same file, and a table can span several files. So how do you design and create such tables, and how do you change the tables' design and optimize their use? The answer to this question, along with others, is found in this chapter. The topics covered in this chapter include the following:

- What is table manipulation?
- Table constraints and column definitions
- Creating and handling indexes

Table Manipulation

The table is the only data structure in SQL. Tables in SQL-92 can be permanent base tables, virtual tables (views), or even temporary, global, and shared tables. Not every database management system vendor implements all these types. However, they all implement the base tables, which are discussed in detail in this chapter. Tables are simply created in SQL with the `CREATE TABLE` statement. After they are created, you can change their design by using the `ALTER TABLE` statement, or drop them from the database with the `DROP TABLE` statement. This section describes in detail the syntax for these two important statements, with examples illustrating how they can be used.

An advantage of having one structure in SQL, the table, is that all SQL operations return the same structure. This makes the SQL language uniform and void of irregularities that might require a good deal of work to convert the structures to one uniform model. Therefore, tables in relational databases are the most important objects. They are usually created by the database administrator and used over and over. Database application developers can also create their own tables, drop them, and manipulate them in the development process.

The `CREATE TABLE SQL` Statement

`CREATE TABLE`, shown in Listing 3.1, is the SQL statement used by all database management systems to create tables.

Note

The table name must be unique in the schema for SQL operations involving tables to succeed. For instance, a CREATE TABLE statement cannot use a table name that already exists in the schema. If it does, an error is returned.

LISTING 3.1 The Basic Syntax of the **CREATE TABLE** SQL Statement

```
CREATE TABLE <table name> (<column and constraint definition list>)
Where:
< column and constraint definition list > =
(<column definition>¦<table constraint definition>,
 <column definition>¦<table constraint definition>,
    .........)
and where:
<column definition> =   <column name><data type>
      <[DEFAULT]><[NOT NULL]>
and:
<constraint definition> =   CONSTRAINT <[constraint name]>
        <primary key constraint>
        <foreign key constraint>
        <uniqueness constraint>
        <check constraint>
        <[NOT]><[DEFERRABLE]>
        <[INITIALLY IMMEDIATE]>
        <[INITIALLY DEFERRED]>
```

Listing 3.1 shows the basic syntax for the CREATE TABLE statement. The statement defines column names and definitions and constraint names and definitions. These items are described in detail in the section "Table Constraints and Column Definitions" later in this chapter.

As a simple example of this statement, let's create a table to hold employee data, and call it tblEmployee. The table includes the following fields and constraints:

- Employee_No: employee number, primary key
- First_Name: employee first name, not null
- Last_Name: employee last name, not null
- Department_ID: department ID to which the employee belongs

- `Phone_No`: employee office phone number
- `Hire_Date`: date of hire
- `Emp_Title`: employee title

Listing 3.2 shows how this table can be created.

LISTING 3.2 Creating the Employee Table (**tblEmployee**)

```
CREATE TABLE tblEmployee
  (Employee_No  INTEGER PRIMARY KEY,
   First_Name  VARCHAR(20) NOT NULL,
   Last_Name  VARCHAR(30) NOT NULL,
   Department_ID  INTEGER,
   Phone_No  CHAR(10),
   Hire_Date  DATETIME,
   Emp-Title  VARCHAR(50))
```

The ALTER TABLE SQL Statement

The ALTER TABLE statement, introduced in the SQL-92 standard, is used to change the definition of the table structure. Such changes include adding a field, dropping a field, changing a field definition, adding a field constraint, and dropping a field constraint. Field definitions and constraints are discussed later in this chapter in the section "Table Constraints and Column Definitions." The basic syntax of this statement is presented in Listing 3.3.

LISTING 3.3 The Basic Syntax of the **ALTER TABLE** SQL Statement

```
ALTER TABLE <table name> <alter table action>
Where:
<alter table action> =
([Add column] <column name><column definition>¦
 [Alter column]<column name><column alter action>¦
 [Drop column]<column name>¦
 [Add table constraint definition]¦
 [Drop constraint]<constraint name><drop behavior>¦
```

Let's take a closer look at the ALTER TABLE statement. The table name has to be a valid name in the schema, or the DBMS returns an error indicating that the requested object does not exist. The `alter table action` part of the statement includes several optional actions, discussed in the following paragraphs.

The Add column option allows adding a new column to the table definition. The column name must also be unique in the table. When adding a column, you can specify the data type, length, and other properties of the table column. Listing 3.4 shows an example for the Add column section.

LISTING 3.4 Adding the Fax and Email Fields to the Employee Table

```
ALTER TABLE   tblEmployee
ADD COLUMN FaxNumber CHAR(10)
ALTER TABLE   tblEmployees
ADD COLUMN emailAddress CHAR(30)
```

The Alter column optional action allows changing certain properties of the columns. These changes vary widely among the different database management systems. However, almost all DBMSs allow changing the column's data type to a compatible one. For example, you can change the column data type from integer to long or from varchar(5) to varchar(40). Generally, however, you cannot change the data type from integer to char(). You can also add the DEFAULT clause to change the column's default value or the CHECK clause to the alter field action. These clauses are discussed later in the chapter (see "Table Constraints and Column Definitions").

> **Note**
>
> Most DBMSs allow changing shorter definitions to longer ones, but not the opposite. For example, you can alter the column data type from char(5) to char(50), but not from char(50) to char(5). The reason for this restriction is to avoid data truncation or loss caused by the conversion process.

The Drop column action allows dropping a column definition from the table. SQL-92 provides two options for this action: the RESTRICT option and the CASCADE option. The RESTRICT option prevents dropping a column that is referenced in other schema objects. The CASCADE option, on the other hand, deletes all objects referencing the dropped column in the schema. These two options are not implemented by all RDBMS vendors. Listing 3.5 illustrates how you can use the Drop column action. Listing 3.5 adds a column called "gender" to the employee table, tblemployee, then removes it.

LISTING 3.5 Dropping the Gender Field from the Employee Table

```
ALTER TABLE tblEmployee
ADD COLUMN gender CHAR(1);
```

LISTING 3.5 CONTINUED

```
ALTER TABLE      tblEmployee
DROP COLUMN gender;
```

> **Tip**
>
> If CASCADE and RESTRICT options are available in the database system you are using, use the RESTRICT option to find out whether any other objects are referencing the column you are dropping in the schema.

The Add table constraint definition option allows you to add a constraint related to the altered field. It is strongly recommended that you name such constraints. This practice makes the constraint easier to drop if you need to in the future. If you don't name your constraint, dropping it involves rebuilding the whole database schema.

Finally, the Drop constraint option drops the constraint referenced by the constraint name part. The options available for the drop behavior option are the RESTRICT and CASCADE options, discussed earlier in this section.

The DROP TABLE SQL Statement

The DROP TABLE statement allows you to remove the table from the database schema. This statement must be used with a great deal of caution. After a table is dropped, all the data it holds is lost. The basic syntax for this statement is shown in Listing 3.6.

LISTING 3.6 The Basic Syntax for the DROP TABLE Statement

```
DROP TABLE <table name> <drop table options>
Where:
<drop table options> =
 [RESTRICT] ¦
 [CASCADE]
```

The table name has to be a valid for the drop operation to succeed. Most DBMS vendors use the DROP TABLE statement without requiring the drop table options. These options include RESTRICT and CASCADE:

- If the RESTRICT option is specified, and another database object references the table to be dropped, the drop operation fails.
- If the CASCADE option is specified, then any schema objects referencing the dropped table are also dropped.

As an example, Listing 3.7 shows the statement used to drop the employee table, tblEmployee.

LISTING 3.7 Dropping the Employee Table (**tblEmployees**) from the Management Schema with the **RESTRICT** Option

```
DROP TABLE management.tblEmployee RESTRICT
```

Table Constraints and Column Definitions

The CREATE TABLE statement defines the fields that need to be created as part of the table definition. It also defines the table constraints that will apply to the table created. Field and constraint definitions can also be defined, or altered, with the ALTER TABLE statement mentioned earlier in this chapter. In this section, I present a detailed description of defining such items.

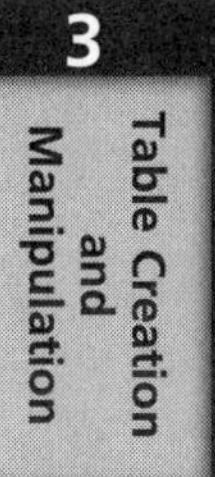
3
Table Creation
and
Manipulation

Field Definitions

Starting with the right column definition is important in database design. Failing to define the table columns adequately results in wasted time and subsequent redesign later in the database application development process. Listing 3.8 shows the basic syntax for column definition.

LISTING 3.8 The Basic Syntax for Column Definition

```
<column definition> =
<column name><data type>
       <[DEFAULT]>
       <<NOT] NULL]>
<[column constraint]>
```

This simple statement indicates that each column must have a valid unique name within the table. It also allows defining a data type for the column. This data type can be changed with the ALTER TABLE statement (see the previous section on the ALTER TABLE statement). SQL data types are explained in detail in Chapter 4, "Data Types." The statement also allows setting a default value for the column with the `DEFAULT` clause. The default value is assigned to the column when new records are created, unless different values are assigned to it. Finally, this statement enables you to add column constraints, explained in the next section. Listing 3.9 presents an example of adding a field to an existing table and assigning a default value to it.

LISTING 3.9 Assigning a Default Value to a Table Column

```
ALTER TABLE   tblEmployee
        ADD Region DEFAULT 'GREAT LAKES'
```

Table Constraints

Table constraints give the database designer great flexibility and power in controlling the data entered in the table. This advantage is possible because each row is validated against all the table's existing constraints. The basic syntax for table constraints is shown in Listing 3.10.

LISTING 3.10 The Basic Syntax of the Table Constraint Definition

```
<constraint definition> =   CONSTRAINT <[constraint name]>
        <primary key constraint>
        <foreign key constraint>
        <uniqueness constraint>
        <check constraint>
        <[NOT>]<[DEFERRABLE]>
        <[INITIALLY IMMEDIATE]>
        <[INITIALLY DEFERRED]>
```

Listing 3.10 shows an optional parameter, the constraint name, followed by the type of the constraint. There are several possible types of constraints, including primary key, foreign key, uniqueness, check, and `NOT NULL` . These constraints are discussed in detail in the following sections.

`NOT NULL` Constraint

`NULL`, a special value in SQL, is available in all data types. It basically means that the value of the field is missing, not determined, or unknown. When used in math calculations, `NULL` produces null values. When used in logical expressions, NULL returns the `UNKNOWN` value, which gives SQL its three logical values: `TRUE`, `FALSE`, and `NULL` (or unknown). Nulls exhibit irregular behavior in SQL; sometimes they group together and sort correctly, but other times they don't group together and don't sort according to the expected way. The

NOT NULL constraint forces a defined non-null value for the column of concern when creating new records in the table, which might help avoid many of these irregularities.

Tip

Always use the NOT NULL constraint as a default for your tables, and then remove it only when you have a good reason. You can also guarantee that a column will not have a NULL as its value when a new record is added by specifying a DEFAULT value for it. However, you still need to use this constraint if you want to prevent users from updating the column value later to NULL.

Note

Although the CREATE TABLE statement specifies that field values can be NULL unless the NOT NULL constraint is used, some commercial database management systems assume the opposite. Sybase and Microsoft SQL Servers assume that all columns have non-null values unless explicitly specified in the CREATE TABLE statement.

Primary Key Constraint

The primary key constraint has been added to the ANSI SQL standard after having been adopted by IBM's DB2 for some time. Most RDBMS vendors added this constraint to their RDBMSs. The primary key constraint defines the column or group of columns that uniquely identify a row in the table. The values in the columns composing the primary key cannot be NULL, and their collective value has to be unique.

The syntax for the primary key constraint is shown in Listing 3.11.

LISTING 3.11 The Basic Syntax of the Primary Key Constraint

```
<Primary Key Constraint> = <column name[,column name[, column name]...]>
```

Listing 3.12 shows how the primary key of the Orders table is defined.

LISTING 3.12 Defining the Primary Key Constraint for the **Orders** Table

```
CREATE TABLE ORDERS
  (ORDER_NO  INTEGER NOT NULL,
   ORDER_DATE  DATE NOT NULL,
```

LISTING 3.12 CONTINUED

```
CUST_ID  INTEGER NOT NULL,
EMPLOYEE_ID  INTEGER,
PRODUCT_ID  INTEGER NOT NULL,
QUANTITY  INTEGER NOT NULL,
PRICE    MONEY NOT NULL,
PRIMARY KEY (ORDER_NO))
```

Foreign Key Constraint

The foreign key constraint defines a foreign key in the table and the relationship it creates to another table in the database. The basic syntax for this constraint is in Listing 3.13.

LISTING 3.13 The Basic Syntax of the Foreign Key Constraint

```
<Foreign Key Constraint> = <column name[,column name[, column name]...]>
  <REFERENCES>table name([column name[, column name]...])
  <MATCH  FULL¦PARTIAL>
  <ON DELETE  CASCADE¦SET NULL¦SET DEFAULT¦NO ACTION>
  <ON UPDATE  CASCADE¦SET NULL¦SET DEFAULT¦NO ACTION>
```

The preceding statement specifies the column (or columns) that form the foreign key constraint. It also references the parent table in the relationship and the columns in the parent table that correspond to the foreign key. A name for the relationship, not used in SQL data manipulation, is optional, but recommended if the key is to be dropped later.

The `MATCH` clause defines how `NULL`s should be treated when found as part of the foreign key. It defines how to match them to the parent table. The `ON DELETE` and `ON UPDATE` clauses specify what to do with the foreign key columns when a parent row is deleted or updated. These are the available options:

- `CASCADE`: If a parent row in this option is deleted or updated, foreign fields in children rows are also deleted or updated accordingly.
- `SET NULL`: If the parent row in this option is deleted or updated, the foreign fields in children rows are set to `NULL`.
- `SET DEFAULT`: If the parent row in this option is deleted or updated, the foreign fields in children rows are set to the default value.
- `NO ACTION`: If the parent row in this option is deleted or updated, the foreign fields in children rows are kept at their current values. This could result in orphan rows in the related table.

As an example of foreign key constraints, let's create the Orders table again, adding to it the appropriate foreign key constraints, as shown in Listing 3.14.

LISTING 3.14 Defining the Foreign Key Constraint for the Orders Table

```
CREATE TABLE ORDERS
  (ORDER_NO  INTEGER NOT NULL,
   ORDER_DATE  DATE NOT NULL,
   CUST_ID  INTEGER NOT NULL,
   EMPLOYEE_ID  INTEGER,
   PRODUCT_ID  INTEGER NOT NULL,
   QUANTITY  INTEGER NOT NULL,
   PRICE    MONEY NOT NULL,
   PRIMARY KEY (ORDER_NO),
 CONSTRAINT  ORDERED_BY
 FOREIGN KEY  (CUST_ID)
 REFERENCES  CUSTOMERS
   ONDELETE  CASCADE,
CONSTRAINT  SALES_REP
 FOREIGN KEY  (EMPLOYEE_ID)
 REFERENCES  EMPLOYEE
   ONDELETE  SET NULL,
CONSTRAINT  PRODUCT_ORDERED
 FOREIGN KEY  (PRODUCT_ID)
 REFERENCES  PRODUCTS
   ONDELETE  NO ACTION)
```


In this example, the Orders table is created with three foreign keys identifying three relationships (see Figure 3.1) with the names ORDERED_BY, SALES_REP, and PRODUCT_ORDERED. The three foreign keys are Cust_ID, which references the Customers table, EMPLOYEE_ID, which references the Employee table, and Product_ID, which references the Products table. When deleting a parent customer in the Customer table, the rows referencing the deleted customer in the Orders table are also deleted because of the ON DELETE CASCADE clause. If a parent row in the Employee table is deleted, the corresponding references to the deleted employee in the children rows of the Orders table are set to NULL. Finally, when a row in the Products table is deleted, the children rows in the Orders table are not affected.

Note

It is always a good idea to name the relationships created by foreign key constraints. Naming these relationships makes it easy to drop them later on.

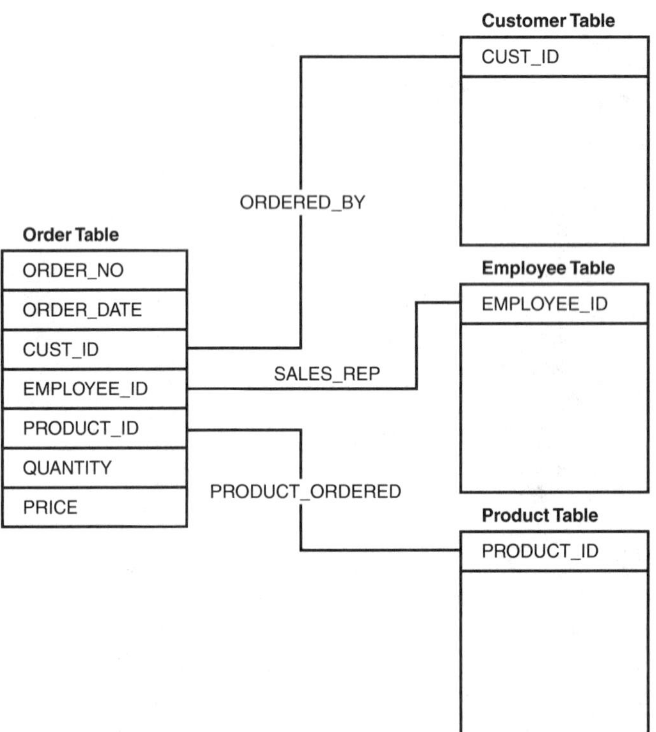

FIGURE 3.1
Foreign key constraints create three relationships between the `Orders` *table and the tables* `Customer`, `Employee`, *and* `Product`.

Unique Constraint

The unique constraint is defined in the `UNIQUE` clause of the `CREATE TABLE` statement. It implies that the column or group of columns referenced in the appropriate clause has a unique value for each row. You might wonder about the difference between the unique and the primary key constraints. There are actually subtle differences between the two constraints. The primary key gets an automatic `NOT NULL` constraint, but the unique constraint allows for a maximum of one `NULL` value in its rows, unless the `NOT NULL` constraint was explicitly used. Also, you can have one primary key constraint on a table, but you can theoretically have multiple unique key constraints in a table.

The syntax for the unique constraint is shown in Listing 3.15.

LISTING 3.15 The Basic Syntax of the Unique Constraint

```
<Unique Constraint> = <column name[,column name[, column name]...]>
```

The following line of a CREATE TABLE statement is an example of a composite unique constraint:

```
UNIQUE (First_Name, Last_Name, Date_Of_Birth)
```

Check Constraint

This constraint, specified in the CREATE TABLE statement, is another integrity feature in SQL-92. It defines a check condition that is checked every time an insert, update, or delete is attempted on the table. If the check constraint remains True after the update, the update is allowed; otherwise, the database engine disallows the update and returns an error. Listing 3.16 shows an example of a simple check constraint, which makes sure an order's price value in the Orders table is greater than $0.00.

LISTING 3.16 Example of Using a Check Constraint to Validate Inserted Values

```
CREATE TABLE ORDERS
  (ORDER_NO  INTEGER NOT NULL,
   ORDER_DATE  DATE NOT NULL,
   CUST_ID  INTEGER NOT NULL,
   EMPLOYEE_ID  INTEGER,
   PRODUCT_ID  INTEGER NOT NULL,
   QUANTITY  INTEGER NOT NULL,
   PRICE    MONEY NOT NULL,
   PRIMARY KEY (ORDER_NO),
 CONSTRAINT  ORDERED_BY
 FOREIGN KEY  (CUST_ID)
 REFERENCES  CUSTOMERS
   ONDELETE  CASCADE,
CONSTRAINT  SALES_REP
 FOREIGN KEY  (EMPLOYEE_ID)
 REFERENCES  EMPLOYEE
   ONDELETE  SET NULL,
CONSTRAINT  PRODUCT_ORDERED
 FOREIGN KEY  (PRODUCT_ID)
 REFERENCES  PRODUCTS
   ONDELETE  NO ACTION,
   CHECK    (Price>=0.00))
```

Notice the last line of code in Listing 3.16. It is the line that identifies the check constraint on the table.

Creating and Handling Indexes

Indexes are provided by most SQL-based database management systems as an important physical storage structure, which allows quick access to certain rows in the table based on the values of one or more columns. I discuss how indexes can be used to enhance query performance in Chapter 19, "Optimizing Query Performance." In this chapter, I focus on creating and dropping these structures. Though present in virtually every implementation, the CREATE/DROP INDEX statement is actually not part of the SQL-92 standard.

Creating Indexes

Indexes in database management systems resemble book indexes. Indexes store the column value along with a pointer to row location on disk, which enables the quick access. Figure 3.2 shows that the `Customer` table has two indexes: the primary key (`Cust_ID`) and the `Phone_Number` column.

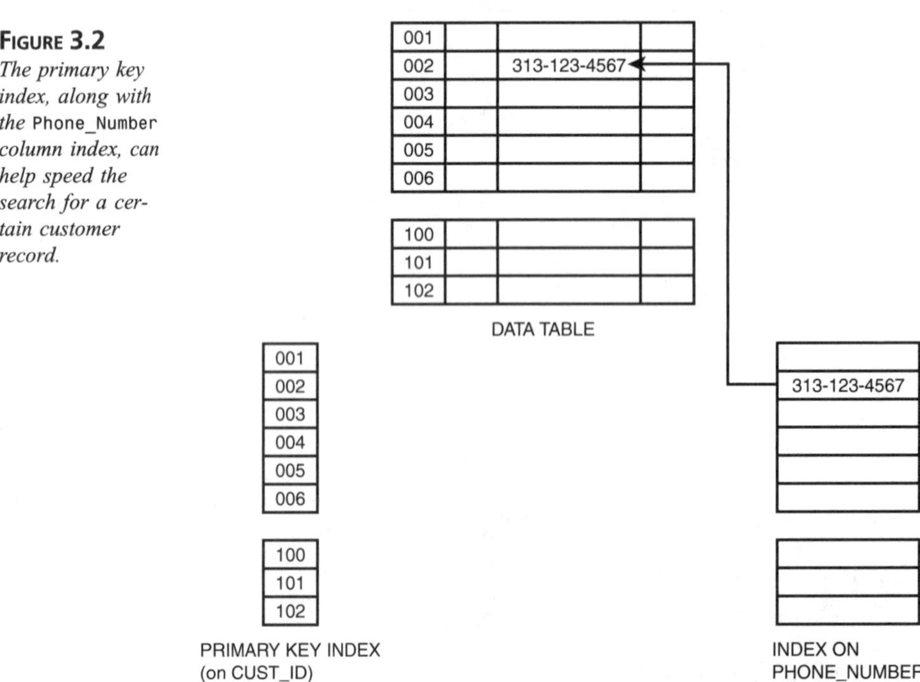

FIGURE 3.2
The primary key index, along with the `Phone_Number` *column index, can help speed the search for a certain customer record.*

For developers using SQL, indexes are transparent, which means, in most cases, they are not aware of using an index in their SQL statements. For example, Listing 3.17 selects a record in the `Customer` table based on the indexed column `Phone_Number`.

LISTING 3.17 Selecting a Row Based on an Indexed Column Is Relatively Fast

```
SELECT   Cust_ID, First_Name, Last_Name,
Address, City, State, Zip, Phone_Number
FROM  customer
WHERE  Phone_Number = '313-123-4567'
```

> **Note**
>
> Some database management systems have tools to monitor the use of indexes in queries issued to the database engine. These systems also offer "hints" that force the use of a particular index. Such hints are placed in the SQL statements themselves, which makes it the developer's responsibility to make sure a particular index is being used.

When it receives this query, the database engine uses the index table to find the value of the phone number supplied in the `WHERE` clause of the SQL statement. This search is usually fast because the index rows are small and ordered. After the phone number is found in the index table, the pointer to the row is used to retrieve the row from disk quickly. If there were no index on the `Phone_Number` column, the database engine would have had to scan the `Customer` table row by row, examining the `Phone_Number` value for each field until it finds a match with the one provided. This process is much slower than using an index.

To create an index, you can use the `CREATE INDEX` SQL statement. The syntax for this statement is described in Listing 3.18.

LISTING 3.18 Syntax for the `CREATE INDEX` Statement

```
CREATE [UNIQUE] INDEX index name ON table name
       (column name [ASC¦DESC][, column name [ASC¦DESC],...])
```

In the statement above, an index name must be specified. The indexed columns are also specified, separated by commas. The statement also allows for ordering the values in the index table in an ascending or descending order if you choose to do so.

The preceding syntax is the generic syntax to create an index. Many RDBMSs add extensions to this statement that allow specifying the disk location of the index, the size of the index pages, the percentage of free space in the index page allocated for new rows, whether the index is clustered, and so forth. These specifications give you added tools for performance tuning.

Note

Clustered indexes are used to arrange the data on disk similarly to its arrangement in the index table. This arrangement makes searching for the data even faster because the data is on the leaf level of the index pages. Sybase and Microsoft SQL Server make extensive use of this feature. However, a maximum of only one clustered index can be allowed for each table, compared to the much larger number of non-clustered indexes allowed.

As an example, to create the index on the `Phone_Number` column in the `Customer` table, you can use the statement in Listing 3.19.

LISTING 3.19 Creating an Index on the `Phone_Number` Column in the `Customer` Table

```
CREATE UNIQUE INDEX idxPhone
ON customer(Phone_Number ASC)
```

Most database management systems index the primary key by default because database engines assume that the primary key field is the most likely field to be used in record searches.

Some of the guidelines for using indexes depend on the type of query you are executing. If you are performing searches and retrieves, indexes are helpful and justify the additional disk space they require. However, if you do a lot of updates, inserts, and deletes, excessive use of indexes could cause problems. Whenever a row is updated, inserted, or deleted, the index must be rebuilt, which affects the database engine's performance.

Choosing the right fields to index is important, too. It does not make much sense to index fields that have few distinct values, such as Boolean fields or fields specifying whether a person is male or female. With such fields, chances are you'll still scan a large portion of the index table.

Dropping Indexes

Dropping indexes is a simple process that can be done with the DROP INDEX statement. You can drop an index to rebuild it or because you don't need it any more. In either case, you use the following syntax:

```
DROP INDEX index name
```

For example, to drop the idxPhone index you created in Listing 3.19, write:

```
DROP INDEX idxPhone
```

Summary

Tables are the basic and only structure in the SQL standard. All other structures resulting from SQL operations have the table's basic architecture. For example, when SELECT statements are used to return recordsets in any programming language, the resulting recordsets have rows and columns similar to the tables they were based on. In this chapter, I explained how to create and manipulate this important structure in SQL. I also discussed how to deal with table columns and constraints and how indexes could be used to speed the search for data in tables. In the next chapter, I talk about the data that can fill the SQL tables, including the SQL standard data types, and the functions used in manipulating them. So sit back and enjoy.

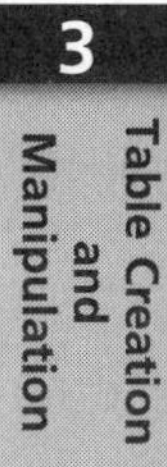
3
Table Creation
and
Manipulation

CHAPTER 4

Data Types

In This Chapter

ANSI SQL-92 introduced new data types that you can use to store data in a relational database that did not exist in the previous SQL standard. The temporal data types are some of these extensions. Today, commercial database management systems add even a wider variety of data types to handle situations stemming from the technical advancement in data storage and manipulation. This chapter discusses the SQL-92 data types that are common to every database management system and briefly discusses some of the newer data types introduced by database management system vendors. The topics covered in this chapter include

- Numeric data types
- Character data types
- Date and time data types
- Data type conversion
- `NULL`s and missing values

Numeric Data Types

Because SQL is not a procedural or object-oriented programming language, it has poor capabilities when it comes to arithmetic and mathematical operations. However, the SQL standard supports a wide array of numeric data types, which makes storing numeric values in a database fairly easy. Database management system vendors also add more numeric types to support certain kinds of data. An example is the `money` data type available in SQL Server, which is actually a decimal that displays a currency sign in its inputs and outputs. The SQL standard also supports some mathematical and statistical functions that you can use in queries to perform some of these operations. The following sections discuss numeric data types supported by the SQL standard and some of mappings to data types available in commercial RDBMSs.

Built-In and Extended SQL Standard Numeric Types

SQL Standard includes several numerical data types. These types are classified as exact or approximate based on their precision (P) and scale (S). Exact numeric types include

- `numeric`
- `decimal`

- `integer`
- `smallint`

Approximate numeric types include

- `float`
- `real`
- `double`

These data types are explained in detail in the following sections.

Note

Precision is a positive number (1 or greater) that identifies the number of significant digits (the maximum total number of digits that can be stored, both to the left and to the right of the decimal point). Scale is a zero or positive number that identifies the number of decimal places available to the right of the decimal point in the numerical value. For example, the number 12345.67 has a precision of 7 and a scale of 2.

Numeric and Decimal

The `numeric` type specifies an exact precision and scale to be used. For example, `numeric(5,2)` specifies that the number will have exactly five significant digits and exactly two decimal places. The `decimal` type specifies a minimum precision and an exact scale to be used. For example, `decimal(5,2)`, abbreviated as `dec(5,2)`, specifies at least five significant digits and exactly two decimal places.

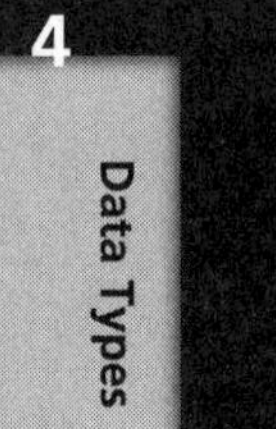

The precision attribute of this data type determines the amount of storage it needs on disk or in memory. Table 4.1 shows the relationship between precision and the amount of storage needed in most database management systems on the Windows NT platform.

TABLE 4.1 Precision and Storage Needs on Windows NT

Precision Range	*Storage (Bytes)*
1 to 9	5
10 to 19	9
20 to 28	13
29 to 38	17

Integer and Smallint

An `integer` (`int`) is a whole number, a `numeric` data type with zero scale, that can be positive, zero, or negative. Examples of this type are -1, 23, 2334, and 0. A `smallint` is an `integer` with smaller storage requirements or a smaller possible range.

> **Note**
>
> The implementation of `int` and `smallint` differs widely among database management systems. For example, in Microsoft SQL Server, an `int` can use up to 4 bytes of storage capacity, but a `smallint` can store only 2 bytes. There is even a third variation of integers in SQL Server, the `tinyint`, which needs 1 byte of storage capacity. In Oracle, just like the SQL-92 standard, an `integer` does not have any size specified.

Float, Real, and Double Precision

The `float`, `real`, and `double` data types are approximate, not exact. They consist of a mantissa and an exponent. The mantissa is a signed numeric value, and the exponent is a signed integer that specifies the magnitude of the mantissa. The value of an approximate number is calculated by multiplying the mantissa by 10 raised to the power of the exponent:

$$1.5E4 = 1.5 \times 10^4 = 15{,}000$$

In this example, the mantissa is 1.5, and the exponent is 4. The precision in these numbers is the number of significant digits in the mantissa. In the example, the precision, P, is 2.

The `float` data type has a binary precision equal to or greater than the value given, whereas the precision of the `decimal` data type is usually defined by its implementation.

> **Note**
>
> Approximate numeric data types do not store the exact values specified. Instead, the value they store is an extremely close approximation of the specified value. Although it may become noticeable in some calculations, the tiny difference between the specified value and the stored approximation is not noticeable in many cases. Because of the nature of the approximate data types, you should not use them when exact numeric behavior is required, such as in financial applications, in operations involving rounding, or in equality checks. Instead, use the exact data types, such as `integer` and `decimal`.

Warning

Do not use fields with approximate data types in the WHERE clause of an SQL statement that uses the equality (=) or inequality (< >) comparison operators. It is likely that no records will match the search criteria in the former case, and all records may match it in the latter. Instead of anApproxColumn = another ApproxColumn, the recommended approach is to use a tolerance, such as ABS(anApproxColumn - anotherApproxColumn) < 0.000001 (where 0.000001 is the tolerance), because the latter approach takes rounding of the approximate data into account.

Additional Commercial RDBMS Numeric Data Types

Database management vendors implement their own data types to facilitate storage and retrieval of certain kinds of numeric data. The most obvious example is the `money` data type implemented in SQL Server. Actually, there is also a `smallmoney` data type. These data types allow for the display of a currency sign in front of the real number. An example of a number in the `money` data type is `$5.30`.

Numeric Conversions and Functions

Numeric data types can be converted from one type to another by using SQL-92 Standard or RDBMS-specific functions. However, before I discuss converting numeric data types to other numeric data types, you need to understand the basics of truncation and rounding in SQL.

Truncation and Rounding

When moving data from numeric columns in one RDBMS to another, you might get some surprises. You might find that the moved data has changed. This happens mostly because the receiving database engine finds that the imported data does not fit in the field it is going into due to the RDBMS-specific storage requirements of the field's data type. Therefore, the receiving database engine truncates the data before accepting it. To avoid such surprises, you need to understand the RDBMS-specific data type implementation and how the database engine performs its truncation and rounding.

In SQL-92, truncation is defined as truncation toward zero. According to this, 1.5 is truncated to 1 and 2.8 is truncated to 2. This is usually consistent among RDBMSs for positive numbers. However, for negative numbers, some systems truncate toward zero, making a -2.5 become -2.0 after truncation, or away from the zero mark, making the same -2.5 become -3.0 after truncation.

Many programming languages have different algorithms for rounding numbers. SQL-92 does not set any rules for rounding numbers in arithmetic calculations. Therefore, rounding follows the individual RDBMS implementation for the most part. However, most RDBMSs agree on the following common method.

Look at the digit to be dropped, and follow either of the following rules:

- If the digit is 0, 1, 2, 3, or 4, drop it and leave the next digit to the left intact. For example, 2.3453 is rounded to 2.345.
- If the dropped digit is 6, 7, 8, or 9, drop it and increment the next digit to the left by one. For example, 2.3456 is rounded to 2.346.
- Finally, if the dropped digit is 5, many rules could apply. The simplest rule is to drop the 5 and increment the next digit to the left by one. The goal of the more complex rules is to round up about half the values. The most popular of these rules is to look at the digit to the left of the dropped digit. If this digit is odd, it is left alone; if it is even, it is incremented by one. For example, 2.345 is rounded to 2.35, and 2.335 is rounded to 2.33.

The `CAST()` Function

The SQL-92 function used to perform data type conversion is the `CAST()` function. You can use it for numeric and non-numeric data types, and therefore, I mention it again in later sections. The general syntax for this function is

```
Converted Number = CAST ( Number AS Data type )
```

In this syntax line, the *`Number`* argument is the number you want to convert its data type. The *`Number`* argument can be a field name, a number, or an expression. It can even be a `NULL` value. The `Data type` argument is the type you want the number to have after the conversion. The following example uses this function:

```
CAST(-2.3 AS INT) = -2
```

Warning

Be careful when you use the `CAST()` function when converting a data type from one numeric type to another. For example, if you try to convert the `numeric24,533,442,323.45` to an `integer` in SQL Server, you will get an overflow error because the value of the number exceeds the storage capacity of the `integer` data type in SQL Server. Note the following code line:

```
SELECT CAST(24533442323.45 AS INT)
```

The server returns the error message:

```
Server: Msg 8115, Level 16, State 3, Line 1
Arithmetic overflow error converting numeric to data type int.
```

RDBMSs introduce many functions to perform data type conversions. These functions allow for more flexibility in how the output is formatted. For example, in SQL Server, the `CONVERT()` function works similar to the `CAST()` function, except that it allows for an additional optional argument called `style`. This argument allows for formatting the output in different ways. Oracle also has its own conversion functions; the one that deals with numeric data is `to_number`. This function converts a valid expression to a number from character types (`char` and `varchar`). The following query illustrates using the Oracle `TO_NUMBER()` function to retrieve a certain employee name and zip code from the Employees table:

```
SELECT   FirstName || ' ' || LastName Name,
TO_NUMBER(ZIP_CODE) ZipCode
FROM   EMPLOYEES
WHERE  EMP_ID = 123;
```

The result of this statement is something like

```
Name           ZipCode
John Smith       44004
```

Arithmetic Operations and Other Functions

SQL supports the four basic arithmetic operations: addition (+), subtraction (-), multiplication (*), and division (/). The order of precedence is multiplication, division, addition, and then subtraction. Just like other programming languages, SQL allows for the use of parentheses, which have priority in deciding the order of operations. In `4 + 5 * 3 = 19`, the multiplication is performed first, followed by the addition. In `(4 + 5) * 3 = 27`, the addition is performed first because of the parentheses, followed by the multiplication.

Warning

When performing arithmetic calculations, pay attention to the order of execution of the arithmetic operations; otherwise, you might get some unwelcome error. For example, let's say that `maxint` is the maximum integer an RDBMS can accept, and let us say you write the operation `maxint + maxint - maxint`. This form will produce an overflow error because the addition is carried out first.

To avoid this error, you might want to write the statement as `maxint + (maxint - maxint)`. This form results in `maxint` and no error because the subtraction will be carried out first.

The different flavors of SQL add many more numeric functions, which are not included in the SQL-92 standard. The following is a list of the most popular of these functions:

- Square root (`SQRT`) calculates the square root of a number. As an example, you can write

  ```
  SELECT SQRT(64) as SQUARE_ROOT;
  ```

  The result is `SQUARE_ROOT = 8`.

- Modulus (`MOD`) calculates the modulus resulting from dividing two numbers. For example, you can write the following statement:

  ```
  SELECT MOD(15, 7) AS MODULUS;
  ```

  The result is `MODULUS = 1`.

- Power (`EXP(num, p)`or `POWER(num, p)`) raises a number (`num`) to a specified power (`p`). The following is an example of using this function:

  ```
  SELECT EXP(2, 3) AS Power_3;
  ```

  The result is `Power_3 = 8`.

- Absolute value (`ABS`) calculates the absolute value of a number:

  ```
  SELECT ABS(-4) AS ABSOLUTE;
  ```

  The result is `ABSOLUTE = 4`.

- `ROUND(num, dig)` rounds a number (`num`) to a specified number of decimal digits (`dig`). See the section "Truncation and Rounding" earlier in this chapter for more details on this function.

- Sine (`SIN`) calculates the sine of an angle.

- Cosine (`COS`) calculates the cosine of an angle.

- Tangent (`TAN`) calculates the tangent of an angle.

- Cotangent (`ATAN`) calculates the cotangent of an angle.

- Logarithm to base 10 (`LOG`) calculates the base 10 logarithm of a number.

- Natural logarithm (`LN`) calculates the base `e` logarithm of a number, where `e` is approximately `2.718281828459`.

There are many other functions. Consult your DBMS documentation to determine which functions are supported.

Date and Time Data Types

Date and time data types, referred to as temporal data types, are well described in SQL-92. The standard has rules for converting from numeric and character strings into these data types. A schema table for global time zone information is used to synchronize all date and time types.

All SQL flavors have a `DATE` data type, and most of them have a `TIME` and `TIMESTAMP` data type. SQL Server combines the two in a `DATETIME` data type. In the following sections, I discuss how SQL handles these data types.

Handling Dates

The ANSI SQL-92 format for dates is called the calendar date format and has a four-digit year, followed by a two-digit month, which is followed by a two-digit day. For example, May 15, 1999, is written as 1999-05-15. With this, SQL-92 adheres to international standards and avoids language-specific abbreviations (such as Aug for August).

If RDBMS vendors stick to the SQL-92 standard in representing dates, they do not have to worry about year 2000 issues. However, very few if any vendors follow the SQL-92 standard. Many represent dates with a two-digit year in the current century. Such representation can lead to serious problems at the end of the 20th century. Many analyses and books and articles have discussed these issues to the extent that they created some kind of panic, making corporations and government agencies spend hundreds of millions of dollars to solve them. Discussing the specifics of these issues is not in the scope of this book.

Note

In the database world, Y2K problems stem not only from date fields, but also from fields that rely on dates in their structure. For example, you might want to create a unique field in a table using the short date (the date with a two-digit year) and append an auto-incrementing counter to it. The problem could arise if the database is replicated among several company branches using the same scheme to create the unique field. If at some point in the future the replicas are merged to form one central database, duplicates are likely to occur. In such situations, the database engine may crash or, worse yet, produce wrong results, attaching child records to the wrong parent record.

Handling Times and Timestamps

SQL-92 handles time and timestamps in great detail. Although not all RDBMS systems go into the same detail, I still discuss how SQL-92 handles these two important issues.

Handling Times

In handling times, you should consider the time zones if the database will span more than one time zone. To do this, you usually store the universal time (GMT) in the time field and add a field that holds the offset between GMT and the local time. For example, let's say an application keeps track of the date and time customers first contact your organization. If a New York customer contacts you on February 1, 1999, at 11:00 local time, you store the time value in the database as 16:00. However, in the offset field, you have the value of -5 hours, the difference between local and GMT time.

> **Note**
>
> It is good practice to use the military time scheme, which expresses time in terms of 24 hours. For instance, 4:00 p.m. is stored as 16:00 hrs. This scheme is less prone to errors than the a.m./p.m. scheme and is easier to read, display, and store.

SQL-92 includes a time data type that is rarely implemented by DBMS vendors. This type is called `INTERVAL`, and as the name implies, it expresses a unit of time duration, rather than a fixed point in time. Duration is measured in `YEAR` or `MONTH` in one class of this data type, called year-month interval, and in other time units (`DAY`, `HOUR`, `MINUTE`, and `SECOND`) in the second class of this data type, which is called day-time interval. Only Oracle Corporation implements this data type in its RDBMS.

Handling Timestamps

A timestamp expresses a fixed point in time to a particular precision, or number of decimal places. This precision depends on the system capabilities. A `timestamp` value is a unique value in a database. For example, `timestamp (6)` expresses time given to the microsecond precision. The minimum precision accepted according to SQL-92 is five decimal places. Timestamps are a good way to mark when a particular event took place. Let's say you need to keep records of the exact times customers submit their orders. In this case, a timestamp is a great way to mark that time and ensure the uniqueness of the record.

Note

In most SQL implementations, the value in the `timestamp`column is updated every time a row containing that column is inserted or updated. This property makes a `timestamp` column a poor candidate for keys, especially primary keys. If a `timestamp` column were made a primary key, any update to a record in the table will change the corresponding key value. This results in creating orphan child records that rely on the original `timestamp` value.

Most SQL implementations require that only one column in a table can be the `timestamp` type. In some implementations, such as Microsoft SQL Server and Sybase SQL Server, the `timestamp` type has nothing to do with dates and times. In these systems, a `timestamp` is a binary number that indicates the relative sequence in which data modifications take place in the database.

Database engines can also use timestamps in recovery algorithms. Such systems stamp every data page with a `timestamp` value, which makes the recovery of such pages in cases of failure an easier job for the database engine.

Using Dates and Time Types in Queries

SQL-92 provides several simple date/time functions that return the current date, time, and timestamp:

- `CURRENT_DATE()` returns the current date of the system.
- `CURRENT_TIME(`*`Precision`*`)` returns the current system time with the required precision.
- `CURRENT_TIMESTAMP(`*`Precision`*`)` returns the current system timestamp with the required precision.
- `EXTRACT(`*`p`*`FROM`*`s`*`)` the date part (day, hour, year, and so on) from the date argument, *`s`*.

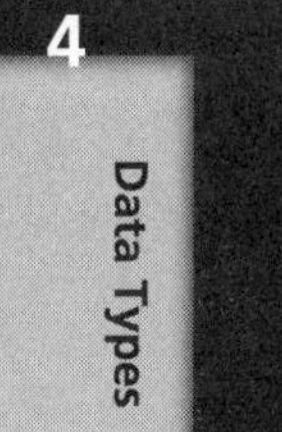

Despite the functions provided by SQL-92 to handle dates and times, RDBMSs handle dates and time data types in queries in different manners. Many of these systems provide a variety of functions to handle date and time queries. For example, in some SQL implementations, such as Oracle, adding a number `x` to a date will yield another date `x` days ahead from the original date. In SQL Server, the same functionality is also provided through the `DateAdd()` function. In this section, I examine how two of the most popular RDBMSs handle dates and times in queries. The two systems are Oracle and Microsoft SQL Server.

Dates and Times in Oracle Queries

Date arithmetic in Oracle is pretty simple. Oracle interprets number constants in arithmetic date expressions as numbers of days. For example, `SYSDATE + 1` is tomorrow. `SYSDATE - 7` is one week ago. `SYSDATE + (30/1440)` is half an hour from now. Subtracting the `HireDate` column of the Employees table from `SYSDATE` returns the number of days since each employee was hired. You cannot multiply or divide date values.

> **Note**
>
> `SYSDATE` is the Oracle function that returns the current system date and time value to the second precision. This value is based on the internal clock of the system Oracle is installed on.

As an example of using date arithmetic in Oracle, the following query returns the employee name and duration of hire in days and years, from the Employees table:

```
SELECT     firstname ¦¦ ' ' ¦¦ lastname EmployeeName,
    HireDate - SYSDATE  DaysDuration,
    (HireDate - SYSDate)/365  YearsDuration
FROM    Employees;
```

The return from this query looks like

```
EmployeeName   DaysDuration    YearsDuration
Mike Doe       1825            5.00
July Smith     1643            4.50
John Smith     120             0.33
```

Oracle provides more useful functions for date and time operations:

- `ADD_MONTHS(`*d*`,` *n*`)` adds a number of months, *n*, to the given date, *d*. As an example, the following query returns the current system date plus one month:

  ```
  SELECT  SYSDATE,
   ADD_MONTHS(SYSDATE, 1) NextMonth
  FROM DUAL;
  ```

  The result of the query is

  ```
  SYSDATE      NextMonth
  20-MAY-99    20-JUN-99
  ```

Note

If the day component of the resulting month is outside the range of that month, the last day of that month is returned. For example, `ADD_MONTH('31-AUG-99', 1)` returns `'30-SEP-99'`.

- `LAST_DAY(d)` returns the last day of the month of the date *d*. For example, use the following query to return the remaining number of days in the current month:

  ```
  SELECT  SYSDATE,
   LAST_DAY(SYSDATE) - SYSDATE DaysRemaining
  FROM DUAL;
  ```

  The result of the query is

  ```
  SYSDATE     DaysRemaining
  20-MAY-99   11
  ```

- `MONTHS_BETWEEN(` *d1*, *d2*`)` returns the number of months between the two given dates, *d1*, and *d2*. The fractional part is calculated based on a 31-day month. The following query returns the number of months between the current system date and three months ahead:

  ```
  SELECT  SYSDATE,
   MONTHS_BETWEEN(ADD_MONTHS(SYSDATE, 3), SYSDATE) MonthsToCome
  FROM DUAL;
  ```

  The result of the query is

  ```
  SYSDATE     MonthsToCome
  20-MAY-99   3
  ```

Other useful time and date functions provided by Oracle include

- `NEW_TIME (`*d*, *zone1*, *zone2*`)` returns the date and time value, *d*, in time zone *zone1* in a different time zone, *zone2*.

- `NEXT_DAY(`*d*, *string*`)` returns something like the date of the first Wednesday after a given date. For example, the following query returns the date of the first Thursday from now:

  ```
  SELECT  SYSDATE,
   NEXT_DAY(SYSDATE, 'THURSDAY') NextThursday
  FROM DUAL;
  ```

  The result of the query is

  ```
  SYSDATE     NextThursday
  20-MAY-99   27-May-99
  ```

- ROUND(*d*[, *format*]) returns the date, *d*, rounded to the unit specified by the format model, *format*. The argument *format* is optional. If it is omitted, *d* is rounded to the nearest day. The next example returns the SYSDATE rounded to the month and year level:

  ```
  SELECT  SYSDATE,
   ROUND(SYSDATE, 'MONTH') FirstOfMonth,
   ROUND(SYSDATE, 'YEAR') FirstOfYear,
   ROUND(TO_DATE('10-OCT-99'), 'YEAR') OCT_Date_Rounded
  FROM DUAL;
  ```

  The result of the query is

  ```
  SYSDATE    FirstOfMonth FirstOfYear OCT_Date_Rounded
  20-MAY-99  01-May-99    01-Jan-99   01-Jan-00
  ```

  As you can see in the previous example, rounding the October 1999 date to the nearest year returned the first day of the year 2000.

- TRUNC(*d*[, *format*]) returns the date, *d*, with the time portion specified by the format model, *format*. The argument *format* is optional. If it is omitted, *d* is truncated to the nearest day. The next query returns the SYSDATE truncated to the month and year level:

  ```
  SELECT  SYSDATE,
   ROUND(SYSDATE, 'MONTH') FirstOfMonth,
   ROUND(SYSDATE, 'YEAR') FirstOfYear,
   ROUND(TO_DATE('10-OCT-99', 'YEAR')) OCT_Date_Rounded
  FROM DUAL;
  ```

  The result of the query is

  ```
  SYSDATE    FirstOfMonth FirstOfYear OCT_Date_Rounded
  20-MAY-99  01-May-99    01-Jan-99   01-Jan-99
  ```

  As you can see in the previous example, rounding the October 1999 date to the nearest year returned the first day of the year 1999.

- TO_CHAR(*d* [, *format* [, *nlsParameters*>), Date conversion converts the date data type, *d*, to a VARCHAR2 data type in the format specified by the date format, *format*. If you omit *format*, *d* is converted to a VARCHAR2 value in the default date format. The following query displays sysdate as a VARCHAR2 data type value in a specific format:

  ```
  SELECT SYSDATE, TO_CHAR(SYSDATE, 'Month dd, yyyy') FormattedDate
  FROM DUAL;
  ```

  The result of the query is

  ```
  SYSDATE    FormattedDate
  20-MAY-99  May 20, 1999
  ```

- TO_DATE(*n* [, *format* [, *nlsParameters*>) converts *n* from a date data type to a CHAR or VARCHAR2 data type. If *format* is omitted, the default date format will be used. The following query shows how you can use this function to convert text to a date data type:

```
INSERT INTO Employees(firstname, lastname, HireDate)
VALUES('John', 'Doe',
TO_CHAR('May 20, 1999, 12:00 P.M.',
'Month dd, yyyy');
```

That list is a summary of most of the date-related functions and their uses in queries in Oracle. Next, I discuss such functions as they are used in Microsoft SQL Server 7.0.

Dates and Times in SQL Server Queries

In SQL Server, the date-related data types are datetimeand smalldatetime. SQL Server also provides a host of functions to deal with dates and time:

- DATEADD(*date part*, *number*, *date*) adds the *number* argument to the *date* argument in terms of the *date part* argument. For example, to add two months to 3/1/1999, you write

  ```
  SELECT DATEADD('month', 2, '3/1/1999')
  ```

  This gives the result '5/1/1999'.

- DATEDIFF(*date part*, *start date*, *end date*) finds the difference between the *start date* and *end date* arguments in terms of the *date part* argument. For example, to find the difference between 12/2/1999 and 12/23/1999 in days, you write

  ```
  SELECT DATEDIFF('day', '12/2/1999', '12/23/1999')
  ```

  The result is 21 days .

- DATENAME(*date part*, *date*) returns a character string representing the *date part* of the passed *date* argument. For example, to return the month of the date 12/2/1999, you write

  ```
  SELECT DATENAME('month', '12/2/1999')
  ```

  The result is December.

- DATEPART(*date part*, *date*) returns an integer representing the specified *date part* of the specified *date*. For example, to get the month date part of the date 12/2/1999, you write

  ```
  SELECT DATEPART('month', '12/2/1999')
  ```

  The result is 12.

- `DAY(date)` returns an integer representing the day date part of the specified date. For example, to find the day in the date 12/2/1999, you write

  ```
  SELECT DAY('12/2/1999')
  ```

  The result is `2`.

- `MONTH(date)` returns an integer representing the month date part of the specified date. For example, to find the month in the date 12/2/1999, you write

  ```
  SELECT MONTH('12/2/1999')
  ```

  The result is `12`.

- `YEAR(date)` returns an integer representing the year date part of the specified date. For example, to find the year in the date 12/2/1999, you write

  ```
  SELECT YEAR('12/2/1999')
  ```

  The result is `1999`.

- `GETDATE()` returns the current system date and time values in the Microsoft SQL Server internal format. For example, to find the system date and time, you write

  ```
  SELECT GETDATE()
  ```

  The result is something like `May 22 1999 1:32 PM`.

Note

It is important to note that you can look up the *date part* argument used by some of the date/time functions in Table 4.2. You can use the name for the *date part* argument or just a proper abbreviation when substituted in the preceding functions. For example, you can use either `year`, `yy`, or even `yyyy` for the *year* date part argument in the preceding functions.

TABLE 4.2 The *date part* Argument

Datepart	*Abbreviations*
year	yy, yyyy
quarter	qq, q
month	mm, m
dayofyear	dy, y
day	dd, d
week	wk, ww
weekday	dw
hour	hh
minute	mi, n

TABLE 4.2 The *date part* Argument

Datepart	*Abbreviations*
second	ss, s
millisecond	ms

Character Data Types

The main character data type used in pre-SQL-92 was the `character(n)` or `char(n)` data type. This data type assumes that a table field has a fixed number of characters equal to *n*. The allowable characters are usually drawn from the ASCII character list, although some SQL implementations allow for control characters, too.

SQL-92 introduced the varying `character(n)`, or `varchar(n)` data type. With this new type, a table field can have a varying number of characters from `1` to *n*. The characters are also drawn from the ASCII character list. Some SQL implementations named this data type differently. For example, Oracle has a `varchar2(n)` data type that equates to the SQL-92 `varchar(n)` type.

SQL-92 also added the `national varying character(n)`, or `nvarchar(n)` data type. This data type is similar to `varchar(n)`, except that the characters are drawn from an ISO-defined foreign language character set. Very few SQL implementations use the `nvarchar(n)` type, and the ones who do, such as SQL Server 7.0 and Oracle 8i, have added their own spin to it.

Note

Note that the SQL-92 standard does not have a zero-length string (a string of zero characters, which is different from `NULL`). Therefore, the value of *n* in `char(n)`, `varchar(n)`, or `nvarchar(n)` data types is always 1 or greater.

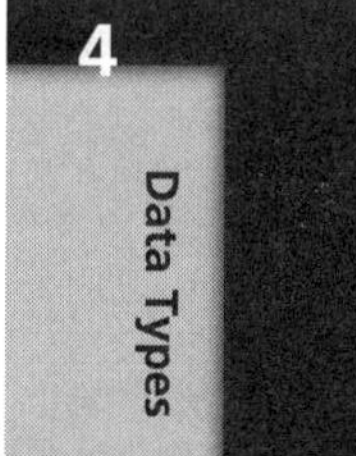

SQL-92 introduced some basic string manipulation functions. These functions are included in most SQL implementations with different formats and with additional functions in most cases. In this section, I discuss the basic SQL-92 string functions and the additional functions introduced by Oracle 8i and Microsoft SQL Server 7.0.

Standard String Functions in SQL-92

SQL-92 supports many string operations. Many functions exist in the standard to handle string conversion to other data types, or vice versa. Also, SQL allows for string manipulations, such as concatenation, trimming, finding the length of a string, searching a string for another string within, etc. The following is a list supported string manipulation functions in the SQL-92 standard.

- String concatenation is done with the "pipe" character (¦¦), taken from PL/I and ADA. For example, to concatenate an employee first name and last name with a space in the middle, you write

```
SELECT Employees.firstname ¦¦ ' ' ¦¦ Employees.lastname
FROM Employees;
```

- You can use the `CAST()` function to convert a data type to a character data type or to convert a character data type to a different type. As mentioned in the section "Numeric Data Types" earlier in this chapter, the syntax for the `CAST()` function is

```
CAST(value AS data_type)
```

  The next example selects employees from the employee table and converts the hire date to character values:

```
SELECT  Employees.firstname ¦¦ ' ' ¦¦ Employees.Lastname AS Name,
 CAST(Employees.HireDate AS VARCHAR(20)) AS Hire_Date
FROM Employees;
```

  The results of this query look like

```
Name           Hire_Date
-----------------------------------------------
john DOE        11-Nov-98 12:00:00
mary DOE        21-Feb-94 12:00:00
terry DAVIS    10-Dec-91 12:00:00
mark SMITH      12-Mar-99 12:00:00
july DAVIS      23-Mar-99 12:00:00
joan SMITH      20-Nov-95 12:00:00
```

- You can also convert a string into another type using the SQL-92 function `CONVERT()`. The syntax for this function is `CONVERT(str USING conv)`. In this function, *str* is the string you want to convert and *conv* is an argument that defines how the conversion process should occur.

- You extract a string from another with the `substring()` function. This function has the following format: `SUBSTRING(A FROM B FOR C)`, where *A* is the string you are searching for the substring, *B* is the search starting point in string *A* where the extracted substring will begin, and c is the length of the extracted substring. In the next example, the first two letters of the employee last name are extracted:

```
SELECT SUBSTRING(Employees.lastname FROM 1 FOR 2)
FROM Employees;
```

Note

If the either the starting point or the length of the substring happen to fall outside the range of the original string, the resulting string will be truncated. For example, `substring('xyz', 4, 2)` will result in the string `''`, but `substring('xyz', 2, 4)` will result in `'yz'`.

- You can convert the string to uppercase or lowercase with either one of the two functions `LCASE(str)` and `UCASE(str)`. *str* is the string to be converted to either lowercase or uppercase. For example, the following query selects the employee name and converts the first name to lowercase and the last name to all uppercase and concatenates the results, adding a space in between:

```
SELECT LCASE(Employees.firstname) || ' ' || UCASE(Employees.lastname)
AS Name
FROM Employees;
```

Sample output of the example follows:

```
Name
------------------------------
john DOE
mary DOE
terry DAVIS
mark SMITH
july DAVIS
joan SMITH
```

- You can trim unwanted characters from either end of a string with the `Trim()` function. The format for this function is `Trim([spec] [ c] FROM [ string])`. *spec* specifies whether the function will trim `LEADING`, `TRAILING`, or `BOTH` occurrences of the trimmed character, *c*. *string* is the original string to be trimmed. The next query selects the names and addresses of employees and trims the addresses:

```
SELECT  Employees.firstname || ' ' || Employees.Lastname AS Name,
 TRIM(BOTH ' ' FROM Employees.Address) AS Address
FROM Employees;
```

A sample output is

```
Name            Address
-----------------------------------------------
john DOE        123 Main St.
mary DOE        123 AnyWhere St.
terry DAVIS     342 Any Street
mark SMITH      345 Secondary St.
july DAVIS      111 Washington Ct.
joan SMITH      654 Any Blvd.
```

Note

The `Trim()` function is general in SQL-92 and applies to any ASCII character. However, almost all of the SQL implementations limit this function to trimming leading or trailing spaces only.

- You finding the length of a string as an integer with the `LENGTH()` function. This function has the format `LENGTH(`*str*`)`, where *str* is the string you want to find its length. The next example shows how you can use this function to find the length of the employee names as a number of characters:

```
SELECT  Employees.firstname ¦¦ ' ' ¦¦ Employees.Lastname AS Name,
 LENGTH(Employees.firstname ¦¦ ' ' ¦¦ Employees.Lastname AS Name) AS Length
FROM Employees;
```

Note

This function can also have the format `CHAR_LENGTH(str)`, where *str* is the string you want to find its length.

A sample output is

```
Name            Length
------------------------------------
john DOE        8
mary DOE        8
terry DAVIS     11
mark SMITH      10
july DAVIS      10
joan SMITH      10
```

- To determine the starting position of a string within another string, you can use the `Position()` function. If the searched string is not found within the source string, the function returns `0`. The format for this function is `Position(`*search* `IN` *src*`)`. *`search`* is the string you are searching for, and *`src`* is the original string that is being searched. Note the following statement:

  ```
  POSITION('xy' IN 'Proxy')
  ```

  The result is `4`.

- One function that SQL-92 introduces, but which no vendor implementation incorporates, is the `Translate()` function. This function uses some kind of character mapping predefined in a schema object called the translation object. This object holds the rules to do this mapping, which can be one character to be replaced by another character or one character to be replaced by many characters.

  The syntax for this function is `TRANSLATE(`*`string`* `USING` *`translation`*`)`. *`string`* is the string to be translated, and *`translation`* is the schema object that holds the rules for this translation.

String Functions in Oracle and SQL Server

Oracle and SQL Server implement many of the SQL-92 character functions and add many more to them. The implementation of these functions is in some cases drastically different between the two database management systems. Table 4.3 summarizes the most important character functions of Oracle and SQL Server.

TABLE 4.3 Character Functions in Oracle 8.x and Microsoft SQL Server 7.0

Function	*Oracle*	*SQL Server*
Convert a character to the ASCII character number	`ASCII(`*`character`*`)`	`ASCII(`*`character`*`)`
Convert ASCII number to a character	`CHR(`*`ASCII`*`)`	`CHAR(`*`ASCII`*`)`
String concatenation	`CONCAT(`*`String1`*`, `*`String2`*`)` or *`String1`* `||` *`String2`*	*`String1`* `+` *`String2`*
Return the difference between the `SOUNDEX` values of two character expressions as an integer	N/A	`DIFFERENCE()`
Greatest character in a list of strings	`GREATEST()`	N/A
Capitalize the initial character of each word in a string	`INITCAP()`	N/A

TABLE 4.3 Character Functions in Oracle 8.x and Microsoft SQL Server 7.0

Function	*Oracle*	*SQL Server*
Find the starting point (from the left) of a character or a pattern in a character string	`ISTR()`	`CHARINDEX()`, `PATINDEX()`
Find the starting point (in bytes) of a character or a pattern in a character string	`INSTRB()`	N/A
The smallest value of a list of characters	`LEAST()`	N/A
Extract a string of several characters from another string starting from the left	N/A	`LEFT()`
Length of a string	`LENGTH()`	`DATALENGTH()`, `LEN()`
Length of a string in bytes	`LENGTHB()`	N/A
Convert a string to lowercase	`LOWER()`	`LOWER()`
Pad the left side of a string with some character	`LPAD()`	N/A
Remove leading blanks from a string	`LTRIM(`*`string`*`)`	`LTRIM(`*`string`*`)`
Remove other leading character from a string	`LTRIM(`*`string`*`, `*`set`*`)`, where *`set`* is the other character	N/A
Convert a string if it's `NULL`	`NVL(`*`String`*`, `*`Value1`*`, `*`Value2`*`)`	`ISNULL(`*`string`*`)`
Return a Unicode string with the delimiters added to make the input string a valid delimited identifier	N/A	`QUOTENAME()`
Replace characters in a string with other characters	`REPLACE()`	`REPLACE()`, `STUFF()`
Repeat a string of characters a specified number of times	N/A	`REPLICATE()`
Reverse the order of characters in a string	N/A	`REVERSE()`
Extract a string of several characters from another string starting from the right	N/A	`RIGHT()`
Pad the right side of a string with some character	`RPAD()`	N/A
Remove trailing blanks from a string	`RTRIM(`*`string`*`)`	`RTRIM(`*`string`*`)`
Remove other trailing character from a string	`RTRIM(`*`string`*`, `*`set`*`)`, where *`set`* is the other character	N/A
Phonetic representation of a string	`SOUNDEX()`	`SOUNDEX()`
Return a string of one or several spaces	N/A	`SPACE()`
Convert numeric or date types to a string	`TO_CHAR()`	`STR()`
Return a substring from within a string	`SUBSTR()`	`SUBSTRING()`
Translate character string	`TRANSLATE()`	N/A

TABLE 4.3 Character Functions in Oracle 8.x and Microsoft SQL Server 7.0

Function	*Oracle*	*SQL Server*
Return the integer value, as defined by the Unicode standard, for the first character of the input string	N/A	`UNICODE(`*`string`*`)`
Convert a string to all uppercase	`UPPER()`	`UPPER()`

Data Type Conversion

Data types are converted for many reasons, such as for comparison and logical and arithmetic operations. For example, if you want to compare a variable `A = 5.1` (`decimal`) to another variable `B = 5` (`integer`), you need to convert one of the two variables to the type of the other because you cannot compare apples to oranges. You might also want to add the two variables to get the sum `A + B`. To do that, the two variables have to be the same type. These basic issues apply to numeric and non-numeric data types alike. For instance, if you want to compare two variables, a string `strDate = '12/12/1999'` and a date `dtmDate = '12/12/1999 12:00 AM'`, you need to convert one of them to the type of the other in all SQL implementations.

Note

`CHAR` and `VARCHAR` data types are usually comparable with no need to convert one to the other's data type as long as the characters are drawn from the same character pool. For example, you can compare ASCII characters to ASCII characters, but not ASCII characters to graphic characters, and you can compare English to English, but not English to Chinese.

Numeric data type conversion usually happens from the lower to the higher data types according to the order `smallint`, `integer`, `decimal`, `numeric`, `real`, `float`, `double precision`. Following this order minimizes the rounding and truncation that may occur during such numeric data conversions.

As you have seen in the section "Numeric Data Types" earlier in this chapter, the `CAST()` function is the main function offered by SQL-92 for converting one data type to another. You have also seen that different implementations have different functions to do more specific data type conversions. The following sections discuss some of the functions used by Oracle and SQL Server for data type conversions.

Data Type Conversion in SQL Server

SQL Server uses the `CONVERT()` and `CAST()` functions for data type conversions. The syntax for the `CAST()` function is `CAST(Arg AS Datatype)`. *Arg* is the argument that needs to be converted to the new type, *datatype*. For example, to convert the employee address to `CHAR(50)` to make the address more readable in a query, you can write the following:

```
SELECT  e.firstname + ' ' + e.lastname AS Name,
  CAST(e.Address AS CHAR(50)) AS Employee_Address
FROM  Employees AS e;
```

The results of this query are

```
Name           Employee_Address
-----------------------------------------------
john DOE       123 Main St.
mary DOE       123 AnyWhere St.
terry DAVIS    342 Any Street
mark SMITH     345 Secondary St.
july DAVIS     111 Washington Ct.
joan SMITH     654 Any Blvd.
```

The same query can be written with the `CONVERT()` function, discussed in the section "Numeric Conversions and Functions" earlier in the chapter. The following example shows how such a query could be written:

```
SELECT  e.firstname + ' ' + e.lastname AS Name,
  CONVERT(CHAR(50), e.Address) AS Employee_Address
FROM  Employees AS e;
```

The results are exactly the same as the `CAST()` function query results.

Note

Sometimes, you use data type conversion functions with some fields so you can use certain predicates in a query. For example, you can convert the employee salary field from the `money` data type to `CHAR(10)` so that you can use the `LIKE` predicate with it. The next example shows the SQL code needed to do this. For a detailed discussion about the `LIKE` predicate and other pattern-matching predicates in SQL, see Chapter 9, "Patterns and Ranges in SQL."

```
SELECT  e.firstname + ' ' + e.lastname AS Name,
  CONVERT(CHAR(10), e.Salary) AS Employee_Salary
```

```
FROM  Employees AS e
WHERE  e.Salary LIKE '2%';
```

The results of this query are

```
Name          Employee_Salary
----------------------------------------------
john DOE      29000
mary DOE      22500
joan SMITH    28000
```

Note

When converting a data type to `datetime` or `smalldatetime`, SQL Server rejects all the values it cannot recognize as dates (including dates earlier than January 1, 1753). You can convert `datetime` values to `smalldatetime` when the date is in the proper range (January 1, 1900, to June 6, 2079). In such conversions, the time value is rounded up to the nearest minute.

Data Type Conversion in Oracle

You have already seen how Oracle converts some data types into the date and time data types. You mainly use the `TO_DATE()`, `TO_CHAR()`, and `TO_NUMBER()` functions for type conversions. All of these functions are discussed earlier in the chapter. These and other conversion functions in Oracle are listed in Table 4.4.

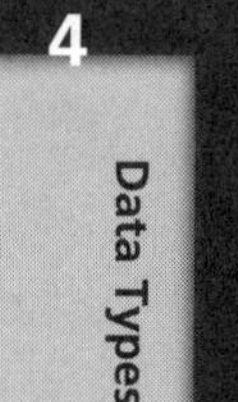

TABLE 4.4 Data Type Conversion Functions in Oracle

Function	*Description*	*Arguments*	*Return Value*
`CHARTOROWID(`*`str`*`)`	Converts *`str`* to type `ROWID`.	*`str`*: `CHAR` or `VARCHAR2`	`ROWID`
`CONVERT(`*`str`*`, `*`set1`*`, `*`set2`*`)`	Converts *`str`* from character *`set1`* to character *`set2`*.	*`str`*: `VARCHAR2` *`set1`*, *`set2`*: `VARCHAR2`	`VARCHAR2`
`HEXTOROW(`*`str`*`)`	Converts *`str`* from `CHAR` or `VARCHR2` to `ROW`.	*`str`*: `CHAR` or `VARCHAR2`	`Row`
`ROWTOHEX(`*`r`*`)`	Converts *`r`* from `row` to `VARCHAR2`.	*`r`*: `row`	`VARCHAR2`
`TO_CHAR(`*`d`*`, [`*`fmt`*`], [`*`nlsparams`*`])`	Converts *`d`* to `VARCHAR2` based on the format *`fmt`*. *`Nlsparams`* decides what language the returned value will have.	*`d`*: `date`, `[`*`fmt`*`]`: `VARCHAR2`, `[`*`nlsparams`*`]`	`VARCHAR2`

Table 4.4 Data Type Conversion Functions in Oracle

Function	*Description*	*Arguments*	*Return Value*
TO_CHAR(*num* [*fmt*], [*nlsparams*])	Converts *num* to VARCHAR2. *fmt* and *nlsparams* can be used to determine the format and currency symbol to use with the returned value.	*num*: NUMBER, [*fmt*]: VARCHAR2, [*nlsparams*]	VARCHAR2
TO_CHAR(*label* [*fmt*])	Converts *label* from MLSLABEL type to VARCHAR2 based on the format *fmt*.	*label*: MLSLABEL, [*fmt* ARCHAR2]	VARCHAR2
TO_DATE()	Converts *str* or *num* to Date based on *fmt*. *fmt* is not optional when converting a number.	*str*: VARCHAR2 or *num*: NUMBER, [*fmt*VARCHAR2], [*nlsparams*]	Date
TO_LABEL(*str*, [*fmt*])	Converts str to the MLSLABEL data type. If *fmt* is omitted, *str* must be in a default label format.	*str*: CHAR or VARCHAR2, [*fmt*VARCHAR2]	MLSLABEL
TO_MULTI_BYTE(*str*)	Converts single byte *str* to multibyte if it exists.	*str*: CHAR or VARCHAR2	CHAR, VARCHAR2
TO_NUMBER(*str* [*nlsparams*])	Converts *str* to NUMBER according to *fmt*. You can define the national language parameters using nlsparams.	*str*: CHAR or VARCHAR2, [*nlsparams*]	NUMBER
TO_SINGLE_BYTE(str)	Opposite of the TO_MULTI_BYTE() function.	*str*: CHAR or VARCHAR2	CHAR, VARCHAR2

A useful function that Oracle uses to converts NULLs to valid values of certain data types is the NVL() function. For a detailed discussion on NULLs in SQL, see the next section, "NULLs and Missing Values."

The syntax for this function is NVL(*A*, *B*). If expression *A* resolves to NULL, expression *B* is returned; otherwise, expression *A* is returned. The following example uses the NVL() function in an Oracle query. In the example, the query returns the names of employees and their salaries. If the salary field for an employee is NULL, the query returns N/A for it.

```
SELECT  e.firstname + ' ' + e.lastname AS Name,
  NVL(TO_CHAR(e.Salary), 'N/A') AS Employee_Salary
FROM  Employees AS e;
```

The results of this query are

```
Name            Employee_Salary
---------------------------------------------
john DOE        29000
mary DOE        22000
terry DAVIS     NA
mark SMITH      NA
july DAVIS      35000
joan SMITH      39000
```

NULLs and Missing Values

SQL-92 uses NULLs to represent currently unknown or missing values that may be replaced later with real values. NULLs have different flavors. A domain NULL, for instance, represents an unknown value of an attribute of an entity where the attribute belongs to a certain domain. For example, if you don't know the eye color of an employee, you can say the value of the corresponding attribute is unknown, or NULL. To represent this, you say John(Eyes) = NULL. If, on the other hand, you don't also know the color of John's hair, you can say John(Hair) = NULL. As you see, the domain-specific NULL is different from the general purpose NULL because you know specifically what is missing or unknown.

Note

Domains are schema objects in SQL-92 and SQL3 that are created with a CREATE DOMAIN statement. Almost no SQL implementation uses this statement yet. Take color as an example on domains: A car color is not the same as the color of an employee's eyes. You say that the eye color domain is different from the car color domain for the same employee.

Another form of NULL is the Not Applicable (N/A) paradigm. You frequently see this paradigm on paper forms and in spreadsheets. SQL-89 assumed NULLs to be Not Applicable. As an example, suppose you are tracking the roof color for employees with convertible cars. For employees who don't have convertibles, the roof color is in the Not Applicable category. If John has a convertible with a red roof, and Mike does not have a convertible, you can say John(Car_Roof) = Red and Mike(NULL) = N/A or NULL. You write Mike(NULL) = NULL because the attribute convertible is missing for Mike.

Another form of NULL that you may encounter is the case where the entity is missing, but the attribute and its values may be known. An example is if you are keeping track of employees with beards. Male employees could have beards, but female employees do not have them. How do you represent this in the database? You can have a `gender` column, and in the beard column, you can make sure with a `CHECK` constraint that the value is `NULL` for female employees. Or you can just have a beard column and make sure that female employees don't have anything other than `NULL` in it. However, you could get into a situation where you need to fill the value of the column without knowing the gender of the employee. For example, the name Kris Doe could be a male or female name. Unless you learn that Kris is a female, you cannot insert `NULL` as the value of the beard column.

Sometimes, even though the value of a table field might not be known (`NULL`), you could still have some information about it. For example, the `Gender` column in the employee table will always have one of two values, male or female. If you are not sure about the gender of an employee, you still know that it is either male or female.

In some instances, `NULL`s are referred to as marked `NULL`s. An example is the checkout date of books in the company library database. You know that the return date has to be greater than the checkout date. If you have some rules—for instance, the maximum checkout period is seven days—you can say that the return date, although `NULL`, is between the checkout date and checkout date plus seven days. As another example, in a travel agency reservation system, you might have certain rules that customers belonging to the same group can only travel together or use certain airlines and hotels.

> **Note**
>
> Building such rules to cover marked `NULL`s in the database is complex, and it is better to have the application code deal with such rules.

Logic and NULLs

The Boolean logical system named after George Boole works well with computer logic because it is based on two values, `TRUE` and `FALSE`, which fits with the computer's binary system.

SQL has three-valued logic, `TRUE`, `FALSE`, and `UNKNOWN`. `UNKNOWN`is not the same as `NULL`, which is a data value. This explains why you write `x IS NULL` or `x IS NOT NULL` instead of `x = NULL` or `x <> NULL`. The SQL truth for the logical operators `AND`, `OR`, and `NOT` are shown in Tables 4.5, 4.6, and 4.7.

TABLE 4.5 SQL Truth Table for the AND Logical Operator

AND	*TRUE*	*UNKNOWN*	*FALSE*
TRUE	TRUE	UNKNOWN	FALSE
UNKNOWN	UNKNOWN	UNKNOWN	FALSE
FALSE	FALSE	FALSE	FALSE

TABLE 4.6 SQL Truth Table for the OR Logical Operator

OR	*TRUE*	*UNKNOWN*	*FALSE*
TRUE	TRUE	TRUE	TRUE
UNKNOWN	UNKNOWN	UNKNOWN	UNKNOWN
FALSE	TRUE	UNKNOWN	FALSE

TABLE 4.7 SQL Truth Table for the NOT Logical Operator

	NOT
TRUE	FALSE
UNKNOWN	UNKNOWN
FALSE	TRUE

NULLs in Math and Comparisons

Most SQL implementations propagate `NULL`s in mathematical and arithmetic expressions. For example, if you add, multiply, subtract, or divide any two variables in an expression, with one of the variables being `NULL`, the value of the whole expression will be `NULL`.

In other words, you might be able to write that

```
X + NULL = NULL,
X - NULL = NULL,
X * NULL = NULL,
```

and

```
x/NULL = NULL.
```

`NULL`s are also propagated in both built-in and user-defined functions. For example, finding the absolute value of a `NULL` value yields `NULL`:

```
ABS(NULL) = NULL
```

Although `NULL` does not belong to any data type, it can replace the values of all data types. In SQL, you can use the `CAST()` function to declare a specific data type for a `NULL`. For instance, you can say `CAST(NULL AS INTEGER)`.

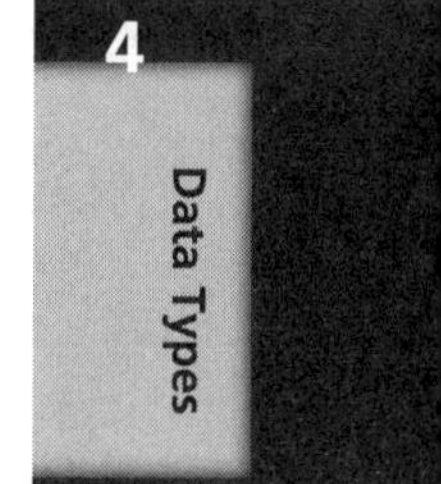

Note

Although most database management systems return a division-by-zero error when a number is divided by zero (with the exception of Oracle and SQL Server, which return `NULL` and an error), most of these systems return `NULL` when a `NULL` is divided by zero.

Converting Values to and from `NULL`

Two SQL-92 functions convert values to `NULL`s and `NULL`s to other values, `NULLIF()` and `COALESCE()`.

`NULLIF()` Function

You can use the `NULLIF()` function to replace an expression with `NULL` and vice versa. The syntax for this function is `NULLIF(`*`Exp1`*`, `*`Exp2`*`)`, where *`Exp1`* and *`Exp2`* are the two arguments for the function. If the two arguments *`Exp1`* and *`Exp2`* are equal, the function returns `NULL`. If the arguments are not equal, the function returns the first argument, *`Exp1`*.

`COALESCE()` Function

You can use the `COALESCE()` function to replace an expression with `NULL` and vice versa. The syntax for this function is `COALESCE (`*`Exp1`*`, `*`Exp2`*`, `*`Exp3`*`, ...)`, where *`Exp1`*, *`Exp2`*, *`Exp3`*, and so on are the arguments of the function. The function returns the first non- `NULL` value of these arguments. If all the arguments are `NULL`, the function returns `NULL`. This function is useful when you are adding some values in a `SELECT` statement. For example, if you are adding the base pay rate for an employee to the overtime pay rate, you write the following SELECT statement:

```
SELECT   Employees.Firstname || ' ' || Employees.Lastname AS Name,
  BaseRate + OTRate AS TotalPay
FROM  EMPLOYEES;
```

However, if the employee does not do any overtime work, the results are `NULL` for the addition. To solve the problem, you can use the `COALESCE()` function to replace a `NULL` with a zero:

```
SELECT   Employees.Firstname || ' ' || Employees.Lastname AS Name,
  COALESCE(BaseRate, 0) + COALESCE(OTRate, 0) AS TotalPay
FROM  EMPLOYEES;
```

Another good use for the `COALESCE()` function is with aggregate functions. With such functions, you usually try to sum the values of a column based on grouping these values relative to another column. If any NULLs exist, the sum yields a NULL. You can use the COALESCE() and NULLIF() functions to solve this problem. Aggregate functions are discussed in detail in Chapter 11, "Sorting and Grouping."

Character Data and NULLs

As with the case of numeric data types, when NULLs are involved in character data functions, they lead to NULL returns of these functions. As an example, concatenating a value to NULL in SQL will yield NULL. In some programming languages, this is handled differently. For instance, in Microsoft Visual Basic and its derivatives, VBA and VBScript, concatenating a zero-length string to a NULL yields a zero-length string. This provides a good advantage in these languages when testing for NULL and zero-length strings. You can test for both cases using a statement like the one shown in the following pseudo code:

```
If '''' & field_name = '''' then
  'DO something
End If
```

In the pseudo code, field_name is a field name of a recordset returned as a result of querying the database. In the test, if field_name is either NULL or a zero-length string, the concatenation yields a zero-length string. With this, you can check against both cases in one statement.

Summary

In this chapter, I presented the different data types that SQL-92 has to offer. These data types are, in some cases, implemented differently among database management systems. I pointed out the major areas of differences when possible, especially with the numeric and date/time data types. I also discussed how to convert one data type to another using the SQL-92 CAST() function or some DBMS-specific functions. Another important topic covered in this chapter is handling NULLs in relation to data types.

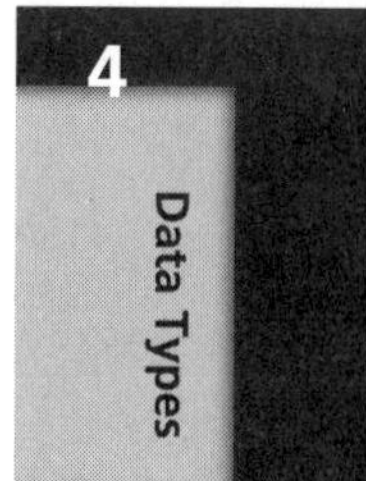

Handling Arrays in SQL

In This Chapter

As you saw in Chapter 2, "Relational Databases," arrays violate the first normal form (1NF) for relational databases, which says that no repeating groups can exist in any columns. Therefore, arrays cannot be represented in standard SQL. However, because most programming uses arrays in some way or another, and SQL was created to be easily used with as many programming languages as possible, there should be some tricks to work around this problem. This chapter represents some of the methods you can use to represent arrays in SQL. This chapter covers array representation and matrix operations in SQL

Array Representation in SQL

As I mentioned earlier, SQL was created to be as simple as possible and to have as many scalar data types as possible. The reason for this is to make is easy to use SQL with any programming language and to transfer data types to these languages.

An *array* is a repeated list of elements that are identified by their subscripts. Some languages start the base subscript at 0, and others at 1. Some even let you decide the lower and upper bounds of the array. In Visual Basic, for instance, you can declare an array with five elements as follows:

```
Dim MyArray(5)
```

The base subscript of this array is 0. You can refer to its elements in this way:

```
Element Number 1:  MyArray(0)
Element Number 2:  MyArray(1)
Element Number 3:  MyArray(2)
Element Number 4:  MyArray(3)
Element Number 5:  MyArray(4)
```

To represent this array in SQL, think of creating a table, such as:

```
CREATE TABLE MyArray(
  Element1 INTEGER NOT NULL,
  Element2 INTEGER NOT NULL,
  Element3 INTEGER NOT NULL,
  Element4 INTEGER NOT NULL,
  Element5 INTEGER NOT NULL);
```

Notice that you immediately lose some of the benefits of using arrays by following this scheme. For example, you cannot refer to the elements in the table by their subscripts. You cannot even loop, as you would in Visual Basic (see Listing 5.1) to set their values to `0`.

LISTING 5.1 Declaring and Looping Through an Array in Visual Basic

```
Dim MyArray(5)
For I = 0 to UBOUND(MyArray)
  MyArray(i) = 0
Next I
```

In SQL, each one of these elements has to be referenced individually. Listing 5.2 shows how to set the five elements to `0` in SQL:

LISTING 5.2 Setting the Values of an Array to `0` in SQL

```
UPDATE MyArray
SET   Element1 = 0,
Element2 = 0,
  Element3 = 0,
  Element4 = 0,
  Element5 = 0;
```

This way of representing arrays can lead to some problems. Let's take a more realistic example. For the company library example you started in Chapter 2, you might want to store what chapters are in each book in the library in the `books` table. This will require changing the structure of the `books` table to include new columns to hold the values for the book chapters. Listing 5.3 shows the SQL code needed to alter the `books` table to accommodate these chapters.

Obviously, some books have more chapters than others. Some have less. So what do you do? If you were to stick with the representation shown previously, you would run into some problems. For instance, assuming that the maximum number of chapters in a book at the time of table design was 10, you have to make enough room for all 10 chapters to be stored. To illustrate some of the problems you might face, say a book has only eight chapters. How do you represent the values in the missing columns? Are you going to use `NULL` values? Or should you modify the structure of the table to accommodate only eight chapters? If you choose the latter solution, what happens to Chapters 9 and 10 of the book with 10 chapters? Do you eliminate them?

LISTING 5.3 Adding Two Columns to the `books` Table

```
ALTER TABLE books ADD (
  Chapter1  VARCHAR    NULL,
  Chapter2  VARCHAR    NULL,
  Chapter3  VARCHAR    NULL,
  Chapter4  VARCHAR    NULL,
```

LISTING 5.3 CONTINUED

```
  Chapter5   VARCHAR    NULL,
  Chapter6   VARCHAR    NULL,
  Chapter7   VARCHAR    NULL,
  Chapter8   VARCHAR    NULL,
  Chapter9   VARCHAR    NULL,
  Chapter10  VARCHAR    NULL);
```

Now say you keep the 10 columns and decide to update the missing columns with `NULL` values. What happens if a book with 12 chapters is added to the library later on? Should you modify the table design again to accommodate the two added chapters? If so, you should remember to update the values in the added columns for the old books with `NULL` values, or maybe you can avoid doing so by explicitly allowing the columns to have `NULL` values. To do that, you need to issue the statements shown in Listing 5.4.

LISTING 5.4 Adding Two More Columns to the `books` Table

```
ALTER TABLE books ADD (
  Chapter11  VARCHAR    NULL,
  Chapter12  VARCHAR    NULL);
```

Now what happens if yet another book is added with 13 chapters? Do you redesign the table? As you can see, this is a very impractical solution. There must be a better way to avoid getting into these problems. The way to do so is by creating a new table for chapters. Let's call it `chapters`. This table will have a column for a `book_id` that serves as a foreign key joining the newly created `chapters` table to the `books` table. Listing 5.5 shows how to create this table.

LISTING 5.5 Creating the `chapters` Table

```
CREATE TABLE chapters (
ChapterID  INTEGER    PRIMARY KEY,
Book_ID    INTEGER    NOT NULL,
  ChapterTitle  VARCHAR    NOT NULL);
```

Every chapter of a given book will have its own record in the new table. Therefore, a book with only two chapters will have two records in the `chapters` table, and a book with 20 chapters will have 20 records in this table. If a new book is added to the library, a number of new records will be inserted into the `chapters` table corresponding to the number of chapters in the added book. On the other hand, if a relatively old book is no longer needed and removed from the library, the records corresponding to its chapters in the `chapters` table will also be deleted. Listing 5.6 shows how inserting a new book in the `books` table leads to inserting a number of records in the `chapters` table to store information about the book's chapters.

> **Note**
>
> With this solution, there will be no `NULL` values in the parent or child tables. More tables are created in the database, but the total storage in the schema is smaller because you are storing only the needed data.

LISTING 5.6 Adding a New Book to the Library

```
INSERT INTO books (
Book_Title,
Book_Topic,
ISBN,
Book_Copy_Right_Year,
Book_Edition,
Publisher_Name,
Purchase_Price,
Date_Purchased,
Shelf_Code,
Cover_Type,
Book_Pages)
VALUES('SQL Unleashed',
  'Computers - Databases',
  '0672317095',
  '1/1/1999',
  2,
  'Sams',
  40,
  '5/24/1999',
  '23A',
  'Soft',
  900)
INSERT INTO chapters (
Chapter_ID
Book_ID,
ChapterTitle)
VALUES (1121,
  '0672317095',
  'Chapter 1: SQL Standards');
```

LISTING 5.6 CONTINUED

```
INSERT INTO chapters (
Chapter_ID
Book_ID,
ChapterTitle)
VALUES (1122,
  '0672317095',
  'Chapter 2: Relational Databases');

INSERT INTO chapters (
Chapter_ID
Book_ID,
ChapterTitle)
VALUES (1123,
  '0672317095',
  'Chapter 3: Table Creation and Manipulation');
................ ................ ................
................ ................ ................
and so on for all the chapters of the added book
```

> **Note**
>
> For more information on the syntax for the `INSERT` or `UPDATE` statements, see Chapter 7, "Inserts, Updates, and Deletes."

Another way to represent an array is to create a table with an integer column to hold the subscripts of the elements in the arrays. You can add a `CHECK` constraint (see Chapter 3, "Table Creation and Manipulation") to limit the values of this integer column to those in the range of subscripts of the array elements. Listing 5.7 shows the syntax for creating this table. Compare this to Listing 5.1.

LISTING 5.7 Creating a Table with an Integer Field to Hold the Value of the Array Subscripts

```
CREATE TABLE MyArray(
  i   INTEGER
 CHECK( i BETWEEN 0 AND 4)
 PRIMARY KEY,
  Element   INTEGER  NOT NULL);
```

The big advantage to this approach is that it allows handling multi-dimensional arrays easily by adding columns to hold the additional subscripts. To demonstrate this, Listing 5.8 shows how a three-dimensional array can be represented with this approach.

LISTING 5.8 Representing a Three-Dimensional Array with a Table in SQL

```
CREATE TABLE MyArray(
  length    INTEGER
 CHECK( length BETWEEN 0 AND 4),
  width    INTEGER
 CHECK( width BETWEEN 0 AND 2),
  height    INTEGER
 CHECK( height BETWEEN 0 AND 3),
  Object    INTEGER  NOT NULL)
PRIMARY KEY (length, width, height);
```

Listing 5.8 shows how to represent an array declared as follows in a language like Visual Basic:

```
Dim MyArray(5,3,4)
```

To use a table with the structure in Listing 5.8, you can use grouping functions.

> **Note**
>
> For detailed information on sorting and grouping and their related functions in SQL, please refer to Chapter 11, "Sorting and Grouping."

LISTING 5.9 Selecting Data from a Table Representing a Three-Dimensional Array

```
SELECT    width,
    height,
    SUM(Object)
FROM    MyArray
GROUP BY  length;
```

This listing sums the values of the `Object` column across the `Length` column. To sum across both `Length` and `Width`, you can use the code in Listing 5.10.

LISTING 5.10 Summing the Values of the Data from a Table Representing a Three-Dimensional Array Across Two Integer Columns

```
SELECT    SUM(height),
    Object
FROM     MyArray
GROUP BY  Object, Length, Width;
```

You have seen two ways to represent arrays in SQL in a simple and practical form. Next you will see how to perform some matrix operations in SQL using the table representations discussed in this section.

Matrix Operations in SQL

Doing matrix operations in SQL is possible but can be very resource intensive. Queries performing such operations usually run for a long time because SQL was not meant to be a language to perform mathematical operations and calculations. SQL was, again, meant to be a universal language for data storage in databases in the simplest possible way to allow for interaction with as many programming languages as possible. This section discusses how mathematical calculations and operations can be performed in SQL.

Note

A matrix is special data structure in which data is arranged in a table-like format. In such an arrangement, data elements have subscripts to indicate their location in the structure. Matrices allow for using a group of data elements together as one unit. An example is a matrix representing the chapters in a book. Let's say the matrix is called chapters. It can have elements such as chapter 1, chapter 2, and so on. An element can be represented as Chapters(i), where i is the index of that element in the matrix. For example, if Chapter 10 is the 10th element in the matrix, we can write Chapters(10) = Chapter 10.

Multiplying a Matrix by a Constant

This operation is simple to perform in SQL. All you need to do is issue an `UPDATE` statement that includes multiplying each element in the table that corresponds to an array element by the constant. For example, Listing 5.11 shows how a table representing the one-dimensional array created in Listing 5.7 can be updated to reflect multiplying the represented array by a constant a.

LISTING 5.11 Multiplying Table Elements Representing an Array by a Constant Value

```
UPDATE MyArray
SET Element = a * Object;
```

The example in Listing 5.12 multiplies the elements in the table created in Listing 5.8 to represent an three-dimensional array by a constant value, x. The example creates a view with the results, instead of storing the results in the original table.

LISTING 5.12 Creating a View That Shows the Results of Multiplying a Three-Dimensional Array Represented by a Table

```
CREATE VIEW MyArrayTimesX (Length, Width, Height, Object)
AS
SELECT Length, Width, Height, Object * x
FROM  MyArray;
```

Note

For information on creating views in SQL, please refer to Chapter 14, "Creating and Using Views."

Transposing a Two-Dimensional Matrix

Listing 5.13 shows how to transpose a two-dimensional matrix. In the listing, a view is created to hold the results of the matrix operation. The view has three columns. The big difference between the view and the original table is the order of the two integer columns, `Length` and `Width`.

LISTING 5.13 Creating a View That Shows the Results of Transposing a Two-Dimensional Matrix

```
CREATE VIEW MyArrayT (Length, Width, Object)
AS
SELECT Length, Width, Object
FROM  MyArray;
```

Adding Two Matrices

To add two matrices, they have to be of the same dimensions. The addition is easily done by adding the matching elements, with respect to the subscripts, in the two matrices. Listing 5.14 shows an example of adding two one-dimensional arrays in SQL. The example assumes that a table represents each array similarly to the approach used in Listing 5.6.

LISTING 5.14 Creating a View That Shows the Results of Two One-Dimensional Arrays

```
CREATE VIEW MyView (Length, Object)
AS
SELECT Length, Object +
  (SELECT Object
 FROM Array2
 WHERE Array2.Length = Array1.Length)
FROM  Array1;
```

In this listing, you are using a subquery to extract the corresponding element from the second array, so that you can add it to the selected element in the first array. Subqueries are explained in detail in Chapter 13, "Subqueries."

> **Warning**
>
> Make sure your tables `Array1` and `Array2` don't have any `NULL` values in them; otherwise, the operation in Listing 5.13 will fail, unless special functions are used to handle `NULL`s.

The next example in Listing 5.15 shows how two two-dimensional arrays can be added. Again, two tables represent the arrays and the two arrays are of the same dimensions.

LISTING 5.15 Adding Two Two-Dimensional Arrays

```
CREATE VIEW MyView (Length, Width, Object)
AS
SELECT Length, Width, Object +
  (SELECT Object
 FROM Array2
 WHERE Array2.Length = Array1.Length
  AND Array2.Width = Array1.Width)
FROM  Array1;
```

Multiplying Two Matrices

To perform matrix multiplication in algebra, the dimensions of the two matrices have to relate to each other according to the following rule:

```
Array1(i, k) * Array2(k, j) = Array(i,j).
```

In other words, the number of columns of one of the two matrices has to be the same as the number of rows in the other. The resulting matrix has the non-matching dimensions of the two multiplied ones. Assuming that you created two tables to represent the matrices `array1` and `array2`, similar to Listing 5.6, you can create a view that holds the result of multiplying the two table elements. Listing 5.16 shows how this can be done.

LISTING 5.16 Multiplying Two Arrays Represented as Tables in SQL

```
CREATE VIEW MyView (Length, Width, Object)
AS
SELECT   Length,
Width,
SUM(Array1.Object * Array2.Object)
FROM  Array1, Array2
WHERE   Array1.Height = Array2.Height
GROUP BY Length, Width;
```

Comparing Arrays in SQL

Often you want to compare some values in a table with other values. In the company library example, assume that you want to keep track of the employees and their check-out material in a new table. The new table will be called `Checkout` and have the following structure:

`Checkout` *Table*	
`Checkout_No`	Integer, `NOT NULL`
`Employee_No`	Integer, `NOT NULL`
`ISBN`	Character data
`Checkout_Date`	Date
`Return_Date`	Date

To create the table, you can use the SQL code in Listing 5.17.

LISTING 5.17 Creating the `Checkout` Table

```
CREATE TABLE checkout(
Checkout_No  INTEGER NOT NULL  PRIMARY KEY,
Employee_No  INTEGER    NOT NULL,
ISBN    INTEGER   NOT NULL,
Checkout_Date  Date,
Return_Date  Date);
```

To be able to use this table, you need an `Employee` table. Listing 5.18 shows how to create one.

LISTING 5.18 Creating the `Employee` Table

```
CREATE TABLE employee(
Employee_No  INTEGER    PRIMARY KEY,
Title    VARCHAR(30)  NULL,
Department_No  INTEGER    NOT NULL,
Fname    VARCHAR(15)  NOT NULL,
Lname    VARCHAR(20)  NOT NULL,
Address    Varchar(50)  NULL,
City    Varchar(30)  NULL,
State    Char(2)    NULL,
Hire_Date  Date    NULL,
Phone_No  Varchar(11)  NULL,
Fax_No    Varchar(11)  NULL,
Email    Varchar(30)  NULL,
Reports_To  INTEGER    NOT NULL,
Birth_Date  Date    NULL);
```

Let's now find out which employees borrowed the same books during a period of time. For example, John might have borrowed `Book1`, `Book2`, and `Book3` in 1999. Also, Alice may have borrowed the same three books in 1999. Such a query will find all the employees that match this criterion.

To solve this problem, create a view that gives the number of books checked out by each employee in 1999. Listing 5.19 shows how this view can be constructed.

LISTING 5.19 Creating a View with the Number of Checkouts Per Employee in 1999

```
/*Create the checkouts table*/
CREATE TABLE checkouts(
Checkout_No INTEGER,
Employee_No INTEGER,
```

LISTING 5.19 CONTINUED

```
Book_ISBN VARCHR,
Checkout_Date Date);

/*Create the view*/
CREATE VIEW EmpCheckouts(Employee_No, Count)
AS
SELECT Employee_No, COUNT(*)
FROM checkouts
WHERE Checkout_Date BETWEEN '1/1/1999' AND '12/31/1999'
GROUP BY Employee_No;
```

Now create another view that gives the pairs of employees having the same number of checkouts during 1999. Listing 5.20 shows how to do this.

LISTING 5.20 Creating a View of Employees with the Same Number of Checkouts in 1999

```
CREATE VIEW SameNumber(Emp1, Emp2, Count)
AS
SELECT  V1.Employee_No AS Emp1,
  V2.Employee_No AS Emp2,
  V1.Count AS Count
FROM  EmpCheckouts AS V1,
  EmpCheckouts AS V2
WHERE  V1.Count = V2.Count;
```

Finally, Listing 5.21 shows the solution to the problem by joining the previous view you had to the checkout table.

LISTING 5.21 Finding Out the Employees Who Checked Out the Same Books

```
SELECT  V1.checkout As Emp1,
V2.checkout As Emp2,
V3.Count AS Count
FROM  EmpCheckouts AS V1,
EmpCheckouts AS V2,
SameNumber AS V3
WHERE  V3.Emp1 = V1.Employee_No
AND V3.Emp2 = V2.Employee_No
AND V1.ISBN = V2.ISBN
GROUP BY Emp1, Emp2, Count
HAVING COUNT(*) = V3.Count;
```

Creating Matrix-Type Reports in SQL

Often you want to create a report from your data that looks like a matrix, which is the opposite of what you have done in the first section of this chapter, "Array Representation in SQL." What you are actually doing here is taking a table and converting it from a one-element, one-column format to an array laid horizontally across a line. Say, for instance, that you want to find out for each employee the number of books she or he checked out per month in 1999. In this case, the year is an array, with the month as the subscript. Every row in this array represents an employee name, and the columns hold the number of books checked out for the corresponding month. Table 5.1 shows sample data of what such an array would look like.

TABLE 5.1 Sample Data for the Array You Need to Get from the Employee `checkout` Table

Employee	*Jan.*	*Feb.*	*Mar.*	*Apr.*	*May*	*Jun.*	*Jul.*	*Aug.*	*Sep.*	*Oct.*	*Nov.*	*Dec.*
John	2	0	1	0	3	3	0	0	2	1	1	0
Mary	0	2	2	1	1	0	1	1	2	2	0	1
Mark	1	2	3	4	0	0	1	0	2	0	2	2

Some SQL vendors make creating these reports easy by integrating special services in their database engine. Microsoft Access and SQL Server 7.0, for instance, allow the use of cross-tabulation and pivot table features that make creating this query very easy. However, assume that you don't have this luxury, and try to build the array by using SQL-92 code.

To do this task, you need to create a table or a view to hold the result. Let's create a view called `monthly`. This view will have a column for the employee name or number, followed by 12 columns for the months of the year. In the following paragraphs, we will build this view, but for now, the definition part of the view looks like this:

```
CREATE VIEW monthly(
  Employee_No, Jan,
Feb, Mar, Apr,
May, Jun, Jul, Aug, Sep)
```

To accomplish this goal, you need to create 12 separate views for the 12 different months in 1999. Then you need to select from all the views to construct the `monthly` target view described previously. The views will be created using the code in Listing 5.22. The listing shows that selecting from two tables, `employee` and `checkout`, and left-joining them on the `employee_no` field create each view. The naming scheme for these views is "V" and the

3-letter abbreviation of the month. For example, for January, the view is VJan, and for February, it is VFeb.

Note

The reason for using a left join on the two tables, employee and checkout, is to list all employees in the left column, whether or not they have checked out any books. This choice makes the job easier when you combine the 12 views into the requested array view. For detailed information on left, right, self, or other joins in SQL, please refer to Chapter 10, "Table Joins."

LISTING 5.22 Creating a Separate View of the Total Checkouts Per Employee in January 1999

```
CREATE VIEW VJan(
  Employee_No)
AS
SELECT T1.Employee_No,
Count(T2.Employee_No) AS Jan,
FROM  Employee AS T1 LEFT JOIN checkout AS T2
ON T1.Employee_No = T2.Employee_No
WHERE  T2.Checkout_Date BETWEEN '1/1/1999' AND
'1/31/1999'
GROUP BY T1.Employee_No
ORDER BY T1.Employee_No;
```

Repeat the code in Listing 5.22 for each month of the year until you get the 12 views. While doing this, make sure you change the WHERE clause appropriately to reflect the corresponding month start and end dates.

Finally, combine the 12 views into your target view. This is shown in Listing 5.23.

LISTING 5.23 Creating the monthly View of the Total Checkouts Per Employee in Each Month of 1999

```
CREATE VIEW monthly(
  Employee_No, Jan,
Feb, Mar, Apr,
May, Jun, Jul, Aug, Sep)
AS
SELECT E.Employee_No,
  VJan.Jan,
```

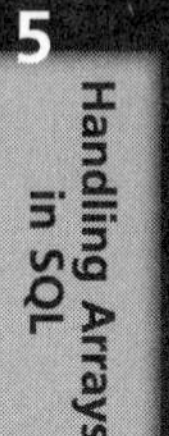
5
Handling Arrays in SQL

LISTING 5.23 CONTINUED

```
  VMar.Mar,
  VApr.Apr,
  VMay.May,
  VJun.Jun,
  VJul.Jul,
  VAug.Aug,
  VSep.Sep,
  VOct.Oct,
  VNov.Nov,
  VDec.Dec,
FROM  Employee AS E,
  VJan,
  VFeb,
  VMar,
  VApr,
  VMay,
  VJun,
  VJul,
  VAug,
  VSep,
  VOct,
  VNov,
  VDec;
```

Summary

In this chapter, you have seen how to represent arrays in SQL and perform basic matrix operations. Two approaches have been suggested to represent arrays, the second of which allows for representing multi-dimensional arrays and makes performing matrix operations easier. Although matrix operations can be done in SQL, I recommend that you don't try to do them because they use a lot of the system resources and might run for a long time. Instead, you can use another programming language with SQL, in which case SQL will be embedded in the other language statements to pull the data from the tables for you.

CHAPTER 6

Other Schema Objects

In This Chapter

In Chapter 3, "Table Creation and Manipulation," you looked at how tables and columns are created in SQL. Few applications operate with only a single table. Most applications require multiple tables, and most implementations support many applications, each with its own set of tables. To avoid table name collisions (that is, two tables using the same name), SQL offers a way to qualify table names with a higher-order name. This higher-order context in which tables exist is called a *schema*. This chapter discusses schema creation and the objects a schema can contain.

A schema is defined as a collection of objects (tables and views, for example) that share a namespace. A schema has a name, such as `MySchema.MyTable`, which can be used to qualify the name of the objects it contains. In SQL-89, a schema could contain only tables and views (a *view*, as discussed in Chapter 14, "Creating and Using Views," is a virtual table). SQL-92 defines other schema objects, which are examined in this chapter. Currently (as of summer 1999), few database vendors have implemented these other schema objects. Many of these schema objects are not implemented, and others do not completely conform to the SQL standard in their implementation. You can see how the most popular database products have implemented some of these other schema objects (such as triggers and stored procedures) in the sections "Triggers" and "Procedures."

Creating Schemas

According to the SQL standard, a schema can contain the following type of objects:

- Base tables and views
- Domains and UDTs
- Constraints and assertions
- Character sets
- Collations
- Translations
- Triggers
- SQL modules
- SQL routines
- Roles

However, as pointed out above, most database products allow only a subset of these elements in their implementation of the `CREATE SCHEMA` statement.

All the schema objects are logically seen as being created in a single statement, and the order in which the object creation statements are written does not matter. The example in Listing 6.1, for example, grants access to a view before the CREATE VIEW statement and creates a view before the creation of the underlying table. It is also possible for a table to declare foreign keys to tables specified later in the CREATE SCHEMA statement.

If an error occurs while creating any schema object, none of the schema objects are created. The example in Listing 6.1 assumes the prior creation of an authorization ID named bob. No schema name is given, so according to the SQL standard, the name defaults to the authorization ID name bob.

LISTING 6.1 Using a Schema to Simultaneously Create Tables and Views and Grant Access

```
-- Filename: 06squ01.sql
-- Purpose: Create a Schema
   CREATE SCHEMA AUTHORIZATION bob
     GRANT SELECT on view1 TO public
     CREATE VIEW view1(id1) AS SELECT id1 from table1
     CREATE TABLE table1 ( id1 INT PRIMARY KEY )
     CREATE TABLE table2 ( id2 INT PRIMARY KEY )
```

You can modify individual schema objects by using the appropriate ALTER statement, such as ALTER TABLE. Although the SQL standard defines a DROP SCHEMA statement, it is not yet implemented in many database products. In this case, to undo a CREATE SCHEMA statement, you must use a DROP statement for each object created within the statement.

Temporary Tables

SQL has several types of tables, some of which are new to SQL-92. SQL-89 provides base tables, discussed in Chapter 3, and views, discussed in Chapter 14. SQL-92 adds temporary tables to this list. I will briefly cover the basics of temporary tables, as they are available in many database products, although not necessarily using the SQL-92 syntax described here. The SQL-92 syntax for creating a temporary table is to use CREATE GLOBAL TEMPORARY TABLE or CREATE LOCAL TEMPORARY TABLE instead of CREATE TABLE, which creates a base table.

The data for base tables is physically stored (usually on disk), but a temporary table materializes only when it is referenced in a SQL session. (*Session* is a term used to describe a connection to a database.) Unlike a base table, the content of a temporary table (neither global nor local) cannot be shared between SQL sessions. The first time a created *global temporary table* is referenced in a SQL session, a new instance is created. The first time a created *local temporary table*is referenced within a SQL module or embedded SQL program, a new instance is created. As a result, two stored procedures cannot share the same local temporary table, even within the same SQL session. This sharing within a session can be accomplished only with a global temporary table.

If you create a temporary table, you can also use the `ON COMMIT` clause to indicate whether you want to empty the table whenever a `COMMIT` statement is executed. If you do not use the `ON COMMIT` clause when creating a temporary table, it defaults to `ON COMMIT DELETE ROWS` . Listing 6.2 shows the creation of a global temporary table that keeps its content after a `COMMIT` statement.

LISTING 6.2 Using the `ON COMMIT` Clause When Creating a Global Temporary Table

```
CREATE GLOBAL TEMPORARY TABLE t1
  ( id1 INT PRIMARY KEY )
ON COMMIT PRESERVE ROWS
```

Temporary tables are a way to give users working space without granting them `CREATE TABLE` privileges. And because each instance of a temporary table exists in isolation, this working space is not subject to interference from other concurrent users.

Assertions

In Chapter 3, you saw that SQL has several types of constraints, which are attached to tables or columns. In addition to these constraints, SQL-92 gives you a type of constraint that is not attached to a particular table or column. This type of constraint, called an *assertion*, is normally used to specify a business rule that affects more than one table. In Listing 6.3, for example, you create an `ASSERTION` to ensure that table `t1` contains as many rows as table `t2`.

LISTING 6.3 Using an Assertion to Ensure Two Tables Contain the Same Number of Rows

```
CREATE ASSERTION t1_equal_t2
  CHECK( (SELECT COUNT(*) FROM t1) = (SELECT COUNT(*) FROM t2) )
```

In Listing 6.4, you create an `ASSERTION` to ensure that table `t3` is never empty. You cannot do this through a constraint because the constraint fires only during a row operation (that is, during an `INSERT` or `UPDATE`).

LISTING 6.4 Using an Assertion to Ensure a Table Is Never Empty

```
CREATE ASSERTION t3_never_empty
  CHECK( (SELECT COUNT(*) FROM t3) > 0 )
```

An ASSERTION is deleted by using the DROP ASSERTION statement. There is no ALTER ASSERTION statement.

Domains

A *domain* is a new SQL-92 schema element that allows you to declare an alias for a specific built-in data type (and, if applicable, size). A domain cannot reference another domain to create a new type.

As you can see in Listing 6.5, using a domain is an acceptable alternative to look up tables because the code to validate all columns with this user-defined data type is conveniently located in one place. Modifying this validation code is just as straightforward as modifying the data in the lookup table.

LISTING 6.5 Using a Domain to Define a Common Column Type

```
CREATE DOMAIN canadian_province
  CHAR(2) NOT NULL
  DEFAULT '??'
  CHECK( VALUE IN
    ('AB', 'BC', 'MB', 'NB', 'NF', 'NS',
    'NW', 'ON', 'PE', 'PQ', 'SK', 'QU', 'YU', '??') )
```

A DOMAIN can have CHECK conditions and DEFAULT conditions associated with it, and you can indicate whether the data type permits NULL values. These conditions are passed on to any columns defined by using that domain. Any condition explicitly specified on a column overrides the domain condition, as shown in Listing 6.6.

LISTING 6.6 A Domain Is Used in a **CREATE TABLE** Statement, Overriding the Domain **DEFAULT**

```
CREATE TABLE t1
  ( c1 canadian_province DEFAULT 'ON' )
```

SQL-92 provides the ALTER DOMAIN and DROP DOMAIN statements to modify and delete domains.

Triggers

A *trigger* is a schema object that's invoked when an attempt is made to modify the table it is associated with. Conceptually, a trigger is an advanced form of a rule, used to enforce more elaborate restrictions on data. Triggers are not part of SQL-92, but are available in many database products, and a standardized form has been proposed in the SQL3 working document.

Triggers are often used to enforce business rules and data integrity or for other complex actions, such as updating summary data. With them, you can perform cascading delete or update actions if a referential integrity violation occurs, and prevent incorrect, unauthorized, or inconsistent changes to data. Triggers are needed because not all database products implement cascading actions using declarative referential integrity.

Triggers are associated with a table, and their execution is automatic. You cannot call a trigger directly; they are invoked whenever modifications are made to a table using INSERT, UPDATE or DELETE. If constraints exist on the "trigger table," they are checked before the trigger execution. If constraints are violated, the data modification statement is not executed and the trigger will not run.

Procedures

Stored procedures are precompiled SQL statements stored in the database. The two major differences between a `TRIGGER` and a `PROCEDURE` are that a stored procedure can accept and return values and that it is invoked by a call from a user session. As with triggers, each database product has its own version of `PROCEDURE`, so you should consult section VII to find out what your particular vendor has given you.

Stored procedures help improve performance when performing repetitive tasks because they are compiled the first time they are executed. Most database products have a procedure cache where a compiled version of the most recently used procedures is kept. This makes subsequent calls to a stored procedure faster and more efficient.

Stored procedures can be used to share application logic to other front-end applications, thus making it easier to change business rules or policies. Finally, stored procedures can be used as a security mechanism. A user can be granted permission to execute a stored procedure even if he or she does not have permissions on the tables or views referenced in that procedure.

Listing 6.7 is an example of the code for creating a stored procedure. Check Section VII to see if this syntax works for your database product.

LISTING 6.7 Creating a Stored Procedure

```
-- Filename: 06squ02.sql
-- Purpose: Create a Procedure

   CREATE PROCEDURE ins_table1( @id1 INT) AS
     INSERT table1 ( id1 ) VALUES( @id1
```

Here is how this stored procedure is called:

```
SELECT * FROM table1

ins_table1 1

SELECT * FROM table1
```

This code returns the following:

```
id1
-----------
(0 row(s) affected)

(1 row(s) affected)

id1
-----------
1

(1 row(s) affected)
```

The previous stored procedure did not return any rows. It is also possible to create a row-returning stored procedure as shown here:

```
   CREATE PROCEDURE get_table1( ) AS
     SELECT * FROM table1
```

The examples of a stored procedure contained a single SQL statement, but a stored procedure can contain a batch of statements.

Summary

A schema is a collection of objects that share a namespace. A schema has a name, such as `MySchema.MyTable`, that can be used to qualify the name of the objects it contains.

While in SQL-89 a schema could contain only tables and views, SQL-92 allows other schema objects, such as:

- Base tables and views
- Domains and UDTs
- Constraints and assertions
- Character sets
- Collations
- Translations
- Triggers
- SQL modules
- SQL routines
- Roles

All the schema objects are logically seen as being created in a single statement, and the order in which the object creation statements are written does not matter. If an error occurs while creating any schema object, none of the schema objects are created.

An `ASSERTION` is a type of constraint that is not attached to a particular table or column, a `DOMAIN` is an alias for a specific built-in data type (and, if applicable, size), and a `TRIGGER` is a schema object that's invoked when an attempt is made to modify the table it is associated with. Stored procedures are precompiled SQL statements stored in the database.

Many of these schema objects are not implemented, and others do not completely conform to the SQL standard in their implementation.

CHAPTER 7

Inserts, Updates, and Deletes

In This Chapter

Data Manipulation Language

The primary purpose of a relational database is to store data and to provide a means to access and manipulate the data. The Data Manipulation Language, or DML as it is commonly referred to, is the set of statements that can be used to manipulate the data stored in the database. The SELECT, INSERT, UPDATE, and DELETE statements compose the Data Manipulation Language. All the DML statements are atomic in nature. Referential integrity checks and constraint violation checks are performed when the INSERT, UPDATE, or DELETE statements are executed. These statements also fire triggers defined on the tables. The implementation of triggers is vendor dependent, and the ANSI standard specifies trigger events that can be fired before or after the statement changes are made. The WHERE clause is used in the SELECT, UPDATE, and DELETE statements to restrict the rows from the target tables that are used to form the resultset for the operation. Now let's look at the ANSI SQL definition of the INSERT, UPDATE, and DELETE statements.

SQL-92 INSERT Statement

The ANSI SQL standard uses the INSERT statement to create new rows in a table. The basic syntax of the INSERT statement is as follows:

```
INSERT INTO <table name> ¦ <view name> (<column list>)
VALUES (<column values list>) ¦ DEFAULT VALUES
¦ <query expression>
```

The <table name> parameter specifies the table into which data is inserted. The <view name> parameter specifies the view into which the data is inserted. If a view is specified, then the columns referred to in the INSERT statement can refer to only one base table in the view. The <column list> parameter is the name of the columns into which the data is being inserted. If <column list> is not specified, then the data is inserted into the columns in the defined order. The <column values list> parameter sets the values for each column specified in the <column list> parameter. The identity column of a table cannot be specified in the <column list> of an INSERT statement. The DEFAULT VALUES option, if used in place of the <column values list> , inserts the default values for all columns as defined in the table definition. The INSERT statement for DEFAULT VALUES is the same as the following:

```
INSERT INTO <table name> (column1, column2, column3)
VALUES (DEFAULT, DEFAULT, DEFAULT)
```

For views defined with the CHECK option, the INSERT statement also validates the data inserted into the base tables through the view. The <query expression> parameter optionally allows a SELECT statement to be provided in place of the column values. The SELECT statement can be used to insert more than one row into the table.

SQL-92 UPDATE Statement

The ANSI SQL standard uses the UPDATE statement to update existing rows in a table. The UPDATE statements are of two types: positioned and searched. A *positioned* UPDATE statement is used to update a row positioned by using a cursor. The *searched* UPDATE statement is used to update data in a table by specifying a search condition. Here is the basic syntax of the UPDATE statement:

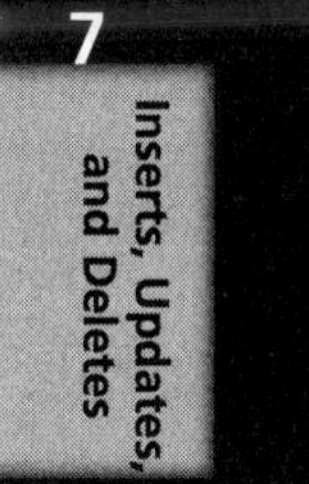
7
Inserts, Updates,
and Deletes

```
UPDATE <table name> ¦ <view name>
SET <column and values list>
WHERE <search condition>
```

The <table name> parameter specifies the table being updated. The <view name> parameter specifies the view that is updated. If a view is specified, then the columns referred to in the UPDATE statement can refer to only one base table in the view. The <column and values list> parameter specifies the column and the new values for the column as a comma-separated string. The general syntax of the parameter is as follows:

```
<column1> = <value1> ¦ DEFAULT
```

The DEFAULT keyword, when used, sets the value of the column to the default specified for the column in the table definition. For views defined with the CHECK option, the UPDATE statement also validates the data being updated in the base table. The <search condition> parameter specifies the conditions that are evaluated to determine the rows to be updated.

SQL-92 DELETE Statement

The ANSI SQL standard defines the DELETE statement to delete rows in a table. The DELETE statements are of two types: positioned and searched. A *positioned* DELETE is used to delete a row positioned by using a cursor. The *searched* DELETE is used to delete data from a table by specifying a search condition. This is the basic syntax of the DELETE statement:

```
DELETE FROM <table name> ¦ <view name>
WHERE <search condition>
```

The <table name> parameter specifies the table from which rows are deleted, and the <view name> parameter specifies the view from which rows are deleted. Rows can be deleted through a view only if the view is based on a single table. The <search condition> parameter specifies the conditions that are evaluated to determine the rows to be deleted.

For more information on positioned updates and deletes, refer to Chapter 18, "Implementing Cursors." The implementation of `INSERT`, `UPDATE`, and `DELETE` statements differs from one database vendor to another. Vendor-specific extensions are provided to enhance and support more features than what's specified in the ANSI SQL standard. Database vendors also supply mechanisms by which a large volume of data can be imported to or exported from a table. This process is usually referred to as *bulk loading and unloading* . In the next two sections of this chapter, you will look at the implementation of the `INSERT`, `UPDATE`, `DELETE`, and bulk loading/unloading statements in Microsoft SQL Server 7.0 and Oracle 8.0.

Inserts, Updates, and Deletes in Microsoft SQL Server

Microsoft SQL Server 7.0 supports the ANSI standard-specific `INSERT`, `UPDATE`, and `DELETE` statements. Apart from this, Transact-SQL extensions are supplied to extend the statements' capabilities. For example, Transact-SQL has extensions that allow data to be inserted into a table on a remote server. Microsoft SQL Server 7.0 supports updatable views that can be referenced in the `INSERT`, `UPDATE`, and `DELETE` statements. The following rules are used to determine whether a view is updatable:

- The `SELECT` statement that makes up the view definition does not contain any aggregate functions in the select list and the `TOP`, `GROUP BY`, `UNION`, or `DISTINCT` clauses. Aggregate functions can, however, be used in subqueries of the `SELECT` statement.
- The `SELECT` statement does not contain any derived columns in the select list. Columns derived by using simple functions or addition or subtraction operators are not considered derived columns.
- The `SELECT` statement references at least one table in the `FROM` clause.
- The select list contains at least one column from a table. The `SELECT` statement cannot contain only system functions or non-tabular columns.

If the `INSERT`, `UPDATE`, or `DELETE` statements reference a view, the statements can operate on only one base table at a time from the view. Depending on the capability of the OLE DB provider, these statements can also be used on remote data sources. Data on a remote server is accessed by using the rowset functions `OPENROWSET` or `OPENQUERY`. The rowset functions can be referenced just like any other table.

Transact-SQL INSERT Statement

The INSERT statement is used to add rows to a table, a view, or a rowset function. The syntax of the INSERT statement is as follows:

```
INSERT INTO
<table name> WITH ( <table hint list>) ¦ <view name>
¦ <rowset function>
[(<column list>)]
VALUES (DEFAULT ¦ NULL ¦ expression) ¦ <select statement>
¦ <execute statement> ¦ DEFAULT VALUES
```

The <table name> parameter specifies the table into which the data is inserted. The <table hint list> parameter specifies the locking mechanism that should be used by the query optimizer. The locking hint can be the following:

- HOLDLOCK or SERIALIZABLE—Places a range lock on the dataset, preventing other transactions from updating or inserting rows into the dataset until the transaction is completed.
- PAGLOCK—Places shared page lock in situations where a single shared table lock is taken.
- READCOMMITTED—Places shared locks on the data being read.
- REPEATABLEREAD—Places locks on data used in the query, preventing other transactions from updating the data.
- ROWLOCK—Places a shared row lock in situations when a single shared page or table lock is taken.
- TABLOCK—Places a shared lock on the table. The lock is held until the end of the statement. If HOLDLOCK is also specified, then the lock is held until the end of the transaction.
- TABLOCKX—Places an exclusive lock on the table. The lock is held until the end of the statement or transaction.

The <view name> parameter specifies the view into which the data is inserted. The <rowset function> parameter can be either the OPENQUERY or the OPENROWSET function. The <column list> parameter specifies the columns into which data is inserted. For every column specified in the <column list> the value is specified in the VALUES clause. The NULL keyword is used to insert NULL into a NULL-able column. The DEFAULT keyword indicates that the column's default value should be inserted. If there's no default on a column and the column allows nulls, NULL is inserted. If the DEFAULT keyword is specified for a column of the time stamp data type, the next time stamp value is inserted. The data values can be specified as a constant, a variable, or an expression. The `<select statement>` parameter is any `SELECT` statement that returns data to be inserted. The columns in the `SELECT` statement should be compatible with the columns specified in the `INSERT` statement. The `<execute statement>` parameter is any Transact-SQL batch or stored procedure that returns data using `SELECT` or `READTEXT` statements. The resultset should be compatible with the columns specified in the `INSERT` statement. The `DEFAULT VALUES` option inserts a row that contains the default values for all columns in the table. If a column is not `NULL`-able and does not have a default value specified, the `INSERT` statement returns an error message. By default, only members of the `sysadmin` fixed server role, members of the `db_owner` fixed database role, and the table owner have permissions to insert into tables. Listing 7.1 shows a few examples of using the `INSERT` statement with the `VALUES` option. The output of `SELECT` statements in all code listings is shown between comments as appropriate.

LISTING 7.1 LST7_1.TXT—INSERT Statement Examples

```
USE Northwind
go
CREATE TABLE SalesPerson(ID int, Last_Name varchar(20) Not Null,
             First_Name varchar(20) Null)
go
/* Insert statement with values in the default column order */
INSERT INTO SalesPerson VALUES(1, 'Smith', 'John')
/* Insert with column list specified */
INSERT INTO SalesPerson (Last_Name, ID) VALUES ('Green', 2)
go
SELECT * FROM SalesPerson
/* Output of SELECT statement:
ID          Last_Name            First_Name
----------- -------------------- --------------------
1           Smith                John
2           Green                NULL
*/
```

The first `INSERT` statement in Listing 7.1 uses an `INSERT` statement with no column list specified, and the values for all columns are specified in the column order in the `VALUES` clause. The second `INSERT` statement specifies that the column list should insert data into only the `Last_Name` and `ID` fields of the table. If the columns are specified in the column list, they don't have to be specified in the same order as in the table. Listing 7.2 shows some examples of using a `SELECT` statement to add data into a table.

LISTING 7.2 LST7_2.TXT—Insert by Using a SELECT Statement

```
USE Northwind
go
CREATE TABLE Orders_USA (CustomerID nchar(10) Not Null, OrderID int Not Null,
             OrderDate datetime Not Null)
go
/* Insert statement orders shipped to USA from the ORDERS table */
INSERT INTO Orders_USA
SELECT CustomerID, OrderID, OrderDate
FROM Orders
WHERE ShipCountry = 'USA'
go
SELECT * FROM Orders_USA
/* Output of the SELECT statement: First six rows shown.
CustomerID OrderID     OrderDate
---------- ----------- ---------------------------
RATTC      10262       1996-07-22 00:00:00.000
WHITC      10269       1996-07-31 00:00:00.000
SPLIR      10271       1996-08-01 00:00:00.000
RATTC      10272       1996-08-02 00:00:00.000
RATTC      10294       1996-08-30 00:00:00.000
OLDWO      10305       1996-09-13 00:00:00.000
*/
```

The SELECT statement can also be used to reference a remote table on a linked server, or it can use the OPENQUERY or OPENROWSET functions. Listing 7.3 uses the SELECT INTO statement to insert rows into a table.

LISTING 7.3 LST7_3.TXT—SELECT INTO Example

```
USE Northwind
go
/* Create a table to hold orders shipped to UK and insert data
  from the ORDERS table */
SELECT CustomerID, OrderID, OrderDate
INTO Orders_UK
FROM Orders
WHERE ShipCountry = 'UK'
go
SELECT * FROM Orders_UK
/* Output of the SELECT statement: First six rows shown.
CustomerID OrderID     OrderDate
---------- ----------- ---------------------------
```

LISTING 7.3 CONTINUED

```
BSBEV    10289      1996-08-26 00:00:00.000
ISLAT    10315      1996-09-26 00:00:00.000
ISLAT    10318      1996-10-01 00:00:00.000
ISLAT    10321      1996-10-03 00:00:00.000
AROUT    10355      1996-11-15 00:00:00.000
SEVES    10359      1996-11-21 00:00:00.000
*/
```

The SELECT INTO statement creates a table and inserts rows retrieved from the SELECT statement into it. The whole statement is one atomic transaction, and the table is not created if the statement fails. Listing 7.4 uses the EXECUTE statement to insert data in a table.

LISTING 7.4 LST7_4.TXT—Insert Example Using an EXECUTE Statement

```
USE Northwind
go
-- If table exists, drop and recreate.
IF OBJECTPROPERTY(OBJECT_ID('Orders_USA'), 'IsTable') = 1

DROP TABLE Orders_USA
GO
CREATE TABLE Orders_USA (CustomerID nchar(10) Not Null, OrderID int Not Null,
             OrderDate datetime Not Null)
go
CREATE PROCEDURE GetUSAOrdersForDate
@OrderDate datetime
AS
SELECT CustomerID, OrderID, OrderDate
FROM Orders
WHERE ShipCountry = 'USA' And OrderDate >= @OrderDate
go
INSERT INTO Orders_USA EXECUTE GetUSAOrdersForDate '1998-05-01 00:00'
go
INSERT  INTO  Orders_USA  EXECUTE('SELECT  ''ZZYY''  AS  CustomerID,  12440  AS
OrderID,
                CURRENT_TIMESTAMP AS OrderDate')
go
SELECT * FROM Orders_USA
/* Output of the SELECT statement:
CustomerID OrderID     OrderDate
---------- ----------- ---------------------------
SAVEA      11064       1998-05-01 00:00:00.000
```

LISTING 7.4 CONTINUED

```
WHITC    11066    1998-05-01 00:00:00.000
RATTC    11077    1998-05-06 00:00:00.000
ZZYY     12440    1999-07-21 23:04:07.660
*/
```

The EXECUTE statement calls a simple stored procedure that returns orders based on a date value. The resultset from the stored procedure is then inserted into the Orders_USA table. If the stored procedure returns multiple resultsets, the columns in the resultset should be the same as the destination columns of the INSERT statement; otherwise, an error is returned. Listing 7.4 also demonstrates an INSERT statement that uses a dynamic SQL statement to insert a row into the Orders_USA table.

Transact-SQL UPDATE Statement

The UPDATE statement can be used to update specific rows in a table, view, or rowset function. Positioned updates can also be performed on rows positioned by using a cursor. For more help on positioned updates, refer to Chapter 18. This is the syntax of the UPDATE statement:

```
UPDATE
<table name> WITH ( <table hint list> ) ¦ <view name>
¦ <rowset function>
SET
<column name> = <expression> ¦ DEFAULT ¦ NULL
¦ @variable = <expression>
¦ @variable = <column name> = <expression>
FROM <table list>
WHERE <search condition>
```

The <table name> parameter specifies the table being updated. The <table hint list> parameter specifies the locking mechanism that should be used by the query optimizer. The locking hint can be HOLDLOCK or SERIALIZABLE, PAGLOCK, READCOMMITTED, REPEATABLE-READ, ROWLOCK, TABLOCK, or TABLOCKX. The <view name> parameter specifies the view that is updated. The <rowset function> parameter can be used to update data on a remote server. The SET clause specifies the columns that are updated. Identity column values cannot be updated. The value for the updated column can be a constant, an expression, a SELECT statement that returns a single value, the DEFAULT keyword, or the NULL keyword. The DEFAULT keyword updates the value of the column with the defined default. The UPDATE statement can also be used to update a local variable with a value from a column or an expression. The variable can be updated with the pre-update value of the column by using the SET @variable = <column name>, <column name> = <expression> clause in the

UPDATE statement. The variable can be updated with the same value as the column by using the SET @variable = <column name> = <expression> clause in the UPDATE statement. The FROM clause specifies the tables that are joined to supply the qualifying rows for the update operation. The <table list> parameter can be a table, view, rowset function, or derived table. The <search condition> parameter limits the rows that are updated. If an update to a row violates a constraint or rule, NULL setting for the column, an arithmetic overflow error or data type conversion error, then the statement is canceled, an error is returned, and no records are updated. Listing 7.5 shows a few examples of the UPDATE statement.

LISTING 7.5 LST7_5.TXT—UPDATE Examples

```
USE Northwind
go
BEGIN TRAN
DECLARE @Shipper nvarchar(80)
SET @Shipper = 'Great Lakes Food Market'
PRINT 'Before Update...'
PRINT ''
SELECT OrderID, OrderDate, ShippedDate, Freight
FROM Orders
WHERE ShipCountry = 'USA' And
   OrderDate > '1998-03-01 00:00' And
   ShipName = @Shipper
/* Output of the SELECT statement:
OrderID     OrderDate                   ShippedDate                  Freight
----------- --------------------------- --------------------------- -------
10936       1998-03-09 00:00:00.000     1998-03-18 00:00:00.000     33.6800
11006       1998-04-07 00:00:00.000     1998-04-15 00:00:00.000     25.1900
11040       1998-04-22 00:00:00.000     NULL                18.8400
11061       1998-04-30 00:00:00.000     NULL                14.0100
*/
PRINT 'Updating Orders for shipper: ' + @Shipper
/*
 The UPDATE statement increases freight value by $1.25, updates null
 shipping date to two days after the Order date. The UPDATE statement
 affects orders placed after 03/01/99 by 'Great Lakes Food Market'
*/
UPDATE Orders
SET Freight = Freight + 1.25,
  ShippedDate = ISNULL(ShippedDate, DATEADD(dd, 2, OrderDate))
WHERE ShipCountry = 'USA' And
   OrderDate > '1998-03-01 00:00' And
   ShipName = @Shipper
```

LISTING 7.5 CONTINUED

```
PRINT 'After Update...'
PRINT ''
SELECT OrderID, OrderDate, ShippedDate, Freight
FROM Orders
WHERE ShipCountry = 'USA' And
   OrderDate > '1998-03-01 00:00' And
   ShipName = @Shipper
/* Output of the SELECT statement:
OrderID     OrderDate                   ShippedDate                 Freight

----------- --------------------------- --------------------------- -------
10936       1998-03-09 00:00:00.000     1998-03-18 00:00:00.000     34.9300
11006       1998-04-07 00:00:00.000     1998-04-15 00:00:00.000     26.4400
11040       1998-04-22 00:00:00.000     1998-04-24 00:00:00.000     20.0900
11061       1998-04-30 00:00:00.000     1998-05-02 00:00:00.000     15.2600
*/
ROLLBACK TRAN
GO
```

The update example shows how system functions can be used in the SET clause of the UPDATE statement. The SELECT statements before and after the UPDATE statement show the change in values. The example uses the orders table in the sample database Northwind, and the update is done in a transaction that is rolled back at the end. Listing 7.6 shows an example of an UPDATE statement that uses variables in the SET clause.

LISTING 7.6 LST7_6.TXT—UPDATE Examples Using Local Variables

```
USE Northwind
go
CREATE TABLE Update_Test (Sequence_Number int)
go
INSERT Update_Test VALUES(1)
INSERT Update_Test VALUES(2)
INSERT Update_Test VALUES(3)
INSERT Update_Test VALUES(4)
go
PRINT 'Before Update...'
PRINT ''
SELECT * FROM Update_Test
/* Output of the SELECT statement:
Sequence_Number
---------------
```

LISTING 7.6 CONTINUED

```
1
2
3
4
*/
go
PRINT 'Updating Sequence numbers with new seed...'
PRINT ''
DECLARE @Sequence int
SET @Sequence = 100
UPDATE Update_Test
SET @Sequence = Sequence_Number = @Sequence + 1
go
PRINT 'After Update...'
PRINT ''
SELECT * FROM Update_Test
/* Output of the SELECT statement:
Sequence_Number
---------------
101
102
103
104
```

The code example demonstrates a powerful feature of the UPDATE statement. The Update_Test table contains sequence numbers starting from one. The UPDATE statement is used to change the sequence numbers of all rows starting with the value 101. Incremental sequence numbers are generated by using a local variable as part of the UPDATE statement that acts as an incremental counter as the update progresses through every row. This problem normally requires a loop to produce the results. However, the UPDATE statement's ability to use local variables as part of the SET clause helps provide an elegant solution to the problem.

Transact-SQL DELETE Statement

The DELETE statement is used to delete rows from a table, view, or rowset function. Positioned deletes can also be performed on rows positioned by using a cursor. For more help on positioned deletes, refer to Chapter 18. The syntax of the DELETE statement is as follows:

```
DELETE FROM
<table name> WITH ( <table hint list>) ¦ <view name>
¦ <rowset function>
FROM <table list>
WHERE <search condition>
```

The `<table name>` parameter specifies the table from which rows are deleted. The `<table hint list>` parameter specifies the locking mechanism that should be used by the query optimizer. The locking hint can be `HOLDLOCK` or `SERIALIZABLE`, `PAGLOCK`, `READCOMMITTED`, `REPEATABLEREAD`, `ROWLOCK`, `TABLOCK`, or `TABLOCKX`. The `<view name>` parameter specifies the view from which rows are deleted. The `<rowset function>` parameter is used to delete data on a remote server. The `WHERE` clause specifies the search condition that limits the rows being deleted. Listing 7.7 shows a few examples of the `DELETE` statement.

LISTING 7.7 LST7_7.TXT—DELETE Examples

```
USE Northwind
go
CREATE TABLE Delete_Test (Sequence_Number int)
go
INSERT Delete_Test VALUES(1)
INSERT Delete_Test VALUES(2)
INSERT Delete_Test VALUES(3)
INSERT Delete_Test VALUES(4)
INSERT Delete_Test VALUES(5)
go
SELECT * FROM Delete_Test
Go
/* Output of the SELECT statement:
Sequence_Number
---------------
1
2
3
4
5
*/
PRINT 'Delete statement with WHERE clause...'
BEGIN TRAN
DELETE FROM Delete_Test WHERE Sequence_Number BETWEEN 2 AND 4
SELECT * FROM Delete_Test
/* Output of the SELECT statement:
Sequence_Number
```

LISTING 7.7 CONTINUED

```
---------------
1
5
*/
ROLLBACK TRAN
GO
PRINT 'Delete statement without WHERE clause...'
BEGIN TRAN
DELETE FROM Delete_Test
SELECT * FROM Delete_Test
/* Output of the SELECT statement:
Sequence_Number
---------------
*/
ROLLBACK TRAN
GO
PRINT 'Truncate Table statement...'
TRUNCATE TABLE Delete_Test
SELECT * FROM Delete_Test
/* Output of the SELECT statement:
Sequence_Number
---------------
*/
GO
```

The first DELETE statement in the code listing deletes rows from the Delete_Test table in which the value in the Sequence_Number column ranges from two to four. By issuing a SELECT statement after the DELETE statement, you can see that the rows are deleted. The second DELETE statement removes all rows from the table by specifying no WHERE clause. The TRUNCATE TABLE statement is similar to a DELETE statement without a WHERE clause. The main difference is that the TRUNCATE TABLE statement records only the deallocation of pages, but the DELETE statement (without the WHERE clause) records the delete of each row. Hence, the TRUNCATE TABLE statement requires less transaction space than the DELETE statement (without the WHERE clause). TRUNCATE TABLE can be used as a fast means of deleting all rows from a table; however, it cannot be issued on a table that is referenced by foreign keys. If the DELETE statement violates a constraint or rule, an arithmetic overflow error, or data type conversion error, then the statement is canceled, an error is returned, and no records are deleted.

Conditions in the WHERE Clause

The WHERE clause is used to restrict the rows that contribute to a statement's resultset. For example, the WHERE clause in a SELECT statement restricts the rows returned by executing the SELECT statement. With the UPDATE and DELETE statements, the WHERE clause restricts the rows in the target table that are affected. Microsoft SQL Server does not impose any limits on the number of predicates in a WHERE clause. A *predicate* is an expression that returns a TRUE, FALSE, or UNKNOWN value. The search condition for the WHERE clause is specified as a series of expressions. This is the general syntax of the search condition:

```
<search condition> =
{ [ NOT ] <predicate> ¦ ( <search condition> ) }
[ {AND ¦ OR} [NOT] {<predicate> ¦ ( <search condition> ) }]
} [,...n]
where <predicate> is
{ <expression> { = ¦ <> ¦ != ¦ > ¦ >= ¦ !> ¦ < ¦ <= ¦ !< }
 <expression>
¦ <string expression> [NOT] LIKE <string expression>
          [ESCAPE '<escape character>']
¦ <expression> [NOT] BETWEEN <expression> AND <expression>
¦ <expression> IS [NOT] NULL
¦ CONTAINS( {<column> ¦ * }, '<search condition>' )
¦ FREETEXT( {<column> ¦ * }, 'freetext string' )
¦ <expression> [NOT] IN (<subquery> ¦ <expression list> )
¦ EXISTS (<subquery>)
¦ <expression> { = ¦ <> ¦ != ¦ > ¦ >= ¦ !> ¦ < ¦ <= ¦ !< }
{ALL ¦ SOME ¦ ANY} (<subquery>)
}
```

The order of precedence for the logical operators is NOT, AND, and OR. The order of evaluation at the same precedence level is always from left to right, but this can be overridden by using parentheses in the search condition. Listing 7.8 shows an example of a WHERE clause and the search conditions used to restrict rows.

LISTING 7.8 LST7_8.TXT—Search Conditions in a WHERE Clause

```
USE pubs
Go
PRINT 'Get titles with ''computer'' in their name... '
SELECT authors.au_lname, authors.au_fname, titles.title
FROM authors
 INNER JOIN titleauthor ON authors.au_id = titleauthor.au_id
 INNER JOIN titles ON titleauthor.title_id = titles.title_id
WHERE (titles.title LIKE '%computer%')
```

LISTING 7.8 CONTINUED

```
ORDER BY authors.au_lname, authors.au_fname
Go
```

For more information on using search conditions, see SQL Server Books Online.

Referential Integrity

Database integrity ensures the accuracy and reliability of the data stored in the database. Data integrity can be broadly classified into four categories: entity, domain, referential, and user-defined integrity. Referential integrity preserves the relationships between tables when rows are added, updated, or deleted, ensuring that the key values are consistent across tables.

Referential integrity is usually defined by defining a parent table that contains a primary key or unique key. The child tables contain foreign keys that reference the primary key or unique key of the parent table. A *primary key constraint* is a column or set of columns that uniquely identify a row in a table. The primary key constraint is not allowed if any of the columns that represent the primary key contain duplicate or `NULL` values. A *foreign key constraint* is a column or set of columns used to link data between two tables. It is linked to the primary key constraint or unique key constraint in the parent table. A foreign key constraint can contain `NULL` values, and the verification of the foreign key constraint is skipped. The constraint is evaluated when the value is changed. For example, in the `Northwind` database, the `Order Details` table contains a link to the `Orders` table. There is a logical relationship between the two tables. The `OrderID` column in the `Orders` table is the primary key, and the `OrderID` column in the `Order Details` table is the foreign key to the `Orders` table. Figure 7.1 shows the diagram for the relationship.

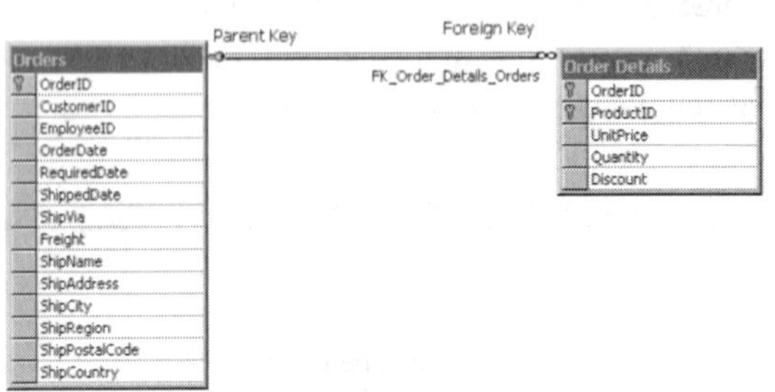

FIGURE 7.1
A relationship diagram.

The primary purpose of a foreign key is to control the changes made to the parent table and control the data stored in the child table. In Microsoft SQL Server, the foreign key constraint is restrictive in nature. It enforces that the changes to the primary key values cannot be made if those changes invalidate the link to data in the foreign key table. If an attempt is made to delete a row in the parent table, the operation will fail if there are foreign keys referencing the value. Similarly, to change the foreign key value, the value should be changed to a different primary key value or `NULL` value or be deleted.

Listing 7.9 shows an example that creates two tables and establishes a logical relationship between them.

LISTING 7.9 LST7_9.TXT—Referential Integrity Example

```
USE Northwind
Go
CREATE SCHEMA AUTHORIZATION dbo
CREATE TABLE Parent_Tbl (ID int NOT NULL IDENTITY(1,1) PRIMARY KEY,
             Value char(1) NOT NULL)
CREATE TABLE Child_Tbl (ID int NULL FOREIGN KEY REFERENCES Parent_Tbl(ID),
            Value char(1) NOT NULL)
GO
PRINT 'Inserting invalid row in the child table...'
INSERT Child_Tbl VALUES(1, 'A')
Go
/*
Server: Msg 547, Level 16, State 1, Line 1
INSERT statement conflicted with COLUMN FOREIGN KEY constraint
'FK__Child_Tbl__ID__6A30C649'. The conflict occurred in
database 'Northwind', table 'Parent_Tbl', column 'ID'.
The statement has been terminated.
*/
Print 'Inserting row in the child table with NULL key value...'
INSERT Child_Tbl VALUES(NULL, 'A')
go
PRINT 'Inserting rows in the parent table...'
INSERT Parent_Tbl VALUES('A')
INSERT Parent_Tbl VALUES('B')
SELECT * FROM Parent_Tbl
/* Output of the SELECT statement:
ID          Value
----------- -----
1           A
2           B
```

LISTING 7.9 CONTINUED

```
*/
go
PRINT 'Updating key value in the child table...'
UPDATE Child_Tbl
SET ID = 1
WHERE Value = 'A'
SELECT * FROM Child_Tbl
/* Output of the SELECT statement:
ID          Value
----------- -----
1           A
*/
Go
PRINT 'Deleting row from the parent table...'
DELETE Parent_Tbl WHERE Value = 'A'
/*
Server: Msg 547, Level 16, State 1, Line 1
DELETE statement conflicted with COLUMN REFERENCE constraint
'FK__Child_Tbl__ID__6A30C649'. The conflict occurred in
database 'Northwind', table 'Child_Tbl', column 'ID'.
The statement has been terminated.
*/
Go
```

The code listing demonstrates two scenarios. In the first scenario, an error message is raised by SQL Server when an invalid foreign key value is inserted in the child table. In the second scenario, SQL Server disallows the delete on a primary key value that is being referenced in the child table. The error messages raised by SQL Server are also shown as part of the script in Listing 7.8. Another Transact-SQL statement that is used in the script is the SQL-92 standard's `CREATE SCHEMA` statement. The `CREATE SCHEMA` statement is used to create a conceptual object under an owner's name that contains tables, views, and permissions. The `CREATE SCHEMA` statement creates all statements within a single statement. This statement is particularly useful in developing scripts that create all the objects as an atomic operation. This statement can also be used to create mutually dependent foreign keys. Listing 7.10 shows examples of the `CREATE SCHEMA` statement.

LISTING 7.10 LST7_10.TXT—CREATE SCHEMA Statement

```
Use NorthWind
GO
PRINT 'Create mutually dependent tables...'
```

LISTING 7.10 CONTINUED

```
go
CREATE SCHEMA AUTHORIZATION dbo
CREATE TABLE Tbl_1 (ID_1 int IDENTITY(1,1) PRIMARY KEY,
          ID_2 int NULL FOREIGN KEY REFERENCES Tbl_2(ID_2))
CREATE TABLE Tbl_2 (ID_2 int IDENTITY(1,1) PRIMARY KEY,
          ID_1 int NULL FOREIGN KEY REFERENCES Tbl_1(ID_1))
GO
Print 'Verify the relationship...'
BEGIN TRAN
DECLARE @ID1 int, @ID2 int
INSERT Tbl_1 VALUES(NULL)
SET @ID1 = @@IDENTITY
INSERT Tbl_2 VALUES(NULL)
SET @ID2 = @@IDENTITY
UPDATE Tbl_1
SET ID_2 = @ID2
WHERE ID_1 = @ID1
UPDATE Tbl_2
SET ID_1 = @ID1
WHERE ID_2 = @ID2
SELECT * FROM Tbl_1
/* Output of the SELECT statement:
ID_1        ID_2
----------- -----------
1           1
*/
SELECT * FROM Tbl_2
/* Output of the SELECT statement:
ID_2        ID_1
----------- -----------
1           1
*/
COMMIT TRAN
Go
```

The CREATE SCHEMA statement, therefore, allows you to easily create tables, views, and complex relationships, and grant permissions in an atomic operation.

Bulk Copy Utility and BULK INSERT Statement

The bulk copy components in SQL Server are used to insert a large number of rows into the database or retrieve a large number of rows from the database. The bulk copy components operate on tables, views, and queries. SQL Server provides the following methods to perform bulk loading:

- Bulk copy utility—**bcp** is a command-line utility that can be used to copy large files into tables or views. The bcp utility can also be used to export data from tables, views, or queries.
- Transact-SQL statement—The `BULK INSERT` Transact-SQL statement is used in stored procedures, batches, and triggers to bulk-copy data from a file into a SQL Server table or view.
- Bulk copy APIs—OLE DB, ODBC, and DB-Library provide APIs for performing bulk copy operations. Data can be loaded in SQL Server tables or views from files or program variables by using the bulk copy APIs.

The bcp utility copies data between a table or view and a data file. The syntax of the bcp utility is as follows:

```
bcp <table name> ¦ <view name> ¦ ''query''
in ¦ out ¦ queryout ¦ format} <data file>
[-m <maximum errors>] [-f <format file>] [-e <error file>]
[-F <first row>] [-L <last row>] [-b <batch size>]
[-n] [-c] [-w] [-N] [-6] [-q] [-C <code page>]
[-t <field terminator>] [-r <row terminator>]
[-i <input file>] [-o <output file>] [-a <packet size>]
[-S <server name>] [-U <login id>] [-P <password>]
[-T] [-v] [-R] [-k] [-E] [-h <hint list>]
```

The bcp utility can bulk copy data into a table or view in the database. The `queryout` option is used to bulk copy data by executing a `SELECT` statement. The `format` option is used to create a format file based on the `-n`, `-c`, `-w`, `-6`, or `-N` options. The format file, used to specify the data in the input file, is used to skip columns from the input file, provide storage information, or save data in different formats. The `-e` option is used to specify the path of an error file used to store rows that cannot be imported successfully into the database. The `-m` option is used to specify the number of errors after which the bcp operation is cancelled. The `-b` option is used to specify the number of rows per batch of data copied by bcp. The `-S` option is used to specify the server running SQL Server. The `-U` option is used to specify the login used to connect to SQL Server. The `-P` option is used to specify the password for the login. For more information on bcp's command-line options, refer to the SQL Server Books Online documentation. The batch file in

Listing 7.11 shows a few examples that use bcp to export data from SQL Server. The batch file should be executed from the DOS command prompt of the SQL Server machine or any machine that has access to SQL Server.

LISTING 7.11 LST7_11.TXT—BCPEXP Batch File

```
@REM Filename: BCPEXP.BAT
@REM Get alphabetical listing of products using the view in
@REM Northwind database.
@REM Specify -S option with the SQL Server name if running
@REM from another machine.
CD\TEMP >NUL
bcp ''Northwind..[Alphabetical list of products]'' out Prods.Dat -c -U sa -P
password
@REM Use trusted connection to connect to SQL Server
@REM Get Top 5 products by sale amount using a query
bcp ''SELECT TOP 5 * FROM Northwind..[Sales Totals by Amount] ORDER BY
SaleAmount DESC'' queryout 5Prods.Dat -c -T
Notepad Prods.dat
Notepad 5prods.dat
Exit
```

The batch file uses the `Northwind` sample database to export data using a view and a query. The batch file in Listing 7.11 uses the character format of bcp to export the data from SQL Server without specifying a format file. The format file can be created interactively by using a simple command line, such as `bcp ''northwind..orders'' out orders.dat`. In the interactive mode, bcp prompts for input for each column in the table or view, and modifications can be made to specify different field terminators, prefix length, and storage type. The `BULK INSERT` Transact-SQL statement can be used to bulk copy data into a SQL Server table or view in a specified format. The `BULK INSERT` statement is executed on the server in the context of the MSSQLServer service, not on the client. It produces the fastest performance when the data file is also located on the server. Here is the syntax of the `BULK INSERT` statement:

```
BULK INSERT <table name> ¦ <view name> FROM <data file>
[WITH (
[ BATCHSIZE [= <batch size>]]
<,] CHECK_CONSTRAINTS]
<,] CODEPAGE [= 'ACP' ¦ 'OEM' ¦ 'RAW' ¦ <code page>]]
<,] DATAFILETYPE [= 'char' ¦ 'native'¦ 'widechar' ¦ 'widenative']]
<,] FIELDTERMINATOR [= <field terminator>]]
<,] FIRSTROW [= <first row>]]
<,] FORMATFILE [= <format file>]]
```

```
[[,] KEEPIDENTITY]
[[,] KEEPNULLS]
[[,] KILOBYTES_PER_BATCH [= <kilobytes per batch>]]
[[,] LASTROW [= <last row>]]
[[,] MAXERRORS [= <maximum errors>]]
[[,] ORDER (<column list> [ASC ¦ DESC])]
[[,] ROWS_PER_BATCH [= <rows per batch>]]
[[,] ROWTERMINATOR [= <row terminator>]]
[[,] TABLOCK]
)]
```

Some of the common options that are used with the `BULK INSERT` statement are `CHECK_CONSTRAINTS`, `DATAFILETYPE`, `FORMATFILE`, `KEEPIDENTITY`, and `ROWS_PER_BATCH`. The `CHECK_CONSTRAINTS` specifies that any constraints on the table into which the data is imported are checked during the bulk copy operation. The `DATAFILETYPE` option specifies the format of the data file. The `'CHAR'`_ option for example performs the bulk copy operation from a data file containing character data. The `FORMATFILE` option describes the contents of the data file. The `KEEPIDENTITY` option specifies that the values for identity columns in a table are present in the data file. If the `KEEPIDENTITY` option is not specified, unique values are generated for the identity column automatically. The `ROWS_PER_BATCH` option specifies the number of rows of data that is imported per batch. This parameter can be used to optimize performance of large bulk load operations.

Listing 7.12 contains a sample data file (`sample.dat`) that is used to load data into a table.

LISTING 7.12 LST7_11.TXT—`Sample.dat` File

```
1,A
2,B
3,C
4,D
5,E
```

The `sample.dat` file should be created in a utility such as Notepad that can work with plain text and saves data in text format. Listing 7.13 shows an example of the `BULK INSERT` statement that loads the sample file created previously.

LISTING 7.13 LST7_13.TXT—`BULK INSERT` Example

```
PRINT 'Create a table to import data from the ''Sample.Dat'' file...'
CREATE TABLE Bulk_Insert_Tbl (ID int NOT NULL, C CHAR(1) NOT NULL)
BULK INSERT Bulk_Insert_Tbl FROM 'C:\Temp\Sample.Dat'
WITH ( FIELDTERMINATOR = ',', ROWTERMINATOR = '\n')
SELECT * FROM Bulk_Insert_Tbl
```

LISTING 7.13 CONTINUED

```
/* Output of the SELECT statement:
ID          C
----------- ----
1           A
2           B
3           C
4           D
5           E
*/
GO
```


The BULK INSERT statement can also be used within a transaction. Rolling back a transaction removes all changes made by the BULK INSERT statement. For more information on using it, refer to the SQL Server Books Online documentation.

In this section, you learned about the INSERT, UPDATE, and DELETE statements in SQL Server and took a brief look at the mechanisms provided by SQL Server to enforce referential integrity. Microsoft SQL Server also supports parallel data load using bulk copy. This feature allows data to be copied into a single table from multiple clients in parallel by using the bcp command-line utility or the BULK INSERT statement.

Inserts, Updates, and Deletes in Oracle

Oracles 8.0 supports the ANSI SQL standard INSERT, UPDATE, and DELETE statements. The INSERT, UPDATE, DELETE, SELECT, and LOCK TABLE statements manipulate data in tables. These statements have additional syntax that is used to extend their functionality. These statements support the use of database links to manipulate data in tables or views on remote databases. The PARTITION and RETURNING clause can also be used with the INSERT, UPDATE, and DELETE statements. The DELETE and UPDATE statements also support table aliases in correlated queries. These statements can be used against an updatable view that contains only one key-preserved table in the join. The UPDATE statement also supports parenthesized lists of columns on the left side of the SET clause. A view cannot be used in INSERT, UPDATE, and DELETE statements if it contains any of the following:

- Set operator
- DISTINCT operator
- Group function

- Flattened subqueries
- Nested table columns
- CAST and MULTISET expressions
- GROUP BY clause
- RETURNING clause

Oracle also supports parallel execution of the DML statements. Optimizer hints can be specified after the INSERT, UPDATE, or DELETE statements to make the operation parallel.

PL/SQL INSERT Statement

The INSERT statement is used to add rows in a table, base table of a view, a partition of a partitioned table, an object table, or the base table of an object's view. Any user with the INSERT privilege or the owner of a table can insert data into it.

```
INSERT INTO [
<table name> [ PARTITION <partition name> ]
¦ <view name>
]
¦ [ THE( <sub query 1> ) ]
[ ( <column list > ) ]
VALUES ( <column values list> ) ¦ (<sub query 2>)
[ RETURNING <expression> INTO <bind variable list> ]
```

The <table name> parameter specifies the table or object table into which rows are inserted. The table can be specified by using the schema.table_name syntax. The <view name> parameter specifies the view into which rows are inserted. The PARTITION clause for the table indicates that inserts that are done in the specified partition. The THE clause is used to perform flattened subqueries. It informs Oracle that the column value returned by the subquery is a nested table, not a scalar value. The <sub query 1> parameter specifies a SELECT statement that is treated like a view, and data can be inserted into the base tables. The <column list> parameter specifies the columns into which data is inserted. For each column in the column list, a value should be supplied in the VALUES clause or the subquery. If a column is omitted from the list, its default value is inserted as specified in the table definition. The <sub query 2> parameter is used to insert rows into a table using a SELECT statement. The RETURNING clause retrieves the rows affected by the INSERT statement and stores the values in bind variables. Only scalar, LOB, ROWID, and REF type values can be retrieved using this clause. The INTO clause is used to store the value of the changed rows in the specified variables. Issuing an INSERT statement against a table fires any INSERT triggers defined on the table.

Listing 7.14 shows a few examples of the INSERT statement.

LISTING 7.14 LST7_14.TXT—INSERT Statement Examples

```
DECLARE DeptNumber dept.DeptNo%TYPE;
    DeptName dept.DName%TYPE;
    DeptLocation dept.Loc%TYPE;
BEGIN
 DeptNumber := 24;
 DeptName := 'SALES';
 DeptLocation := 'MIAMI';
 INSERT INTO dept VALUES (DeptNumber, DeptName, DeptLocation);
 INSERT INTO dept VALUES (43, 'SUPPLIES', 'TAMPA');
 COMMIT;
END;
/
EXEC DBMS_OUTPUT.PUT_LINE('Insert data using column list...');
INSERT INTO emp (empno, ename, job, sal, deptno)
  VALUES (8463, 'SMITH', 'CLERK', 1650, 40);
EXEC DBMS_OUTPUT.PUT_LINE('Insert using system functions, pseudo-
columns...');
CREATE SEQUENCE empseq;
INSERT INTO emp
  VALUES (empseq.nextval, 'CULLEN', 'CLERK', 7566, SYSDATE, 1300, NULL, 20);
EXEC DBMS_OUTPUT.PUT_LINE('Inserting data using a SELECT statement...');
INSERT INTO (SELECT empno, ename, job, sal, deptno FROM emp)
  VALUES (8375, 'GREEN', 'MANAGER', 3500, 20);
COMMIT;
/
DBMS_OUTPUT.PUT_LINE('Inserting data into emp table on a remote data-
base...');
INSERT INTO scott.emp@newyork (emp, empname, job, sal, deptno)
  VALUES (5976, 'SMITH', 'CLERK', 1250, 15);
COMMIT;
/
```

The example demonstrates various uses of the INSERT statement. The INSERT statement can also be used against a remote table, as demonstrated in the script. The database link has to be configured separately for this example to work. For more details on configuring database links, see the Oracle 8.0 Documentation. Listing 7.15 shows the use of the PARTITION clause of the INSERT statement.

LISTING 7.15 LST7_15.TXT—An INSERT Example with the PARTITION Clause

```
INSERT INTO sales PARTITION (June99)
  SELECT * FROM Monthly_Data;
```

The script in Listing 17.15 inserts data from a monthly table into a specific partition of the sales table. The INSERT statement with partitions improves performance and gives you a way to manage very large tables. Listing 17.16 shows the use of bind variables with INSERT statements.

LISTING 7.16 LST7_16.TXT—An INSERT Example with Bind Variables

```
VARIABLE sal NUMBER;
VARIABLE job CHAR(9);
CREATE SEQUENCE empseq;
INSERT INTO emp VALUES (empseq.nextval, 'ROGER', 'MANAGER',
            2359, SYSDATE, 4200, 15)
  RETURNING sal/5, job INTO :sal, :job;
PRINT sal;
PRINT job;
CREATE TYPE emptype AS OBJECT(empno INTEGER, ename VARCHAR2(20))
/
CREATE TABLE emps OF emptype
/
DECLARE
 employee REF emptype;
BEGIN
 INSERT INTO emps e VALUES (emptype(4512, 'MARY'))
  RETURNING REF INTO employee;
 COMMIT;
END;
/
```

The INSERT statement with the RETURNING clause returns the values of the inserted rows into output bind variables. The REF function on a table returns the reference value for the inserted row that is stored in the example's bind variable.

The CREATE TABLE statement supports an extension that can be used to create a table and insert data into the table in one atomic operation. The syntax of the statement is as follows:

```
CREATE TABLE <table name> AS <query>
```

Listing 7.17 shows an example of the CREATE TABLE statement with a SELECT statement as the input.

LISTING 7.17 LST7_17.TXT—CREATE TABLE Example Using SELECT Statement

```
/* Create a table that contains all employees with deptno 44 */
CREATE TABLE emp_20
AS SELECT empno, ename FROM emp WHERE deptno = 20;
SELECT * FROM emp_20
/* Output of the SELECT statement:
  EMPNO    ENAME
--------- ---------
   7369    SMITH
   7566    JONES
   7788    SCOTT
   7876    ADAMS
   7902    FORD
   8375    GREEN
*/
```

The created table will have the same data type as the fields specified in the SELECT statement. The CREATE TABLE privilege is required to create the table.

PL/SQL UPDATE Statement

The UPDATE statement is used to change existing values in a table or in a view's base table. Optimizer hints can be passed by enclosing them in comments in the UPDATE statement. For example, the parallel hint can be specified immediately after the UPDATE keyword to parallelize both the underlying scan and UPDATE operations. The UPDATE statement can be performed only by the table owner or any user with the UPDATE privilege. If the SQL92_SECURITY initialization parameter is set to TRUE, then SELECT privilege is also required on the table whose column values are referenced in the WHERE clause to perform an UPDATE. This is the syntax of the UPDATE statement:

```
UPDATE [
<table name> [ PARTITION ( <partition name> )
¦ <view name>
]
¦ [ THE ( <sub query 1> ) ]
SET <column list> ¦ ( <columns> ) =
  <value list> ¦ <sub query2> ¦ ( <sub query 3> )
WHERE <search condition>
[ RETURNING <expression> INTO <bind variable list> ]
```

The <table name> parameter specifies the table or object table being updated. The table can be specified with the schema.table_name syntax. The <view name> parameter specifies the view that is updated. The PARTITION clause for the table specifies that updates are done in the specified partition. The `THE` clause is used to perform flattened subqueries. It informs Oracle that the column value returned by the subquery is a nested table, not a scalar value. The `<sub query 1>` parameter specifies a `SELECT` statement that is treated like a view, and data can be updated in the base tables. The `SET` clause determines which columns are updated and what values are stored in them. The columns can be specified as a list or a set of columns. The `<sub query 2>` is a `SELECT` statement that returns a value assigned to the corresponding column. The `<sub query 3>` is a `SELECT` statement that returns new values assigned to the corresponding columns when the column list is specified in parentheses. The `WHERE` clause restricts the rows updated to those for which the specified condition is `TRUE`. The search condition can reference the table and contain a subquery. For each row that satisfies the `WHERE` clause, the columns to the left of the equals (=) operator in the `SET` clause are set to the values of the corresponding expressions on the right. The expressions are evaluated as the row is updated. The `RETURNING` clause is used to retrieve the rows affected by the `UPDATE` statement. The `INTO` clause indicates that the values of the changed rows are to be stored in the variable(s) specified in the `<bind variable list>` parameter. Listing 7.18 shows an example of the `UPDATE` statement.

LISTING 7.18 LST7_18.TXT—UPDATE **Statement Example**

```
DECLARE
  SalInc NUMBER;
BEGIN
SalInc := 100;
UPDATE emp
  SET comm = NULL, sal = sal + SalInc
  WHERE job = 'CLERK';
DBMS_OUTPUT.PUT_LINE('Updating data using parenthesized columns...');
UPDATE emp
  SET (deptno, sal) = (SELECT 20, 4500 FROM DUAL)
  WHERE ename = 'JONES' And job = 'MANAGER';
COMMIT;
END;
/
```

Listing 7.19 shows an `UPDATE` statement used to update a table on a remote database.

LISTING 7.19 LST7_19.TXT—UPDATE **Statement Example on a Remote Table**

```
EXEC DBMS_OUTPUT.PUT_LINE('Updating data in a remote table...');
UPDATE emp@boston
SET sal = sal + 1000
```

LISTING 7.19 CONTINUED

```
WHERE job = 'MANAGER';
/
```

Listing 7.20 shows an UPDATE statement that uses correlated subqueries.

LISTING 7.20 LST7_20.TXT—UPDATE Statement Using Correlated Subqueries

```
EXEC DBMS_OUTPUT.PUT_LINE('Update statement using correlated
subqueries...');
UPDATE emp a
SET a.deptno = (SELECT d1.deptno FROM dept d1 WHERE d1.loc = 'DETROIT'),
  a.sal = (SELECT AVG(e.sal) * 2.5 FROM emp e
      WHERE e.deptno = a.deptno And e.job = 'MANAGER')
WHERE a.deptno IN (SELECT d2.deptno FROM dept d2
         WHERE d2.loc = 'DALLAS') And
    a.job = 'MANAGER';
ROLLBACK;
```

The script in Listing 7.20 updates the department number and salary of all employees whose job type is MANAGER and are located in DALLAS. The code in Listing 7.21 shows an example of an UPDATE statement with the RETURNING clause and bind variables.

LISTING 7.21 LST7_21.TXT—UPDATE Statement Using RETURNING Clause

```
Variable Salary NUMBER;
Variable EName CHAR(10);
Variable DeptNo NUMBER;
UPDATE emp
 SET job = 'MANAGER', sal = sal + 1200, deptno = 40
 WHERE ename = 'SMITH'
 RETURNING sal, ename, deptno INTO :Salary, :EName, :DeptNo;
ROLLBACK;
PRINT Salary;
PRINT ENAME;
PRINT DeptNo;
```

If the RETURNING clause is used with UPDATE statements that affect multiple rows, then the bind variables should be specified as arrays to hold the values.

PL/SQL DELETE Statement

The DELETE statement is used to remove rows from a table, a partitioned table, a view's base table, or a view's partitioned base table. It can be issued by any user with the DELETE privilege or the owner of the table. If the SQL92_SECURITY initialization parameter is set to TRUE, then SELECT privilege is required on the table whose columns are referenced in the WHERE clause. The syntax of the DELETE statement is as follows:

```
DELETE FROM [
<table name> [ PARTITION ( <partition name> )
¦ <view name>
]
¦ [ THE ( <sub query> ) ]
WHERE <search condition>
[ RETURNING <expression> INTO <bind variable list> ]
```

The <table name> parameter specifies the table or object table being updated. The table can be specified with the schema.table_name syntax. The <view name> parameter specifies the view that is updated. The PARTITION clause for the table indicates that updates are done in the specified partition. The THE clause is used to perform flattened subqueries. It informs Oracle that the column value returned by the subquery is a nested table, not a scalar value. The <sub query> parameter of the THE clause specifies which data is selected for deletion. Oracle executes the subquery and then uses the resulting rows as a table in the FROM clause. The subquery cannot query a table that appears in the same FROM clause as the subquery. The <search condition> parameter of the WHERE clause restricts the rows that are deleted. The search condition can reference the table and contain a subquery. All table and index space released by the deleted rows is retained by the table and index. Issuing a DELETE statement against a table fires any DELETE triggers defined on the table.

Listing 7.22 shows a few examples of the DELETE statement.

LISTING 7.22 LST7_22.TXT—DELETE Statement Examples

```
CREATE TABLE Delete_Test(ID NUMBER NOT NULL, C char(1) NOT NULL);
INSERT INTO Delete_Test VALUES(1, 'A');
INSERT INTO Delete_Test VALUES(2, 'B');
INSERT INTO Delete_Test VALUES(3, 'C');
COMMIT;
SELECT * FROM Delete_Test;
/* Output of the SELECT statement:
       ID C
--------- -
        1 A
        2 B
```

LISTING 7.22 CONTINUED

```
    3 C
*/
EXEC DBMS_OUTPUT.PUT_LINE('Deleting data with a WHERE clause...');
DELETE FROM Delete_Test WHERE ID = 2;
SELECT * FROM Delete_Test;
/* Output of the SELECT statement:
       ID C
--------- -
        1 A
        3 C
*/
ROLLBACK;
EXEC DBMS_OUTPUT.PUT_LINE('Deleting data without a WHERE clause...');
DELETE FROM Delete_Test;
SELECT * FROM Delete_Test;
/* Output of the SELECT statement:
no rows selected
*/
ROLLBACK;
EXEC DBMS_OUTPUT.PUT_LINE('Deleting all rows with a TRUNCATE statement...');
TRUNCATE TABLE Delete_Test;
SELECT * FROM Delete_Test;
/* Output of the SELECT statement:
no rows selected
*/
```


A DELETE statement without a WHERE clause deletes all rows from a table, as seen in the script's output. The TRUNCATE TABLE statement is an alternative way of removing all rows from a table. The TRUNCATE TABLE statement is a DDL command and generates no rollback information. It does not fire the table's DELETE triggers. The TRUNCATE command allows you to optionally deallocate the space freed by the deleted rows by using the DROP STORAGE option. The TRUNCATE statement cannot be used on a table that is part of a cluster. The parent table of an enabled referential integrity constraint cannot be truncated.

Listing 7.23 shows examples of the DELETE statement with subqueries.

LISTING 7.23 LST7_23.TXT—DELETE Statement with Subqueries and Remote Tables

```
SELECT * FROM emp WHERE job = 'CLERK' And sal < 1500;
/* Output of the SELECT statement:
EMPNO ENAME    JOB        MGR HIREDATE    SAL    COMM  DEPTNO
```

LISTING 7.23 CONTINUED

```
----- ---------- --------- --------- --------- --------- --------- ---------
 7369 SMITH      CLERK     7902      17-DEC-80       900        20
 7876 ADAMS      CLERK     7788      23-MAY-87      1200        20
 7900 JAMES      CLERK     7698      03-DEC-81      1050        30
 7934 MILLER     CLERK     7782      23-JAN-82      1400        10
*/
EXEC DBMS_OUTPUT.PUT_LINE('Delete clerks with salary < 1500');
DELETE FROM emp
  WHERE job = 'CLERK'
  AND sal < 1500;
SELECT * FROM emp WHERE job = 'CLERK' And sal < 1500;
/* Output of the SELECT statement:
no rows selected
*/
ROLLBACK;
EXEC DBMS_OUTPUT.PUT_LINE('Delete clerks with salary < 1500 using sub-
query');
DELETE FROM (SELECT * FROM emp)
  WHERE job = 'CLERK'
  AND sal < 1500;
SELECT * FROM emp WHERE job = 'CLERK' And sal < 1500;
/* Output of the SELECT statement:
no rows selected
*/
ROLLBACK;
/
```

Listing 7.24 shows some advanced examples of the `DELETE` statement using remote tables and the `THE` clause.

LISTING 7.24 LST7_24.TXT—DELETE **Statement with Subqueries and Remote Tables**

```
EXEC DBMS_OUTPUT.PUT_LINE('Delete data from the remote emp table');
DELETE FROM scott.emp@boston;
ROLLBACK;
EXEC DBMS_OUTPUT.PUT_LINE('Delete data from a nested table');
DELETE THE(SELECT projects
      FROM Offices o WHERE o.id = 2454) AS p
WHERE p.budget > 500;
ROLLBACK;
EXEC DBMS_OUTPUT.PUT_LINE('Delete data from a partitioned table');
DELETE FROM MonthlySales PARTITION (June99)
```

LISTING 7.24 CONTINUED

```
 WHERE sale < 1000;
/
```

For more information on how to create and configure database links for remote database access and creating nested tables, see the Oracle 8 Documentation.

The `RETURNING` clause is used to return values from deleted columns, and thereby eliminate the need to perform a `SELECT` following the `DELETE` statement. When deleting a single row, a `DELETE` statement with a `RETURNING` clause can retrieve column expressions using the deleted row, `ROWID`, and references to the deleted row and store them in PL/SQL variables or bind variables. When using a `DELETE` statement with the `RETURNING` clause to remove multiple rows, values from expressions, `ROWID`, and references involving the deleted rows are stored in bind arrays. For host binds, the data type and size of the expression must be compatible with the bind variable.

Bulk Loading and Unloading

Bulk loading is performed in Oracle 8 by using the SQL*Loader component, which loads data from external operating system files into tables in an Oracle database. SQL*Loader takes a control file as its input, which describes the load to SQL*Loader. The control file also specifies the input data files. During execution, SQL*Loader produces a log file where it writes information about the load. If records are rejected because of any error, it produces a bad file containing the rejected records. It also discards a file containing records that did not meet the specified selection criteria. SQL*Loader can perform the following functions:

- Load data from multiple input data files of different file types.
- Load multiple tables.
- Load data files in fixed-format, delimited-format, and variable-length format.
- Manipulate data fields with SQL functions before inserting the data into database columns.
- Perform various transformations on the data. For example, multiple physical records can be combined into a single logical record before inserting into the database, or a single physical record can be split as multiple logical records.
- Generate unique, sequential key values for specified columns.
- Load data from disk, tape, or named pipes.

The SQL*Loader control file is written in the SQL*Loader Data Definition Language (DDL). The control file specifies the format of the data, what tables and columns to insert the data into, and transformations to be performed on the data. Listing 7.25 shows an example of the control file format.

LISTING 7.25 LST7_25.TXT—Example of Control File Format

```
-- Control file example 1
INTO TABLE dept
   WHEN recordtype = 'D'
   (recordtype POSITION(1:1) CHAR EXTERNAL,
    deptno POSITION(3:6) INTEGER EXTERNAL,
    ename POSITION(8:17) CHAR)
INTO TABLE emp
   WHEN recordtype <> 'E'
   (recordtype POSITION(1:1)  CHAR EXTERNAL,
    empno POSITION(3:6)  INTEGER EXTERNAL,
    ename POSITION(8:17) CHAR)
-- End of example 1
```

SQL*Loader uses the conventional and direct load methods to load data into the database. The conventional path method uses the standard SQL `INSERT` statements to insert data into tables. A direct path load parses the input data according to the description given in the loader control file, converts the data for each input field to its corresponding Oracle column data type, and builds an array of the column values. SQL*Loader then uses the column array to format Oracle data blocks and build index keys. The newly formatted database blocks are then written directly to the database.

The conventional data load method can be used in the following situations:

- Loading data with SQL*Net across heterogeneous platforms. Direct path load cannot be used over Net8 unless both systems belong to the same family of computers, and both are using the same character set.
- Accessing an indexed table concurrently with the load, or when applying inserts or updates to a non-indexed table concurrently with the load.
- Loading data into a clustered table.
- Loading a small number of rows into a large indexed table.
- Loading a small number of rows into a large table with referential and column-check integrity constraints.
- While using SQL functions on the data fields.

The direct path load method is used in the following situations:

- Loading a large number of rows quickly.
- Loading data in PARALLEL for maximum performance.
- Load data in a character set that cannot be supported in your current session, or when the conversion to the database character set would cause errors.

For more information on using SQL*Loader, see the Oracle8 Utilities documentation.

Oracle8 also provides the Export and Import utilities. The Export utility is used to write data from the database into operating system files. Export provides a simple way to transfer data objects between Oracle databases. Export extracts the object definitions and table data from an Oracle database and stores them in an Oracle binary format. The data can be read only by the Import utility. The Export utility can be used at the table level or at the database level. The Import utility inserts the data objects extracted from one Oracle database by the Export utility into another Oracle database. The Import utility can read only data files saved by the Export utility. It cannot be used on ASCII data files. For a complete discussion on the features of the Export and Import utility, see the Oracle 8 documentation.

Summary

In this chapter, you took a brief look at the INSERT, UPDATE, and DELETE statements as specified in the SQL-92 standard. You also looked at the implementation of the INSERT, UPDATE, and DELETE statements in Microsoft SQL Server 7.0 and Oracle 8.0, and saw how referential integrity is implemented in SQL Server.

Transactions in SQL

IN THIS CHAPTER

What Is a Transaction?

A *transaction* can be defined as a logical sequence of data manipulation operations performed as a single unit of work. Either all the changes in the transaction are made or none of them are. Transactions maintain the ACID properties: atomicity, consistency, isolation, and durability.

- Atomicity ensures that all the data manipulations completed in a specific transaction are committed or they get aborted and rolled back to their previous state.
- Consistency ensures that the database is transformed from one correct state to another at the end of the transaction.
- Isolation ensures that concurrent transactions do not see each other's partial and uncommitted changes.
- Durability ensures that the effect of the transaction persists in case of system failures.

Relational database systems use locking and logging mechanisms to enforce the physical integrity of a transaction. Locking resources preserves transaction isolation. Exclusive locks are obtained for data manipulation operations and held until the end of the transaction. Logging the database changes ensures the transaction's durability. Relational databases use a *write-ahead log* to perform transactions, which ensures that no data modifications are written to the disk before the associated log record is created. The write-ahead log helps recover individual transactions and incomplete transactions. The log records all changes made by the transaction. Programming constructs help enforce a transaction's atomicity and consistency by allowing the programmer to perform conditional error checking and decide the eventual outcome of the transaction.

A transaction essentially goes through several phases. Before the transaction starts, the database is in a consistent state. Either the application starts the transaction by issuing a database command or the database starts a transaction implicitly. The application then performs data manipulation commands that leave the database in a logical and consistent state. After the changes are made as a permanent part of the database, the transaction is committed. If any error is encountered during the transaction, all data modifications are rolled back and the database is returned to the point of consistency when the transaction started.

Example of a Transaction

The transaction process can be explained by looking at a simple account balance transfer scenario. In this transaction, money from a savings account has to be transferred to a credit card account. This is a typical database problem that uses transactions to make sure the operation runs correctly and the accounts are left in a consistent state in case of an error. Typically, the transaction also prevents other transactions from reading or updating the accounts during the transfer operation. Listing 8.10 contains the pseudocode for the balance transfer operation without a transaction.

LISTING 8.1 LST8_10.TXT—Account Balance Transfer Pseudocode without Transaction

```
Deduct $500 from Savings Account
If Error Then Add $500 to Savings Account
Credit $500 to Credit Card Account
If Error Then Add $500 to Savings Account and Credit Card Account
```

From the pseudocode it is evident that the error handling required is cumbersome. The error handling routine should take care of restoring the data to a consistent state. Without transactions in relational databases, it is not possible to perform the two operations as an atomic unit and the programming required to achieve the same is more. Now let us take a look at the same operation performed within a transaction.

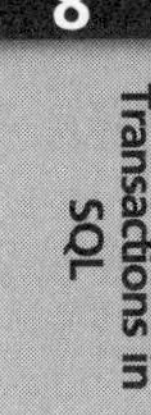

Listing 8.2 contains the pseudocode of an account balance transfer operation.

LISTING 8.2 LST8_1.TXT—Account Balance Transfer Pseudocode

```
Begin Transaction Account_Transfer
Deduct $500 from Savings Account
If Error Then Roll Back Transaction Account_Transfer
Credit $500 to Credit Card Account
If Error Then Roll Back Transaction Account_Transfer
Commit Transaction Account_Transfer
```

The database system guarantees the transaction's atomicity. In this case, both the debit and credit operations are completed to ensure a successful transfer, or neither operation is completed. While the transfer operation is in progress, another transaction cannot read the intermediate values of the accounts. After the transaction is committed, the effects of the transaction persist if a database failure occurs. This is also true in the case of a failure that happens before the commit operation.

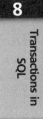

Now consider each operation in its entirety. The `begin transaction` command creates a record in the log that indicates the start of the transaction. The `update` operation that

deducts $500 from the savings account is logged as a series of changes to the data pages. The `update` operation that adds $500 to the credit card account is logged in the same way. After both the `update` operations, the log record contains the old and new values of the accounts. The final `commit` operation marks the end of the transaction in the log. The log then contains a record of all changes made to the database to perform the transfer operation. If an error occurs after the savings account has been deducted, the log is used to undo the changes made to the savings account. The database is thus restored to a consistent state, as it was before the account balance transfer operation started. If a system failure happens after the commit operation is recorded in the log, the database system can ensure that the account balance transfer operation is consistent and the values are correct by analyzing the log records.

Most relational database systems also have features that enable programmers to set a marker called *savepoint*within a transaction. The savepoint defines the location to which a transaction can return if part of the transaction is cancelled based on some logical condition. If a transaction is rolled back to the point of the marker, it must be either committed or rolled back subsequently.

Transaction Isolation Levels

SQL-92 specifies transaction isolation levels that allow programmers to define different types of behavior in a transaction. A *transaction isolation level* is the level to which a transaction can see inconsistent data. It is the degree to which one transaction can be isolated from other transactions. A lower isolation level increases concurrency but can result in data inconsistency. Conversely, a higher isolation level results in lock contention. These are the four isolation levels defined by SQL-92:

- **Read Uncommitted:** This is the lowest isolation level that provides maximum concurrency by allowing transactions to perform dirty reads. A dirty read allows a transaction to read uncommitted changes made by other transactions.
- **Read Committed:** This isolation level allows transactions to read-only changes that have been permanently made in the database.
- **Repeatable Read:** This isolation level locks data read by the transaction, but new phantom rows (included later in the current transaction) can be inserted by another transaction.
- **Serializable:** This is the highest isolation level; transactions are completely isolated from one another. It's the most restrictive of the four isolation levels, and concurrency is low.

Database systems provide transaction isolation levels as a way for the programmer to control concurrency and the data's correctness. Based on a transaction's isolation level, any of the following conditions can occur during the duration of a transaction:

- **Dirty Reads:** Changes made by another transaction that are not yet committed can be read by other transactions. As a result, a transaction could read data that might no longer exist when the other transaction commits.
- **Non-Repeatable Reads:** If data is repeatedly read from the database, the transaction's dataset could be inconsistent. Another transaction can modify or delete the data read by the transaction.
- **Phantom Reads:** A transaction can insert new rows in a dataset that are included in later reads in the current transaction.

Table 8.1 shows the conditions that can occur in the four isolation levels.

TABLE 8.1 Transaction Isolation Level Conditions

Isolation Level	*Dirty Read*	*Non-Repeatable Read*	*Phantom*
Read Uncommitted	Yes	Yes	Yes
Read Committed	No	Yes	Yes
Repeatable Read	No	No	Yes
Serializable	No	No	No

What Is a Distributed Transaction?

A transaction is distributed in nature if it spans two or more data sources with transactional capabilities. Distributed transactions enable programmers to make changes to distributed data on two or more network-connected systems in a single transaction. A distributed transaction involves two or more data sources or resources and a coordinator. The data sources are commonly referred to as *resource managers*, and the coordinators, as *transaction managers* or *transaction monitors*. A distributed transaction can be client initiated, server initiated on behalf of the client application, or initiated by a transaction monitor.

The data sources perform the local transactions as requested by the application. Examples of data sources that can participate in a distributed transaction are Microsoft SQL Server and Oracle. The coordinator is responsible for initiating the transaction process in the participating data sources, and committing or rolling back the transaction as necessary. In addition, the coordinator provides transactions with the ACID properties. Examples of coordinators are Microsoft Distributed Transaction Coordinator, Tuxedo, and Encina.

Two-Phase Commit Protocol

The coordinator uses the two-phase commit (2PC) protocol to ensure the transaction's all-or-nothing property. It consists of two stages:

- **Prepare:** The coordinator sends a "prepare to commit" request to each data source participating in the distributed transaction. The data source in turn performs operations required to complete the commit process, holds the locks required to maintain the transaction's integrity, and returns a success message to the coordinator. If any of the data sources can't complete the prepare request, the coordinator requests all data sources to roll back the local transactions.
- **Commit:** In this stage, the coordinator sends the actual commit request to all the data sources after they have returned "success" to the prepare request. The data sources in turn record the transaction and release all locks held by the transaction.

Example of a Distributed Transaction

Figure 8.1 shows a typical distributed transaction operation initiated by a client application. In the figure, the data sources are Microsoft SQL Server and Oracle, and the coordinator is Microsoft Distributed Transaction Coordinator (MS DTC). For illustration purposes, use the pseudocode for the account balance transfer example shown in Listing 8.1. The modified version for the distributed transaction will look like Listing 8.3.

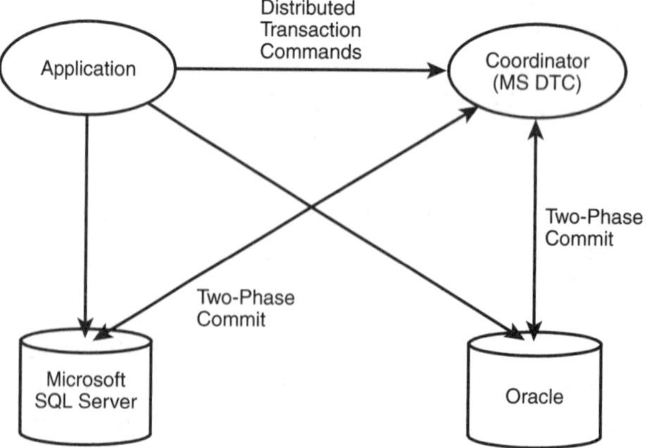

FIGURE 8.1
Client-Initiated Distributed Transaction.

LISTING 8.3 LST8_2.TXT—Account Balance Pseudocode with a Distributed Transaction

```
Begin Distributed Transaction Account_Transfer
Deduct $500 from Savings Account on SQL Server
If Error Then Rollback Distributed Transaction Account_Transfer
Credit $500 to Credit Card Account on Oracle
If Error Then Rollback Distributed Transaction Account_Transfer
Commit Distributed Transaction Account_Transfer
```

The "Begin Distributed Transaction" command starts a DTC transaction. The application then requests the two data sources, SQL Server and Oracle, to register with MS DTC as the participants in the distributed transaction. The update operations are then performed on each data source. If any fatal error or logical error occurs during the course of the update operations, the application issues a rollback command to MS DTC. The application issues a "commit transaction" command to MS DTC if all the operations are successful. In the prepare phase of the two-phase commit protocol, MS DTC sends a prepare request to SQL Server and Oracle. The data sources in turn perform the work necessary to make the transaction durable by logging all the changes made. The data sources then send a successful prepared message to MS DTC. Now both the data sources are in an in-doubt mode in which the outcome of the transaction is not known. If any of the data sources send an abort message to the prepare request, MS DTC aborts the transaction. During the commit phase, MS DTC makes a record of the commit operation in its log file. This commit record helps determine the outcome of the transaction in case of a system failure and can be used to reconcile any in-doubt transactions. MS DTC then sends a commit request to SQL Server and Oracle, and the data sources in turn record the commit in their log files and release all locks held by the transaction. The data sources then respond to MS DTC indicating that the transaction was successfully committed.

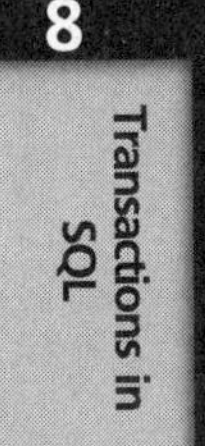

Transactions in Microsoft SQL Server

The discussion in this section is specific to Microsoft SQL Server 7. Transactions in SQL Server can contain both data definition and data manipulation commands. SQL Server uses a dynamic locking mechanism that determines the most cost-effective locks for a statement to preserve transaction isolation. Transaction logs ensure the durability of transactions. Transactions can be started as autocommit, explicit, or implicit transactions.

- **Autocommit Transactions:** In this mode, each individual Transact-SQL statement in SQL Server is committed when it completes. This is the default setting for SQL Server.

- **Explicit Transactions:** Applications use the `BEGIN TRANSACTION` statement to start a transaction locally. The `BEGIN DISTRIBUTED TRANSACTION` statement is used to start a distributed transaction. Both statements optionally allow the programmer to specify a name for the transaction.
- **Implicit Transactions:** The `SET IMPLICIT_TRANSACTIONS ON` statement is used to set this mode. In this mode, executing any of the following Transact-SQL statements will start a transaction automatically if one does not exist: `ALTER`, `CREATE`, `DELETE`, `DROP`, `FETCH`, `GRANT`, `INSERT`, `OPEN`, `REVOKE`, `SELECT`, `TRUNCATE`, and `UPDATE`. The transaction must be explicitly committed or rolled back by the application.

SQL Server 7 supports the four SQL-92 isolation levels: read uncommitted, read committed (default), repeatable read, and serializable. The `SET TRANSACTION ISOLATION LEVEL` command allows the programmer to set the isolation level at which transactions operate.

The Transact-SQL `SAVE TRANSACTION` statement can be used to set a savepoint within a transaction and supply a name for the savepoint. Savepoints are not supported in distributed transactions.

The SQL-92-compatible `COMMIT WORK` and `ROLLBACK WORK` statements and the Transact-SQL `COMMIT TRANSACTION` and `ROLLBACK TRANSACTION` statements control transactions in SQL Server. Explicit transactions can be nested, and the current nesting level can be determined from the `@@TRANCOUNT` global variable. Each `BEGIN TRANSACTION` statement increments `@@TRANCOUNT` by one. A trigger in SQL Server is considered to be an implicit transaction and `@@TRANCOUNT` is always incremented after execution begins inside the trigger. Each `COMMIT TRANSACTION` or `COMMIT WORK` statement decrements `@@TRANCOUNT` by one.

If transactions are nested, only the outermost `COMMIT TRANSACTION` statement commits all changes made by the transaction. The `ROLLBACK TRANSACTION` command always rolls back the entire transaction, even with nested transactions. In both cases, the `ROLLBACK TRANSACTION` command sets the `@@TRANCOUNT` value to zero. `ROLLBACK TRANSACTION` can be used to roll back to a savepoint by specifying the savepoint name. If a `ROLLBACK TRANSACTION` command is issued in a trigger, then the current transaction is rolled back to the outermost `BEGIN TRANSACTION` statement.

The `@@ERROR` global variable is used for error handling in Transact-SQL. `@@ERROR` returns the error number for the last Transact-SQL statement that was executed. It is set to zero if the statement executed successfully. Because the `@@ERROR` value is cleared after each Transact-SQL statement, it has to be checked after every statement that needs to check for an error condition.

Now take the account balance transfer problem and analyze the transaction implementation details in SQL Server. For syntax and information on creating stored procedures and executing in SQL Server, refer to the SQL Server Books Online. For the example, the data for the transaction is assumed to be in two tables: `Account_Savings` for the savings account information and `Account_Visa` for the Visa account. Listing 8.4 shows the Transact-SQL stored procedure and the batch used to execute the stored procedure.

Note

The code required to create the sample tables and data is in the file `LST_8_10.TXT`.

LISTING 8.4 `LST8_3.TXT`—Stored Procedure with Explicit Transactions

```
Create Procedure Account_Transfer_Explicit
(@Account_Number int, @Amount money)
As
Begin Transaction Account_Transfer
Update Account_Savings Set Balance = Balance - @Amount
Where Account_Number = @Account_Number
If @@Error <> 0 Goto Error_Handler
Update Account_Visa Set Balance = Balance + @Amount
Where Account_Number = @Account_Number
If @@Error <> 0 Goto Error_Handler
Commit Transaction Account_Transfer
Return(0)
Error_Handler:
Rollback Transaction Account_Transfer
Return(-1)
Go
Declare @Return_Status int
Exec @Return_Status = Account_Transfer_Explicit 2413, 500
Select @Return_Status AS Return_Status
Go
```

The transaction is started explicitly by using the `BEGIN TRANSACTION` command. After each `UPDATE` statement, the global variable `@@ERROR` is checked to see if there was an error in the `UPDATE` statement, and the procedure flow branches to the error handler. The error handler performs the `ROLLBACK TRANSACTION` command and returns an error code to the calling routine. If both the `UPDATE` statements are successfully executed, the transaction is committed using the `COMMIT TRANSACTION` command. The stored procedure shown in

Listing 8.5 performs the same transaction but uses SQL Server's implicit transaction feature.

LISTING 8.5 LST8_4.TXT—Stored Procedure with Implicit Transactions

```
Create Procedure Account_Transfer_Implicit
(@Account_Number int, @Amount money)
As
Update Account_Savings Set Balance = Balance - @Amount
Where Account_Number = @Account_Number
If @@Error <> 0 Goto Error_Handler
Update Account_Visa Set Balance = Balance + @Amount
Where Account_Number = @Account_Number
If @@Error <> 0 Goto Error_Handler
Commit Transaction
Return(0)
Error_Handler:
Rollback Transaction
Return(-1)
Go
Set Implicit_Transactions On
Go
Declare @Return_Status int
Exec @Return_Status = Account_Transfer_Implicit 2413, 500
Select @Return_Status AS Return_Status
Go
```

In this example, the application issues the `SET IMPLICIT_TRANSACTIONS ON` command to set the connection in implicit transaction mode before calling the stored procedure. When the stored procedure execution begins, the first `UPDATE` statement starts the transaction. One important point to remember when an implicit transaction is in effect is that any `BEGIN TRANSACTION` command within the implicit transaction will only increment the `@@TRANCOUNT` global variable, thereby increasing the nesting level of the transaction. Now look at a modified version of the account balance transfer example shown in Listing 8.6 that illustrates nested transactions. You will create two different stored procedures—one to perform the savings account transaction and another to perform the Visa account transaction—and encapsulate them in an account balance transfer stored procedure.

LISTING 8.6 LST8_5.TXT—Stored Procedure with Nested Transactions

```
Create Procedure Account_Savings_Debit
(@Account_Number int, @Amount money)
As
```

LISTING 8.6 CONTINUED

```
Begin Transaction Savings_Debit
Update Account_Savings Set Balance = Balance - @Amount
Where Account_Number = @Account_Number
If @@Error <> 0 Goto Error_Handler
Commit Transaction Savings_Debit
Return(0)
Error_Handler:
Rollback Transaction Savings_Debit
Return(-1)
Go
Create Procedure Account_Visa_Credit
(@Account_Number int, @Amount money)
As
Begin Transaction Visa_Credit
Update Account_Visa Set Balance = Balance + @Amount
Where Account_Number = @Account_Number
If @@Error <> 0 Goto Error_Handler
Commit Transaction Visa_Credit
Return(0)
Error_Handler:
Rollback Transaction Visa_Credit
Return(-1)
Go
Create Procedure Account_Transfer_Nested
(@Account_Number int, @Balance money)
As
Declare @Return_Status int
Begin Transaction Account_Transfer
Exec @Return_Status = Account_Savings_Debit @Account_Number, @Balance
If @@Error <> 0 Or @Return_Status <> 0 Goto Error_Handler
Exec @Return_Status = Account_Visa_Credit @Account_Number, @Balance
If @@Error <> 0 Or @Return_Status <> 0 Goto Error_Handler
Commit Transaction Account_Transfer
Return(0)
Error_Handler:
If @@Trancount > 0 Rollback Transaction Account_Transfer
Return(-1)
Go
Declare @Return_Status int
Exec @Return_Status = Account_Transfer_Nested 2413, 500
Select @Return_Status AS Return_Status
Go
```

In this listing, the transaction control is in the main account balance transfer stored procedure, which demonstrates some of the error-handling tasks that need to be performed. The return status and @@ERROR check after each stored procedure trap all error conditions. The return status value can be used primarily to check the status of the update operation. The @@ERROR check handles any statement-level error (for example, a missing stored procedure or modifications such as adding more parameters to the stored procedure that could result in an execution error or deadlocks in the database) that happens with the stored procedure execution call.

This error handling is important in Transact-SQL's default method of executing statements in SQL Server—that is, the batch execution continues to the next statement in a transaction if an error occurs. The error handler in the account balance transfer stored procedure is also different in that it includes the check for the @@TRANCOUNT global variable. This check is required to ensure that the rollback happens only if a transaction is active when an error occurs. This prevents SQL Server from raising warning messages if a ROLLBACK TRANSACTION command is issued when there is no active transaction.

Transact-SQL also enables the programmer to control runtime error conditions in a transaction. The SET XACT_ABORT ON statement can be used to automatically roll back a transaction if a runtime error occurs in a Transact-SQL statement. This setting, when turned on, terminates the entire transaction if there's an error, and the batch execution stops. The SET XACT_ABORT ON statement should be issued before executing the account balance transfer stored procedure or after establishing the connection to the database.

Let's take the account balance transfer scenario a step further to illustrate distributed transactions in SQL Server. For this example, assume that the Visa account information resides on a different SQL Server. The Transact-SQL code is shown in Listing 8.7. The example uses a remote SQL Server named sqlsrvr01. For configuring remote servers in SQL Server, refer to the topic of remote servers in SQL Server Books Online.

LISTING 8.7 LST8_6.TXT—Stored Procedure with Distributed Transactions

```
-- Procedure on remote SQL Server sqlsrvr01 that hosts the database for
-- the Visa account information
Create Procedure Account_Visa_Credit
(@Account_Number int, @Amount money)
As
Begin Transaction Visa_Credit
Update Account_Visa Set Balance = Balance + @Amount
Where Account_Number = @Account_Number
If @@Error <> 0 Goto Error_Handler
Commit Transaction Visa_Credit
Return(0)
```

LISTING 8.7 CONTINUED

```
Error_Handler:
Rollback Transaction Visa_Credit
Return(-1)
Go
-- Procedure on local server that starts the distributed transaction
Create Procedure Account_Transfer_Distributed
(@Account_Number int, @Amount money)
As
Declare @Return_Status int
Begin Distributed Transaction Account_Transfer_Distributed
Update Account_Savings Set Balance = Balance - @Amount
Where Account_Number = @Account_Number
If @@Error <> 0 Goto Error_Handler
Exec  @Return_Status  =  sqlsrvr01...Account_Visa_Credit  @Account_Number,
@Amount
If @@Error <> 0 or @Return_Status <> 0 Goto Error_Handler
Commit Transaction Account_Transfer_Distributed
Return(0)
Error_Handler:
Rollback Transaction Account_Transfer_Distributed
Return(-1)
Go
Declare @Return_Status int
Exec @Return_Status = Account_Transfer_Distributed 2413, 500
Select @Return_Status AS Return_Status
Go
```

A distributed transaction can be started explicitly in SQL Server by using the `BEGIN DISTRIBUTED TRANSACTION` statement. Alternatively, SQL Server can be configured to start distributed transactions automatically when a local transaction calls a remote stored procedure. This can be configured at the connection level by using the `SET REMOTE_-PROC_TRANSACTIONS ON` statement and at the server level by setting the Remote Proc Trans configuration option. The Microsoft Distributed Transaction Coordinator coordinates distributed transactions started in that way. This is an example of a server-initiated distributed transaction. The two-phase commit protocol is transparent to the application invoking the stored procedure and handled by MS DTC.

Bound Connections

SQL Server also supports bound connections that allow two or more connections to share the same transaction space and locks with the restriction that only one connection can be active at any time. This feature allows bound connections to work on the same data without any locking conflicts. The bound connections can be either local or distributed. Local bound connections share transaction space on a single server. Distributed bound connections share transaction space across two or more servers that participate in the distributed transaction. Bound connections are useful in developing applications that incorporate business logic in separate programs that work together. For more information, refer to the "Using Bound Connections" topic in the SQL Server Books Online.

Transactions in Oracle

The discussion in this section is specific to Oracle 8. In Oracle, a transaction begins with the first data definition and data manipulation statement. The transaction ends when a `COMMIT` or `ROLLBACK` without the `SAVEPOINT` option is issued or a data definition statement, such as `CREATE`, `ALTER`, `DROP`, or `RENAME`, is executed. A data definition statement always commits the existing transaction and starts a new single statement transaction. A transaction holds exclusive row locks on all affected rows to provide isolation. Oracle also has data lock conversion mechanisms to provide higher data concurrency. Rollback segments are used to record transactional changes.

Oracle supports the two SQL-92 transaction isolation levels: read committed and serializable. Apart from these isolation levels, Oracle also has a read-only isolation level. Oracle uses a multiversion concurrency mechanism to give queries read consistency. All the data for a query is consistent from a single point in time. The data for the query is constructed from the rollback segments that contain the old values of data that has been changed by concurrent transactions. In this feature's default behavior, any query that reads data neither acquires any locks nor waits for other locks to be released before reading the data. This feature provides statement-level read consistency and improves concurrency. Oracle also provides transactional-level read consistency when all queries within the transaction see only changes that were committed at the time the transaction began. Read-only transactions are restricted to `SELECT` statements. The isolation level for a transaction is set by using the `SET TRANSACTION ISOLATION LEVEL` statement. Using the `FOR UPDATE` clause on a `SELECT` statement, the `LOCK TABLE` statement, and the `SET TRANSACTION ISOLATION LEVEL` statement can change the locking behavior.

The `SAVEPOINT`command is used to set a savepoint within a transaction. Savepoints are used with the `ROLLBACK` command to roll back portions of a transaction. The `COMMIT` and `ROLLBACK` commands are used to control transactions. Both commands optionally allow the programmer to supply a comment for the transaction. The `COMMIT` and `ROLLBACK` commands also allow administrators to manually commit or roll back in-doubt distributed transactions. None of the transactional commands can be used inside triggers in Oracle.

Exceptions are used for handling errors in PL/SQL stored procedures. Predefined exceptions are available in the global PL/SQL package STANDARD. Exceptions can be user-defined and raised programmatically. The `PRAGMA EXCEPTION_INIT` is a compiler directive used in PL/SQL stored procedures to associate a name with an Oracle error number. This allows a specific error handler to be written for any Oracle error number.

Now take the account balance transfer problem discussed earlier and analyze the transaction implementation details in Oracle. For syntax and information on creating stored procedures and executing in Oracle, refer to the Oracle documentation. Take a look at the PL/SQL stored procedure and the PL/SQL anonymous block shown in Listing 8.8.

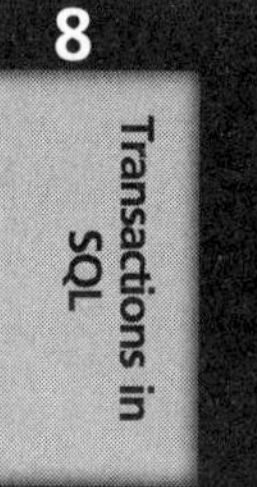

Note

The code required to create the sample tables and data is in the file `LST_8_11.TXT`.

LISTING 8.8 `LST8_7.TXT`—Stored Procedure with a Transaction

```
Create or Replace Procedure Account_Transfer
(Account_Number IN int, Amount IN number, Return_Status OUT int)
As
deadlock_error EXCEPTION;
PRAGMA EXCEPTION_INIT(deadlock_error, -60);
Begin
Update Account_Savings Set Balance = Balance - Amount
Where Account_Number = Account_Number;
Update Account_Visa Set Balance = Balance + Amount
Where Account_Number = Account_Number;
Commit;
Return_Status := 0;
Exception
When deadlock_error Then
Return_Status := -2;
Rollback;
When Others Then
Return_Status := -1;
Rollback;
end;
```

LISTING 8.8 CONTINUED

```
/
/* PL/SQL block that executes the stored procedure and returns the status. */
Set serveroutput on;
Declare return_status int := 0;
Begin
 Account_Transfer( 2413, 500, return_status );
 DBMS_OUTPUT.PUT_LINE('Return status is ' || return_status);
end;
/
```

The transaction is automatically started by Oracle when the first update statement on the `Account_Savings` table gets executed. The transaction is first assigned to an available rollback segment. Any concurrent transactions that read the rows being updated by the account transfer transaction would see the old values constructed from the rollback segments. Error handling is done by defining exceptions. In the example, an exception for deadlock error is defined by using the `PRAGMA EXCEPTION_INIT` directive. All other error conditions are handled by the predefined error `OTHERS`. The `SET SERVEROUTPUT ON` statement in the PL/SQL block for executing the stored procedure enables the client to display messages printed by the `DBMS_OUTPUT.PUT_LINE` procedure.

A distributed transaction is automatically started by Oracle if changes are made to two or more networked databases. The remote database is set up in Oracle by establishing a database link. After the transaction becomes distributed in nature, the two-phase commit mechanism is used to make the changes permanent across the participating databases. In this case, the Oracle server that accesses the remote database initiates the distributed transaction, and the `COMMIT` and `ROLLBACK` statements control the outcome of the transaction. The server also acts as the coordinator of the distributed transaction. In the event of a system failure, administrators can manually commit or roll back the distributed transactions that are in doubt as a result of the failure. The `COMMIT WORK` or `ROLLBACK WORK` statement with the `FORCE` clause is used to manually commit or roll back the in-doubt transaction. The `FORCE` clause requires the name of the transaction that is identified by the local or global transaction identifiers. The data dictionary view `DBA_2PC_PENDING` is used to identify the in-doubt distributed transactions. The account balance transfer example can be modified to illustrate distributed transaction in Oracle. The PL/SQL stored procedure is shown in Listing 8.9.

LISTING 8.9 `LST8_8.TXT`—Stored Procedure with a Distributed Transaction

```
Create or Replace Procedure Account_Transfer_Distributed
(Account_Number IN int, Amount IN number, Return_Status OUT int)
As
```

LISTING 8.9 CONTINUED

```
deadlock_error EXCEPTION;
PRAGMA EXCEPTION_INIT(deadlock_error, -60);
Begin
Update Account_Savings Set Balance = Balance - Amount
Where Account_Number = Account_Number;
/* Update the Visa account balance on a remote oracle database, orasvr01 */
Update Account_Visa@orasvr01 Set Balance = Balance + Amount
Where Account_Number = Account_Number;
Commit;
Return_Status := 0;
Exception
When deadlock_error Then
Return_Status := -2;
Rollback;
When Others Then
Return_Status := -1;
Rollback;
end;
/
/* PL/SQL block that executes the stored procedure and returns the status. */
Set serveroutput on;
Declare return_status int := 0;
Begin
 Account_Transfer_Distributed ( 2413, 500, return_status );
 DBMS_OUTPUT.PUT_LINE('Return status is ' || return_status);
end;
/
```

The distributed transaction is automatically initiated by Oracle in this case. The transaction is transparent to the application and is handled by Oracle. The `COMMIT` statement uses the two-phase commit mechanism to commit the distributed transaction. The Visa account information is updated on the remote server `orasvr01`. The remote procedure is executed by supplying the database link as part of the stored procedure name. For details on setting up and configuring remote servers in Oracle and using database links, refer to the Oracle documentation.

To increase the performance of short, non-distributed transactions, Oracle uses the `BEGIN_DISCRETE_TRANSACTION` system procedure. Discrete transactions, however, introduce a few restrictions:

- Only a few database blocks can be modified
- Cannot modify the same database block again within the same transaction
- Cannot modify data used by long-running queries
- Cannot read the new values of the data being updated
- Cannot modify tables containing the `LONG BLOB` data type
- Cannot participate in distributed transactions

All changes made by discrete transactions are deferred until the transaction commits. When the transaction issues a `COMMIT` statement, the changes made to the database are applied directly. This eliminates the need to generate undo information for the transaction because the changes are not made until the transaction is committed. Any errors encountered while processing a discrete transaction cause the predefined exception `DISCRETE_TRANSACTION_FAILED` to be raised. The `BEGIN_DISCRETE_TRANSACTION` procedure must be called before the first statement in the transaction and is effective only for the duration of the transaction. All subsequent transactions are processed as normal transactions. Listing 8.10 shows the modified PL/SQL stored procedure for the account transfer that uses discrete transactions.

LISTING 8.10 `LST8_9.TXT`—Stored Procedure with a Discrete Transaction

```
Create or Replace Procedure Account_Transfer_Discrete
(Account_Number IN int, Amount IN number, Return_Status OUT int)
As
Begin
DBMS_TRANSACTION.BEGIN_DISCRETE_TRANSACTION;
Update Account_Savings Set Balance = Balance - Amount
Where Account_Number = Account_Number;
Update Account_Visa Set Balance = Balance + Amount
Where Account_Number = Account_Number;
Commit;
Return_Status := 0;
Exception
When DBMS_TRANSACTION.DISCRETE_TRANSACTION_FAILED Then
Return_Status := -2;
Rollback;
When Others Then
Return_Status := -1;
Rollback;
end;
/
```

LISTING 8.10 CONTINUED

```
/* PL/SQL block that executes the stored procedure and returns the status. */
Set serveroutput on;
Declare return_status int := 0;
Begin
 Account_Transfer_Discrete( 2413, 500, return_status );
 DBMS_OUTPUT.PUT_LINE('Return status is ' || return_status);
end;
/
```

The `BEGIN_DISCRETE_TRANSACTION` procedure in the `DBMS_TRANSACTION` system package is used to start the discrete transaction. Because each data block in the transaction can be changed only once, certain combinations of data manipulation statements on the same table are not allowed. Using an `INSERT` and `UPDATE` statement together is least likely to affect the same block. Multiple `INSERT` statements, however, are more likely to affect the same database block. For more information on the system packages, locking features, and transaction management features, refer to the Oracle product documentation.

Summary

The discussion of transactions in Microsoft SQL Server and Oracle gives you some insight into the features available in two of the mainstream database products. You can get more details on the locking implementation and transaction management features from the following products' documentation and white papers:

"A Relational Model of Data for Large Shared Data Banks," by Dr. E. F. Codd

Oracle8 Distributed Database Systems, Release 8.0 documentation

"MS SQL Server: An Overview of Transaction Processing Concepts and the MS DTC," a white paper from the Desktop and Business Systems Division, Microsoft. This white paper can be found in MS Technet Online and MSDN Online.

Patterns and Ranges in SQL

In This Chapter

The SELECT statement in SQL carries a great deal of flexibility. It allows adding filters and criteria that help narrow down the search criteria when retrieving data and selecting only needed data. This chapter examines some of the tools and predicates that can be used in the SELECT statement to achieve this goal.

More About the SELECT Statement

As you already know, the SELECT statement has several parts, or clauses. In the first part, you define the fields you want to retrieve from the database tables. In the second part, you define the tables you want to retrieve data from. In the third part, you can define criteria and add predicates to specify a certain pattern or range to the data you want to retrieve. Another optional part allows you to group the data based on a certain field. Finally, you can also add a section at the end that defines the sort order of the retrieved fields. Therefore, the syntax for the SELECT statement looks like this example:

```
SELECT Field1[, Field2, ... Fieldn]
FROM Table1[, Table2, ... Tablem]  (m<=n)
WHERE Criteria [and Joins may be defined here]
GROUP BY (Fields defined here)
ORDER BY (Fields defined here);
```

This chapter focuses mostly on the WHERE clause of the SELECT statement. You will see how the search criteria can be defined to help you quickly get to the records you want. While doing so, you will see the tools and predicates that can be used in this clause to achieve that goal. The criteria and predicates help define some patterns in the SQL statement. It is these patterns that the statement returns. The simplest type of criteria is some equality or inequality between the data you want and a certain value. For example, Listing 9.1 returns all records from the Employee table in which the state is Michigan.

LISTING 9.1 Adding Criteria in the WHERE Clause

```
SELECT Emp_Fname || ' ' || Emp_Lname AS Name
FROM Employee
WHERE State = 'MI';
```

The LIKE Predicate

The LIKE predicate is one of the most powerful predicates in SQL. It is basically a string pattern-matching test with this syntax:

```
Field LIKE Match Value
```

or

```
Field NOT LIKE Match Value
```

In this code, `Match Value` is an expression or a single value.

Two wild characters can be used with the `LIKE` predicate: the percent sign (`%`) and the underscore character (_). The `%` character represents an arbitrary substring of characters that can be of zero length or higher. The _ character represents only one arbitrary character.

> **Note**
>
> According to the SQL-92 standard, SQL patterns are case sensitive. Therefore, saying `Like 'app%'` is not the same as `Like 'App%'`. However, most SQL implementations allow you to set case sensitivity on or off at the database system level.

As an example of using the `LIKE` predicate with the `%` wild character, Listing 9.2 retrieves all employees whose last name starts with `'Mc'`.

LISTING 9.2 Retrieving All Employees Whose Last Name Starts with `'Mc'`

```
SELECT Emp_Fname || ' ' || Emp_Lname AS Name
FROM Employee
WHERE Emp_Lname LIKE 'Mc%';
```

Here are the results of this query:

```
Name
--------------
John McCarthy
Dave McKinley
Susan McQueen
```

When dealing with patterns, you have to be careful. Sometimes an extra character can lead to breaking the pattern you intend to establish. For example, if you are looking for the pattern `L%N`, you will find that words such as `LOAN`, `LEAN`, `LAN`, and `LASERATION` all fit the pattern. However, the word `LOANS` does not because of the letter `S` at the end, which breaks the intended pattern.

Note

Using the underscore wild character is usually faster than the percent sign. The reason is obvious: Although the database engine has to look ahead for subsequent characters with the `%` wild character, it has to look at only one character for the _ wild character.

Using the `LIKE` predicate does take some resources and slows down the database engine search, so you need to be wise when using it. For instance, to retrieve all names of employees from the `Employee` table, Listing 9.3 will run very slowly compared to Listing 9.4.

LISTING 9.3 Retrieving Employee Names from the **`Employee`** Table Using the **`LIKE`** Predicate

```
SELECT emp_FName || ' ' || emp_Lname AS Name
FROM employee
WHERE emp_FName Like '%' AND emp_Lname LIKE '%';
```

LISTING 9.4 Retrieving Employee Names from the **`Employee`** Table Without Using the **`LIKE`** Predicate

```
SELECT emp_FName || ' ' || emp_Lname AS Name
FROM employee;
```

You can also use the `NOT` logical operator with the `LIKE` predicate to exclude certain results from being returned by the `SELECT` statement. For example, Listing 9.5 shows a statement for retrieving a list of employees whose last names don't start with `'Mc'`.

LISTING 9.5 Retrieving the Employee Name Using the **`NOT LIKE`** predicate

```
SELECT Emp_Fname || ' ' || Emp_Lname AS Name
FROM Employee
WHERE Emp_Lname NOT LIKE 'Mc%';
```

A partial list of results to this query would include names such as the following:

```
Name
--------------
John Doe
Dave Smith
Susan Mackenzie
```

I mentioned earlier that the _ wild character represents one character only and the % wild character represents zero or more characters. To enforce a one or more character pattern, you can use the combination of both wild characters. Listing 9.6 shows how to do this, and Listing 9.7 shows the same statement using only the % wild character.

LISTING 9.6 Retrieving All Employees Whose Last Name Starts with 'John' Using Both Wild Characters

```
SELECT Emp_Fname || ' ' || Emp_Lname AS Name
FROM Employee
WHERE Emp_Lname LIKE 'John_%';
```

The results of this query would look like this:

```
Name
-------------
John Johnston
Dave Johnson
```

LISTING 9.7 Retrieving All Employees Whose Last Name Starts with 'John' Using Only the % Character

```
SELECT Emp_Fname || ' ' || Emp_Lname AS Name
FROM Employee
WHERE Emp_Lname LIKE 'John%';
```

The results of this query would look like this:

```
Name
-------------
John Johnston
Dave Johnson
Susan John
```

As you can see, Listing 9.6 did not retrieve the name `Susan John` because it does not match the pattern of one or more characters after the substring `John`.

Note

It is important to note that the `LIKE` predicate does not mean equality between two expressions. It actually sets a pattern for one expression and finds the matches in the other. For example, the string "John" is not like the string "John" which has a trailing blank character, even though the two strings are equal in SQL.

Phonic Matching: SOUNDEX and METAPHONE

A group of my old friends and I participated in a Web community. We used this community to communicate with each other and discuss the issues of the day. We also had a lot of email going between us in which we continued our discussions. One of my friends had my email address in his address book missing a letter—`syounes@some_isp.com` instead of `syouness@some_isp.com`. Suddenly, we all received an email from someone whose address was the one used incorrectly by my friend. The email begged us to remove the sender from our email list. Of course, none of us intended to add this poor guy to our heated discussions, but the proximity of his mail address to mine did it.

The reason I am telling this story is that names have the potential to create mix-ups and misunderstandings, especially in this country's population, which has a huge diversity in ethnic backgrounds. Ignoring the issue of mix-ups in names can only make things worse. Therefore, SQL-92, like many other programming languages, tried to solve this problem by introducing the functions `SOUNDEX` and `METAPHONE`, which introduce phonetic algorithms to find similar-sounding names.

SOUNDEX

This function accepts a name as an input argument and produces a 4-digit alphanumeric character code corresponding to a list of names that sound roughly similar to the input name. Margaret O'Dell and Robert C. Russel created the original `SOUNDEX` algorithm in 1918, long before computers. Their algorithm served as the basis for many modifications afterward. The following is one of the most powerful of these algorithms:

1. Capitalize all letters in the input name and pad the name with blanks to the right as needed during each step.
2. Look for all vowels and replace the ones that are not leading with the letter `A`.
3. Use the following table to change the prefix to the word:

   ```
   MAC = MCC
   KN = MN
   K = C
   PF = FF
   SCH = SSS
   PH = FF
   ```
4. Take the part of the input name after the first letter and transform certain letter combinations according to the following table:

   ```
   transform DG   to GG
   transform CAAN to TAAN
   transform D    to T
   transform NST  to NSS
   ```

```
transform AV  to AF
transform Q   to G
transform Z   to S
transform M   to N
transform KN  to NN
transform K   to C
```

5. Replace any occurrence of `H` with `A` after the first letter, unless the `H` is preceded and followed by `A` (such as `AHA`).
6. After the first letter, replace every `AW` with `A`.
7. Replace `PH` with `FF` after the first letter.
8. Replace `SCH` with `SSS` after the first letter.
9. Drop the letters `A` and `S` if they happen to be at the end of the resulting string.
10. Pad the resulting string with blanks to the right as needed.
11. Replace `NT` with `TT` at the end of the string.
12. Strip the string of `A` characters (except if `A` is the first letter) and pad the string with spaces to the right as needed.
13. Find any repeating adjacent characters and delete them, leaving only the first character of such substrings, and pad the resulting string with spaces to the right as needed.
14. Take the first four characters. This will be the resulting string.

As an example, take my name, Sakhr. According to this algorithm, the `SOUNDEX` function would return `SKR` .

METAPHONE

`METAPHONE` is an improved version of the `SOUNDEX` function. It first appeared in an article by Lawrence Philips in the December 1990 issue of *Computer Language*. With this function, an input word is reduced to a 1- to 4-character code using relatively simple phonetic rules for typical spoken English. `METAPHONE` reduces the alphabet to 16 consonant sounds— `B X S K J T F H L M N P R 0 W Y` —and uses the following transformation rules:

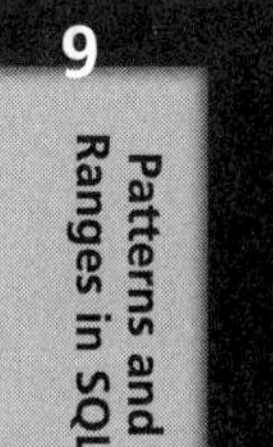
9
Patterns and Ranges in SQL

- Except for `C`, keep only one of repeated adjacent characters.
- Remove vowels unless they are the first character.
- Leave `B` as is unless it's at the end of a word after `M`, as in "dumb," and then transform it to `silent`.
- Transform `C` to:

  `X` (sh) if followed by "ia" or "h"

`S` if followed by "i", "e," or "y"

`K` otherwise, including "sch"

- Transform `D` to:

`J` if followed by "ge," "gy," or "gi"

`T` otherwise

- Leave `F` as is.
- Transform `G` to:

`silent` if followed by "h" and not at the end or before a vowel, or if followed by "n" or "ned"

`J` if before "I," "e," or "y," if not double "gg"

`K` otherwise

- Transform `H` to:

`silent` if after vowel and no vowel follows

`H` otherwise

- Leave `J` as is.
- Transform `K` to:

`silent` if after "c"

`K` otherwise

- Leave `L` as is.
- Leave `M` as is.
- Leave `N` as is.
- Transform `P` to:

`F` if before "h"

`P` otherwise

- Transform `Q` to:

`K`

- Leave `R` as is.
- Transform `S` to:

`X` (sh) if before "h" or if followed by "io" or "ia"

`S` otherwise

- Transform `T` to:

  `X` (sh) if followed by "ia" or "o"

  `O` (th) if before "h"

  `silent` if followed by "ch"

  `T` otherwise

- Transform `V` to:

  `F`

- Transform `W` to:

  `silent` if not followed by a vowel

  `W` if followed by a vowel

- Transform `X` to:

  `KS`

- Transform `Y` to:

  `silent` if not followed by a vowel

  `Y` if followed by a vowel

- Transform `Z` to:

  `S`

According to the algorithm above, my name, `SAKHR`, would return `SKR`, and some phonetically matching names are `SECOR` and `SOCORRO`.

BETWEEN and OVERLAPS Predicates

These two predicates indicate that a value lies between the boundaries of a range of values. `BETWEEN` works with scalar range limits, and `OVERLAPS` checks whether two time periods overlap. The time periods can be identified by a start and end point in time or by a start point and duration. This section discusses these two predicates and their effects in detail.

The BETWEEN Predicate

This predicate is used in the `WHERE` clause of the `SELECT` statement with the following syntax:

```
WHERE Expression Value BETWEEN Low Value AND High Value
```

This is equivalent to saying

```
WHERE Value <= High Value AND Value >= Low Value
```

In the expression above, `Low Value` is the lower boundary of the range and `High Value` is the higher boundary of the range you are seeking.

The OVERLAPS Predicate

This predicate is harder to implement because of excessive use of date/time data types, so only a few SQL implementations included it in their SQL library. This function uses a SQL-92-specific data type called `INTERVAL`, which expresses a duration of time with a starting point and a finishing point. The starting point has to be of the `DATE/TIME` data type, but the finishing point can be either a `DATE/TIME` data type or a duration measured in a date or time unit, such as days, hours, and so forth. If the starting and finishing points are both of the `DATE/TIME` data type and are equal, an *event* is said to occur.

The following rules apply when comparing two intervals:

- The two intervals overlap if a common interval exists for both of them. For example, if the first interval started at 11:00 and ended at 15:00 today, and another interval started at 13:00 and ended at 18:00 on the same day as the first interval, there is an overlap period between 13:00 and 15:00 for the two intervals.
- If one of the intervals is an event, the event is said to have occurred within the other interval if its time is between the boundaries of that interval.
- For two events to overlap, they have to be equal.
- If the starting point of an interval is `NULL`, the ending point is considered both the starting and ending point and the interval is treated as an event.

Because of the difficulty in implementing the `OVERLAPS` predicate, many programmers find ways around it by using the `BETWEEN` predicate with other tricks as demonstrated in the following example.

Say that you have a table that lists the special events at a college. You can create this table with the code in Listing 9.8.

LISTING 9.8 Creating a Table to Store a List of Special College Events

```
CREATE TABLE events
  (event  CHARACTER(50)  PRIMARY KEY,
   event_Start  DATE,
   event_End  DATE);
```

The data in the table is presented as follows:

Event	*Event_Start*	*Event_End*
Winter Registration	1/5/1999	1/12/1999
Winter Semester	1/13/1999	5/15/1999
Spring/Summer Break	5/16/1999	8/31/1999
Fall Registration	8/25/1999	9/1/1999
Fall Semester	9/1/1999	12/20/1999
Holiday Break	12/21/1999	1/4/2000

Let's now keep track of the teachers who took vacations during 1999 in a table called `vacations`. Listing 9.9 shows the code needed to create such a table.

LISTING 9.9 Creating a Table to Store a List of Teacher Vacations During 1999

```
CREATE TABLE vacations
  (teacher  CHARACTER(50)  PRIMARY KEY,
   vac_Start  DATE,
   vac_End  DATE);
```

The data in the table is presented as follows:

Teacher	*Vac_Start*	*Vac_End*
Mike	3/5/1999	3/12/1999
Mary	7/10/1999	7/24/1999
David	5/4/1999	5/7/1999
Wayne	10/2/1999	10/3/1999
John	11/1/1999	11/10/1999
Sally	12/15/1999	12/19/1999

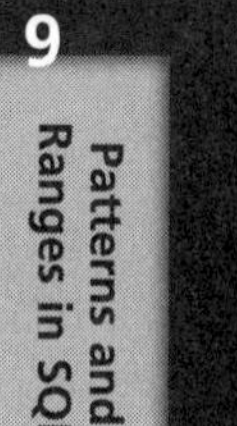
9
Patterns and Ranges in SQL

First, examine the simple case of dealing with one end of the range, the start date of the vacation, and map the date to the list of events to find the names of teachers and the events corresponding to the start date of their vacations. You can use a simple `SELECT` statement with the `BETWEEN` predicate to solve this problem. The code is shown in Listing 9.10.

LISTING 9.10 Retrieving the Names of Teachers Who Had Vacations and the Events Corresponding to the Start of Their Vacations

```
SELECT teacher, event As ''Vacation Started During:''
FROM  vacations, events
```

LISTING 9.10 CONTINUED

```
WHERE  vac_start BETWEEN event_start AND event_end
  AND vac_start <> event_End;
```

The data in the table is shown here:

Teacher	*Vacation Started During*
Mike	Winter semester
Mary	Spring/summer break
David	Winter semester
Wayne	Fall semester
John	Fall semester
Sally	Fall semester

Now try to compare both ends of the vacations to the college events. Using the BETWEEN predicate in this case becomes more difficult, as you can see in Listing 9.11.

LISTING 9.11 Retrieving the Names of Teachers Who Had Vacations and the Events Corresponding to both Ends of Their Vacations

```
SELECT teacher, event As ''Vacation Started During:''
FROM  vacations, events
WHERE  vac_start BETWEEN event_start AND event_end
  AND vac_start <> event_End;
```

Now, if you want to find out what college events the teachers' vacations coincided with, taking into account both the start and end of the vacation range, use code similar to Listing 9.12.

LISTING 9.12 Retrieving Events Corresponding to the Vacations Taken by the Teachers

```
SELECT teacher, event As ''Vacation Started During:''
FROM  vacations, events
WHERE  vac_start BETWEEN event_start AND event_end
  OR vac_End BETWEEN event_start AND event_End
OR event_start BETWEEN vac_start AND vac_End;
```

This code assumes that a vacation and a college event will overlap if

- The start of the vacation is within the boundaries of the event, or
- The end of the vacation is within these boundaries, or
- The start of the event (or its end) is within the boundaries of the vacation

The last condition corresponds to the vacation starting before the event started and ending after the event ended.

> **Note**
>
> In many cases, views make it easier to deal with overlapping ranges. You can create views that can be used to build other views or by your SQL statements to find different pieces of information about overlapping intervals in your data, such as finding the number of teachers taking vacations during each event. Views are discussed in detail in Chapter 14, "Creating and Using Views."

`IN` and `NOT IN`

The `IN` (or `NOT IN`) predicate is used in the `WHERE` clause to limit the search criteria based on a list of compatible values. These values can be scalar or row values in SQL-92. The general syntax for this predicate is as follows:

```
WHERE VALUE IN(Value(1), Value(2), .. , Value(n))
```

The `IN(Value(1), Value(2) .. Value(n))` is equivalent to saying `ANY(Value(1), Value(2), .. ,Value(n))`. Also, `Expression NOT IN(List of values)` is equivalent to `NOT Expression IN(List of values)`.

> **Note**
>
> In most SQL implementations, the `IN` predicate uses working, or temporary, tables to build a list of values usually returned from a subquery. Such working tables generally are not indexed and allow duplicate values to be entered. This makes the `IN` predicate less efficient compared to other ones, such as the `EXISTS` and `NOT EXISTS` predicates, which use indexes to find their values. Therefore, it is recommended that you convert statements using the `IN` predicate to make them use the `EXISTS` and `NOT EXISTS` predicates. The `EXISTS` and `NOT EXISTS` predicates are discussed in more detail in Chapter 13, "Subqueries."

Say you want to find the books in the company library database (described in detail in Chapter 2, "Relational Databases") written by authors who lived in Europe. The code you would write is shown in Listing 9.13.

LISTING 9.13 Listing the Books by Authors Who Lived in Europe

```
SELECT t.book_title, a.author_name
FROM  titles t, authors a, author_title ta
WHERE    t.ISBN = ta.ISBN
AND   ta.author_id = a.author_id
AND  a.country IN (SELECT DISTINCT country
 FROM countries
 WHERE continent='Europe');
```

> **Note**
>
> Notice that the subquery of Listing 9.13 uses the keyword `DISTINCT` to make sure no duplicates are returned. Old database engines allowed duplicates to be returned in a subquery like this one, which dramatically affected the performance of the `IN`/`NOT IN` predicates.

In the previous example above, you are assuming that a `country` table exists that has a field called `continent`. The table can be created with the code in Listing 9.14.

LISTING 9.14 Creating a `country` Table for the Company Employee Database

```
CREATE TABLE country(
    Country_code integer PRIMARY KEY,
    Country
    Continent);
```

In most cases, replacing the `IN` predicate with a join operation improves the query performance. In Listing 9.13, if you replace the `IN` predicate and the subquery with a join between the `country` table and the `author` table, you will definitely improve the query's performance. Another benefit of using joins instead of `IN` predicates is that duplicates are not returned, and indexes can be used. Listing 9.15 shows the same code as Listing 9.13, but uses a join on the `author` and `country` tables instead of the `IN` predicate.

LISTING 9.15 Using a Join Operation to List the Books Written by Authors Who Lived in Europe

```
SELECT t.book_title, a.author_name
FROM  titles t, authors a, author_title ta, country c
WHERE    t.ISBN = ta.ISBN
AND   ta.author_id = a.author_id
AND  a.country_code = c.country_code;
```

NULLs and Empty Strings in Ranges and Patterns

So far I have discussed several predicates that help define ranges and patterns in SQL statements. In this section, I cover general rules for handling NULLs when introduced with some of these predicates:

- For the LIKE predicate, the NULL can be the escape character, the pattern, or the match value. In any case, the predicate returns UNKNOWN as a result.
- In the case of the LIKE predicate, if the pattern, P, and match value, M, are both strings with zero length, then the expression M LIKE P returns TRUE. If at least one of the two values has a length greater than zero, you use the regular rules to test the predicate.
- For the BETWEEN predicate, if the expression value is NULL, the predicate returns UNKNOWN as the result. If the expression value is not NULL, and both the low value and high values are NULL, then the predicate returns UNKNOWN too. If the expression value is not NULL and only one of the high and low values is NULL, then the predicate returns the result from comparing the non-NULL end-value (high or low value) to the expression value.

Note

Please note that the terminology used in this discussion is based on the syntax definitions of these predicates in their corresponding sections. For example, the syntax for the BETWEEN predicate is expression value BETWEEN low value and high value.

Summary

In this chapter, you have seen how SQL gives you great tools to make data selection more flexible and to allow you to establish patterns for the data you want to retrieve. It is these predicates, such as `LIKE`, `IN`, `BETWEEN`, and so on, that make SQL popular. The benefit of these tools is that they are so easy to understand and use across the many SQL implementations.

CHAPTER

Table Joins

In This Chapter

What Are Table Joins?

Table joins are used to retrieve data from two or more related tables in a database based on a search condition. Table joins are done with the SQL-92 SELECT statement, which is used to specify the join conditions, the columns to be retrieved, and the search conditions. The basic form of the SELECT statement is as follows:

```
SELECT <field list>
FROM <joined table list>
WHERE <search conditions>
```

The <field list> parameter specifies the fields retrieved from the tables in the FROM clause. If a field is common to two or more tables, then the field name has to be qualified by the table name or the alias of the table. An asterisk (*) can denote that the fields from all tables in the join are retrieved. The <joined table list> parameter specifies the tables that are joined together. The table referenced in the FROM clause can also be a derived table. The <search conditions> parameter further restricts the rows in the joined tables based on the conditions specified. Let's look at the SELECT statement's FROM clause and how to create the joins. This is the syntax of the FROM clause:

```
FROM <table> [AS <table alias>]
[, <table> [AS <table alias>]...]
```

In this code, <table> can be a derived table, view, or joined table, and <table alias> is a short name given to a table for convenience's sake or to distinguish it from duplicate tables in a self-join. The simplest form of a SELECT statement is this:

```
SELECT * FROM Table1
```

This SELECT statement retrieves all rows and columns from the table Table1. The joined table is specified as follows:

```
<joined table> =
{<table1> CROSS JOIN <table2>} |
{<table1> [NATURAL]
[INNER | UNION | [LEFT | RIGHT | FULL] OUTER]
<table2>
[ON <search condition>] | [USING (<join column list)]}
```

If NATURALis the join type, then a join specification cannot be specified—that is, the ON clause or USING clause cannot be used. If UNION is used, then neither NATURAL nor a join condition can be specified. Otherwise, a join condition is mandatory. If a join type—INNER, LEFT, RIGHT, or FULL—is not specified, then INNER is the default. The USING clause indicates that the join is based on the common columns between the joined tables. The `NATURAL` join is really a special type of `INNER` join that performs the join based on a single common column in the joined tables. It cannot be used if the joined tables have duplicate common column names. The order of the tables in a join is not important. In the following sections, you will examine each join type and see a few examples that use ANSI SQL statements. The tables shown in Listing 10.1 are used in all the examples. These examples can be executed using Microsoft SQL Server versions 6.0 and above with a few exceptions as noted.

LISTING 10.1 LST10_1.TXT—Tables for the Join Examples

```
CREATE TABLE Customers (CustomerID INTEGER,
       Customer CHARACTER(10), Address CHARACTER(50),
       CONSTRAINT PK_Customers PRIMARY KEY (CustomerID))
CREATE TABLE Orders (CustomerID INTEGER, OrderID INTEGER, OrderDate DATE-
TIME,
       CONSTRAINT PK_Orders PRIMARY KEY (OrderID),
       CONSTRAINT FK_Orders FOREIGN KEY (CustomerID) REFERENCES Customers)
CREATE TABLE Special_Customers (SpecialID INTEGER,
       Customer CHARACTER(10), OrderNumber INTEGER, OrderDate DATETIME)
INSERT INTO Customers VALUES(1, 'Customer1', 'Address1')
INSERT INTO Customers VALUES(2, 'Customer2', 'Address2')
INSERT INTO Customers VALUES(3, 'Customer3', 'Address3')
INSERT INTO Orders VALUES(1, 1, '01/01/1999')
INSERT INTO Orders VALUES(1, 2, '02/01/1999')
INSERT INTO Orders VALUES(2, 3, '01/21/1999')
INSERT INTO Orders VALUES(2, 4, '02/21/1999')
INSERT INTO Special_Customers VALUES(1, 'Special1', 1, '01/02/1999')
INSERT INTO Special_Customers VALUES(1, 'Special1', 2, '03/02/1999')
INSERT INTO Special_Customers VALUES(1, 'Special1', 3, '03/08/1999')
INSERT INTO Special_Customers VALUES(2, 'Special2', 4, '03/02/1999')
INSERT INTO Special_Customers VALUES(2, 'Special2', 5, '02/22/1999')
INSERT INTO Special_Customers VALUES(3, 'Special3', 6, '04/02/1999')
INSERT INTO Special_Customers VALUES(3, 'Special3', 7, '03/08/1999')
INSERT INTO Special_Customers VALUES(3, 'Special3', 8, '03/02/1999')
```

The tables in the examples and the `SELECT` statements can be tested in any database that supports ANSI SQL, with the exception of the `NATURAL` join and `USING` clause, which aren't widely used.

Inner Joins

The simplest form of a join is the inner join that retrieves all the matching rows from the specified tables. The ON clause specifies the column or columns in one table that should match the corresponding columns in the second table. Listing 10.2 shows a few examples of INNER JOIN using the Customers and Orders tables from Listing 10.1. The inner join examples retrieve all customers who have placed orders.

LISTING 10.2 LST10_2.TXT—Inner Join Examples

```
/* Example #1, Inner join */
SELECT A1.CustomerID, A1.Customer, A2.OrderID, A2.OrderDate
FROM Customers AS A1 INNER JOIN Orders AS A2
ON A1.CustomerID = A2.CustomerID
go
/* Example #2, Natural join based on the common column CC1 */
/* NATURAL JOIN clause is not implemented in SQL Server. */
SELECT A1.CustomerID, A1.Customer, A2.OrderID, A2.OrderDate
FROM Customers AS A1 NATURAL JOIN Orders AS A2
go
/* Example #3, Inner join with USING clause */
/* USING clause is not implemented in SQL Server. */
SELECT A1.CustomerID, A1.Customer, A2.OrderID, A2.OrderDate
FROM Customers AS A1 INNER JOIN Orders AS A2
USING (CustomerID)
go
/* Example #4, Inner join with WHERE clause */
SELECT A1.CustomerID, A1.Customer, A2.OrderID, A2.OrderDate
FROM Customers AS A1 INNER JOIN Orders AS A2
ON A1.CustomerID = A2.CustomerID
WHERE A2.OrderDate > '01/01/1999'
```

The inner join is used to retrieve rows from the Customers and Orders tables based on the column CustomerID, as shown in Example #1 in the listing. The inner join can be formulated as a NATURAL join that implicitly performs the join based on the common column CustomerID, as shown in Example #2. The USING clause can be alternatively used to specify the common column or columns on which the join conditions have to be based, as shown in Example #3. The WHERE clause can be used to further restrict the rows retrieved by the SELECT statement, as shown in Example #4. From the output of the inner join examples, you can see that the CustomerID with the value 3 is not retrieved because there is no order for that customer.

Outer Joins

The outer join is used to retrieve all data from one table and the corresponding records from the second table. In the Customers table, the CustomerID with the value 3 does not have any orders placed. The inner join will not return this CustomerID based on the join condition. An outer join can be used instead to list all customers, including those with no orders. Listing 10.3 shows a few examples of the outer join.

LISTING 10.3 LST10_3.TXT—Outer Join Examples

```
/* Example #1, Left outer join */
SELECT A1.CustomerID, A1.Customer, A2.OrderID, A2.OrderDate
FROM Customers AS A1 LEFT OUTER JOIN Orders AS A2
ON A1.CustomerID = A2.CustomerID
/* Example #2, Right outer join */
SELECT A1.CustomerID, A1.Customer, A2.OrderID, A2.OrderDate
FROM Orders AS A2 RIGHT OUTER JOIN Customers AS A1
ON A1.CustomerID = A2.CustomerID
```

The LEFT OUTER JOIN, as you can see in Example #1, also retrieves the customer with the CustomerID value of 3. The LEFT OUTER JOIN can also be used as a RIGHT OUTER JOIN by reversing the tables specified. The right outer join can be treated as a left outer join, for all practical purposes. The FULL OUTER JOIN returns rows from both the joined tables that do not have matching column values.

Union Joins

The UNION join is used to gather data from different SELECT statements and present it as a single resultset. The general syntax of the UNION join is as follows:

```
SELECT <field list1> FROM <table list1>
UNION [ALL]
SELECT <field list2> FROM <table list2>
```

The number of SELECT statements that can be joined in this manner is specific to the implementation. The ALL keyword indicates that duplicate rows should be returned from the SELECT statements. The UNION join's default behavior is to eliminate duplicate rows from the resultset. Listing 10.4 shows an example of a UNION join.

LISTING 10.4 LST10_4.TXT—Union Join Examples

```
/* Example #1 */
SELECT A1.CustomerID, A1.Customer, A2.OrderID, A2.OrderDate
FROM Customers AS A1 INNER JOIN Orders AS A2
```

LISTING 10.4 CONTINUED

```
ON A1.CustomerID = A2.CustomerID
UNION ALL
SELECT SpecialID, Customer, OrderNumber, OrderDate
FROM Special_Customer
/* Example #2 */
SELECT A1.CustomerID, A1.Customer, A2.OrderID, A2.OrderDate
FROM Customers AS A1 INNER JOIN Orders AS A2
ON A1.CustomerID = A2.CustomerID
UNION ALL
SELECT SpecialID AS CustomerID, Customer, OrderNumber AS OrderID, OrderDate
FROM Special_Customers
WHERE OrderDate > '01/10/1999'
```

The number of columns in each `SELECT` statement should be the same, and the data types should be compatible.

Self-Joins and Range Joins

A range join is one that returns all values between two specified values for a column. Inclusive ranges return any values that match the two specified values. Exclusive ranges do not return any values that match the two specified values. The range search can also be used to find a row outside the range. Listing 10.5 shows some examples of range joins.

LISTING 10.5 `LST10_5.TXT`—Range Join Examples

```
/* Example #1, Inclusive range */
SELECT A1.CustomerID, A1.Customer, A2.OrderID, A2.OrderDate
FROM Customers AS A1 INNER JOIN Orders AS A2
ON A1.CustomerID = A2.CustomerID
WHERE A2.OrderDate BETWEEN '01/01/1999' AND '02/01/1999'
/* Example #2, Exclusive range */
SELECT A1.CustomerID, A1.Customer, A2.OrderID, A2.OrderDate
FROM Customers AS A1 INNER JOIN Orders AS A2
ON A1.CustomerID = A2.CustomerID
WHERE A2.OrderDate > '01/01/1999' AND A2.OrderDate < '02/01/1999'
/* Example #3, Outside specified range */
SELECT A1.CustomerID, A1.Customer, A2.OrderID, A2.OrderDate
FROM Customers AS A1 INNER JOIN Orders AS A2
ON A1.CustomerID = A2.CustomerID
WHERE A2.OrderDate NOT BETWEEN '01/01/1999' AND '02/01/1999'
```

In a self-join, a table is joined to itself. The tables in the FROM clause must be differentiated by using different aliases. Listing 10.6 shows the table used in the self-join example.

LISTING 10.6 LST10_6.TXT—Table for the Self-Join Example

```
CREATE TABLE Employees (EmployeeID INTEGER, EmployeeName CHARACTER(20),
            SupervisorID INTEGER NULL)
INSERT INTO Employees VALUES(1, 'GREEN', NULL)
INSERT INTO Employees VALUES(2, 'JONE', 1)
INSERT INTO Employees VALUES(3, 'SMITH', 1)
INSERT INTO Employees VALUES(4, 'ROGER', 2)
INSERT INTO Employees VALUES(5, 'BARRY', 2)
INSERT INTO Employees VALUES(6, 'ALAN', 1)
```

Listing 10.7 shows two examples of a self-join that retrieves the employees' names and their supervisors from the Employees table.

LISTING 10.7 LST10_7.TXT—Self-Join Examples

```
/* Example #1 */
SELECT A1.EmployeeName, A2.EmployeeName AS Supervisor
FROM Employees A1 INNER JOIN Employees A2
ON A1.SupervisorID = A2.EmployeeID
/* Example #2 */
SELECT A1.EmployeeName, COALESCE(A2.EmployeeName, '(None)') AS Supervisor
FROM Employees A1 LEFT OUTER JOIN Employees A2
ON A1.SupervisorID = A2.EmployeeID
```

In Example #1, only employees who have supervisors are retrieved by INNER JOIN. In Example #2, LEFT OUTER JOIN is used to get all employees whether they have a supervisor or not. The COALESCE function is used to show the supervisor value as (None) for employees who do not have a supervisor.

In this section, you have seen the types of joins in the SQL-92 standard. You will now look at the implementation of joins, specifically the SELECT statement in Microsoft SQL Server 7.0 and Oracle 8.0. Both database systems have extensions to the SELECT statement that are not in the SQL-92 standard.

Table Joins in Microsoft SQL Server

The SELECT statement is used to perform joins in SQL Server. The joins can be written using the Transact-SQL syntax or the ANSI-92 SQL syntax. The preferred syntax for writing queries in Microsoft SQL Server 7.0 is the ANSI syntax. Transact-SQL also has extensions to the SELECT statement that can be used, for instance, to perform multidimensional analysis of the data. The basic syntax of the SELECT statement is as follows:

```
SELECT [DISTINCT ¦ ALL] <field list> ¦ *
FROM <table list>
[WHERE <search conditions>]
[GROUP BY [ALL] <group list> [WITH CUBE ¦ROLLUP>
[HAVING <search conditions>]
[ORDER BY <order list> [ASC ¦ DESC>
[OPTION <query hints>]
```

The <field list> parameter describes the columns of the resultset. It is a comma-separated list of expressions or column names. Each column name defines the data type, size, and source of the data for the resultset column. The select list expression can also be any other expression, such as a constant or a Transact-SQL function. If an asterisk is specified as the field list, then all columns in the table list are included. The DISTINCT keyword ensures that only unique values of the specified columns are retrieved. The ALL keyword indicates that all values of the specified column should be retrieved. The optional ALL keyword is the default behavior of the SELECT statement. The <table list> parameter of the FROM clause contains a list of the tables from which the resultset is retrieved. The WHERE clause is a filter that defines the conditions each row in the source tables must satisfy to qualify for the SELECT statement. Only rows that meet the conditions contribute data to the resultset.

The GROUP BY clause groups the resultset into groups based on the values in the columns specified in the <group list> parameter. When ALL is specified for the GROUP BY clause, all groups and resultsets that do not match the search condition in the WHERE clause are returned. The ALL option cannot be used with CUBE or ROLLUP operators. The CUBE operator specifies that, in addition to the usual rows provided by GROUP BY, summary rows are introduced into the resultset. A GROUP BY summary row is returned for every possible combination of group and subgroup in the resultset. A GROUP BY summary row is displayed as NULL in the resultset, but is used to indicate all values. The GROUPING function determines whether null values in the resultset are GROUP BY summary values. The number of summary rows in the resultset is determined by the number of columns included in the GROUP BY clause. Each column in the GROUP BY clause is bound under the grouping NULL, and grouping is applied to all other columns. Because CUBE returns every possible combination of group and subgroup, the number of rows is the same, regardless of the order in which the grouping columns are specified. The ROLLUP operator indicates that, in addition to the usual rows provided by GROUP BY, summary rows are introduced into the resultset. Groups are summarized in a hierarchical order, from the lowest level in the group to the highest. The group hierarchy is determined by the order in which the grouping columns are specified.

The number of rows produced in the resultset depends on the order of the grouping columns.

The HAVING clause is an additional filter applied to the resultset. It is typically used with the GROUP BY clause. Aggregate functions on columns of the table can be used in the HAVING clause.

The ORDER BY clause defines the order in which the rows in the resultset are sorted. The <order list> parameter determines the resultset columns that form the sort list. The ASCand DESC keywords indicate whether the rows are sorted in ascending or descending sequence. The ORDER BY clause must be used in any SELECT statement in which the order of the resultset rows is important.

The FROM clause specifies the tables, views, derived tables, and joined tables used in the SELECT statement. It supports the SQL-92 syntax for joined tables and derived tables. This is the syntax of the FROM clause:

```
[ FROM <source table> [,...n] ]
<source table> =
<table> [ ¤ <alias> ] [ WITH ( <hint list>) ]
¦ <view> [ ¤ <alias> ]
¦ <rowset function> [ ¤ <alias> ]
¦ <derived table> ¤ <alias> [ (<column alias list>) ]
¦ <joined table>
<joined table> =
<table> CROSS JOIN < table>
¦ <table> [ INNER ¦
{ { LEFT ¦ RIGHT ¦ FULL } [OUTER] } ]
[ <join hint> ]
JOIN <table> ON <search_condition>
```

The <source table> parameter can be a table or view. The alias name is not necessary if the table names are unique. The FROM clause can reference up to 256 tables. If the table or view exists in another database on the same computer running SQL Server, a fully qualified name in the form of database.owner.object_name is required. If the table or view exists outside the local server on a linked server, a four-part name in the form of linked_server.catalog.schema.object is required. The order of the tables and views after the FROM keyword does not affect the resultset returned. The <rowset function> parameter is used to reference a resultset from a remote server. The <derived table> parameter is a subquery that retrieves rows from the database. The <alias> name is given to a <source table> either for convenience or to distinguish a table or view in a self-join or subquery. An alias is often a shortened table name used to qualify columns of the tables in a join. If there are duplicate column names, then the column name must be qualified by a table name or alias. The WITH clause is used to specify a table scan, one or more indexes to be used by the query optimizer, or a locking method to be used by the query optimizer with this table and for the SELECT statement. The <column alias list> parameter determines a column name in for each column in the derived table.

The <joined table> parameter is a resultset that is the product of two or more tables. If multiple CROSS joins are specified, then parentheses can be used to change the natural order of the joins. The <join type> parameter indicates the type of join operation. The INNER JOIN specifies that all matching pairs of rows be returned. This is the default if no join type is mentioned. In the FULL OUTER JOIN, a row from either the left or the right table that does not meet the join condition is included in the resultset, and output columns that correspond to the other table are set to NULL. This includes all rows usually returned by the INNER JOIN. The LEFT OUTER JOIN indicates that all rows from the left table not meeting the join condition are included in the resultset, and output columns from the other table are set to NULL, in addition to all rows returned by the inner join. In the RIGHT OUTER JOIN, all rows from the right table not meeting the join condition are included in the resultset, and output columns that correspond to the other table are set to NULL, in addition to all rows returned by the inner join. The <join hint> parameter specifies that the SQL Server query optimizer use one *join hint*, or execution algorithm, per join specified in the query's FROM clause. The ON clause states the condition on which the join is based. The condition can use any predicate. When the condition specifies columns, the columns do not have to have the same name or same data type; however, if the data types are not identical, they must be compatible or types that SQL Server can implicitly convert. If the data types cannot be implicitly converted, the condition must explicitly convert the data type by using the CAST function. The CROSS JOIN or Cartesian product specifies the cross product of two tables.

The <hint list> parameter specifies a table scan, indexes to be used by the query optimizer, or a locking method to be used by the query optimizer. The hint applies to the specified table and for the SELECT statement only. SQL Server does not allow more than one table hint from each of the following groups:

- Granularity hints: PAGLOCK, NOLOCK, ROWLOCK, TABLOCK, or TABLOCKX
- Isolation level hints: HOLDLOCK, NOLOCK, READCOMMITTED, REPEATABLEREAD, or SERIALIZABLE

The syntax of the <hint list> parameter is as follows:

```
<hint list> =
{ INDEX(<index values>)
¦ FASTFIRSTROW
¦ HOLDLOCK
¦ NOLOCK
```

```
¦ ROWLOCK
¦ PAGLOCK
¦ UPDLOCK
¦ TABLOCK
¦ TABLOCKX
¦ READCOMMITTED
¦ READPAST
¦ READUNCOMMITTED
¦ REPEATABLEREAD
¦ SERIALIZABLE
}
```

For an explanation of the index hints, please refer to the SQL Server Books Online documentation.

The `<join hint>` parameter is used to enforce a join strategy between two tables listed in the `FROM` clause. If a join hint is specified for any two tables, the query optimizer automatically enforces the join order for all joined tables in the query, based on the position of the `ON` keywords. For a `FULL OUTER JOIN`, when the `ON` clauses are not used, parentheses can be used to indicate the join order. The join hints can be one of the following: `LOOP`, `HASH`, `MERGE`, or `REMOTE`. The `REMOTE` hint indicates that the join operation is performed on the site of the right table. This is useful when the left table is a local table and the right table is a remote table. `REMOTE` should be used only when the left table has fewer rows than the right table. If the right table is local, the join is performed locally. If both tables are remote but from different data sources, `REMOTE` causes the join to be performed on the right table's site. If both tables are remote tables from the same data source, `REMOTE` is not necessary.

The `OPTION` clause specifies that the indicated query hint be used throughout the entire query. Each query hint can be used only once, although multiple query hints are permitted. The `OPTION` clause must use the outermost query of the statement. The query hint affects all operators in the statement. If a `UNION` is involved in the main query, only the last query involving a `UNION` operator can have the `OPTION` clause. If one or more query hints causes the query optimizer to not generate a valid plan, SQL Server recompiles the query without the specified query hints. These are the query hints that can be used:

- `HASH ¦ ORDER GROUP` Hashing or ordering is used to perform aggregations in the `GROUP BY` or `COMPUTE` clause of the `SELECT` statement.
- `MERGE ¦ HASH ¦ CONCAT UNION` Merging, hashing, or concatenating union sets for all `UNION` operations. If more than one `UNION` hint is specified, the optimizer selects the least expensive strategy from those hints.
- `LOOP ¦ MERGE ¦ HASH JOIN` All join operations are performed by loop join, merge join, or hash join in the `SELECT` statement. If more than one join hint is used, the

optimizer selects the least expensive join strategy for the allowed ones. If, in the same query, a join hint is also indicated for a specific pair of tables, it takes precedence when joining the two tables.

- FAST <*n* rows>   The query is optimized for fast retrieval of the first <*n* rows> specified. After the first <*n* rows> are returned, the query continues running and produces its full resultset.
- FORCE ORDER   The join order indicated by the syntax of the SELECT statement is preserved during query optimization.
- MAXDOP number   Specifies the maximum degree of parallelism for the SELECT statement. It overrides the default configuration value.
- ROBUST PLAN   Forces the query optimizer to attempt a plan that works for the maximum potential row size.
- KEEP PLAN   Forces the query optimizer to relax the estimated recompile threshold for a query. The estimated recompile threshold is the point at which a query is automatically recompiled when the estimated number of update, delete, or insert operations has been made to a table. Specifying KEEP PLAN ensures that a query is not recompiled as often when there are multiple updates to a table.

The processing order of the WHERE, GROUP BY , and HAVING clauses in a SELECT statement is as follows:

- WHERE clause   The search condition excludes rows not meeting the conditions.
- GROUP BY clause   Groups rows into one group for each unique value of the columns in the GROUP BY clause. The aggregate functions, if specified in the select list, are then performed for each group.
- HAVING clause   The search condition in the HAVING clause further excludes rows.

All the examples in Listings 10.1, 10.2, 10.3, 10.4, 10.5, 10.6, and 10.7 will work in SQL Server, with the exception of the NATURAL JOIN and the INNER JOIN with the USING clause.

Inner Joins

Listing 10.8 shows four Transact-SQL examples of inner joins. The examples use the Northwind sample database installed with SQL Server.

LISTING 10.8 LST10_8.TXT—Inner Join Examples

```
/* Example #1, Lists products and categories */
Use Northwind
```

LISTING 10.8 CONTINUED

```
Go
SELECT Products.ProductName, Categories.CategoryName
FROM Categories INNER JOIN Products
ON Categories.CategoryID = Products.CategoryID
/* Example #2, Lists categories and number of products in each */
SELECT Categories.CategoryName, COUNT(*) AS [Number Of Products]
FROM Categories INNER JOIN Products
ON Categories.CategoryID = Products.CategoryID
GROUP BY Categories.CategoryName
ORDER BY Categories.CategoryName
/* Example #3, Lists categories that have more than 10 products in each */
SELECT Categories.CategoryName, COUNT(*) AS [Number Of Products]
FROM Categories INNER JOIN Products
ON Categories.CategoryID = Products.CategoryID
GROUP BY Categories.CategoryName
HAVING COUNT(*) > 10
ORDER BY Categories.CategoryName
/* Example #4, Lists sales for Beverage products for month of July in 1996 */
SELECT Products.ProductName,
    '$' + CAST(Sum(CONVERT(money,
         ([Order Details].UnitPrice*Quantity*(1-Discount)/100))*100)
       AS varchar) AS Sales
FROM Categories
INNER JOIN Products
INNER JOIN Orders
INNER JOIN [Order Details]
 ON Orders.OrderID = [Order Details].OrderID
 ON Products.ProductID = [Order Details].ProductID
 ON Categories.CategoryID = Products.CategoryID
WHERE Month(Orders.ShippedDate) = 7 AND
   YEAR(Orders.ShippedDate) = 1996 AND
   Categories.CategoryName = 'Beverages'
GROUP BY Products.ProductName
/* Example #5, LOOP join using optimizer hint */
SELECT Products.ProductName, Categories.CategoryName
FROM Categories INNER LOOP JOIN Products
ON Categories.CategoryID = Products.CategoryID
/* Example #6, MERGE join using optimizer hint */
SELECT Products.ProductName, Categories.CategoryName
FROM Categories INNER MERGE JOIN Products
ON Categories.CategoryID = Products.CategoryID
/* Example #7, Lists categories and number of products in each */
```

LISTING 10.8 CONTINUED

```
SELECT Categories.CategoryName, COUNT(*) AS [Number Of Products]
FROM Categories INNER JOIN Products
ON Categories.CategoryID = Products.CategoryID
GROUP BY Categories.CategoryName
ORDER BY Categories.CategoryName
OPTION (HASH GROUP)
```

In Example #1, an inner join is used to get all products and category names. Example #2 retrieves the number of products in each category by using the `COUNT (*)` function with the `GROUP BY` clause. In Example #3, the `HAVING` clause is used to get categories that have more than 10 products. Example #4 uses a different syntax of the `SELECT` statement `is used`. In this format, the order of the `ON` clause is important, and the tables in the `INNER JOIN` clauses are opened from the last `INNER JOIN` clause to the first. The results are the same as a `SELECT` statement with typical inner joins. Examples #5, #6, and #7 demonstrate how to specify join hints and the `OPTION` clause in the `SELECT` statement.

Outer Joins

Listing 10.9 shows two Transact-SQL examples of a left join and a right join. Internally, a right outer join is treated as a left outer join by swapping the tables.

LISTING 10.9 `LST10_9.TXT`—Outer Join Examples

```
/* Example #1 using left join */
SELECT
  E.EmployeeID,
  E.LastName + ' ' + E.FirstName AS EmployeeName,
  COALESCE(S.FirstName + ' ' + S.LastName, 'No Supervisor') AS SupervisorName
FROM Employees AS E
LEFT JOIN Employees AS S
ON E.ReportsTo = S.EmployeeID
Order By SupervisorName
/* Example #2 using right join */
SELECT
  E.EmployeeID,
  E.LastName + ' ' + E.FirstName AS EmployeeName,
  COALESCE(S.FirstName + ' ' + S.LastName, 'No Supervisor') AS SupervisorName
FROM Employees AS S
RIGHT JOIN Employees AS E
ON E.ReportsTo = S.EmployeeID
Order By SupervisorName
```

The keyword OUTER is optional in a LEFT or RIGHT join.

Derived Table Join

Listing 10.10 shows a Transact-SQL example that uses derived tables to get the employees and their supervisor names.

LISTING 10.10 LST10_10.TXT—Derived Table Example

```
SELECT
  E.EmployeeID,
  E.LastName + ' ' + E.FirstName AS EmployeeName,
  S.SupervisorName
FROM Employees AS E
INNER JOIN
(SELECT DISTINCT ISNULL(E2.ReportsTo, -1),
        COALESCE((SELECT E1.FirstName + ' ' + E1.LastName
              FROM Employees E1
              WHERE E1.EmployeeID = E2.ReportsTo),
             'No Supervisor')
 FROM Employees E2) AS S(ReportsTo, SupervisorName)
ON ISNULL(E.ReportsTo, -1) = S.ReportsTO
Order By SupervisorName
```

The DISTINCT keyword in the derived table's SELECT statement retrieves unique values from the ReportsTo field. The ISNULL function in the example returns -1 for NULL values in the ReportsTo column. This ensures that the inner join can be performed between the Employees table and the derived table. This example is only for demonstrating the use of derived tables, and the performance of this SELECT statement is not the same as the outer join example.

Union Joins

Listing 10.11 shows some Transact-SQL examples that perform union joins.

LISTING 10.11 LST10_11.TXT—Union Join Examples

```
/* Example #1, Get all company names from the customers & suppliers table */
SELECT CompanyName, ContactName
FROM Customers
WHERE country = 'USA'
UNION
SELECT CompanyName, ContactName
FROM Suppliers
```

LISTING 10.11 CONTINUED

```
WHERE country = 'USA'
UNION
SELECT CompanyName, '(None)'
FROM Shippers
/* Example #2, Gets the procedures and tables in the database */
SELECT Name, 'Table' AS [Object Type] FROM sysobjects WHERE Type = 'U'
UNION ALL
SELECT Name, 'View' AS [Object Type] FROM sysobjects WHERE Type = 'V'
UNION ALL
SELECT Name, 'Procedure' AS [Object Type] FROM sysobjects WHERE Type = 'P'
```

All select lists in the statements being combined with `UNION` must have the same number of expressions. The expressions can be column names, functions, and other expressions. The order of the columns should also be the same because `UNION` compares the columns one-to-one in the order given in the individual `SELECT` statements. When different data types are combined in the union join, they are converted using the rules of data type precedence. If a conversion is not successful, an error message is raised.

Cross Joins

A cross join, or Cartesian product between tables, returns all possible combinations of the rows. For example, if a cross join is performed between two tables—one with 12 rows and another with 3 rows—the resultset will contain 36 rows. Listing 10.12 shows an example of a `CROSS JOIN` used to generate sequence numbers for rows in a table.

LISTING 10.12 `LST10_12.TXT`—Cross Join Example

```
Use Northwind
Go
CREATE TABLE Test (Description CHAR(5))
INSERT Test VALUES('AAAAA')
INSERT Test VALUES('BAAAB')
INSERT Test VALUES('HAAAB')
INSERT Test VALUES('MMMMM')
INSERT Test VALUES('TAAAR')
INSERT Test VALUES('XXXXZ')
INSERT Test VALUES('ZZZZA')
Go
/* Generate all possible combinations of data using a CROSS JOIN */
SELECT t1.Description, t2.Description
FROM Test t1 CROSS JOIN Test t2
Go
```

LISTING 10.12 CONTINUED

```
/* Now use the CROSS JOIN to generate sequence numbers for the rows */
SELECT t1.Description,
SUM(CASE WHEN t2.Description <= t1.Description THEN 1 ELSE 0 END) AS Sequence
FROM Test t1 CROSS JOIN Test t2
GROUP BY t1.DESCRIPTION
ORDER BY t1.DESCRIPTION
```

In this example, `CROSS JOIN` is used in a unique way to generate the row numbers by summing the rows up to a value. This is possible because of the way `CROSS JOIN` generates all possible combinations of rows in the table and the self-join. The `CROSS JOIN` returns all rows from `t1` for each row in `t2`. The `SUM` aggregate function is used to count only rows matching the description of the current row and this process is repeated for all rows in the table `t1`. The `CROSS JOIN` thus effectively provides a method to loop through the table `t1` for each value of the description and generate a sequence for every row.

Transact-SQL Extensions

In this section, you will look at the `SELECT` statement's `CUBE` and `ROLLUP` operators. Listing 10.13 shows two examples of the `SELECT` statement with a `CUBE` operator.

LISTING 10.13 `LST10_13.TXT`—`CUBE` Operator Example

```
Use Northwind
Go
CREATE TABLE PC_Products(Product CHAR(10), Type CHAR(10), Units INTEGER)
INSERT PC_Products VALUES('Desktop', 'Intel', 2000)
INSERT PC_Products VALUES('Desktop', 'AMD', 575)
INSERT PC_Products VALUES('Desktop', 'Cyrix', 450)
INSERT PC_Products VALUES('Laptop', 'Intel', 1200)
INSERT PC_Products VALUES('Laptop', 'AMD', 200)
GO
/* Example #1, generate aggregations based on product and type */
SELECT Product, Type, SUM(Units) AS [Units Sold]
FROM PC_Products
GROUP BY Product, Type
WITH CUBE
Go
/* Example #2, Use GROUPING function to denote sales of a particular type */
SELECT CASE WHEN GROUPING(Product) = 1 THEN '(All Products)'
      ELSE Product END AS Product,
    CASE WHEN GROUPING(Type) = 1 THEN '(All Types)'
      ELSE Type END AS Type,
```

LISTING 10.13 CONTINUED

```
    SUM(Units) AS [Units Sold]
FROM PC_Products
GROUP BY Product, Type
WITH CUBE
```

Example #1 in Listing 10.13 generates a resultset that contains all possible combinations of the values in the dimension columns (such as `Product` and `Type`) along with the aggregate values from the underlying rows that match that combination of dimension values. The `NULL` value in the `Product` and `Type` columns specifies the aggregate for any value of that column. The `GROUPING` function can be used to distinguish this `NULL` value. Example #2 uses the `GROUPING` function to print text indicating that the aggregate value belongs to all values of that column. The `CUBE` operator generates a resultset showing aggregates for all combinations of the values in the dimension columns. Listing 10.14 uses the `ROLLUP` operator on the `PC_Products` table to generate a multidimensional report of the units sold.

LISTING 10.14 LST10_14.TXT—ROLLUP Operator Example

```
Use Northwind
Go
SELECT CASE WHEN GROUPING(Product) = 1 THEN '(All Products)'
      ELSE Product END AS Product,
    CASE WHEN GROUPING(Type) = 1 THEN '(All Types)'
      ELSE Type END AS Type,
    SUM(Units) AS [Units Sold]
FROM PC_Products
GROUP BY Product, Type
WITH ROLLUP
```

From the example, you can see that the `ROLLUP` operator generates aggregates only for a hierarchy of values in the dimension columns.

Listing 10.15 shows another example that uses the `CUBE` operator to solve a typical problem.

LISTING 10.15 LST10_15.TXT—CUBE Operator Example

```
Use Northwind
Go
CREATE TABLE Person (PersonID INTEGER, FirstName CHAR(20), LastName
CHAR(20))
INSERT Person VALUES(1, 'GREEN', 'SMITH')
INSERT Person VALUES(2, 'JONES', 'KENNY')
```

LISTING 10.15 CONTINUED

```
SELECT CASE
   WHEN GROUPING(PersonID) = 0 AND GROUPING(Firstname) = 1 AND
   GROUPING(Lastname) = 1
   THEN 'PersonID'
   WHEN GROUPING(PersonID) = 1 AND GROUPING(Firstname) = 0 AND
   GROUPING(Lastname) = 1
   THEN 'FirstName'
   WHEN GROUPING(PersonID) = 1 AND GROUPING(Firstname) = 1 AND
   GROUPING(Lastname) = 0
   THEN 'LastName'
   END AS FieldName,
   CASE
   WHEN GROUPING(PersonID) = 0 AND GROUPING(Firstname) = 1 AND
   GROUPING(Lastname) = 1
   THEN LTRIM(STR(PersonID))
   WHEN GROUPING(PersonID) = 1 AND GROUPING(Firstname) = 0 AND
   GROUPING(Lastname) = 1
   THEN firstname
   WHEN GROUPING(PersonID) = 1 AND GROUPING(Firstname) = 1 AND
   GROUPING(Lastname) = 0
   THEN LastName
   END AS FieldValue
FROM Person
GROUP BY PersonID, Firstname, Lastname
WITH CUBE
HAVING (GROUPING(PersonID) = 0 AND GROUPING(Firstname) = 1 AND
GROUPING(Lastname) = 1)
     OR
     (GROUPING(PersonID) = 1 AND GROUPING(Firstname) = 0 AND GROUPING
     (Lastname) = 1)
     OR
     (GROUPING(PersonID) = 1 AND GROUPING(Firstname) = 1 AND GROUPING
     (Lastname) = 0)
```

The `SELECT` statement in Listing 10.15 transposes the values in the table's columns as rows in the resultset. This is achieved by using the `CUBE` operator to generate the combinations of the columns and the `GROUPING` function to filter only the values that correspond to all values of a column. The `CUBE` and `ROLLUP` operators are extensions to the `SELECT` statement that are specific to Microsoft SQL Server. The `SELECT` statements using these extensions are not portable across different database systems.

Table Joins in Oracle

The SELECT statement is used to retrieve data from one or more tables, views, object tables, object views, or snapshots. The SQL-92 support in Oracle is limited, but the SELECT statement has unique PL/SQL extensions, such as the START WITH and CONNECT BY clauses. This is the basic syntax of the SELECT statement:

```
SELECT [DISTINCT ¦ ALL] <field list> ¦ *
FROM [
<table name> [ PARTITION <partition name> ]
¦ <view name>
]
¦ [ THE( <sub query> ) ]
[WHERE <search condition>]
<GROUP BY <group by list>]
[HAVING <search condition>>
¦
[START WITH <start condition>
 CONNECT BY <connect condition>
]
[ORDER BY <order list> [ASC ¦ DESC>
```

The DISTINCT keyword tells the SELECT statement to return only one copy of each set of duplicate rows selected. The ALL keyword, which is the default, specifies that the SELECT statement returns all rows selected, including all copies of duplicates. The <field list> parameter indicates which fields are retrieved from the tables in the FROM clause. It can also be a constant, an expression, or a system function. If an asterisk (*) is used for <field list>, all columns from all tables, views, or snapshots listed in the FROM clause are returned. The asterisk can be qualified with a particular table, view, or snapshot to return all columns only from that element. A different name for the column expression can be supplied in the <field list> parameter. The alias effectively renames the select list item for the duration of the SELECT statement. The alias can be used in the ORDER BY clause, but not other clauses in the query.

The FROM clause determines from which table, view, or snapshot the data is retrieved. The table, view, or snapshot can be written as a three-part name in the form of schema.owner.object_name. If the schema is omitted, Oracle assumes that the table, view, or snapshot is in your own schema. A remote table, view, or snapshot can be referenced by using a database link. The <partition name> parameter specifies the partition from which the table data is retrieved. The THE clause is used to perform flattened subqueries. It informs Oracle that the column value returned by the subquery is a nested table, not a scalar value. The <sub query> of the THE clause determines which data is selected for deletion.

A subquery can also be used in the FROM clause. In this case, Oracle executes the subquery and then uses the resulting rows as a view in the FROM clause. An alias can be supplied for the table, view, snapshot, or subquery. It is most often used in a correlated query or self-joins. The WHERE clause restricts the rows selected to those for which the <search condition> evaluates to TRUE. The START WITH ... CONNECT BY clause returns rows in a hierarchical order. The GROUP BY clause groups the selected rows based on the value of the columns for each row, and returns a single row of summary information for each group. The HAVING clause restricts the groups of rows returned to those groups for which the <search condition> evaluates to TRUE. The ORDER BY clause orders rows returned by the statement. The columns on which the resultset is ordered are specified in the <order by list> parameter. Each column in the ORDER BY clause can be ordered in ascending or descending order by using the ASC or DESC keywords. Listing 10.16 shows some examples of the SELECT statement in Oracle.

LISTING 10.16 LST10_16.TXT—SELECT Statement Examples

```
/* Example #1, Get employees and department name */
SELECT ename, dname
FROM emp, dept
WHERE empno.deptno = dept.deptno;
/* Example #2 Get employee details for depertments in Dallas */
SELECT empno, sal, comm
FROM emp, dept
WHERE job = 'CLERK' AND emp.deptno = dept.deptno AND loc = 'DALLAS';
/* Example #3, Get lowest and highest salaries of all employees */
SELECT deptno, MIN(sal), MAX (sal)
FROM emp
GROUP BY deptno;
/* Example #4, Get data from the partition June99 of the table MonthlyData */
SELECT * FROM Monthly_Data PARTITION (June99);
/* Example #5, Cross join query */
SELECT ename, dname
FROM emp e, dept d
```

Oracle does not support the SQL-92 syntax for INNER JOINS, OUTER JOINS, and CROSS JOINS. So in the subsequent sections, you will look at how equijoins, self-joins, outer joins, union joins, and range joins are performed with the PL/SQL syntax of the SELECT statement.

Joins

A join is a query that combines rows from two or more tables, views, or snapshots. Oracle performs a join whenever multiple tables appear in the SELECT statement's FROM clause. The select list of the SELECT statement can select any columns from any of these tables. If any two of these tables have a column name in common, then the column has to be qualified by the table name or alias to avoid ambiguity.

In a join condition, two columns, each from a different table, are compared. Oracle executes a join by combining pairs of rows, each containing one row from each table, for which the join condition evaluates to TRUE. It is not necessary for the columns in the join condition to appear in the select list also. Oracle executes a join of three or more tables by first joining two of the tables based on the join conditions, comparing their columns, and then joining the result to another table, based on join conditions, that contains columns of the joined tables and the new table. Oracle continues this process until all tables are joined into the result. The optimizer determines the order in which Oracle joins tables, based on the join conditions, indexes on the tables, and statistics for the tables. In addition to join conditions, the WHERE clause of a join query can contain other conditions that refer to columns of only one table. These conditions can further restrict the rows returned by the join query.

An equijoin has a join condition containing an equality operator. It combines rows that have equivalent values for the specified columns. Listing 10.17 shows a few examples of equijoins in Oracle.

LISTING 10.17 LST10_17.TXT—Equijoin Examples

```
SELECT e.deptno, dname, loc, ename, job
FROM emp e, dept d
WHERE e.deptno = d.deptno;
SELECT e.deptno, dname, ename, job
FROM emp e, dept d
WHERE e.deptno = d.deptno and dname = 'SALES'
ORDER BY ename DESC;
SELECT e.deptno, dname, ename, job
FROM emp e, dept d
WHERE e.deptno = d.deptno and loc = 'DALLAS'
ORDER BY ename;
```

A self-join is a join of a table to itself. This table is listed twice in the FROM clause and is followed by table aliases that qualify column names in the join condition. Oracle performs a self-join by combining and returning rows of the table that satisfy the join condition.

Listing 10.18 shows an example of a self-join that returns the employees and the name of their managers.

LISTING 10.18 LST10_18.TXT—Self-Join Examples

```
/* Example #1, Self join */
SELECT e.ename Employee, m.ename Manager
FROM emp e, emp m
WHERE e.mgr = m.empno;
/* Example #2, Self join using derived table*/
SELECT e.ename Employee, m.manager
FROM emp e, (SELECT empno Mgr, ename Manager FROM emp) m
WHERE e.mgr = m.mgr;
```

The join condition for the `SELECT` statement uses the aliases `e` and `m` for the `EMP` table and specifies the join condition between the `Mgr` and `Empno` fields of the `EMP` table. In Example #2, the self-join is performed using a derived table from `emp`.

Listing 10.19 shows some examples of a range join in Oracle.

LISTING 10.19 LST10_19.TXT—Range Join Examples

```
/* Example #1, Inclusive range */
SELECT e.ename Employee, e.Job, e.Sal Salary
FROM emp e
WHERE e.sal BETWEEN 1200 AND 2000;
/* Example #2, Exclusive range */
SELECT e.ename Employee, e.Job, e.Sal Salary
FROM emp e
WHERE e.sal > 1200 AND e.sal < 2000;
/* Example #2, Outside specified range */
SELECT e.ename Employee, e.Job, e.Sal Salary
FROM emp e
WHERE e.sal NOT BETWEEN 1200 AND 2000;
```

Outer Joins

The outer join extends the result of a simple join by returning all rows that satisfy the join condition and those rows from one table for which no rows from the other satisfy the join condition. To perform an outer join of tables `Table1` and `Table2` and return all rows from `Table1`, the outer join operator `(+)`is applied to all columns of `Table2` in the join condition. For all rows in `Table1` that have no matching rows in `Table2`, Oracle returns `NULL` for any select list expressions containing columns of `Table2`. The basic syntax for an outer join of two tables is as follows:

```
SELECT <select list>
FROM <table list>
WHERE [table1.Column1 (+) = table2.Column1]
¦ [table1.Column1 = (+) table2.Column1 ]
```

The following rules and restrictions apply to using outer join operators in `SELECT` statements:

- If two tables are joined by multiple join conditions, the `(+)` operator must be used in all these conditions
- The `(+)` operator can appear only in the `WHERE` clause and can be applied only to a column of a table or view
- The `(+)` operator can be applied only to a column, not to an arbitrary expression
- A join condition containing the `(+)` operator cannot be combined with another condition using the `OR` logical operator
- Any column marked with the `(+)` operator cannot be used with the `IN` comparison operator to compare with another expression
- Any column marked with the `(+)` operator in a condition cannot be compared with a subquery

If the `WHERE` clause contains a condition that compares a column from `Table2` with a constant, the `(+)` operator must be applied to the column so that Oracle returns the rows from table A for which it has generated `NULL`s for this column. In a query that performs outer joins of more than two pairs of tables, a single table can be the `NULL`-generated table for only one other table. The `(+)` operator cannot be applied to columns of `Table2` in the join condition for `Table1` and `Table2` and the join condition for `Table2` and `Table3`.

Listing 10.20 shows some examples of the outer join operator.

LISTING 10.20 `LST10_20.TXT`—Outer Join Examples

```
SELECT e.deptno, d.dname, e.ename, e.job
FROM emp e, dept d
WHERE e.deptno (+) = d.deptno;
SELECT e.deptno, d.dname, e.ename, e.job
FROM emp e, dept d
WHERE e.deptno (+) = d.deptno AND e.job (+) = 'CLERK';
```

Set Operators

The UNION, INTERSECT, and MINUS operators combine the resultsets of two queries into a single result. SELECT statements using THE or MULTISET keywords cannot be used with these set operators. If more than two queries are combined with set operators, adjacent pairs of queries are evaluated from left to right. You can use parentheses to specify a different order of evaluation. The UNION operator returns all rows selected by either query. The UNION ALL operator returns all rows selected by either query, including all the duplicate rows. The INTERSECT operator returns the distinct rows selected by both queries. The MINUS operator returns all distinct rows selected by the first query only.

Consider the two tables in Listing 10.21.

LISTING 10.21 LST10_21.TXT—Tables for Set Operators Example

```
CREATE TABLE Table1 (ID1 NUMBER(2), C1 VARCHAR2(4));
CREATE TABLE Table2 (ID2 NUMBER(2), C2 VARCHAR2(4));
INSERT INTO Table1 VALUES(1, 'AAAA');
INSERT INTO Table1 VALUES(2, 'BBBB');
INSERT INTO Table1 VALUES(3, 'CCCC');
INSERT INTO Table2 VALUES(1, 'AAAA');
INSERT INTO Table2 VALUES(1, 'ABAB');
INSERT INTO Table2 VALUES(2, 'BCBC');
INSERT INTO Table2 VALUES(4, 'DADA');
```

Listing 10.22 uses Table1 and Table2 to demonstrate the use of the set operators.

LISTING 10.22 LST10_22.TXT—Set Operators Examples

```
/* Example #1, UNION operator */
SELECT ID1, C1 FROM Table1
UNION
SELECT ID2, C2 FROM Table2;
/* Example #2, UNION operator */
SELECT ID1, C1 FROM Table1
UNION ALL
SELECT ID2, C2 FROM Table2;
/* Example #3, INTERSECT operator */
SELECT ID1, C1 FROM Table1
INTERSECT
SELECT ID2, C2 FROM Table2;
/* Example #4, MINUS operator */
SELECT ID1, C1 FROM Table1
MINUS
```

LISTING 10.22 CONTINUED

```
SELECT ID2, C2 FROM Table2;
/* Example #5, MINUS operator */
SELECT ID2, C2 FROM Table2
MINUS
SELECT ID1, C1 FROM Table1;
```

The number of columns in each of the SELECT statements used with the set operators should be the same. The columns' data types should be the same or any compatible data type that Oracle can implicitly convert.

Hierarchical Queries

In Oracle, if a table contains hierarchical data, the SELECT statement can be used to select rows in a hierarchical order with the START WITH and CONNECT BY clauses. The START WITH clause specifies the root row(s) of the hierarchy. The CONNECT BY clause indicates the relationship between the parent rows and child rows of the hierarchy. You can use the WHERE clause to restrict the rows returned by the SELECT statement without affecting other rows of the hierarchy. The hierarchy is formed based on the conditions in the START WITH and CONNECT BY clauses. Oracle uses the these steps to build the hierarchy:

- The condition in the START WITH clause is used to select the root row(s) of the hierarchy.
- The child rows of each root row are then selected. Each child row must satisfy the condition of the CONNECT BY clause with respect to one of the root rows.
- Successive generations of child rows are selected by evaluating the CONNECT BY condition with respect to a current parent row.
- If a WHERE clause is specified, then rows from the hierarchy that do not satisfy the conditions are eliminated. The condition is evaluated for each individual row in a hierarchy.

The rows are then returned in the order shown in Figure 10.1. You can use the ORDER BY clause in the SELECT statement to change the order in which the rows are returned. In the diagram, the root row is denoted by 1 and the children of each row appear below their parents.

A SELECT statement that performs a hierarchical query cannot participate in a normal join or select data from a view that contains a join.

The START WITH clause identifies the rows to be used as the root of a hierarchical query. If this clause is omitted, then all rows in the table are used as root rows. The condition in the

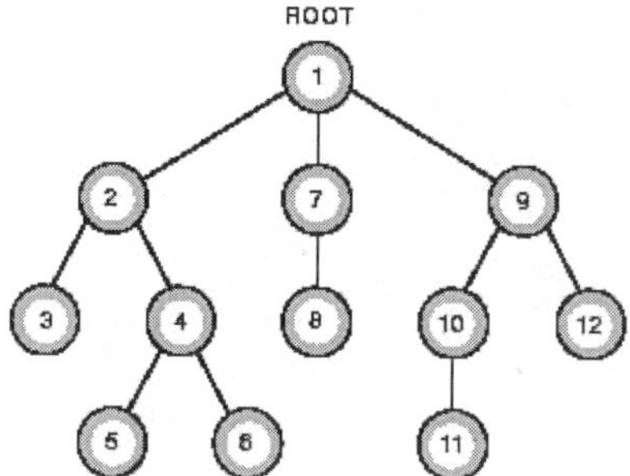

FIGURE 10.1
Hierarchical queries.

START WITH clause can contain a subquery also. The CONNECT BY clause determines the relationship between the parent and child rows in a hierarchical query. The condition in the CONNECT BY clause defines this relationship. The PRIOR operator is used in the condition to refer to the parent row. The part of the condition containing the PRIOR operator must have following syntax:

```
PRIOR <expression> <operator> <expression>
¦ <expression> <operator> PRIOR <expression>
```

The children of a parent row are determined by evaluating the PRIOR expression for the parent row and the other expression for each row in the table. Rows that satisfy the condition are the children of the parent. The CONNECT BY clause can contain other conditions to further restrict the rows selected by the query. However, it clause cannot contain a subquery. Oracle returns an error if the CONNECT BY clause results in a loop in the hierarchy. A loop can occur if one row is both the parent (or grandparent or direct ancestor) and a child (or a grandchild or a direct descendent) of another row. The following CONNECT BY clause defines a hierarchical relationship in which the EMPNO value of the parent row is equal to the MGR value of the child row:

```
CONNECT BY PRIOR empno = mgr;
```

In the following CONNECT BY clause, the PRIOR operator applies only to the EMPNO value. To evaluate this condition, Oracle evaluates EMPNO values for the parent row and MGR and SAL values for the child row:

```
CONNECT BY PRIOR empno = mgr AND sal > 1200;
```

With this condition, the child row is determined based on the MGR value and SAL value greater than 1,200. SELECT statements that perform hierarchical queries can use the LEVEL pseudocolumn, which returns the value 1 for a root node, 2 for a child node of a root node, 3 for a grandchild, and so on. A root node is the highest node within an inverted tree. A child node is any non-root node, a parent node is any node that has children, and a leaf node is any node without children. The number of levels returned by a hierarchical query might be limited by available system memory.

Listing 10.23 shows some examples of retrieving employees in a hierarchical order.

LISTING 10.23 LST10_23.TXT—Hierarchical Queries

```
/* Example #1 Return all employees working under managers */
SELECT LPAD(' ',2*(LEVEL-1)) || ename AS Employee, empno, mgr, job, sal
FROM emp
START WITH job = 'MANAGER'
CONNECT BY PRIOR empno = mgr;
/* Example #2 Return all employees except clerks working,*/
/* starting from president */
SELECT LPAD(' ',2*(LEVEL-1)) || ename AS Employee, empno, mgr, job, sal
FROM emp
WHERE job != 'CLERK'
START WITH job = 'PRESIDENT'
CONNECT BY PRIOR empno = mgr;
/* Example #3 Return all employees starting from president and*/
/*  up to the 3rd level in the hierarchy */
SELECT LPAD(' ',2*(LEVEL-1)) || ename AS Employee, empno, mgr, job, sal
FROM emp
WHERE sal > 1400
START WITH job = 'PRESIDENT'
CONNECT BY PRIOR empno = mgr AND LEVEL <= 3;
```

In Example #1, the root row is identified as the employee whose job is `MANAGER`. The child rows of a parent row are defined as those who have the employee number of the parent row as their manager number. In Example #2, the root row is identified as the employee whose job is `PRESIDENT`. The child rows are further restricted by getting only employees whose job is not `CLERK`. In Example #3, the root row is identified as the employee whose job is `PRESIDENT`. The child row is restricted to employees with a salary greater than $1,400, and the level of hierarchy is restricted to 3. The `START WITH ... CONNECT BY` clause is an extension specific to the Oracle implementation of the `SELECT` statement and is not portable across different database systems.

Optimizer Hints

You can use optimizer hints in `SELECT` statements to specify different access paths, parallelism options, and so forth. The hints are applied only to the optimization of the statement block in which they appear. You indicate the hints by enclosing them in a comment within the `SELECT` statement. A `SELECT` statement can have only one comment containing hints; that comment should follow the SELECT keyword. Here are some of the hints that can be used in the SELECT statement:

- ALL_ROWS Forces the optimizer to choose the cost-based approach to optimize the SELECT statement block and provide the best throughput
- FIRST_ROWS Forces the optimizer to choose the cost-based approach to optimize the SELECT statement block and provide the best response time to return the first row
- CHOOSE Forces the optimizer to choose between the rule-based approach and the cost-based approach for the SELECT statement based on the availability of statistics for the tables accessed by the statement

In general, if the data dictionary contains statistics for at least one of the tables in the SELECT statement, the optimizer uses the cost-based approach and optimizes with the goal of best throughput. If the data dictionary contains no statistics, then default statistics values based on the allocated storage of the tables are used. If the CHOOSE hint is specified, the optimizer uses the rule-based approach in case of missing statistics.

Hints can be used in the SELECT statement to suggest various access methods. If a hint is supplied for the access path, the optimizer chooses it only if the access path is available based on the existence of an index or cluster and the syntactic constructs of the SQL statement. The hint is ignored if there is no available access path as specified. You must indicate the table to be accessed exactly as it appears in the statement. If the statement uses an alias for the table, you must use the alias, rather than the table name, in the hint. The table name within the hint cannot include the schema name if the schema name is present in the statement. The following hints can be used for access methods:

- FULL
- ROWID
- CLUSTER
- HASH
- HASH_AJ
- INDEX
- INDEX_ASC
- INDEX_COMBINE
- INDEX_DESC
- INDEX_FFS

- MERGE_AJ
- AND_EQUAL
- USE_CONCAT

For a more detailed discussion of the hints for access methods, please refer to the Oracle8 documentation.

Join orders can be enforced in SELECT statements by using hints. The ORDERED hint is used to enforce a join order as specified in the SELECT statement. If the ORDERED hint is omitted from the SELECT statement performing a join, the optimizer chooses the order in which to join the tables. The STAR hint forces a star query plan to be used for the SELECT statement. In a star plan, the largest table in the query is joined last in the join order and with a nested loop join on a concatenated index. The STAR hint is used only if there are at least three tables and the largest table's concatenated index has at least three columns.

Hints can be specified to force the optimizer to use a specific join strategy. The following hints can be used for join operations:

- USE_NL Forces the optimizer to join each specified table to another row source with a nested loop join, using the specified table as the inner table.
- USE_MERGE Forces the optimizer to join each specified table with another row source using the sort-merge join strategy.
- USE_HASH Forces the optimizer to join each specified table with another row source using the hash join strategy.
- DRIVING_SITE Forces the SELECT statement to be executed at a different site from that selected by Oracle. This hint is used in SELECT statements that involved remote tables, views, or snapshots.

Oracle supports parallel execution of queries, so the optimizer considers parallelism when compiling a query. Hints can be used in SELECT statements to change the parallel execution behavior. These are the valid hints:

- PARALLEL
- NOPARALLEL
- APPEND
- NOAPPEND
- PARALLEL_INDEX
- NOPARALLEL_INDEX

The PARALLEL hint, for instance, lets you determine the number of concurrent servers that can be used for a parallel operation. Listing 10.24 shows some examples of SELECT statements that use optimizer hints to control the execution of a query.

LISTING 10.24 LST10_24.TXT—SELECT Statements with Optimizer Hints

```
/* Example #1 Use FIRST_ROWS to optimize data retrieval */
SELECT /*+ FIRST_ROWS */ empno, deptno, ename, sal, job
FROM emp
WHERE empno = 7788;
/* Example #2 Use hint for parallelism */
SELECT /*+ FULL(emp) PARALLEL(emp, 3) */ e.ename, m.ename AS Manager
FROM emp e, emp m
WHERE e.mgr = m.empno(+)
ORDER BY e.ename;
/* Example #3 Use DRIVING_SITE hint on remote table */
SELECT /*+DRIVING_SITE(dept)*/ e.empno, e.ename, e.deptno, d.dname, d.loc
FROM emp e, dept@newyork d
WHERE e.deptno = d.deptno;
/* Example #4 Use the ORDERED hint to force join in a particular order   */
/* The order of the retrieved data can indicate to some extent the order in
*/
/* which the join was performed.                       */
SELECT /*+ ORDERED */ e1.empno, e1.ename, d.deptno, d.dname, e1.mgr,
e2.ename AS manager
FROM emp e1, emp e2, dept d
WHERE e1.mgr = e2.empno(+) AND e1.deptno = d.deptno;
/* Example #5 Another SELECT statement with the ORDERED hint */
SELECT /*+ ORDERED */ e1.empno, e1.ename, d.deptno, d.dname, e1.mgr,
e2.ename AS manager
FROM emp e1, emp e2, dept d
WHERE e1.mgr = e2.empno(+) AND e1.deptno = d.deptno;
```

Optimizer hints, therefore, give the experienced user a way to control the execution plan of a query. The use of optimizer hints should be restricted only to situations in which the user has complete knowledge of the data and the query. For more information on using optimizer hints, see the "Tuning" topic in the Oracle8 documentation.

Summary

In this chapter, you looked at the various types of SQL-92-style joins. You also looked at the implementation of the ANSI joins in Microsoft SQL Server and Oracle. By using SQL-92-style joins, the application code is portable across database systems that implement them. The SQL-92-style joins are also more readable and give you better control over the formulation of the `SELECT` statement.

CHAPTER

Sorting and Grouping

In This Chapter

This chapter introduces powerful tools that allow you to use SQL to work with data in a flexible manner. With these tools, you can create reports that make sense of the data piling up in your database. You can, for example, sort the data you retrieve by certain fields, or you can group the data based on certain fields, which opens a number of possibilities for the arithmetic and statistical operations you perform. For example, you can run reports on a monthly, quarterly, or annual basis to see your organization's sales by department or even by salesperson. You can identify points of weakness in your organization and work on strengthening them. This chapter discusses these features in SQL that allow you to use your collected data for planning a better future for your organization

ORDER BY Clause

As you have previously seen, the last part of the `SELECT` statement is the optional `ORDER BY` clause. The general syntax for this clause is as follows:

```
ORDER BY field1, field2, .., fieldn ASC¦DESC
```

In this code, `field1, field2, .., fieldn` are the fields you use to indicate in what order you want the data sorted. `ASC¦DESC` can be used to specify whether the sorting is ascending (the default for most SQL databases if ASC and DESC are omitted) or descending. For example, say you want to retrieve a list of employees ordered by their state, then by their city, and finally by their last name. The SQL statement for this task is in Listing 11.1.

LISTING 11.1 Using the **ORDER BY** Clause to Retrieve a List of Employees Ordered According to Three Different Fields

```
SELECT  emp_Lname ¦¦ ', ' ¦¦ emp_Fname AS Name,
    Address,
    City,
    State,
FROM    employee
ORDER BY  State, City, emp_Lname ASC;
```

Table 11.1 shows the list of retrieved employees.

TABLE 11.1 Results of the Query in Listing 11.1

Name	*Address*	*City*	*State*
Ice Man	200 Ice Ave.	Anchorage	AL
John Doe	111 Main St.	Oakland	CA
Susan Davis	120 Clue	Sacramento	CA
July Sloan	300 Circle St.	Sacramento	CA

TABLE 11.1 Results of the Query in Listing 11.1

Name	*Address*	*City*	*State*
Mary Smith	123 North Ave.	Miami	FL
James Jamison	400 James St.	Detroit	MI

Note

SQL-89 allowed the sorting to be done by the columns based on their ordinal location in the `SELECT` statement. For the preceding example, the `ORDER BY` clause could have been written as `ORDER BY 4,3,1` . Although SQL-92 still supports this deprecated feature, whenever possible, try to avoid it.

SQL-92 supports sorting by the synonym given to concatenated columns. For example, in Listing 11.1, you could have written the `ORDER BY` clause as `ORDER BY state, city, name`. Notice that you are using `name`, which is not a column in the employee table by itself, but a concatenation of two columns. This feature becomes important when the `ORDER BY` clause is used in combination with aggregate functions, such as `SUM`, which are explained in the "Aggregate Functions" section of this chapter. Used in this way, it allows you to sort the results of a sales report by the total sales column and quickly see which employee had the highest sales.

GROUP BY and HAVING

As I mentioned at the beginning of this chapter, the data in the database does not become meaningful and useful until you summarize and simplify it. One efficient way to do this is with the `GROUP BY` clause. With `GROUP BY`, you can summarize the data based on certain columns, calculating aggregations of the data and presenting it in a useful form. Another clause used in combination with the `GROUP BY` clause is the `HAVING` clause, which allows you to limit the data summaries produced by the `GROUP BY` clause by certain criteria. In this section, you will see how these two clauses are used and optimized.

GROUP BY Clause

If you have basic experience with SQL, you should have already used the `GROUP BY` clause several times. Here is the general syntax for this clause, which is an optional part of the `SELECT` statement:

```
GROUP BY column(1), column(2), .., column(n)
[HAVING expression]
```

In these syntax lines, `columns(1)`, `column(2)`, `column(n)` are the columns used to group the data in the order of the grouping. The `HAVING` clause has an expression that sets the criteria for limiting the data returned by the `GROUP BY` clause.

The `GROUP BY` clause arranges the results of the `SELECT` and `WHERE` statement in groups, with each group having the same value in the grouping column. All operations are then defined on groups rather than on rows. Say you have a table called `city` with a column called `state` in it. The `city` table can be created with the code in Listing 11.2.

LISTING 11.2 Creating the City Table

```
CREATE TABLE city
  (city  CHAR(50)  NOT NULL,
   state CHAR(2)  NOT NULL,
   PRIMARY KEY(city, state));
```

Now say you populate the table with some city names in the U.S. To find out the number of cities in the table for each state, issue the SQL statement shown in Listing 11.3.

LISTING 11.3 Finding the Number of Cities in Each `state` in the `city` Table Using the `GROUP BY` Clause and the `COUNT` Aggregate Function

```
SELECT   State, COUNT(*) AS NumberOfCities
FROM    city
GROUP BY   state;
```

Note

In Listing 11.3, you used the function `COUNT()`. This function along with some other functions are called aggregate functions and are explained in detail in the "Aggregate Functions" section.

The results of the preceding query would tell you that there are 10 cities from Michigan listed in the `city` table, 5 cities from New York, and so forth.

The `GROUP BY` clause is often used with aggregate functions, such as the `COUNT()` function shown in Listing 11.3. To explain why, take a look at the previous example. Say that the query returns two cities in Ohio, `Cleveland` and `Toledo`. The `GROUP BY` clause arranges the data as (`OH`, `Cleveland`) and (`OH`, `Toledo`). The `GROUP BY` clause does not present the arranged rows as you see them here, however. If that is what you wanted, you could execute a normal `SELECT` statement `sorting` on the `state` and `city` columns, respectively.

The GROUP BY wants to find some characteristic of the groups it constructed. These characteristics are usually returned with aggregate functions, which are explained later in the chapter.

NULLs in Groups

Before SQL-92, NULLs were treated by different SQL implementations as separate groups. In other words, if you have a table with employees that has a field for state of birth, not all employees will have that field filled. If you select the employees and group on the state field, each NULL value will be treated as a group by itself. This makes sense because chances are the NULL values could actually be different states.

SQL-92 treated all NULLvalues as one group. This change also makes sense in some cases. If all you are interested in for the preceding example is the number of employees who don't have the state of birth field filled in, then one group for all NULLs in this field is sufficient.

If you still want to have each NULL in its own group, you can use a set operation in your SQL statement. Listing 11.4 shows how you can use the UNION ALL clause to have a separate group for every NULL value in your data.

> **Note**
>
> Set operations involve combining two datasets according to certain rules. You might want to find the common data among the two sets (INTERSECT), you could find the data that belongs to one but not to the other (MINUS), or you might want to find the data in both sets (UNION). All these actions, called *set operations* , are discussed in detail in Chapter 12, "Sets and Subsets Operations."

LISTING 11.4 Separating NULLs in Their Own Groups Using the UNION ALL Clause

```
SELECT   count(*) AS Number_of_births_in_state,
state_of_birth
FROM     employee
WHERE    state IS NOT NULL
GROUP BY  state_of_birth
UNION ALL
SELECT   1,
state_of_birth
FROM     employee
WHERE    state IS NOT NULL;
```

You can clearly see in Listing 11.4 that the first part selects all records, which have non-NULL values in the state field, and groups them according to their state. In the second part, it selects all records that have NULL in the state field individually without grouping them. The two parts are combined by the UNION ALL statement.

A possible list of results for this statement is in Table 11.2.

TABLE 11.2 Results of Grouping the Data Excluding the Records with NULLs and Recombining Them with the UNION ALL Statement

Number_of_births_in_state	state
3	CA
5	IL
2	MI
3	OH
2	WI
1	NULL
1	NULL
1	NULL
1	NULL
1	NULL

This table indicates that five employees had NULL in their state field. The same query written in Listing 11.5 would produce the results in Table 11.3.

LISTING 11.5 Grouping Employees Based on Their State of Birth

```
SELECT   count(*) AS Number_of_births_in_state,
state_of_birth
FROM     employee
GROUP BY  state_of_birth;
```

TABLE 11.3 Results of Grouping the Data on the state Field in the employee Table

Number_of_births_in_state	state
3	CA
5	IL
2	MI
3	OH
2	WI
4	NULL

Sorting and GROUP BY

The SQL-92 standard does not require sorting in the GROUP BY operation. However, most SQL implementations do sort the results of the grouped query. Usually, the reason is that they sort the table by the grouping column before they build their groups. Therefore, using ORDER BY with the GROUP BY clause is not recommended if the sorting is to happen according to the grouping columns.

> **Note**
>
> If you want to use ORDER BY with the GROUP BY clause to make sure you sort by the grouping columns, make sure the order of the sort is the same as that in the GROUP BY clause. If the orders are different, the query will most likely take longer to run.

The HAVING Clause

As you saw in the previous sections, the GROUP BY clause helps organize the data in groups for summary reports. To limit the data returned in each group, SQL offers the HAVING clause. The general syntax for this clause was shown in the previous section.

> **Note**
>
> In standard SQL-89 and SQL-92, HAVING is not required to accompany a GROUP BY clause. If a GROUP BY clause is not included, the whole table is treated as one group by the HAVING clause. Many SQL implementations require that the HAVING clause be used with the GROUP BY clause. This is not standard SQL, but is a recommended practice.

As an example of using the HAVING clause, Listing 11.6 shows a list of employees grouped by their states. The results are limited to states in which five or more employees were born.

LISTING 11.6 Listing Employees Grouped by State of Birth in States Where Five or More Employees Were Born

```
SELECT  COUNT(*) AS Number_Of_Employees,
    State
FROM    employee
GROUP BY  state
HAVING  count(*) > 4;
```

One of the difficult things to understand in SQL is the difference between HAVING and WHERE clauses and when and where to use each of them. To make this concept easy to understand, keep in mind that HAVING applies only to grouped tables or recordsets. Therefore, HAVING can reference only the grouping columns or aggregate functions that apply to the group. According to this rule, a query such as the one in Listing 11.7 will fail because it does not conform to this rule.

LISTING 11.7 Query Will Fail Because of Non-Conformance to GROUP BY Rules

```
SELECT  COUNT(*) AS Number_Of_Employees,
    State
FROM    employee
GROUP BY  state
HAVING  hair_color='brown';
```

To fix this query, you can rewrite it according to Listing 11.8.

LISTING 11.8 This Query Fixes the One in Listing 11.7 by Moving the Condition to the WHERE Clause

```
SELECT  COUNT(*) AS Number_Of_Employees,
    State
FROM    employee
WHERE    hair_color='brown'
GROUP BY  state;
```

In this listing, the WHERE clause is performed first and the grouping takes place on the resulting filtered recordset.

Multiple Grouping Levels

Often you need to generate a report based on hierarchical or nested groupings. For example, in an auto company, sales can be grouped under a salesclerk, and then rolled up to be grouped by dealership. The dealership sales summary data is then rolled up into regional summary data, and finally, a company sales summary can be generated. This scheme of multiple grouping is common in the business world where quarterly and annual reports are generated for all these levels to help in decision making.

Unfortunately, SQL-92 does not directly allow for nesting the grouping operation. However, SQL allows using views, which can be constructed to reflect hierarchies, in which each view is created from the view underneath it. It is worth mentioning that many tools are on the market to do just this task. These tools might be even more effective than using SQL views in generating business reports.

Now let's see how views can be used to summarize the sales data for an auto company on different levels. Listing 11.9 shows how the first view, which summarizes the sales on the salesperson's level, can be created.

LISTING 11.9 Summarizing the Sales at the Salesclerk's Level of an Auto Company

```
CREATE VIEW salesclerk_summary(region, dealership, salesclerk, Amount)
AS
SELECT   region,
dealership,
salesclerk,
SUM(sales_amount)
FROM     sales
GROUP BY  region, dealership, salesclerk;
```

For the dealership sales report, the view created in Listing 11.10 can be used.

LISTING 11.10 Summarizing the Sales at the Dealership's Level of an Auto Company

```
CREATE VIEW dealership_summary(region, dealership, Amount)
AS
SELECT   region,
dealership,
SUM(amount)
FROM     salesclerk_summary
GROUP BY  region, dealership;
```

Continuing to the regional level, you can create the view given in Listing 11.11.

LISTING 11.11 Summarizing the Sales at the Regional Level of an Auto Company

```
CREATE VIEW region_summary(region, Amount)
AS
SELECT   region,
SUM(amount)
FROM     dealership_summary
GROUP BY  region;
```

Finally, to get the sales for the whole company, use the query in Listing 11.12.

LISTING 11.12 Summarizing the Sales for the Auto Company Based on the Views Created in Listings 11.9 Through 11.11

```
SELECT   SUM(amount)
FROM     region_summary_summary;
```

> **Note**
>
> Many corporate database administrators choose to permanently store the views in the database instead of creating them every time a management report needs to be generated. Storing the views allows much faster execution, and consumes little disk space (about 1K per view). With disk space becoming more affordable, the gains of fast execution outweigh the drawbacks of the disk space required to store these views.

Aggregate Functions

Aggregate functions are usually used with the grouping operations to produce data aggregates that make more sense than row data. In SQL-92, aggregate (or summary) functions include the following:

- `COUNT`: Used to tally values in a table column
- `AVG`: Used to get the average value of some values in a column
- `SUM`: Used to get the total amount of values in a column
- `MAX` and `MIN`: Used to get the maximum and minimum values of a field

This section explores the different functions that SQL-92 has to offer, with many examples of how to best use these functions.

The `COUNT` Function

One of the most important and often used aggregate functions is the `COUNT` function, used to get the number of rows in a table that satisfy the criteria given in the `WHERE` and `GROUP BY` / `HAVING` clauses. The basic syntax for using the `COUNT` function is as follows:

```
SELECT COUNT([DISTINCT] [Field], [*]) FROM table_name
```

You must provide an argument to this function, which could be the asterisk (`*`) or a field name. If you use the asterisk, all rows will be counted. If you use the keyword `DISTINCT`, duplicate values in the column will be ignored. As an example of this function, in a company employee table, to find the number of employees in a certain region, such as the Midwest, you can write the query shown in Listing 11.13.

LISTING 11.13 Finding the Number of Employees in a Certain Region Using the COUNT Function

```
SELECT  COUNT(*) AS Number_Of_Employees
FROM    employee
WHERE    region = 'midwest';
```

Note

The COUNT(*) function is the only aggregate function that allows using the asterisk as an argument. When used, it returns the number of rows regardless of whether some fields in these rows are NULL.

Using the COUNT function is not as easy as it looks. In some cases you might get the wrong answer if you don't pay attention to the details of the data you are querying. As an example, look at Table 11.4, which includes a list of people who used a certain computer at a school library. This list is saved in a database table called tblUserLog. Assume that the users log on the system, which triggers a record to be inserted with the data and time of login. When the user is done with the computer, he or she logs out, which triggers a database trigger to update the EndUse field. Listing 11.14 shows the code needed to create this table.

LISTING 11.14 Creating the User Log Table (tblUserLog)

```
CREATE TABLE tblUserLog
  (FirstName  CHARACTER(30) NOT NULL,
   LastName  CHARACTER(30) NOT NULL,
   StartUse  DATE  NOT NULL,
   EndUse  DATE);
```

TABLE 11.4 Data in the Computer Library User Log

FirstName	LastName	StartUse	EndUse
Karen	Johnson	6/22/1999 12:00:00	6/22/1999 12:30:00
Karen	Michel	6/22/1999 08:45:00	6/22/1999 11:00:00
Silva	Carlson	6/21/1999 14:15:00	6/21/1999 15:00:00
Karen	Johnson	6/20/1999 09:45:00	6/20/1999 13:00:00
Denise	Long	6/20/1999 14:10:00	6/20/1999 14:15:00
Denise	Long	6/20/1999 15:00:00	6/20/1999 16:30:00

TABLE 11.4 Data in the Computer Library User Log

FirstName	LastName	StartUse	EndUse
David	Ruling	6/19/1999 11:00:00	6/19/1999 11:45:00
David	Ruling	6/18/1999 09:00:00	6/18/1999 12:00:00

If you use the query shown in Listing 11.15 to get the number of people who used this particular computer between 6/18/1999 and 6/22/1999, you will get the wrong result. The value returned from this query is 8, which is the total number of rows in the table. This result does not really reflect the actual number of people who used the computer. If this does not work, then how do you get the number of users who used the computer? Try to change the query passing the FirstName field as an argument into the COUNT function, and use the DISTINCT keyword to make sure duplicates are not counted in the result. The modified query is in Listing 11.16.

LISTING 11.15 Getting the (Wrong) Number of Users of the Computer Library

```
SELECT   COUNT(*) AS NumOfUsers
FROM     tblUserLog
WHERE     StartUse BETWEEN '6/18/1999' AND '6/22/1999';
```

LISTING 11.16 Getting the (Wrong—Again!) Number of Users of the Computer Library

```
SELECT   COUNT(DISTINCT FirstName) AS NumOfUsers
FROM     tblUserLog
WHERE     StartUse BETWEEN '6/18/1999' AND '6/22/1999';
```

The result of the query in Listing 11.16 is 4, which is still not the right answer to the question. So what went wrong this time? Notice that there are two people with the first name Karen. If you include only the FirstName column in the COUNT function, these two people are counted as one because of the DISTINCT keyword. The solution to this issue is easy. You can generate a unique value to tally on by concatenating the FirstName and LastName fields. The final query that produces the right answer of 5 is shown in Listing 11.17.

LISTING 11.17 Getting the Correct Number of Users of the Computer Library

```
SELECT   COUNT(DISTINCT firstname || ' ' || lastname) AS NumOfUsers
FROM     tblUserLog
WHERE     StartUse BETWEEN '6/18/1999' AND '6/22/1999';
```

The SUM Function

This function is used more than any other aggregate function, especially in summary queries and reports. The function simply sums the values in a column according to a certain grouping provided in the GROUP BY clause. This is the general syntax for this function:

```
SELECT SUM([ALL]/[DISTINCT] [field_name])
FROM table_name
GROUP BY another_field;
```

You can use the keyword ALL or DISTINCT. ALL is the default if you just include the field name as the argument to the function. If you use the keyword DISTINCT, all NULLs and duplicate values are excluded from the summation process.

Note

SQL implementations differ in the precision they seek for the results of this function. They also differ in the way they implement the rounding and truncation of results. Therefore, it is a good idea to have an extra decimal place when declaring your numeric data types.

As an example of using this function, consider the data in the sales table shown in Table 11.5, and try to find the total sales per salesperson over time.

TABLE 11.5 Employee sales Table

Salesclerk	sale_amount	Date	Customer_ID
Linda Walters	$2,000.00	6/21/1999	4
Michael Smith	$1,200.50	6/20/1999	21
Linda Walters	$350.00	6/20/1999	3
Linda Walters	$875.00	6/19/1999	78
James Michell	$900.00	6/19/1999	34
July Edwards	$675.00	6/19/1999	23
Linda Walters	$250.00	6/18/1999	278
Michael Smith	$1,150.50	6/18/1999	26
Michael Smith	$1,800.00	6/20/1999	25
Linda Walters	$50.00	6/17/1999	8
Linda Walters	$875.00	6/17/1999	7
Michael Smith	$3,200.50	6/17/1999	43
James Michell	$2900.00	6/16/1999	30
Linda Walters	$870.00	6/17/1999	53
James Michell	$900.00	6/19/1999	43
James Michell	$2,300.00	6/19/1999	65

Listing 11.18 can be used to accomplish your goal.

LISTING 11.18 Sales Per Salesclerk

```
SELECT   salesclerk,
SUM(sales_amount) as Total_Sale
FROM     sales
GROUP BY  salesclerk;
```

Table 11.6 shows the results of this query.

TABLE 11.6 Results of the Query in Listing 11.18

Salesclerk	Total_Sale
July Edwards	$675.00
James Michell	$7000.00
Linda Walters	$5,270.00
Michael Smith	$7351.50

These results could be summarized over time, such as annual, quarterly, or monthly sales.

Note

If the field that the SUM function is summing has empty values, it does not return zero. Instead, it returns NULL.

The Average Function (AVG)

This function returns the average of a set of values in a table column. The basic syntax for the function is as follows:

```
SELECT AVG([ALL]¦[DISTINCT] expression)
FROM table_name ...
```

The ALL operator is optional, but when used, gets the average of all the values in expression, including redundant values. The DISTINCT operator includes only the non-redundant values in the averaging process. If neither operator is specified, ALL is used implicitly by default.

Note

The expression `AVG(values)` is not equivalent to the expression `SUM(values)/COUNT(values)`. The reason is that the `COUNT` function includes `NULL`s when it returns its answer, but the `SUM` function does not.

The problems with the `SUM` function for precision, rounding, and truncation apply for the `AVG` function, too. Different implementations of SQL handle these issues differently. Therefore, be aware of that issue, especially when you have to transfer your SQL code from one implementation to another.

As an example of using the `AVG` function, consider Table 11.4, which includes the sales of salespeople in a store. Use the query in Listing 11.19 to try to get the average sales per employee at the store over time.

LISTING 11.19 Average Sales Per Salesclerk

```
SELECT   salesclerk,
AVG(sale_amount) as Average_Sale
FROM    sales
GROUP BY  salesclerk;
```

Table 11.7 gives the results of this query.

TABLE 11.7 Results of the Query in Listing 11.19

Salesclerk	Average_Sale
July Edwards	$675.00
James Michell	$1,750.00
Linda Walters	$752.86
Michael Smith	$1,837.86

MIN and MAX Functions

As the names of these functions imply, they are used to find the highest and lowest values in a set of values that refers to a table field or to an expression. Here is the basic syntax for these two functions:

```
SELECT MAX/MIN([ALL¦DISTINCT] expression)
FROM table_name...
```

Note

MAX and MIN are the only aggregate functions that work on non-numeric or temporal data types because these functions also work on CHARACTER data.

Although the ALL and DISTINCT operators are included in the syntax, they are hardly ever used because the expression MAX(ALL expression) is the same as MAX(expression) and MAX(DISTINCT expression). I included these two operators only for completeness.

NOTE

If the expression in the basic syntax of the MIN and MAX functions returns an empty set, the functions return NULL.

As an example of using the MAX/MIN functions, consider Table 11.4, which includes the sales of salespeople in a store. Use the query in Listing 11.20 to get the maximum and minimum sales per employee at the store over time.

LISTING 11.20 Maximum and Minimum Sales Per Salesclerk

```
SELECT   salesclerk,
MAX(sale_amount) as Max_Sale,
MIN(sale_amount) as Min_Sale
FROM    sales
GROUP BY  salesclerk;
```

Table 11.8 shows the results of this query.

TABLE 11.8 Results of the Query in Listing 11.20

Salesclerk	Max_Sale	Min_Sale
July Edwards	$675.00	$675.00
James Michell	$2,900.00	$900.00
Linda Walters	$2,000.00	$50.00
Michael Smith	$3,200.50	$1,150.50

Grouped Subqueries

Subqueries are an effective tool in SQL-92 because they provide the flexibility to do tasks that could not be easily done without them. Subqueries are discussed in detail in Chapter 13, "Subqueries." However, I will discuss one feature of subqueries that relates to grouping and aggregation of data here. If you are not familiar with subqueries yet, or haven't experimented with them long enough, you might want to consider skipping this section for now and reading Chapter 13.

Subqueries can be used in the `FROM` clause of the `SELECT` statement if they return a table of values. Scalar subqueries, on the other hand, can be used anywhere in the `SELECT` statement. Some SQL implementations have restrictions on the use of subqueries. You need to check the documentation of the SQL flavor you are using before you try the examples in this section.

With the auto dealership example you have been using, you can build multilevel aggregations in a simple query. Listing 11.21 shows an example of this feature.

LISTING 11.21 Building Multilevel Aggregations Using Subqueries and Grouping Together

```
SELECT   region,
dealership,
salesclerk,
SUM(sales_amount) AS total_sales,
(SELECT  SUM(sales_amount)
 FROM    Sales AS S1
 WHERE  S1.region = S2.region
    AND
    S1.dealership = S2.dealership)
AS dealership_sales
FROM    sales AS S2
GROUP BY  salesclerk,
dealership,
region,
dealership_sales;
```

This query would return a constant value of `dealership_sales` for every salesperson belonging to a dealership. This is illustrated in Table 11.9.

TABLE 11.9 Partial Results of the Query in Listing 11.21

Region	Dealership	Salesclerk	Total_ Sales	Dealership_ Sales
Midwest	Ford-1	J. Edwards	$105,675.00	$236,175.00
Midwest	Ford-1	J. Smith	$130,500.00	$236,175.00
Midwest	Toyota-1	M. Doe	$120,000.00	$730,000.00
Midwest	Toyota-1	L. Cool	$130,000.00	$730,000.00
Midwest	Toyota-1	F. Franks	$180,000.00	$730,000.00
Midwest	Toyota-1	E. Edwards	$200,000.00	$730,000.00
Midwest	Toyota-1	R. Robin	$100,000.00	$730,000.00
Northeast	GM-1	S. Stevens	$100,000.00	$330,000.00
Northeast	GM-1	D. Rules	$230,000.00	$330,000.00
Northeast	GM-2	D. Davis	$190,000.00	$340,000.00
Northeast	GM-2	S. Kools	$150,000.00	$340,000.00
Northeast	GM-3	S. Schultz	$130,000.00	$130,000.00
Northeast	Ford-3	W. Bills	$100,000.00	$430,000.00
Northeast	Ford-3	B. Coral	$180,000.00	$430,000.00
Northeast	Ford-3	L. Holmes	$150,000.00	$430,000.00
Southeast	Ford-4	M. Clay	$170,000.00	$600,000.00
Southeast	Ford-4	A. Andrews	$190,000.00	$600,000.00
Southeast	Ford-4	C. Charles	$240,000.00	$600,000.00
Southeast	Ford-5	W. Franky	$310,000.00	$510,00000
Southeast	Ford-5	M. Moon	$200,000.00	$510,00000

More interesting things can be done with the data when it comes to using grouped subqueries. For instance, you can mix the aggregate functions used to get custom reports. Listing 11.22 shows a query that retrieves the average dealership sales per region. In other words, you can use this query to get the average total sales for all the dealerships in the Midwest versus that in the Northeast, and so on. In the query, you sum up the sales grouping by dealership, and then use the resulting table to get the average sales for the dealerships per region grouping by region.

LISTING 11.22 Mixing Aggregate Functions to Get Some Interesting Results

```
/*This is the start of the big query that gets
the averages of the results of the subquery*/
SELECT   D.region,
      AVG(D.dealership_sales) AS
region_average_sales
/*Build the subquery that would return a table to be used in the
  original query*/
FROM    (SELECT region,
dealership,
SUM(sales_amount)
```

LISTING 11.22 CONTINUED

```
FROM   Sales
GROUP BY region, dealership) AS
D(region, dealership, dealership_sales)
/*The following grouping belongs to the original query*/
GROUP BY  D.region;
```

Don't be surprised if your SQL implementation does not include this feature because it is fairly new in SQL-92. However, you can still get the same result by building a view to hold the data in the table created in the preceding subquery, and then you can use the view to get the same result as the previous query. Listing 11.23 shows how this can be done.

LISTING 11.23 Using Views to Simulate Mixing Aggregate Functions

```
/*Create the view*/
CREATE View D(region, dealership, dealership_sales)
AS
SELECT  region,
dealership,
SUM(sales_amount)
FROM     Sales
GROUP BY   region,
Dealership;
/*Now use the view above to retrieve the required results*/
SELECT   D.region,
      AVG(D.dealership_sales) AS
region_average_sales
FROM    D
GROUP BY  D.region;
```

In either case, the results of Listing 11.22 or 11.23 are given in Table 11.10.

TABLE 11.10 Average Total Dealership Sales Per Region as Retrieved from Listings 11.22 and 11.23

region	region_average_sales
Midwest	$483,087.50
Northeast	$307,500.00
Southeast	$555,000.00

Note

The parameter to an aggregate function cannot be another aggregate function. Hence, unlike most programming languages, you cannot write something like `SELECT salesclerk, AVG(SUM(sales_amount)) ...` . This query is not valid in SQL-92 and will fail.

Note

Although grouped subqueries can be used to create flexible reports, they are not always the best solution to selecting data. Creating the view in Listing 11.23 and storing it in the database makes it more efficient at retrieving the final results sought in that listing than using the query in Listing 11.22.

Relational Divisions

The idea of relational divisions is that a table can be partitioned based on data in another table. The best way to understand this concept is by creating an example. Say you have a storage system where companies or individuals can store goods for a given fee. The managers of the storage facility organized it in the following fashion: They constructed a table that holds the customer names and the type of items they stored. For instance, someone might have stored boxes of file folders; another could have stored furniture or even light machinery. The tables created to store the data are in Listings 11.24 and 11.25.

LISTING 11.24 Creating the Table to Store Customer Unit Storage Information

```
CREATE TABLE CustomerStorage
  (CustomerName CHARACTER(30) NOT NULL,
   UnitType CHARACTER(20) NOT NULL,
   PRIMARY KEY (CustomerName, UnitType);
```

LISTING 11.25 Creating the Table to Store Storage Warehouses

```
CREATE TABLE warehouses
  (warehouse CHARACTER(30) PRIMARY KEY);
```

A sample of the data in these two tables is presented in Tables 11.11 and 11.12.

TABLE 11.11 Sample Data Stored in the `CustomerStorage` Table

`CustomerName`	`UnitType`
Mike Smith	Boxes of folders
David Bulk	Furniture
Mike Smith	Small machinery
George Small	Small machinery
Frank Jones	Boxes of folders
Julia Peters	Boxes of folders
Rob Zoo	Clothing
John Richards	Small machinery
Bill Kemp	Furniture
Linda Smith	Furniture
Linda Smith	Boxes of folders
David Bulk	Small machinery
Rosa Foo	Boxes of folders
Julia Peters	Furniture
Mike Smith	Furniture
Linda Smith	Small machinery

TABLE 11.12 Sample Data Stored in the `warehouses` Table

`Warehouse`
Boxes of folders
Furniture
Small machinery

Table 11.13 shows the table resulting from this expression:

```
CustomerStorage DIVIDED BY warehouses
```

TABLE 11.13 Result of `CustomerStorage DIVIDED BY warehouses`

`Customer`
Mike Smith
Linda Smith

According to this result, only Mike Smith and Linda Smith have items stored in all three warehouses.

Two kinds of divisions are available: division with a remainder and exact division. Division with a remainder allows the dividend table to have more values than the divisor table. For example, in the previous example, you might have a customer who can store a fourth kind of goods, such as clothing (see Rob Zoo in Table 11.11). This criterion does not exist in the warehouse table, which is the divisor in this case. In exact division, on the other hand, the dividend and divisor have to match exactly without extra values in the dividend table.

More about division is discussed in the next chapter, "Sets and Subsets Operations."

Summary

In this chapter, you have learned about the important features of grouping and sorting in SQL. These features give you a great deal of flexibility in generating a variety of reports, especially hierarchical reports. I also discussed aggregate functions that go with grouping data. These functions allow you to summarize data and roll it up to higher levels. The next chapters augment this chapter by discussing sets and subsets operations, which allows you to know more about how different sets of data compare and can be divided.

CHAPTER

Sets and Subsets Operations

In This Chapter

Join operators (discussed in Chapter 10, "Table Joins,") combine tables in some horizontal fashion, but set and pseudo-set operators allow you to combine the output of two or more queries end to end.

Set and pseudo-set operators can combine only those query outputs that have identical layouts in terms of number and types of columns retrieved. Therefore, if the first query returns a number, a character, and a date column, the second query must return a number, a character, and a date as well, or an error will result.

Run `crpeople.sql`to create and load the tables `people1` and `people2`.

Most examples in this chapter use the `people1` and `people2` tables. They are similar, except `people2` includes wealth data. It has five rows, two of which overlap with `people1`. Listing 12.1 displays the content for both `people1` and `people2`.

LISTING 12.1 Displaying the Content of Two Tables

```
-- Filename: 12squ01.sql
-- Purpose: Display contents of people1 and people2 tables

SELECT * FROM people1

SELECT * FROM people2
```

This code returns the following:

```
pk_id       last_name      first_name     age         gender
----------- -------------- -------------- ----------- ------
1           Jones          David N.       34          M
2           Martinelli     A. Emery       92          M
3           Talavera       F. Espinosa    19          F
4           Kratochvil     Mary T.        48          F
5           Melsheli       Joseph K.      14          M

(5 row(s) affected)

pk_id       last_name      first_name     age         gender wealth
----------- -------------- -------------- ----------- ------ -----------
1           Jones          David N.       34          M      -143000
2           Martinelli     A. Emery       92          M      645000
6           Robinson       Faye M.        31          F      2000
```

LISTING 12.1 CONTINUED

```
7          Kazen        M. Okechuku    23     F     281990
8          Rochblatt    Harold T.      32     M     24000
(5 row(s) affected)
```

Set Operators

The three set operators (UNION, EXCEPT, and INTERSECT) behave like their mathematical counterparts and return elements of a set that are distinctly different from all other elements in the resultset. In other words, redundant rows are not returned. Conforming to set theory, this section therefore uses the term *element* to denote a non-redundant row. Here are the three set operators:

- UNION returns all elements of all queries
- EXCEPT selects those elements that exist in one table but not the other
- INTERSECT displays matching elements only

Returning All Elements: UNION

Two queries combined through the UNION operator return all elements from both queries. The database retrieves all rows into the temporary workspace that is used for sorting and returns the distinct set. Listing 12.2 shows a UNION operator joining two queries on people1 and people2.

LISTING 12.2 Using a UNION Operator to Join Two Queries

```
-- Filename: 12squ02.sql
-- Purpose: Union operator joining people1 and people2
SELECT
  pk_id,
  last_name,
  first_name,
  gender
FROM people1
UNION
SELECT
  pk_id,
  last_name,
  first_name,
  gender
FROM people2
```

This code returns the following:

```
pk_id       last_name      first_name     gender
----------- -------------- -------------- ------
6           Robinson       Faye M.        F
7           Kazen          M. Okechuku    F
8           Rochblatt      Harold T.      M
3           Talavera       F. Espinosa    F
1           Jones          David N.       M
2           Martinelli     A. Emery       M
4           Kratochvil     Mary T.        F
5           Melsheli       Joseph K.      M

(8 row(s) affected)
```

As you can see, the rows with `pk_id` values of `1` or `2`, which occur in both queries, are displayed only once.

Figure 12.1 illustrates the behavior of the `UNION` operator in the standard set theory way. Two sets of elements are returned by the subquery. These sets overlap; in this case, the rows with the `pk_id` values `1` and `2` are represented in both sets. The query returns the elements that occur only in the first set, those that occur only in the second set, and those that occur in both.

Even if the redundant rows originate in one table, the `UNION` operator strips them out, just as a `SELECT DISTINCT` would. Listing 12.3 demonstrates this by inserting the rows with the `pk_ids` of `4` and `5` into the table `people1` and then reruns the query of the previous example. At the end, the insert is rolled back to revert `people1` to its original state, as discussed in Chapter 8, "Transactions in SQL."

LISTING 12.3 Using the `UNION` Operator to Join Two Queries with Redundant Rows

```
-- Filename: 12squ03.sql
-- Purpose: Union operator joining people1 and people2
--      additional redundant rows
BEGIN TRANSACTION
INSERT people1
SELECT * FROM people1
WHERE pk_id > 3
SELECT * FROM people1
SELECT
  pk_id,
  last_name,
  first_name,
```

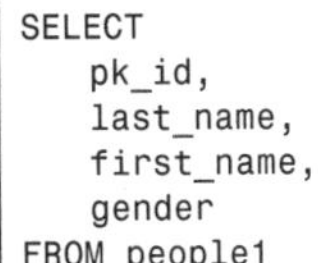

UNION

```
SELECT
    pk_id,
    last_name,
    first_name,
    gender
FROM people2
```

Area Included

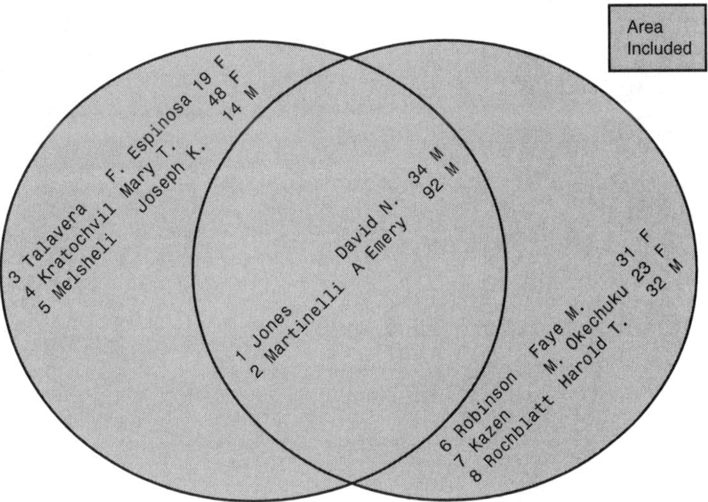

FIGURE 12.1
The UNION *set operator.*

LISTING 12.3 CONTINUED

```
  gender
FROM people1
UNION
SELECT
  pk_id,
  last_name,
  first_name,
  gender
FROM people2
ROLLBACK TRANSACTION
```

As you can see from the following results, the `UNION` query returns the same result as `12squ02.sql`.

```
(2 row(s) affected)
pk_id       last_name       first_name      age         gender
----------- --------------- --------------- ----------- ------
1           Jones           David N.        34          M
```

```
2          Martinelli    A. Emery      92       M
3          Talavera      F. Espinosa   19       F
4          Kratochvil    Mary T.       48       F
5          Melsheli      Joseph K.     14       M
4          Kratochvil    Mary T.       48       F
5          Melsheli      Joseph K.     14       M

(7 row(s) affected)

pk_id      last_name     first_name    gender
---------- ------------- ------------- ------
6          Robinson      Faye M.       F
7          Kazen         M. Okechuku   F
8          Rochblatt     Harold T.     M
3          Talavera      F. Espinosa   F
1          Jones         David N.      M
2          Martinelli    A. Emery      M
4          Kratochvil    Mary T.       F
5          Melsheli      Joseph K.     M

(8 row(s) affected)
```

Returning All Elements That Exist in One Table But Not the Other: EXCEPT

Two queries combined through the EXCEPT operator return all elements of the first query that do not occur in the second one. The EXCEPT operator strips out redundant rows of the first table as well. In some database products, such as Oracle and Sybase, the EXCEPT operator is available under the name MINUS.

Figure 12.2 illustrates the behavior of the EXCEPT operator in the standard set theory. The query returns those elements that occur only in the first set. It does not return those that occur only in the second set or those that occur in both.

Listing 12.4 demonstrates the workings of the EXCEPT set operator. The 12squ04.sql script contains the same example with redundant rows in the first table.

LISTING 12.4 Using the **EXCEPT** Operator to Join Two Queries

```
-- Filename: 12squ04.sql
-- Purpose: Except operator joining people1 and people2
--      additional redundant rows
-- Note: Oracle uses MINUS instead
SELECT
```

FIGURE 12.2
The EXCEPT *set operator.*

MINUS

```
SELECT
   pk_id,
   last_name,
   first_name,
   gender
FROM people2
```

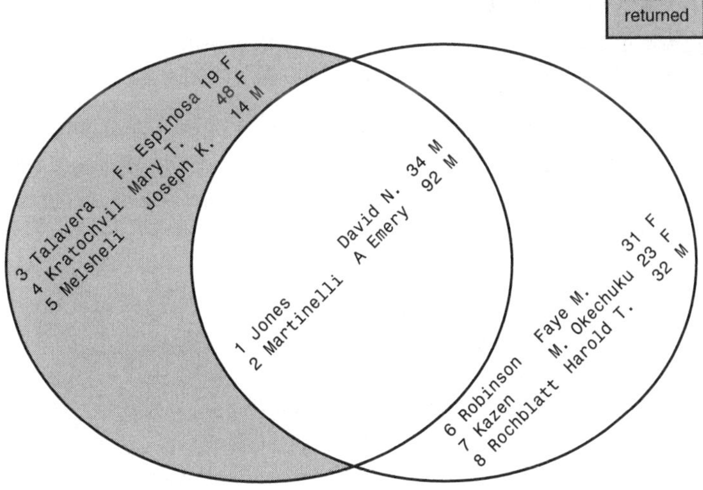

LISTING 12.4 CONTINUED

```
  pk_id,
  last_name,
  first_name,
  gender
FROM people1
EXCEPT SELECT
  pk_id,
  last_name,
  first_name,
  gender
FROM people2
```

This code returns the following:

```
pk_id       last_name       first_name      gender
----------- --------------- --------------- ------
```

```
3           Talavera        F. Espinosa     F
4           Kratochvil      Mary T.         F
5           Melsheli        Joseph K.       M

(3 row(s) affected)
```

An Alternative to EXCEPT with Outer Joins

There are other ways to get the same result, either with an outer join or through the use of a subquery. The next chapter covers using a subquery to get the same result.

If the tables are joined on `pk_id` through a left outer join (see Chapter 10, "Table Joins"), each row in `people1` that does not have a match in `people2` is represented in a combined row where the `people2` columns are `NULL`. Therefore, selecting the `people1` columns of all rows where the `people2` columns are `NULL` returns the same rows an `EXCEPT` would. Listing 12.5 uses that approach to get the same results as `12squ04.sql`.

LISTING 12.5 Using the LEFT OUTER JOIN to Join Two Queries

```
-- Filename: 12squ05.sql
-- Purpose: An alternative to the EXCEPT operator
--     joining people1 and people2
--     additional redundant rows
SELECT
  people1.pk_id,
  people1.last_name,
  people1.first_name,
  people1.gender
FROM people1
  LEFT OUTER JOIN people2
  ON (people1.pk_id = people2.pk_id)
WHERE people2.pk_id IS NULL
```

This code returns the following:

```
pk_id       last_name       first_name      gender
----------- --------------- --------------- ------
3           Talavera        F. Espinosa     F
4           Kratochvil      Mary T.         F
5           Melsheli        Joseph K.       M

(3 row(s) affected)
```

The difference with the EXCEPT operator is that duplicate rows in people1 are selected with this approach, which the next part of the example shows:

```
BEGIN TRANSACTION

INSERT people1
SELECT * FROM people1
WHERE pk_id > 3

SELECT * FROM people1

SELECT
  people1.pk_id,
  people1.last_name,
  people1.first_name,
  people1.gender
FROM people1
  LEFT OUTER JOIN people2
  ON (people1.pk_id = people2.pk_id)
WHERE people2.pk_id IS NULL

ROLLBACK TRANSACTION
```

This code returns the following:

```
(2 row(s) affected)
pk_id       last_name       first_name      age         gender
----------- --------------- --------------- ----------- ------
1           Jones           David N.        34          M
2           Martinelli      A. Emery        92          M
3           Talavera        F. Espinosa     19          F
4           Kratochvil      Mary T.         48          F
5           Melsheli        Joseph K.       14          M
4           Kratochvil      Mary T.         48          F
5           Melsheli        Joseph K.       14          M

(7 row(s) affected)

pk_id       last_name       first_name      gender
----------- --------------- --------------- ------
3           Talavera        F. Espinosa     F
4           Kratochvil      Mary T.         F
5           Melsheli        Joseph K.       M
4           Kratochvil      Mary T.         F
5           Melsheli        Joseph K.       M
```

```
(5 row(s) affected)
```

Therefore, if redundant rows are a possibility, a `SELECT DISTINCT` has to be used, as shown here:

```
SELECT DISTINCT
  people1.pk_id,
  people1.last_name,
  people1.first_name,
  people1.gender
FROM people1
  LEFT OUTER JOIN people2
  ON (people1.pk_id = people2.pk_id)
WHERE people2.pk_id IS NULL
```

This code returns the same result as the first statement in the example (`12squ04.sql`):

```
pk_id       last_name      first_name     gender
----------- -------------- -------------- ------
3           Talavera       F. Espinosa    F
4           Kratochvil     Mary T.        F
5           Melsheli       Joseph K.      M
(3 row(s) affected)
```

How fast each option runs depends on the way the database is set up. If you want to test the statements, you can do what's explained in Chapter 19, "Optimizing Query Performance."

Returning Matching Elements Only: INTERSECT

Two queries combined through an `INTERSECT` operator return all the elements of the first query that also occur in the first one. The `INTERSECT` operator also strips out redundant rows in the matching set.

Figure 12.3 illustrates the query returning those elements that occur in both sets, expressed by the overlapping area of the circles.

Listing 12.6 shows the effect of combining two queries through the `INTERSECT` set operator.

LISTING 12.6 Using the `INTERSECT` Operator to Join Two Queries

```
SELECT
  pk_id,
  last_name,
  first_name,
  gender
FROM people1
```

FIGURE 12.3
The INTERSECT *set operator.*

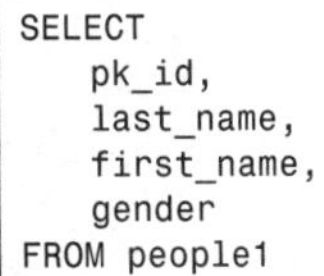

INTERSECT

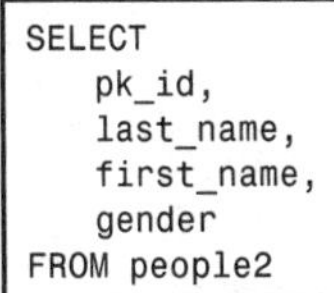

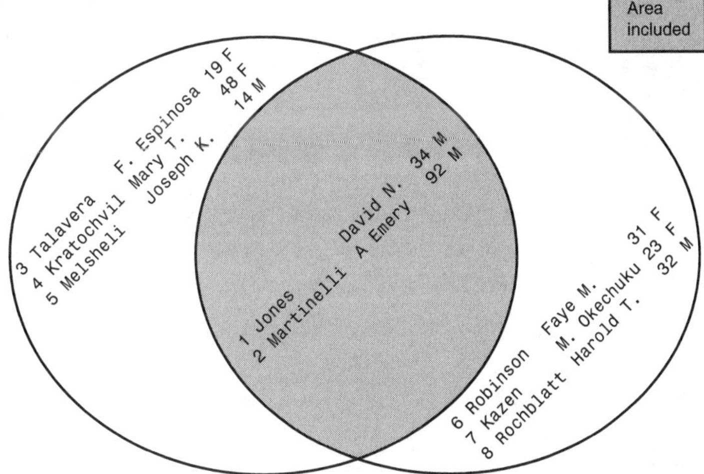

LISTING 12.6 CONTINUED

```
INTERSECT
SELECT
  pk_id,
  last_name,
  first_name,
  gender
FROM people2
```

This code returns the following:

```
pk_id       last_name       first_name      gender
----------- --------------- --------------- ------
1           Jones           David N.        M
2           Martinelli      A. Emery        M
```

The example contains a second statement with redundant rows that returns the same output as the statement printed here.

An Alternative to INTERSECT with Inner Joins

As is the case with EXCEPT, you can get the INTERSECT results in other ways. Besides a subquery, which is discussed in the next chapter, a SELECT DISTINCT on an inner join of tables works fine.

An inner join on pk_id keeps only the rows that have matches in both tables. Therefore, it's enough to create only the inner join and select all people1 columns from the qualifying rows. This is what Listing 12.7 does.

LISTING 12.7 Using an INNER JOIN to Join Two Queries

```
-- Filename: 12squ07.sql
-- Purpose: An alternative to the INTERSECT operator
--      joining people1 and people2
--      additional redundant rows

SELECT
  people1.pk_id,
  people1.last_name,
  people1.first_name,
  people1.gender
FROM people1
  INNER JOIN people2
  ON (people1.pk_id = people2.pk_id)
```

This code returns the following:

```
pk_id       last_name       first_name      gender
----------- --------------- --------------- ------
1           Jones           David N.        M
2           Martinelli      A. Emery        M
```

Duplicate matching rows are returned if this approach is used, just as they are with the preceding outer join example. The following statements show that:

```
INSERT people1
SELECT * FROM people1
WHERE pk_id < 3
SELECT
  people1.pk_id,
  people1.last_name,
  people1.first_name,
  people1.gender
FROM people1
```

```
  INNER JOIN people2
  ON (people1.pk_id = people2.pk_id)
```

This code returns the following:

```
pk_id       last_name      first_name     gender
----------- -------------- -------------- ------
1           Jones          David N.       M
2           Martinelli     A. Emery       M
1           Jones          David N.       M
2           Martinelli     A. Emery       M

(4 row(s) affected)
```

If, however, both tables have duplicate rows, each of them in the first table is joined with each matching one in the second table, and many rows end up being returned, as the following statements demonstrate:

```
INSERT people2
SELECT * FROM people2
WHERE pk_id < 3

SELECT
  people1.pk_id,
  people1.last_name,
  people1.first_name,
  people1.gender
FROM people1
  INNER JOIN people2
  ON (people1.pk_id = people2.pk_id)
```

This code returns the following:

```
pk_id       last_name      first_name     gender
----------- -------------- -------------- ------
1           Jones          David N.       M
1           Jones          David N.       M
2           Martinelli     A. Emery       M
2           Martinelli     A. Emery       M
1           Jones          David N.       M
1           Jones          David N.       M
2           Martinelli     A. Emery       M
2           Martinelli     A. Emery       M

(8 row(s) affected)
```

Again, a SELECT DISTINCT takes care of duplicate rows. The last statement of the example uses the following:

```
SELECT DISTINCT
  people1.pk_id,
  people1.last_name,
  people1.first_name,
  people1.gender
FROM people1
  INNER JOIN people2
  ON (people1.pk_id = people2.pk_id)
```

This returns the same rows as the first SELECT statement at the beginning of the example.

Exclusive Union

As is the case with the exclusive or, there is no corresponding exclusive union set operator either. An exclusive union contains all the elements retrieved by the first query or the second query, but not both. Figure 12.4 shows the area of interest—all elements in the combined set, with the exception of the matching elements.

If all non-matching rows of both tables are to be selected, you must use a compound statement. There are two straightforward ways to do that:

- By combining a UNION of the queries and an INTERSECT of the queries through an EXCEPT operator, as follows:

  ```
  (query1 UNION query2) EXCEPT (query1 INTERSECT query2)
  ```

  The UNION operator returns the entire set, and the INTERSECT operator returns only the matching set. By subtracting the latter from the former, the non-overlapping portion remains.

- By combining an EXCEPT of the queries and an EXCEPT of the reversed queries through a UNION operator, as follows:

  ```
  (query1 EXCEPT query2) UNION (query2 EXCEPT query1)
  ```

  Here, (query1 EXCEPT query2) returns the non-overlapping portion that pertains to the first query only. Then, (query2 EXCEPT query1) returns the non-overlapping portion that pertains to the second query only. The two combined with the UNION operator returns the complete, non-overlapping set.

FIGURE 12.4
The output of two queries combined with an exclusive union.

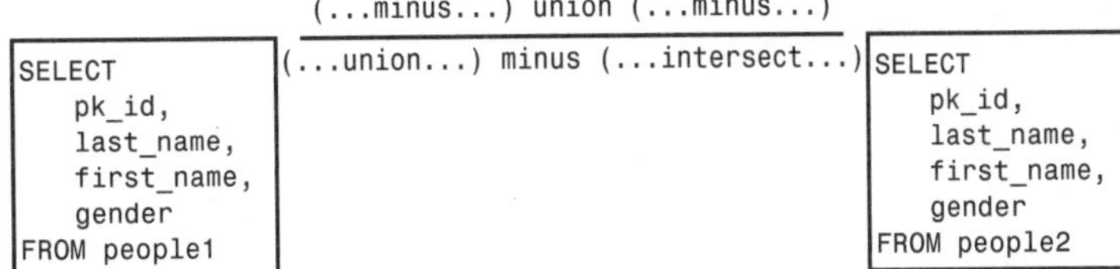

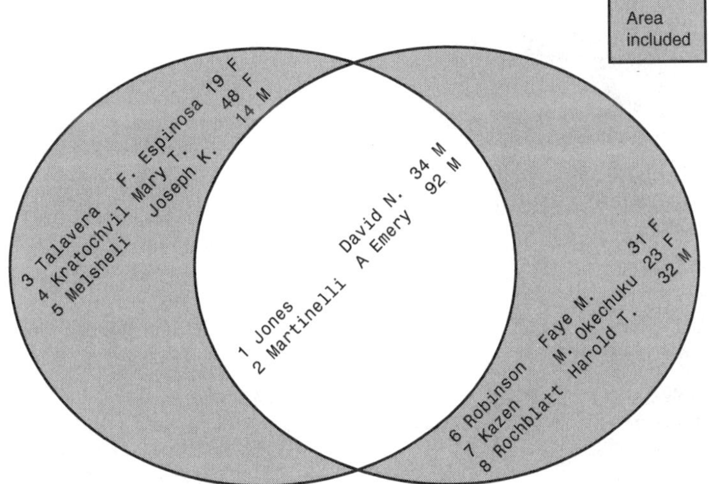

Listing 12.8 uses both approaches.

LISTING 12.8 Using Compound Statements to Join Two Queries

```
-- Filename: 12squ08.sql
-- Purpose: Union Except Intersect operator
--      Except Union Except operator
--      joining people1 and people2
--      additional redundant rows

INSERT people1
SELECT * FROM people1

INSERT people2
SELECT * FROM people2
WHERE pk_id < 3

(SELECT
```

LISTING 12.8 CONTINUED

```
  pk_id,
  last_name,
  first_name,
  gender
FROM people1
UNION
SELECT
  pk_id,
  last_name,
  first_name,
  gender
FROM people2)
EXCEPT
(SELECT
  pk_id,
  last_name,
  first_name,
  gender
FROM people1
INTERSECT
SELECT
  pk_id,
  last_name,
  first_name,
  gender
FROM people2)

(SELECT
  pk_id,
  last_name,
  first_name,
  gender
FROM people1
EXCEPT
SELECT
  pk_id,
  last_name,
  first_name,
  gender
FROM people2)
UNION
(SELECT
```

LISTING 12.8 CONTINUED

```
  pk_id,
  last_name,
  first_name,
  gender
FROM people2
EXCEPT
SELECT
  pk_id,
  last_name,
  first_name,
  gender
FROM people1)
```


Both queries return the following:

```
pk_id       last_name       first_name      gender
----------- --------------- --------------- ------
6           Robinson        Faye M.         F
7           Kazen           M. Okechuku     F
8           Rochblatt       Harold T.       M
3           Talavera        F. Espinosa     F
4           Kratochvil      Mary T.         F
5           Melsheli        Joseph K.       M

(6 row(s) affected)
```

If your database product has only the `UNION` operator, then you can use the following statement to return the same result. It does the equivalent of `(query1 EXCEPT query2) UNION (query2 EXCEPT query1)`.

```
(SELECT DISTINCT
  people1.pk_id,
  people1.last_name,
  people1.first_name,
  people1.gender
FROM people1
  LEFT OUTER JOIN people2
  ON (people1.pk_id = people2.pk_id)
WHERE people2.pk_id IS NULL)
UNION
(SELECT DISTINCT
  people2.pk_id,
  people2.last_name,
```

```
  people2.first_name,
  people2.gender
FROM people2
  LEFT OUTER JOIN people1
  ON (people1.pk_id = people2.pk_id)
WHERE people1.pk_id IS NULL)
```

Pseudo-Set Operations

Pseudo-set operators do not follow the mathematical rules of set theory because they return redundant rows. They are characterized by the addition of `ALL` directly following the set operator: `UNION ALL`, `EXCEPT ALL`, and `INTERSECT ALL`.

Keeping All Rows Retrieved by All Multiple Queries: `UNION ALL`

The `UNION ALL` pseudo-set operator simply returns the output of the first query followed by the output of the second query. Listing 12.9 illustrates the use of the `UNION ALL` operator to join `people1` and `people2`.

LISTING 12.9 Using a `UNION ALL` to Join Two Queries

```
-- Filename: 12squ08.sql
-- Purpose: Union all operator joining people1 and people2

SELECT
  pk_id,
  last_name,
  first_name,
  gender
FROM people1
UNION ALL
SELECT
  pk_id,
  last_name,
  first_name,
  gender
FROM people2
```

This code returns the following:

```
pk_id       last_name      first_name     gender
----------- -------------- -------------- ------
1           Jones          David N.       M
2           Martinelli     A. Emery       M
3           Talavera       F. Espinosa    F
4           Kratochvil     Mary T.        F
5           Melsheli       Joseph K.      M
1           Jones          David N.       M
2           Martinelli     A. Emery       M
6           Robinson       Faye M.        F
7           Kazen          M. Okechuku    F
8           Rochblatt      Harold T.      M

(10 row(s) affected)
```

Figure 12.5 illustrates the workings of the `UNION ALL` operator in typical set graphics. The left square encloses the output of the first query, and the right square encloses the output of the second query. Because the overlapping lines are returned once for each query, they are repeated on the figure as well.

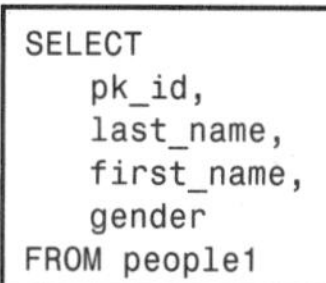

FIGURE 12.5 *The output of two queries combined with the* `UNION ALL` *pseudo-set operator.*

Typical Errors Occurring with Set Operators

Set and pseudo-set operators can combine only those query outputs that have identical layouts in terms of number and types of columns retrieved.

Unequal Number of Columns

If the queries do not return the same number of columns, an error will result, as shown in Listing 12.10.

LISTING 12.10 Joining Queries with an Unequal Number of Columns

```
SELECT
  *
FROM people1
UNION
SELECT
  *
FROM people2
```

This code returns the following:

```
Server: Msg 205, Level 16, State 1, Line 1
All queries in an SQL statement containing a UNION operator must have
an equal number of expressions in their target
lists.
```

The reason for the error is that `people1` and `people2` are not identical in their layout. The `people2` table has one more column, `wealth`:

```
SQL> sp_help people1

Column_name
--------------
pk_id
last_name
first_name
age
gender

SQL> sp_help people2
```

```
Column_name
--------------
pk_id
last_name
first_name
age
gender
wealth
```

Inconsistent Data Types

An error also results if the queries return the same number of columns but the data types of these columns are inconsistent across queries. Therefore, if the first query returns a number, a character, and a date column, the second query must return a number, a character, and a date column as well, or an error results. This requirement is actually quite forgiving; for its purposes, CHAR data types match with VARCHAR, and any number data type can be combined with the same or any other number data type. The example in Listing 12.11 explores some UNIONs with inconsistent data types.

LISTING 12.11 Joining Queries with Inconsistent Data Types

```
-- Filename: 12squ11.sql
-- Purpose: Union operator joining people1 and people2
--      Inconsistent data types

SELECT
  pk_id,
  last_name,
  first_name,
  age,
  gender
FROM people1
UNION
SELECT
  1,
  2,
  3,
  4,
  5
FROM people2
```

The statement returns an error because first_name and last_name are VARCHAR, gender CHAR, but all five constants of the second query are numbers:

```
Server: Msg 245, Level 16, State 1, Line 1
Syntax error converting the varchar value 'M' to a column
of data type int.
```

To fix that error, just enclose 2, 3, and 5 in single quotes:

```
SELECT
  pk_id,
  last_name,
  first_name,
  age,
  gender
FROM people1
UNION
SELECT
  1,
  '2',
  '3',
  4,
  '5'
FROM people2
```

Doing so returns the following:

```
pk_id       last_name       first_name      age         gender
----------- --------------- --------------- ----------- ------
1           2               3               4           5
5           Melsheli        Joseph K.       14          M
4           Kratochvil      Mary T.         48          F
1           Jones           David N.        34          M
3           Talavera        F. Espinosa     19          F
2           Martinelli      A. Emery        92          M

(6 row(s) affected)
```

The first line was generated from the second query.

Another issue is raised by `NULL` constants. The following statement of the example has `NULL` constants in the columns corresponding to `pk_id` and `last_name`:

```
SELECT
  pk_id,
  last_name,
  first_name,
  age,
  gender
```

```
FROM people1
UNION
SELECT
  NULL,
  NULL,
  '3',
  4,
  '5'
FROM people2
```


It might return an error on your database, but this error can be fixed by typecasting the NULLs through to CAST functions. These functions still return NULLs, but NULLs of type number or type CHAR, which suffices to create consistency of data types. This is shown in the following:

```
SELECT
  pk_id,
  last_name,
  first_name,
  age,
  gender
FROM people1
UNION
SELECT
  CAST(NULL AS int),
  CAST(NULL AS VARCHAR(15)),
  '3',
  4,
  '5'
FROM people2
```

This code returns the following:

```
pk_id       last_name       first_name      age         gender
----------- --------------- --------------- ----------- ------
NULL        NULL            3               4           5
5           Melsheli        Joseph K.       14          M
4           Kratochvil      Mary T.         48          F
1           Jones           David N.        34          M
3           Talavera        F. Espinosa     19          F
2           Martinelli      A. Emery        92          M

(6 row(s) affected)
```

The number data type, on the other hand, is very forgiving. Numerical columns of any sort—integer, fixed-point, or floating point—can be combined. Dividing wealth by 1,000 (thus rendering a fixed-point number) and combining that with the integer `pk_id` works, as the following statement shows:

```
SELECT
  pk_id
FROM people1
UNION
SELECT
  wealth/1000.0
FROM people2
```

This code returns the following:

```
pk_id
-------------------
24.000000
281.990000
645.000000
4.000000
2.000000
1.000000
3.000000
5.000000

(8 row(s) affected)
```

Ordering Output Retrieved Through Set and Pseudo-Set Operators

Output combined through set and pseudo-set operators can be ordered, but two limitations apply:

- Only one order by subclause can be used for the entire statement.
- The columns listed in the order by comma list must be included in the select comma list. This is different from a one-shot select, in which any column in any accessed table can be used for querying, whether included in the select comma list or not.

Ordering by Column Number

Listing 12.12 orders the output from `12squ03.sql` by the second and third columns.

LISTING 12.12 Ordering Output When Joining Queries

```
-- Filename: 12squ12.sql
-- Purpose: Union operator joining people1 and people2
--      Ordering Output
SELECT
  pk_id,
  last_name,
  first_name,
  gender
FROM people1
UNION
SELECT
  pk_id,
  last_name,
  first_name,
  gender
FROM people2
ORDER BY 2, 3
```

This code returns the following:

```
pk_id       last_name       first_name      gender
----------- --------------- --------------- ------
1           Jones           David N.        M
7           Kazen           M. Okechuku     F
4           Kratochvil      Mary T.         F
2           Martinelli      A. Emery        M
5           Melsheli        Joseph K.       M
6           Robinson        Faye M.         F
8           Rochblatt       Harold T.       M
3           Talavera        F. Espinosa     F

(8 row(s) affected)
```

If two `ORDER BY` clauses are used in one statement, as in Listing 12.13, an error results.

LISTING 12.13 Using Two **ORDER BY** Clauses in One Statement

```
-- Filename: 12squ13.sql
-- Purpose: Union operator joining people1 and people2
```

LISTING 12.13 CONTINUED

```
--      Ordering Output
--      *** THIS CODE IS NOT CORRECT SQL!
SELECT
  pk_id,
  last_name,
  first_name,
  gender
FROM people1
ORDER BY 2, 3
UNION
SELECT
  pk_id,
  last_name,
  first_name,
  gender
FROM people2
ORDER BY 2, 3
```

This is the error that results:

```
Server: Msg 156, Level 15, State 1, Line 11
Incorrect syntax near the keyword 'UNION'.
```

This is not a helpful error message. What it means is that SQL expects the statement to end after the `ORDER BY` section, so it is confused to see `UNION`.

Subset Operations

This section contains a collection of tricks for extracting subsets from a table. The standard way of extracting subsets from a table is to use the `WHERE` clause, but sometimes the requirements are not easily defined using such a simple predicate.

Returning Top-*n* Values

Say you want to extract the two people with the most wealth from the `people2` table. In this example, there is a tie for second place. The simplest approach is to use an `ORDER BY` clause and ignore the extra rows, as shown in Listing 12.14.

LISTING 12.14 Retrieving All Rows Instead of Top-*n*

```
-- Filename: 12squ14.sql
-- Purpose: Subset Operators
```

LISTING 12.14 CONTINUED

```
SELECT *
FROM people2
ORDER BY wealth DESC
```

This code returns the following:

```
pk_id       last_name       first_name      age         gender wealth
----------- --------------- --------------- ----------- ------ -----------
2           Martinelli      A. Emery        92          M      645000
7           Kazen           M. Okechuku     23          F      281990
8           Rochblatt       Harold T.       32          M      281990
1           Jones           David N.        34          M      24000
6           Robinson        Faye M.         31          F      2000

(5 row(s) affected)
```

However, this query must sort the whole table, which can take some time if the table is large.

Some vendors supply extensions that allow you to return the top-*n* rows. Microsoft SQL Server 7, for example, allows you to write

```
SELECT TOP 2 WITH TIES *
FROM people2
ORDER BY wealth DESC
```

This code returns the following:

```
pk_id       last_name       first_name      age         gender wealth
----------- --------------- --------------- ----------- ------ -----------
2           Martinelli      A. Emery        92          M      645000
7           Kazen           M. Okechuku     23          F      281990
8           Rochblatt       Harold T.       32          M      281990

(3 row(s) affected)
```

It gets quite complicated to retrieve the top-*n* rows in an efficient manner using standard SQL. A good way to achieve the desired result uses a `GROUP BY` clause along with the idea of nested sets. The idea is to take each amount and build a group of other amounts that are greater than or equal to it:

```
SELECT larger_eq_count = COUNT(*), w1.pk_id, w1.wealth
FROM people2 AS w1, people2 AS w2
WHERE (w1.wealth >= w2.wealth)
GROUP BY w1.pk_id, w1.wealth
```

This returns the original set, with a counter indicating how many rows have a smaller or equal amount:

```
larger_eq_count pk_id       wealth
--------------- ----------- -----------
2               1           24000
5               2           645000
1               6           2000
4               7           281990
4               8           281990

(5 row(s) affected)
```

By adding one to that count and subtracting the number of rows in the table, you get the rank of the amount in the table, properly accounting for the possible duplicates. The solution query, therefore, is this:

```
SELECT w1.pk_id, w1.wealth
FROM people2 AS w1, people2 AS w2
WHERE (w1.wealth >= w2.wealth)
GROUP BY w1.pk_id, w1.wealth
HAVING (SELECT COUNT(*) FROM people2) - COUNT(*) + 1 <= 3
```

This code returns the following:

```
pk_id       wealth
----------- -----------
2           645000
7           281990
8           281990

(3 row(s) affected)
```

Returning Every *n*th Item

It is easy to return every *n*th item in a table that has a column with consecutive numbers, as the `people1` table does. You simply compute the `pk_id` `modulo` *n*, which is `2` in this example. The `modulo` function is found in many database products, but is not part of SQL-92. The SQL-3 working document proposes the `MOD(m,n)` syntax, which is used here:

```
SELECT *
FROM people1
WHERE MOD(pk_id, 2) = 0
```

This code returns the following:

```
pk_id       last_name       first_name      age         gender
----------- --------------- --------------- ----------- ------
2           Martinelli      A. Emery        92          M
4           Kratochvil      Mary T.         48          F

(2 row(s) affected)
```

This approach does not work with the people2 table, however, because the numbers in the pk_id column are not consecutive. Here again, the approach is to use a GROUP BY clause along with the idea of nested sets. The idea is to take each pk_id and build a group of other pk_ids that are less than or equal to it:

```
SELECT Row_Counter = COUNT(*), p1.pk_id
FROM people2 AS p1, people2 AS p2
WHERE (p1.pk_id >= p2.pk_id)
GROUP BY p1.pk_id
```

This code returns the following:

```
Row_Counter pk_id
----------- -----------
1           1
2           2
3           6
4           7
5           8

(5 row(s) affected)
```

You now have consecutive numbers, as with the people1 table, and can use the modulo function to retrieve every *n*th item.

```
SELECT p1.pk_id
FROM people2 AS p1, people2 AS p2
WHERE (p1.pk_id >= p2.pk_id)
GROUP BY p1.pk_id
HAVING MOD(COUNT(*), 2) = 0
```

This code returns the desired rows:

```
pk_id
-----------
2
7

(2 row(s) affected)
```

Summary

Set and pseudo-set operators allow you to combine the output of two or more queries end to end. These operators can combine only those query outputs that have identical layouts in terms of number and types of columns retrieved. Numerical columns of any sort—integer, fixed-point, or floating-point—can be combined. Output from `CHAR` and `VARCHAR` columns can be combined as well.

The three set operators behave like their mathematical counterparts and return elements of a set that are distinctly different from all other elements in the set (in other words, redundant rows are not allowed):

- `UNION` returns all elements of all queries.
- `EXCEPT` selects those elements that exist in one table but not in the other. You can get the same result with a left outer join when only those rows of a table are selected that do not have a match in another table. Such rows can be identified as those combined rows in which the second table's columns are all `NULL`s.
- `INTERSECT` displays matching elements only. You can get the same results with an inner join when the columns of only one table are included in the select comma list.

The pseudo-set operator `UNION ALL` does not follow the mathematical rules of set theory. It simply returns the output of the first query followed by the output of the second query.

Set operators can combine simple and compound queries alike. The queries can be enclosed between parentheses as applicable. Using such compound statements, exclusive union output can be generated.

The exclusive union is generated with the statement

```
(query1 UNION query2) EXCEPT (query2 INTERSECT query1)
```

or with

```
(query1 EXCEPT query2) UNION (query2 EXCEPT query1)
```

Output combined through set and pseudo-set operators can be ordered, but only one order by subclause must be used for the entire statement, and all `ORDER BY` columns must be included in the select comma list.

CHAPTER 13

Subqueries

In This Chapter

SQL allows for the use of subqueries, which give you a number of convenient, although not necessarily efficient, options for more complex tasks. This chapter will be devoted to subqueries. Two options are available:

- Subqueries are nested when a subquery is executed and its results are inserted into the `WHERE` condition of the main query. This chapter starts with subqueries that return exactly one value.
- Correlated subqueries present the opposite case—the main query is executed first and a subquery is executed for every row retrieved by the main query.

Nested Subqueries

Most conditions for the `WHERE` or `HAVING` subclauses are static, such as `WHERE AGE > 30`. If, however, the question is to find everybody who is older than the average person in the table, then two queries are necessary: one to find the average age and the other to find all records where age is greater than the average age. The following query shows that approach:

```
select avg(age) from pers1;
```

Note

All the tables used in this chapter are created with scripts included on the CD-ROM.

Crpers1.sql	Creates and populates the pers1 table
Crpers3.sql	Creates and populates the pers3 table
Crlawyer1.sql	Creates and populates the lawyer1 table
Crlawyer2.sql	Creates and populates the lawyer2 table

The preceding code returns the following output:

```
 AVG(AGE)
---------
     41.4
```

This value is then inserted into the `WHERE` clause of the second query to retrieve the desired rows, as shown in Listing 13.1.

LISTING 13.1 Retrieve Rows Where Age > Average Age, Which Is 41.4

```
select *
from pers1
where age > 41.4
;
```

The preceding code returns the following output:

```
       ID LNAME          FMNAME         SSN        AGE       S
--------- -------------- -------------- --------- --------- -
        2 Martinelli     A. Emery       312331818 92        M
        4 Kratochvil     Mary T.        969825711 48        F
```

The second query is the important one; it returns the information you wanted in the first place. The first query is subsidiary to it; it retrieves only a value that was necessary to fit into the second one—the average age.

Note

Throughout this chapter, one of Oracle's SQL utilities, SQL*Plus, is used (see Chapter 24, "Oracle SQL," for more information on SQL*Plus). Although most of the SQL will work in any ANSI-compliant database, the Oracle formatting is used to make the output easy to read. You will notice formatting lines similar to this code:

```
column rate format 999.99 heading 'Hourly¦ Rate'

column avrate format 999.99 heading 'Average¦Hourly Rate'

clear columns
```

You will also notice that the errors are from Oracle, such as the following error:

```
ERROR:

ORA-01427: single-row subquery returns more than one row

no rows selected
```

Subqueries allow you to do exactly the same, but in a one-shot process. The statement begins with the outer query. The value `41.4` in the `WHERE` subclause, however, is replaced by the subquery or inner query, which returns this value. The statement in Listing 13.2 performs that task.

LISTING 13.2 Retrieve Rows Where Age > Average Age

```
select *
from pers1
where age >
  (select avg(age) from pers1)
;
```

The preceding code returns exactly the same output:

```
       ID LNAME          FMNAME          SSN       AGE       S
--------- -------------- --------------- --------- --------- -
        2 Martinelli     A. Emery        312331818 92        M
        4 Kratochvil     Mary T.         969825711 48        F
```

Just as with the initial example, the query is executed in two stages, except that SQL does all the work. SQL executes the inner query first to find the average age. Then it executes the outer query, using the value returned by the inner query in the `WHERE` subclause (see Figure 13.1).

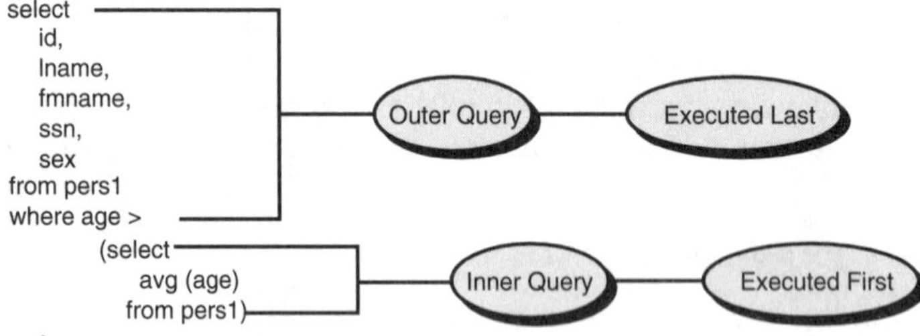
select
id,
lname,
fmname,
ssn,
sex
from pers1
where age >
(select
avg (age)
from pers1)
;
Outer Query
Executed Last
Inner Query
Executed First

FIGURE 13.1
The execution order of a nested query.

Caution

Although SQL does all the work, you still need to make sure your subquery returns exactly one value. If you are not absolutely sure, test it first.

The statement in Listing 13.3 includes a subquery that retrieves no rows.

LISTING 13.3 Retrieve Rows Where Age > Age of Person with ID of 6

```
select *
 from pers1
 where age >
  (select age from pers1 where id = 6)
;
```

Instead of just returning to the SQL> prompt, the database server returns a message that lets you know that no rows matched the query.

```
no rows selected
```

The last line is a SQL-style terse statement, which does not indicate an error. Go figure. No rows are selected because no rows fulfill the condition in the subquery. The next statement, in Listing 13.4, uses a subquery that returns too many values.

LISTING 13.4 Invalid Query That Returns More Than One Subquery Row

```
select *
 from pers1
 where age >
   (select age from pers1 where age > 20)
;
```

This query returns the following message:

```
ERROR:
ORA-01427: single-row subquery returns more than one row
no rows selected
```

The resulting error message is a no-brainer; SQL tells you exactly what's wrong.

The final statement in Listing 13.5 uses a subquery that returns too many columns.

LISTING 13.5 Invalid Subquery That Returns Too Many Columns

```
select *
 from pers1
 where age >
   (select min(age), max(age) from pers1)
;
```

This query generates the following message for the user:

```
  (select min(age), max(age) from pers1)
```

```
  *
ERROR at line 4:
ORA-00913: too many values
```

The last error message is not quite as clear, but mercifully, the offending line is printed too.

Properties of Conditional Subqueries

The preceding subqueries could have also been called *conditional subqueries* because what they return is subsequently inserted into a condition within the outer query. The inner queries of conditional subquery statements must have the following two conditions:

- They must be enclosed in parentheses.
- They must be on the right side of conditions.

Listing 13.6 shows the errors that result if these rules are violated.

LISTING 13.6 Invalid Query with Subquery on Left Side of Condition

```
select *
from pers1
where (select avg(age) from pers1) < age
;
```

The preceding code returns the following error:

```
where (select avg(age) from pers1) < age
     *
ERROR at line 3:
ORA-00936: missing expression
```

This is another case in which an error message returned by SQL is a bit terse. The same message results from omitting the parentheses, as shown in Listing 13.7.

LISTING 13.7 Invalid Query with Missing Parentheses

```
select *
 from pers1
 where age >
   select avg(age) from pers1 where id = 6
;
```

When entering the preceding query, you will then see the following error message:

```
  select avg(age) from pers1 where id = 6
  *
ERROR at line 4:
ORA-00936: missing expression
```

Note

Subqueries and the outer query can retrieve information from different tables or sets of those tables.

Single-Row Comparison Operators

As their name says, *single-row subqueries* must return one and only one row. They can be used with the six comparison operators that compare exactly one value (expression) with another one.

TABLE 13.1 Single-Row Comparison Operators

Operator	*Meaning*
=	Equal to
<>	Not equal to
>	Greater than
>=	Greater than or equal to
<	Less than
<=	Less than or equal to

Listing 13.8 runs six sets of queries with subqueries, one set for each operator.

LISTING 13.8 Subquery Using the = Operator

```
select '= ' op,
    id,
    lname,
    fmname,
    ssn,
    age,
    sex
from pers1
where age =
```

LISTING 13.8 CONTINUED

```
  (select avg(age) from pers1)
;
```

The preceding code returns the following output:

```
no rows selected
```

It makes perfect sense that the query does not retrieve any rows because no person in the table is exactly as old as the average. For the same reason, the not equal to (<>) condition returns all five rows, as shown in Listing 13.9.

LISTING 13.9 Subquery Using the <> Operator

```
select '<>' op,
    id,
    lname,
    fmname,
    ssn,
    age,
    sex
from pers1
where age <>
  (select avg(age) from pers1)
;
```

The preceding code returns the following output:

```
OP         ID LNAME           FMNAME          SSN       AGE       S
-- --------- --------------- --------------- --------- --------- -
<>          1 Jones           David N.        895663453 34        M
<>          2 Martinelli      A. Emery        312331818 92        M
<>          3 Talavera        F. Espinosa     533932999 19        F
<>          4 Kratochvil      Mary T.         969825711 48        F
<>          5 Melsheli       Joseph K.        000342222 14        M
```

The greater than condition (>) returns the same rows as the greater equal condition (>=) for the same reason, as you can see in Listing 13.10.

LISTING 13.10 Subquery Using the > Operator

```
select '> ' op,
    id,
    lname,
    fmname,
```

LISTING 13.10 CONTINUED

```
    ssn,
    age,
    sex
from pers1
where age >
  (select avg(age) from pers1)
;
```

The preceding code returns the following output:

```
OP         ID LNAME           FMNAME          SSN       AGE       S
-- --------- --------------- --------------- --------- --------- -
>          2 Martinelli      A. Emery        312331818 92        M
>          4 Kratochvil      Mary T.         969825711 48        F
```

The statement in Listing 13.11 returns the same output.

LISTING 13.11 Subquery Using the >= Operator

```
select '>=' op,
    id,
    lname,
    fmname,
    ssn,
    age,
    sex
from pers1
where age >=
  (select avg(age) from pers1)
;
```

Similarly, the less than condition (<) returns the same as the less equal condition (<=), as illustrated in Listing 13.12.

LISTING 13.12 Subqueries Using the < and <= Operators

```
select '< ' op,
    id,
    lname,
    fmname,
    ssn,
    age,
    sex
```

LISTING 13.12 CONTINUED

```
from pers1
where age <
  (select avg(age) from pers1)
;

select '<=' op,
    id,
    lname,
    fmname,
    ssn,
    age,
    sex
from pers1
where age <=
  (select avg(age) from pers1)
;
```

Both SQL statements return the same row output as shown here.

```
OP         ID LNAME           FMNAME          SSN        AGE       S
-- --------- --------------- --------------- --------- --------- -
<=          1 Jones           David N.        895663453 34        M
<=          3 Talavera        F. Espinosa     533932999 19        F
<=          5 Melsheli        Joseph K.       000342222 14        M
```

Parallel Subqueries

A further enhancement is the possibility of including more than one subquery in a statement. You can nest the query so that a main query is dependent on the results of a subquery, which in turn depends on the results of another one. A nested subquery is not limited to three levels.

Tip

Although it might be appealing, you are well advised to keep the complexity of expressions down. You might feel smart and excited about that eight-level nested query with at least two parallel branches per level. These feelings will quickly subside if you—or worse, somebody else—must debug a tiny logical error in the statement a year later. Unless you have a major performance reason, keep it as simple as possible.

Further subqueries that are parallel to the first are much more frequent. The main query has a compound WHERE clause, more than one component of which has subqueries attached.

The following query retrieves names, age, wealth, and income of every record in pers3 where the age, wealth, and income are greater than average. But first, recapitulate the averages for these three variables by themselves. To do that, type these two SQL statements as shown:

```
select avg(wealth) from pers3;
select avg(interest + salary + profit + royalty) from pers3;
```

The SQL statements and their output are shown in Listing 13.13.

LISTING 13.13 Averages

```
SQL> select avg(wealth) from pers3;
AVG(WEALTH)
-----------
     622680
SQL>
SQL> select avg(interest + salary + profit + royalty) from pers3;

AVG(INTEREST+SALARY+PROFIT+ROYALTY)
-----------------------------------
                              75786
```

The query for retrieving that information consists of a main, or outer, query whose WHERE condition has three parts. Each of them has a subquery attached to it. They are parallel because they are executed at approximately the same time. The results are put into their respective places in the outer query, which is executed next (see Listing 13.14).

LISTING 13.14 A Parallel Subquery

```
select
  lname,
  fmname,
  age,
  wealth,
  (interest + salary + profit + royalty) income
from pers3
where age >
  (select avg(age) from pers1)
and  wealth >
  (select avg(wealth) from pers3)
```

LISTING 13.14 CONTINUED

```
and  (interest + salary + profit + royalty) >
  (select avg(interest + salary + profit + royalty) from pers3)
;
```

The preceding code returns the following output:

```
LNAME           FMNAME          AGE       WEALTH    INCOME
--------------- --------------- --------- --------- ---------
Martinelli      A. Emery        92        645000    92900
Kratochvil      Mary T.         48        2400600   188800
```

Incidentally, the code returns the same two people.

Figure 13.2 shows the execution order of the next statement. The inner queries are executed first, followed by the outer query.

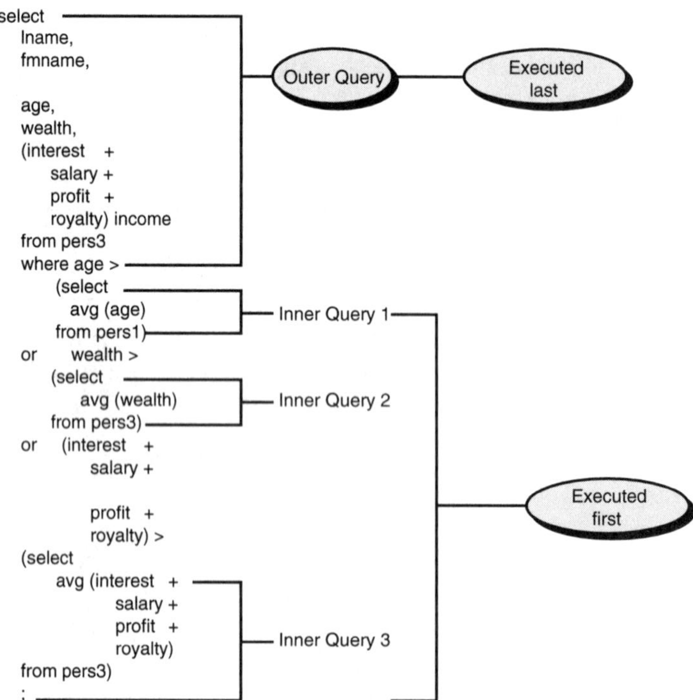
select
lname,
fmname,
age,
wealth,
(interest +
salary +
profit +
royalty) income
from pers3
where age >
(select
avg (age)
from pers1)
or wealth >
(select
avg (wealth)
from pers3)
or (interest +
salary +
profit +
royalty) >
(select
avg (interest +
salary +
profit +
royalty)
from pers3)
;
Outer Query
Executed last
Inner Query 1
Inner Query 2
Inner Query 3
Executed first

FIGURE 13.2
The execution order of parallel subqueries.

If, however, the Boolean operators are set to `OR`, a third row is retrieved, as the example in Listing 13.15 shows.

LISTING 13.15 Three Subqueries Against Different Tables

```
select
  lname,
  fmname,
  age,
  wealth,
  (interest + salary + profit + royalty) income
from pers3
where age >
  (select avg(age) from pers1)
or  wealth >
  (select avg(wealth) from pers3)
or  (interest + salary + profit + royalty) >
  (select avg(interest + salary + profit + royalty) from pers3)
;
```


The preceding code returns the following output:

```
LNAME           FMNAME          AGE       WEALTH    INCOME
--------------- --------------- --------- --------- ---------
Jones           David N.        34        43000     92200
Martinelli      A. Emery        92        645000    92900
Kratochvil      Mary T.         48        2400600   188800
```

Mr. Jones, who is clearly younger than average and who has much less wealth, is nevertheless retrieved because his income is higher than average.

Multiple-Row Subqueries

Subqueries can also retrieve more than one value by using special multiple-row comparison operators. Imagine a situation in which you need to list all lawyers from the `lawyer1` table who work in offices that yield a larger-than-average hourly rate (weighted by hour). The answer to this question could be found by executing three queries.

The first query, in Listing 13.16, finds the average hourly rate per lawyer.

LISTING 13.16 Determine Average Hourly Rate Per Lawyer

```
select
  avg(bgross/bhrs)
```

LISTING 13.16 CONTINUED

```
from lawyer1
;
```

The output of this query is

```
AVG(BGROSS/BHRS)
----------------
                152.7733
```

The second query, in Listing 13.17, shows the average hourly rate per office in descending order.

LISTING 13.17 Determine Average Hourly Rate Per Office

```
select
  office,
  avg(bgross/bhrs)
from lawyer1
group by office
order by office desc
;
```

The output of this query is

```
OFFICE          AVG(BGROSS/BHRS)
--------------- ----------------
New York        201.52445
Los Angeles     155.55272
Houston         110.55293
Boston          107.26889
```

If you insert the first query as a subquery for the second, you can filter out the offices that average a higher billable rate than the average over all billed hours, as shown in Listing 13.18.

LISTING 13.18 Determine Office Averaging Higher Billable Rate Than Average of All Hours

```
select
  office,
  avg(bgross/bhrs)
from lawyer1
having avg(bgross/bhrs) >
  (select
```

LISTING 13.18 CONTINUED

```
   avg(bgross/bhrs)
  from lawyer1)
group by office
order by avg(bgross/bhrs) desc
;
```

The output of this query is

```
OFFICE          AVG(BGROSS/BHRS)
--------------- ----------------
New York        201.52445
Los Angeles     155.55272
```

Those offices, it turns out, are New York and Los Angeles. Finally, using the `IN` operator, you can adapt the whole statement and insert it as a multi-row subquery to identify the lawyers in those cities and their average hourly earnings, as shown in Listing 13.19.

LISTING 13.19 Multi-Row Subquery Using the `IN` Operator

```
column rate format 999.99 heading 'Hourly¦ Rate'
select
   office,
   name,
   bgross/bhrs rate
 from lawyer1
 where office in
     (select
       office
      from lawyer1
      having avg(bgross/bhrs) >
         (select
           avg(bgross/bhrs)
         from lawyer1)
      group by office)
 order by
   office,
   bgross/bhrs desc
;
clear columns
```

The output of this query is

```
                                      Hourly
OFFICE          NAME                    Rate
--------------- --------------- -------
Los Angeles     Easton                172.32
Los Angeles     Howe                  163.60
Los Angeles     Miller                159.72
Los Angeles     Roll                  155.51
Los Angeles     Martinez              151.74
Los Angeles     Ming                  144.07
Los Angeles     Chandler              141.91
New York        Frankie               220.17
New York        Chatham               209.18
New York        Bonin                 206.73
New York        Cheetham              200.60
New York        Earl                  187.41
New York        Chabot                185.06
13 rows selected.

columns cleared
```

Note that Martinez, Ming, and Chandler made the list despite making less than the average hourly rate—their offices made more, and that is the key criterion here.

Figure 13.3 illustrates the execution order of a multiple-row subquery combined with a nested subquery.

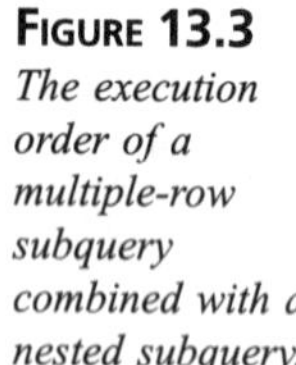

FIGURE 13.3
The execution order of a multiple-row subquery combined with a nested subquery.

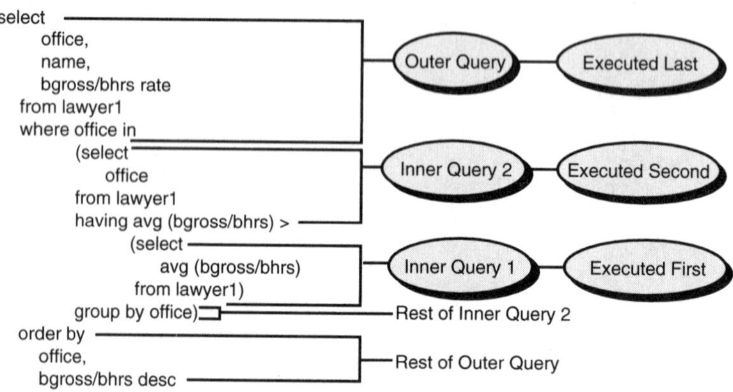
select
office,
name,
bgross/bhrs rate
from lawyer1
where office in
(select
office
from lawyer1
having avg (bgross/bhrs) >
(select
avg (bgross/bhrs)
from lawyer1)
group by office)
order by
office,
bgross/bhrs desc
;
Outer Query
Executed Last
Inner Query 2
Executed Second
Inner Query 1
Executed First
Rest of Inner Query 2
Rest of Outer Query

Caution

Although SQL does all the work, you still need to make sure your subqueries return what they are supposed to. They should return exactly one value for inner query 1, which calculates the average `bgross/bhrs`, and exactly two values for inner query 2, which identifies the offices that do better than that average. If you are not absolutely sure, test.

Correlated Subqueries

Correlated subqueries use the opposite approach of nested subqueries. Nested subqueries are executed first. Their result(s) is then used as part of the `WHERE` clause of the statement that includes the subquery. Depending on this result, a row in the main (outer) query is or is not retrieved.

With correlated subqueries, on the other hand, the outer query retrieves all rows as candidate rows, which are then qualified through a subquery that is executed once per row of the outer query.

The correlated subquery execution is illustrated in Figure 13.4. They are processed as follows:

- The outer query retrieves a candidate row.
- For each candidate row, the correlated inner query is executed once.
- The results of this query then are used to determine whether the candidate rows should be accepted and printed or rejected and omitted.
- The next row of the outer query is retrieved.

Returning to the `lawyer1` table, a nested subquery could be used to find all lawyers who achieve a higher than average hourly rate. The solution to this question is shown in Listing 13.20.

LISTING 13.20 Retrieve Lawyers Who Achieve a Higher Than Average Billable Rate

```
column rate format 999.99 heading 'Hourly¦ Rate'
column avrate format 999.99 heading 'Average¦Hourly Rate'

select
  avg(bgross/bhrs) avrate
from lawyer1;
```

LISTING 13.20 CONTINUED

```
select
  office,
  name,
  bgross,
  bhrs,
  bgross/bhrs rate
from lawyer1
where bgross/bhrs >=
   (select
     avg(bgross/bhrs)
   from lawyer1)
order by bgross/bhrs desc
;

clear columns
```

The inner query returns an average hourly rate of $152.77, as shown in the following code:

```
Average
Hourly Rate
-----------
     152.77
```

The second statement retrieves the 10 lawyers whose rates are above average:

```
                                      Hourly
OFFICE           NAME                 BGROSS       BHRS    Rate
--------------- --------------- --------- --------- -------
New York         Frankie              469843       2134  220.17
New York         Chatham              367944       1759  209.18
New York         Bonin                346892       1678  206.73
New York         Cheetham             280435       1398  200.60
New York         Earl                 434801       2320  187.41
New York         Chabot               310897       1680  185.06
Los Angeles      Easton               654832       3800  172.32
Los Angeles      Howe                 569338       3480  163.60
Los Angeles      Miller               503582       3153  159.72
Los Angeles      Roll                 498084       3203  155.51
10 rows selected.
```

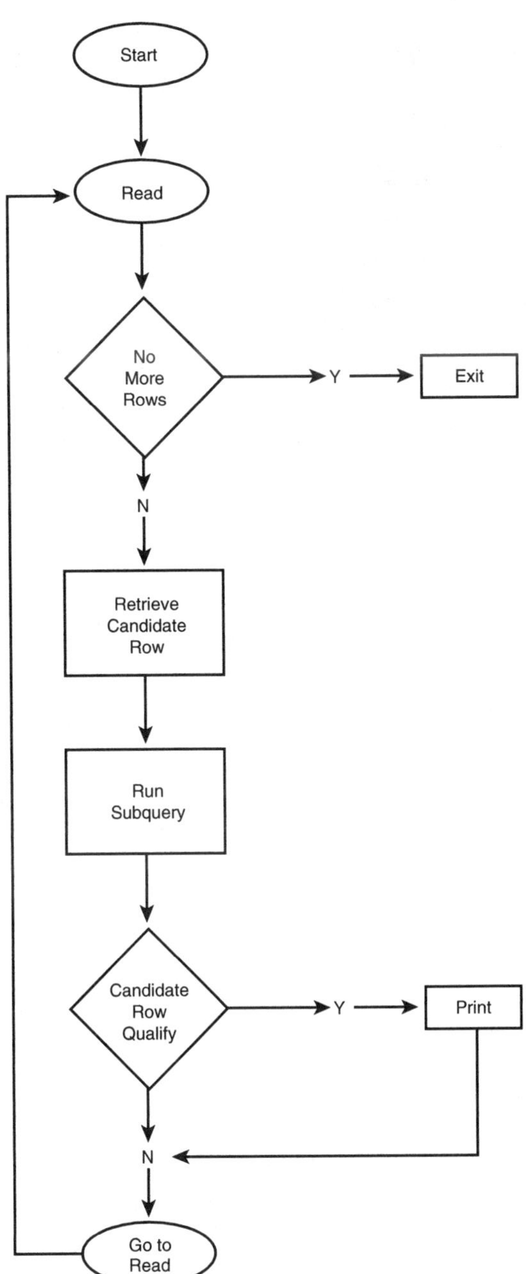

FIGURE 13.4
The correlated subquery execution order.

A correlated subquery comes into play when the question is slightly modified, such as when you want to find lawyers who achieve a higher billable rate than the average rate for their office, as the example in Listing 13.21 does.

LISTING 13.21 Retrieve Lawyers with Higher Billable Rates Than Their Office Average

```
column rate format 999.99 heading 'Hourly¦ Rate'
column avrate format 999.99 heading 'Average¦Hourly Rate'

select
  office,
  avg(bgross/bhrs) avrate
from lawyer1
group by office
order by office;

select
  office,
  name,
  bgross,
  bhrs,
  bgross/bhrs rate
from lawyer1 outer
where bgross/bhrs >=
   (select
     avg(bgross/bhrs)
   from lawyer1
   where office = outer.office)
order by
  office,
  bgross/bhrs desc
;

clear columns
```

The output of the first query displays the average rates for all four offices, as shown here:

```
                    Average
OFFICE          Hourly Rate
--------------- -----------
Boston               107.27
Houston              110.55
Los Angeles          155.55
```

```
New York                201.52
```

The output of the second query shows the high achievers per office:

```
                                           Hourly
OFFICE          NAME               BGROSS      BHRS    Rate
--------------- --------------- --------- --------- -------
Boston          Dewey              426800      2856  149.44
Boston          Paul               239855      2198  109.12
Houston         Roach              269844      2349  114.88
Los Angeles     Easton             654832      3800  172.32
Los Angeles     Howe               569338      3480  163.60
Los Angeles     Miller             503582      3153  159.72
New York        Frankie            469843      2134  220.17
New York        Chatham            367944      1759  209.18
New York        Bonin              346892      1678  206.73
9 rows selected.
```

Note

In most cases you have to use an alias (such as `outer` in the example for the outer table). The only exception is when the outer and inner tables are different and use mutually exclusive column names. The default, where no table is specified, is the inner table.

All columns of the example can and should be fully qualified through table aliases, as shown in Listing 13.22.

LISTING 13.22 Retrieve Lawyers with Higher Billable Rates Than Their Office Average Using Correlated Subquery and Alias for Each Column

```
column rate format 999.99 heading 'Hourly¦ Rate'
column avrate format 999.99 heading 'Average¦Hourly Rate'

select
  outer.office,
  outer.name,
  outer.bgross,
  outer.bhrs,
  outer.bgross/outer.bhrs rate
from lawyer1 outer
where outer.bgross/outer.bhrs >=
```

LISTING 13.22 CONTINUED

```
    (select
      avg(inner.bgross/inner.bhrs)
    from lawyer1 inner
    where inner.office = outer.office)
order by
  outer.office,
  outer.bgross/outer.bhrs desc
;

clear columns
```

The result is exactly the same as the previous query. Although aliasing appears redundant and cluttered in this case, it might help when more than two levels of queries are combined in a statement; however, even more complex statements work with minimum aliasing. The next example in Listing 13.23 retrieves lawyers who achieve a higher than average billable rate by using a correlated subquery and minimum aliasing.

LISTING 13.23 Retrieve Averages for Each Office

```
column rate format 999.99 heading 'Hourly¦ Rate'
column avgross format 999,999.99 heading 'Average¦Gross¦Receipts'
column avhrs format 9,999.99 heading 'Average¦Hours¦Billed'

select
  office,
  avg(bgross) avgross,
  avg(bhrs)  avhrs
from lawyer1
group by office order by office
;
clear columns
```

The output of the first query lists the average gross receipts and billable hours by office.

```
                    Average   Average
                      Gross     Hours
OFFICE             Receipts    Billed
--------------- ----------- ---------
Boston           287,635.00  2,678.20
Houston          229,944.50  2,069.00
Los Angeles      487,460.43  3,110.57
New York         368,468.67  1,828.17
```

The second query retrieves those lawyers who exceed *both* the average gross receipts *and* the average billable hours of their respective offices, as shown in Listing 13.24.

LISTING 13.24 Retrieve Lawyers with Higher Billable Hours and Higher Gross Receipts Than Their Office Average

```
select
  office,
  name,
  bgross,
  bhrs,
  bgross/bhrs rate
from lawyer1 outer
where bgross >=
   (select
     avg(bgross)
   from lawyer1
   where office = outer.office)
and bhrs >=
   (select
     avg(bhrs)
   from lawyer1
   where office = outer.office)
order by
  office,
  bgross/bhrs desc
;

clear columns
```

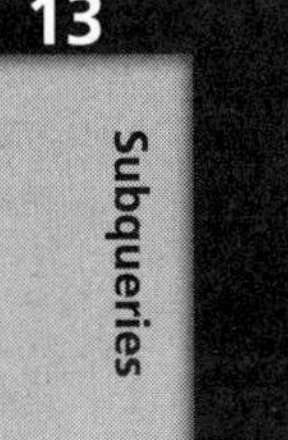

The second query returns the following output:

```
                                      Hourly
OFFICE          NAME                  BGROSS       BHRS    Rate
--------------- --------------- ---------- ---------- -------
Boston          Dewey                426800       2856  149.44
Boston          Greene               289435       2854  101.41
Houston         Roach                269844       2349  114.88
Los Angeles     Easton               654832       3800  172.32
Los Angeles     Howe                 569338       3480  163.60
Los Angeles     Miller               503582       3153  159.72
Los Angeles     Roll                 498084       3203  155.51
New York        Frankie              469843       2134  220.17
New York        Earl                 434801       2320  187.41
```

```
9 rows selected.
```

Correlated Subqueries Versus Views

Another approach—a temporary view that displays the averages per office—yields the same result as corresponding statements that include correlated subqueries. This temporary view can then be joined to the original table (from which, in this case, it originates itself) and rows retrieved by simply using a `WHERE` clause.

The following example retrieves the information by using a view. First, a view with average gross receipts, average hours billed, and average hourly rates is created, as shown in Listing 13.25.

LISTING 13.25 Create the View

```
column rate format 999.99 heading 'Hourly¦ Rate'
column avgross format 999,999.99 heading 'Average¦Gross¦Receipts'
column avhrs format 9,999.99 heading 'Average¦Hours¦Billed'

create or replace view avgoff as
select
  office,
  avg(bgross) avgross,
  avg(bhrs)  avhrs,
  avg(bgross/bhrs) avrate
from lawyer1
group by office
;
clear columns
```

This code returns the output:

```
View created.
```

Next is a query, shown in Listing 13.26, against a join of the original table and the aggregate view just created. The `WHERE` clause has three components, which limit the rows to those that

- Have a gross receipt value larger than the average gross receipt value for the office

- Have a billable hours value larger than the average billable hours value for the office
- Have matching office values for view and table

LISTING 13.26 Retrieve Lawyers with Higher Billable Rates Than Their Office Average Using Views

```
select
  l.office,
  l.name,
  l.bgross,
  l.bhrs,
  l.bgross/l.bhrs rate
from lawyer1 l, avgoff a
where
  l.bgross >= a.avgross and
  l.bhrs   >= a.avhrs  and
  l.office = a.office
order by
  l.office,
  l.bgross/l.bhrs desc;
```

This query returns the following output:

```
                                        Hourly
OFFICE          NAME                    BGROSS       BHRS    Rate
--------------- --------------- --------- --------- -------
Boston          Dewey                   426800       2856  149.44
Boston          Greene                  289435       2854  101.41
Houston         Roach                   269844       2349  114.88
Los Angeles     Easton                  654832       3800  172.32
Los Angeles     Howe                    569338       3480  163.60
Los Angeles     Miller                  503582       3153  159.72
Los Angeles     Roll                    498084       3203  155.51
New York        Frankie                 469843       2134  220.17
New York        Earl                    434801       2320  187.41
```

This is the familiar output of the correlated subquery.

Performance Considerations for Correlated Subqueries

On a little table, such as the one used for these examples, there is no practical difference in the performance when using any option. All the blocks of the table are likely in memory, which produces an almost instant response.

The correlated query can be comparably efficient if

- Only relatively few rows are retrieved through the outer query, especially if the `WHERE` clause, which limits the number of rows returned, can use an index.
- The correlated inner queries are performed through an index scan. This is especially important if the table(s) against which the inner query is performed is large and the index scan has to retrieve only a small portion of its rows.

EXISTS/NOT EXISTS Operators

The `EXISTS` operator and its counterpart `NOT EXISTS` have some subtle advantages over their closest relatives—`IN` and `NOT IN` in terms of speed, and when logic that includes `NULL` values is involved.

EXISTS Versus IN

The `EXISTS` operator provides the first example of a recursive relationship, in which one row in a table contains a column that refers to another row of the same table. A typical situation is a boss column that contains the ID of the person reported to in the same table.

Only one query is required to answer the question of which person somebody reports to as identified by the boss's own personal `id` value. To retrieve the name of the boss, a second query, or a join, is necessary. Answering the question of who has lawyers reporting to him or her requires a query with at least one join or a subquery because the status of a boss is not included in the row of a lawyer; it has to be taken from all other rows.

The first query, shown in Listing 13.27, is the straightforward multiple-value subquery; generate a list of all boss ID values and insert the list into the `WHERE` clause of the main query.

LISTING 13.27 Retrieve Lawyers Who Have At Least One Report Using IN Operator

```
select
  name,
  office
from lawyer2
```

LISTING 13.27 CONTINUED

```
where id in
   (select distinct boss
    from lawyer2 )
order by
  office,
  name
;
```

The result of the preceding code is as follows:

```
NAME            OFFICE
--------------- ---------------
Dewey           Boston
Greene          Boston
Paul            Boston
Roach           Houston
Easton          Los Angeles
Howe            Los Angeles
Miller          Los Angeles
Ming            Los Angeles
Roll            Los Angeles
Bonin           New York
Earl            New York
Frankie         New York

12 rows selected.
```


The next case, shown in Listing 13.28, is a correlated subquery that uses the `EXISTS` operator. The main query retrieves candidate rows. For each candidate row, a subquery is executed. As soon as this subquery finds only one occurrence where the outer ID is used in the `boss` column, it stops execution and returns a true value to the outer query, which then qualifies the candidate row.

LISTING 13.28 Retrieve Lawyers Who Have At Least One Report Using a Correlated Subquery

```
select
  name,
  office
from lawyer2 outer
where exists
   (select 1
    from lawyer2 inner
```

LISTING 13.28 CONTINUED

```
    where inner.boss = outer.id)
order by
  office,
  name
;
```

The output is the same as in the first statement of this example.

> **Tip**
>
> When only the row count matters, not the content of a row, you can simply select a constant. A constant subquery is more efficient.

The last option, demonstrated in Listing 13.29, is to join the table to itself, which can then easily return the number of employees who report to each boss.

LISTING 13.29 Retrieve Lawyers Who Have At Least One Report Using a Recursive Join

```
select
  m.name,
  m.office,
  count(e.name)
  from lawyer2 m, lawyer2 e
 where m.id = e.boss
 group by
  m.name,
  m.office
 order by
  m.office,
  m.name
;
```

This code returns the following output:

```
NAME            OFFICE          COUNT(E.NAME)
--------------- --------------- -------------
Dewey           Boston                      2
Greene          Boston                      1
Paul            Boston                      1
Roach           Houston                     1
```

```
Easton          Los Angeles                5
Howe            Los Angeles                1
Miller          Los Angeles                1
Ming            Los Angeles                1
Roll            Los Angeles                1
Bonin           New York                   1
Earl            New York                   2
Frankie         New York                   2
12 rows selected.
```

Again, the preferred solution in most cases is the recursive join.

NOT EXISTS Versus NOT IN

The alternative question asks for all lawyers who are not bosses. Trying this query with the NOT IN operator returns an incorrect result because Easton in Los Angeles does not report to anybody. Hence, the boss entry in his or her row is NULL. If the subquery retrieves at least one NULL value, the entire WHERE condition evaluates to unknown. As a result, not a single row is returned, when in fact eight lawyers do not have reports. The first statement, shown in Listing 13.30, illustrates this problem.

LISTING 13.30 Retrieve Lawyers Who Do Not Have At Least One Report Using the NOT IN Operator

```
select
  name,
  office
from lawyer2
where id not in
   (select boss
    from lawyer2 )
order by
  office,
  name
;
```

The preceding code returns the following output:

```
no rows selected
```

The NOT EXISTS operator, as used in Listing 13.31, remedies the problem. Note that in this example it is only important whether the query returns rows at all; what it returns is of no concern.

LISTING 13.31 Retrieve Lawyers Who Do Not Have At Least One Report Using the `NOT EXISTS` Operator

```
select
  name,
  office
from lawyer2 outer
where not exists
    (select 1
     from lawyer2
     where boss = outer.id )
order by
  office,
  name
;
```

The preceding code returns the following:

```
NAME            OFFICE
--------------- ---------------
Cardinal        Boston
Wright          Boston
Clayton         Houston
Chandler        Los Angeles
Martinez        Los Angeles
Chabot          New York
Chatham         New York
Cheetham        New York

8 rows selected.
```

Again, there is a recursive join solution, which is demonstrated in Listing 13.32. The table is joined to itself by the `boss` field when looking at employees and the `ID` field when looking at bosses. The outer join indicator `(+)` after `e.boss` indicates that all the rows in the table aliased with `e` should be preserved even if no match in the other table can be found. From this joined set, you select all boss names who don't have a single employee name entry.

LISTING 13.32 Retrieve Lawyers Who Do Not Have At Least One Report Using a Recursive Join

```
select
  m.name,
  m.office,
  count(e.name)
```

LISTING 13.32 CONTINUED

```
  from lawyer2 m, lawyer2 e
where m.id = e.boss (+)
having count(e.name) = 0
group by
  m.name,
  m.office
order by
  m.office,
  m.name
;
```

This code returns the same eight rows with a count of employees reporting to that person. It isn't necessary to display this count because only those people who are not bosses are selected in the query.

```
NAME            OFFICE          COUNT(E.NAME)
--------------- --------------- -------------
Cardinal        Boston                      0
Wright          Boston                      0
Clayton         Houston                     0
Chandler        Los Angeles                 0
Martinez        Los Angeles                 0
Chabot          New York                    0
Chatham         New York                    0
Cheetham        New York                    0

8 rows selected.
```

Summary

This chapter has introduced the first cases of SQL statements that consisted of more than one query. The subquery (or inner query, as it is often referred to) is executed first and returns exactly one value. This value is then inserted into the `WHERE` condition of the second query.

These conditional subqueries must be enclosed in parentheses and must be on the right side of conditions. They can be used with the six comparison operators that compare exactly one value (expression) with another one: =, <>, >, >=, <, and <=.

Next, the chapter discussed the useful multiple-row subqueries, which return one or more rows and can then be incorporated into the main query's `WHERE` statement by means of special multiple-row comparison operators. The most important of these are `IN` and `NOT IN`.

Finally, the chapter introduced correlated subqueries. Correlated subqueries retrieve all rows of the outer query as candidate rows to be qualified through one subquery each. They are useful if the values of a column are to be compared with an aggregate value for a group of which that row is a part.

Correlated subqueries can take advantage of the `EXISTS` operator, which qualifies an outer query row as soon as a single inner query that fulfills the condition is retrieved. The opposite operator `NOT EXISTS` can be used to overcome the problem of the `NOT IN` operator. The `NOT IN` operator does not return any rows if a single value of the inner query compared in the `WHERE` statement is `NULL`. Other options, namely a recursive outer join, retrieve the same information.

CHAPTER

Creating and Using Views

In This Chapter

In this chapter, you take a look at database views. There are several different types of views that you can create, and some allow you to update the underlying tables behind the view. Implementation of database views for both Oracle and SQL Server are covered. To begin the chapter, you will take a look at what a database view actually is and how it can be of use to you in your database design.

Next, this chapter gets into the technical side of things by documenting the `CREATE VIEW` command and giving a good number of examples of how to create the different types of database views.

You will finish up by taking a look at the other SQL view maintenance commands: `ALTER VIEW` and `DROP VIEW`.

What Is a View?

There are more than a few definitions of the word *view* in the dictionary. A view can be a personal opinion, a field of vision, or an inspection. In the database world, a *view* can best be described as a different look for existing information in your databases.

In more technical terms, a database view is a custom-designed table, or *virtual* table. The columns of the view point to columns or selected rows of columns in already existing tables. No data is actually stored in the view. The pre-existing tables are called the *base* tables of the view. After the view is created, you use the `SELECT` statement to read data from the view. You can update the base table data through the view, if you have that type of access when you create the view.

There are many types of views and many reasons you might want to use them. This chapter covers how database views are implemented in the Oracle database. Let's take a look at some of the advantages of using views and at the different types of database views you can create.

Reasons for Using Database Views

Some of the many reasons for implementing database views are discussed in this section:

- **Database security:** Implementing table security with views is quick and easy. When creating the view, you can specify it as `READ_ONLY`. This way, users and applications can use the `SELECT` statement with the view, but all `INSERT`, `UPDATE`, and `DELETE` statements are rejected.

Another security option available in views is to allow access to certain non-sensitive columns of a table and restrict access to the more sensitive data in the same table. This is accomplished by leaving out those columns when creating the view. You will see an example of this option later in the chapter.

- **To hide data complexity:** You can create a view by including columns from the same table, different tables, or even different tables that reside in different databases. The remote database access is accomplished through the use of database links. Users could specify each component in their queries, making for a long and complicated statement. If a database view were created, however, the query would appear as though it was reading data from a single table.
- **To present data in a different way:** When creating a database view, you can define how names of the columns appear, making them different from the original column names, if you like. The default is to keep the same name, but in many cases, especially when creating a view from multiple table sources, you should changes the names to make the view appear more like a single table than a collection of semi-related columns.
- **To reduce maintenance on applications:** Often, when changing the structure of a database table, the applications that access that table need to be checked and recoded if necessary. When using database views, however, this is usually unnecessary because the changes to the base table would be hidden from the view. At most, you would need to recompile only the view.

Different Types of Views

Aside from the basic view that is created with a single `AS SELECT` clause, the following types of views are available to you:

- **Join view:** A *join view* uses more than one table or view in the `FROM` clause in the `CREATE VIEW` statement. You are restricted when creating a join view in that the query creating the view cannot contain any of the following clauses: `DISTINCT`, `AGGREGATION`, `GROUP BY`, `START WITH`, `CONNECT BY`, `ROWNUM`, or any set operators.
- **Updatable join view:** An *updatable join view* must follow the same rules as a regular join view, plus additional rules that involve changing the data in the base tables from the view. The general rule specifies that you can modify only one base table at a time with any `INSERT`, `UPDATE`, or `DELETE` statement specifying a view in the `FROM` clause. These additional rules are covered later in the chapter when you create a sample updatable join view.
- **Partition view:** A *partition view* is composed of a group of individual tables, partitioned from the original master table, that are linked in the view. The individual

tables have their own unique indexes, which helps database performance when performing queries on the partition view.

- **Object view:** In Oracle, with the objects option installed, you can create a view that is composed of Oracle object types (BLOB, CLOB, REF, and so on). With object views, you can also create views of relational data that you can manipulate as though it were object-oriented data.

View Features and Restrictions

In this section you take a quick look at the features and restrictions of using database views.

Privileges

To create a database view in an Oracle database, you need the `CREATE VIEW` system privilege. To create a view in a schema other than your own, you need the `CREATE ANY VIEW` system privilege. You create views in other schemas by specifying the schema name and the view name, separated by a period, in the `CREATE VIEW` command.

Updating Rows Through the View

In some cases you can update the rows in the base tables from the database view. The section "Join Views" later in this chapter covers the requirements for doing this. In all cases, the owner of the view needs access to the base tables to perform `SELECT`, `INSERT`, `UPDATE`, and `DELETE` operations. If this access is not granted, then those operations error out.

A view is inherently updatable if it can be inserted, updated, or deleted without using `INSTEAD OF` triggers and if it conforms to the following restrictions:

- No set operators
- No group functions
- No `GROUP BY`, `CONNECT BY`, or `START WITH` clauses
- No use of the `DISTINCT` operator
- No table joins (a subset of join views is updatable, though)

On the other hand, if the view query contains any of these restrictions, it is not inherently updatable, so you can perform `INSERT`, `UPDATE`, and `DELETE` operations on the view only through `INSTEAD OF` triggers.

ROWID Selection (Oracle Specific)

You can select on the ROWID pseudocolumn from a join view, given that there is one and only one key-preserved table in the join. The ROWID of that table then becomes the ROWID of the view.

The CREATE VIEW Command

Now that you know the different types of views that you can create in SQL Server and Oracle, let's take a look at the command that makes it all happen: the CREATE VIEW command. The basic form of the command (with no optional clauses specified) is as follows:

```
CREATE VIEW view_name AS SELECT columns FROM base_tablename;
```

This example would create a simple view composed of a subset of the columns that are part of the base table.

Note

The example views created in this chapter were created using Oracle. Although the SQL commands will work with Oracle or SQL Server, the output of the SQL commands may be slightly different when using SQL Server than what appears in the chapter text.

CREATE VIEW Syntax

The *view name* parameter of the CREATE VIEW command specifies the name of the view as it will be stored in the database. You can specify the name alone, or the schema name (owner) and view name separated by a period.

The AS SELECT clause creates the subquery that will actually create the view. It is the rows selected from this query that populate the view.

There are quite a few optional clauses. Table 14.1 lists them, and they are explained in the section that follows.

TABLE 14.1 CREATE VIEW Command Optional Clauses

Name	*Description*
OR REPLACE	You can use CREATE or CREATE OR REPLACE to create the view.
FORCE	Does not do any checking on the tables specified as the base tables.
NO FORCE	Creates the view only if the base tables exist and are accessible.

TABLE 14.1 `CREATE VIEW` Command Optional Clauses

Name	*Description*
`alias`	Uses an alias to change the name of a column as it appears in the view.
`OF`	Used when creating object views.
`WITH OBJECT OID`	Used when creating object views.
`DEFAULT`	Used when creating object views.
`WITH READ ONLY`	Disallows any changes to the base tables through the view.
`WITH CHECK OPTION`	Specifies the types of updates that can be made through the view.
`CONSTRAINT`	Used with the `CHECK_OPTION` clause.
`WITH ENCRYPTION`	Encrypts text of query that created view. (SQL Server only)

OR REPLACE

You have two options when it comes to the `CREATE VIEW` command itself. When creating a new view, you can use either the `CREATE VIEW` or `CREATE OR REPLACE VIEW` command. The `CREATE VIEW` command creates a new view as specified, but errors out if the view already exists. When using `CREATE OR REPLACE`, the view is created whether the view already exists or not. If the view does exist already, the view is overwritten and re-created.

It might be a good habit to use `CREATE OR REPLACE VIEW` for all view creations, so that you never get the error stating that the view already exists. Be careful, however, that you don't end up accidentally overwriting someone else's view that uses the same name you picked.

FORCE

The `FORCE` clause tells the `CREATE VIEW` command not to do any checking on the base tables specified in the command. The view is created regardless of whether the base tables exist or whether the view has read access to the base tables. Even though the view exists, you can't do any operations on it, even `SELECT`, until the base tables exist and are accessible by the view.

NO FORCE

The `NO FORCE` clause is rarely used in `CREATE VIEW` statements because it is the default. By specifying `NO FORCE` (or not specifying `FORCE`), the `CREATE VIEW` command checks whether the base tables in the view exist and whether the view can perform the specified operations on the base tables. If either of those checks fails, the view is not created and the `CREATE VIEW` command returns an error.

Alias

You couldn't really call the alias element of the `CREATE VIEW` command a clause. It is specified after any or all column names that appear in the `FROM` clause of the subquery that defines the view. The alias changes how the column is named in the view. The default is to use the same name as the base table; you use the alias to customize the view's column names.

This method is useful when your view is composed of columns from different tables (a join view). It is unlikely that the names of different columns would look like they were from the same table in the view. By using an alias, you can fix this.

OF

The `OF` clause is used when creating views of *object* types. An object, in Oracle, is a user-defined type. Objects contain columns and attributes as database tables do. When creating a view of an object type, the columns of the view are derived from the object's attributes or the columns of the relational tables.

WITH OBJECT OID

The `WITH OBJECT OID` clause specifies the attributes of the object type to be used as the key in the object view. Usually these attributes are defined as the primary key columns of the view's base table.

DEFAULT

The `DEFAULT` clause is also used when creating an object view. It specifies that the intrinsic object identifier of the base object table or object view is used to uniquely identify each row in the view.

WITH READ ONLY

You use the `WITH READ ONLY` clause to prevent any changes to the base tables through the view. This is a great security feature. `INSERT`, `UPDATE`, and `DELETE` operations on the rows in the view aren't performed and return an error if you attempt them.

WITH CHECK OPTION

The `WITH CHECK OPTION` clause is interesting. It guarantees that any `INSERT` or `UPDATE` operations on the view data result in a row that can be queried from the view. For example, suppose you created a view of the employee table and included employees with a base salary between $20,000 and $30,000. Let's also suppose you allow changes of the base table through the view. If you add or update a row in the view, you can specify a salary only between $20,000 and $30,000. Any other value is not part of the view data set, and the operation is rejected.

CONSTRAINT

The CONSTRAINT clause assigns a name to the CHECK OPTION constraint discussed previously. All constraints have names in the Oracle database. If you specify CHECK OPTION and leave out the CONSTRAINT clause, Oracle generates a unique constraint name of the form *SYS_Cn*; *n* is a sequence number. This constraint name is stored in the database.

WITH ENCRYPTION

The WITH ENCRYPTION clause is specific to SQL Server and is used as a security device. If you specify the WITH ENCRYPTION clause in your CREATE VIEW command, then the SQL command that created the view will be encrypted when it is stored in the *syscomments* system table.

> **Note**
>
> Not all the clauses listed here will work on both Oracle and SQL Server. Of the clauses listed above, the OR REPLACE, FORCE, NO FORCE, CONSTRAINT, WITH READ ONLY, and all the clauses relating to objects are specific to Oracle.
>
> The WITH ENCRYPTION clause is specific to SQL Server and has no counterpart in the Oracle Server.

Preparations Before Creating Your Views

Let's get right into the "how to" part of the chapter and start by discussing everything you need to know to be able to create some of the types of views discussed in this chapter's opening section.

For these examples, you are going to use the demo tables available with the Oracle database. Oracle supplies a script with its database software that creates tables it uses as examples throughout Oracle's documentation. If you are using Oracle, all you need to do to create these tables in your own schema is to execute the demobld.sql script in the sqlplus/demo directory under ORACLE_HOME.

So that non-Oracle readers are not left out in the cold, the table definitions and descriptions for the sample employee tables are included here:

```
SQL> describe bonus;
 Name                              Null?    Type
 -------------------------------- -------- ----
 ENAME                                      VARCHAR2(10)
```

```
 JOB                                       VARCHAR2(9)
 SAL                                       NUMBER
 COMM                                      NUMBER
SQL> describe dept;
 Name                           Null?    Type
 ------------------------------ -------- ----
 DEPTNO                                  NUMBER(2)
 DNAME                                   VARCHAR2(14)
 LOC                                     VARCHAR2(13)
SQL> describe emp;
 Name                           Null?    Type
 ------------------------------ -------- ----
 EMPNO                          NOT NULL NUMBER(4)
 ENAME                                   VARCHAR2(10)
 JOB                                     VARCHAR2(9)
 MGR                                     NUMBER(4)
 HIREDATE                                DATE
 SAL                                     NUMBER(7,2)
 COMM                                    NUMBER(7,2)
 DEPTNO                                  NUMBER(2)
SQL> describe salgrade;
 Name                           Null?    Type
 ------------------------------ -------- ----
 GRADE                                   NUMBER
 LOSAL                                   NUMBER
 HISAL                                   NUMBER
```

Tables 14.2 through 14.5 describe each of the fields in these sample tables.

TABLE 14.2 BONUS Table Column Descriptions

Column Name	*Description*
ENAME	Employee name
JOB	Job title
SAL	Salary
COMM	Commission rate

TABLE 14.3 DEPT Table Column Descriptions

Column Name	*Description*
DEPTNO	Department number
DNAME	Name of the department (such as Data Processing)
LOC	City in which the department is located

TABLE 14.4 EMP Table Column Descriptions

Column Name	*Description*
EMPNO	Employee's ID number
ENAME	Employee's last name
JOB	Employee's job title
MGR	ID number of employee's boss
HIREDATE	First day on the job
SAL	Monthly salary
COMM	Sales commission rate
DEPTNO	ID number of department in which the employee works

TABLE 14.5 SALGRADE Table Column Descriptions

Column Name	*Description*
GRADE	Salary grade level
LOSAL	Low end of the grade's salary range
HISAL	High end of the grade's salary range

All you have to do is create the table as specified in the definitions and populate the tables with a few rows.

Creating Some Simple Views

For starters, let's create some very simple views. Create a database view called EMP_VIEW_LOWSAL that's composed of all employees with a salary less than $2,000 per month:

```
SQL> CREATE OR REPLACE VIEW EMP_VIEW_LOWSAL
 2> AS SELECT * FROM EMP
 3> WHERE SAL < 2000;
```

```
View created.
```

Use the DESCRIBEcommand to show all the columns available in the view. It should be the same as the column names in the EMP table.

```
SQL> describe EMP_VIEW_LOWSAL
 Name                              Null?    Type
 ------------------------------ -------- ----
 EMPNO                             NOT NULL NUMBER(4)
 ENAME                                      VARCHAR2(10)
 JOB                                        VARCHAR2(9)
 MGR                                        NUMBER(4)
 HIREDATE                                   DATE
 SAL                                        NUMBER(7,2)
```

```
COMM                                               NUMBER(7,2)
DEPTNO                                             NUMBER(2)
```

Now let's write a query to print out the employee numbers, names, and salaries that are stored in the view:

```
SQL> SELECT EMPNO, ENAME, SAL FROM EMP_VIEW_LOWSAL;

    EMPNO  ENAME             SAL
---------- ---------- ----------
     7369  SMITH             800
     7499  ALLEN            1600
     7521  WARD             1250
     7654  MARTIN           1250
     7844  TURNER           1500
     7876  ADAMS            1100
     7900  JAMES             950
     7934  MILLER           1300

8 rows selected.
```

Since all you are concerned with is the employee's number, name, and salary, change the view so that those are the only columns available:

```
SQL> CREATE OR REPLACE VIEW EMP_VIEW_LOWSAL
  2 AS SELECT EMPNO, ENAME, SAL FROM EMP
  3 WHERE SAL < 2000;

View created.
```

Verify that the three columns are the only ones available by using the DESCRIBE command:

```
SQL> DESCRIBE EMP_VIEW_LOWSAL;
 Name                            Null?    Type
 ------------------------------- -------- ----
 EMPNO                           NOT NULL NUMBER(4)
 ENAME                                    VARCHAR2(10)
 SAL                                      NUMBER(7,2)
```

14
Creating and Using Views

Take a look at the rows in the view by using the SELECT statement:

```
SQL> SELECT * FROM EMP_VIEW_LOWSAL;
    EMPNO  ENAME             SAL
---------- ---------- ----------
     7369  SMITH             800
     7499  ALLEN            1600
     7521  WARD             1250
```

```
    7654     MARTIN            1250
    7844     TURNER            1500
    7876     ADAMS             1100
    7900     JAMES              950
    7934     MILLER            1300

8 rows selected.
```

As you can see, there is no access to the other columns of the EMP table. This is a good example of one of the row access restriction security options discussed earlier in this chapter.

For the next example, use two *aliases* to change the name of the ENAME and SAL columns as they appear in the view. In the view, the ENAME column will be called NAME, and the SAL column will be called SALARY.

```
SQL> CREATE OR REPLACE VIEW EMP_VIEW_LOWSAL
 2 AS SELECT EMPNO ID_NUMBER, ENAME NAME, SAL SALARY
 3 FROM EMP
 4 WHERE SAL < 2000;

View created.
```

To see the changed column names, use DESCRIBE with the new view:

```
SQL> DESCRIBE EMP_VIEW_LOWSAL;
 Name                           Null?    Type
 ------------------------------ -------- ----
 ID_NUMBER                      NOT NULL NUMBER(4)
 NAME                                    VARCHAR2(10)
 SALARY                                  NUMBER(7,2)
```

When doing INSERTS, UPDATES, and DELETES from the view, you use the column names listed here, not the column names in the base table.

Creating Read Only and Constrained Views

Now that you can create some basic views, let's get a little creative and start exploring what the optional clauses can do for you. First, re-create the EMP_VIEW_LOWSAL view that you saw in the previous section, this time making it read

```
SQL> CREATE OR REPLACE VIEW EMP_VIEW_LOWSAL
 2 AS SELECT EMPNO ID_NUMBER, ENAME NAME, SAL SALARY
 3 FROM EMP
 4 WHERE SAL < 2000
 5 WITH READ ONLY;
```

```
View created.
```

The view that was just created does not allow INSERT, UPDATE, or DELETE operations. Let's test that right now with three SQL statements:

```
SQL> INSERT INTO EMP_VIEW_LOWSAL
 2 VALUES (1234, 'JOE', 2050);
INSERT INTO EMP_VIEW_LOWSAL
*
ERROR at line 1:
ORA-01733: virtual column not allowed here

SQL> DELETE FROM EMP_VIEW_LOWSAL
 2 WHERE NAME='JONES';
DELETE FROM EMP_VIEW_LOWSAL
*
ERROR at line 1:
ORA-01733: virtual column not allowed here

SQL> UPDATE EMP_VIEW_LOWSAL
 2* SET SALARY = 9999
SET SALARY = 9999
  *
ERROR at line 2:
ORA-01733: virtual column not allowed here
```

That is how read-only views work. Now take a look at the WITH CHECK OPTION clause. By creating a new view with this clause specified, you can use INSERT, UPDATE, and DELETE from the view, as long as the salary value is below $2,000. Take a look at these examples:

```
SQL> CREATE OR REPLACE VIEW EMP_VIEW_LOWSAL
 2 AS SELECT EMPNO ID_NUMBER, ENAME NAME, SAL SALARY
 3 FROM EMP
 4 WHERE SAL < 2000
 5 WITH CHECK OPTION
 6 CONSTRAINT LOWSAL;

View created.

SQL> INSERT INTO EMP_VIEW_LOWSAL
 2 VALUES (2345,'DUER',1750);

1 row created.

SQL> UPDATE EMP_VIEW_LOWSAL
```

```
 2 SET SALARY = 1800
 3 WHERE NAME = 'DUER';

1 row updated.

SQL> UPDATE EMP_VIEW_LOWSAL
 2 SET SALARY = 2500
 3 WHERE NAME='DUER';
UPDATE EMP_VIEW_LOWSAL
    *
ERROR at line 1:
ORA-01402: view WITH CHECK OPTION where-clause violation

SQL> INSERT INTO EMP_VIEW_LOWSAL
 2 VALUES (2346,'DUER2',3000);

INSERT INTO EMP_VIEW_LOWSAL
       *
ERROR at line 1:
ORA-01402: view WITH CHECK OPTION where-clause violation
SQL> DELETE FROM EMP_VIEW_LOWSAL
 2 WHERE NAME='DUER';
1 row deleted.
```

As you can see from these sample queries, you were able to add a new record for DUER that had a salary value of 1750. You were then able to update it to change to 1800. When you tried to update it to 2500, the constraint was violated and the row was not changed. Then you tried to insert a new employee with a salary that was out of range for the view. That INSERT operation was not allowed.

Join Views

A *join view* is a database view that contains a table join within the subquery that defines the view. In English, this means that a join view contains columns from multiple tables.

For the sample join view called EMP_VIEW_FULL, you will create a new view composed of columns from the EMP and DEPT tables:

```
CREATE OR REPLACE VIEW EMP_VIEW_FULL AS
    SELECT e.empno, e.ename, e.job, d.dname, d.loc, e.sal
     FROM emp e, dept d
     WHERE e.deptno = d.deptno;
```

This database view allows the user to print out the more descriptive columns of the two tables—for example, the full department name rather than the department number, and the location (city) that the employee works in. Take a look at this query of the EMP_VIEW_FULL view:

```
SQL> SELECT EMPNO ''ID Number'', ENAME ''Name'',
 2 JOB ''Title'', DNAME ''Department'', LOC ''City'',
 3 SAL ''Salary''
 4 FROM EMP_VIEW_FULL;

ID Number  Name       Title     Department     City          Salary
---------- ---------- --------- -------------- ------------- ----------
   7782    CLARK      MANAGER   ACCOUNTING     NEW YORK            2450
   7839    KING       PRESIDENT ACCOUNTING     NEW YORK            5000
   7934    MILLER     CLERK     ACCOUNTING     NEW YORK            1300
   7369    SMITH      CLERK     RESEARCH       DALLAS               800
   7876    ADAMS      CLERK     RESEARCH       DALLAS              1100
   7902    FORD       ANALYST   RESEARCH       DALLAS              3000
   7788    SCOTT      ANALYST   RESEARCH       DALLAS              3000
   7566    JONES      MANAGER   RESEARCH       DALLAS              2975
   7499    ALLEN      SALESMAN  SALES          CHICAGO             1600
   7698    BLAKE      MANAGER   SALES          CHICAGO             2850
   7654    MARTIN     SALESMAN  SALES          CHICAGO             1250

 ID Number Name       Title     Department     City          Salary
---------- ---------- --------- -------------- ------------- ----------
   7900    JAMES      CLERK     SALES          CHICAGO              950
   7844    TURNER     SALESMAN  SALES          CHICAGO             1500
   7521    WARD       SALESMAN  SALES          CHICAGO             1250

14 rows selected.
```

Notice that the SQL query used aliases to bypass the view's column names, which produces a much nicer-looking report. You could have used the aliases when creating the view, but the ID number would have had to be ID_NUMBER and the column names would have all been displayed in uppercase.

In terms of being to modify the rows in the join view, the following rule applies: If at least one column in the subquery join has a unique index, then it might be possible to modify one base table in a join view. You can query the USER_UPDATABLE_COLUMNS table to see whether the columns in a join view are updatable, as shown in the following example:

```
SQL> SELECT COLUMN_NAME, UPDATABLE
 2 FROM USER_UPDATABLE_COLUMNS
```

```
 3 WHERE TABLE_NAME='EMP_VIEW_FULL';

COLUMN_NAME                    UPD
------------------------------ ---
EMPNO                          NO
ENAME                          NO
JOB                            NO
DNAME                          NO
LOC                            NO
SAL                            NO

6 rows selected.
```

From the query's output, it's obvious that you can only use `SELECT` on the view. `INSERT`, `UPDATE`, and `DELETE` operations do not work. Any changes to the rows that appear in the view must be done through the base tables.

After creating a unique index on the `DEPTNO` column of the `DEPT` table, the output from `USER_UPDATABLE_COLUMNS` changes:

```
SQL> SELECT COLUMN_NAME, UPDATABLE
 2 FROM USER_UPDATABLE_COLUMNS
 3 WHERE TABLE_NAME='EMP_VIEW_FULL';

COLUMN_NAME                    UPD
------------------------------ ---
EMPNO                          YES
ENAME                          YES
JOB                            YES
DNAME                          NO
LOC                            NO
SAL                            YES

6 rows selected.
```

Now you can insert, update, and delete rows as well as use `SELECT` from the `EMP_VIEW_FULL` view.

Partition Views

A *partition view* is composed of several tables that behave as a single table. Partition views are generally created for performance reasons. They were introduced into Oracle in version 7.3, but are looked at as obsolete because the data partitioning option that Oracle offers has replaced it. For those of you who don't use Oracle version 8 or don't have the partitioning option (it's expensive!), let's discuss how partition views work.

To create a partition view, you first have to split up your data into multiple tables based on a constraint value. For example, EMP1 contains employees with salaries from $0 to $1,000, EMP2 contains employees with salaries from $1,001 to $2,000, and so on. You should also add constraints to each table with the salary ranges.

When all the tables are created, you then need to create a unique index on each of the tables. Create the index on the constrained column (salary) of your tables.

Next, use the CREATE VIEW command to create the view, specifying multiple SELECT statements as your subquery and adding the UNION ALL clause. Listing 14.1 shows PARTITIONVIEW.SQL, a script that creates the base tables and indexes needed before you can create the partition view.

LISTING 14.1 PARTITIONVIEW.SQL—How to Create the Tables and Indexes for a Partition View

```
DROP TABLE EMP1;
DROP TABLE EMP2;
DROP TABLE EMP3;
DROP TABLE EMP4;
DROP TABLE EMP5;

CREATE TABLE EMP1 AS
SELECT * FROM EMP
WHERE EMPNO >= 0
AND EMPNO < 1000;

CREATE TABLE EMP2 AS
SELECT * FROM EMP
WHERE EMPNO >=1000
AND EMPNO < 2000;

CREATE TABLE EMP3 AS
SELECT * FROM EMP
WHERE EMPNO >= 2000
AND EMPNO < 3000;

CREATE TABLE EMP4 AS
SELECT * FROM EMP
WHERE EMPNO >= 3000
AND EMPNO < 4000;
```

LISTING 14.1 CONTINUED

```
CREATE TABLE EMP5 AS
SELECT * FROM EMP
WHERE EMPNO >= 4000
AND EMPNO <= 9999;

ALTER TABLE EMP1 ADD CONSTRAINT
C1 CHECK (SAL >=0 AND SAL < 1000);

ALTER TABLE EMP2 ADD CONSTRAINT
C1 CHECK (SAL >=1000 AND SAL < 2000);

ALTER TABLE EMP3 ADD CONSTRAINT
C1 CHECK (SAL >=2000 AND SAL < 3000);

ALTER TABLE EMP4 ADD CONSTRAINT
C1 CHECK (SAL >=3000 AND SAL < 4000);

ALTER TABLE EMP5 ADD CONSTRAINT
C1 CHECK (SAL >=4000 AND SAL <= 9999);

CREATE UNIQUE INDEX
EMP1_INDEX
ON EMP1 (EMPNO ASC);

CREATE UNIQUE INDEX
EMP2_INDEX
ON EMP2 (EMPNO ASC);

CREATE UNIQUE INDEX
EMP3_INDEX
ON EMP3 (EMPNO ASC);

CREATE UNIQUE INDEX
EMP4_INDEX
ON EMP4 (EMPNO ASC);

CREATE UNIQUE INDEX
EMP5_INDEX
ON EMP5 (EMPNO ASC);
```

Now all you need to do is bring them together with the `CREATE VIEW` command:

```
SQL> CREATE OR REPLACE VIEW EMPVIEW AS
2 SELECT * FROM EMP1 UNION ALL
3 SELECT * FROM EMP2 UNION ALL
4 SELECT * FROM EMP3 UNION ALL
5 SELECT * FROM EMP4 UNION ALL
6 SELECT * FROM EMP5;
View created.
```

As I mentioned earlier, partition views are created for performance reasons, more often than not. Here are the features of partition views:

- You can overlap partitions.
- Each table in the view has its own index.
- The partition tables can be scanned in parallel (parallel query and multiple CPUs required).
- Partitions that do not meet the specification of a SQL statement are not scanned.
- The underlying tables cannot be updated through the view.
- Partition tables work best on DSS (decision-support systems), rather than on transaction-based OLTP systems.

In Oracle version 8, you would create a partition table, rather than a view. Oracle8 still supports partition views, however.

Object Views

An *object view* simulates a user-defined object type. You use the `CREATE TYPE` command (Oracle objects option required) to create the object base type. Then you create the view with the special clauses `OF` and `WITH OBJECT OID`:

```
CREATE TYPE employee_t AS OBJECT
 ( empno    NUMBER(4),
  ename    VARCHAR2(20),
  job      VARCHAR2(9),
  mgr      NUMBER(4),
  hiredate  DATE,
  sal      NUMBER(7,2),
  comm     NUMBER(7,2) );

CREATE OR REPLACE VIEW emp_object_view OF employee_t
 WITH OBJECT OID (empno)
```

```
AS SELECT empno, ename, job, mgr, hiredate, sal, comm
  FROM emp;
```

In the previous example, the SELECT AS clause was replaced by the OF clause. The OF clause specifies that the view being created is going to be a view of an object type. In the WITH OBJECT OID clause, you specify the attribute of the object that will be used to uniquely identify each row in the object. This is usually defined as the primary key columns of the base table.

If you do not include the WITH OBJECT OID clause, Oracle uses a default, which is an internal object identifier, to identify the object's individual rows.

Using FORCE to Create Views

Sometimes you might want to create a database view that includes objects that don't exist yet. For example, you could have a particular table and view that are constantly being dropped and re-created. At times, the base tables are not there when the view is created.

Normally, the CREATE VIEW command would return an error and the view would not be created. However, you do have the option of adding the FORCE clause to the CREATE VIEW command in this situation. This option tells Oracle to create the view without checking for the existence of the base tables. Instead of returning an error, Oracle creates the view and returns a warning that there were compilation errors creating the view. Let's try it now and take a look at what happens.

First, create a view called SPORTS that includes all columns and rows from the BASEBALL table. The BASEBALL table does not exist, so the CREATE VIEW command errors out:

```
SQL> CREATE OR REPLACE VIEW SPORTS
 2 AS
 3 SELECT * FROM BASEBALL;

SELECT * FROM BASEBALL
              *
ERROR at line 3:
ORA-00942: table or view does not exist
```

Now try to create the same database view, using the FORCE clause:

```
SQL> CREATE OR REPLACE FORCE VIEW SPORTS
 2 AS
 3 SELECT * FROM BASEBALL;
Warning: View created with compilation errors.
```

Trying to select on this view returns an error, as shown:

```
SQL> SELECT * FROM SPORTS
 2 ;
SELECT * FROM SPORTS
       *
ERROR at line 1:
ORA-04063: view ''JDUER.SPORTS'' has errors
```

You can also see from the USER_OBJECTS database table that the view is invalid:

```
SQL> COLUMN OBJECT_NAME FORMAT A25
SQL> SELECT OBJECT_TYPE, OBJECT_NAME, STATUS
 2 FROM USER_OBJECTS
 3 WHERE OBJECT_NAME='SPORTS';

OBJECT_TYPE     OBJECT_NAME               STATUS
--------------- ------------------------- -------
VIEW            SPORTS                    INVALID
```

To resolve the problem, all you need to do is create the BASEBALL table and recompile the view with the ALTER VIEW COMPILE command. You do not need to drop and re-create the view.

Views on Tables That Reside on Different Systems

The last type of database view you will look at is a view composed of columns from databases residing on different systems. Creating this type of view is not complicated. The only new thing you need to know is how to link the two databases so that you can create the view. To link two databases, you use the CREATE DATABASE LINK command.

Suppose that the EMP table was on the remote system called carpathia.joeduer.com in a database named jdbase and a schema named EMP_SCHEMA. You would create the database link with this command:

```
CREATE DATABASE LINK JDBASE_LINK
  CONNECT TO EMP_SCHEMA IDENTIFIED BY BASEBALL
  USING JDBASE_SERV;
```

In the previous example, jdbase_serv is a Net8 service name that points to the jdbase instance on host carpathia.joeduer.com.

Creating the database view is actually rather simple after you have the database link created. Here is one of the previous examples modified to use the database link to create the view:

```
CREATE OR REPLACE VIEW EMP_VIEW_FULL AS
    SELECT e.empno, e.ename, e.job, d.dname, d.loc, e.sal
     FROM emp@jdbase_link e, dept@jdbase_link d
     WHERE e.deptno = d.deptno;
```

The view will have the same access and restrictions as though the base tables were in the local database. This type of view is a good example of complexity hiding. You can use the DESCRIBE and SELECT commands to look at the view structure and rows, and you would never know that the actual tables are in a remote database.

```
SQL> DESCRIBE EMP_VIEW_FULL
Name                                Null?    Type
 ----------------------------- -------- ----
 EMPNO                              NOT NULL NUMBER(4)
 ENAME                                       VARCHAR2(10)
 JOB                                         VARCHAR2(9)
 DNAME                                       VARCHAR2(14)
 LOC                                         VARCHAR2(13)
 SAL                                         NUMBER(7,2)
SQL> SELECT COUNT(*) FROM EMP_VIEW_FULL;
 COUNT(*)
----------
    14
```

Altering and Dropping Database Views

Along with the CREATE VIEW command, which you have learned quite a bit about, there are two other commands you need to be familiar with when dealing with database views.

Suppose you create a database view and someone drops one of the base tables that composed the view. The view would become invalid. Even if the base table was re-created, you would need to recompile the view to make it usable again.

The ALTER VIEW command exists for this purpose. Before you look at that, query the USER_OBJECTS table (Oracle only) to see if any invalid views are currently in the schema:

```
SQL> COLUMN OBJECT_NAME FORMAT A15
SQL> SELECT OBJECT_TYPE, OBJECT_NAME, STATUS
 2 FROM USER_OBJECTS
 3 WHERE OBJECT_TYPE ='VIEW';
OBJECT_TYPE      OBJECT_NAME      STATUS
--------------- --------------- -------
```

```
VIEW            ED              VALID
VIEW            EMPVIEW         VALID
VIEW            EMP_VIEW        INVALID
VIEW            EMP_VIEW_FULL   VALID
VIEW            EMP_VIEW_LOWSAL VALID
VIEW            JOE             VALID
6 rows selected.
```

As you can see in the previous example, the `EMP_VIEW` view has a status of `INVALID`. To recompile this view, simply use the `ALTER VIEW` statement as shown here:

```
SQL> ALTER VIEW EMP_VIEW COMPILE;

View altered.
```

Now query `USER_OBJECTS` again and look at the status:

```
SQL> SELECT OBJECT_TYPE, OBJECT_NAME, STATUS
 2 FROM USER_OBJECTS
 3 WHERE OBJECT_TYPE ='VIEW';

OBJECT_TYPE     OBJECT_NAME     STATUS
--------------- --------------- -------
VIEW            ED              VALID
VIEW            EMPVIEW         VALID
VIEW            EMP_VIEW        VALID
VIEW            EMP_VIEW_FULL   VALID
VIEW            EMP_VIEW_LOWSAL VALID
VIEW            JOE             VALID
6 rows selected.
```

If you want, you can get view information from the `USER_VIEWS` table. This available information is shown in the following `DESCRIBE` command:

```
SQL> DESCRIBE USER_VIEWS;
 Name                              Null?    Type
 ------------------------------ -------- ----
 VIEW_NAME                         NOT NULL VARCHAR2(30)
 TEXT_LENGTH                                NUMBER
 TEXT                                       LONG
 TYPE_TEXT_LENGTH                           NUMBER
 TYPE_TEXT                                  VARCHAR2(4000)
 OID_TEXT_LENGTH                            NUMBER
 OID_TEXT                                   VARCHAR2(4000)
 VIEW_TYPE_OWNER                            VARCHAR2(30)
 VIEW_TYPE                                  VARCHAR2(30)
```

Only the first three columns apply to views that do not involve object types. Let's take a look at the contents of that table now:

```
SQL> SELECT VIEW_NAME, TEXT_LENGTH, TEXT FROM USER_VIEWS;
VIEW_NAME       TEXT_LENGTH TEXT
--------------- ----------- ----------------------------------------
ED                       94 SELECT e.empno, e.ename, d.deptno, d.loc
                            FROM emp e, dept d
                            WHERE e.deptn
EMPVIEW                 430 select ''EMPNO'',"ENAME'',"JOB'',"MGR'',"HIRE

                            DATE'',"SAL'',"COMM'',"DEPTNO'' from EMP1 UN
EMP_VIEW                 92 SELECT ''EMPNO'',"ENAME'',"JOB'',"MGR'',"HIRE

                            DATE'',"SAL'',"COMM'',"DEPTNO'' FROM EMP
                            WIT
VIEW_NAME       TEXT_LENGTH TEXT
--------------- ----------- ----------------------------------------
EMP_VIEW_FULL           118 SELECT e.empno, e.ename, e.job, d.dname,
                              d.loc, e.sal
                                       FROM emp e, dept
EMP_VIEW_LOWSAL          91 SELECT EMPNO ID_NUMBER, ENAME NAME, SAL
                            SALARY
                            FROM EMP
                            WHERE SAL < 2000
                            WITH CH
VIEW_NAME       TEXT_LENGTH TEXT
--------------- ----------- ----------------------------------------
JOE                      77 SELECT ''EMPNO'',"ENAME'',"JOB'',"MGR'',"HIRE

                            DATE'',"SAL'',"COMM'',"DEPTNO'' FROM EMP
6 rows selected.
```

As you can see, all that's stored for the database view is essentially the text of the query that created it.

If you want to delete a view completely, use the `DROP VIEW` command. Its syntax is simple. All you need to do is specify the view name:

```
SQL> DROP VIEW EMPVIEW;
View dropped.
```

The `DROP VIEW` command does not alter or drop any of the base tables. It simply removes the view definition from the data dictionary.

Summary

In this chapter you were introduced to database views. You learned that database views did not contain any physical data; they simply pointed to the selected rows that reside in the view's base tables. You learned about the different types of views that you can create: join views, partition views, and object views. You also learned what it takes to be able to update the base tables through the view.

You learned that database views have many potential uses and are a useful tool in database and application design.

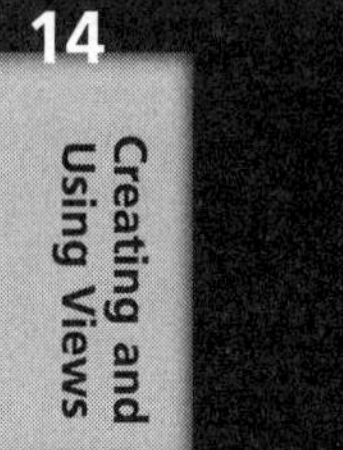
14
Creating and
Using Views

CHAPTER 15

Trees and Hierarchies

In This Chapter

In Chapter 13, "Subqueries," you learned about correlated subqueries by working with a recursive table, `lawyer2`, which includes a column named `boss` that refers back to the ID column in the same table. The information you retrieved from this table was everyone who did or did not have reports, or to join the table with itself so that information about the boss could be retrieved.

These queries, then, were limited to two levels—a boss and a working bee—without considering that many bosses in turn work for another boss.

The purpose of the queries in this chapter is to retrieve information about the entire set of relationships, which is commonly referred to as a *tree*.

Tables Joined to Themselves: Recursive Joins and *N*-Level Queries

A *hierarchical table* contains a column that references another column in the same table. An example is `lawyer2`, whose `boss` column references its own ID column.

```
describe lawyer2
```

This SQL statement returns the following:

```
Name                              Null?    Type
 -------------------------------- -------- ----
 ID                               NOT NULL NUMBER(2)
 BOSS                                      NUMBER(2)
 NAME                                      VARCHAR2(15)
 OFFICE                                    VARCHAR2(15)
 BHRS                                      NUMBER(4)
 BGROSS                                    NUMBER(7)
```

Note

Throughout this chapter, Oracle's SQL utility, SQL*Plus, is used. Although almost all of the SQL works in any ANSI-compliant database, I use the Oracle formatting to make the output easy to read. You will notice formatting lines similar to the following code:

```
set pagesize 40

break on idb skip 1
```

```
clear columns

column rate format 999.99 heading 'Hourly¦ Rate'

column avrate format 999.99 heading 'Average¦Hourly Rate'
```

The table used in this chapter is created with the `crlawyer2.sql` script included on the CD-ROM.

Two-Level Queries

Using the reference of the `boss` column to the `id` column and an outer join with an `nvl` function allows you to retrieve the worker-bee information on the left side of the vertical bar and the boss information on the right, as shown in Listing 15.1.

LISTING 15.1 Two-Level Query

```
set pagesize 40
break on idb skip 1

select
  w.id,
  w.name bee_name,
  w.office,
  '¦',
  b.id idb,
  nvl(b.name,'  NOBODY') boss_name,
  b.office
from
  lawyer2 w,
  lawyer2 b
where nvl(w.boss,-9) = b.id (+)
order by w.boss
;

clear columns
clear breaks
set pagesize 24
```

This code returns the following:

```
ID BEE_NAME   OFFICE      ' IDB BOSS_NAME  OFFICE
--- --------- ----------- - --- ---------- -----------
10 Greene     Boston      ¦  1  Dewey      Boston
11 Cardinal   Boston      ¦     Dewey      Boston
6  Roll       Los Angeles ¦  3  Howe       Los Angeles
4  Clayton    Houston     ¦  5  Roach      Houston
12 Chandler   Los Angeles ¦  6  Roll       Los Angeles
3  Howe       Los Angeles ¦  7  Easton     Los Angeles
9  Frankie    New York    ¦     Easton     Los Angeles
17 Miller     Los Angeles ¦     Easton     Los Angeles
20 Paul       Boston      ¦     Easton     Los Angeles
5  Roach      Houston     ¦     Easton     Los Angeles
2  Cheetham   New York    ¦  8  Bonin      New York
8  Bonin      New York    ¦  9  Frankie    New York
14 Earl       New York    ¦     Frankie    New York
15 Wright     Boston      ¦ 10  Greene     Boston
16 Chabot     New York    ¦ 14  Earl       New York
19 Chatham    New York    ¦     Earl       New York
18 Ming       Los Angeles ¦ 17  Miller     Los Angeles
13 Martinez   Los Angeles ¦ 18  Ming       Los Angeles
1  Dewey      Boston      ¦ 20  Paul       Boston
7  Easton     Los Angeles ¦     NOBODY

20 rows selected.
```

By using aggregate functions, you could create similar queries to return information such as the number of direct reports.

N-Level Queries

If you want to have more than two levels in your query, each level has to be covered with its own query, as Listing 15.2 shows. It runs a three-level query first, and then a four-level query.

LISTING 15.2 Display Contents of `lawyer2` Table Three-Level Query

```
column id    format 99
column idb    format 99
column office  format a11
column bee_name format a10
column low_manag format a10
column mid_manag format a10
column boss_name format a10
```

LISTING 15.2 CONTINUED

```
set pagesize 40
break on idb skip 1

select
  w.id,
  w.name bee_name,
  '¦',
  m.id,
  nvl(m.name,'  NOBODY') mid_manag,
  '¦',
  b.id idb,
  nvl(b.name,'  NOBODY') boss_name
from
  lawyer2 w,
  lawyer2 m,
  lawyer2 b
where nvl(w.boss,-9) = m.id (+) and
   nvl(m.boss,-9) = b.id (+)
order by
  m.boss,
  w.boss
;
```

The three-level query returns the following:

```
 ID BEE_NAME   ' ID  MID_MANAG  ' IDB BOSS_NAME
--- ---------- - --- ---------- - --- ----------
 15 Wright     ¦ 10  Greene     ¦  1  Dewey
 12 Chandler   ¦ 6   Roll       ¦  3  Howe
 6  Roll       ¦ 3   Howe       ¦  7  Easton
 4  Clayton    ¦ 5   Roach      ¦     Easton
 8  Bonin      ¦ 9   Frankie    ¦     Easton
 14 Earl       ¦ 9   Frankie    ¦     Easton
 18 Ming       ¦ 17  Miller     ¦     Easton
 1  Dewey      ¦ 20  Paul       ¦     Easton
 2  Cheetham   ¦ 8   Bonin      ¦  9  Frankie
 16 Chabot     ¦ 14  Earl       ¦     Frankie
 19 Chatham    ¦ 14  Earl       ¦     Frankie
 13 Martinez   ¦ 18  Ming       ¦ 17  Miller
 10 Greene     ¦ 1   Dewey      ¦ 20  Paul
 11 Cardinal   ¦ 1   Dewey      ¦     Paul
```

```
3   Howe      ¦ 7   Easton    ¦        NOBODY
17  Miller    ¦ 7   Easton    ¦        NOBODY
20  Paul      ¦ 7   Easton    ¦        NOBODY
5   Roach     ¦ 7   Easton    ¦        NOBODY
9  Frankie    ¦ 7   Easton    ¦        NOBODY
7  Easton     ¦     NOBODY    ¦        NOBODY

20 rows selected.
```

The next part, in Listing 15.3, extends the statement to four levels:

LISTING 15.3 Display Contents of `lawyer2` Table Four-Level Query

```
select
  w.id,
  w.name bee_name,
  '¦',
  l.id,
  nvl(l.name,'  NOBODY') low_manag,
  '¦',
  m.id,
  nvl(m.name,'  NOBODY') mid_manag,
  '¦',
  b.id idb,
  nvl(b.name,'  NOBODY') boss_name
from
  lawyer2 w,
  lawyer2 l,
  lawyer2 m,
  lawyer2 b
where nvl(w.boss,-9) = l.id (+) and
   nvl(l.boss,-9) = m.id (+) and
   nvl(m.boss,-9) = b.id (+)
order by
  m.boss,
  l.boss,
  w.boss
;
clear columns
clear breaks
set pagesize 24
```

It returns the following:

```
ID BEE_NAME   ¦ ID  LOW_MANAG  ¦ ID  MID_MANAG  ¦ IDB BOSS_NAME
--- --------- - --- ---------- - --- ---------- - --- ---------
12 Chandler   ¦ 6   Roll       ¦ 3   Howe       ¦ 7   Easton
2  Cheetham   ¦ 8   Bonin      ¦ 9   Frankie    ¦     Easton
16 Chabot     ¦ 14  Earl       ¦ 9   Frankie    ¦     Easton
19 Chatham    ¦ 14  Earl       ¦ 9   Frankie    ¦     Easton
13 Martinez   ¦ 18  Ming       ¦ 17  Miller     ¦     Easton
10 Greene     ¦ 1   Dewey      ¦ 20  Paul       ¦     Easton
11 Cardinal   ¦ 1   Dewey      ¦ 20  Paul       ¦     Easton
15 Wright     ¦ 10  Greene     ¦ 1   Dewey      ¦ 20  Paul
6  Roll       ¦ 3   Howe       ¦ 7   Easton     ¦     NOBODY
4  Clayton    ¦ 5   Roach      ¦ 7   Easton     ¦     NOBODY
8  Bonin      ¦ 9   Frankie    ¦ 7   Easton     ¦     NOBODY
14 Earl       ¦ 9   Frankie    ¦ 7   Easton     ¦     NOBODY
18 Ming       ¦ 17  Miller     ¦ 7   Easton     ¦     NOBODY
1  Dewey      ¦ 20  Paul       ¦ 7   Easton     ¦     NOBODY
3  Howe       ¦ 7   Easton     ¦     NOBODY     ¦     NOBODY
20 Paul       ¦ 7   Easton     ¦     NOBODY     ¦     NOBODY
17 Miller     ¦ 7   Easton     ¦     NOBODY     ¦     NOBODY
5  Roach      ¦ 7   Easton     ¦     NOBODY     ¦     NOBODY
9  Frankie    ¦ 7   Easton     ¦     NOBODY     ¦     NOBODY
7  Easton     ¦     NOBODY     ¦     NOBODY     ¦     NOBODY

20 rows selected.
```

Two more levels could be performed: The first one would show `NOBODY` as Easton's boss in the first seven rows and `Easton` as Paul's boss in row 8. The last level would show `NOBODY` as Easton's boss in row 8 as well as in the first seven rows.

The Hierarchical SELECT Statement: Using CONNECT BY PRIOR and START WITH

Oracle has its own approach to tree queries, using the keywords `CONNECT BY PRIOR` and `START WITH`. They allow you to retrieve the entire tree structure in one query. The chapter works mostly with that approach.

Whereas the *n*-level queries in the previous section list the bosses and superbosses of all employees of a table side by side, the hierarchical `SELECT` statement is used to answer similar questions with a slightly different tack:

- Who are the people who report to a person, or to anyone reporting to that person?
- Who are the people to whom a person reports and the people to whom those people report?

In other words, a hierarchical query allows you to choose one node in the hierarchy and to select from that node, up or down, to identify the entire subtree to which this node belongs.

The `CONNECT BY PRIOR` keyword replaces the join condition. In contrast to the join condition, the order of the columns following this keyword matter because they direct the query to go either upward or downward from the node identified with the `START WITH` keyword. Listing 15.4 first selects Greene, with the employee ID 10, and all people to whom he reports. Then it selects Greene and all people who report to him. The difference is that in the first case, the condition after `prior` is listed as `boss = id`; in the second, it is `id = boss`.

LISTING 15.4 Display Contents of `lawyer2` Table Hierarchical Query

```
column id    format 99
column office  format a11
column name   format a10
column boss   format 99
set pagesize 40

select
  id,
  name,
  office,
  boss
from
  lawyer2
connect by prior boss = id
start with id=10
;

select
  id,
  name,
  office,
  boss
from
  lawyer2
connect by prior id = boss
start with id=10
```

LISTING 15.4 CONTINUED

```
;

clear columns
clear breaks
set pagesize 24
```

It returns the following:

```
ID NAME        OFFICE      BOSS
--- --------- ---------- ----
10 Greene      Boston      1
1  Dewey       Boston      20
20 Paul        Boston      7
7  Easton      Los Angeles

ID NAME        OFFICE      BOSS
--- --------- ---------- ----
10 Greene      Boston      1
15 Wright      Boston      10
```

Level of a Node in the Hierarchy: The `level` Pseudocolumn

The `level` pseudocolumn returns the level of a node relative to the node listed after `START WITH`, which gets level 1. Every step away from that node adds 1 to `level`. The query starts with lawyer number 20, which leads to different rows being returned; for example, all subtrees reporting to Paul are now listed as shown in Listing 15.5.

LISTING 15.5 Hierarchical Query Displaying Levels

```
column id    format 99
column office  format a11
column name   format a10
column boss   format 99
set pagesize 40

select
  level,
  id,
  name,
  office,
  boss
```

LISTING 15.5 CONTINUED

```
from
  lawyer2
connect by prior boss = id
start with id=20;
select
  level,
  id,
  name,
  office,
  boss
from
  lawyer2
connect by prior id = boss
start with id=20
;

clear columns
clear breaks
set pagesize 24
```

The code returns this:

```
  LEVEL   ID  NAME       OFFICE      BOSS
--------- --- ---------- ----------- ----
    1     20  Paul       Boston      7
    2     7   Easton     Los Angeles

  LEVEL   ID  NAME       OFFICE      BOSS
--------- --- ---------- ----------- ----
    1     20  Paul       Boston      7
    2     1   Dewey      Boston      20
    3     10  Greene     Boston      1
    4     15  Wright     Boston      10
    3     11  Cardinal   Boston      1
```

A second subtree, consisting of Cardinal (who reports to Dewey), is now included.

Formatting Hierarchical Reports Using `lpad`

The `lpad` function usually has three arguments:

- The string to be padded.

- The display length of the output in characters.
- The *padset*, which is a string that's repeated by the function until it reaches the specified display length. If this argument is omitted, a single blank is used as the default.

By using a calculated length that depends on `level` as the second argument, indentations by level can be created. The following examples in Listing 15.6 use this approach.

LISTING 15.6 Display Contents of `lawyer2` Table Hierachical Query Displaying Levels

```
column id    format 99
column office  format a11
column name   format a10
column boss   format 99
column distance format a15
set pagesize 40

select
  lpad(level-1,level*4-3,'===>') distance,
  id,
  name,
  office,
  boss
from
  lawyer2
connect by prior boss = id
start with id=20
;

select
  lpad(level-1,level*4-3,'===>') distance,
  id,
  name,
  office,
  boss
from
  lawyer2
connect by prior id = boss
start with id=20
;

clear columns
```

LISTING 15.6 CONTINUED

```
clear breaks
set pagesize 24
```

The code returns this:

```
DISTANCE        ID  NAME       OFFICE      BOSS
--------------- --- ---------- ----------- ----
0               20  Paul       Boston      7
===>1           7   Easton     Los Angeles

DISTANCE        ID  NAME       OFFICE      BOSS
--------------- --- ---------- ----------- ----
0               20  Paul       Boston      7
===>1           1   Dewey      Boston      20
===>===>2       10  Greene     Boston      1
===>===>===>3   15  Wright     Boston      10
===>===>2       11  Cardinal   Boston      1
```

The same trick can be used to create a stylized organizational chart that indents names according to reporting relationship and then lists level and office, as shown in Listing 15.7.

LISTING 15.7 Display Stylized Organizational Chart

```
column office   format a11
column fake_chart format a35
column level   format 99 heading 'LV'
set pagesize 40

select
  lpad(' ',(level-1)*4) || name FAKE_CHART,
  level,
  office
from
  lawyer2
connect by prior id = boss
start with boss is NULL
;

clear columns
clear breaks
set pagesize 24
```

This query returns the following:

```
FAKE_CHART                          LV  OFFICE
----------------------------------- --- ----------
Easton                              1   Los Angeles
  Howe                              2   Los Angeles
    Roll                            3   Los Angeles
      Chandler                      4   Los Angeles
  Roach                             2   Houston
    Clayton                         3   Houston
  Frankie                           2   New York
    Bonin                           3   New York
      Cheetham                      4   New York
    Earl                            3   New York
      Chabot                        4   New York
      Chatham                       4   New York
  Miller                            2   Los Angeles
    Ming                            3   Los Angeles
      Martinez                      4   Los Angeles
  Paul                              2   Boston
    Dewey                           3   Boston
      Greene                        4   Boston
        Wright                      5   Boston
      Cardinal                      4   Boston

20 rows selected.
```

The name `fake_chart` is chosen to indicate that an organizational tree is usually represented in a graphically more pleasing fashion. On the other hand, retrieving the whole tree in a graphic approximation is actually a handy feature.

The output of a hierarchical query can be ordered by using an `ORDER BY` subclause.

Caution

According to relational theory, the ordering of rows in a database, and generally in output, is in no way facilitated or guaranteed. A hierarchical subquery with levels and indenting expresses meaning with the ordering of the rows, in particular that a node dependent on another node is indented in a row after the row it depends on, but before the next node on which it does not depend. Reordering might destroy that relationship.

In the lawyer2 table, the reporting lines are consistent with office lines. It is, therefore, possible to order the output by office and then by level, which then produces organizational charts per office (see Listing 15.8).

LISTING 15.8 Display Stylized Organization Chart Order by Office

```
column office   format a11
column fake_chart format a35
column level   format 99 heading 'LV'
column boss    format 99 heading 'BS'
column id     format 99

set pagesize 40
break on office skip 1

select
  office,
  lpad(' ',(level-1)*4) || name FAKE_CHART,
  level,
  id,
  boss
from
  lawyer2
connect by prior id = boss
start with boss is NULL
order by office, level
;

clear columns
clear breaks
set pagesize 24
```

This script returns the following:

```
OFFICE      FAKE_CHART                          LV  ID  BS
----------- ----------------------------------- --- --- ---
Boston      Paul                                2   20  7
            Dewey                               3   1   20
            Greene                              4   10  1
            Cardinal                            4   11  1
            Wright                              5   15  10
Houston     Roach                               2   5   7
            Clayton                             3   4   5
```

```
Los Angeles Easton                      1   7
            Howe                        2   3   7
            Miller                      2   17  7
            Roll                        3   6   3
            Ming                        3   18  17
            Chandler                    4   12  6
            Martinez                    4   13  18
New York    Frankie                     2   9   7
            Bonin                       3   8   9
            Earl                        3   14  9
            Cheetham                    4   2   8
            Chabot                      4   16  14
            Chatham                     4   19  14
```

Tip

If you reorder the output as shown here, always display the columns that establish the relationship—in this case, `boss` and `id`. The top line of each office reports to 7, or Easton. This indicates that the reordering has not compromised the information of levels and ordering.

Eliminating Branches: Using `CONNECT BY PRIOR...AND`

The examples so far have presented two possibilities:

- Displaying the entire tree
- Displaying a subtree

There are two more options for the partial representation of trees—eliminating whole branches, which is done by adding a second condition to the `CONNECT BY PRIOR` subclause, and eliminating single rows, which is done with a `WHERE` subclause.

[ic:cd] The `CONNECT BY PRIOR` subclause enables using logical and conditional operators beyond the join condition. In particular, combined with an `AND`, it can be used to include entire branches in the output or exclude them from it. You can use the previous example, which is already ordered by office, to demonstrate this. The first query retrieves the East Coast offices, and the second query, the South(west)ern ones. Because everyone knows that Easton is the big boss, he will be eliminated from the query altogether, and the level indentations will be adjusted accordingly. A SQL script that will accomplish this task is provided in Listing 15.9.

LISTING 15.9 Using the CONNECT BY PRIOR Clause to Eliminate Branches

```
column office   format a11
column fake_chart format a35
column level   format 99 heading 'LV'
column boss    format 99 heading 'BS'
column id     format 99

set pagesize 40
break on office skip 1

select
  office,
  lpad(' ',(level-2)*4) || name FAKE_CHART,
  level,
  id,
  boss
from
  lawyer2
where name <> 'Easton'
connect by prior id = boss and
    office in ('Los Angeles','Houston')
start with boss is NULL
order by office, level
;

select
  office,
  lpad(' ',(level-2)*4) || name FAKE_CHART,
  level,
  id,
  boss
from
  lawyer2
where name <> 'Easton'
connect by prior id = boss and
    office not in ('Los Angeles','Houston')
start with boss is NULL
order by office, level
;
```

LISTING 15.9 CONTINUED

```
clear columns
clear breaks
set pagesize 24
```

This query returns the following:

```
OFFICE      FAKE_CHART                         LV  ID  BS
----------- ---------------------------------- --- --- ---
Houston     Roach                              2   5   7
            Clayton                            3   4   5
Los Angeles Howe                               2   3   7
            Miller                             2   17  7
            Roll                               3   6   3
            Ming                               3   18  17
            Chandler                           4   12  6
            Martinez                           4   13  18

8 rows selected.

OFFICE      FAKE_CHART                         LV  ID  BS
----------- ---------------------------------- --- --- ---
Boston      Paul                               2   20  7
            Dewey                              3   1   20
            Greene                             4   10  1
            Cardinal                           4   11  1
            Wright                             5   15  10
New York    Frankie                            2   9   7
            Bonin                              3   8   9
            Earl                               3   14  9
            Cheetham                           4   2   8
            Chabot                             4   16  14
            Chatham                            4   19  14

11 rows selected.
```

Summary

The purpose of hierarchical queries is to retrieve information about the entire set of relationships, which is commonly referred to as a *tree*.

Queries of two or more levels can be performed through one or more outer joins with `nvl` functions, which allows you to retrieve the information about a node as well as information about the nodes above it. With this approach, however, each level has to be covered with its own query.

Hierarchical queries, on the other hand, allow you to choose a node and to retrieve all information pertaining to a subtree above or below that node. Hierarchical queries in Oracle use the keywords `CONNECT BY PRIOR` and `START WITH`. The `CONNECT BY PRIOR` keywords replace the join condition. Depending on the order of the columns, the query is directed either upward or downward from the node identified with the `START WITH` keywords.

Another useful feature of hierarchical subqueries is the `level` pseudocolumn, which indicates the level in the subtree, starting with 1 for the node listed after `START WITH`. You can use this to create indentations using the `lpad` function by passing a calculated length that depends on the level as the second argument into `lpad`.

The output of a hierarchical query can be ordered by using an `ORDER BY` subclause. This, however, might destroy the inherent meaning of the rows' order.

Finally, whole subtrees can be eliminated through a second condition added to the `CONNECT BY PRIOR` subclause. Single nodes/rows can be omitted through a `WHERE` subclause.

CHAPTER 16

Dynamic SQL

In This Chapter

What Is Dynamic SQL?

Dynamic SQL has the means to execute a batch of SQL statements at runtime on the database server. The SQL statements composing the call are parsed and executed by the database engine at runtime. The dynamic SQL statements are not embedded in the client application; rather, they are generated by the application at runtime. This allows the client application to be more flexible and add generic functionality. For example, dynamic SQL can be used to write an application that builds ad hoc `SELECT` statements for tables in the database based on the parameters supplied by the user. This application can build the `WHERE` clause for the `SELECT` statement based on the user's input, and by using industry-standard data access APIs, such as ODBC, the application can work against a variety of data sources. Dynamic SQL statements can be processed using various methods by the database engine. It can be broadly classified into two categories:

- Client-side programming constructs—The commands necessary to execute the dynamic SQL statements on the database are coded in the client side.
- Server-side programming constructs—The client sends the dynamic SQL statement to the server and the statements are processed using server commands. The dynamic SQL can also be built entirely on the server side and executed.

Dynamic SQL statements are usually processed in two stages:

- `PREPARE`—The database engine parses the statements. The statements are checked for syntax errors, the objects referred to in the statements are validated, database access rights are checked, and the execution strategy is determined.
- `EXECUTE`—The client supplies values for any input parameters to the dynamic SQL. The database engine then executes the actual statement.

For example, consider the following dynamic SQL statement that deletes an order from the `Orders` table:

```
Delete Orders Where Order_Number = ?
```

The question mark (`?`) is the parameter marker that acts as a holder for the input data. The parameter marker helps optimize the statement if it is executed multiple times with different values for the parameters. It also avoids having to prepare the dynamic SQL statement for each execution of the statement. In the `PREPARE` phase, the `DELETE` statement is checked for any syntax errors and the permissions for the client connection on the `Orders` table are checked. The client then uses the `EXECUTE` statement to execute the parsed statement. The syntax for the `PREPARE` and `EXECUTE` statements are as follows:

```
EXEC SQL PREPARE <STATEMENT> FROM <VARIABLE>
```

```
EXEC SQL EXECUTE <STATEMENT> [USING <VARIABLE_LIST>]
```

STATEMENT is the name given to the prepared statement. VARIABLE contains the dynamic SQL statement that needs to be prepared by the database engine. It can be a literal string containing the dynamic SQL statement or a client variable that contains the statement. VARIABLE_LIST is one or more host variables that contain the values for any parameters specified in the dynamic SQL statement. The general syntax for using dynamic SQL statements is described in this chapter. The implementation specifics vary depending on the programming language being used to write the client application.

The dynamic SQL statement can be executed in a single step by using the EXECUTE IMMEDIATE statement, which is useful for statements typically run only once. A good candidate for using this command is any data definition statement, such as CREATE TABLE or DROP TABLE. In this case, the dynamic SQL statement is parsed and executed. The syntax of the EXECUTE IMMEDIATE statement is as follows:

```
EXEC SQL EXECUTE IMMEDIATE <VARIABLE>
```

VARIABLE contains the dynamic SQL statement to be executed. The dynamic SQL statement used in the EXECUTE IMMEDIATE method cannot contain any parameter markers or client variables.

Dynamic SQL statements that contain SELECT statement can be executed on the database engine by using a cursor. This method allows retrieving data from the database a row at a time. These are the statements used to perform this operation:

```
EXEC SQL PREPARE <STATEMENT> FROM <VARIABLE>
EXEC SQL DECLARE <CURSORNAME> CURSOR FOR <STATEMENT>
EXEC SQL OPEN <CURSORNAME> [USING <VARIABLE_LIST>]
EXEC SQL FETCH <CURSORNAME> INTO <VARIABLE_LIST>
EXEC SQL CLOSE <CURSORNAME>
```

The PREPARE statement prepares the SELECT statement specified in VARIABLE and gives it the name used in STATEMENT. The DECLARE statement defines the cursor by giving it the name determined in CURSORNAME and associates it with the specified statement. The OPEN statement allocates a server-side cursor, binds any variables specified in the VARIABLE_LIST, executes the query, and builds the resultset. The OPEN statement also positions the cursor on the first row of the resultset. The FETCH statement returns a row from the cursor and assigns the values of the columns returned to the variables supplied in the VARIABLE_LIST. The CLOSE statement frees all resources used by the cursor and closes it. All the methods discussed so far have one restriction: The fields that can be specified in a SELECT statement used in the dynamic SQL are fixed. These statements cannot be used to execute dynamic SQL statements that contain an unknown number of fields in the select list of the SELECT statement. Say you have a client application with a function that retrieves data from the table storing the employees' information. Based on user input, the field list can be different for the SELECT statement, as shown in Listing 16.1.

LISTING 16.1 LST16_1.TXT—Dynamic SQL Statements with a Variable Field List

```
SELECT First_Name, Last_Name, Salary FROM Employees
SELECT First_Name, Last_Name, Join_Date FROM Employees
SELECT First_Name, Last_Name, Job FROM Employees
```

In this scenario, because the field list is not known at design time, the PREPARE, EXECUTE, and DECLARE methods cannot be used. To execute dynamic SQL statements of this nature, the select list items and/or the parameter markers for the bind variables are stored in a structure called the *SQL Descriptor Area* (*SQLDA*). The SQLDA data structure defines the type of data to be passed from the database to the client, or vice versa. The DESCRIBE statement populates the SQLDA structure with information about the prepared statement. Its syntax is as follows:

```
EXEC DESCRIBE [SELECT LIST FOR] <STATEMENT> INTO <SQLDA>
EXEC DESCRIBE BIND VARIABLES FOR <STATEMENT> INTO <SQLDA>
```

The DESCRIBE SELECT LIST FOR statement processes the prepared statement specified in STATEMENT and populates the SQLDA structure determined by the variable <SQLDA > with the name, data type, constraints, length, scale, and precision of the fields in the SELECT statement. A select descriptor stores descriptions of select list items and the addresses of output buffers that hold the names and values of the fields in the SELECT statement. The DESCRIBE BIND VARIABLES FOR statement processes the statement for parameter markers and bind variables and populates the SQLDA structure. A bind descriptor stores descriptions of the parameter markers, bind variables, and addresses of the input buffer where the names and values of the parameter markers and bind variables are stored. The following sequence shows one way of executing a dynamic SQL statement that can contain an unknown number of fields and variables:

```
EXEC PREPARE <STATEMENT> FROM <VARIABLE>
EXEC DECLARE <CURSOR> FOR <STATEMENT>
EXEC DESCRIBE BIND VARIABLES FOR <STATEMENT> INTO <BIND_DA>
EXEC OPEN <CURSOR> USING DESCRIPTOR <BIND_DA>
EXEC DESCRIBE SELECT LIST FOR <STATEMENT> INTO <SQL_DA>
EXEC FETCH <CURSOR> USING DESCRIPTOR <SQL_DA>
EXEC CLOSE <CURSOR>
```

```
Or the sequence:
EXEC PREPARE <STATEMENT> FROM <VARIABLE>
EXEC DESCRIBE BIND VARIABLES FOR <STATEMENT> INTO <BIND_DA>
EXEC EXECUTE <STATEMENT> USING DESCRIPTOR <SQLDA>
```

Dynamic SQL, therefore, has methods for writing applications that give you more flexibility and improved functionality over static SQL. Dynamic SQL statements can be built interactively with input from users having little or no knowledge of SQL.

Most databases also have programming constructs on the server side for building and executing dynamic SQL statements. How they are used varies from vendor to vendor, but the general concept of processing dynamic SQL statements remains the same. The dynamic SQL statements are built as strings by stored procedures. The statement is then parsed and executed at runtime from the stored procedure, which enables programmers to create stored procedures that are more general. For example, a stored procedure for deleting all the foreign key constraints defined on a table can be written by using dynamic SQL. With this method, it is possible to write stored procedures that do not know which table they are going to operate on until runtime.

Where Can Dynamic SQL Be Used?

Dynamic SQL is used in applications that are more general-purpose and flexible. It is used when one of the following criteria is met:

- Portions of the SQL statement or its entire text is not known at design time or compilation time.
- References to database objects, such as tables, views, and columns, can change dynamically in the application, based on user input.
- You need to automate tasks that operate on certain objects. For example, dynamic SQL can be used to write an application that periodically gets a list of tables in a database and re-creates the indexes.
- You want to build applications that work against different data sources. For example, by using the ODBC syntax for SQL statements, an application can provide the functionality to query data from different databases.
- Applications such as reporting tools that use ad hoc queries can use dynamic SQL.

There are a few points to keep in mind while using dynamic SQL, though:

- Application code maintenance becomes an issue when using dynamic SQL. If a change is made to the database structure, the application has to be modified and retested.

- The capabilities of the database server cannot be used completely if an application is written to use dynamic SQL against different data sources.
- If the dynamic SQL statement is used to enforce business rules, it is preferable to move the code to a stored procedure.
- The dynamic SQL statements should not be used to implement larger and more complex statements. The bigger the dynamic SQL statements, the longer they take to get compiled by the database engine.

Now let's look at the implementation of dynamic SQL in Oracle and Microsoft SQL Server with specific examples.

Dynamic SQL in Oracle PL/SQL

Oracle supports dynamic SQL on the client side and server side. The client-side programming constructs are available through the `EXEC` commands, as discussed in the first section. In this section, let's look at how dynamic SQL statements can be executed on the database server from PL/SQL stored procedures. From PL/SQL V2.1, the `DBMS_SQL` system package can be used to execute dynamic SQL statements, stored procedures, and anonymous PL/SQL blocks. This gives the programmer the ability to process any data manipulation or data definition language statements. For executing dynamic SQL statements, take the following steps:

- Open a cursor on the server.
- Parse the string containing the dynamic SQL statement.
- Bind the variables required.
- Execute the dynamic SQL statement.
- Fetch a record from the result of the dynamic SQL statement.
- Close the cursor.

The `DBMS_SQL` package allows the programmer to work with arrays of data using the PL/SQL data type. This feature can be used to perform bulk selects, inserts, updates, and deletes that can considerably enhance the performance of applications. The `DBMS_SQL` package can execute a DML statement multiple times, each time with a different value for the variables. The `BIND_ARRAY` procedure allows you to bind an array of values, each of which is used as input per `EXECUTE` statement call. If the `DBMS_SQL` procedure is called from an anonymous PL/SQL block, the privileges of the connected user are used to execute the dynamic SQL statements. If the procedure is called from a stored procedure, then it is executed using the privileges of the stored procedure's owner. Therefore, if a user creates a procedure and grants EXECUTE privilege to another user, the second user must be granted privileges for all operations performed in the stored procedure. The flowchart in Figure 16.1 and Table 16.1 illustrate the series of steps required to parse and execute a dynamic SQL statement by using the DBMS_SQL procedures.

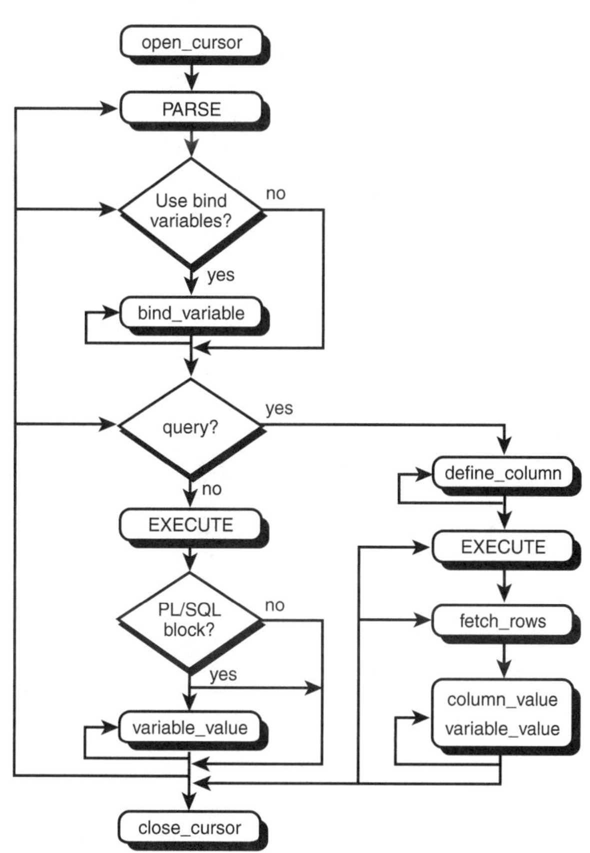

FIGURE 16.1
Illustration of DBMS_SQL *Flow (Taken from the Oracle Documentation).*

TABLE 16.1 DBMS_SQL Package Functions and Procedures

Function/Procedure	*Description*
OPEN_CURSOR	Opens a new cursor and returns the ID
PARSE	Parses the given statement
BIND_VARIABLE	Binds a value to a variable
DEFINE_COLUMN	Defines a column to be selected from the cursor
EXECUTE	Executes the cursor
EXECUTE_AND_FETCH	Executes the cursor and fetches rows
FETCH_ROWS	Fetches rows from the cursor

TABLE 16.1 DBMS_SQL Package Functions and Procedures

Function/Procedure	*Description*
COLUMN_VALUE	Returns the value of the column in the cursor
VARIABLE_VALUE	Returns the value of the variable for the cursor
IS_OPEN	Returns true if the cursor is open
DESCRIBE_COLUMNS	Describes the columns for the cursor
CLOSE_CURSOR	Closes the cursor and frees resources
LAST_ERROR_POSITION	Returns the position where the error occurred in the dynamic SQL statement
LAST_ROW_COUNT	Returns cumulative number of rows fetched from the cursor
LAST_ROW_ID	Returns the internal ROW_ID of the last processed row
LAST_SQL_FUNCTION_CODE	Returns the SQL function code for the dynamic SQL statement

Variations of the BIND_VARIABLE, DEFINE_COLUMN, COLUMN_VALUE, and VARIABLE_VALUE are supplied to handle the data types supported by Oracle.

Listing 16.2 is a simple PL/SQL procedure that uses dynamic SQL to drop the specified table.

LISTING 16.2 LST16_2.TXT—PL/SQL Stored Procedure with Dynamic SQL

```
Create Or Replace Procedure Drop_Table (Table_Name IN Varchar) AS
 Dyn_Cursor Integer;
Begin
 Dyn_Cursor := DBMS_SQL.OPEN_CURSOR;
 DBMS_SQL.PARSE(Dyn_Cursor, 'DROP TABLE ' ¦¦ Table_Name, DBMS_SQL.NATIVE);
 DBMS_SQL.CLOSE_CURSOR(Dyn_Cursor);
Exception
When Others Then
 DBMS_SQL.CLOSE_CURSOR(Dyn_Cursor);
End;
/
/* Call the Drop_Table procedure with a valid table name. */
Execute Drop_Table('Emp');
```

Data definition statements used in the dynamic SQL statements are executed at parse time. Hence, the call to the EXECUTE function of the DBMS_SQL package is not necessary here. The simple PARSE statement takes three parameters: the cursor name, the dynamic SQL statement, and a flag indicating how Oracle should handle the SQL statement. The flag takes the following values:

- V6 Oracle version 6 behavior
- V7 Oracle version 7 behavior
- NATIVE Normal behavior of the database the program is connected to

Additionally, the PARSE statement supplies parameters to parse strings larger than 32KB.

Now let's look at the example in Listing 16.3 that illustrates using the other DBMS_SQL functions.

LISTING 16.3 LST16_3.TXT—PL/SQL Stored Procedure with DBMS_SQL Functions

```
Create or Replace Procedure GetEmployeeName (Employee_Number IN Number) AS
 Dyn_Cursor Integer;
 Employee_Name Char(20);
 Row_Count Integer;
 Fetch_Status Integer;
Begin
 Dyn_Cursor := DBMS_SQL.OPEN_CURSOR;
 DBMS_SQL.PARSE(Dyn_Cursor, 'SELECT ename FROM emp WHERE empno = :empno',
DBMS_SQL.NATIVE);
 DBMS_SQL.BIND_VARIABLE(Dyn_Cursor, ':empno', Employee_Number);
 DBMS_SQL.DEFINE_COLUMN_CHAR(Dyn_Cursor, 1, Employee_Name, 20);
 Row_Count := DBMS_SQL.EXECUTE(Dyn_Cursor);
 Fetch_Status := DBMS_SQL.FETCH_ROWS(Dyn_cursor);
 DBMS_SQL.COLUMN_VALUE_CHAR(Dyn_Cursor, 1, Employee_Name);
 DBMS_SQL.CLOSE_CURSOR(Dyn_cursor);
 If Fetch_Status = 0 Then
   DBMS_OUTPUT.PUT_LINE('Unable to locate the employee number!');
 Else
   DBMS_OUTPUT.PUT_LINE('Employee name is '¦¦ Employee_Name);
 End If;
Exception
When Others Then
 DBMS_SQL.CLOSE_CURSOR(Dyn_Cursor);
End;
/
SET SERVEROUTPUT ON;
/* Call the GetEmployeeName procedure with a valid employee number. */
Execute GetEmployeeName(7369);
/* Output from the stored procedure is:
** Employee name is SMITH
*/
/* Call the GetEmployeeName procedure with an invalid employee number. */
```

LISTING 16.3 CONTINUED

```
Execute GetEmployeeName(2413);
/* Output from the stored procedure is:
** Unable to locate the employee number!
*/
```

The example uses dynamic SQL to build a `SELECT` statement that retrieves the name of the employee. If a dynamic SQL statement is used to process a query, the following extra steps must be followed:

- Use the `BIND_VARIABLE` function to bind values to the variables defined in the cursor
- Use the `DEFINE_COLUMN` function to define the variables that will contain the values returned by the `SELECT` statement
- Use the `EXECUTE` function to execute the `SELECT` statement
- Use `FETCH_ROWS` or `EXECUTE_AND_FETCH` to retrieve the rows
- Use the `COLUMN_VALUE` function to determine the value of a column retrieved by the `FETCH` statements

The `FETCH_ROWS` status returns a status value indicating the success of the `FETCH` operation. In the preceding stored procedure, the fetch status is checked after the operation, and the user is notified if the employee number was not found. The `DBMS_SQL` package, therefore, has programming constructs that can be used in PL/SQL stored procedures to execute SQL statements at runtime.

Dynamic SQL in Microsoft Transact-SQL

Microsoft SQL Server supports the client-side `EXEC` programming constructs discussed in the beginning of this chapter. The Transact-SQL programming language offers dynamic SQL functionality on the server side that can be used in stored procedures. At the database engine level, SQL Server has a feature called Automatic Parameterization. Most databases allow precompilation of code and storing the execution plan, such as compiling a stored procedure, for example. Precompiling is more efficient because it allows reuse of the execution plan. The execution plan allows the user to submit variables as parameters to the plan. Many applications, such as reporting tools that generate ad hoc queries, use dynamic SQL. SQL Server 7.0 implements a new feature, called *automatic parameters*, that caches a plan created for dynamic SQL, turning constants into parameters. The result is less compilation effort, providing many of the efficiencies of stored procedures, even for those applications that don't use stored procedures. Consider the ad hoc SELECT statements in the following example that are sent from a client application:

```
SELECT Title_Name, Author_Name FROM Books WHERE state = 'FL'
SELECT Title_Name, Author_Name FROM Books WHERE state = 'TN'
```

The values for the search on the state field can be specified as a parameter. The database engine builds the execution plan, taking this into account, and parameterizes the SELECT statement, as shown here:

```
SELECT Title_Name, Author_Name FROM Books WHERE state = ?State
```

This auto-parameterization improves performance because queries of the same type with different values will reuse the existing execution plan.

Transact-SQL supports two methods of building dynamic SQL statements at runtime in Transact-SQL scripts, stored procedures, and triggers:

- EXECUTE—a statement to execute a character string.
- sp_executesql—a system-stored procedure to execute a Unicode string. This procedure supports parameter substitution also.

The Transact-SQL batch shown in Listing 16.4 uses both methods to build a dynamic SQL statement and execute it.

LISTING 16.4 LST16_4.TXT—T-SQL Batch That Uses Dynamic SQL

```
Declare @Dynamic_SQL nVarchar(500), @State char(2)
Set @State = 'Fl'
Set @Dynamic_SQL = N'SELECT au_lname, au_fname FROM Authors ' +
CHAR(13)
Set @Dynamic_SQL = @Dynamic_SQL + 'WHERE state = ''' + @State + ''''
Execute(@Dynamic_SQL)
Go
Declare @Dynamic_SQL nVarchar(500)
Set @Dynamic_SQL = N'SELECT au_lname, au_fname FROM Authors ' +
CHAR(13)
Set @Dynamic_SQL = @Dynamic_SQL + 'WHERE state = @State'
Exec sp_executesql @Dynamic_SQL, N'@State Char(2)', @State = 'FL'
Go
```

When using the EXECUTE statement to execute the dynamic SQL statement, the entire statement has to be passed as a string. That means the parameters must be converted to string data type and concatenated appropriately with the dynamic SQL statement. If there are more parameters, then the complexity increases for the statements required to build the dynamic SQL string. The same dynamic SQL, using the `sp_executesql` system stored procedure, can be executed more efficiently and reused multiple times. Because the actual text of the Transact-SQL statement does not change between executions, the query optimizer reuses the existing plan.

Now let's look at using the `EXECUTE` statement in detail. Its syntax for executing a character string or stored procedure is as follows:

```
EXEC[UTE] (@Dynamic_SQL ¦ [N]'Transact-SQL String' + [+...n])
```

`@Dynamic_SQL` is the name of a local variable. The variable can be defined as `CHAR`, `VARCHAR`, `NCHAR`, or `NVARCHAR` data type. If the dynamic SQL statement is longer than 4,000 characters, multiple strings can be concatenated. A constant string can also be specified directly for execution. The Transact-SQL batch in Listing 16.5 builds a dynamic SQL statement by concatenating three strings to form a complete `SELECT` statement.

LISTING 16.5 `LST16_5.TXT`—Dynamic SQL Execution Using `EXECUTE` Statement

```
Declare @Select_Stmt nvarchar(255), @Where_Clause nvarchar(255), @State
char(2)
Set @Select_Stmt = 'SELECT au_lname, au_fname FROM authors '
Set @Where_Clause = 'WHERE State = '
Set @State = 'FL'
EXEC(@Select_Stmt + @Where_Clause + '''' + @State + '''')
Go
```

The permissions for any statement used in the `EXECUTE` string are checked at the time of execution only. The permissions are always checked in the context of the user executing the dynamic SQL statement. The `EXECUTE` statement can be used with a local variable to execute a stored procedure, as shown in Listing 16.6.

LISTING 16.6 `LST16_6.TXT`—`EXECUTE` Statement Example for Calling a Stored Procedure

```
Declare @Dyn_Proc varchar(128), @State char(2)
Set @Dyn_Proc = 'GetAuthorForState'
Set @State = 'FL'
Execute @Dyn_Proc @State
Go
```

The stored procedure name is supplied in a variable and evaluated at the time of execution only. The permissions for executing the stored procedure, the parameters, and other validations are also checked at the time of execution. If a `SET` statement is used in a dynamic SQL batch, it is valid only for the execution of the `EXECUTE` or the `sp_executesql` statement. The setting does not affect statements that follow the dynamic SQL statement. For example, the Transact-SQL batch in Listing 16.7 raises an error after the dynamic SQL statement is finished.

LISTING 16.7 LST16_7.TXT—EXECUTE Statement That Demonstrates Effect of Settings in Dynamic SQL

```
Use master
Go
Exec('Use pubs Select au_lname, au_fname From Authors')
/* The following SELECT statement raises an error because the database
context
** is reset to master after the dynamic SQL statement completes */
Select au_lname, au_fname From Authors
Go
```

Any variables declared outside the `EXEC` statement are not visible inside the dynamic SQL batch, and vice versa. But any setting before the `EXEC` statement can affect the dynamic SQL statements, including settings such as `SET TRANSACTION ISOLATION LEVEL`, `SET ANSI_DEFAULTS`, or `SET ROWCOUNT`. Any local temporary table created in the dynamic SQL statement gets destroyed after the `EXECUTE` statement is done.

The `sp_executesql` system stored procedure is used to execute a Transact-SQL statement or batch that has been built dynamically. This stored procedure also supports using embedded parameters in the dynamic SQL statements. The syntax of the `sp_executesql` system stored procedure is as follows:

```
Exec sp_executesql @stmt = SQL, [
   {, [@params =] N'@parameter_name data_type [,...n]' }
   {, [@param1 =] 'value1' [,...n] } ]
```

The first parameter `@stmt` is a Unicode string representing the Transact-SQL statement or batch. The string can be specified as a constant or a local variable. Character constants are not allowed. If a constant needs to be specified, it must be converted into a Unicode string by prefixing it with an `N`. The dynamic SQL statement can contain parameters with a variable name, as shown in this example:

```
Declare @Dyn_SQL nvarchar(255)
Set @Dyn_SQL = N'Select au_lname, au_fname From Authors Where au_fname Like
@First_Name'
```

The parameters specified this way in the SQL string must be passed in the `@params` parameter value and the parameter values list. The `@params` parameter is a string containing the definitions of all the parameters that have been embedded in the dynamic SQL string.

The string must be either a Unicode string or a variable that can be converted to Unicode. The parameter definition consists of the parameter name as specified in the dynamic SQL string and the data type. Additional parameter definitions can be included as needed. The `@param1` parameter is a value for the first parameter defined in the parameter definition list. The value can be a constant or another variable. Parameter values should be supplied for every parameter embedded in the dynamic SQL string. Additional parameter values can be supplied as needed. The `sp_executesql` procedure has the same behavior as `EXECUTE` regarding database contexts, scope of variables, and permission checks. The SQL string is compiled only when the `sp_executesql` statement is executed. The contents of the dynamic SQL string are compiled and an execution plan is generated. The `sp_executesql` stored procedure can be used instead of stored procedures to execute a Transact-SQL statement a number of times when the change in parameter values to the statement is the only variation. This increases performance because the query optimizer reuses the execution plan generated for the first execution.

Summary

Dynamic SQL statements in the client application and in the server give programmers the ability to build complex logic on-the-fly and make the application more flexible. The optimization techniques used by databases to execute dynamic SQL increases the performance of ad hoc queries that are used by a majority of client tools.

CHAPTER

Embedded SQL

In This Chapter

SQL is a unique language in that it can be used directly against database management systems for ad hoc queries. SQL can also be used through other programming languages for database access. Its dual nature resulted in great advantages for database and client/server application developers. The most important of these advantages is that developers can access databases more easily than ever by using SQL directly in their code or by making calls to an application programming interface (API) that facilitates access. Developers can also use integrated APIs with abstraction layers, such as ODBC and ADO, which take care of the connection and data transfer between the database and the client applications, allowing them to write their SQL code as though they are doing that interactively with the database server. Chapter 21, "Call Level Interface (CLI)," covers using APIs to access the database server. This chapter specifically deals with embedded SQL.

Concepts of Embedded SQL

Although SQL is a language, it cannot be considered a programming language. Standard SQL lacks the basic components of a good programming language, such as looping structures, conditions and other logic, or even variable and constant declarations. Different database vendors tried to extend SQL by adding these features to their SQL flavors, but even then, the resulting languages were strictly used for direct database access through stored procedures and triggers.

With embedded SQL, SQL statements are intermixed with statements written in the host programming language, referred to as *host language* from here on. Host language variables and constants can be used to construct the SQL statements and to get the results of the SQL statements. The host language uses special variables and functions to handle `NULL` values, allowing for insertion and retrieval of column values. The embedded SQL statements are submitted to a SQL precompiler that processes the statements before submitting them to the database engine. This precompiler takes a file with embedded SQL code and transforms it into pure host language (calling the native database API for the database operations). When the host language is C, the source file with embedded SQL conventionally has an .SQC extension.

First Look at an Embedded SQL Program

The possibilities and scenarios for using embedded SQL are endless. With embedded SQL you can retrieve records from a database based on criteria you establish in your code. You can also execute DML statements, such as inserting new records and updating or deleting existing records. Listing 17.1 shows a C program that uses embedded SQL to pass an employee ID to the database engine to retrieve other employee attributes, such as name, address, department, and phone number.

LISTING 17.1 Using Embedded SQL with the C Programming Language

```
main()
{
  exec sql include sqlca;
  exec sql begin declare section;
    int employee_id; /*employee id from user*/
    char name[30];    /*employee name*/
    char address[40];   /*employee address*/
    char city[20];    /*employee city*/
    char state[2];    /*employee state*/
    char phone_number[12] /*employee phone number*/
    char department[20]  /*employee department name*/
  exec sql end declare section;
  /*error handling*/
  exec sql whenever sqlerror goto q_error;
  exec sql whenever not found goto bad_id;
  /*prompt user for employee id*/
  printf(''Enter employee id: '');
  scanf(''%d'', &employee_id);
  /*run the embedded sql statement*/
  exec sql select name,
         address,
         city,
         state,
         phone_number,
         department_name
       from  employee, department
       where employee.department_id =
         department_department_id and
         employee.employee_id = :employee_id
       into  :name,
         :address,
         :city,
```

LISTING 17.1 CONTINUED

```
         :state,
         :phone_number
         :department;
  /*displaying the results*/
  printf(''Name: %s\n'') name);
  printf(''Address: %s\n'') address);
  printf(''City: %s\n'') city);
  printf(''State: %s\n'') state);
  printf(''Phone: %s\n'') phone_number);
  printf(''Department: %s\n'') department);
  exit();
  /*q_error error handler*/
  printf(''SQL error encountered: %ld\n'', sqlca.sqlcode);
  exit();
  /*bad_id error handler (no employee found with passed id)*/
  printf(''Employee ID not found. Make sure you pass a valid ID. \n'');
  exit();
}
```

Don't worry if you don't understand every statement in this example. By the end of this chapter, you should be able to. However, you might notice that the program is a mix of two languages: C and SQL. To understand it, you have to know both languages. You might also notice new statements specifically used with embedded SQL, such as the `WHENEVER` and `INTO` constructs. One more thing you might notice in Listing 17.1 is that the programming language variables are used within the SQL statement to store the returned values from the statement, and one variable was also used as an input in the `WHERE` clause.

Note

SQLCA stands for *SQL Communication Area* . This is a special data structure that contains error variables and status indicators. This structure helps the application learn the status of the SQL statement—success or failure. It also provides the application with the error code, if any, and the appropriate message. For more information on SLQCA and error handling, see the error handling section of this chapter.

How Does It Work?

Embedded SQL (*ESQL*), SQL-92 standard API for SQL database access, requires a two-step compilation process. The first step involves compiling the code without the SQL statements to an executable that is consistent with the host language format; the second step involves turning the SQL code into an execution plan stored in the database in a format consistent with that of the DBMS. These two steps are discussed in more detail:

- A special precompiler translates embedded SQL statements into commands in the programming language used to write the application. The generated statements are specific to the database that supplied the precompiler. Therefore, although the original source is generic to embedded SQL, the generated statements and the final executable file are specific to one database vendor.

Note

Precompilers are available for host languages, such as C, Pascal, FORTRAN, ADA, PL/I, RPG, and some assembly languages. A DBMS might have precompilers for only one or more of these languages. For example, Microsoft SQL Server has an embedded SQL precompiler for C programs. The SQL Server precompiler translates embedded SQL statements as calls to the appropriate DB-Library API functions, which are a group of functions that can be accessed from C or Microsoft Visual Basic to a limited extent.

- The precompiler produces two files as its output. One file has the host language program without the embedded SQL statements. The statements are substituted with DBMS-specific routines that supply the runtime link between the DBMS and the program. The second file has a copy of all SQL statements used in the host language program. This file is usually called the database request module.
- The source generated by the precompiler is then compiled using the compiler for the host language. This process produces the object code for the program.
- The linker then processes the object modules generated by the host language compiler, linking them with various library routines, including the DBMS-specific routines described previously. An executable is produced as a result of this step.
- A special `BIND` program processes the database request module described previously. The `BIND` program validates the SQL statements, parses, and optimizes them producing an execution plan for each of them.

As a result, the embedded SQL and source code are turned into two executable files: the executable for the host language code, excluding the SQL code, and an executable application plan stored in the database in a format understood by the DBMS.

Note

Embedded SQL has a simpler syntax than other database access abstraction tools, such as COM APIs, including OLE DB or Call-Level Interfaces such as ODBC. Therefore, it is easier to learn and program with embedded SQL. However, embedded SQL is less flexible than OLE DB or ODBC, in which well-written applications can switch from one database management system (DBMS) to another by simply switching drivers or providers. OLE DB and ODBC are also better at dealing with environments in which the SQL statements are not known when the application is compiled, such as when developing ad hoc query tools.

Figure 17.1 summarizes the steps needed to run a program with embedded SQL, illustrating the two-step compilation process.

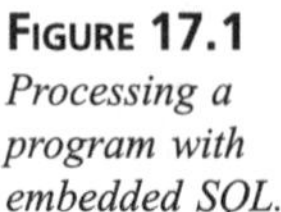

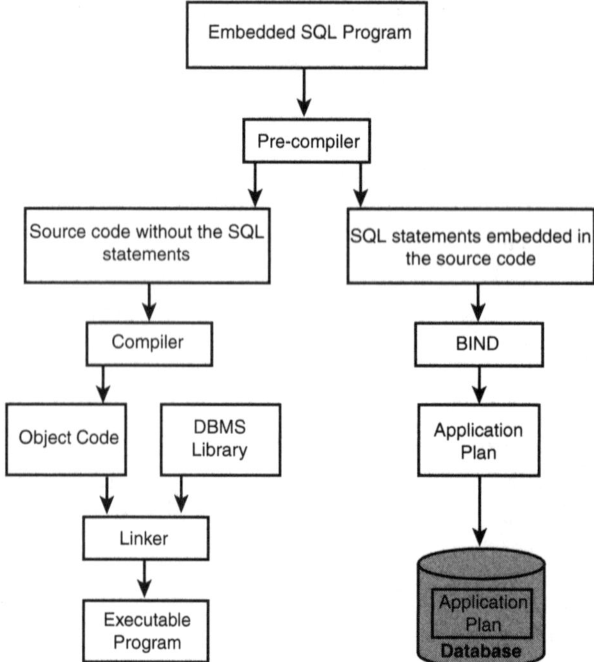

FIGURE 17.1
Processing a program with embedded SQL.

Embedded SQL Syntax and Statements

Embedded SQL is a mix of two languages: SQL and the host language. Therefore, the SQL-92 standard had to introduce special statements to make using embedded SQL as consistent among programming languages as possible. The general syntax for this mix usually follows that of the host language. This section discusses, with examples, the syntax of embedded SQL, error handling, and the statements introduced by the SQL-92 standard.

Embedded SQL Syntax

Because embedded SQL is a mix of SQL statements and the host language code, special considerations should be followed to make sure the syntax of the mix does not go bad. The following general rules apply when writing embedded SQL:

- Embedded SQL statements usually follow the host language requirements when it comes to their case (upper or lower).
- An embedded SQL statement is flagged at the beginning by an introducer, which can differ from one DBMS to another. However, the introducer `EXEC SQL` is adopted by the SQL-92 standard and supported by most DBMSs.
- Line continuation follows the host language rules. In `C`, for instance, a SQL statement can extend over multiple lines. A new line begins only after the line end (;) is encountered. In `FORTRAN`, a line continuation character `C` must be placed in the sixth column of the second and subsequent lines.
- SQL statements end with terminators, which flag the end of the SQL statement. This terminator differs according to the host language and usually follows the language's line ending scheme. For instance, in `C`, a terminator is the semicolon, and in FORTRAN, the terminator does not introduce any more line continuation characters.

Listing 17.2 shows a sample C program that has embedded SQL. The SQL deletes records in the `employee` table for employees who have been terminated. The code assumes that terminated employees will have a non-`NULL` value in the `termination_date` field of the `employee` table. For current employees, this value is `NULL`. The SQL used in the program is simple:

```
DELETE FROM employee
WHERE termination_date IS NOT NULL;
```

LISTING 17.2 Sample C Program with a Simple Embedded Sql Statement

```
main()
{
  exec sql include sqlca;
  exec sql declare employee table
        (employee_id integer not null,
         name varchar(30) not null,
         address varchar(50),
         city varchar(30),
         state varchar(2),
         zip varchar(11),
         phone_number varchar(12),
         hire_date date,
         termination_date char(12);
  /*Execute the SQL statement*/
  exec sql delete from employee
          where termination_date is not null;
  /*display message*/
  printf(''Deleted records..\n'');
  exit();
}
```

> **Note**
>
> Please note that in Listing 17.2, the DECLARE TABLE statement is an optional statement and is not executable. The reason it can be added is to help the precompiler parse the SQL statement faster and more easily. It can also serve for documentation purposes.

The same program shown in Listing 17.2 is presented in Listing 17.3 using FORTRAN instead of C. Notice how the general rules established previously for the embedded SQL syntax apply here.

LISTING 17.3 Sample FORTRAN Program with a Simple Embedded Sql Statement

```
PROGRAM SAMPLE
   EXEC SQL INCLUDE SQLCA
   EXEC SQL DECALRE EMPLOYEE TABLE
  C         (EMPLOYEE_ID INTEGER NOT NULL,
  C         NAME VARCHAR(30) NOT NULL,
```

LISTING 17.3 CONTINUED

```
  C         ADDRESS VARCHAR(50),
  C         CITY VARCHAR(30),
  C         STATE VARCHAR(2),
  C         ZIP VARCHAR(10),
  C         PHONE_NUMBER VARCHAR(11),
  C         HIRE_DATE DATE,
  C         TERMINATION_DATE DATE)
* Execute the SQL statement
   EXEC SQL DELETE FROM EMPLOYEE
  C         WHERE TERMINATION_DATE IS NOT NULL
* Display message
     WRITE(6,100) 'Records deleted...'
 100 FORMAT(' ', A40)
     RETURN
     END
```


Error Handling

Error handling in embedded SQL is the responsibility of the host application. Just like any programming code, embedded SQL statements can generate compile errors and runtime errors. Compile errors usually have to do with not using the right syntax, like missing the terminator character or the line continuation character. These errors are usually picked up by the precompiler and reported to the application when an attempt is made to compile it.

Runtime errors, on the other hand, can be linked to so many things, such as not having the security privileges to execute the SQL statement on the given table or database, not being able to connect to the database, not finding the table you are using in the database, and so forth. These errors are best handled by the application. The application should be written in such a way that it anticipates the errors and traps them and directs the execution to special error handlers.

Using `SQLCODE` for Error Handling

As mentioned earlier, the SQLCA data structure is used by the application to determine the success or failure of the embedded SQL statements. If an error is indicated, the application is directed to respond according to the error code. `SQLCODE` is the variable used internally within SQLCA to indicate the error code, if any. Although SQLCA can vary slightly from one DBMS implementation to another, this variable is common in most implementations.

Note

In Listings 17.1, 17.2, and 17.3, SQLCA was included at the beginning of the program. This tells the precompiler to include it with the compiled program. If you want to use the benefits of `SQLCODE`, you must include this data structure.

`SQLCODE` can have zero, positive, or negative values. These values indicate the seriousness of the errors as follows:

- A zero indicates that the SQL statement was executed successfully without errors or warnings.
- A positive value indicates a warning condition, such as truncating the results returned from the SQL statement.
- A negative value indicates a serious error that's preventing the SQL statement from executing. Each runtime error has a different value.

The general scheme for using `SQLCODE` in error handling is shown in Listing 17.4.

LISTING 17.4 A C Program Using the `SQLCODE` Variable in Error Handling

```
/*SQL statement goes here followed by the error check below*/
exec sql insert into table1
   values(val1, val2, ..);
If (sqlca.sqlcode < 0)
  goto error_handler;
...
...
...
error_handler:
  printf(''SQL Error: %ld\n, sqlca.sqlcode);
  exit();
...
...
...
```

Using SQLSTATE for Error Handling

The `SQLCODE` variable became popular among database management systems and was used in almost all of them by the time the SQL-92 standard came about. However, the implementation of this variable and the error numbers it represented varied widely among these DBMSs. Therefore, SQL-92 came up with a new variable intended to eventually replace the SQLCODE variable. This new variable was called SQLSTATE. DBMSs are now required to report errors in terms of both variables for backward compatibility and to conform to the new standard. This variable was meant to make error numbers and their meanings consistent among SQL implementations. The variable consists of five characters that form two distinct parts:

- The first two characters to the left represent an error class to indicate the general error type or classification. For example, the code 01 indicates a general warning, and the code 0A means the feature used is not supported. The first character of this part of the SQLSTATE variable can be a digit from 0 to 4 or a letter from A to H. The SQL-92 standard allows the use of the digits 5 through 9 and the letters I through Z as non-standardized DBMS-specific error codes. This scheme allows for differences in DBMSs to continue. However, all the most common SQL error codes are included in the standardized codes.
- The next three characters identify an error subclass, a specific error within the error class. For example, within the general warning error class, you might find the subclass 004, which warns the user that the data has been truncated. The SQLSTATE variable value for this error subclass is 01004. Also, the SQLSTATE value 01S02 means that the optional value has changed.

The general scheme for using SQLSTATE in error handling is shown in Listing 17.5.

LISTING 17.5 A C Program Using the SQLSTATE Variable in Error Handling

```
/*SQL statement goes here followed by the error check below*/
exec sql insert into table1
   values(val1, val2, ..);
If (strcmp(sqlca.sqlstate, ''00000''))
  goto error_handler;
...
...
...
error_handler:
  printf(''SQL Error: %ld\n, sqlca.sqlstate);
  exit();
...
...
...
```

Note

Notice the use of the function `strcmp`, which is usually used to compare two strings. Therefore, the statement using it in Listing 17.5 compares the `sqlca.sqlstate` error code to the value `00000`. If the two values are different, execution goes to the error handler. It is assumed that your code will include the header file `string.h`.

Embedded SQL Statements

SQL-92 introduced many statements targeted for embedded SQL programs. You have already seen some of these statements in Listing 17.1. This section discusses them in more detail.

Using the GET DIAGNOSTICS Statement

SQL-92 provides this statement for additional error diagnostic information. It allows an embedded SQL program to find one or more items of information about the raised error condition. The general syntax for this statement is two-fold. To retrieve diagnostic information on the statement level to determine how many diagnostic errors occurred, the syntax is as follows:

```
GET DIAGNOSTICS  [variable = NUMBER]
[, variable = MORE]
[, variable = COMMAND_FUNCTION]
[, variable = DYNAMIC_FUNCTION]
[, variable = ROW_COUNT];
```

To retrieve information about an individual diagnostic error, this is the syntax:

```
GET DIAGNOSTICS EXCEPTION err_number
[variable = CONDITION_NUMBER]
[, variable = RETURNED_SQLSTATE]
[, variable = CLASS_ORIGIN]
[, variable = SERVER_NAME]
[, variable = CONNECTION_NAME]
[, variable = CONSTRAINT_CATALOG]
[, variable = CONSTRAINT_SCHEMA]
[, variable = CONSTRAINT_NAME]
[, variable = CATALOG_NAME]
[, variable = SCHEMA_NAME]
[, variable = SERVER_NAME]
```

```
[, variable = TABLE_NAME]
[, variable = COLUMN_NAME]
[, variable = CURSOR_NAME]
[, variable = MESSAGE_TEXT]
[, variable = MESSAGE_LENGTH]
[, variable = MESSAGE_OCTET_LENGTH];
```

Listing 17.6 shows an example of how this statement is used.

LISTING 17.6 A C Program Using the `GET DIAGNOSTICS` Statement with `SQLSTATE`

```
/*A DELETE SQL statement goes here followed by the error check*/
  exec sql delete from employee
where termination_date is not null;
  If (strcmp(sqlca.sqlstate, ''00000''))
    goto error_handler;
/*if the deletion is successful, you need to find out how
 many rows were deleted*/
  exec sql get diagnostics :numrows = ROW_COUNT;
  printf(''%ld rows deleted\n'', numrows);
...
...
...
error_handler:
  /*find out how many errors reported*/
  exec sql get diagnostics :errcount = NUMBER;
  /*loop through reported errors to get
   additional information*/
  for (i=1; i<errcount;i++) {
    exec sql get diagnostics EXCEPTION :I
        :errnumber = RETURNED_SQLSTATE,
        :errmsg = MESSAGE_TEXT;
  printf(''SQL Error # %d: error code: %s error message: %s/n'',
        i, errnumber, errmsg);
  }
  exit();
...
...
...
```

Listing 17.6 checks to see if the delete statement is successful. If it is, you use the `GET DIAGNOSTICS` statement to get the number of deleted rows. If an error occurred during executing the `DELETE` statement, the error handler retrieves and prints the number errors reported. Then it loops through these errors retrieving additional information about them individually, such as error code and message. The `GET DIAGNOSTICS` statement is used for this purpose.

The `WHENEVER` Statement

To avoid checking for exceptions after every SQL statement in your embedded SQL program, SQL-92 introduced the `WHENEVER` statement, which tells the precompiler to automatically generate error handling code after each statement, according to what's specified in the statement. Three situations are covered with the `WHENEVER` statement:

- `WHENEVER SQLERROR` indicates to the precompiler that error handling code should be generated. This is the case when `SQLCODE` is negative.
- `WHENEVER SQLWARNING` tells the pre-compiler that code should be generated to handle a warning, which is when `SQLCODE` is positive. This statement is not included in the SQL-92 standard, but most SQL implementations support it.
- `WHENEVER NOT FOUND` indicates to the precompiler that code should be generated to handle a specific warning. This specific warning is generated by the DBMS when you try to retrieve records that don't exist, such as when you go past the end of the recordset.

This is the general syntax for the `WHENEVER` statement:

```
WHENEVER SQLERROR¦SQLWARNING¦NOT FOUND
     CONTINUE¦GOTO label¦GOTO;
```

Because the `WHENEVER` statement indicates to the precompiler what to do in cases of errors, these statements can supersede each other. In other words, the second `WHENEVER` statement in an embedded SQL program overrides the first `WHENEVER` statement from the point of the second statement in the program.

Note

Based on the previous paragraph, the `WHENEVER ... CONTINUE` statement can be used to cancel the effect of a previous `WHENEVER` statement.

To illustrate this concept, look at Listing 17.7. It has three SQL statements: a delete, an update, and an insert. If an error happens in the delete, the code in `err_handler1` is executed. If an error occurs in the update statement, however, the next statement in the program is executed because of the `WHENEVER ... CONTINUE` statement. Finally, if an error occurs in the insert statement, the code in `err_handler2` is executed.

LISTING 17.7 A C Program Demonstrating the Use of the **WHENEVER** Statement

```
/*If a SQLERROR is raised, redirect to err_handler1*/
  exec sql whenever sqlerror goto err_handler1;
/*A DELETE SQL statement goes here*/
  exec sql delete from employee
where termination_date is not null;
...
...
...
/*If a SQLERROR is raised, go to next statement*/
  exec sql whenever sqlerror continue;
/*Update statement goes here*/
  exec sql update employee
       set department_id = 2
       where employee_id=233;
...
...
...
/*If a SQLERROR is raised, go to err_handler2*/
  exec sql whenever sqlerror goto err_handler2;
/*Insert statement goes here*/
  exec sql insert into employee(
       employee_id, name, hire_date)
       values(343, 'John Doe', '1-DEC-1999');
...
...
...
err_handler1:
  printf(''SQL DELETE Error: %dl\n'', sqlca.sqlcode);
  exit();
err_handler2:
  printf(''SQL INSERT Error: %dl\n'', sqlca.sqlcode);
  exit();
...
...
...
```

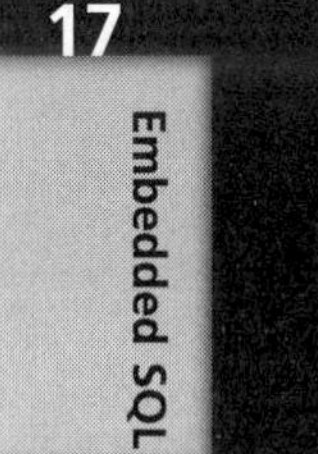

Mixing SQL with the Host Language

This section examines how the mix of SQL and host language code works together. In particular, you will see how host language features and elements can be used in the SQL statements. For example, you will learn how to declare and use host variables and constants in SQL statements.

Declaring and Using Host Language Variables

Variables in the host language can be used in SQL in an embedded SQL program. Some of the examples you have seen already use this feature of embedded SQL. For example, in Listing 17.1, you saw that the host language variable, `name`, is used to store the value of the name field retrieved from the query.

To use host variables in the SQL statements, you need to declare them using the host language declaration methods. Listing 17.8 presents a C program that declares host variables and later uses them in the embedded SQL statements.

SQL-92 introduces two statements to tell the precompiler when variable declarations start and when they end. These statements are `BEGIN DECLARE SECTION` and `END DECLARE SECTION`. These two statements are not executable; their only purpose is to bracket the beginning and end of variable declarations. Although they are in the SQL-92 standard, they are not required in all SQL implementations.

Note

Variable declarations can take place at any point in the program, especially in a block-structured program, such as C and Pascal. Therefore, any time you have variable declarations, you need to use the `BEGIN DECLARE SECTION` and `END DECLARE SECTION` statements.

LISTING 17.8 Example of Declaring Host Variables in an Embedded SQL Program

```
main()
{
  exec sql include sqlca;
  exec sql begin declare section;
    int department_id;  /*dept id from user*/
    char department;    /*department name*/
exec sql end declare section;
  /*error handling*/
```

LISTING 17.8 CONTINUED

```
  exec sql whenever sqlerror goto q_error;
  exec sql whenever not found goto bad_id;
  /*prompt user for department id*/
  printf(''Enter department id: '');
  scanf(''%d'', &department_id);
  /*run the embedded sql statement*/
  exec sql select department_name
       from  department
       where department_id = :dept_id
       into  :department;
  /*displaying the results*/
  printf(''Department Name: %s\n'') department);
  exit();
  /*q_error error handler*/
  printf(''SQL error encountered: %ld\n'', sqlca.sqlcode);
  exit();
  /*bad_id error handler (no employee found with passed id)*/
  printf(''Department ID not found. Make sure you pass a valid ID. \n'');
  exit();
}
```


In Listing 17.8, the two variables `dept_id` and `department` are declared in the declaration section. The variable `dept_id` is then used in the `WHERE` clause of the embedded SQL statement. The second variable, `department`, is used to hold the retrieved value of the department name from the SQL statement. This is done using the `INTO` clause. In this clause, you can determine what variables hold the output of the query in the order of the returned columns.

Note

When dealing with host variables in embedded SQL programs, you have to be careful about what your SQL implementation supports. Some SQL implementations, for instance, accept constants defined in the host language just like the host variables. Some implementations, on the other hand, return errors when such constants are used.

Host Language Variables and Data Types

Host language variables play a unique role. They are variables that should conform to the rules and types of the host programming language, such as C or FORTRAN, as well as to the SQL standard limitations and types. For example, if a variable is declared as an integer in a C program, then when it's used in an embedded SQL statement in the program, it should correspond to an integer column in the SQL statement, or it will fail. Therefore, host variable data types should map to equivalent SQL data types. Table 17.1 shows a list of available SQL data types and their mappings to C and FORTRAN data types.

TABLE 17.1 SQL Data Types Mapped to Some Host Language Data Types

SQL Data Type	*C Data Type*	*FORTRAN Data Type*
Smallint	short	Integer*2
Integer	long	Integer*4
Real	float	Real*4
Double Precision	double	Real*8
Numeric(p,s)	double	Real*8
Decimal(p,s)	double	Real*8
Char(n)	char[n+1]	Character*n
Varchar(n)	char[n+1]	Not supported
Bit	char[1]	Character*m
Varying(n)	char[1]	Not supported
Date	Not supported	Not supported
Time	Not supported	Not supported
Timestamp	Not supported	Not supported
Interval	Not supported	Not supported

Note that the SQL data types in Table 17.1 that aren't directly supported in the host language, such as SQL `DATE`, require conversion to some character data type in that language. Also note that the SQL `Char(n)` data type's equivalent in FORTRAN is `Character*m`; `m` is length of the host character string. This length is the number of bits for the string divided by the number of bits per character for this host language. The table shows that data type mapping between SQL and the host language is not always an automatic and straightforward task. As an example, Listing 17.9 shows update statements that use host variables of different types.

LISTING 17.9 An Example of Data Type Mapping of Host Variables to SQL Data Types

```
main()
{
  exec sql include sqlca;
  exec sql begin declare section;
    int employee_id;        /*employee id from user*/
```

LISTING 17.9 CONTINUED

```
    char name = 'John Doe';      /*employee name*/
    char address = '123 Main St.'; /*employee address*/
    char city = 'New York';      /*employee city*/
    char state = 'NY';         /*employee state*/
    char hire_date = '01-Jan-1999'; /*employee hire date*/
    float salary = '60000.00';    /*employee salary*/
  exec sql end declare section;
  /*error handling*/
  exec sql whenever sqlerror goto sql_error;
  exec sql whenever not found goto id_not_found;
  /*prompt user for employee id*/
  printf(''Enter employee id: '');
  scanf(''%d'', &employee_id);
  /*run the embedded sql statement*/
  exec sql update employee set
          name = :name,
          address = :address,
          city = :city,
          state = :state,
          hire_date = :hire_date,
          salary = :salary
  where employee.employee_id = :employee_id;
  exit();
  /*sql_error error handler*/
  printf(''SQL error encountered: %ld\n'', sqlca.sqlcode);
  exit();
  /*id_not_found error handler (no employee found with passed id)*/
  printf(''Employee ID not found. Make sure you pass a valid ID. \n'');
  exit();
}
```

The C program in Listing 17.9 shows how SQL data types can be mapped to C types. The update statements use fields with the SQL types `integer`, `char`, `date`, and `money`. As for the integer type, the DBMS automatically converts the C `integer` (`short`) type to a SQL integer. As for the `char` type, the mapping is also automatic according to Table 17.1. There is no `DATE` type in C. Therefore, you should declare an array of character data and fill the array with a string representing an acceptable data format to the DBMS. The `money` data type does not exist in C, either, so you should use a floating-point variable, which is translated automatically by most DBMS systems to the appropriate `money` type.

Note

Always check the documentation of the specific DBMS you are using for data type mapping and conversion with the SQL standard data types. Doing so could keep you from running into some unpleasant surprises.

Handling `NULL` in Host Language Variables

Many programming languages, such as C and FORTRAN, don't have the concept of `NULL`. These languages require that their variables always have values and that no variables can be "unknown." Therefore, embedded SQL programs using such host languages could face significant problems if `NULL` values are not handled appropriately. To avoid these problems, the SQL standard came up with an indicator variable whose purpose is to indicate the host variable's appropriate value to the DBMS and host language. When specifying host variables in an embedded SQL program, indicator variables should follow the host variable immediately if it is used.

The following is an example of using indicator variables in a C embedded SQL program:

```
Exec sql update employee
    set salary = :salary :salary_ind,
    hire_date = :hiredate :hiredate_ind
     where employee_id = 122;
```

The rules for indicator variables are as follows:

- If the host variable has a known, non-`NULL` value, the indicator variable is set to zero. Taking the previous example, if the host variables `salary` and `hireDate` are `NULL`, then the statement is equal to writing this:

  ```
  Exec sql update employee
     set salary = :salary,
     hire_date = :hiredate
      where employee_id = 122;
  ```

- If the indicator variable has a negative value, the host variable is assumed to have a `NULL` value. In this case, the actual value of the host variable can be ignored. Again, taking the previous example, if the host variable is `NULL`, the statement is equal to the following:

  ```
  Exec sql update employee
     set salary = null,
  ```

```
hire_date = null
 where employee_id = 122;
```

- If the indicator variable has a positive value, the host variable is likely to have a valid value that is rounded up or down or truncated.

Note

Indicator variables cannot be used in WHERE clauses because you cannot search on a NULL. In other words, it makes no sense to say WHERE employee_id = NULL because NULL means unknown, and you cannot search for an unknown value. Instead, if you want to use NULL in a search criteria, you need to use the IS NULL function.

As an example of the situation mentioned in the Note box, the following statement is not valid and will return an error:

```
exec sql delete from employee
     where hire_date = :hiredate :hiredate_ind;
```

Instead, you need to write the code like this:

```
If (hiredate_ind<0){
  exec sql delete from employee
     where hire_date is null;
)
else {
  exec sql delete from employee
     where hire_date = :hire_date;
}
```

In this example, the first statement used the indicator variable `hiredate_ind` in the `WHERE` clause's search criteria. If the host variable is `NULL`, the statement fails because the search criteria is now unknown. The second statement, however, checks for the indicator variable as indicated in the preceding example. If the value is negative, the `IS NULL` function is used in the `WHERE` clause. If the indicator variable is not `NULL`, the `WHERE` clause is written as usual, without the indicator variable.

Data Retrieval

So far, what you have learned about embedded SQL will allow you to insert, update, and delete data from the database using these programs. However, if you want to retrieve data, things become rather tricky because SQL `SELECT` statements could return a set of records as a whole. These sets of records cannot be handled as they are in many host languages, such as C and FORTRAN. Those languages expect individual values or, at best, individual records to handle.

To solve this problem, the SQL standard classified retrieving data from the database in embedded SQL programs in two major categories: single-row queries and multiple-row queries. With single-row queries, data is retrieved one row at a time, such as retrieving an employee whose ID is 143. Multiple-row queries, on the other hand, return a set of records, such as retrieving the list of employees in the Detroit area. Interactive SQL does not make this distinction, so the `SELECT` statement is the same whether it returns one row or multiple rows.

Single-Row Queries

Single-row queries are used in data entry programs and online transaction processing programs. In these programs, one record at a time is retrieved and worked on by the user. The single `SELECT` statement is used in embedded SQL for these types of queries. This statement resembles the regular interactive `SELECT` statement in that it has `SELECT` and `FROM` clauses and an optional `WHERE` clause. It does not, however, have a `GROUP BY` or `ORDER BY` clause because only one record is retrieved. This statement introduces a new clause, the `INTO` clause, which allows introducing host language variables that store the values of the retrieved columns. The general syntax of the single `SELECT` statement is shown here:

```
SELECT [ALL¦DISTINCT] field list
INTO host variable list
FROM table names
WHERE search condition;
```

Listing 17.11 shows an example of using the single `SELECT` statement in an embedded SQL program. The program prompts the user for an order number, and then uses a single query to retrieve the status of the entered customer order number. The query also retrieves the customer ID and salesperson name associated with the sale. The query uses the famous NorthWind database that ships with Microsoft Access (all versions) and Microsoft SQL Server (version 7.0).

LISTING 17.11 Using the Single `SELECT` Statement to Retrieve the Order Status and Salesperson's Name

```
main()
{
  exec sql include sqlca;
  exec sql begin declare section;
   int orderid;      /* Employee ID (from user)     */
```

LISTING 17.11 CONTINUED

```
   int custid;      /* Retrieved customer ID     */
   char salesperson[10]; /* Retrieved salesperson name   */
   char status[6];    /* Retrieved order status    */
  exec sql end declare section;
  /* Set up error processing */
  exec sql whenever sqlerror goto query_error;
  exec sql whenever not found goto bad_number;
  /* Prompt the user for order number */
  printf (''enter order number: '');
  scanf (''%d'', &orderid);
  /* Execute the SQL query */
  exec sql select custid,
          employeeid,
          status
   into :custid,
      :salesperson,
      :status
   from orders
   where orderid = :orderid;
  /* Display the results */
  printf (''Customer number: %d\n'', CustID);
  printf (''Salesperson: %s\n'', SalesPerson);
  printf (''Status: %s\n'', Status);
  exit();
query_error:
  printf (''SQL error: %ld\n'', sqlca.sqlcode);
  exit();
bad_number:
  printf (''Invalid order number.\n'');
  exit();
}
```


Note

The host language variables used in the INTO clause of the single query serve as output variables. The number of these variables, as specified in the INTO clause, should be equal to the number of retrieved fields, and their data types should correspond to those of the retrieved fields.

NULL in Embedded SQL Queries

If the single SELECT in an embedded SQL program returns NULL values, chances are the host language will not be able to handle the results. This is true if the host language, such as C or FORTRAN, does not support NULL values. To handle this issue, the single SELECT uses indicator variables in the INTO clause. For a definition of the indicator variables, please refer to the section "Handling NULL in Host Language Variables" earlier in this chapter.

This solution is similar to the one you saw earlier with INSERT and UPDATE queries, where the indicator variables were used in the VALUES clause of the INSERT statement and in the SET clause of the UPDATE statement.

The indicator variable immediately follows the host variable name in the INTO clause. Listing 17.12 shows the same example in Listing 17.11 but uses indicator variables. In this program, you check the value of the indicator variable `status_ind`. If the value is negative, you know that the returned value for the field from the database is NULL, and you print this to the user, instead of printing the actual value of the `status` variable.

> **Note**
>
> Note that the fields `customerid` and `salesperson` are defined as NOT NULL in the database, so they do not need any indicator variables.

LISTING 17.12 Using Indicator Variables in the Single SELECT Statement

```
main()
{
  exec sql include sqlca;
  exec sql begin declare section;
   int orderid;      /* Employee ID (from user)*/
   int customerid;      /* Retrieved customer ID*/
   char salesperson[10]; /* Retrieved salesperson name*/
   char status[6];     /* Retrieved order status*/
   short status_ind [3]; /*indicator variable for status*/
  exec sql end declare section;
  /* Set up error processing */
  exec sql whenever sqlerror goto query_error;
  exec sql whenever not found goto bad_number;
  /* Prompt the user for order number */
  printf (''enter order number: '');
  scanf (''%d'', &orderid);
```

LISTING 17.12 CONTINUED

```
  /* Execute the SQL query */
  exec sql select custid,
          employeeid,
          status
   into :customerid,
      :salesperson,
      :status :status_ind
   from orders
   where orderid = :orderid;
  /* Display the results */
  printf (''Customer number: %d\n'', customerid);
  printf (''Salesperson: %s\n'', salesperson);
  if (:status_ind < 0){
    printf (''status is null\n'');
    }
  else
    printf (''status: %s\n'', status);
  exit();
query_error:
  printf (''SQL error: %ld\n'', sqlca.sqlcode);
  exit();
bad_number:
  printf (''Invalid order number.\n'');
  exit();
}
```


Note

In single SELECT queries, if the query returns no records in its results, a NOT FOUND warning is returned in the SQLCA.SQLCODE variable (value is +100), and a NO DATA class is returned for the SQLCA.SQLSTATE variable.

On the other hand, if more than one row is returned in the single SELECT statement result, an error is raised and a negative SQLCA.SQLCODE value is returned.

Using Data Structures in Data Retrieval

Some host languages use data structures to represent a related set of data of different types. The embedded SQL precompilers of these languages may allow the use of such structures in the embedded SQL code. This actually acts as a shortcut, with the structure name being used in the INTO clause instead of using the individual variable names. The precompiler replaces the structure with a list of the variables in the structure in the same order they were declared. Therefore, it is important that the number, names, and types of the variables declared in the data structure correspond to the list of columns retrieved in the single SELECT statement.

Listing 17.13 shows the same example in Listing 17.12 but with a data structure used instead of the list of output variables.

LISTING 17.13 Using Data Structures in the Single SELECT Statement

```
main()
{
  exec sql include sqlca;
  exec sql begin declare section;
   int orderid;      /* Employee ID (from user)*/
struct {
   char customerid[10];  /* Retrieved customer id */
char salesperson[10];  /* Retrieved salesperson name */
   char status[6];     /* Retrieved order status */
    } results;
   short results_ind[1];  /*results indicator variable array*/
  exec sql end declare section;
  /* Set up error processing */
  exec sql whenever sqlerror goto query_error;
  exec sql whenever not found goto bad_number;
  /* Prompt the user for order number */
  printf (''enter order number: '');
  scanf (''%d'', &orderid);
  /* Execute the SQL query */
  exec sql select custid,
          employeeid,
          status
   into customerid:results :results_ind
   from orders
   where orderid = :orderid;
  /* Display the results */
  printf (''Customer number: %d\n'', results.customerid);
  printf (''Salesperson: %s\n'', results.salesperson);
```

LISTING 17.13 CONTINUED

```
  if (:results_ind[1] < 0){
    printf (''Status is NULL\n'');
    }
  else
    printf (''Status: %s\n'', results.status);
  exit();
query_error:
  printf (''SQL error: %ld\n'', sqlca.sqlcode);
  exit();
bad_number:
  printf (''Invalid order number.\n'');
  exit();
}
```


Multiple Row Queries (Cursors)

Often an embedded SQL statement returns more than one record, creating the need to find a way for the host language to handle the resulting recordset one record at a time. To help solve this issue, the SQL standard introduced the *cursor*, which provides a pointer to the record being processed in the recordset. It also allows you to scroll up and down the recordset to access a certain record in some cases. Cursors also fetch the needed record from the database.

Using a cursor involves declaring it with the `DECLARE CURSOR` statement. This declaration associates the cursor with the query. After declaring the cursor, it has to be opened with the `OPEN` statement so that the DBMS generates the results. The `OPEN` statement positions the cursor before the first record in the returned recordset. The `FETCH` statement can be used to advance the cursor to the next row, get the values of the query fields for the corresponding record, and store them in host variables. Finally, when the results have been processed, the `CLOSE` statement closes the cursor, breaking its association with the query result.

Listing 17.14 shows an embedded SQL program written in C that retrieves the name, department, hire date, and salary of the employees in the employee table. Notice how the cursor declaration includes the interactive SQL statement that would have been used directly against the DBMS. Also notice how the `OPEN`, `FETCH`, and `CLOSE` statements are used in the program in relation to the cursor. These statements are explained in more detail in the following sections.

LISTING 17.14 A Sample C Program Showing How Cursors Can Be Used to Retrieve Multiple Records

```
Main()
{
  exec sql include sqlca;
  /*begin declarations*/
  exec sql begin declare section;
    char  empname[30];  /*employee name*/
    char  dept[20];    /*employee department*/
    char  hiredate[12]  /*employee hire date*/
    float  salary;     /*employee salary*/
    short  salary_ind;   /*salary indicator variable*/
  exec sql end declare section;
/*declare the cursor to be used for the query*/
  exec sql declare empcursor cursor for
      select employee_name,
          department,
          hire_date,
          salary
      from employee, department
      where employee.department_id =
          department.department_id
      order by employee_name;
/*set up error handling*/
  whenever sqlerror goto sql_error;
whenever not found goto no_records_left;
/*open the cursor*/
  exec sql open empcursor;
/*loop through the resulting recordset*/
  for(;;) {
  /*fetch the next row*/
    exec sql fetch empcursor
      into :empname,
         :dept,
         :hiredate,
         :salary
         :salary_ind;
  /*print the retrieved values*/
    printf(''Name: %s\n'', empname);
    printf(''Department: %s\n'', dept);
    printf(''Hire Date: %s\n'', hiredate);
    if (salary_ind < 0){
      printf(''Salary is null\n'');
```

LISTING 17.14 CONTINUED

```
      }
    else
      printf(''Salary: %s\n'', salary);
  }
exit();
/***Error handling***/
sql_error:
  printf(''SQL Error: %ld\n'', sqlca.sqlcode);
  exit();
no_records_left:
  exec sql close empcursor;
  exit();
```


In Listing 17.14, variables were declared to hold the results of the returned recordset. It is assumed that `salary` is the only field that can be `NULL`, so an indicator variable was declared for it.

In the cursor declaration section, the query is entered as though it were an interactive query. The query joins the `department` and `employee` tables to retrieve the employee's information and his or her department name. The cursor is then opened and the records are fetched one at a time. While the records are being fetched, they are printed out. Notice that for the `salary` field, the indicator variable `salary_ind` is checked to see whether the value is `NULL`. When all records have been fetched and printed out, the `NOT FOUND` condition is then met. The execution shifts to the corresponding error trap where the cursor is closed.

Note

Cursors provide flexibility to the embedded SQL program. For instance, by opening multiple cursors, you can manipulate data in several tables and query several tables at once. However, cursors carry a big overhead performance-wise because the DBMS has to process the query. Also, SQL cursors are sequential; they do not provide random access to the data like some programming languages deal with files in a file system. Accessing a record involves scrolling through the records one by one until the record is fetched.

In the following sections, you will take a closer look at the cursor-related statement and how it is used.

Declaring a Cursor

As you saw in Listing 17.14, a cursor has the following syntax in embedded SQL programs:

```
DECLARE cursor_name CURSOR FOR select_query;
```

In this code, `cursor_name` is the name the cursor is referenced by. It becomes the name associated with the select query itself throughout the program. `Select_query` is the multi-row query you want to execute in your embedded SQL program.

> **Note**
>
> Technically, a cursor declaration can be placed anywhere in the program before any statement referencing it because the declaration is not an executable element. In other words, the precompiler does not include it in the object code or the application plan. The declaration indicates to the precompiler that the cursor name be used in association with the SQL query it represents throughout the embedded SQL program.

The select query can be any valid interactive query. The `SELECT` and `FROM` clauses are mandatory, but the `WHERE`, `GROUP BY`, `ORDER BY`, and `UNION` clauses are optional. This gives developers flexibility in what they can query for and return from the database tables by allowing them to use the power and capabilities available in interactive queries.

Just like insert, update, delete, and single `SELECT` queries, the select query in the cursor declaration can include input host variables in the `WHERE` clause or anywhere a constant is allowed. The select query, however, does not include an `INPUT` clause because no output variables are used in it. The `INPUT` clause comes as part of the `FETCH` statement (explained later in the chapter).

Some SQL implementations don't treat the `DECLARE CURSOR` statement as declarative only. Their precompiler might generate some object code for it in the compiled program. No matter how your SQL flavor implements cursors in embedded SQL programs, it is recommended that you make sure the cursor declaration is always taking place before the cursor `OPEN` statement, and that the `OPEN` statement is located before the `FETCH` and `CLOSE` statements. Always consult the documentation of your SQL implementation when it comes to using cursors, among other things, in embedded SQL programs.

Opening a Cursor

The OPEN statement used in Listing 17.14 has the following syntax:

```
OPEN cursor_name;
```

In this code, cursor_name is the name of the cursor to be opened. This name has to refer to a valid cursor that has already been declared in the embedded SQL program before the OPEN statement. If the cursor declaration follows the OPEN statement, an error will be returned in the form of a negative SQLCODE value.

> **Note**
>
> The OPEN statement is the statement that causes the DBMS to execute the query. It prepares the requested recordset, but does not show any records yet because the cursor at that point is located before the first record.

The OPEN statement is an important one in the cursor implementation. Many of the connection errors that can take place are trapped at this level. Therefore, any time you get SQLCODE values indicating invalid table name, permissions denied, or column names not recognized, these errors are raised at the OPEN statement. Fixing these errors, however, involves work on the DECLARE CURSOR 's select query part, making sure you have the right table and field names, and on the part of database security, making sure you have the required access to the tables or views in the select query.

Fetching the Data with a Cursor

Now that you have declared and opened your cursor, you are ready to start fetching the records one at a time to do what you need to do with them. You can do this with the FETCH statement, which has the following general syntax:

```
FETCH cursor_name INTO list_of_host_variables;
```

The FETCH statement fetches rows returned by the SELECT statement defined in a cursor. It reads the values in the specified row from the open cursor and places them in the host data variables defined in the INTO clause. Host variables are subject to the same conditions you have seen in the previous sections of this chapter. For instance, you can always use indicator variables along with the host variables to take care of NULL conditions, as demonstrated in Listing 17.14, where the variable salary_ind is used in combination with the host variable salary, which is designed to store the salary field of the returned recordset.

The number of host variables in the INTO clause of the FETCH statement should be equal to that of the fields returned in the SQL statement. Also, their data type and length should be the same as the table fields they correspond to.

The FETCH statement should follow the OPEN statement; if it comes before it, negative SQLCODE values are returned, indicating SQL errors.

The way the FETCH statement works is illustrated in Table 17.2.

TABLE 17.2 Flow of Execution of the Cursor-Related Statements

Statement	*Effect*
`OPEN cursor_name`	Opens the cursor and causes the DBMS to execute the SQL statement and produce a recordset of the results.
`FETCH`	Positions the cursor at the first record, causing the record to be viewed and the values of its fields to be assigned to the corresponding host variables.
`Next FETCH statements`	Moves the cursor one record at a time, reassigning the values of the retrieved fields to the host variables.
`NOT FOUND condition met`	The cursor is positioned past the last record in the returned recordset, and it has no current record. In this case, you should write your code in the error trap that corresponds to this condition so that you close the cursor.
`CLOSE cursor_name`	Closes the cursor and ends access to the returned recordset.

Note

If the returned recordset from the SQL statement is empty, the OPEN statement still positions the cursor before the empty recordset. The first FETCH statement causes the program to detect the NOT FOUND condition and positions the cursor after the end of the empty recordset. This behavior explains why in some cases, when an empty recordset is returned, you don't get an error message until you try to move to some record in the recordset. In this case, the movement causes the FETCH statement to be carried out.

Scrollable Cursors

The cursors you have been dealing with so far are forward-only sequential cursors. They move only one record forward at a time. If your program wants to move back to a record that has already been fetched, you have to close the cursor, open it again, and fetch up to the record you are interested in. This limitation caused major performance issues because the DBMS had to run the SQL statement every time this process was required. This kind of cursor was supported by the SQL-89 standard, and for quite some time, it was the only type of cursor supported by the SQL-92 standard.

Beginning in the early 1990s, some implementations introduced what's called a *scrollable cursor*. This cursor allows the program to move freely to practically any record in the recordset. This kind of cursor proved to be practical and helpful, especially in programs that require a lot of browsing in the database. Browsing often requires moving randomly from record to record. The advantages of this new type of cursor made the SQL-92 standard adopt it as a requirement for the intermediate and full conformance levels. As for entry-level conformance with SQL-92, the old unidirectional cursors were still the only type required.

The SQL-92 standard defined scrollable cursors by specifying the type in the `DECLARE CURSOR` statement and by adding an extension to the `FETCH` statement. Based on this, to declare a scrollable cursor, you have to write:

```
DECLARE CURSOR cursor_name SCROLL CURSOR FOR sql_query;
```

This is the syntax for the `FETCH` statement of this cursor:

```
FETCH [FIRST¦LAST¦PRIOR¦NEXT¦ABSOLUTE record_number¦RELATIVE
+/- number_of_records]
FROM cursor_name INTO list_of_host_variables;
```

Based on the above, to declare the cursor in Listing 17.14 as a scrollable cursor, you need to modify the declaration to the following:

```
/*declare the cursor to be used for the query*/
  exec sql declare empcursor scroll cursor for
      select employee_name,
             department,
             hire_date,
             salary
      from employee, department
      where employee.department_id =
            department.department_id
      order by employee_name;
```

As the FETCH statement syntax indicates, you can now move to

- The first record in the recordset, using FETCH FIRST
- The next record in the recordset, using FETCH NEXT
- The previous record in the recordset, using FETCH PRIOR
- The last record in the recordset, using FETCH LAST
- An absolute record by providing the row number for that record in the FETCH ABSOLUTE clause
- A record relative to the current record by specifying the offset number of records and adding that or subtracting it from the current absolute record number, using the clause FETCH RELATIVE

Note

Although scrollable cursors are useful and give you flexibility in browsing and navigating through the returned recordset, they still impose a lot of overhead on some DBMS systems. The reason is that the DBMS needs to track the current record during the FETCH operation and needs to resolve any lock and concurrency issue that might arise. Therefore, it is recommended that you use scrollable cursors prudently and only when you are certain you need them. In other words, if the work your program is doing can be satisfied by a unidirectional cursor, use that instead of a scrollable cursor.

Closing a Cursor

To close a cursor, you can use the CLOSE statement, which has the following syntax:

```
CLOSE cursor_name;
```

In this code, cursor_name has to reference a valid cursor name that has been both declared and opened before the CLOSE statement. You can close the cursor before fetching all the records in the resulting recordset. After the cursor has been closed, all references to the resulting recordset end and become invalid. Also, all cursors are automatically closed when a transaction is committed or rolled back. You will learn more about cursors in transactions later in the chapter.

Using Cursors for Updates and Deletes

Often when users are browsing records in a table or a view, using a cursor in your application behind the scenes, they might find that a value need to be updated or a record needs to be deleted. For example, in Listing 17.14, if a manager is using the cursor to browse a list of his employees, he might discover that an employee who quit five years ago still has an existing record that takes up space in the database, so he might want to be able to delete the record. Maybe as the manager browses through the records, he spots the wrong salary value for one of his employees, and he might want to update it on the spot.

Embedded SQL allow the manager to do so if the program uses what is called *positioned deletes* and *positioned updates*. They are special versions of the DELETE and UPDATE statements that work with cursors. The syntax for these statements is shown here:

```
/*Syntax of positioned DELETE in SQL-92*/
DELETE FROM table_name WHERE CURRENT OF cursor_name;
```

```
/*Syntax of positioned UPDATE in SQL-92*/
UPDATE table_name SET (list of columns and their new values)
WHERE CURRENT OF cursor_name;
```

The SQL-89 standard put strict conditions on using positioned updates and deletes. These restrictions included the following:

- The SQL query in the cursor declaration can use only one table.
- The SQL query in the cursor declaration cannot use the ORDER BY clause.
- The SQL query in the cursor declaration cannot use the GROUP BY clause and the HAVING subclause.
- The SQL query in the cursor declaration cannot use the DISTINCT keyword.

Because of the popularity of positioned updates and deletes, the SQL-92 standard adopted them with an additional change to the syntax of the DECLARE CURSOR statement. This change declares that the cursor will be used for updates. Here is the syntax for that change:

```
DECLARE CURSOR cursor_name FOR select_SQL
  [FOR UPDATE [OF column list>;
```

In short, the statement ends with an optional FOR UPDATE clause and could include a list of the columns that will change. This syntax makes it easier and more efficient for the DBMS to perform the query because it knows beforehand whether the query is for updates and which columns are expected to change as a result of the cursor use.

According to the SQL-92 standard, if the `FOR UPDATE` clause is not used, the cursor is automatically declared for update unless it is a scroll cursor or explicitly declared for read only.

Finally, Listing 17.15 shows an example of a positioned update cursor in which the user is prompted to change the employee's `salary` field. If the user answers with a `Y` or `y`, he or she is prompted to update the field and a positioned update statement is issued.

LISTING 17.15 An Example of Positioned Updates in Cursors

```
Main()
{
  exec sql include sqlca;
  /*begin declarations*/
  exec sql begin declare section;
      char    empname[30];     /*employee name*/
      char    dept[20];        /*employee department*/
      char    hiredate[12]     /*employee hire date*/
      float   salary;          /*employee salary*/
      short   salary_ind;      /*salary indicator variable*/
  exec sql end declare section;

  char intbuffer[101]          /*character entered by user*/
  float newsalary;             /*New salary value entered by user*/

/*declare the cursor to be used for the query*/
    exec sql declare empcursor cursor for
            select employee_name,
                   department,
                   hire_date,
                   salary
           from employee, department
           where employee.department_id =
                 department.department_id
           order by employee_name
             for update of salary;

/*setup error handling*/
    whenever sqlerror goro sql_error;
    whenever not found goto no_records_left;

/*open the cursor*/
  exec sql open empcursor;
```

LISTING 17.15 CONTINUED

```
/*loop through the resulting recordset*/
  for(;;) {

  /*fetch the next row*/
    exec sql fetch empcursor
      into    :empname,
              :dept,
              :hiredate,
              :salary
              :salary_ind;

  /*print the retrieved values*/
    printf(''Name: %s\n'', empname);
    printf(''Department: %s\n'', dept);
    printf(''Hire Date: %s\n'', hiredate);
    if (salary_ind < 0){
      printf(''Salary is null\n'');
      }
    else
      printf(''Salary: %s\n'', salary);

  /*prompt user to see if she needs to update salary*/
  printf(''Do you want to update salary?\n'');
  scanf(''%d'', &intbuffer)

  /*if the user enters ''y'' then prompt for new value*/
  if (intbuffer == ''y'') {
    printf(''Enter new value:\n'');
    scanf(''%d'', &newsalary)
    exec sql update employee set
            salary = :newsalary
         where current of empcursor;
  /*Inform user of success*/
  printf(''Update successful.\n'');
    }
  /*end of for loop*/
  }

exit();

/***Error handling***/
```

LISTING 17.15 CONTINUED

```
sql_error:
    printf(''SQL Error: %ld\n'', sqlca.sqlcode);
    exit();

no_records_left:
    exec sql close empcursor;
    exit();
```

In Listing 17.15, the user scrolls through the records retrieved and presented by the cursor (forward-only in this case). As she or he scrolls, the program prompts the user, asking whether a salary update for the current record is wanted. If the user's answer to the prompt is `y`, a second prompt asks the user about the new value of the `salary` field. The user enters the new salary value, and then the program updates the record with the new value before going to the next record.

Cursors in Transactions

Data has to remain consistent during a transaction, according to the SQL-92 standard. This is one of the fundamental principles in SQL transactions. Therefore, when you open a cursor and retrieve a recordset, then close it, and then reopen it, you should expect to see the same data you saw the first time you opened the cursor. Furthermore, if your cursor scrolls through the recordset, you should see the same data when you scroll to a particular record, then away from it, and then back to it. To take this a little further, if you open the same recordset with two different cursors, you should see the same data.

This consistency is maintained at the expense of performance. The database management system does a great deal of work to accomplish this goal. Mainly, the DBMS locks the records retrieved by your cursor declaration from other users until you commit your changes, if you have any. If your cursor allows for user interaction, the impact will be worse because the user could take a long time responding to prompts offered by your program, which means locking the records for a longer period from other users who might need access to them. Also, if your transaction is long and includes opening several cursors for a long time and performing many actions before committing or rolling back the changes, the lock will be held longer.

To minimize the effects of locking and concurrency issues associated with transactions, you might want to consider the following recommendations:

- Keep transactions as short as possible.
- Use forward-only and read-only cursors whenever you can.

- Avoid introducing user interaction in your program during a transaction unless you absolutely have to.
- Use more restrictive isolation levels as much as possible to unlock the rows as soon as you fetch the next one.
- Minimize the number of statements included in a transaction by issuing `COMMIT` or `ROLL BACK` statements as early as possible.
- If you have to use scrollable cursors, try to optimize performance and minimize locking by taking other precautions.

Note

One last note on cursors and transaction that you might have already figured out: After you commit or roll back a transaction, all cursors are closed.

Summary

In this chapter, you looked at embedded SQL, a powerful tool that allows database access right from your own programs, which are written in the language of your choice (with some limitations). You saw how inserts, updates, and deletes can be conducted with embedded SQL programs. Then you looked at querying data and retrieving single rows and multiple rows. With single-row retrieval, you looked at the single `SELECT` statement and, in the process, learned how to handle `NULL`s in the query results. In multiple-row retrieval queries, you looked at the cursor concept and learned how to declare cursors, open them, use them to fetch the records one at a time, and close them when you are done with them. You also learned how cursors can be used in updates, deletes, and transactions.

CHAPTER 18

Implementing Cursors

In This Chapter

What Is a Cursor?

A relational database usually works with a set of data. A cursor can be defined as the **CUR**rent **S**et **O**f **R**ows the client application is working with. A cursor thus allows the client application to work with each individual row or one set of rows at a time and optionally update or delete the data. Cursors are typically used in interactive applications when the user wants to scroll up and down the resultset.

Cursor Types

This section discusses the cursor implementation as defined in the SQL-92 specification. The DECLARE CURSOR statement specifies a cursor; its syntax is as follows:

```
DECLARE <cursor_name> SENSITIVE ¦ INSENSITIVE
[SCROLL] CURSOR [WITH HOLD]
FOR <select_statement>
FOR READ ONLY ¦ UPDATE OF <columns>
```

In the DECLARE statement, <cursor_name> represents the name given to the cursor, and <select_statement> represents the SELECT statement that forms the data for the cursor. You can set attributes for the cursor in the DECLARE statement. The SENSITIVE option allows the cursor to see changes made to the rows that qualify the SELECT statement or any new rows added that meet the requirements of the SELECT statement. The INSENSITIVE option allows the cursor to work with a temporary copy of data, isolated from any changes happening to the qualifying rows. The SCROLL option for the INSENSITIVE cursor allows the application to traverse the cursor in an up or down direction. It allows backward, relative, and absolute positioning in the resultset. The READ ONLY option allows only reading rows from the cursor. If the INSENSITIVE, SCROLL, or SELECT statement with ORDER BY is used, then the cursor is READ ONLY by default. The UPDATE OF option is used to indicate what columns in the SELECT statement can be updated by the positioned UPDATE statement. The WITH HOLD option allows the cursor to be open when a SQL transaction is terminated with a commit operation. A cursor created with the HOLD option is closed if the SQL transaction is terminated with a rollback operation. A cursor declared without the HOLD option is closed when the SQL transaction in which it was created is terminated. A cursor is in either the open state or the closed state. Issuing the OPEN statement opens the cursor. The syntax of the OPEN statement is as follows:

```
OPEN <cursor_name>
```

The OPEN statement executes the SELECT statement specified in the DECLARE statement, acquires locks as necessary on the qualifying rows (the locking mechanism is implementation dependent), and positions the row pointer before the first row. Issuing the

FETCH statement subsequently positions the open cursor on a specific row and retrieves the values of that row's columns. The FETCH statement returns a status value indicating the operation's outcome. This is its syntax:

```
FETCH NEXT ¦ PRIOR ¦ FIRST ¦ LAST ¦
[ABSOLUTE ¦ RELATIVE] <number_of_rows>
[FROM] <cursor_name>
INTO <variable_list>
```

The NEXT, PRIOR, FIRST, and LAST options allow positioning within the resultset based on the options you have when declaring the cursor. The ABSOLUTE and RELATIVE options allow positioning within the resultset by indicating the number of rows to move from the current location. The ABSOLUTE option positions the cursor on a row from the front or the end of the cursor. The RELATIVE option positions the cursor on a row either forward or backward from the current position. The name of the cursor from which to fetch the data is specified in <cursor_name>. The <variable_list> parameter determines the variables that hold the values of the columns in the row. You can use a positioned UPDATE statement to update the columns of the current row based on the cursor position. A positioned DELETE statement can be used to delete the same. Issuing the CLOSE statement closes the open cursor and frees any resources used by the cursor. Here is the syntax of the CLOSE statement:

```
CLOSE <cursor_name>
```

All cursors work with the four SQL-92 transaction isolation levels.

Cursor Implementation in Oracle 8.0

Oracle uses work areas to execute SQL statements and store the processing information. A PL/SQL construct called a *cursor* lets you name a work area and access its stored information. There are two kinds of cursors: implicit and explicit. PL/SQL implicitly declares a cursor for all SQL data manipulation statements, including queries that return only one row. For queries that return more than one row, you can declare an explicit cursor to process the rows individually. In Oracle, any resultset from a SELECT statement is treated as a forward-only cursor when fetched in the client application. This holds true whether you are using Oracle Forms, ODBC, OCI, or Embedded SQL as your development tool. Every FETCH command issued by the client application results in a call to the server. If a client application wants to fetch more than one row at a time across the network, it must set up an array in its program and perform an array fetch. Between fetches, no locks are held at the server for a read-only cursor because of Oracle's multiversioning concurrency model. When a SELECT statement with the FOR UPDATE clause specifies an updatable cursor, all the requested rows in the SELECT statement are locked when the statement is opened. These row-level locks remain in place until a COMMIT or ROLLBACK statement is issued. Oracle supports only forward-scrolling cursors. The fetch operations can be performed only in the forward direction. Scrollable cursors can, however, be used while developing applications with ODBC or ADO, if the Oracle ODBC driver supports client cursors.

Implicit Cursors

PL/SQL maintains an implicit cursor by the name *SQL* that is defined and initialized every time a SQL command is executed. An implicit cursor is maintained for all data manipulation commands, too. After each stage of execution, the cursor retains enough information about the SQL statement to re-execute the statement without starting over, as long as no other SQL statement has been associated with that cursor. By opening several cursors, the parsed representation of several SQL statements can be saved. Repeated execution of the same SQL statements is possible, then, without parsing the statements again. The implicit cursor thus created by Oracle is named SQL. The OPEN, FETCH, and CLOSE statements cannot be used on the SQL cursor. The SQL cursor has attributes, however, that can be used in PL/SQL code to return information about executing an INSERT, UPDATE, DELETE, or SELECT INTO statement. The values of the cursor attributes always refer to the most recently executed SQL statement. Before Oracle opens the SQL cursor, the implicit cursor attributes, shown in the following list, are initialized to NULL:

- %FOUND Until a SQL data manipulation statement is executed, %FOUND returns NULL. If an INSERT, UPDATE, or DELETE statement affected one or more rows, or a SELECT INTO statement returned one or more rows, then %FOUND returns TRUE. Otherwise, %FOUND returns FALSE.

- %ISOPEN Always returns FALSE because Oracle automatically closes the SQL cursor after executing the associated SQL statement.

- %NOTFOUND %NOTFOUND is the logical opposite of %FOUND. If an INSERT, UPDATE, or DELETE statement affected no rows, or a SELECT INTO statement returned no rows, then %NOTFOUND returns TRUE. Otherwise, %NOTFOUND returns FALSE.

- %ROWCOUNT Returns the number of rows affected by an INSERT, UPDATE, or DELETE statement, or returned by a SELECT INTO statement. %ROWCOUNT yields 0 if an INSERT, UPDATE, or DELETE statement affected no rows or if a SELECT INTO statement returned no rows. If a SELECT INTO statement returns more than one row, PL/SQL raises the predefined exception TOO_MANY_ROWS, and %ROWCOUNT yields 1, not the actual number of rows that satisfy the query.

The PL/SQL code in Listing 18.1 shows an example of how to use the implicit cursor variables.

LISTING 18.1 LST18_1.TXT—PL/SQL Code Showing Implicit Cursors

```
CREATE or REPLACE PROCEDURE DeleteDept
(DeptNumber IN int)
AS
BEGIN
DELETE FROM dept WHERE DeptNo = DeptNumber;
IF SQL%ROWCOUNT = 0 THEN
 DBMS_OUTPUT.PUT_LINE('No departments were deleted.');
END IF;
COMMIT;
END;
/
Set serveroutput on;
Execute DeleteDept( 2413 );
```

The values of the cursor attributes always refer to the most recently executed SQL statement, wherever that statement is. It might be in a different scope (for example, in a different stored procedure). If the attribute value is required later, then it needs to be assigned to a Boolean variable immediately after executing the statement.

Explicit Cursors

Explicit cursors can be declared for SELECT statements. They can be declared in the declarative part of any PL/SQL block, subprogram, or package. The OPEN, FETCH, and CLOSE statements manipulate the cursor. A cursor can be declared in PL/SQL by using the following syntax:

```
CURSOR <cursor_name> [<parameter_list>]
  [RETURN <return_type>] IS <select_statement>;
```

In this statement, <cursor_name> is the name of the cursor, <parameter_list> is the list of parameters passed to the cursor, <select_statement> is the SELECT statement that returns the resultset for the cursor, and <return_type> represents the record or row in the SELECT statement. The <select_statement> can use the FOR UPDATE clause to lock the data being read from the cursor for updating. The %ROWTYPE attribute can be used in the RETURN clause to provide a record type that represents the row in a table or a row returned by a previously declared cursor. The %TYPE attribute can be used with a previously declared record. The parameter list is set up with the following syntax:

```
<cursor_parameter > [IN] datatype [{:= ¦ DEFAULT} <value>]
```

The cursor's parameters can be used in the SELECT statement, but they cannot be used to return values. The cursor parameters can also be initialized to a default value. The scope of the parameters is local to the cursor only. They can be used only in the SELECT statement specified for the cursor. The PL/SQL block in Listing 18.2 shows some examples of declaring cursors.

LISTING 18.2 LST18_2.TXT—PL/SQL Code for Declaring Cursors

```
DECLARE
 CURSOR EmpCursor IS SELECT empno, ename, sal FROM emp WHERE job = 'MANAGER';
 CURSOR DeptCursor10 RETURN dept%ROWTYPE IS
  SELECT * FROM dept WHERE deptno = 30;
 /* cursor declared with select statement using local variable */
 DeptNumber INT := 40;
 CURSOR DeptCursor40 RETURN dept%ROWTYPE IS
  SELECT * FROM dept WHERE deptno = DeptNumber;
 /* cursor declared with parameters */
 CURSOR EmpSalCursor (LowSalary INTEGER DEFAULT 500,
           HighSalary INTEGER DEFAULT 2000) IS
SELECT * FROM emp WHERE sal >= LowSalary AND sal <= HighSalary;
BEGIN
 NULL;
END;
/
```

The OPEN statement is used to pass parameters to a cursor. Unless a default value is supplied for the cursor parameters, you must provide values for the parameters when the OPEN statement is issued. The syntax of the OPEN statement is as follows:

```
OPEN <cursor_name> [(<parameter_list>)];
```

The FETCH statement is used to retrieve a row from the resultset into local variables. After each FETCH statement, the cursor position moves to the next row in the resultset. Here is the FETCH statement's syntax:

```
FETCH <cursor_name> INTO <variable_list>;
```

For each column returned by the SELECT statement for the cursor, the <variable_list> should contain a corresponding variable. A PL/SQL record that identifies the row in the resultset can also be specified in the INTO clause. The data types of all variables must be compatible with those in the resultset's columns.

The CLOSE statement closes the cursor and disassociates it from the resultset. Here is its syntax:

```
CLOSE <cursor_name>;
```

You can reopen a cursor again after closing it. Any operation performed on a closed cursor raises the predefined exception INVALID_CURSOR. Listing 18.3 shows a PL/SQL block that declares a cursor with parameters and reads data from it.

LISTING 18.3 LST18_3.TXT—Cursor using OPEN, FETCH, and CLOSE statements

```
DECLARE
 /* cursor declared with parameters */
 CURSOR EmpSalCursor (LowSalary INTEGER DEFAULT 500,
           HighSalary INTEGER DEFAULT 2000) IS
SELECT ename FROM emp WHERE sal >= LowSalary AND sal <= HighSalary;
 EmployeeName emp.ENAME%TYPE;
BEGIN
 OPEN EmpSalCursor(1000);
 FETCH EmpSalCursor INTO EmployeeName;
 DBMS_OUTPUT.PUT_LINE('Employee Name is: ' || EmployeeName);
 CLOSE EmpSalCursor;
END;
/
```


The explicit cursor can be used with the FOR LOOP instead of the OPEN, FETCH, and CLOSE statements. A cursor FOR LOOP implicitly declares its loop index as a %ROWTYPE record, opens a cursor, repeatedly fetches rows of values from the resultset into fields in the record, and closes the cursor when all rows have been processed. Listing 18.4 is an example of a PL/SQL block that uses a FOR LOOP to open and fetch data from a cursor.

LISTING 18.4 LST18_4.TXT—Cursor Using FOR LOOP

```
DECLARE
 NewSalary INTEGER;
 Bonus INTEGER := 500;
 JobType emp.job%TYPE;
 CURSOR EmpSalCursor IS
  SELECT sal FROM emp WHERE job = JobType;
BEGIN
 FOR Employee IN EmpSalCursor LOOP
  NewSalary := Employee.sal + Bonus;
 END LOOP;
END;
/
```

In Listing 18.4, the SELECT statement refers to a PL/SQL variable to get all employees of the specified job type. Local variables can be used in the SELECT statement everywhere a regular expression can be used.

The SELECT statement can also be used with the FOR UPDATE clause to explicitly lock the rows being fetched from the cursor, ensuring that the data cannot be updated or deleted by other transactions. You can use the UPDATE and DELETE statement with the CURRENT OF clause perform positioned updates or deletes on the cursor. The FOR UPDATE clause identifies rows to be updated or deleted, and then locks each row in the resultset. This method is useful when you want to base an update on the existing values in a row. In this case, the FOR UPDATE clause makes sure the row is not changed by another user before the update.

The optional keyword NOWAIT tells Oracle not to wait if another user has locked the table. Control is immediately returned to your program so that it can do other work before trying again to acquire the lock. If you omit the keyword NOWAIT, Oracle waits until the table is available. The wait has no limit unless the table is remote, in which case the Oracle initialization parameter DISTRIBUTED_LOCK_TIMEOUT sets a limit. All rows are locked when you open the cursor, not as they are fetched. The rows are unlocked when the transaction is committed or rolled back. FETCH statements cannot be performed on a cursor declared with the FOR UPDATE clause after the transaction has ended. When querying multiple tables, the FOR UPDATE clause can be used to restrict row locking to particular tables. Rows in a table are locked only if the FOR UPDATE OF clause refers to a column in that table. For example, the PL/SQL code in Listing 18.5 declares a cursor that locks only the emp table in the SELECT statement.

LISTING 18.5 LST18_5.TXT—Cursor Using the FOR UPDATE Clause

```
DECLARE
 CURSOR EmpSalCursor IS
  SELECT e.ename, d.dname, e.sal FROM emp e, dept d WHERE e.job = 'CLERK'
  FOR UPDATE OF sal;
BEGIN
 NULL;
END;
/
```

Now let's look at an example that uses the CURRENT OF clause to update the data in a cursor. Listing 18.6 shows a PL/SQL block that updates the salary information for all managers in the emp table.

LISTING 18.6 LST18_6.TXT—Update Using CURRENT OF Clause

```
DECLARE
 NewSalary INTEGER;
 Bonus INTEGER := 500;
 JobType emp.job%TYPE;
 CURSOR EmpSalCursor IS
  SELECT empno, sal FROM emp WHERE job = JobType FOR UPDATE;
BEGIN
 JobType := 'ANALYST';
 FOR Employee IN EmpSalCursor LOOP
  DBMS_OUTPUT.PUT_LINE('Empno : ' || TO_CHAR(Employee.Empno) ||
            ', Old Salary: ' || TO_CHAR(Employee.Sal));

  NewSalary := Employee.sal + Bonus;
  UPDATE emp SET sal = NewSalary WHERE CURRENT OF EmpSalCursor;
 END LOOP;
 /* re-open cursor to see the updated data */
 FOR Employee IN EmpSalCursor LOOP
  DBMS_OUTPUT.PUT_LINE('Empno : ' || TO_CHAR(Employee.Empno) ||
            ', New Salary: ' || TO_CHAR(Employee.Sal));

 END LOOP;
 ROLLBACK;
END;
/
```


Explicit cursor attributes return information about the execution of the SELECT statement for the cursor. The cursor attributes %FOUND, %ISOPEN, %NOTFOUND, and %ROWCOUNT could be used with explicit cursors. The %ROWTYPE attribute can be used with the cursor declaration to declare record variables of the same row type as the cursor. Listing 18.7 shows an example of the declaration.

LISTING 18.7 LST18_7.TXT—Using %TYPE with a Declared Cursor

```
DECLARE
 JobType emp.job%TYPE;
 CURSOR EmpSalCursor IS
  SELECT empno, sal FROM emp WHERE job = JobType;
 EmpRecord EmpSalCursor%ROWTYPE;
BEGIN
JobType := 'ANALYST';
OPEN EmpSalCursor;
LOOP
```

LISTING 18.7 CONTINUED

```
 FETCH EmpSalCursor INTO EmpRecord;
 EXIT WHEN EmpSalCursor%NOTFOUND;
 DBMS_OUTPUT.PUT_LINE('Empno : ' || TO_CHAR(EmpRecord.Empno) || ',
Salary: ' ||
           TO_CHAR(EmpRecord.Sal));
 END LOOP;
END;
/
```

Oracle PL/SQL, therefore, has extensions to the basic cursor loops using the `OPEN`, `FETCH`, and `CLOSE` statements. The cursor attributes also help write code that is easy to read and use.

Cursor Variables

A cursor variable can be used to pass resultsets between PL/SQL stored procedures and other clients. It is declared as a reference data type, and its value can be passed from one scope to another. A cursor variable can refer to different SQL work areas. Cursor variables are declared in two steps:

- Define a `REF CURSOR` type
- Declare variables of that type

The syntax for defining `REF CURSOR` types is as follows:

```
TYPE <type_name> IS REF CURSOR RETURN <return_type>;
```

The `<type_name>` parameter is the name for the type definition, and `<return_type>` represents the record or row in the table. A cursor variable is then declared based on the type definition. After a `REF CURSOR` type has been defined, cursor variables of that type can be declared in any PL/SQL block or subprogram. Cursor variables can also be used as parameters to functions and stored procedures, but they cannot be declared in a package. Cursor variables do not have persistent state because they are pointers. Listing 18.8 shows some examples of cursor variable declarations.

LISTING 18.8 LST18_8.TXT—Cursor Variable Declarations

```
/* Declare using the return type and the %ROWTYPE attribute for
the dept table row */
DECLARE
 TYPE DeptCursorType IS REF CURSOR RETURN dept%ROWTYPE;
 DeptCursor DeptCursorType;
BEGIN
```

LISTING 18.8 CONTINUED

```
 NULL;
END;

/* Declare using the return type with a record variable */
DECLARE
 DeptRecord dept%ROWTYPE;
 TYPE DeptCursorType IS REF CURSOR RETURN DeptRecord%TYPE;
 DeptCursor DeptCursorType;
BEGIN
 NULL;
END;
/* Declare cursor variables as parameters to stored procedures */
DECLARE
 TYPE DeptCursorType IS REF CURSOR RETURN dept%ROWTYPE;
 PROCEDURE GetDepartments (DeptCursor IN OUT DeptCursorType);
BEGIN
 NULL;
END;
```


The `OPEN` statement associates a cursor variable with a `SELECT` statement, executes the `SELECT` statement, and creates the resultset. Here is its syntax:

```
OPEN <cursor_variable> FOR <select_statement>;
```

The `<cursor_variable>` parameter can be a PL/SQL cursor variable or a host variable. Cursor variables do not take parameters while opening the cursor. The `<select_statement>` can, however, refer to PL/SQL variables, host variables, parameters, and functions. The `<select_statement>` cannot use the `FOR UPDATE` clause also. Listing 18.9 shows how cursor variables can be declared in a Pro*C program.

LISTING 18.9 LST18_9.TXT—Using Cursor Variables in a Pro*C Program

```
EXEC SQL BEGIN DECLARE SECTION;
  /* Declare host cursor variable. */
  SQL_CURSOR DeptCursor;
EXEC SQL END DECLARE SECTION;

/* Initialize host cursor variable. */
EXEC SQL ALLOCATE :DeptCursor;

/* Pass host cursor variable to PL/SQL block to open a cursor. */
EXEC SQL EXECUTE
BEGIN
```

LISTING 18.9 CONTINUED

```
  OPEN :DeptCursor FOR SELECT * FROM dept;
END;
END-EXEC;
```

The host cursor variables are compatible with any query return type—that is, they are weakly typed. A cursor variable can be used in a PL/SQL packaged procedure, as shown in Listing 18.10.

LISTING 18.10 LST18_10.TXT—Using Cursor Variables in a PL/SQL Package

```
CREATE PACKAGE Departments AS
 TYPE DeptCursorType IS REF CURSOR RETURN dept%ROWTYPE;
 PROCEDURE GetDepartments (DeptCursor IN OUT DeptCursorType);
END Departments;
/

CREATE PACKAGE BODY Departments AS
 PROCEDURE GetDepartments (DeptCursor IN OUT DeptCursorType) IS
 BEGIN
  OPEN DeptCursor FOR SELECT * FROM dept;
 END;
END Departments;
/
```

You can also create a standalone procedure that refers to the `REF CURSOR` type `DeptCursor` defined in the package departments. Any variables in the `SELECT` statement are evaluated only when the cursor variable is opened. To change the resultset or the values of the variable in the query, the cursor has to be reopened.

The `FETCH` statement retrieves one row at a time from the resultset. Its syntax is shown here:

```
FETCH <cursor_variable>
INTO <variable_list> ¦ <record_name>;
```

Listing 18.11 shows a PL/SQL example that declares cursor variables and fetches data into a record.

LISTING 18.11 LST18_11.TXT—Fetching Data Using Cursor Variables

```
DECLARE
 TYPE DeptCursorType IS REF CURSOR RETURN dept%ROWTYPE;
 DeptRecord dept%ROWTYPE;
 DeptCursor DeptCursorType;
```

LISTING 18.11 CONTINUED

```
BEGIN
 OPEN DeptCursor FOR SELECT * FROM dept;
 LOOP
 FETCH DeptCursor INTO DeptRecord;
 EXIT WHEN DeptCursor%NOTFOUND;
 DBMS_OUTPUT.PUT_LINE('Department Name: ' || DeptRecord.DNAME);
 END LOOP;
 CLOSE DeptCursor;
END;
/
```

The return type of the cursor variable should be compatible with the INTO clause of the FETCH statement. For each column value returned by the query associated with the cursor variable, there must be a corresponding, type-compatible field or variable in the INTO clause. Also, the number of fields or variables must equal the number of column values. The error occurs at compile time, if the cursor variable is strongly typed, or at runtime, if it is weakly typed. At runtime, PL/SQL raises the predefined exception ROWTYPE_MISMATCH before the first fetch. So if you trap the error and execute the FETCH statement using a different INTO clause, no rows are lost. The predefined exception INVALID_CURSOR is raised if a FETCH statement is issued on a closed cursor or a never-opened cursor.

The CLOSE statement releases the cursor used by the variable. The resultset is not available after the CLOSE statement is issued. Here is the syntax of the CLOSE statement:

```
CLOSE <cursor_variable>;
```

The predefined exception INVALID_CURSOR is raised if the CLOSE statement is used on an already closed cursor or a never-opened cursor. Cursor variables have the following restrictions when used in PL/SQL blocks:

- Cursor variables cannot be declared in a package because they do not have any persistent storage space.
- Remote stored procedures cannot accept the cursor variables as parameters.
- If a host cursor variable is passed to a PL/SQL block, the cursor has to be reopened again on the server side before any FETCH operation can be performed.
- The SELECT statement used in the OPEN statement cannot use the FOR UPDATE clause.
- Cursor variables cannot be used with operators to check, for example, nullability or equality.
- NULL values cannot be assigned to cursor variables.

- Cursor variables cannot be used with dynamic SQL.
- Cursors and cursor variables are not interoperable. For example, cursor variables cannot be used in the cursor `FOR LOOP`.
- `REF CURSOR` types cannot be used as column types in `CREATE TABLE` or `CREATE VIEW` statements.

The cursor attributes `%FOUND`, `%ISOPEN`, `%NOTFOUND`, and `%ROWCOUNT` could be used with cursor variables.

Cursor Implementation in Microsoft SQL Server 7.0

The cursor support in Microsoft SQL Server 7.0 can be broadly classified into two categories: server-side cursors and client-side cursors. The server-side cursors are made up of the Transact-SQL cursors and API server cursors. The client API implements the client-side cursors.

- **Transact-SQL cursors** Transact-SQL cursors can be used in Transact-SQL batches, stored procedures, and triggers. Transact-SQL cursors are implemented on the server and are compliant with SQL-92 cursor syntax.
- **API server cursors** API server cursors are implemented on the server. The API cursor functions are used in ADO (Microsoft ActiveX Data Object), OLE DB, ODBC (open database connectivity), and DB-Library.
- **Client-side cursors** Client-side cursors are implemented on the client side by the DB-Library DLL, ADO DLL, or the SQL Server ODBC DLL. The resultset is cached on the client-side, and the cursor operations are performed on the client.

With server-side cursors, server resources are used to manage the resultset. These are the advantages offered by server-side cursors:

- Server-side cursors eliminate the need for the client to cache the data for the resultset and the resources required for maintaining the cursor.
- Multiple statements can be active at the same time when using server-side cursors because no results are pending on the connection between cursor operations.
- Positioned updates and deletes on the resultset are more reliable and accurate with server-side cursors.

- Keyset-driven and dynamic cursors can be used with server-side cursors. These cursors offer rich functionality in terms of scrolling, updating data, and ensuring transaction isolation.
- Performance is improved if only a subset of the resultset is fetched by the application from time to time.

The client-side cursors are maintained on the client machine. Their advantages are as follows:

- Better cursor performance for small resultsets.
- Cursor functionality can be provided to applications when connecting to data sources that do not implement server-side cursors or do not implement certain cursor features.
- They allow applications to work in a disconnected mode, where the connection to the server is not maintained.
- Support for operations like sorting, filtering, and find data on the client side.

A cursor type is chosen based on the following variables:

- Percentage of data needed from a resultset
- Size of the resultset
- Performance of the cursor
- Transaction isolation level at which the cursor operates

Microsoft SQL Server has several ways to use cursors:

- Microsoft OLE DB Provider for SQL Server supports the cursor functionality of the ADO and OLE DB APIs
- Microsoft SQL Server ODBC driver supports the cursor functionality of ODBC, RDO, DAO, and MFC Database Classes APIs
- DB-Library DLL supports the cursor functionality of the DB-Library APIs
- Transact-SQL supports the SQL-92-compatible cursors and extended functionality
- Microsoft Embedded SQL for C supports the Embedded SQL standard cursor functionality

Microsoft SQL Server supports four concurrency options for server cursors that affect all cursor operations and performance. These are the options:

- `READ_ONLY` No locks are held on the rows of the resultset. Positioned updates or deletes are not allowed on the cursor.

- `OPTIMISTIC WITH VALUES` No locks are held on the rows of the resultset. Positioned updates are allowed on the cursor. At the time of the update, the current values in the row are compared against the values fetched. If any of the values have changed, then the update operation is disallowed.
- `OPTIMISTIC WITH ROW VERSIONING` The server uses a timestamp column in the table to detect changes. It is updated when a modification is made to a row in the table. This improves performance because only the timestamp column needs to be checked for any changes.
- `SCROLL LOCKS` This is a pessimistic approach in which the server locks the rows as they are read into the resultset of the cursor. An update lock is placed on the row fetched from the cursor. The lock is held for the duration of the transaction if the cursor is opened within a transaction or until the next row is fetched from the cursor.

Transact-SQL Cursors

Microsoft SQL Server by default sends data to the client as a resultset. This type of processing is used when the cursor attributes are the default values and there is no cursor processing on the server. In this mode, SQL Server sends network packets containing data to the client. The network packets are then cached in the client's network buffers. When the client application fetches the rows, the API DLL gets the data from the network buffers and transfers it to the client. This allows the client application to fetch data in the same manner by using the API fetch commands. Therefore, default resultsets can be used for any `SELECT` statement; it's the most efficient way to send results to the client. Transact-SQL cursors are used in batches, stored procedures, and triggers to perform row-based operations. The process of using a Transact-SQL cursor is as follows:

- Use the SQL-92-compatible `DECLARE CURSOR` statement to associate a `SELECT` statement with a cursor and define the cursor's attributes. Or use the cursor data type to declare a variable and define the cursor.
- Use the `OPEN` statement to execute the `SELECT` statement and get the rows for the cursor.
- Use the `FETCH` statement to fetch data for the columns from the current row into local variables declared in the Transact-SQL script.
- Use the `CLOSE` statement to close the cursor and free certain resources, such as locks on the current row and the resultset. At this time, the cursor can be reopened again by issuing the `OPEN` statement.
- Use the `DEALLOCATE` statement to free all resources used by the cursor.

The DECLARE CURSOR or the SET command can be used to define the cursor's characteristics and the query used to build the resultset for the cursor. The DECLARE CURSOR statement can be used with the SQL-92 syntax:

```
DECLARE <cursor_name> [INSENSITIVE] [SCROLL] CURSOR
FOR <select_statement>
[FOR [READ ONLY ¦ UPDATE [OF <column_list>>]
```

Or with the Transact-SQL syntax:

```
DECLARE <cursor_name> CURSOR
[LOCAL ¦ GLOBAL]
[FORWARD_ONLY ¦ SCROLL]
[STATIC ¦ KEYSET ¦ DYNAMIC ¦ FAST_FORWARD]
[READ_ONLY ¦ SCROLL_LOCKS ¦ OPTIMISTIC]
[TYPE_WARNING]
FOR <select_statement>
[FOR UPDATE [OF <column_list>>
```

The name of the Transact-SQL cursor is specified in <cursor_name>. The name should conform to the rules for identifiers in Transact-SQL. The LOCAL option scopes the cursor to the stored procedure, trigger, or batch where the cursor was created. The cursor can be referenced by local variables or passed as a parameter to other stored procedures. The cursor is automatically deallocated when the batch, stored procedure, or trigger terminates. The GLOBAL option scopes the cursor to the connection, and it is automatically deallocated when the connection is terminated. The default setting for the cursor if LOCAL or GLOBAL is specified is controlled by the default to local cursor database option.

The FORWARD_ONLY option for the cursor allows only fetch operations from the first to the last row. If the STATIC, KEYSET, or DYNAMIC option is not used, the cursor is dynamic in nature. The STATIC option makes a temporary copy of the cursor's resultset, and all cursor operations are performed on this copy. The STATIC option does not allow modifications to the resultset, and modifications made to the base tables are not reflected by the FETCH statements.

The KEYSET option for the cursor fixes the membership and order of the rows when the OPEN statement is executed. Modifications to nonkey values in the base tables, made by the connection that created the cursor or by other connections, are visible when the FETCH statement is executed. Modifications to key values by the connection that created the cursor are visible when the FETCH statement is executed. Inserts made by other connections are not visible when the FETCH statement is executed. If a row is deleted and the FETCH statement attempts to retrieve that row, a status value indicating the operation's failure is returned. The FETCH operation's status can be determined from the global variable @@FETCH_STATUS. The DYNAMIC option allows the cursor to see all data changes made as the FETCH operations are performed. The READ_ONLY option does not allow positioned updates or deletes to be performed using the cursor. The FAST_FORWARD option makes the cursor a FORWARD_ONLY, READ_ONLY cursor with performance benefits.

The SCROLL_LOCKS option ensures positioned updates or deletes through the cursor by locking the rows that are fetched. The OPTIMISTIC option specifies that the timestamp column or a checksum of the data be used to determine whether the data has been changed when performing a positioned update. The update operation fails if the data was changed by other connections. No locks are obtained on the rows as FETCH operations are performed on the cursor with the OPTIMISTIC option. The TYPE_WARNING option requests SQL Server to send a warning message to the client if the cursor is implicitly converted from one type to another. The <select_statement> option specifies the SELECT statement that provides the resultset of the cursor. The cursor is implicitly converted from one type to another if the clauses in the SELECT statement conflict with the type of cursor requested. The UPDATE option specifies the columns that can be updated by using positioned updates. If no column list is specified, then all columns can be updated. Cursor variables can also be declared in Transact-SQL scripts. The syntax for declaring a CURSOR variable is as follows:

```
DECLARE @cursor_variable CURSOR
```

A variable contains a reference to the cursor and can be passed to stored procedures. You initialize the cursor variable by assigning the name of a cursor to it or by using the SET statement, which has the following syntax:

```
SET @cursor_variable = @cursor_variable ¦ cursor_name
¦ CURSOR [FORWARD_ONLY ¦ SCROLL]
[READ_ONLY ¦ SCROLL_LOCKS ¦ OPTIMISTIC]
[TYPE_WARNING]
FOR <select_statement>
[FOR [READ ONLY ¦ UPDATE [OF <column_list>>]
```

The SQL-92-compatible FETCH statement retrieves a row from the cursor. This is its syntax:

```
FETCH [
[FIRST ¦ NEXT ¦ PRIOR ¦ LAST ¦
ABSOLUTE {<num_rows> ¦ <variable>} ¦ RELATIVE {<num_rows> ¦ <variable>}
] FROM]
[GLOBAL] <cursor_name> ¦ <cursor_variable>
[INTO <variable_list>]
```

The FETCH statement with the FIRST option returns the first row from the cursor. The NEXT option returns the subsequent row from the current row and increments the cursor's position. If the FETCH statement with the NEXT option is the first statement issued, then it returns the first row from the cursor. The NEXT option is also the default for FETCH operations.

The PRIOR option returns the previous row from the current row and decrements the cursor's position. The LAST option returns the last row of the cursor. The ABSOLUTE option returns the row *n* rows from the beginning or end of the cursor. You can indicate the number of rows as a constant or as a local Transact-SQL variable. A negative value for the number of rows implies that the row is returned from the end of the cursor. The RELATIVE option returns the row from the cursor's current position. The number of rows can be specified as a constant or as a local Transact-SQL variable. A negative value for the number of rows implies that the row is returned from before the cursor's current position.

The GLOBAL option is used to refer to a global cursor specified in <cursor_name>. You can also refer to the cursor by a Transact-SQL cursor variable and specify it in <cursor_variable>. The INTO option assigns the data from the columns of the fetched row into local variables. The data from the columns is assigned starting from the leftmost variables and their corresponding columns. The data type of each variable should match the data type of the column or be a data type that SQL Server can implicitly convert. If the INTO option is not specified, then the fetched row is returned as a resultset to the client application. Table 18.1 lists the options that can be used with the SQL-92-style DECLARE CURSOR statement and the Transact-SQL-style DECLARE CURSOR or SET statement.

TABLE 18.1 DECLARE CURSOR Options

FETCH *Option*	*SQL-92-Style Cursor Options*	*Transact-SQL-Style Cursor Options*
FIRST, NEXT, PRIOR, LAST, ABSOLUTE, RELATIVE	SCROLL	KEYSET, STATIC, or SCROLL without DYNAMIC, FORWARD_ONLY, or FAST_FORWARD options
FIRST, NEXT, PRIOR, LAST, RELATIVE	N/A	DYNAMIC SCROLL
NEXT	Without SCROLL	FORWARD_ONLY or FAST_FORWARD

The @@FETCH_STATUS global variable returns the status of the last FETCH operation performed on a cursor by the connection. These are the values returned by @@FETCH_STATUS:

- 0 Indicates that the FETCH statement was successful
- -1 Indicates that the FETCH statement failed or the position of the row is beyond the cursor's resultset
- -2 Indicates that the fetched row has been deleted from the base table

The @@CURSOR_ROWS global variable returns the rows that qualified for the last opened cursor. The values returned by @@CURSOR_ROWS are as follows:

- -*n* Indicates that the cursor is being populated asynchronously. The absolute value of -*n* is the number of rows currently in the keyset for the cursor.
- -1 Indicates that the cursor is dynamic.
- 0 Indicates that no resultset was generated for the last opened cursor, no cursors were opened, or the last opened cursor is closed or deallocated.
- *n* Indicates the total number of rows in the cursor.

The CURSOR_STATUS system function can be used to determine the validity of a cursor name or a cursor variable. This is its syntax:

```
CURSOR_STATUS ('local', '<cursor_name>' ¦
'global', '<cursor_name>' ¦ 'variable', <cursor_variable>')
```

The first parameter to the function is a constant specifying whether the cursor is local, global, or represented by a variable. The second parameter supplies the name of the cursor for the local or global option or a cursor variable for the variable option. These are the return values of the CURSOR_STATUS function:

- 1 Indicates that the opened cursor represented by <cursor_name> or <cursor_variable> contains at least one row.
- 0 Indicates that the opened cursor referenced by <cursor_name> or <cursor_variable> is empty. This option is applicable for cursors created without the DYNAMIC option.
- -1 Indicates that the cursor represented by <cursor_name> or <cursor_variable> is closed.
- -2 Indicates that no cursor has been assigned to the <cursor_variable>.
- -3 Indicates that the cursor represented by <cursor_name> or <cursor_variable> does not exist.

The CLOSE statement releases the cursor's resultset and the locks held on the rows where the cursor is positioned. The cursor can be reopened by issuing the OPEN statement. This is the syntax of the CLOSE statement:

```
CLOSE [GLOBAL] <cursor_name> ¦ <cursor_variable>
```

The DEALLOCATE statement removes the reference to the cursor and releases all resources the cursor used. Here is its syntax:

```
DEALLOCATE [GLOBAL] <cursor_name> ¦ <cursor_variable>
```

The script in Listing 18.12 shows how to use Transact-SQL cursors with the SQL-92 style of the `DECLARE` statement and a cursor variable.

LISTING 18.12 LST18_12.TXT—Sample Script for Using Cursors

```
DECLARE @LastName nvarchar(10), @EmployeeID int, @CursorVar CURSOR
DECLARE SQL92Cursor CURSOR FOR
SELECT EmployeeID, LastName FROM Northwind..Employees
-- Create reference to the SQL92Cursor
SET @CursorVar = SQL92Cursor
OPEN SQL92Cursor
PRINT '"Fetching using the cursor name..."'
WHILE('FETCH-IS-OK'='FETCH-IS-OK')
BEGIN
 FETCH NEXT FROM SQL92Cursor INTO @EmployeeID, @LastName
 IF @@FETCH_STATUS < 0 BREAK
  PRINT '"Employee ID: ''' + STR(@EmployeeID) + ''', Last Name: ''' +
@Last_Name
END
CLOSE SQL92Cursor
-- Find out the status of the cursor variable
PRINT '"Cursor status of the variable: ''' +
   CURSOR_STATUS('variable', '@CursorVar')
-- Now open the cursor again by using the cursor variable
OPEN @CursorVar
PRINT '"Fetching using the cursor variable..."'
WHILE('FETCH-IS-OK'='FETCH-IS-OK')
BEGIN
 FETCH NEXT FROM @CursorVar INTO @EmployeeID, @LastName
 IF @@FETCH_STATUS < 0 BREAK
  PRINT '"Employee ID: ''' + STR(@EmployeeID) + ''', Last Name: ''' +
@Last_Name
END
CLOSE @CursorVar
DEALLOCATE SQL92Cursor
GO
```

Listing 18.12 also demonstrates how a cursor variable creates a reference to a cursor. The `WHILE` loop is used to fetch rows from the cursor until you reach the end of the resultset. For more help on the `WHILE` loop construct, refer to the SQL Server Books Online. The `CURSOR_STATUS` function is used in the script to show the status of the cursor variable before performing the `OPEN` operation on the cursor.

Listing 18.13 shows how to define a Transact-SQL cursor with the SET statement and the SCROLL option.

LISTING 18.13 LST18_13.TXT—Using Cursors in Stored Procedures

```
-- A procedure to fetch data from a cursor.
CREATE PROCEDURE FetchFromCursor
( @ProcCursorVar CURSOR VARYING OUTPUT )
AS
DECLARE @LastName nvarchar(10), @EmployeeID int
SET @ProcCursorVar = CURSOR SCROLL
         FOR SELECT EmployeeID, LastName FROM Northwind..Employees
         ORDER BY EmployeeID
OPEN @ProcCursorVar
WHILE('FETCH-IS-OK'='FETCH-IS-OK')
BEGIN
 FETCH NEXT FROM @ProcCursorVar INTO @EmployeeID, @LastName
 IF @@FETCH_STATUS < 0 BREAK
 PRINT 'Employee ID: ' + STR(@EmployeeID) + ', Last Name: ' + @Last_Name
END
GO

DECLARE @RowCount int, @CursorVar CURSOR
PRINT 'Fetching rows using the stored procedure...'
Exec FetchFromCursor @CursorVar OUTPUT

PRINT 'Retrieving the first row again...'
FETCH FIRST FROM @CursorVar

PRINT 'Retrieving the last row again...'
FETCH LAST FROM @CursorVar

PRINT 'Retrieving the fifth row from the beginning...'
FETCH ABSOLUTE 5 FROM @CursorVar

PRINT 'Retrieving the second row prior to the current (fifth) row...'
SET @RowCount = -2
FETCH RELATIVE @RowCount FROM @CursorVar

DEALLOCATE @CursorVar
GO
```

This example declares a scrollable cursor with the SET statement and uses the different FETCH options possible. The stored procedure FetchFromCur is also used to declare the cursor and fetch all rows from the cursor initially. The Transact-SQL batch then issues FETCH commands without the variable list to get certain rows from the cursor. For more help on the syntax of the CREATE PROCEDURE statement, refer to Chapter 26, "Microsoft Transact-SQL," or the SQL Server Books Online. The scrollable cursor used in the example allows all FETCH options to be used as demonstrated.

The SET TRANSACTION ISOLATION LEVEL statement determines the transaction isolation level under which the SELECT statements of the CURSOR operate. The transaction isolation level can also be set by using locking hints in the SELECT statement. The SET CURSOR_CLOSE_ON_COMMIT statement controls whether an open cursor is closed when a transaction is committed. The ON setting for the statement closes any open cursor when a transaction is committed using the COMMIT statement. This behavior is compliant with the SQL-92 specification. All open cursors are closed when a transaction is rolled back using the ROLLBACK statement, regardless of this setting. SQL Server has system stored procedures for monitoring cursor activity on the server:

- sp_cursor_list Supplies a list of cursors for the current connection and the attributes of the cursors
- sp_describe_cursor Determines the attributes of the server cursor
- sp_describe_cursor_columns Sets the attributes of the resultset's columns, such as name, data type, and length of the columns
- sp_describe_cursor_tables Sets the attributes of the base tables specified in the SELECT statement of the cursor

The data in the cursor can be updated by issuing positioned update and delete statements. The syntax of the positioned UPDATE statement is as follows:

```
UPDATE <table> ¦ <view> SET <column_values>
WHERE CURRENT OF GLOBAL <cursor_name> ¦ <cursor_variable>
```

This is the syntax of the positioned DELETE statement:

```
DELETE [FROM] <table> ¦ <view>
WHERE CURRENT OF GLOBAL <cursor_name> ¦ <cursor_variable>
```

The WHERE CURRENT OF clause indicates that the update or delete is performed on the current row fetched from the cursor.

API Server Cursors

The OLE-DB, ODBC, and DB-Library APIs create the API Server cursors. These APIs also support creating cursors for resultsets returned by stored procedures and `SELECT` statements. The application calls API cursor functions to perform all cursor operations. The following restrictions apply when using API server cursors:

- Transact-SQL batches, stored procedures, or triggers cannot return multiple resultsets
- Transact-SQL stored procedures cannot contain more than one `SELECT` statement
- `SELECT` statements cannot use clauses like `COMPUTE`, `COMPUTE BY`, `GROUP BY`, `HAVING`, and `UNION`
- Server cursors cannot be created on Transact-SQL statements that SQL Server does not support in cursors
- Execute statements cannot call a remote stored procedure

The API cursor functions use system stored procedures in SQL Server to perform cursor operations. These system stored procedures are stubs used to call the actual cursor implementation code in SQL Server. Ultimately, Transact-SQL cursors and API server cursors use the same code on the server. These are the system stored procedures provided by SQL Server:

- `sp_cursoropen` Used to declare the `SELECT` statement associated with the cursor, set the cursor's attributes, and create the resultset for the cursor
- `sp_cursorprepare` Used to compile the execution plan for the Transact-SQL batch where the cursor is created
- `sp_cursorunprepare` Used to remove the execution plan created by the `sp_cursorprepare` stored procedure
- `sp_cursoroption` Used to set the options for the cursor
- `sp_cursorexecute` Used to execute the prepared statement and create the resultset for the cursor
- `sp_cursorfetch` Used to fetch a row or block of rows from the cursor
- `sp_cursor` Used to perform positioned updates or deletes on the cursor
- `sp_cursorclose` Used to close the cursor and deallocate all resources

The use of server-side cursors is initiated on the client; the driver determines whether the statement to be executed is a `SELECT` statement or a stored procedure. If it is one of these, instead of sending the SQL string directly to Microsoft SQL Server, the driver invokes an extended stored procedure called sp_cursoropen and uses the SQL statement and other options as its arguments. This is the syntax of the sp_cursoropen stored procedure:

```
sp_cursoropen(cursor_handle, statement, scroll_option,
concurrency_option, number_of_rows)
```

The parameters to the stored procedure are as follows:

- `cursor_handle` A handle returned by the procedure and mapped to the current statement handle in the driver.
- `statement` The SELECT statement or a stored procedure that provides the resultset for the cursor. The stored procedure must contain a single SELECT statement only.
- `scroll_option` Cursor types can be KEYSET, STATIC, DYNAMIC, or FORWARD_ONLY.
- `concurrency_option` Concurrency control option can be READ_ONLY, LOCK, ROWVER, or VALUES.
- `number_of_rows` The number of rows in the resultset. The server provides this parameter if the resultset is materialized entirely when the cursor is opened.

The sp_cursoropen stored procedure causes the SQL statement to be executed and the metadata of the resultset to be returned. The sp_cursorfetch stored procedure is used by the API cursor engine to retrieve the next row set; this is its syntax:

```
sp_cursorfetch(cursor_name, fetch_type, row_number,
number_of_rows, value_list)
```

These are the parameters to the stored procedure:

- `cursor_handle` Handle returned by sp_cursoropen.
- `fetch_type` Can be NEXT, PREV, FIRST, LAST, ABSOLUTE, RELATIVE, BY_VALUE, REFRESH, or INFO.
- `row_number` The absolute or relative number of the row to fetch. It is used only when the fetch type is ABSOLUTE or RELATIVE.
- `number_of_rows` The number of rows to fetch. This value corresponds to the rowset size.
- `value_list` Optional parameter that specifies the data values used only with BY_VALUE fetches. This option allows the application to retrieve a specific row in the resultset by value.

The ABSOLUTE option for the fetch_type can be used only if the cursor was declared as keyset-driven or static. The BY_VALUE option requires the optional values parameters. FORWARD_ONLY cursors can use only the INFO, FIRST, NEXT, and REFRESH options. The positions for NEXT, PREV, and RELATIVE are determined with respect to the cursor position, which is considered to be the first row in the previous fetch operation. If the current fetch is the first fetch, the cursor position is considered to be before the start of the resultset. If a fetch operation fails because the requested cursor position is beyond or before the resultset, the cursor position is set to beyond the last row or before the first row, respectively.

The server manages and maintains the keys for keyset-driven cursors. The sp_cursor extended stored procedure performs the operations, such as updating, inserting, explicit locking, and deleting rows. When scrollable cursors are used, updates or deletes of fetched rows are usually initiated by some action of the end user. Typically, the user presses an arrow key or clicks the mouse to select a particular row and then types in the new values for the row. The application can perform a positioned update or delete and have considerable flexibility in handling concurrency control issues. The extended stored procedures are provided only as a way for the API functions to use SQL Server's cursor functionality. These stored procedures are not meant to be used in Transact-SQL batches or stored procedures.

Client-Side Cursors

The ODBC, ADO, and DB-Library APIs support client cursors that are implemented on the client. Client cursors use default resultsets to cache the resultset on the client and perform the cursor operations against this cached data. Only forward-only and static cursors can be used with client cursors. Client cursors can be used to avoid the restrictions that server cursors impose on certain Transact-SQL batches, such as when a client application wants to provide a disconnected resultset. Listing 18.14 shows Visual Basic code that uses ADO to implement a disconnected resultset.

LISTING 18.14 LST18_14.TXT—Example for a Disconnected Resultset

```
Dim SQLConnection As ADODB.Connection
Dim ResultSet As ADODB.Recordset

' Create the connection object and open the connection.
Set SQLConnection = New ADODB.Connection
SQLConnection.Open ''DSN=localserver'', ''sa'', ''''
  ' Create the recordset object and open the recordset object
Set ResultSet = New ADODB.Recordset

' Set the cursor location to client side to get a disconnected recordset.
ResultSet.CursorLocation = adUseClient
ResultSet.Open ''Select Last_Name from Northwind..Employees'', _
        SQLConnection, ADODB.adOpenForwardOnly, _
```

LISTING 18.14 CONTINUED

```
        ADODB.adLockOptimistic

' Disconnect the connection for the resultset and close the connection
Set ResultSet.ActiveConnection = Nothing
SQLConnection.Close

' Show value of a field from the disconnected resultset
Debug.Print ''Field value is: '' & ResultSet.Fields(0).Value

Set ResultSet = Nothing
Set SQLConnection = Nothing
```

The client cursor engine for ADO caches the resultset from the server after the recordset is opened. The application can then close the connection and work locally. This is demonstrated in the code by printing the value of a field in the recordset after the connection is closed. The recordset can also be updated later by connecting to the server again and issuing the `UPDATE` statement.

Cursor Implementation in Data Access Technologies

Data access technologies provide connectivity between the client application and the server. Some of the commonly used ones are ODBC, OLE DB, ADO, and JDBC. Data access technologies are characterized by the following:

- Generic methods to access data from disparate data sources
- Portability of applications
- Functions to use the server's features efficiently and easily

Data access technologies have cursor types programmers can use, depending on their needs and requirements. These are some of the cursor types:

- Static The membership, order, and values of the cursor's resultset are fixed when the cursor is opened. This cursor does not reflect any changes made to the resultset by other users.
- Dynamic The membership, order, and values of the cursor's resultset are always changing. All changes made to the resultset are reflected by the cursor the next time data is fetched.

- Keyset The membership and order of the cursor's resultset are fixed when the cursor is opened. Most changes made to the resultset are reflected by the cursor the next time data is fetched.
- Mixed (keyset/dynamic) The keyset of the cursor is smaller than the resultset, but larger than the rowset. Within the boundaries of the keyset, a mixed cursor has all the characteristics of a keyset cursor. When the fetch statement scrolls beyond the keyset's boundaries, it becomes dynamic and retrieves the next rowset. This is a unique type of cursor supported by the ODBC and ADO APIs.

All the cursors can be made forward-only, in which case the fetch statements can be used in a serial manner only. The SQL-92/ISO behavior for cursors are contained in the defined cursor types, and each API has methods for setting the cursor type accordingly. The typical default cursor type is forward-only or a non-scrollable cursor that can only move forward in the resultset. With some forward-only cursors, all insert, update, and delete operations made by the current user or by other users to the rows in the resultset are visible as the rows are fetched. A scrollable cursor is used to move forward and backward through the resultset.

Cursor Implementation in ODBC

ODBC is a standard API that can be used to access data in relational databases, flat-file databases, and other data sources. The ODBC architecture consists of four components:

- Application This is the program written in programming languages such as C and Visual Basic that calls ODBC functions to communicate with a data source.
- Driver Manager Manages communication between the application and its ODBC drivers.
- Driver Performs the actual calls to the data source. It is also responsible for translating the ODBC commands sent by the application into the data source's native format.
- Data Source Supplies the information required for the driver to access the data in a data source.

The ODBC driver manager always creates a cursor when a resultset is returned from the server. ODBC supports several types of cursors, scrolling and positioning within a cursor, concurrency options for a cursor, and positioned update/deletes. The cursor's attributes are set by using functions. The `SQLExecuteDirect` and `SQLExecute` functions execute the statement specified and open a cursor for the resultset. The `SQLFetch` and `SQLExtendedFetch` functions fetch data from the cursor. The `SQLSetPos` function and `WHERE CURRENT OF` clause performs positioned updates or deletes on the cursor. The `SQLCloseCursor` function is used to close the cursor and free the resources used by the cursor. The ODBC API has two different methods for setting a cursor's attributes using the SQLSetStmtAttr function:

- Cursor types   Set using the SQL_ATTR_CURSOR_TYPE attribute of SQLSetStmtAttr. The supported ODBC cursor types are forward-only, static, keyset-driven, mixed, and dynamic.
- Cursor behavior   Set using the SQL_ATTR_CURSOR_SCROLLABLE and SQL_ATTR_-CURSOR_SENSITIVITY attributes of SQLSetStmtAttr. These options are SQL-92 and ISO SQL compatible.

The ODBC driver uses two methods of binding when dealing with more than one row.

- Column binding   Each column is bound to an array of variables. The size of each array is the same as the rowset size.
- Row binding   Each row is bound to a structure that holds the data for the row. The structure is present in an array that's the same size as the rowset size.

All cursor operations are affected by the concurrency options set by the application. The SQL_ATTR_CONCURRENCY option of SQLSetStmtAttr is used to set the concurrency type. These are the valid concurrency types:

- Read-only   SQL_CONCUR_READONLY
- Column values   SQL_CONCUR_VALUES
- Row version   SQL_CONCUR_ROWVER
- Lock   SQL_CONCUR_LOCK

The locking behavior of cursors is based on an interaction between concurrency attributes and the transaction isolation level set by the client. The SQL_ATTR_TXN_ISOLATION option of SQLSetStmtAttr sets the transaction isolation level. The ODBC API supports the following cursor transaction isolation levels:

- SQL_TXN_READ_COMMITTED   Read committed
- SQL_TXN_READ_UNCOMMITTED   Read uncommitted
- SQL_TXN_REPEATABLE_READ   Repeatable read
- SQL_TXN_SERIALIZABLE   Serializable

Table 18.2 shows the cursor models in ODBC and their relative advantages.

TABLE 18.2 ODBC Cursor Types

Cursor Type	*Performance*	*Consistency*	*Concurrency*	*Accuracy*
Static	Dependent	Excellent	Good	Poor
Keyset	Good	Good	Good	Good
Dynamic	Dependent	Poor	Excellent	Excellent
Mixed	Good	Fair	Good	Dependent

ODBC has two functions for fetching rows from a resultset: the `SQLFetch` function, for retrieving rows from forward-only cursors one row at a time, and the `SQLExtendedFetch` function, designed to fetch rows from scrollable cursors. For scrolling operations, `SQLExtendedFetch` has the following options, which are compatible with the SQL-92 `FETCH` options:

- `SQL_FETCH_FIRST` Fetches the first rowset.
- `SQL_FETCH_NEXT` Fetches the next rowset.
- `SQL_FETCH_PRIOR` Fetches the prior rowset.
- `SQL_FETCH_LAST` Fetches the last rowset.
- `SQL_FETCH_RELATIVE` Fetches the rowset *n* rows from the current position in the cursor. The value *n* can be positive or negative to indicate forward or backward direction.
- `SQL_FETCH_ABSOLUTE` Fetches the rowset beginning at the *n*th row in the resultset. The value *n* can be positive or negative to specify forward or backward direction.

The `SQLExtendedFetch` options also allow an application to fetch either a single row or multiple rows. This capability depends on the data source. The Microsoft SQL Server ODBC driver, for example, supports specifying the rowset sizes for the fetch operation. One of the new features in ODBC 2.0 is the support for *bookmarks*, values used to reposition a cursor to a particular row in a resultset. Each bookmark is a 32-bit value that the application requests from the ODBC driver for a particular row. The application repositions the cursor to that row by calling `SQLExtendedFetch` with the special fetch type of `SQL_FETCH_BOOKMARK`. In interactive applications, a bookmark is used when the user clicks on a particular displayed row to update it, but then, before doing the update, the user moves the focus to another row or rowset. For example, when the user edits the contents of a row, the focus remains on the row the user was working with, and that row must be fetched again.

There are many ways to implement bookmarks. For example, an application could use a fully keyset-driven cursor and store the key value for the row that was clicked on. When it needs to return to the row, the application could search the keyset for the key value previously stored. The application can also maintain an array of logical row numbers (for each row), store the row number and the key of the row clicked on, and use the row number for a relative offset from the current row. Either case involves a fair amount of coding for the application that can be handled by the driver. Also, this approach works only with fully keyset-driven and static cursors; dynamic cursors are much harder to manage because their membership is not fixed. Bookmarks were designed to allow applications to store a specific row and return to that row with a minimum of effort on the application programmer's part. They are independent of the cursor model used (static, keyset-driven, or dynamic). Not all drivers support bookmarks, so the application needs to check for this capability before assuming it can be used.

ODBC supports two methods for performing positioned updates in a cursor: the `SQLSetPos` function and the `WHERE CURRENT OF` clause. The `SQLSetPos` function has the following options:

- `SQL_POSITION` Positions the cursor on a specific row in the current rowset
- `SQL_REFRESH` Refreshes data in the program variables bound to the resultset columns with the values from the row the cursor is currently positioned on
- `SQL_UPDATE` Updates the current row in the cursor with the values stored in the program variables bound to the resultset columns
- `SQL_DELETE` Deletes the current row in the cursor

The `SQLSetPos` function can be used with any statement resultset when the statement handle cursor attributes are set to use server cursors. The resultset columns must be bound to program variables. After the application has fetched a row, it calls `SQLSetPos` with the `SQL_POSITION` option to position the cursor on the row. The application could then call `SQLSetPos` with the `SQL_DELETE` option to delete the current row, or it can change the data values in the bound program variables and call `SQLSetPos` with the `SQL_UPDATE` option to update the current row. Applications can update or delete any row in the rowset with `SQLSetPos`, which is a convenient alternative to constructing and executing a SQL `UPDATE` or `DELETE` statement. `SQLSetPos` operates on the current rowset and can be used only after a call to `SQLFetchScroll`. Rowset size is set by a call to `SQLSetStmtAttr` with an attribute argument of `SQL_ATTR_ROW_ARRAY_SIZE`. The first row in the rowset is row number 1. The `RowNumber` argument in `SQLSetPos` must identify a row in the rowset; that is, its value must be in the range between `1` and the number of rows most recently fetched (which could be less than the rowset size). If `RowNumber` is `0`, the operation applies to every row in the rowset. The delete operation of `SQLSetPos` makes the data source delete one or more selected rows of a table. To delete rows with SQLSetPos, the application calls SQLSetPos with the SQL_DELETE option and RowNumber set to the number of the row to delete. If RowNumber is 0, all rows in the rowset are deleted. After SQLSetPos returns, the deleted row is the current row, and its status is SQL_ROW_DELETED. The row cannot be used in any further positioned operations, such as calls to SQLGetData or SQLSetPos. When deleting all rows of the rowset (RowNumber is equal to 0), the application can prevent the driver from deleting certain rows by using the row operation array in the same way as for the update operation of SQLSetPos. Every row that is deleted should be a row that exists in the resultset.

Positioned updates can also be done using the WHERE CURRENT OF clause on UPDATE, DELETE, and INSERT statements. The WHERE CURRENT OF clause requires a cursor name, which ODBC generates when the SQLGetCursorName function is called. Optionally, this clause can be specified when calling SQLSetCursorName. The following steps have to be used to perform a WHERE CURRENT OF update in an ODBC application:

- Call SQLSetCursorName to set a cursor name for the statement to be executed.
- Construct the SELECT statement with a FOR UPDATE OF clause and execute it.
- Call SQLFetchScroll to retrieve a rowset or SQLFetch to retrieve a row.
- Call SQLSetPos with the SQL_POSITION option to position the cursor on the row.
- Build and execute an UPDATE statement with a WHERE CURRENT OF clause using the cursor name set with SQLSetCursorName.

The SQLGetCursorName function can be called after executing the SELECT statement to get the default cursor name assigned by ODBC. SQLSetPos is preferred over WHERE CURRENT OF when using server cursors. If you are using a static, updatable cursor with the ODBC cursor library, the cursor library implements WHERE CURRENT OF updates by adding a WHERE clause with the key values for the underlying table.

Cursor Implementation in ADO

Microsoft ActiveX Data Objects (ADO) is a data access interface used to communicate with OLE DB-compliant data sources, such as Microsoft SQL Server 7.0. The discussion in this section is specific to ADO version 2.0. Applications can use ADO to connect to OLE DB data sources and to retrieve, manipulate, and update data from them. ADO is the application-level interface to OLE DB, a library of COM interfaces that enables universal access to diverse data sources. ADO is built on top of OLE DB and shields the application developer from the necessity of programming COM interfaces. ADO clients that communicate with OLE DB need an OLE DB provider, a dynamic link library that uses OLE DB interfaces and methods to query a SQL data source. ADO and OLE DB map cursors over the resultsets of executed SQL statements. SQLOLEDB implements these operations through the use of server cursors, which are cursors implemented on the server and managed by API cursor functions. By default, an ADO application does not use the API server cursors with SQLOLEDB. An ADO application can control the cursor functionality through the following `Recordset` properties:

- `CursorType` Indicates the type of cursor to be used. Valid options are `adOpenForwardOnly` (forward-only/read-only), `adOpenStatic` (static), `adOpenKeyset` (keyset), and `adOpenDynamic` (dynamic).
- `CursorLocation` Indicates the location of the cursor. Valid options are `adUseServer` (server cursor) and `adUseClient` (client cursor).
- `LockType` Indicates the type of locks placed on the rows of the cursor. Valid options are `adLockReadOnly` (read-only), `adLockPessimistic` (pessimistic locking), and `adLockOptimistic` or `adLockBatchOptimistic` (optimistic locking).
- `CacheSize` Specifies the number of records to be cached in the client's memory.

To use a server cursor, an application can set these properties to anything other than the default value and set the `CursorLocation` property to `adUseServer`. Server cursors are created only for statements that begin with the following:

```
SELECT
EXEC[UTE] <procedure_name>
{call <procedure_name>}
```

Even if an application explicitly requests a server cursor, server cursors are not created for other statements such as `INSERT`. Server cursors cannot be used with statements that generate more than one resultset. The sample Visual Basic code in Listing 18.15 opens a keyset cursor.

LISTING 18.15 LST18_15.TXT—ADO Sample Code That Uses a Server Cursor

```
Dim SQLConnection As ADODB.Connection
Dim ResultSet As ADODB.Recordset
Dim FieldValue

' Create the connection object and open the connection.
Set SQLConnection = New ADODB.Connection
SQLConnection.Open ''DSN=localserver'', ''sa'', ''''
' Create the recordset object and open the recordset object
Set ResultSet = New ADODB.Recordset
' Set the cursor location to server
ResultSet.CursorLocation = adUseServer
```

LISTING 18.15 CONTINUED

```
' Open a keyset-driven cursor with optimistic locking
ResultSet.Open ''Select LastName from Northwind..Employees'', _
        SQLConnection, ADODB.adOpenKeyset, _
        ADODB.adLockOptimistic
' Loop through the rows in the cursor
ResultSet.MoveFirst
Do While Not ResultSet.EOF
 Debug.Print ''Last Name of employee: '' & ResultSet!LastName
 ResultSet.MoveNext
Loop

' Close the recordset and connection
Set ResultSet = Nothing
Set SQLConnection = Nothing
```

The `Open` method opens a cursor for the `SELECT` statement and executes it on the server. Its syntax is discussed later in the chapter. The ADO `Supports` method determines what types of functionality are supported when a `Recordset` object is opened against the current OLE DB provider. The `Supports` method returns a Boolean value that indicates whether the provider supports the features identified by the various `CursorOptions` constants. The OLE DB Cursor Service retrieves data from a rowset, stores the data locally, and makes the data available, along with rich data-manipulation functionality, through rowset functions. The Cursor Service handles all rowsets independently. Rowsets do not share common data, and no integrity constraints are enforced. The Cursor Service doesn't try to replicate the provider data model, its integrity restrictions, or its data. Instead, it manipulates independent data sets as defined and required by the application. The Cursor Service has the following functions: data fetching, data manipulation, local updates, and local rowsets. Now let's look at some of the advanced features that ADO 2.0 offers when using client-side cursors.

With large resultsets, fetching can take a long time, so ADO has a way to fetch the resultset asynchronously. With asynchronous fetching, the user can see some results almost immediately, and then the rest can be retrieved in the background. Asynchronous fetching in ADO is implemented only for client cursors by setting the recordset's `CursorLocation` location property to `adUseClient`. The actual background fetching is implemented with the Remote Data Service cursor engine. There are two types of asynchronous fetches: blocking and nonblocking. The main difference between these two methods is how they handle any rows that need to be fetched. With the blocking type, the function being requested is executed and the control is returned to the application. For example, if the `MoveLast` function is called and the last row is not available in the cache currently, ADO waits until the last row has been made available, and then returns control to the application. For the nonblocking type, the `MoveLast` operation returns immediately, but the current row is changed to the last one fetched; the user is placed on the last row currently fetched, not on the last row of the resultset. Thus, the user can see that row and all the other rows already fetched.

Let's look at an application containing a grid in which 25 rows are displayed from a resultset at a time. When the form loads, the first 25 rows are fetched before control is returned to the user. The number of rows to return initially is controlled with the `Initial Fetch Size` property in the `RecordsetProperties` collection. Asynchronous fetching can be requested only by using the `Recordset` object, through the `Open` method's `Options` parameter. The Visual Basic code in Listing 18.16 shows how to perform asynchronous fetching with an initial fetch size.

LISTING 18.16 LST18_16.TXT—Asynchronous Fetching with Initial Fetch Size

```
Dim ResultSet As ADODB.Recordset
Sub Form_Load()
Dim SQLConnection as New ADODB.Connection

' Create the connection object and open the connection.
Set SQLConnection = New ADODB.Connection
SQLConnection.Open ''DSN=localserver'', ''sa'', ''''

' Create the recordset object and open the recordset object
Set ResultSet = New ADODB.Recordset
Set ResultSet.ActiveConnection = conn
ResultSet.CursorLocation = adUseClient
ResultSet.Properties(''Initial Fetch Size'') = 1
ResultSet.Open ''SELECT LastName, FirstName FROM NorhtWind..Employees'', _
        SQLConnection, , , adAsyncFetch

Debug.Print ''Fetching Started...''
Debug.Print ''Last Name: '' & ResultSet!LastName & '', First Name: '' & _
       ResultSet!FirstName
End Sub

Private Sub ResultSet_FetchComplete(ByVal pError As ADODB.Error, _
    adStatus As ADODB.EventStatusEnum, ByVal pRecordset As ADODB.Recordset)
  Debug.Print ''Fetching of all rows completed.''
End Sub
```

The `Open` method in the example uses a blocking (`adAsyncFetch`) asynchronous fetch mechanism to get the data. The `Open` method on a `Recordset` object opens a cursor for the records returned by executing a command on the data source. The syntax of the `Open` method is as follows:

```
Recordset.Open <Source>, <ActiveConnection>, _
        <CursorType>, <LockType>, <Options>
```

The `<Source>` parameter specifies the `SELECT` statement, stored procedure, or table name or filename of a persisted recordset. `<ActiveConnection>` is the connection that should be used for executing the statement. `<CursorType>` indicates the type of cursor to open. `<LockType>` determines the type of locking to use for the cursor. `<Options>` specifies how the `<Source>` parameter should be evaluated or how the recordset should be retrieved. The following list of valid values can be specified as arguments to control the asynchronous fetching of rows from the resultset:

- `adAsyncExecute` The command specified in `<Source>` is executed asynchronously.
- `adAsyncFetch` After the number of rows in the `Initial Fetch Size` property is fetched, any remaining rows are fetched asynchronously. If a row is required that has not been fetched, the main thread is blocked until the requested row becomes available.
- `adAsyncFetchNonBlocking` In this method, the main thread never blocks while fetching. If the requested row has not been fetched, the current row automatically moves to the end of the file.

The `FetchComplete` event for the recordset is called after all the rows have been fetched from the cursor. In Listing 18.16, the `RecordSet_FetchComplete` event prints the message indicating the end of the fetch operation after all the rows have been retrieved from the cursor. The `FetchProgress` event for the recordset can be used to determine the number of rows that have been fetched from the cursor.

ADO 2.0 also has sorting and finding features in recordsets that can be used with cursors. With these features, users can perform desktop-style data manipulation against any data source from within ADO. `Find` and `Sort` are implemented to use support from the data source. If the data source does not support the proper OLE DB interfaces, ADO carries out these operations at the client. If client cursors are being used, indexes are built on sorted columns to optimize the `Find` and `Filter` operations. You can sort a recordset by setting the `Sort` property to the name of the column or columns the recordset should be sorted by. The Visual Basic code in Listing 18.17 shows an example that sorts data in the cursor.

LISTING 18.17 LST18_17.TXT—Sorting Using a Client Cursor

```
Sub main()

  Dim SQLConnection As New ADODB.Connection
  Dim ResultSet As New ADODB.Recordset

  ' Create the connection object and open the connection.
  Set SQLConnection = New ADODB.Connection
  SQLConnection.Open ''DSN=localserver'', ''sa'', ''''

  Set ResultSet.ActiveConnection = SQLConnection
  ResultSet.CursorLocation = adUseClient
  ResultSet.Open ''SELECT LastName, FirstName FROM NorhtWind..Employees'', _
         adOpenStatic, adLockBatchOptimistic

  'Print records as retrieved
  While Not ResultSet.EOF
   Debug.Print ''Last Name: '' & ResultSet!LastName & _
         '', First Name: '' & ResultSet!FirstName
   ResultSet.MoveNext
  Wend

  'Set sorting by the last name and first name fields
  'Setting the Sort property positions cursor in the first row
  ResultSet.Sort = ''LastName, FirstName''

  While ResultSet.EOF <> True
   Debug.Print ''Last Name: '' & ResultSet!LastName & _
         '', First Name: '' & ResultSet!FirstName
   ResultSet.MoveNext
  Wend
End Sub
```

The columns can also be sorted in descending order by using the `DESC` option after the column:

```
ResultSet.Sort = ''LastName DESC, FirstName DESC''
```

After retrieving the resultset from the data source, the `Find` method can be used to search for a specific value in a row. Here's its syntax:

```
RecordSet.Find (<Criteria>, [<RecordsToSkip>], _
        [<SearchDirection>], [<StartRow>])
```

The <Criteria> method indicates that the Find expression is supplied. The syntax for supplying the expression is the fieldname operator value. The fieldname value must be the name of a field, as found in the resultset or the ADO Fields collection. <RecordsToSkip> is used to offset the search by a particular row. By default, Find searches from the current row. A value of 1 for this parameter starts the search with the next row (in the direction you are searching). A value of -1 starts the search with the previous row. <SearchDirection> indicates the direction of the search from the current row. <StartRow> specifies the row from which to start the search; it's indicated by using a bookmark. The Visual Basic code in Listing 18.18 uses the Find method on the resultset of a cursor.

LISTING 18.18 LST18_18.TXT—Find Data Using a Client Cursor

```
Sub main()

  Dim SQLConnection As New ADODB.Connection
  Dim ResultSet As New ADODB.Recordset

  ' Create the connection object and open the connection.
  Set SQLConnection = New ADODB.Connection
  SQLConnection.Open ''DSN=localserver'', ''sa'', ''''

  Set ResultSet.ActiveConnection = SQLConnection
  ResultSet.CursorLocation = adUseClient
  ResultSet.Open ''SELECT LastName, FirstName FROM NorhtWind..Employees'', _
         adOpenStatic, adLockBatchOptimistic
 'Search from the beginning and find an author named Ringer
  ResultSet.Find ''LastName = 'Fuller'''
  'Search from the beginning and find an author named Green
  ResultSet.Find ''LastName = 'King''', , , adBookmarkFirst

  'Search from the end and find an author named Ringer
  ResultSet.Find ''LastName = 'Fuller''', , adSearchBackward, adBookmarkLast

End Sub
```

The Find method works only with a single column. It does not support searching multiple columns. If Find does not find a match, it positions the cursor at end-of-file (EOF) if the search is forward or beginning-of-file (BOF) if the search is backward. Resync gives the developer a way to find the current values on the server for the specified records in the recordset, without requiring a complete reexecution of the original query.

The `Resync` method can be used to find the current values on the data source for the specified rows without having to reissue the `SELECT` statement that created the cursor. The syntax of the `Resync` method is as follows:

```
Recordset.Resync <AffectRecords>, <ResyncValues>
```

The optional `<AffectRecords>` parameter tells how many rows the method will affect. Here are the valid values:

- `adAffectCurrent` Only the current row is refreshed.
- `adAffectGroup` The rows are refreshed based on the `Filter` property setting.
- `adAffectAll` All rows are refreshed regardless of the `Filter` property condition. This is the default setting.
- `adAffectAllChapters` All chapter rows are refreshed.

`<ResyncValues>` is also an optional parameter that indicates whether the values of the columns in the data source are overwritten. These are the valid values:

- `adResyncAllValues` Data is overwritten, and pending updates are canceled. This is the default setting.
- `adResyncUnderlyingValues` Data is not overwritten, and pending updates are not canceled.

The `Resync` method is useful if the cursor is either static or forward-only but you want to see any changes in the data source. If the `CursorLocation` property is set to `adUseClient`, `Resync` is available only for non-read-only `Recordset` objects.

ADO 2.0, along with the RDS Cursor Service, provides a mechanism to create empty recordsets by supplying column information and calling the `Open` method. The Visual Basic code in Listing in 18.19 is an example of using a creatable recordset.

LISTING 18.19 LST18_19.TXT—Creatable Recordset Using a Client Cursor

```
Dim ResultSet As New ADODB.Recordset
ResultSet.CursorLocation = adUseClient

'Add Fields to the recordset
ResultSet.Fields.Append ''EmployeeID'', adInteger
ResultSet.Fields.Append ''LastName'', adVarChar, 20
ResultSet.Fields.Append ''FirstName'', adVarChar, 10, adFldIsNullable

'Create the recordset
ResultSet.Open , , adOpenStatic, adLockBatchOptimistic
```

LISTING 18.19 CONTINUED

```
'Add Rows
ResultSet.AddNew Array(''EmployeeID'', ''LastName'', ''FirstName''), _
        Array(10, ''Murray'', ''Bill'')

ResultSet.MoveFirst
Debug.Print ''Last Name: '' & ResultSet!LastName & _
      '', First Name: '' & ResultSet!FirstName &_
      ''Employee ID: '' & ResultSet!EmployeeID
```

The creatable recordset can also be saved to a disk file by using the `Save` method of the `Recordset` object. The `Recordset` object's `Open` method used with the `adCmdFile` argument allows the `Recordset` to be loaded later for use. The `RecordsetPersistence` mechanism in ADO 2.0 also allows the client cursor created from the data source to be saved to a file and reused later. This allows applications to work in a disconnected mode from the data source, make changes to the data, and resync the changes by connecting to the data source later. For more information on using creatable recordsets, persistent recordsets, and other advanced features, refer to the ADO 2.0 documentation.

Summary

You have looked at the cursor implementations in Oracle 8.0 and Microsoft SQL Server 7.0. The implementation and adherence to the SQL-92 standard depend on the DBMS. Data access technologies have been discussed; they offer another way to use cursors in client applications without affecting server performance. The Java Database Connectivity (JDBC) technology also works like ODBC and can be used to access data sources such as Oracle and SQL Server.

CHAPTER 19

Optimizing Query Performance

In This Chapter

SQL is flexible enough that there are almost always alternative ways to formulate the same request if retrieval of data is involved. In fact, one of the first operations carried out by a SQL optimizer is to rewrite the query. On the other hand, the degrees of freedom for SQL data updates are much more limited. Most of this chapter, therefore, illustrates and deals with SQL retrieval enhancement.

Query performance is a vendor-specific attribute of a query. That doesn't mean some vendors have higher or lower average query performance. It means that the way they implement optimizations is different. It also means that for a specific query, performance might be better on one system than on another, but for a different query the reverse could be true given the same choice of databases.

In this chapter, specific products and vendors are named when necessary because query optimization is subject to strong reality checks—it is not a theoretical subject. The manner in which the RDBMS implements optimization influences what a programmer must do to improve and "tune up" SQL queries. The most significant names are Sybase, Oracle, IBM, and Microsoft, but the material is applicable to other vendors.

The following points are noteworthy:

- Up to and including SQL Server 6.0—the name originated at Sybase—Microsoft SQL Server and Sybase SQL Server were virtually identical products.
- Since the advent of SQL Server 6.5, particularly in SQL Server 7 (SQL7), Microsoft has changed some of the optimization techniques in terms that are worth mentioning and that differentiate the product.
- The cost-based optimizer found in SQL7 derives most of its core technology from Sybase, but has been enhanced with a number of peripheral index application and index storage techniques.
- Sybase basically has two products now: Adaptive Sybase Anywhere (ASA), whose roots are in the original Watcom SQL technology, and Adaptive Server Enterprise (ASE), a renamed form of its original SQL Server. Both these products handle SQL optimization differently.
- Query optimization strategies native to the RDBMS are becoming an increasingly important marketing tool because of the issue of data warehousing for decision support, where—unlike online transaction processing (OLTP) production machines—queries more often tend to be long and complex.
- In effect, the increasing weight given by vendors to internal query optimization renders a programmer's efforts to improve queries manually less important than it used to be in OLTP—but increasingly important in data warehousing.

- An understanding of how the optimizer works and of the tools available to measure its effect on critical queries are useful backgrounds.
- Oracle7 and Oracle8 support rule-based optimizer hints that are based on syntax rules, operator precedence, subquery nesting, and so forth. I believe this approach can be disregarded in favor of cost-based optimization mentioned previously, where index cardinality, selectivity and density, disk I/O times, data volumes, and so on are taken into account.
- I have read one case study in which Oracle rule-based optimization caused severe degradation in retrieval performance when compared to the same query with default cost-based optimization.

General Considerations

Almost without exception, physical storage in an RDBMS is by row. (Thinking Machines Inc is one exception—its product stores data by columns; so does Sybase IQ, to some extent.) This is probably the most significant determinant of overall performance capabilities because it affects physical access. However, the vendor controls most of the features that could affect query performance in this area. For example, after Adaptive Server Anywhere has placed a row on disk, it stays there until deleted, even if it is modified afterward; Adaptive Server Enterprise, however, moves the row if it changes in size because of modifications.

Finding out about Thinking Machines recently in a book about data warehousing was interesting. I wrote a multiuser RDBMS in the mid-'80s (in C, on UNIX) that stored data by column. The idea was to be able to access related data quickly and to have "narrow" data paths because most reports did not have many columns in them. More than that, some of the columns in the database were not data, but record IDs for foreign tables—that is, referential keys. In a sense, that covered the concept of nested tables. Such a system really flies. We clocked close to 200 parent/child insertions per second on a 386, using (I think) ST506 disk technology and a whopping 16MB of RAM. It didn't have much mass appeal, though, because I picked an interface (QBE—which looked good on the recently announced Macintosh at that time) that didn't appeal to the venture capitalists. They also thought UNIX was going to die. But that's another story, whose moral probably is that you can't just pick a good horse—the jockey is also important.

In general, most of the deep-down physical storage subsystem is not tunable. But there are some (global) parameters that should be considered before any other (local) performance tuning is undertaken.

Another area you might not have much control over as a query designer is concurrency. The more users, the slower things are. However, there are some precautions you can take, as explained in the section "Transactions" later in this chapter.

To some extent, what you can do to improve a SQL query depends on whether your system uses compile-time as opposed to runtime optimization during query execution. In compile-time optimization, not all the necessary data may be available to make the best optimization decisions; most systems use this technology. ASA uses runtime optimization, which seems a superior method but is more costly. I believe ASA is alone here; its real optimization work starts after `OPEN CURSOR` is called—that is, after the data manager is activated. It uses the preliminary cost-based estimates after it rewrites the query as a rough guide. Ironically, I'll disregard this feature in the following sections because its effect is to merely (!) improve the query.

However, a programmer's strategy is more likely to be influenced by the environment he or she is immersed in. For example, some programmers might be coding against OLTP systems, others against data warehouses. Some could be writing SQL from scratch; others need to improve SQL generated by a query tool.

SQL RDBMSs have been in existence since the 1970s; their optimizers have been under development for a long time. It is safe to start by assuming that the optimizer is good, and to code SQL accordingly—that is, to achieve the required result. All optimizers rewrite your query under most circumstances, anyway. They change the syntax but preserve the semantics of the query. Regardless of your system, some general principles are discussed in more detail later:

- Normalize the database reasonably well, but try to avoid taking it to the point where there are more than four-way joins to run heavily-used queries.
- Keep resultsets to a minimum; for example, instead of shipping large amounts of data to the client for filtering and analysis, try to do as much as possible on the server to reduce the resultset.
- Keep indexes narrow and try to avoid multicolumn indexes; optimizers have difficulty using indexes to an advantage if the degrees of freedom in the index are constrained.
- Avoid expressions in the `WHERE` clause if possible—expressions cause sequential scans of a table—and let the client evaluate the expressions after the resultset has been returned; this applies to older RDBMSs only.
- Avoid inequalities in `WHERE` clauses. Some of them cannot be used to advantage in creating fast search arguments by the optimizer; also for older systems only.

- Avoid local variables in `WHERE` clauses if possible; sometimes procedural clauses are better.
- Whatever else you do, avoid unnecessary joins, particularly involving `OR` clauses.
- Avoid aggregation comparisons if they cannot be easily optimized; they can also be performed on the client's resultset afterward, using report generator features or procedural code.

If the query is still thought to be underperforming, it might have to be split up differently; for example, complex `OR` clauses can sometimes be replaced by simpler unions. Splitting a query beyond that, into separate queries, might work only for non-distributed data requests; this method is also subject to transaction integrity problems.

Rewriting a query is best done on the basis of feedback from the optimizer:

- Oracle: explain plan
- ASA: select plan(<query>)
- DB2: explain
- SQL Server: set showplan

If you have to decide on a SQL query tool for users, make sure it permits access to the SQL code it generates—you can't optimize what you can't see. My current project is a query generator (DBsurfer) that tries to generate the best possible SQL, given an English query. The problem with this kind of product is that you must do what the user says—exactly and all within the one query. Such a product relies strongly on the optimizer to polish the query because the translator is hard-coded. The translator's main job is to make sure there are no major gaffes in its generated SQL. But it isn't perfect, so one of the things I want to do here is learn with you some of the techniques that might affect its future performance.

Some of the topics I'll discuss here are relevant to this software, others are not. As a complex query generator the product has to present a uniform interface across different RDBMSs; it's not concerned with preliminary database design or database updates. However, my consulting work involves just those topics.

I have nine different database systems on my desk. Some, like Access, Interbase, and Pervasive, are not appropriate targets because they are non-ANSI, unconventional, or under-powered—or all three of the above. I deal only in conventional ANSI databases. I term an ANSI database *conventional* if it is rational to the extent that it implements mechanisms not directly documented by ANSI in a manner that is logical and similar to what others do. For example, to disallow `UNION` in a view is unconventional, as is a requirement to manually cast corresponding `UNION` columns; casting should be automatic (known as *implicit* data type conversion). My version of Access does not allow `ORDER BY`

`<column #>`. It's easy to tweak SQL generators to handle that (even for expressions), but it's probably a harbinger of bigger problems. Few of these systems can be optimized.

To illustrate some of the optimization issues, I chose the DB2 UDB V5 `explain` facility because it gives you a textual representation of the optimizer rewrites. Using optimizer rewrites rather than I/O graphs of logical versus physical page accesses, for example, has the advantage of allowing you to design a database and test your design without the need to populate it.

However, the choice of visualization tool depends on your environment: If your database is already populated, you can take advantage of the runtime statistics. In fact, the results from the optimizer can be quite different for populated and empty databases. Take a look at this example:

```
select b1.DEPTNO as ''DEPTNO'', b1.DEPTNAME as ''DEPTNAME''
from MIKE.DEPARTMENT b1
where b1.DEPTNO in
  (select c1.WORKDEPT
  from MIKE.EMPLOYEE c1)
```

It uses a referential key to link the two tables, but on a small database, the DB2 optimizer decides that paging indexes isn't worth it, so it stays exclusively with full table scans. This can be misleading. The Oracle8 optimizer is more stable here; it always does a full table scan on `EMPLOYEE` for the preceding query. If you want to take advantage of indexing in Oracle8, you have to rewrite the query as follows:

```
select b1.DEPTNO as ''DEPTNO'', b1.DEPTNAME as ''DEPTNAME''
from MIKE.DEPARTMENT b1
where exists
  (select c1.WORKDEPT
  from MIKE.EMPLOYEE c1
  where b1.DEPTNO = c1.WORKDEPT)
```

The DB2 optimizer treats both queries identically by forming a join.

The single most useful result of examining optimizer rewrites is that you can learn how to write good SQL by comparing execution times for different forms of the same query. Most systems use cost-based optimizers, which optimize for maximum speed.

Tip

If you run against large databases, remember to turn off result generation before you start testing. This technique can save you a lot of time.

Tip

If you are using embedded dynamic SQL and iterative SQL calls, you should turn off or minimize optimization to reduce the SQL "prepare stage" delay associated with optimization. This is particularly true after the SQL has been redesigned to be as efficient as you can—or want—to make it.

There are several reasons for keeping the width of resultsets to a minimum:

- To reduce the amount of temporary table storage for work files and merging operations on them.
- To decrease communications overhead—WAN connections can be a scarce resource.
- To increase the likelihood that sorts don't run out of space and cancel a long job.
- To increase the visibility of data and not dilute precious information in a soup of data. This last point applies particularly to seasoned users who are used to legacy batch reports and don't realize the surgical precision and informational power of ad hoc query systems.

If you choose a query tool for your users, make sure it supports asynchronous execution—that is, make sure the user can cancel a query. I had an embarrassing moment during a presentation when I forgot that my laptop database didn't support multithreading; I fired off a query I knew would take a long time—and there was no cancel button!

Indexing

In this chapter I am going to consider OLTP-type indexing, not special indexing features such as bitmapped indexes offered by Sybase IQ. This product has probably one of the fastest—if not the fastest—(patented) indexing technologies on the market, but it's specialized for data warehousing and requires special update techniques.

While on the subject, note that Oracle8 OLTP also allows bitmap index creation and is faster for retrieval; however, its locking granularity is high and could cause update slowdowns in busy environments. It's better kept for data warehousing applications as well.

One of the tunable parameters for proper indexing is page size because it has an effect on fanout. The larger the fanout, the more node separators per page and the fewer the pages that have to be read. Available RAM and memory reserved by the system for temporary table page caching, hash buffers, and data caching place a limit on page size. Small pages are good for intelligently used ad-hoc query systems, but bad for massive sequential updates.

Although most systems now hash large keys in index nodes, it is wise to keep indexes narrow. Multi-column indexes should be avoided. For example, clustered unique index keys in SQL7 are part of the data for any non-clustered indexes. The fanout for the latter can decrease dramatically if the clustered keys are wide.

ASA hashes all keys, so queries such as the following, in which `DEPTNO` is an index, run slower under ASA than other systems like DB2 because DB2 just scans the index, without visiting the data tables:

```
select c1.DEPTNO as ''department numbers''
from MIKE.DEPARTMENT c1
where c1.DEPTNO between 'A00' and 'C01'
```

Other design considerations for indexing center on the type and number of indexes. Indexing everything in sight can be counterproductive in most systems because it can cause the following:

- Slows down updates
- Increases the learning curve load on the optimizer subsystem

Consider a column likely to be modified often. If it is indexed, not only does the base data have to be updated, but so does its index. If the index is updated, the optimizer statistics for the column also must be re-learned. Current optimizers rely on a relatively new technique pioneered by Sybase whereby the RDBMS keeps statistics of the data distribution in indexes to track the data's cardinality and density. If you use SQL7, you would be particularly unpopular because the contents of secondary non-clustered keys depend on the values in clustered indexes, so there is additional work propagation.

Apart from primary keys, you can always add indexes later as needed. Primary index organization is subject to the rule that if it is a multi-column key, the most likely search argument should be placed first. This enables most systems to at least use the index for partial searches. In the following, the `LASTNAME` search will access the index even if it is a composite `LASTNAME, FIRSTNAME` index:

```
select f1.SALARY as ''SALARY''
from MIKE.EMPLOYEE f1
where f1.LASTNAME = 'LUCCHESSI '
```

If this index were defined on only the single column LASTNAME, all systems would search by index for this query. If the equality comparison is replaced with a different comparison operator, however, systems such as Oracle8 and ASA6 need to do a full table scan. On the other hand, DB2 is still able to limit itself to indexed access, as is SQL7.

A nifty piece of jargon in discussing indexing techniques is the term *sargable*. It stems from the phrase *search argument*. Search arguments, or SARGs, are WHERE clause predicates that use indexing. A predicate is sargable if it can be used for searching an index.

Obviously, I didn't invent this term; I picked it up in the literature. This reminds me to caution the reader about picking up too much on optimizers by reading random material about them—at the risk of shooting myself in the foot. There is copyrighted material right up to 1999 discussing sargability. Much of it is obsolete, however, because optimizers change rapidly due to technological leap-frogging and cross-pollination between vendors.

For example, the recently announced SQL7 specifically mentions *constant folding* as a feature. Although it's not defined, I believe it refers to casting constants so they become sargable. For example, in the following example, MIKE.STAFF.ID is a primary integer index:

```
select e1.NAME as ''STAFF NAME''
from MIKE.STAFF e1
where e1.ID = 20
```

In the past, if you used 20.0 as the constant value, the equality would not be sargable because the constant's precision is higher and the optimizer didn't cast dynamically. Now they all do. A similar condition holds if the index were defined as CHAR(x) and you used a longer, blank-padded string or a shorter string to search it. Of course, if you are using an older database, you should still be aware of these idiosyncrasies.

A quick check with the DB2 optimizer confirmed that this dynamic casting technique also extends to functions, so the following example, in which MIKE.DEPARTMENT.DEPTNO is a character index CHAR(3), is sargable:

```
The following statement works - it just may not retrieve any records, which
is immaterial to the discussion - MS
select h1.DEPTNAME as ''DEPTNAME''
from MIKE.DEPARTMENT h1
where h1.DEPTNO = char(1234)
```

In older versions, this example would not be sargable unless the function returned the same data type and length as the index.

It's gratifying to find that even certain complex built-in functions in SQL would qualify as sargable, according to the documentation. For example, the year() function in the following code, if applied to the indexed column MIKE.EMPLOYEE.HIREDATE, is sargable:

(Full name of employees hired more than 10 years ago. Oracle query)

```
select l1.FIRSTNME || ' ' || l1.MIDINIT || ' ' || l1.LASTNAME as '''Full
name'''
from MIKE.EMPLOYEE l1
where ( year( current date ) - year(l1.HIREDATE)) > 10
```

The sargability rules—as mentioned previously—differ from system to system. Exploring your optimizer and its documentation can pay off. For example, in ASA6, *<column id> IS NOT NULL* is not sargable, but *<column id> > 0* is; hence, if you know that EDLEVEL is numeric, constrained to be greater than or equal to 0 but NULLABLE, then the following is faster than searching for *EDLEVEL IS NOT NULL* :

```
select y1.SALARY as ''SALARY''
from MIKE.EMPLOYEE y1
where y1.EDLEVEL >= 0
```

Similarly, normalization can pay off. Comparing an indexed column to a non-indexed column in the same table is always non-sargable, but if the non-indexed column is in a second table, the operation is sargable and uses the index. If the second table is narrower—remember that storage is by row—its rows are retrieved more quickly.

Actually, I am a bit puzzled why even DB2 doesn't treat this condition as sargable. It could depend on the level of selectivity of the indexed column, although a primary key has maximum selectivity. Or it might depend on the fact that the database size and the SYSCAT.TABLESPACES disk I/O parameters skewed access costs to sequential access (I use SCSI disks).

In some older optimizers (such as Watcom), I have found that placing the highest selectivity condition first in an AND clause increases performance. For example, the following query is better than the same query with a selection on BONUS before a selection on EMPNO because EMPNO is an index and BONUS is not:

```
select f1.SALARY as ''SALARY''
from MIKE.EMPLOYEE f1
where f1.EMPNO > '000030'
and f1.BONUS < 900.00
```

This sequencing of selectivity conditions is based on the fact that additional AND conditions are not evaluated if the first one fails. In the preceding example, this would reduce data table I/O. However, newer optimizers equalize both choices automatically with rewrites.

If you are going to access a table based on an index and want to avoid sargability because of low index selectivity (it's not a primary key), then you can fool the optimizer with a dummy condition, such as this:

```
select *
from MIKE.EMPLOYEE b1
where b1.DEPTNO = 'B01' or 1=0
```

Here the optimizer could perform an argument search on the secondary index DEPTNO and then fetch to get the remaining data without the dummy condition; with it, you force a table scan. This is good for narrow tables and to bypass an otherwise useful index operation. You'll think of other dummy conditions. I have not tried this on a low selectivity index with a modern optimizer—they might be too smart to be tricked this easily. In Oracle8 you can guarantee subversion by using the appropriate optimizer hint as a comment beside the SELECT clause.

A good reason for using this technique is that it can avoid looping when the optimizer has decided that it will use nested loops to examine an inner table index to compare it with an outer table column. This method can be sub-optimal and is detectable by examining optimizer results. It's difficult to predict when it will happen—you could be using a simple join or a complex correlated subquery.

With SQL7 we are seeing what promises to be a powerful new approach in indexing. RDBMS index set operations, such as union and intersect, add a new complexion to what you can do with indexes. The need for composite indexes can now disappear except for special situations. Until this technology appeared, a query could use only a single index per table at a time; now you can use several separate indexes. Matches on different indexes are *intersected* for AND conditions, and a *set union* is invoked for OR conditions. Sargability has increased considerably, and I'm sure the technique will spread quickly to other vendors.

I have already mentioned that almost any operation involving an indexed column is now sargable. The notable exception of comparing an indexed column to a non-indexed column within the same table can now be made sargable by instantiating an index on the latter and letting the optimizer perform an index intersect.

Joins and Subqueries

Almost everybody's optimizer does join analysis pairwise, so *n*-table joins cost about *n*-factorial combinations to test for optimality. Red Brick's STAR join is an exception, but it's specialized to data warehousing. Since V5, DB2 UDB also supports star joins under special schema conditions detected by the optimizer; so does Oracle 8, but it has to be given an optimizer hint first (`/*+ STAR */`).

Use joins only when it's absolutely necessary. Joins are necessary only if data output has to come from more than one table. Looking at your optimizer documentation, you might be misled by the optimizer rewriting nested subqueries as joins. Most do, but that does not mean joins are a good idea when they are fed to the optimizer. Generally, they are useful only if the optimizer itself generates them.

I am going to spend a little time on this topic because it's a major subject; for my product, it's almost religion. The problem with joins, whether at the top level or in a subquery, is that they do not guide the optimizer. The optimizer is guided by what your query is trying to say—its semantics. Raw joins (`FROM <list>`) do not convey any semantic information. Yes, the `WHERE` clause says how to use the join—after it has been formed—but it doesn't shed any light on the choice of the *n*-factorial combinations possible—and particularly not the order in which they should be chosen.

I have met people with years of "experience" in SQL still using unnecessary joins to which conditions are applied, instead of using subqueries. Most query and reporting tools do it as well. Their excuse is that they are looking at denormalized warehouse tables anyway—and besides, there are the fast star- and bitmapped joins. But the truth is that data warehouses are becoming more complex, with many dimension tables linked to a number of huge fact tables. So the fact tables are starting to split and proliferate...

On the other hand, if the optimizer takes your query and converts subqueries to joins, that's different. It knows more than you do about the query's environment. The following example illustrates this conversion.

(Display department numbers for departments that have every project with responsible employees less than `000320` and with project numbers starting with MA.)

```
select c1.DEPTNO as ''DEPTNO''
from MIKE.DEPARTMENT c1
where c1.DEPTNO in
  (select e1.WORKDEPT
  from MIKE.EMPLOYEE e1
  where ( e1.EMPNO in
   (select d1.RESPEMP
   from MIKE.PROJECT d1
   where not exists
     (select *
     from MIKE.PROJECT d3
     where d3.RESPEMP >= '000320' and
```

```
        d1.RESPEMP = d3.RESPEMP) and not
      exists
    (select *
    from MIKE.PROJECT d4
    where d4.PROJNO not like 'MA%' escape
        '\' and d1.RESPEMP =
  d4.RESPEMP))))
```

The DB2 optimizer rewrite follows. Surprising at first glance is that the optimizer chose joins for the outer tables. The final negation is subtle; the original query had two parallel NOT EXISTS clauses. Both were asserted and the comparisons inverted by the optimizer. Based on experience with the database, this query works well.

```
SELECT DISTINCT Q7.DEPTNO AS ''DEPTNO''
FROM MIKE.PROJECT AS Q1, MIKE.EMPLOYEE AS Q6,
    MIKE.DEPARTMENT AS Q7
WHERE (Q6.EMPNO = Q1.RESPEMP) AND (Q7.DEPTNO =
    Q6.WORKDEPT) AND EXISTS(SELECT $RID$
FROM MIKE.PROJECT AS Q2
WHERE (Q1.RESPEMP = Q2.RESPEMP) AND ('000320' <=
    Q2.RESPEMP)) AND EXISTS(SELECT $RID$
FROM MIKE.PROJECT AS Q4
WHERE (Q1.RESPEMP = Q4.RESPEMP) AND
    NOT((Q4.PROJNO LIKE 'MA%')))
```

Don't attempt to execute this kind of code optimizer; output cannot always be fed back into the optimizing stage. For example the RID above refers to a record id (tuple id) and is not recognized by the SQL parser.

Now let's take a look at what happens when joins are abused. First, write a query correctly, as shown here:

(Birth dates for employees that either work in the Development Center or are responsible for Project MA2110.)

```
select w1.BIRTHDATE as ''BIRTHDATES''
from MIKE.EMPLOYEE w1
where ( w1.WORKDEPT in
  (select x1.DEPTNO
  from MIKE.DEPARTMENT x1
  where x1.DEPTNAME = 'DEVELOPMENT CENTER      ')
or w1.EMPNO in
  (select y1.RESPEMP
  from MIKE.PROJECT y1
  where y1.MAJPROJ = 'MA2110'))
```

This query takes 132 time units on a small database and was rewritten by the optimizer as follows:

```
SELECT Q5.BIRTHDATE AS ''BIRTHDATES''
FROM MIKE.EMPLOYEE AS Q5
WHERE ((((Q5.WORKDEPT >= $C0) AND (Q5.WORKDEPT <=
    $C1)) AND Q5.WORKDEPT = ANY
  (SELECT DISTINCT Q3.DEPTNO, $C0, $C1
  FROM MIKE.DEPARTMENT AS Q3
  WHERE (Q3.DEPTNAME = 'DEVELOPMENT CENTER ')
  ORDER BY Q3.DEPTNO) ) OR (((Q5.EMPNO >= $C2)
    AND (Q5.EMPNO <= $C3)) AND Q5.EMPNO = ANY
  (SELECT DISTINCT Q1.RESPEMP, $C2, $C3
  FROM MIKE.PROJECT AS Q1
  WHERE (Q1.MAJPROJ = 'MA2110')
  ORDER BY Q1.RESPEMP) ))
```

Now let's write it in a simpleminded way:

```
select w1.BIRTHDATE as ''BIRTHDATES''
from MIKE.EMPLOYEE w1, MIKE.DEPARTMENT x1,
MIKE.PROJECT y1
where w1.WORKDEPT = x1.DEPTNO
and x1.DEPTNAME = 'DEVELOPMENT CENTER      '
or w1.EMPNO = y1.RESPEMP
and y1.MAJPROJ = 'MA2110'
```

This time the query took 10,303 time units. Changing the join order had no effect. There was no significant rewrite by the optimizer.

Rewriting it manually as a DB2 union costs 150 time units; this is vastly preferable but still not as good as the original (classical) form.

The Oracle8 optimizer documentation promises to rewrite the previous form as a union and it seems to do very well indeed; however, I find the Oracle8 `explain plan` facility fairly primitive, quite clumsy, and hard to understand for complex queries. Acyclic directed graphs don't translate well into single columns. Like SQL Plus, it could benefit from modernization.

The following example is a demonstration of what can go wrong if you assume that joins on primary keys are cheap and start taking a cavalier attitude toward them:

It is also worth mentioning that the worst performer for the last (joined) form of this query was the ASA5 optimizer, whose result led to execution times literally thousands of times worse than that of the classic form. This may be a specific weakness of the ASA5 optimizer. I did not try it on ASA6.

```
select w1.BIRTHDATE
from MIKE.EMPLOYEE w1
where w1.WORKDEPT in
  (select x1.DEPTNO
  from MIKE.DEPARTMENT x1
  where x1.DEPTNAME = 'DEVELOPMENT CENTER    ')
union all
select w1.BIRTHDATE
from MIKE.EMPLOYEE w1
where w1.EMPNO in
  (select y1.RESPEMP
  from MIKE.PROJECT y1
  where y1.MAJPROJ = 'MA2110')
```

In an ad hoc query system there are certain high-level considerations; one of them is that the user should be allowed to generate logical (OR/AND) combinations of what are basically WHERE and HAVING clauses. As you know, these things don't mix well—in my opinion, a severe orthogonality failure in SQL—so DBsurfer does its best by inhibiting HAVING whenever possible.

As a result, instead of implementing the HAVING clause used in the following query, which expresses "department numbers for projects with the latest starting date equal to Feb 15, 1998"

```
select t1.DEPTNO as ''DEPARTMENT NUMBERS''
from MIKE.PROJECT t1
group by t1.DEPTNO
having max(t1.PRSTDATE) = '1982-02-15'
```

it generates code using this correlated subquery with identical semantics:

```
select t1.DEPTNO as ''DEPTNO''
from MIKE.PROJECT t1
where date('1982-02-15') =
  (select max(t3.PRSTDATE)
  from MIKE.PROJECT t3
  where t1.DEPTNO = t3.DEPTNO)
```

This correlated subquery costs about six times more in CPU time and twice as much in I/O. In this particular instance, the reason is that the ASA runtime optimizer detected hardly any difference between these two queries (48 versus 50 I/O operations), and that was my original basis for a decision. This situation highlights the influence different optimizers can have, as I mentioned earlier. My SQL code generation algorithms are being improved on the basis of this finding.

I should close this section with a quick comment on clustering because it has a mixed and confusing genealogy. This is an index management tool that sorts record IDs physically, using the logical order of key values. In SQL7, ASA, and ASE, it applies to single tables; in Oracle7 and Oracle8, it applies to both single and multiple tables.

The Oracle mechanism seems more interesting because it can speed up searches that involve joins, but it is expensive to update—that is, it is not a cheap update, as explained in the next section. It also slows down scans of single tables involved in the cluster. I'm not sure the mechanism is not just another name for referential integrity in Oracle.

For example, the employee/department couple is probably a good candidate for clustering if you often use them together (and your company doesn't have a high turnover ratio). On the other hand, the customer/orders pair is not because it is updated quite often.

Transactions

As in other sections in this chapter, much depends on the tuning knobs available on your particular database. I am going to lean toward database update (data update, insert, and delete) transactions in this section. This topic deals primarily with OLTP systems. This is fairly "white" technology, and not much has changed since Jim Gray (then at IBM, now at Microsoft) was publishing typed notes back in '77. OLTP systems need some form of locking protocol; data warehousing applications don't use locking because they are batch-updated.

Okay, some things have changed; so now you have a fiber channel SCSI RAID share-nothing (or share-everything if Windows NT) MPP architecture, and your transaction rate is still going nowhere. Let's take a look at what you might do with the database software to match your fancy hardware, but parallel execution hints are beyond my scope here.

The log device should be different from the database device. This is a small step toward disk striping, where you try to minimize disk latency by judicious placement of heavily used database regions. The data pages (including indexes) and the log are big; they have separate functions but are used simultaneously, so you should minimize disk seeks with physical separation. This is particularly important if you cannot avoid *expensive* updates, as opposed to *cheap* updates.

In a *cheap* (fast) update, the data row size doesn't change after the update, so the data manager (DM) goes through a minimal sequence: Find the data to be changed, write the log, and update the data and indexes. It immediately comes to mind that you should use `CHAR()` instead of `VARCHAR[2]()` as a column storage attribute if possible.

The column being updated cannot be the key, or part of the key, of a clustered index; because the rows in a clustered index are stored in key order, a change to the key almost always means that the row changes location. This applies to most systems, but not to ASA6 (ASA6 prefers to split a row across pages rather than move it). Neither can the column be involved in referential integrity. And yes, you cannot bypass the latter condition with a trigger either because the effect is the same. Neither can the update statement involve a join. Of course, after the previous section, you shouldn't be able to even imagine a join in an update.

In an *expensive* update, the data for deletes and inserts has to be located, for each hit the log is written, then the log is read and all deletes take place based on it, and then the log is reread and all inserts take place. This happens when you use joins in the update statement or when you update referential keys.

Updates can become extremely expensive if you ask for user input during updates in a multi-user system, but everybody knows you shouldn't hold locks longer than absolutely necessary. Just make sure you use either `COMMIT` or `ROLLBACK` each time before asking for user input.

What might not be quite as obvious is that cursors could be wasteful because they can behave similarly. Open cursors in a WAN also tie up valuable traffic channels. The most efficient strategy for using cursors is the get-in-and-out-fast approach and the use of more complicated one-pass SQL. If you must hold locks, try to avoid unnecessary cursor stability by not requiring isolation levels 2 or 3 (repeatable read and serializable update, respectively).

In the following I'll stay away from using complete code because the syntax varies between systems in picky little details. For example, a typical application I have come across is updating the customer record with payment data. You can do this update by using different operators simultaneously on the same database or with a single operator. A payment can be applied to a specific invoice or to the account. If applied to the account, it should go to the oldest invoice. I won't go into details on overpayments, however. They don't add to the example, and neither do associated general ledger financial details.

Incorrectly designed, this application would open a cursor that executes a join on the customer header row and the invoice row using the payment information in a loop. It would hold the cursor and update each customer account with the following:

- A modification to the customer header account balance
- A modification of the invoice unpaid balance
- An insertion into the payment table for the customer
- An update of the cursor's payment log table status to "posted"

A correct version uses the payment log table that already exists as a free cursor. It reads the table into a read-only cursor once (unless it wants to go on posting forever as new payments come in), and then just runs the `customer_payments` stored procedure. In skeletal form, the procedure looks something like this:

```
CREATE PROC customer_payments
(@custid char(4), @amount FLOAT, @invoice INT,
@when TIMESTAMP)
AS
UPDATE cust_hdr
where cust = @custid
set cust_bal = cust_bal - @amount
update cust_inv
where invcust = @custid
set inv_bal = inv_bal - @amount
INSERT cust_pay
VALUES(@custid, @amount, @invoice)
UPDATE paylog
where logged = @when
set status = ''Y''  -- means Yes, posted
```

Obviously, I've forgotten the date; it can be extracted from the timestamp. Note that the last update goes back into the data supporting my cursor—hence the need for the timestamp, to make each log row unique. There are `IDENTITY` techniques to achieve the same effect, but the timestamp is useful here.

One last item: If you must hold cursor locks, use row locking, not table locks.

In the "Ancillary Topics" section later in this chapter, I discuss some uses for the `CASE` statement. Here is an illustration of its application in efficient updates:

```
UPDATE MIKE.EMPLOYEE
SET SALARY =
CASE
```

```
WHEN WORKDEPT = 'C001'
AND BONUS + COMM > SALARY
THEN SALARY * 1.1
WHEN WORKDEPT = 'D001'
AND BONUS + COMM > SALARY
THEN SALARY * 1.2
ELSE SALARY
END
WHERE WORKDEPT IN ('C001', 'D001')
```

Batching worked for me as a consultant, when there was good top-down control in a smaller (around 100 employees) company; I just asked management to lay down a policy of dedicating specific time slots for postings. Then we turned off isolation—and ran at maximum speed. Of course, I knew which programs you could use that method with and those you could not.

I mentioned the importance of choosing good page sizes earlier. This parameter also has update implications for data pages. If your rows are large or have much variability in width, the page size should be as large as possible to accommodate a generous amount of free space. This prevents row splitting in ASA or row migration in other systems during subsequent updates.

The percentage of free space per page is, therefore, an important tunable parameter. It is worth testing empirically because too large a value can cause immediate page chaining, even during initial inserts.

Temporary Tables

The previous cursor example could have used a temporary table, but you would be controlling it. Another term is *worktable*.

Temporary tables most often are instantiated by the relational data system when sorts are required or at the behest of the optimizer to store temporary results for looping or re-examination. Some systems like ASE and SQL7 might also decide to build temporary indexes on these tables to avoid rescanning them too often. One system that tries to avoid using temporary tables internally is ASA, which is designed to have a small footprint.

SQL7 allows different types of temporary tables; some are dropped automatically, and others only on demand or on database shutdown. Because they are all created in the `tempdb` database, they are more visible and can be better managed.

Sometimes, when it's difficult to get a complex query to work properly, you have another choice: You can create a temporary table with the result of part of the query in it, and then apply the remainder of the query to the temporary table. If you do this, some systems might not be able to optimize access to the temporary table. Using two stored procedures, one to create the table and the second to scan it, can solve this problem.

Ancillary Topics

You can save about 5% of CPU cycles required to evaluate `LIKE` clauses by rewriting them, so instead of

```
select t1.SEX as ''Gender''
from MIKE.EMPLOYEE t1
where t1.FIRSTNME like 'fr%' escape '\'
```

you could try

```
select t1.SEX as ''Gender''
from MIKE.EMPLOYEE t1
where t1.FIRSTNME >= 'fr' and t1.FIRSTNME < 'fs'
```

The Sybase Adaptive Server Enterprise (ASE) optimizer does this; DB2 doesn't bother.

The following examples fall under the title "Keep your thinking cap on." For example, using `ALL` predicates is usually best rethought by using aggregation comparisons:

(Commission of staff who aren't clerks that earn more commission than each of the clerks.)

```
select k1.COMM as ''COMM''
from MIKE.STAFF k1
where k1.job <> 'Clerk'
and k1.COMM >all
  (select k2.COMM
  from MIKE.STAFF k2
  where k2.JOB = 'Clerk')
```

This example is better—and more easily —expressed as follows:

```
select k1.COMM as ''COMM''
from MIKE.STAFF k1
where k1.job <> 'Clerk'
and k1.COMM >
  (select max (k2.COMM)
  from MIKE.STAFF k2
  where k2.JOB = 'Clerk')
```

This method is better because as a limit, a MAX operation is sargable if its argument is an index. On the other hand, the preceding ALL comparison is subject to all kinds of NULL checks, as shown by this optimizer rewrite:

```
SELECT Q4.COMM AS ''COMM''
FROM
  (SELECT MAX(Q2.$C0), MAX(CASE
  WHEN Q2.$C0 IS NULL
  THEN 1
  ELSE 0 END )
  FROM
   (SELECT Q1.COMM
   FROM MIKE.STAFF AS Q1
   WHERE (Q1.JOB = 'Clerk')) AS Q2) AS Q3,
    MIKE.STAFF AS Q4
WHERE (Q4.JOB <> 'Clerk') AND ((Q4.COMM > Q3.$C0)
    OR Q3.$C1 IS NULL ) AND ((Q4.COMM IS NULL
    AND Q3.$C1 IS NULL ) OR (Q4.COMM >=
CASE
WHEN Q3.$C1 IS NULL
THEN -99999.99
WHEN (Q3.$C1 = 0)
THEN Q3.$C0
ELSE NULL END ))
```

The following example shows you shouldn't reprogram by rote if you need to optimize:

(Job categories for staff that *consistently* make less than $15,000.00 in that category)

```
select t1.JOB as ''JOB category''
from MIKE.STAFF t1
where not exists
  (select *
  from MIKE.STAFF t3
  where t3.SALARY >= 15000.00
  and t1.JOB = t3.JOB)
```

Hence, the following would read "*...do not consistently...* " instead:

```
select t1.JOB as ''JOB description''
from MIKE.STAFF t1
where exists
  (select *
  from MIKE.STAFF t3
  where t3.SALARY >= 15000.00
```

```
  and t1.JOB = t3.JOB)
```

This query is programmed much more efficiently as follows:

```
select t1.JOB as ''JOB''
from MIKE.STAFF t1
where t1.SALARY >= 15000.00
```

Writing good SQL is like playing chess: Your performance improves as you store good moves and combinations in your subconscious. Serendipity plays an important part in this process. Recently a customer asked if he could include a `CASE` statement in machine-generated SQL. The knee-jerk answer was yes, but you have to cut and paste it into the `SELECT` list generated by the program. Since then, I started looking more closely at this statement and realized it has SQL optimization possibilities apart from improving output readability.

The following query requires two complete table scans to separate employees by seniority:

```
SELECT EMPNO, LASTNAME, 'Junior' AS SENIORITY
FROM MIKE.EMPLOYEE
WHERE (YEAR( CURRENT DATE) - YEAR( HIREDATE)) < 10
UNION ALL
SELECT EMPNO, LASTNAME, 'Senior' AS SENIORITY
FROM MIKE.EMPLOYEE
WHERE (YEAR( CURRENT DATE) - YEAR( HIREDATE)) >= 10
```

The following query, however, requires only one table scan:

```
SELECT EMPNO, LASTNAME,
CASE
WHEN (YEAR( CURRENT DATE) - YEAR( HIREDATE)) < 10
THEN 'Junior'
WHEN (YEAR( CURRENT DATE) - YEAR( HIREDATE)) >= 10
THEN 'Senior'
ELSE 'Unclassifiable'
END AS SENIORITY
FROM MIKE.EMPLOYEE
```

This approach can obviously lead to savings that increase linearly for additional classifications. When applied to queries involving aggregations, you can get even more mileage out of this clause, as in the following query (number of employees, by gender, with commission greater than salary):

```
SELECT SUM( CASE WHEN SEX = 'F'
AND COMM IS NOT NULL AND SALARY IS NOT NULL
AND COMM > SALARY THEN 1 ELSE 0 END)
```

```
AS ''Female emps'',
SUM( CASE WHEN SEX = 'M'
AND COMM IS NOT NULL AND SALARY IS NOT NULL
AND COMM > SALARY THEN 1 ELSE 0 END)
AS ''Male emps''
FROM MIKE.EMPLOYEE
```

In DB2 the `CASE` statement is part of SQL proper; in other systems, it can be programmed as part of a stored procedure.

Along a similarly serendipitous vein, I recently came across some material that I'd like to share with you because it's quite interesting, appropriate to this chapter, and highly functional. A company called Synamic, in the UK, sources it. They call their method *characteristic functions*. (Unlike their namesakes in wave/quantum mechanics, these are easier to understand.) Synamic presented this material originally in 1997 as a closed-session paper.

I'm not going to copy it verbatim here—you can read all about it at `www.synamic.co.uk`. I'd just like to sift through the highlights so they are conveniently available for reference. Essentially, they describe a way of achieving pivot table generation on the server with an economical resource consumption level. Their implementation is based on Transact-SQL (hence, ASE SQL), but it can easily be adapted to almost any database.

I have rewritten their main example from the original ASE form shown here:

```
select product_id,
sum(list_price * (1-abs(sign(to_char(end_date,'MM')-1))))
as ''jan_rev'',
sum(list_price * (1-abs(sign(to_char(end_date,'MM')-5))))
as ''may_rev'',
sum(list_price * (1-abs(sign(to_char(end_date,'MM')-12))))
as ''dec_rev''
from demo.price
group by product_id
```

In Oracle8 SQL (and most others), you write it as follows:

```
select product_id,
sum(min_price * (1-abs(sign(to_char(end_date,'MM')-1))))
as ''jan_rev'',
sum(min_price * (1-abs(sign(to_char(end_date,'MM')-5))))
as ''may_rev'',
sum(min_price * (1-abs(sign(to_char(end_date,'MM')-12)))) as ''dec_rev''
from demo.price
group by product_id
```

Like the previous examples related to the CASE statement, these functions serve a similar purpose in providing a powerful single-statement filter that can produce a result in one pass, instead of multiple table scans or horrendously inefficient joins.

Because the contents of Web pages can be changeable, I am only going to reproduce some critical data on other functions they describe. There is no copyright notice on the source material.

These are for numeric values:

```
d[A=B] = 1-abs(sign(A-B))
d[A!=B] = abs(sign(A-B)) {NB = 1-d[A=B]}
d[A<B] = 1-sign(1+sign(A-B))
d[A<=B] = sign(1-sign(A-B))
d[A>B] = 1-abs(1-sign(A-B))
d[A>=B] = sign(1+sign(A-B))
d[A is NULL] = isnull(0*A,1)
d[A is NOT NULL] = 1-isnull(0*A,1)
d[NOT A] = 1-d[A]
d[A AND B] = d[A]*d[B] {NB where d[A] and d[B] are never NULL}
d[A OR B] = sign(d[A]+d[B]) {NB where d[A] and d[B] are never NULL}
```

These are for string values:

```
d[A=B] = charindex(A,B)*charindex(B,A)
d[A!=B] = 1-charindex(A,B)*charindex(B,A)
d[A is NULL] = isnull(0*ascii,1)
d[A is NOT NULL] = 1-isnull(0* ascii,1)
```

As another example of its applicability, this code would use `instr()` instead of `charindex()` in Oracle8.

And these are for date values:

```
d[A=B] = 1-abs(sign(datediff(dd,B,A))
d[A!=B] = abs(sign(datediff(dd,B,A))
d[A<B] = 1-sign(1+sign(datediff(dd,B,A)))
d[A<=B] = sign(1-sign(datediff(dd,B,A)))
d[A>B] = 1-abs(1-sign(datediff(dd,B,A)))
d[A>=B] = sign(1+sign(datediff(dd,B,A)))
d[A is NULL] = isnull(0*datepart(yy,A),1)
d[A is NOT NULL] = 1-isnull(0* datepart(yy,A),1)
```

I'll leave it as an exercise for readers to transcribe the rest of these conditions to their favorite SQL dialect.

I'm going to close by mentioning one more detail. As you know by now, SQL optimizers are highly nonlinear and unpredictable. It appears that if you are interested in only the first few lines of output from a query, you'll be helping them by saying so. In DB2, for example, you can invoke `optimize for <x> rows`; `x` is a small number, ideally 1. SQL7 might benefit from the use of the `TOP` clause or the `FAST <x>` query optimizer hint.

A good ad hoc query tool will invoke these optimizer hints when the user limits output within the query, but they are relatively new and not universally available (both the tools and the optimizer hints).

Summary

I have tried to be as wide-ranging as possible in this chapter in order to not only illustrate the kinds of techniques to use in optimization, but also the fact that SQL optimization depends on your environment.

In general, retrieval optimization is controlled indirectly by the optimizer based on the specifications (code) you give it. Update optimization is based on your understanding of the storage mechanisms used by the RDBMS.

The optimizer's performance is a figure of merit of the RDBMS. If you are fortunate enough to have discretion over the choice of RDBMS, make the optimizer a serious factor. Just as nobody would seriously consider an IDE (integrated development environment) without a good debugger and associated display tools, you should give weight not only to the optimizer, but also to the visualization tools it offers.

Optimizer technology is probably the cheapest way for RDBMS vendors to improve the performance of their products. In my opinion, a rationally designed product would have a rock-solid relational engine with a very fluid optimizing layer. By changing the way this layer works, vendors could keep improving its performance and some features of their software. Regardless of how the RDBMS is designed, it appears to behave this way. You have to be prepared for differences in the optimizer when porting between versions and across vendors.

Optimizing for (old) OLTP and for (new) data warehousing may be quite different, not only because the metadata is different, but because the RDBMS designs themselves are changing and exhibiting new features.

Finally, SQL programs operate within vast parametric ranges: from being optimized on empty, nascent databases to running on multi-gigabyte data regions. These parameters also determine their design and subsequent optimization. Fortunately SQL—with all its shortcomings—is flexible enough to allow a considerable latitude of expression for a given semantic set.

I doubt that any individual can call himself or herself an expert in SQL optimization—the subject is too reliant on constant experimentation. The best you can do is study SQL idioms, learn how to weave them together, then learn how to take them all apart and rephrase them. That is how you learned your spoken language. Without the subconscious use of idioms you wouldn't be able to communicate at a fraction of your current speed, or efficiency.

CHAPTER 20

Security Issues

In This Chapter

Security is a major concern for any large database. Corporations entrust their data to a database management system and expect that data to be kept safe from a number of possible threats. A good security policy should cover not only possible data theft but also the following areas:

- Accidental damage—Because of the interactive nature of relational database systems, it is possible for someone to issue a query that could destroy or invalidate an entire database. Tight control over who has access to specific data should, therefore, be central to any security policy.
- Availability—Data should be not only accurate, but also accessible if it's to be of value.
- Theft or malicious damage—Of course, there is always the possibility of data theft or malicious damage. These problems should be considered in any potential plan.

There are four main lines of security in a relational database management system (see Figure 20.1). First, there is the operating system. As in most multiuser systems, the first line of defense, if you will, is the login. To be able to gain access to anything, you first need to log in to the operating system. Second is the username for the database management system. The third line of defense is the object permissions, controlling who has access to specific objects in the database.

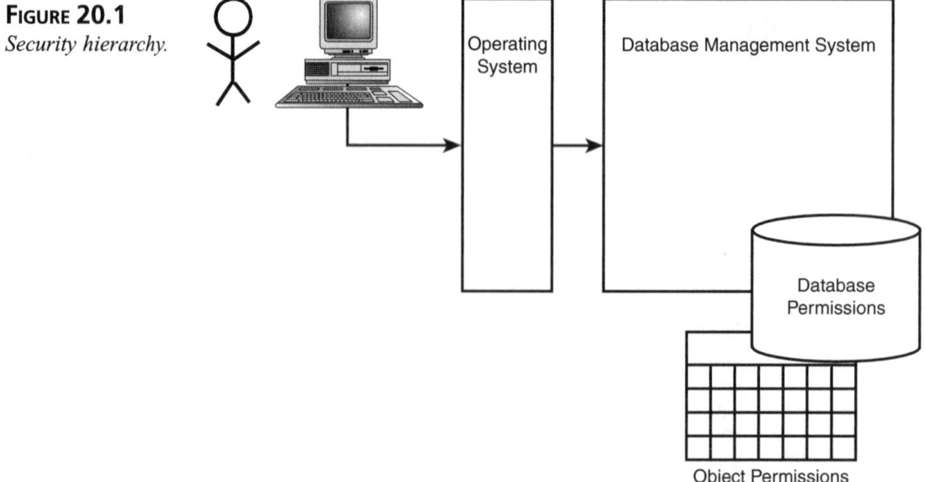

FIGURE 20.1
Security hierarchy.

Permissions can be granted and revoked not only on databases and tables, but also on other objects, such as views, stored procedures, and even whole applications. The last line of defense is object privileges, which control what a user can do within an object. For example, a user might be given `SELECT` permission on one table and `DELETE` on another.

Note

Most remote access methods, such as ODBC, JDBC, or SQL*Net, bypass the operating system login and authenticate the user at the database level.

This chapter covers user security first, explaining how to create and drop users. It goes on to look at object permissions and roles, covering the granting and revoking of privileges, followed by a look at the methods of securing database access with views and stored procedures. The chapter finishes up with a look at how to enable auditing for your database sessions.

Database Users

User security is one of the most important lines of defense for any multiuser database system. ANSI SQL uses the term *authorization ID* to describe users or user IDs, and you will come across this term in some database documentation. For your purposes here, the terms are interchangeable. Anyone who needs access to the database needs a user ID. It is common practice to assign one user ID per person; there are, however, exceptions. If, for example, Fred works in Accounting for three days a week but works as a part-time administrator for the rest of the week, it makes sense to give Fred two user IDs—`FredAcct` and `FredAdmin`—each with its own permissions and rights. This system reduces the chance of accidentally executing a query with administrative privileges.

User Security in Oracle

To create a user in Oracle, use the following command:

```
create user user_name identified by password;
```

This command creates a new user account as soon as it runs. The user can't log in, however, because he or she hasn't been assigned the `CREATE SESSION` privilege yet.

> **Note**
>
> Oracle 8 also supports external authentication of users. To take advantage of this feature, user IDs are typically prefixed with OPS$ and the keyword EXTERNALLY is used in place of a password in the CREATE USER statement.

Listing 20.1 shows how to create a user account.

LISTING 20.1 Creating a User Account

```
drop user fred cascade;

create user fred identified by fred;
```

The first statement drops the user fred. By using the CASCADE option, all objects in the user's schema are deleted, too. This procedure can't be rolled back, however, so use it with caution! Note, too, that attempting to drop fred when the user doesn't exist returns an error. The second statement creates a new user, fred, with the password fred. If you try to login with this user, you see the following:

```
Connect fred/fred
ERROR:
ORA-01045: user FRED lacks CREATE SESSION privilege; logon denied

Warning: You are no longer connected to ORACLE.
```

For the user to be allowed to log in, you need to assign fred the CREATE SESSION privilege. You can do this by logging in to an existing account:

```
Connect sys/sys
grant create session to fred;

Grant succeeded.
```

Managing Database Users in Oracle

Inevitably, at some point you have to change a password or find out what permissions a user has been granted.

To change a user's password, use the ALTER USER statement, as shown here:

```
ALTER USER fred IDENTIFIED BY fred2 PASSWORD EXPIRE;

Statement Processed.
```

This changes the password for `fred` to `fred2`, and uses the `PASSWORD EXPIRE` statement to force the user to change the password the next time he logs in.

To generate a report of what permissions a user has been granted, you need to query the `DBA_SYS_PRIVS` view. Although it won't tell you who granted the permissions, it does list what permissions have been granted. Since `fred` doesn't have any permissions granted, this example uses the built-in user `SCOTT`.

LISTING 20.2 Reporting on a User's Permissions

```
SELECT * FROM dba_sys_privs WHERE grantee = 'SCOTT';
```

This statement returns the following:

```
GRANTEE                        PRIVILEGE                                ADM
------------------------------ ---------------------------------------- ---
SCOTT                          CREATE TABLE                             NO
SCOTT                          UNLIMITED TABLESPACE                     NO
```

User Security in SQL Server

In SQL Server the process is similar, except you need to create both a login and a user. SQL Server operates in two authentication modes: Windows NT Authentication and Mixed Mode. The mode you choose depends on how your network is configured. To add an existing Windows NT user to SQL Server, use the `sp_grantlogin` stored procedure as follows:

```
sp_grantlogin ' login_name'
```

The *`login_name`* parameter is the name of the Windows NT user or group to be added, qualified with the Windows domain.

Listing 20.3 demonstrates adding a login to SQL Server 7.0.

LISTING 20.3 Adding a Login to SQL Server 7.0

```
USE Master
GO
Sp_grantlogin 'NTDOMAIN\'Fred'
GO
```

This listing returns

```
Granted database access to 'NTDOMAIN\'Fred'.
```

This statement creates a login for `Fred`.

Warning

Windows NT allows longer usernames than SQL Server's 128-character limit for the domain and username combination.

This statement just creates a login and does not allow `Fred` to connect to SQL Server. Attempting to do so results in the following error:

```
Unable to connect to server \\SQL1:

Server: Msg 18456, Level 16, State 1
[Microsoft][ODBC SQL Server Driver][SQL Server]Login failed for user
''fred'.
```

To create a new SQL Server login not related to a Windows NT account, use the `sp_addlogin` stored procedure:

```
sp_addlogin 'login_name','password'[,'default_database']
```

In this statement, you must provide a password as well as a login name. You can also specify a default database for the login, as shown here:

```
sp_addlogin ''fred2',''fred2'
```

This returns

```
New login created
```

This command creates a login called `fred2` with a password of `fred2` in the current database.

Two stored procedures can be used to stop a user from logging in: `sp_revokelogin`, which removes the login from SQL Server, and `sp_denylogin`, which actually prevents a user or group from connecting to SQL Server.

To be able to connect to SQL Server, a login has to be assigned to a user. This is done using the `sp_grantdbaccess` stored procedure. The following example, Listing 20.4, shows assigning the login created in Listing 20.3 to a user within the database.

LISTING 20.4 Assigning a Login to a User

```
USE Northwind
GO
sp_grantdbaccess 'NTDOMAIN\'Fred',''Fred'
GO
```

LISTING 20.4 CONTINUED

```
Sp_grantdbaccess ''Fred2',''Fred2'
GO
```

This statement creates two users called `Fred` and `Fred2` in the Northwind database and assigns the logins `Fred` and `Fred2`, respectively.

Managing Database Users in SQL Server

Managing database users is an important part of database administration. Being able to see what users have access to and being able to change those users' attributes are essential day-to-day administration tasks.

To generate a report of users for the current database—in this case, `master`—use the code in Listing 20.5.

LISTING 20.5 Listing All Users in the Current Database

```
USE master
GO
EXEC sp_helpuser
GO
```

To list all logins and users for the system, use the `sp_helplogin` stored procedure, as shown in Listing 20.6.

LISTING 20.6 Listing All Logins and Users

```
USE master
GO
EXEC sp_helplogins
GO
```

This script returns

```
LoginName                  SI   DefDBName  DefLangName      AUser ARemote
-----------------------  ----------------------  ------------
------------------- ----- -------
NTDOMAIN\Administrator   0x0105000000000000051500000  master      us_english
NO  no
BUILTIN\Administrators   0x0102000000000000052000000  master      us_english
NO  no
sa           0x01          master    us_english yes  no
```

```
(3 row(s) affected)
LoginName         DBName            UserName          UserOrAlias
----------------- ----------------- ----------------- -----------
NTDOMAIN\fred     master            Northwind         User
sa                master            db_owner          MemberOf
sa                master            dbo               User
sa                model             db_owner          MemberOf
sa                model             dbo               User
sa                msdb              db_owner          MemberOf
sa                msdb              dbo               User
sa                Northwind         db_owner          MemberOf
sa                Northwind         dbo               User
sa                pubs              db_owner          MemberOf
sa                pubs              dbo               User
sa                tempdb            db_owner          MemberOf
sa                tempdb            dbo               User

(13 row(s) affected)
```

Two stored procedures manage database access: `sp_revokedbaccess` and p_change_users_login. To remove a user from the database, use the `sp_revokedbaccess` stored procedure:

```
sp_revokedbaccess ''Fred2'
```

This procedure removes the user `Fred2` from the current database. To change the relationship between a login and a SQL Server user, use `sp_change_users_login`, as shown in Listing 20.7. First it adds a new login, `NewFred`, and then updates the user `Fred`, relating it to `NewFred`.

LISTING 20.7 Changing the Link Between a User and Login

```
--Add the new login.
USE master
GO
EXEC sp_addlogin '''NewFred'
GO
--Change the user account to link with the '''NewFred' login.
USE Northwind
go
EXEC sp_change_users_login 'Update_One', '''Fred', '''NewFred'
```

The `sp_password` procedure is used to change a user's password. The following procedure executed at `fred2` changes the `fred2`'s password to `jam`:

```
sp_password 'fred2','jam'
```

The system administrator can change a password without having to know the previous password, as shown here:

```
sp_password NULL,'fred2','fred'
```

This procedure changes `fred`'s password back to `fred2`.

Permissions and Privileges

In the previous section, you granted users access to the database. However, they still can't do much in the database itself. For that, you need to grant the relevant permissions to the user.

There are two types of permissions in most database systems: server or statement, and object permissions. Server or statement permissions allow you to create, alter, or drop actual database objects. Object permissions, on the other hand, allow you to execute commands on specific objects.

Server Permissions

You have two built-in users when you create a database in Oracle: `SYS` and `SYSTEM`. These two users have *all* the system permissions and the ability to grant them to other users.

Oracle offers many system permissions (see the following list), so deciding which one to assign to which user is a tricky task. You need to decide which users can grant permissions to another user, too. If you grant a permission with the `ADMIN OPTION` or give users the `GRANT ANY PERMISSION` server permission, they can in turn grant that permission to other users. If this is not kept in check, it can quickly get out of control, undermining your entire security policy.

To grant the `CREATE TABLE` permission to `fred` and allow him to assign `CREATE TABLE` to others, use the following statement:

```
GRANT create table TO fred WITH ADMIN OPTION;
```

You can also assign permissions to `PUBLIC`, thereby allowing all users to essentially be granted that permission. Use with care!

If, for example, you decide that all users in your database should be able to create tables, you can use the following:

```
GRANT create table TO PUBLIC
```

System Permissions

ALTER ANY CLUSTER	CREATE SESSION
ALTER ANY INDEX	CREATE SNAPSHOT
ALTER ANY PROCEDURE	CREATE SYNONYM
ALTER ANY ROLE	CREATE TABLE
ALTER ANY SEQUENCE	CREATE TABLESPACE
ALTER ANY SNAPSHOT	CREATE TRIGGER
ALTER ANY TABLE	CREATE TYPE
ALTER ANY TRIGGER	CREATE VIEW
ALTER ANY TYPE	DELETE ANY TABLE
ALTER DATABASE	DROP ANY CLUSTER
ALTER PROFILE	DROP ANY DIRECTORY
ALTER RESOUCE COST	DROP ANY INDEX
ALTER ROLLBACK SEGMENT	DROP ANY LIBRARY
ALTER SESSION	DROP ANY PROCEDURE
ALTER SYSTEM	DROP ANY ROLE
ALTER TABLESPACE	DROP ANY SEQUENCE
ALTER USER	DROP ANY SNAPSHOT
ANALYZE ANY	DROP ANY SYNONYM
AUDIT ANY	DROP ANY TABLE
AUDIT SYSTEM	DROP ANY TRIGGER
BACKUP ANY TABLE	DROP ANY TYPE
BECOME USER	DROP ANY VIEW
COMMENT ANY TABLE	DROP LIBRARY
CREATE ANY CLUSTER	DROP PROFILE
CREATE ANY DIRECTORY	DROP PUBLIC DATABASE LINK
CREATE ANY INDEX	DROP PUBLIC SYNONYM
CREATE ANY LIBRARY	DROP ROLLBACK SEGMENT
CREATE ANY PROCEDURE	DROP TABLESPACE
CREATE ANY SEQUENCE	DROP USER
CREATE ANY SNAPSHOT	EXECUTE ANY PROCEDURE
CREATE ANY SYNONYM	EXECUTE ANY TYPE
CREATE ANY TABLE	FORCE ANY TRANSACTION
CREATE ANY TRIGGER	FORCE TRANSACTION

```
CREATE ANY TYPE
CREATE ANY VIEW
CREATE CLUSTER
CREATE DATABASE LINK
CREATE ANY LIBRARY
CREATE PROCEDURE
CREATE PROFILE
CREATE PUBLIC DATABASE LINK
CREATE PUBLIC SYNONYM
CREATE ROLE
CREATE ROLLBACK SEGMENT
CREATE SEQUENCE
GRANT ANY ROLE
INSERT ANY TABLE
LOCK ANY TABLE
MANAGE TABLESPACE
RESTRICTED SESSION
SELECT ANY SEQUENCE
SELECT ANY TABLE
SYSDBA
SYSOPER
UNLIMITED TABLESPACE
UPDATE ANY TABLE
```

The following example demonstrates the `CREATE TABLE` permission. Running the script in Listing 20.8 creates two new users called `fred` and `sam`. It then assigns the `CREATE TABLE` and `CREATE SESSION` permissions to `fred` and gives `sam` only the `CREATE SESSION` permission.

LISTING 20.8 Creating a New User

```
drop user fred cascade;
drop user sam cascade;

create user fred identified by fred
 default tablespace user_data
 temporary tablespace temp_data
 quota unlimited on user_data
 quota unlimited on temp_data;

create user sam identified by sam
 default tablespace user_data
 temporary tablespace temp_data
 quota unlimited on user_data
 quota unlimited on temp_data;

grant create session to sam;
grant create session, create table, create view to fred;
```

This listing returns the following:

```
User dropped.
```

```
User dropped.
User created.
User created.
Grant succeeded.
Grant succeeded.
```

First, sam attempts to create a table in his schema, as shown in Listing 20.9.

LISTING 20.9 Table Creation in a Schema

```
connect sam/sam

Create table test1(
 id number(2) not null,
 uname varchar2(15),
 real_name varchar2(30)
);
```

This listing returns

```
Create table test1 (
       *
ERROR at line 1:
ORA-0131: insufficient privileges
```

Because sam doesn't have the CREATE TABLE permission, the script fails. However, if you try to create a table connecting as fred, as shown in Listing 20.10, the script succeeds.

LISTING 20.10 Creating a Table in a Schema with Sufficient Permissions

```
connect sam/sam
Create table test1(
 id number(2) not null,
 uname varchar2(15),
 real_name varchar2(30)
);

insert into test1 values (1, ''fred',''''fred');
insert into test1 values (2, ''sam',''''sam');
insert into test1 values (3, 'jack','jack');

commit;
```

This returns

```
Statement processed
1 row processed
```

After you have granted a permission to someone, you can always revoke it. For example, if you want to allow a developer to create a selection of tables while you are developing an application, but don't want any more tables created when the application is deployed, you could just revoke the permission.

In Listing 20.8, you assigned `fred` the `CREATE VIEW` permission. If you decide he no longer needs that permission, you can revoke it by using the following:

```
Connect sys/sys
revoke create view from fred;
```

> **Warning**
>
> System permissions can be dangerous. Grant only the level of permission required to get a job done, and revoke that permission as soon as it's no longer needed. Pay special attention to any permission granted with the `ADMIN OPTION`.

In SQL Server, most of the server permissions are handled by granting roles. For more information on roles, see the next section, "Object Permissions." When SQL Server is installed, the `sa` login and any members of the `sysadmin` role are equivalent to the `SYS` and `SYSTEM` users in Oracle. They can do anything in SQL Server, including grant permissions to other users.

There are a limited number of server permissions that can be granted without the use of roles under SQL Server. These permissions, shown in the following list, can be granted by members of the `sysadmin`, `securityadmin`, or `db_owner` roles.

- ALTER DATABASE
- CREATE DATABASE
- CREATE DEFAULT
- CREATE PROCEDURE
- CREATE RULE
- CREATE TABLE
- CREATE VIEW
- BACKUP DATABASE
- BACKUP LOG

Listing 20.11 illustrates granting the `CREATE TABLE` permission.

LISTING 20.11 Creating a New User and Assigning Initial Permissions

```
USE master
GO
EXEC sp_addlogin ''fred',''''fred'
EXEC sp_addlogin ''sam',''''sam'
GO
USE Northwind
GO
EXEC sp_grantdbaccess ''fred',''''fred'
EXEC sp_grantdbaccess ''sam',''''sam'
GO
grant CREATE TABLE to fred
```

This listing returns

```
New login created.
New login created.
Granted database access to ''fred'.
Granted database access to ''sam'.
```

If `sam` connects and attempts to create a table, as shown in Listing 20.12, essentially the same as Listing 20.10's table created in Oracle, then it fails because of lack of privileges.

LISTING 20.12 Creating a Table

```
Create table test1(
 id int(2) not null,
 uname varchar(15),
 real_name varchar(30)
);
```

This listing returns

```
Server:Msg 262, Level 14, State 1, Line 1
CREATE TABLE permission denied, database 'Northwind', owner 'dbo'.
```

If `fred` tries to run the same script, it works with no problems because he has been granted the `CREATE TABLE` permission.

Warning

Remember that permissions are assigned to a username or role, not the login name.

If you later realize that `fred` doesn't need the `CREATE VIEW` permission, it can be revoked using the ANSI standard revoke syntax:

```
revoke CREATE VIEW from fred
```

This statement returns the following:

```
The Command(s) completed successfully.
```

After you have a few users in a database, it can become a nightmare to try to remember who has been assigned which permissions. To keep track of what has been assigned, you can use the `sp_helprotect` stored procedure. Like most of SQL Server's administration stored procedures, what it reports depends on what parameters are passed to it. For example, to see what permissions have been assigned on a table, use this:

```
sp_helprotect 'test1'
```

This procedure returns all the permissions assigned on the `test1` table. To see what permission a user has, pass a username to the procedure:

```
sp_helprotect NULL, 'fred'
```

You can also see what permissions a user has granted, a useful feature when you're trying to track down a potential security breach:

```
sp_helprotect NULL, NULL, 'fred'
```

This procedure returns all the permissions granted by `fred` in the current database.

Note

SQL Server supports the `WITH GRANT` option for `GRANT` only with object permissions, not server permissions. There is no equivalent to Oracle's `ADMIN OPTION` .

Object Permissions

Contrary to system permissions, object permissions apply to single objects only. For example, the right to insert data into the `SALES` table doesn't give you any access to the `INVENTORY` table. This provides a specific level of security, allowing people access to only the functions they need.

The SQL1 ANSI standard supports the four basic commands:

- The `SELECT` privilege allows you to query a table to view and retrieve data from it.
- The `DELETE` privilege allows you to delete data from a table or view.

- The INSERT privilege allows you to insert rows of data into a table or view.
- The UPDATE privilege allows you to update specific rows of data in a table or view.

The SQL2 standard augments these basic features with several new commands, including the following:

- The REFERENCES privilege allows you to restrict the ability to create a reference to a table from a foreign key in another table.
- The EXECUTE privilege allows you to execute a specific stored procedure.

As well as these new commands, the SQL2 standard also extends the INSERT and UPDATE commands, allowing them to be specified on a column-level basis. For more details on column-level security, see the section "Column-Level Permissions."

To assign these privileges in Oracle, use the standard GRANT statement. The following examples demonstrate how to use these privileges

This following statement allows fred to query data in the sales_data table. For example, if fred just needed to generate reports from the sales data, this is the privilege to grant.

```
GRANT SELECT ON sales_data TO fred
```

The following query grants SELECT, DELETE, and UPDATE privileges on the sales_data table, which allows sam to modify and delete data in that table. This privilege is the one to grant if sam has to check and correct data in the sales_data table.

```
GRANT SELECT, DELETE, UPDATE ON sales_data TO sam
```

The next query is similar to the preceding one; it grants SELECT permission on the sales_data table. It also allows a user to create a foreign key that references the dept column in the sales_dept table.

```
GRANT SELECT ON sales_data REFERENCES (dept) ON sales_dept TO sam
```

The following example in Listing 20.13 demonstrates using some of these privileges.

LISTING 20.13 Create a New User and Grant Privileges

```
drop user fred cascade;
drop user jack cascade;
drop user sam cascade;

create user fred identified by fred
 default tablespace user_data
 temporary tablespace temp_data
 quota unlimited on user_data
```

LISTING 20.13 CONTINUED

```
 quota unlimited on temp_data;
create user jack identified by jack
 default tablespace user_data
 temporary tablespace temp_data
 quota unlimited on user_data
 quota unlimited on temp_data;

create user sam identified by sam
 default tablespace user_data
 temporary tablespace temp_data
 quota unlimited on user_data
 quota unlimited on temp_data;

grant create session to fred;
grant create session to sam;
grant create session, create table to jack;
```

This listing creates three new users. Note the `DROP` with the `CASCADE` option at the top of the script.All three users were assigned `CREATE SESSION` permissions, and `jack` was given `CREATE TABLE` permission as well.

The user `jack` then creates a table, as shown in Listing 20.14, and assigns `SELECT` privileges to `fred`; note the `WITH GRANT OPTION` that allows `fred` to assign `SELECT` privileges to other users.

LISTING 20.14 Creating a Table and Granting Permissions

```
connect jack/jack

Create table test1(
 id number(2) not null,
 uname varchar2(15),
 real_name varchar2(30)
);

insert into test1 values (1, ''fred',''''fred');
insert into test1 values (2, ''sam',''''sam');
insert into test1 values (3, 'jack','jack');

commit;

GRANT SELECT ON test1 TO fred WITH GRANT OPTION;
```

The user `fred` can now select from the `test1` table, as shown in Listing 20. 15.

LISTING 20.15 Testing the **SELECT** Privilege

```
connect fred/fred
select * from jack.test1;
```

The listing returns this:

```
ID  UNAME            REAL_NAME
--- ---------------- ------------------------------
1   fred             fred
2   sam              sam
3   jack             jack
```

Note the use of `jack.test1`. Because the `test1` table is in `jack`'s schema, `fred` needs to refer to its full name. For more information about schemas, see the "Databases Versus Schemas" section later in this chapter.

As `fred` has been granted the `SELECT` privilege only, he cannot perform inserts, updates, or deletes. The script in Listing 20.16 shows `fred` trying to test his privileges.

LISTING 20.16 Testing **DELETE**, **INSERT**, and **UPDATE** Privileges

```
connect fred/fred
delete from jack.test1;
insert into jack.test1 values (4,'judy','judy');
update jack.test1 set uname='richard', real_name='richard' where id = 1;
```

This listing returns the following:

```
delete from jack.test1;
            *
ERROR at line 1:
ORA-01031: insufficient privileges

insert into jack.test1 values (
            *
ORA-01031: insufficient privileges

update jack.test1 set uname='richard'
            *
ORA-01031: insufficient privileges
```

Say `jack` grants the `INSERT` privilege to `fred`, by using the following commands:

```
connect jack/jack
GRANT INSERT ON test1 to fred;
```

When fred attempts to insert data into test1, as shown here

```
connect fred/fred
insert into jack.test1 values (4,'judy','judy');
```

It returns this:

```
Connected.
1 row updated.
```

If sam later discovers he needs the data in test1 and tries to query the table, as shown here

```
Connect sam/sam
select * from jack.test1;
```

the following is returned:

```
Connected.
select * from jack.test1
              *
ERROR at line 1:
ORA-00942: table or view does not exist
```

Because jack granted fred the SELECT privilege with the GRANT OPTION , fred can now assign it to other users:

```
Connect fred/fred
GRANT SELECT on jack.test1 TO SAM;
```

If sam attempts to retrieve the data again, he finds he now has the correct privilege:

```
Connect sam/sam
select * from jack.test1;
```

The preceding command now returns this:

```
ID  UNAME           REAL_NAME
--- --------------- ------------------------------
1   fred            fred
2   sam             sam
3   jack            jack
4   judy            judy
```

If jack then decides that the data in test1 is of a sensitive nature and wants to revoke fred's SELECT privilege, the REVOKE statement does the job:

```
REVOKE SELECT ON jack.test1 FROM fred
```

This statement automatically revokes the privilege from anyone `fred` has assigned it to—in this case, `sam`. Oracle does this automatically.

Note

The `WITH GRANT OPTION` is much like the `ADMIN OPTION`. It can be useful, enabling you to delegate administrative tasks to select users. It is, however, dangerous. Be careful to whom you assign these privileges.

Databases Versus Schemas

Before you take a look at SQL Server's implementation of object privileges, it will be helpful to take a look at the idea of schemas in Oracle and databases in SQL Server.

In Oracle when a user creates a table without specifying a schema, the table is created in the user's default schema. To access a table in another schema, even if he or she has been granted the relevant privileges, a user must specify the schema name and the table name.

Using the users and table created in Listings 20.13 and 20.14, this can be demonstrated as follows. In Listing 20.15, `fred` could select from `test1` by using the table name prefixed with the schema name. In the following example, `fred` attempts to select from `test1` first without using the schema name and then using the schema name:

```
connect fred/fred
select * from test1;
select * from jack.test1;
```

This code returns the following:

```
Connected
Select * from test1;
       *
ERROR at line 1:
ORA-00942: table or view does not exist
ID  UNAME           REAL_NAME
--- --------------- ----------------------------
1   fred            fred
2   sam             sam
3   jack            jack
4   judy            judy
```

In SQL Server there is no concept of a schema. The closest equivalent concept is database and object owner. When users create a database, they become the object owner of any objects they create. By default, when an object is first created, only the owners have access to it. As object owners, they are implicitly granted all privileges to allow them to perform all tasks in those objects. To allow anyone else to access the object, the owner must grant the specific privileges to other users.

Object privileges in SQL Server are similar to those in Oracle. SQL Server also uses the SQL standard grant and revoke statements:

```
USE master
GO
CREATE DATABASE test
ON
(NAME = test_dat,
 FILENAME = 'c:\mssql7\data\test.mdf')

GO
USE test
GO
EXEC sp_addlogin 'fred',''fred'
GO
EXEC sp_addlogin 'sam',''sam'
GO
EXEC sp_addlogin 'jack','jack'
GO
EXEC sp_grantdbaccess 'fred',''fred'
GO
EXEC sp_grantdbaccess 'sam',''sam'
GO
EXEC sp_grantdbaccess 'jack','jack'
GO
GRANT CREATE TABLE TO sam
GO
```

This code returns the following:

```
The CREATE DATABASE process is allocating 0.75MB on disk 'test_dat'.
The CREATE DATABASE process is allocating 0.49MB on disk 'test_log'.
New login created.
New login created.
New login created.
Granted database access to ''fred'.
Granted database access to ''sam'.
```

```
Granted database access to 'jack'.
```

Say sam then logs in and creates a table using the following script:

```
USE test
GO
create table sam.test1 (
 id int not null,
 uname varchar(15),
 real_name varchar(30))
GO
insert into test1 values (1,'''fred','''fred')
insert into test1 values (1,'''sam','''sam')
insert into test1 values (1,'jack','jack')
```

This script creates and populates the test1 table in the test database. Note that sam has the insert privilege because he is the object owner and therefore implicitly gains all the privileges associated with that object.

Now say fred needs access to the data stored in the test1 table and attempts to query it as follows:

```
USE test
GO
SELECT * from sam.test1
GO
```

It returns

```
Server: Msg 229, Level 14, State 5, Line 1
SELECT permission denied on object 'test1', database 'test', owner ''sam'
```

If fred then asks sam for SELECT privileges and sam decides that fred is going to be in charge of who can query test1, sam issues the following grant:

```
GRANT select ON sam.test1 TO fred with GRANT OPTION
```

So fred is now able to query the table and can also assign others the privilege.

Connecting as fred:

```
USE test
GO
SELECT * from sam.test1
GO
```

It returns the following:

```
Id          uname          real_name
----------- -------------- -------------------------
1           fred           fred
2           sam            sam
3           jack           jack

(3 row(s) affected)
```

If `jack` then asks `fred` to be able to query `test1`, `fred` can grant him the privilege as follows:

```
GRANT SELECT on sam.test1 TO jack
```

And `jack` can now query the table, too. If `sam` then decides that `fred` wasn't a good choice to be in charge of who can access the table, he might try running the following:

```
REVOKE SELECT on sam.test1 FROM fred
```

But he forgot the `CASCADE` keyword, so it returns the following:

```
Server: Msg 4611, Level 16, State 1, Line 1
To revoke grantable privileges, specify the CASCADE option with REVOKE.
```

Seeing his error, `sam` then reissues the query as follows:

```
REVOKE SELECT on sam.test1 FROM fred CASCADE
```

The query executes, and the `SELECT` permission is removed from both `fred` and `jack`.

If `fred` or `jack` now attempt to query the table, as follows,

```
select * from sam.test1
```

the query returns

```
Server: Msg 229, Level 14, State 5, Line 1
SELECT permission denied on object 'test1', database 'test', owner ''sam'.
```

If `sam` then agrees that `jack` should have access to the data, all he needs to do is grant that privilege to `jack` directly:

```
GRANT SELECT on sam.test1 TO jack
```

In SQL Server, not only can you revoke a privilege, but you can also deny them. `REVOKE` removes the privilege from the user in much the same way as `REVOKE` works with Oracle.

Note

REVOKE removes the privilege from the user. However, if the user belongs to a role that has the privilege, the revoke is essentially overridden.

There is now a new level of security with SQL Server 7.0. You can not only revoke, but also actually deny a user access to a privilege. If you don't want to take any chances with a user, then DENY gives you the level of security you need.

Note

The DENY statement overrides any privileges or permissions that might have been assigned to a user or to a role he or she belongs to.

If fred decides that the data in test1 is of a sensitive nature and wants to revoke jack's SELECT privilege, the REVOKE statement does the job:

```
REVOKE SELECT ON sam.test1 FROM jack
```

SQL, unlike Oracle, does not automatically revoke privileges for users who have been given privileges by a user with the GRANT OPTION . To revoke cascade-granted privileges, you need to use the CASCADE keyword, as shown here:

```
REVOKE SELECT on sam.test1 FROM jack CASCADE
```

This has the same effect as Oracle's automatic revoke.

The situation gets more complex if fred belongs to a role that has been granted SELECT privileges to test1:

```
USE test
GO
EXEC sp_addrole Managers, sam
GO
EXEC sp_addrolemember Managers, fred
GO
GRANT SELECT on sam.test1 TO Managers
```

This code adds a role— Managers—and assigns fred to that role. It then grants the SELECT privilege to the role. If sam relents and grants fred the SELECT permission directly again, as shown in the following line, it allows fred to access test1 and query the data:

```
GRANT SELECT on sam.test1 to fred
```

If sam subsequently realizes that fred doesn't need SELECT permission for the test1 table, he can revoke it as follows:

```
REVOKE SELECT ON sam.test1 FROM fred
```

As far as sam is concerned, fred should now be denied access to test1. However, when fred goes to query test1 as follows:

```
USE test
GO
SELECT * from sam.test1
GO
```

It still returns this:

```
Id          uname           real_name
----------- --------------- -------------------------
1           fred            fred
2           sam             sam
3           jack            jack
```

What sam should have done is deny fred the SELECT privilege. This overrides any other privileges fred has, either directly or through membership to a role. To deny fred that privilege, sam runs the following:

```
DENY SELECT ON sam.test1 TO fred
```

Now when fred attempts to query the test1 table, as shown here,

```
USE test
GO
SELECT * from sam.test1
GO
```

the query returns this:

```
Server: Msg 229, Level 14, State 5, Line 1
SELECT permission denied on object 'test1', database 'test', owner ''sam'.
```

For more information about the use of roles, see the following section, "Using Roles to Simplify Administration."

Column-Level Permissions

You can make security even more restrictive by using column-level access to tables or views.

Oracle uses a slight variation on the ANSI standard GRANT statement:

```
GRANT privilege column1,column2 on table/view to user/role;
```

Oracle supports a subset of object privileges that can be granted on a column-by-column basis. INSERT, UPDATE, and REFERENCES are the only privileges supported at the column level. Oracle doesn't support the SELECT statement because this function is available through views. Of course, DELETE isn't supported; it wouldn't make much sense to be able to delete only specific columns.

SQL Server also uses a variation of the ANSI SQL standard GRANT statement. The privileges that can be granted are, however, different in SQL Server than Oracle. SQL supports SELECT, UPDATE, and REFERENCES privileges at the column level. SQL Server does not support the INSERT privilege, but it does support the SELECT privilege.

To be able to list all column privileges for a table, you can use the sp_column_privileges stored procedure:

```
EXEC sp_column_privileges test1
```

For example, say you grant the following privileges to fred:

```
GRANT SELECT uname ON sam.test1 TO fred
```

Now fred can select only from the uname column of test1. If he issues the following statement,

```
SELECT uname FROM sam.test1
```

it returns this:

```
uname
---------------
fred
sam
jack
```

If fred tries to query the entire table as follows:

```
USE test
GO
SELECT * from sam.test1
GO
```

it returns this:

```
Server: Msg 229, Level 14, State 5, Line 1
SELECT permission denied on object 'test1', database 'test', owner ''sam'.
```

If fred then tries to alter any value in the uname column, as shown here:

```
USE test
GO
UPDATE sam.test1 set uname = 'judy' where uname = ''fred'
```

it also returns the following:

```
Server: Msg 229, Level 14, State 5, Line 1
SELECT permission denied on object 'test1', database 'test', owner ''sam'.
```

Using Roles to Simplify Administration

After users can connect to the database, they still need to be granted the requisite privileges to be able to do anything productive. Grouping users into a single unit means that permissions can be granted to the unit as a whole, which simplifies administration.

Most database management systems use *roles* for grouping users together. Any permission granted, revoked, or denied to a role applies to all the members of that role, too. Normally, roles are created to reflect job roles, such as defining roles for each department in your organization. When a user changes departments, it's simply a matter of removing the user from one role and adding him or her to another.

Oracle includes a small number of built-in roles, listed in Table 20.1.

TABLE 20.1 Built-In Roles

Role	*Permission*
CONNECT	Very basic permissions for most users
RESOURCE	Basic permissions for a developer
DBA	All the basic administration permissions granted with the ADMIN OPTION
EXP_FULL_DATABASE	Permissions for users of the Export utility
IMP_FULL_DATABASE	Permissions for users of the Import utility

Oracle relies on user-defined roles, set up with the CREATE ROLE statement. A user must have the CREATE ROLE permission to be able to execute the following statement, for example:

```
CREATE ROLE Managers
```

This statement creates the Managers role. You can assign privileges to roles and can also assign roles to other roles, creating *meta-roles*.

To grant a role to a user, use the GRANT statement in much the same way as you assign an object privilege. For example, to assign sam to the DBA role, run the following:

```
GRANT DBA TO sam;
```

To remove a role from a user, use the REVOKE statement as you do for revoking an object permission.

After a user has been assigned to a role, you must enable the role with the SET ROLE command before the user can use any of the permissions assigned to the role. For sam to enable the DBA role, you use the following command:

```
Connect sam/sam
SET ROLE DBA;
```

SQL Server has three types of role: fixed server roles, fixed database roles, and user-defined roles.

There are seven fixed server roles, listed in Table 20.2.

TABLE 20.2 Fixed Server Roles

Role	*Permission*
Sysadmin	Perform any activity
Dbcreator	Create and alter databases
Diskadmin	Manage disk files
Processadmin	Manage the SQL Server processes
Serveradmin	Configure server-wide settings
Setupadmin	Install replication
Securityadmin	Manage and audit server logins

To grant a server role, use the sp_addsrvrolemember system stored procedure. To assign fred to the dbcreator role, issue the following command:

```
EXEC sp_addsrvrolemember ''fred', dbcreator
```

After users are assigned to a role, they can, of course, be removed with the sp_dropsrvrolemember system stored procedure.

There are 10 fixed database roles in SQL Server, listed in Table 20.3.

TABLE 20.3 Fixed Database Roles

Role	*Permission*
Public	Used to maintain all default permissions
db_owner	Perform any database role activity
db_accessadmin	Add and remove database users, roles, and groups
db_ddladmin	Add, modify, and drop database objects
db_securityadmin	Assign statement and object permissions

TABLE 20.3 Fixed Database Roles

Role	Permission
db_backupoperator	Back up and restore database
db_datareader	Read data from any table
db_datawriter	Add, change, or delete any data in any table
db_denydatareader	Cannot read from any table
db_denydatawriter	Cannot write to any table

To grant a database role, use the sp_addrolemember stored procedure. The following example adds jack to the db_ddladmin role:

```
EXEC sp_addrolemember db_ddladmin, 'Jack'
```

To remove a user from a role, use the sp_droprolemember procedure.

Note

Any member of a fixed server or database role can add other users to that role.

Assigning Permissions to Roles

When a database grows to contain hundreds of users and possibly thousands of tables, stored procedures, and other database objects, it can become impossible to administer. By grouping users into roles and then assigning permissions to those roles, you can make your administrative tasks far simpler.

Under Oracle, you can assign system and object privileges to roles with the same GRANT statement you use to assign privileges to a user. To be able to grant a privilege to a role, you need the GRANT ANY ROLE system privilege or the ADMIN OPTION on the role. The creator of a role implicitly gains the ADMIN OPTION for that role. As soon as a privilege has been granted to a role, anyone who has the role enabled can use those privileges.

SQL Server uses exactly the same GRANT syntax as when granting privileges to a user. Replacing the username with the name of the role is the only change necessary.

Application Roles

SQL Server also enables you to assign a role to an application. This feature restricts users from accessing the data directly, forcing them to access the data indirectly, through the application. For example, you might have an order entry clerk who uses a Visual Basic application to enter customer orders into an underlying SQL Server database. You don't want to let the order clerk access the database except through the application.

Application roles differ from the other roles available because they cannot have any members and they require a password. The application is granted permissions, and the application then connects to the database. Users lose all their existing permissions, and the application role's permissions override any assigned to the user directly.

The `sp_addapprole` procedure creates an application role. Only members of the `db_owner`, `db_securityadmin`, and `sysadmin` roles can execute the `sp_addapprole` procedure, shown here:

```
EXEC sp_addapprole 'OrderEntryApp', 'password'
GO
GRANT SELECT ON inventory TO OrderEntryApp
GO
```

To activate the application role, the application runs the `sp_setapprole` procedure:

```
EXEC sp_setapprole 'OrderEntryApp', {ENCRYPT N'password'}'ODBC'
```

This procedure activates the role and gives the application all granted privileges.

Using Views and Stored Procedures

Views and stored procedures, as shown in Figure 20.2, can be used to abstract users away from the data, thereby providing an extra level of security. You can remove all privileges from the underlying tables and assign only those necessary to the views or procedures.

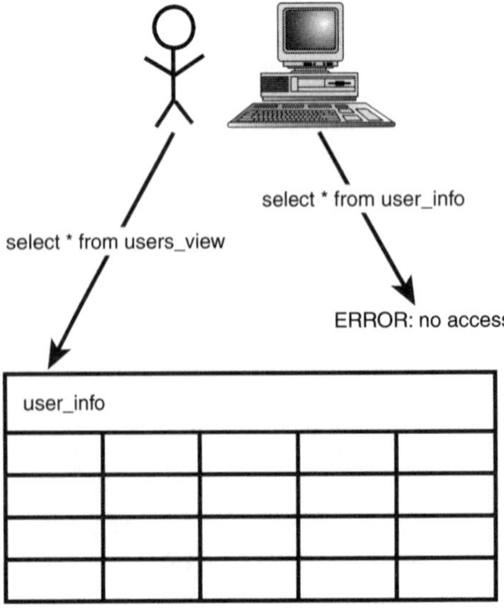
select * from user_info
select * from users_view
ERROR: no access
user_info

FIGURE 20.2
Using views and stored procedures to enhance security.

Take the following example:

```
Create table user_info (
 User_id int not null,
 Fname varchar(30),
 Lname varchar(50),
 Dept_id int,
 Salary float,
 Birthday datetime);
```

For example, the salary column in this table contains confidential employee information. The rest of the table has information all users need access to. To protect the sensitive information from users, a view can be used, as shown here:

```
CREATE VIEW users_view AS
SELECT User_id,Fname,Lname,Dept_id,Birthday FROM user_info
```

After the view has been created, you can grant `SELECT` permissions on `users_view` and remove all permissions from the underlying table.

You can use a similar principle with stored procedures. Instead of creating a view, use a procedure as shown here:

```
CREATE PROCEDURE sp_users AS SELECT User_id,Fname,Lname,Dept,Birthday FROM
user_info
```

Again, you can remove all permissions from the table and assign the `EXECUTE` permission to users.

Summary

As in other multiuser systems, relational database systems have multiple levels of security—controlling who has access to the system and then, at finer levels of granularity, who accesses what and who can manipulate objects.

Remember that security is based on authentication and privileges. If you follow some simple procedures, you should be able to secure your system.

- Decide if you are going to use external or operating system authentication.
- Create only those accounts that are needed. Always remove any user accounts that are no longer needed to avoid any security breaches.
- Grant only those system permissions that a user needs, or even better, assign the permissions to a role and then assign users to the roles.

- Be careful with `ADMIN OPTION` and `GRANT OPTION`. It is easy to lose control of a system if a user is granted too high a privilege.
- Use views and stored procedures to hide sensitive data and to create a level of abstraction from the data.

CHAPTER 21

Call Level Interface (CLI)

In This Chapter

As you have already seen in Chapter 17, "Embedded SQL," SQL can be used through other programming languages for database access, just as easily as it can be used interactively against the database management system (DBMS). Chapter 17 covered how database and client/server application developers could access their databases by embedding SQL statements in the code of the language they are using to write the application. In this chapter, you will see how to access data in the database by making calls to an application programming interface (API) extended by the SQL-92 standard.

The International Standard Organization (ISO) ISO/IEC 9075 created a standard that included a definition and detailed description of this API. This standard defines the structures and procedures that can be used to execute SQL statements from within an application written in a standard programming language. The structures and procedures defined are independent of the SQL statements to be executed. This chapter discusses this standard, mentioning the resources and data structures it uses as well as how it can be used to execute SQL statements. The topics covered in this chapter include the following:

- CLI routines and resources (data structures)
- CLI statement execution

CLI Routines and Resources (Data Structures)

The call level interface (SQL/CLI) is an alternative mechanism for executing SQL statements against the DBMS through routines written in a regular programming language. SQL/CLI consists of routines called from the programming language that pass parameters acting as the messenger between the application and the DBMS. These routines perform the following functions:

- Allocate and deallocate resources needed to manage a SQL environment, a SQL connection, a CLI descriptor area, or a SQL statement. A detailed description of these resources follows later in this chapter.
- Control connections to SQL servers.
- Execute SQL statements using mechanisms similar to dynamic SQL.
- Get diagnostic information.
- Control transaction termination.

SQL/CLI Resources (Data Structures)

When using SQL/CLI, several resources are allocated to allow the routines written in the regular programming language to establish sessions and connections to the database and pass the parameters and SQL statements that need to be executed. To make this process happen, resources are defined by allocating handles to them. The main resources in the SQL/CLI standard include the following:

- **SQL environment:** This resource is established to maintain a remote session with the database management system in which SQL statements can be executed. It is the top-level data structure within which database access can take place. SQL/CLI uses this data structure to keep track of the programs and applications that are using it.
- **SQL connection:** This resource is allocated in the context of the SQL environment. The SQL connection defines parameters that allow the actual connection to the database to happen. SQL/CLI enables a certain application to connect to several database servers concurrently. Each of these connections has its data structure that helps SQL/CLI keep track of its status, among other things.
- **CLI descriptor area:** This resource is allocated in the context of a SQL connection. The CLI descriptor area is a special data structure used to pass parameters dynamically from the application to the DBMS. This data structure is used specifically when the number of parameters to be passed or their data types are not known.
- **SQL statement:** This resource is allocated in the context of a SQL connection and translates directly to the executable SQL statement, which the DBMS executes. Each program can issue several SQL statements against the database management system. Each of these statements goes through several stages of compilation, error checking, execution, and, in case of a query, returning the resultset to the calling application. SQL/CLI uses a separate data structure for each statement to keep track of its progress.

Figure 21.1 shows the relationship between these resources. In the figure, you can see that several connections can be allocated in the context of the same SQL environment. These connections can be concurrent. In the context of each connection, CLI descriptor areas and/or SQL statements can be allocated.

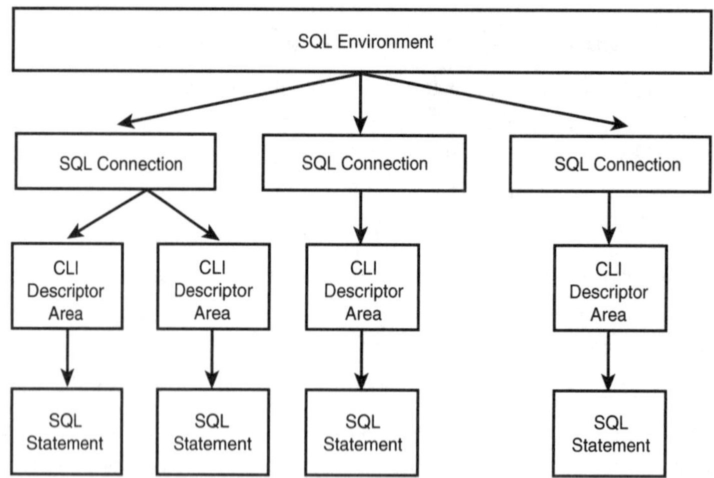

FIGURE 21.1 *The relationship between the SQL/CLI data structures.*

A separate handle, which is a pointer to the data structure, is associated with the SQL environment, each connection to the database, the CLI descriptor areas, and the SQL statements. When a handle to a SQL connection is allocated, the handle of the SQL environment is also passed to the allocating routine so that the connection can run in its context. Similarly, when a handle is allocated to a SQL descriptor area or SQL statement, the handle of the SQL connection is passed to the allocating routine so that the CLI descriptor and SQL statement can run in its context.

This scheme ensures that the subsequent data structures, such as a SQL connection, run in the context of the parent data structure, such as the SQL environment. This scheme also allows for multiple threads of execution to concurrently access the SQL/CLI from the same program or from different programs. SQL/CLI uses these handles to keep track of each thread at all times.

When a data structure is no longer needed, its handle is freed by using special CLI routines. This frees any resources reserved for the structure and makes them available for use by other data structures.

SQL Environment

This is the main data structure in SQL/CLI. In its context, other structures are formed and run. An application can have one SQL environment, which can host several connections in multithreaded applications, and only one connection in single-threaded applications. If a data environment has multiple SQL connections, these connections can be used to connect to one or several databases. These databases can be from the same vendor or from different vendors. An application can also have multiple data environments maximized for multiple and parallel threading.

Besides the general-purpose routines used for allocating and deallocating handles to the SQL/CLI data structures, such as `AllocHandle` and `FreeHandle`, several SQL environment–specific routines include `AllocEnv` and `FreeEnv`.

SQL Connections

A SQL connection is the link that allows the application to connect to the database server. It is actually a virtual network connection to the database server located on a remote computer or on the same machine as the application. As you have already seen, an application can have multiple connections to the same or different databases within the context of the same SQL environment.

Besides the general-purpose routines used for allocating and deallocating handles to the SQL/CLI data structures, several SQL connection–specific routines include `AllocConnect`, `FreeConnect`, `Connect`, `SQLDisconnect`, and `DataSources`.

SQL/CLI Descriptor Area

When you make a call to a SQL/CLI routine to execute a SQL statement, you can pass parameters to the routine dynamically. In this case, the CLI descriptor area serves as the interface for describing the dynamic parameters, dynamic parameter values, the resulting columns of a dynamic select statement or dynamic single-row select statement, and the target specifications for the resulting columns.

A CLI descriptor area for each type of interface is automatically allocated when a SQL statement is allocated.

SQL Statements

As mentioned previously, this is the final statement executed at the database server. The SQL statements are usually dynamic, which means they can have parameters that help define the number of fields in the resultset and specify what fields they are. These parameters are usually passed to the statements in the routine as native programming language variables. Every SQL statement in the context of a connection has its own handle and is allocated its own resources and data structures to help the application keep track of its status.

SQL/CLI Routines

SQL/CLI defines general-type routines as well as routines specific for each data structure. There are also routines for exception handling and error processing. These routines are discussed in detail later in this section. The following is a general overview of these routines.

Main SQL/CLI Routines

The following list of the most important SQL/CLI routines describes each of their functions:

- The `SQLAllocHandle` routine is a general-type routine used to allocate the resources for managing a SQL environment, a SQL connection, a CLI descriptor area, or a SQL processing statement.
- The `SQLFreeHandle` routine deallocates a specified resource.
- The `SQLReleaseEnv` routine deallocates all the allocated SQL connections within a specified SQL environment.

Note

One of the most popular applications of the SQL/CLI is the ODBC API, designed and written by Microsoft.

- `SQLSetEnvAttr`is used by the application to set the value of the attribute of the allocated SQL environment. This attribute determines whether output character strings are `NULL` terminated by the SQL-specific implementation.
- `SQLGetEnvAttr` retrieves the current value of the SQL environment attribute.
- The `SQLConnect`routine establishes a SQL connection.

- The `SQLDisconnect` routine terminates an established SQL connection. Switching between established SQL connections occurs automatically whenever the application switches processing to a dormant SQL connection.
- The `SQLExecDirect` routine is used for a one-time execution of a SQL statement.
- The `SQLPrepare` routine prepares a SQL statement for subsequent execution using the `Execute` routine. In each case, the executed SQL statement can contain dynamic parameters.
- `SQLSetStmtAttr` is used by the application to allocate a CLI descriptor area for each interface every time it allocates a SQL statement. This routine can be used by the application to allocate additional CLI descriptor areas and nominate them for use as the interface for describing dynamic parameter values or target specifications.
- The application uses the routine `SQLGetStmtAttr` to retrieve the value of the handle of the CLI descriptor area currently being used for a specific interface.
- `SQLGetDescField` is used by the application to retrieve field information of the tables in the query from a CLI descriptor area.
- `SQLGetDescRec` is used by the application to retrieve information about the rows from a CLI descriptor area.
- `SQLCopyDesc` copies the contents of a CLI descriptor area to another CLI descriptor area.
- `SQLDescribeCol` can be used by the application to retrieve information about a single column in the query's resultset.

Note

When a dynamic select statement or dynamic single-row select statement is prepared or executed immediately, a description of the resulting columns is automatically provided in the applicable CLI descriptor area if this facility is supported by the current SQL connection.

- The application can use the routine `SQLNumResultCols` to retrieve information about the column count in the query's resultset.
- `SQLSetDescField` is used by the application to explicitly set values in the CLI descriptor area for describing the corresponding table column or dynamic parameter values. These parameters are passed to the dynamic SQL statement.

- `SQLSetDescRec` is used by the application to explicitly set values in the CLI descriptor area for describing the corresponding table row or dynamic parameter values.
- `SQLBindCol` is used by the application to implicitly set values in the CLI descriptor area for describing the corresponding table target specification.
- `SQLBindParam` is used by the application to implicitly set values in the CLI descriptor area for describing the dynamic parameter values when dynamic or immediate SQL statements are being issued.
- `SQLGetConnectAttr` is used by the application to check whether the current SQL connection supports the facility described in the previous Note. In other words, it checks whether the SQL connection supports supplying a description of the resultset in the CLI descriptor area when a dynamic statement is prepared or executed.
- `SQLSetCursorName` is used by the application to supply the implicitly declared cursor name. The cursor is implicitly declared and opened when a dynamic SQL statement is executed.

Note

If a cursor name is not supplied by the application, an implementation-dependent cursor name is generated. The same cursor name is used for each implicit cursor within a single allocated SQL statement.

- `SQLGetCursorName` can be used to retrieve the implicit cursor name, which is generated when a dynamic SQL statement is executed.
- `SQLFetch` positions an open cursor on the next row and retrieves the values of bound columns for that row.

Note

A bound column is one whose target specification in the specified CLI descriptor area defines a location for the target value. Values for unbound columns can be individually retrieved by using the `GetCol` routine.

- `SQLGetCol` allows retrieving the values of unbound columns individually. This routine also enables you to retrieve the values of character string columns piece by piece.

> **Note**
>
> The current row of a cursor can be deleted or updated by executing a prepared dynamic positioned delete or positioned update statement for that cursor under a different allocated SQL statement than the one that opened the cursor. For more information on positioned update and positioned delete statements, please refer to Chapter 17.

- `SQLCloseCursor` closes the current cursor.
- `SQLGetDiagField` gets diagnostic information about the most recent routine operating on a particular field.
- `SQLGetDiagRec` gets diagnostic information about the most recent routine operating on a particular row.
- `SQLEndTran` routine is used to end a SQL transaction.

> **Note**
>
> Neither a `COMMIT` statement nor a `ROLLBACK` statement can be executed with the ExecDirect or `Execute` routines.

- `SQLCancel` cancels the execution of a concurrently executing SQL/CLI routine.

CLI Routine Format

The CLI routine, a predefined routine written in a standard programming language, is invoked by a compilation unit of the same standard programming language, such as ADA, C, COBOL, FORTRAN, MUMPS, Pascal, and PL/I.

> **Note**
>
> Just like other programming languages, a CLI routine that contains a CLI returns clause is called a *CLI function* , and a CLI routine without that clause is called a *CLI*

procedure. Actually, for each CLI function, there is a corresponding CLI procedure with the same name and parameter list, except for one additional parameter in the function to hold the return value. This parameter is declared as `ReturnCode OUT SMALLINT`. The host language should support invoking either of these forms.

When using the SQL/CLI routines, you need to follow their general format, as shown here:

```
CLI routine ::= CLI routine name(CLI parameter list)
          [ <CLI returns clause> ]

Where:
     CLI routine name ::= CLI name prefix + CLI generic name
  Where:
     CLI name prefix ::=
       CLI by-reference prefix (SQLR)¦CLI by-value prefix (SQL)
  And:
     CLI generic name::= one valid CLI routine name, such as:
        SQLAllocHandle
        ¦SQLBindCol
        ¦SQLBindParam
        ¦SQLCancel
        ¦SQLCloseCursor
        ¦SQLConnect
        ¦SQLCopyDesc
        ¦SQLDescribeCol
        ¦SQLDisconnect
        ¦SQLEndTran
        ¦SQLExecDirect
        ¦SQLExecute
        ¦SQLFetch
        ¦SQLFreeHandle
        ¦SQLGetCol
        ¦SQLGetConnectAttr
        ¦SQLGetCursorName
        ¦SQLGetDescField
        ¦SQLGetDescRec
        ¦SQLGetDiagField
        ¦SQLGetDiagRec
        ¦SQLGetEnvAttr
        ¦SQLGetStmtAttr
        ¦SQLNumResultCols
        ¦SQLPrepare
```

```
        ¦SQLReleaseEnv
        ¦SQLSetCursorName
        ¦SQLSetDescField
        ¦SQLSetDescRec
        ¦SQLSetEnvAttr
        ¦SQLSetStmtAttr
AND
      CLI parameter list ::=
        (CLI parameter1 [,CLI parameter2 [, CLI parameter3...>)
  Where:
      CLI parameter(i) ::=
        (CLI parameter name CLI parameter mode CLI parameter data type)
    Where:
         CLI parameter name ::= !! Differs according to CLI routine
         CLI parameter mode ::=
                     IN¦OUT¦DEFIN¦DEFOUT¦DEF

         CLI parameter data type ::= INTEGER¦SMALLINT¦ANY¦
                       CHARACTER(n)
AND
  CLI returns clause ::= RETURNS SMALLINT
```

The CLI parameter mode defines whether the parameter passed to the DBMS is one of the following:

- `IN`: The parameter is called an *input parameter* and should have a value coming in.
- `OUT`: The parameter is called an *output parameter* and should have a value when the routine is executed.
- `DEFIN`: This is called a *deferred input parameter* . Its value for a CLI routine is not established by executing the routine in which it is declared, but by the execution of a related CLI routine.
- `DEFOUT`: This is called a *deferred output parameter* . Its value for a CLI routine is not established by executing the routine in which it is declared, but by the execution of a related CLI routine.

The first 12 characters of CLI routine names should be unique. Any implementation that requires routine names to be unique with less than 12 characters should replace the CLI routine name with an abbreviated name, according to the following rules:

- Any CLI by-value prefix remains unchanged.

- Any CLI by-reference prefix is replaced by SQR.
- The CLI generic name is replaced by an abbreviated version. For example, the CLI routine SQLAllocateHandle is abbreviated to AH, and SQLNumResultCode is abbreviated to NRC.

Examples of Using CLI Routines

The following examples, which are all written in C, show how to use the major CLI routines. The first one illustrates the SQLAllocHandle routine and how parameters are passed to it:

```
short SQLAllocHandle (
  short hdlType,   /*integer dor the handle type*/
  long inHandle,   /*Handle to SQL environment or SQL connection*/
  long *rtnHandle); /*returned handle*/
```

To free a previously allocated handle by SQLAllocHandle, you can use the SQLFreeHandle routine:

```
short SQLFreeHndle(
  short HdlType,   /*integer dor the handle type*/
  long inHandle) /*handle to be freed*/
```

You can use the following example to allocate a handle to a SQL environment:

```
short SQLAllocEnv(
  long *envHandle);/*returned environment handle*/
```

To free the handle you just allocated with SQLAllocEnv, you can use this routine:

```
short freeEnv(
  long envHandle); /*environment handle to be freed*/
```

To connect to a database server, use this routine:

```
short SQLConnect(
  long connHandle,   /*connection handle*/
  char svrName, /*name of database server*/
  short svrNameLen,  /*length of server name*/
  char username,    /*user name*/
  short userNameLen, /*length of user name*/
  char password,    /user password*/
  short passwordLen); /*length of user password*/
```

To disconnect from the database server you just connected to, use this routine:

```
short SQLDisconnect(
```

```
longConnHandle);  /*connection handle to the server*/
```

CLI Statement Execution

When SQL statements are passed to CLI routines, they are executed similarly to dynamic embedded SQL statements. The SQL statement is passed to the routine in text form to be executed in one or two steps.

The application starts by calling the `SQLAllocHandle` function to get a handle to the SQL statement. This handle is used by other routines that execute the statement, such as `SQLExecDirect` (in one-step processing), `SQLPrepare`, and `SQLExecute` (in two-step processing). Use the CLI routine `SQLFreeHandle` to free the statement handle when there is no more need for it.

When `SQLExecuteDirect` is used, the statement is passed to the function as a parameter. The DBMS processes the statement and returns a status code to the application through the CLI call.

In the two-step execution, the statement is passed to the DBMS as a parameter of the `SQLPrepare` function. The DBMS analyzes the statement and keeps the results of the analysis for future encounters of the `SQLExecute` statement. The advantage of this method over the one-step method is evident when you want to call the statement repeatedly. In that case, `SQLPrepare` makes the DBMS analyze the statement only once, instead of analyzing it several times, once for each call.

The order of the SQL statement execution is shown in Figure 21.2.

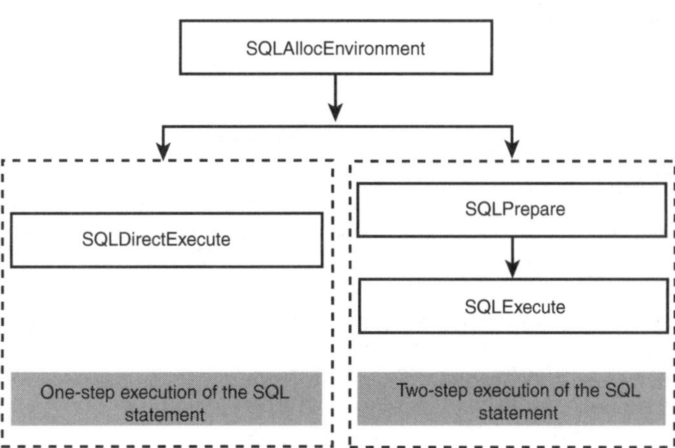

FIGURE 21.2
The order of the execution of a SQL statement through SQL/CLI calls.

SQL Statement with Parameters

Sometimes you might want to execute the SQL statement repeatedly with only simple changes in some of its attributes. For example, you might want to insert data in a department table, changing only the name of the department in each statement. In this case, passing parameters to the SQL statement itself helps to a great extent. To do that, you need to pass the statement to the `SQLPrepare` routine with a question mark (`?`) in place of each attribute you want to parameterize.

The CLI routine `SQLBindParam`can be used to supply parameter values to the statement. Each call to this routine establishes a link between the application program and one of the parameter markers in the SQL statement. These markers are now identified by numbers to easily indicate their address in memory.

`SQLExecute` is called to execute the SQL statement after the association between the application and the parameters has been established. `SQLParamData` and `SQLPutData` can then be used to pass parameter data at runtime to the DBMS. This process is called *deferred parameter passing*. The selection of this technique is indicated in the CLI call to the `SQLBindParam` function. There are two main advantages to using deferred parameters instead of directly binding the values to the application: The application waits until the last possible moment to supply the data, and with repeated calls to `SQLPutData`, the application can pass long data types one chunk at a time.

Figure 21.3 shows an outline of the steps needed to execute a parameterized SQL statement. It is assumed in the figure that the connection between the application and the database has already been established.

Processing Query Results

Processing query results can be done simply with the `SQLBindCol`and `SQLFetch`routines. Assuming your application has already established a connection to the database, the application goes through the following steps to process a query-type SQL statement:

- Using `SQLAllocHandle`, a statement handle is allocated.
- `SQLPrepare` is then called to have the DBMS analyze and prepare the execution plan for the passed SQL statement.
- `SQLExecute` is then called to carry out the query.
- `SQLBindCol` is then called once for each column of the query resultset, associating a separate program buffer area with each data column.

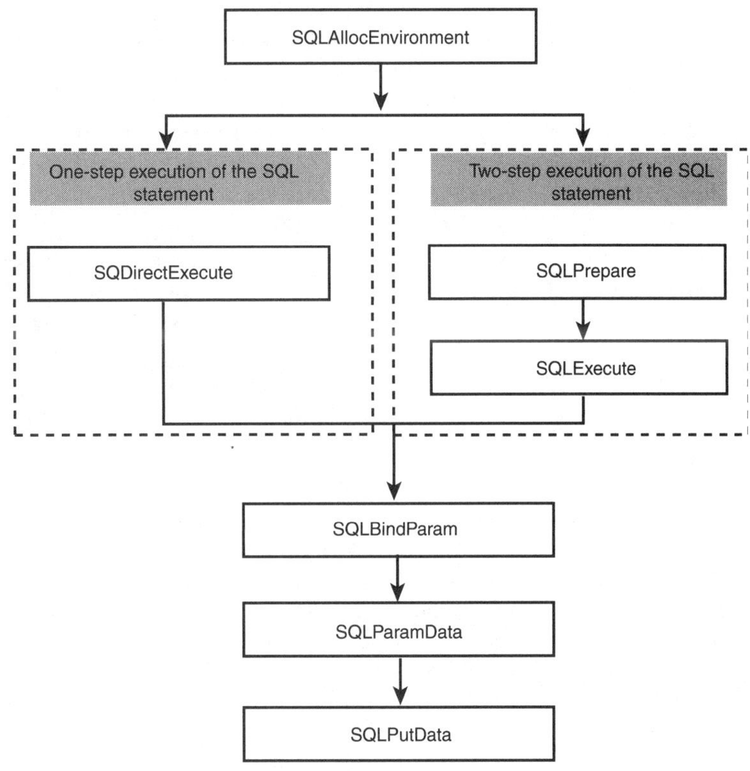

FIGURE 21.3
The order of the execution of a parameterized SQL statement through SQL/CLI calls.

- The application then calls `SQLFetch` to fetch a row of the query result. This step is repeated until there are no more rows to fetch. This is usually indicated by the value `100` (no data found) for the CLI routine return code.
- The application calls `SQLCloseCursor` to close the implicitly created cursor and end the query results when the query processing is done.

Listing 21.1 shows an example of using CLI to process a query that retrieves the names of employees and their salaries.

LISTING 21.1 Example of Using SQL/CLI to Process Query Results

```
#include <stdio.h>      // We use printf()
#include <string.h>      // We use strcat() and strcpy()
#include ''sqlcli.h''     // Header file with CLI definitions

// Function prototype
int example1(SQLCHAR *svr_name, SQLCHAR *user_name, SQLCHAR *user_pwd);
```

LISTING 21.1 CONTINUED

```
int main()
{
  SQLHENV     env_handle;        //SQL environment handle
  SQLHDBC     conn_handle;        //Connection handle
  SQLHSTMT     stmt_handle;        //statement handle
  SQLCHAR     svr_name[] = ''kangaroo'';   //Server name
  SQLCHAR     user_name[] = ''mfekete'';   //User name
  SQLCHAR     user_pwd[] = ''pumpkin'';   //User password
  char      *emp_name[30];        //retrieved employee name
  float     salary;          //retrieved employee salary
  SQLINTEGER     salary_ind;        //NULL salary indicator variable
  SQLCHAR     stmt_buffer[256];     //Buffer for SQL statement

   //Allocate handle and connect to database server
  SQLAllocHandle(SQL_HANDLE_ENV, SQL_NULL_HANDLE, &env_handle);
  SQLAllocHandle(SQL_HANDLE_DBC, env_handle, &conn_handle);
  SQLAllocHandle(SQL_HANDLE_STMT, conn_handle, &stmt_handle);
  SQLConnect(conn_handle, svr_name, SQL_NTS,
             user_name, SQL_NTS,
             user_pwd, SQL_NTS);

   //Start query execution by requesting it
  strcpy((char*)stmt_buffer, ''select fname || ' ' || lname as name'');
  strcat((char*)stmt_buffer, '', salary from employee'');

  SQLExecDirect(stmt_handle, stmt_buffer, SQL_NTS);

   //Bind retrieved columns to application buffer
  SQLBindCol(stmt_handle, 1, SQL_C_CHAR, emp_name, 30, NULL);
  SQLBindCol(stmt_handle, 2, SQL_C_FLOAT, &salary, 0, &salary_ind);

   //Loop through rows of the query result
  for (; ;) {
    //Fetch next row
    if (SQLFetch(stmt_handle) != SQL_SUCCESS) {
      break;
    }
    //display retrieved data
    printf(''Name: %s\n'', emp_name);
    if (salary_ind < 0) {
      printf(''Salary is NULL\n'');
    }
```

LISTING 21.1 CONTINUED

```
      else {
        printf(''Salary: %f\n'', salary);
      }
    }
     //Disconnect from database server, deallocate handles, and exit
    SQLDisconnect(conn_handle);
    SQLFreeHandle(SQL_HANDLE_STMT, stmt_handle);
    SQLFreeHandle(SQL_HANDLE_DBC, conn_handle);
    SQLFreeHandle(SQL_HANDLE_ENV, env_handle);

    return(0);
}
```

This program shows how the CLI routines can be used to query the database and retrieve and display the data. It starts by allocating handles to the SQL environment, SQL connection, and SQL statement. Then it opens a connection to the database server, `kangaroo`, passing the user name `mfekete` and password `pumpkin`.

After the connection is established, the SQL statement is built with the C functions `strcpy()` and `strcat()`. The `SQLExecuteDirect()` function is then called to execute the statement at the DBMS. After the statement has been executed, the fields are bound to the application buffer area by using the function `SQLBindCol()` for each retrieved field (two in this case). Then there's a loop through the result of the query in which the rows are fetched one at a time with the call `SQLFetch()`. At the end, the connection is closed and the handles released.

> **Note**
>
> Note that the `NULL` indicator variable was used for the `salary` field to guard against retrieving a `NULL` value for it. If the value of the `NULL` indicator variable is negative, this means a `NULL` salary has been retrieved. To learn more about this technique, please refer to Chapter 17.

Scrolling Cursors

SQL/CLI supports scrolling cursors just as embedded SQL does. The function `SQLFetchScroll()` can be used to scroll forward, backward, to an absolute, or to a relative position in the query result. This function serves as an extension to the `SQLFetch()` function. One of its parameters specifies the statement handle, and the other specifies the scroll direction (`NEXT`, `PREVIOUS`, `FIRST`, and so forth). `SQLBindCol` and `SQLGetData` are still used with this function, similarly to the way they are used with the regular `SQLFetch()` function.

Named Cursors

SQL/CLI supports cursors implicitly, so there is no declarative statement for cursors. A cursor in the SQL/CLI scheme is the same as the statement handle, and by default, does not have a name. This works great for data retrieval. However, if you want to perform positioned updates and deletes, you need a cursor name in the SQL statement. To let you do that, the SQL/CLI standard provides a function, `SQLSetCursorName()`, to assign a cursor name specified as one of the function parameters to a set of query results. The function `SQLGetCursorName()` can then be used in subsequent statements to retrieve the preassigned cursor name.

Transaction Management with SQL/CLI

SQL/CLI recognizes transactions just as embedded SQL does. However, because it needs to know when a transaction has ended, it cannot just use the `COMMIT` and `ROLLBACK` functions. Instead, these two functions are replaced by the calls `SQLEndTran()` and `SQLCancel()`. `SQLEndTran()` tells the application that the transaction started with the previous `SQLExecute` or `SQLExecuteDirect` has ended and data needs to be committed. The `SQLCancel()` call can be used to cancel a previously started `SQLExecute`/ `SQLExcecuteDirect` statement. This call also works in multithreaded environments, but its implementation is very SQL implementation-specific, so it is not discussed here.

Return Codes and Diagnostics

The execution of a CLI routine causes one or more conditions to be raised. The execution's basic result is indicated by a code returned as the result of a CLI function or as the value of the `ReturnCode` argument of a CLI procedure.

The values and meanings of the return codes are as follows:

- A value of `0` indicates "Success."
- A value of `1` indicates "Success with information." The CLI routine executed successfully, but a warning was raised as a completion condition.
- A value of `100` indicates "No data found." The CLI routine executed successfully but a completion condition was raised: no data.

- A value of `-1` indicates "Error." The CLI routine did not execute successfully because an exception condition other than a CLI-specific, condition-invalid handle was raised.
- A value of `-2` indicates "Invalid handle." The CLI routine did not execute successfully because an exception condition was raised.

Note

Different SQL implementations have their own ways to set values of the CLI routine's output arguments if the CLI routine does not execute successfully. This is the case unless explicitly defined by the SQL ANSI standard.

SQL implementations provide the return code for all CLI routines other than `SQLGetDiagField` and `SQLGetDiagRec`. These implementations also record information about completion conditions and exception conditions (other than invalid handle) in the application program's diagnostics area associated with the resource being used.

Each application diagnostics area has header fields with general information about the routine that was executed and zero or more status records with information about individual conditions that occurred during the CLI routine's execution. A condition that causes a status record to be generated is referred to as a *status condition*.

Note

The resource being used by a routine is the resource identified by its input handle: SQL environment, SQL connection, or SQL statement. In the case of `SQLCopyDesc`routine, which has two input handles, the resource being used is deemed the one identified by the `SQLTargetDescHandle` routine.

At the beginning of the execution of any CLI routine, the diagnostics area for the resource being used is cleared. This is true for all routines except `SQLGetDiagField` and `SQLGetDiagRec`. If the execution of such a routine does not result in the CLI-specific exception condition "invalid handle," then the following happens:

- Header information is generated in the diagnostics area.
- No status records are generated if the routine's return code indicates SQL success.

- If the routine's return code indicates "Success with information," which indicates a warning, or "Error," then one or more status records are generated.
- If the routine's return code indicates "No data found," then no status record is generated corresponding to `SQLSTATE` value `02000`, but there might be status records generated corresponding to `SQLSTATE` value `02nnn`; `nnn` is an implementation-defined subclass value. For more information on `SQLSTATE`, please refer to Chapter 17.
- The routines `SQLGetDiagField` and `SQLGetDiagRec` retrieve information from a diagnostics area. The application identifies which diagnostics area is accessed by supplying the handle of the relevant resource as an input argument to these two routines. The two routines return a result code but do not modify the identified diagnostics area.

CLI Sample C Program

Listing 21.2 is a sample program taken from the SQL/CLI standard documentation. I opted to use this example, adding many in-line code comments to it, because it is a comprehensive example that shows the use of many of the SQL/CLI functions to insert records, retrieve records, and report status. The program uses the CLI functions to interactively execute a SQL statement supplied as an argument. In this program, the user types a `SELECT` statement, and the function fetches and displays all rows of the resultset.

This example also illustrates the use of the routine `SQLGetDiagField` to identify the type of SQL statement executed and, for SQL statements where the row count is defined on all implementations, it illustrates the use of the routine `SQLGetDiagField` to get the row count.

LISTING 21.2 Sample Program Using SQL/CLI Functions to Access the Database Interactively

```
/*
* Sample program - uses concise CLI functions to execute
* interactively an ad hoc statement.
*/

#include <stdio.h>
#include <stddef.h>
#include <string.h>
#include <stdlib.h>
#include ''sqlcli.h''

#define MAXCOLS 100
#define max(a,b) (>?:)
```

LISTING 21.2 CONTINUED

```
int print_err(SQLSMALLINT handletype, SQLINTEGER handle);
int build_indicator_message(SQLCHAR *errmsg, SQLPOINTER *data,
   SQLINTEGER collen, SQLINTEGER *outlen, SQLSMALLINT colnum);
   SQLINTEGER display_length(SQLSMALLINT coltype, SQLINTEGER collen,
   SQLCHAR *colname);

int  example2(SQLCHAR  *server,  SQLCHAR  *uid,  SQLCHAR  *authen,  SQLCHAR
*sqlstr)
{
   int i;
   SQLHENV henv;        /*SQL environment handle*/
   SQLHDBC hdbc;        /*SQL connection handle*/
   SQLHSTMT hstmt;     /*SQL statement handle*/
   SQLCHAR errmsg[256];     /*variable to hold error message*/
   SQLCHAR colname[32];     /*table column name*/
   SQLSMALLINT coltype;     /*table column data type*/
   SQLSMALLINT colnamelen;   /*column name length*/
   SQLSMALLINT nullable;     /* nullable column - Boolean*/
   SQLINTEGER collen[MAXCOLS];   /*array holding length of columns*/
   SQLSMALLINT scale;     /*scale value*/
   SQLINTEGER outlen[MAXCOLS];   /*length of output arguments*/
   SQLCHAR *data[MAXCOLS];   /*column data value*/
   SQLSMALLINT nresultcols;   /*number of returned columns*/
   SQLINTEGER rowcount;     /*number of returned rows*/
   SQLINTEGER stmttype;     /*type of SQL statement*/
   SQLRETURN rc;        /*SQL return code value*/

   /* allocate an environment handle */
   SQLAllocHandle(SQL_HANDLE_ENV, SQL_NULL_HANDLE, &henv);

   /* allocate a connection handle */
   SQLAllocHandle(SQL_HANDLE_DBC, henv, &hdbc);

   /* connect to database */
   if (SQLConnect(hdbc, server, SQL_NTS, uid, SQL_NTS, authen, SQL_NTS)
        != SQL_SUCCESS )
     /*Connection error*/
     return(print_err(SQL_HANDLE_DBC, hdbc));

   /* allocate a statement handle */
   SQLAllocHandle(SQL_HANDLE_STMT, hdbc, &hstmt);
```

LISTING 21.2 CONTINUED

```
/* execute the SQL statement */
if (SQLExecDirect(hstmt, sqlstr, SQL_NTS) != SQL_SUCCESS)
  return(print_err(SQL_HANDLE_STMT, hstmt));

/* see what kind of statement it was */
SQLGetDiagField(SQL_HANDLE_STMT, hstmt, 0,
  SQL_DIAG_DYNAMIC_FUNCTION_CODE,
  (SQLPOINTER)&stmttype, 0, (SQLSMALLINT *)NULL);

switch (stmttype) {
  /* SELECT statement */
  case SQL_DIAG_SELECT_CURSOR:
     /* determine number of result columns */
     SQLNumResultCols(hstmt, &nresultcols);

     /* display column names */
     for (i=0; i<nresultcols; i++) {
       SQLDescribeCol(hstmt, i+1, colname, sizeof(colname),
          &colnamelen, &coltype, &collen[i], &scale, &nullable);

       /* assume there is a display_length function which
       computes correct length given the data type */
       collen[i] = display_length(coltype, collen[i], colname);

       (void)printf(''%*.*s'', (int)collen[i], (int)collen[i],
       (char *)colname);

       /* allocate memory to bind column */
       data[i] = (SQLCHAR *) malloc(collen[i]);

       /* bind columns to program vars, converting all types
       to CHAR */
       SQLBindCol(hstmt, i+1, SQL_CHAR, data[i], collen[i],
          &outlen[i]);
     }
     /* display result rows */
     while ((rc=SQLFetch(hstmt))!=SQL_ERROR) {
       errmsg[0] = '\0';
       if (rc == SQL_SUCCESS_WITH_INFO) {
          for (i=0; i<nresultcols; i++) {
          if (outlen[i] == SQL_NULL_DATA
```

LISTING 21.2 CONTINUED

```
            || outlen[i] >= collen[i])
          build_indicator_message(errmsg,
          (SQLPOINTER *)&data[i], collen[i],
          &outlen[i], i);

        (void)printf(''%*.*s '', (int)outlen[i], (int)outlen[i],
          (char *)data[i]);
        } /* for all columns in this row */

      /* print any truncation messages */
      (void)printf(''\n%s'', (char *)errmsg);
      }
    } /* while rows to fetch */
    SQLCloseCursor(hstmt);
    break;
  /* searched DELETE, INSERT or searched UPDATE statement */
  case SQL_DIAG_DELETE_WHERE:
  case SQL_DIAG_INSERT:
  case SQL_DIAG_UPDATE_WHERE:
    /* check rowcount */
    SQLGetDiagField(SQL_HANDLE_STMT, hstmt, 0,
    SQL_DIAG_ROW_COUNT, (SQLPOINTER)&rowcount, 0,
    (SQLSMALLINT *)NULL);
    if (SQLEndTran(SQL_HANDLE_ENV, henv, SQL_COMMIT)
      == SQL_SUCCESS) {
      (void) printf(''Operation successful\n'');
    }
    else {
    (void) printf(''Operation failed\n'');
    }
    (void)printf(''%ld rows affected\n'', rowcount);
    break;
  /* other statements */
  case SQL_DIAG_ALTER_TABLE:
  case SQL_DIAG_CREATE_TABLE:
  case SQL_DIAG_CREATE_VIEW:
  case SQL_DIAG_DROP_TABLE:
  case SQL_DIAG_DROP_VIEW:
  case SQL_DIAG_DYNAMIC_DELETE_CURSOR:
  case SQL_DIAG_DYNAMIC_UPDATE_CURSOR:
  case SQL_DIAG_GRANT:
  case SQL_DIAG_REVOKE:
```

LISTING 21.2 CONTINUED

```
        if (SQLEndTran(SQL_HANDLE_ENV, henv, SQL_COMMIT)
        == SQL_SUCCESS) {
        (void) printf(''Operation successful\n'');
        }
        else {
        (void) printf(''Operation failed\n'');
        }
        break;
     /* implementation-defined statement */
     default:
        (void)printf(''Statement type=%ld\n'', stmttype);
        break;
   }

   /* free data buffers */
   for (i=0; i<nresultcols; i++) {
     (void)free(data[i]);
   }

   /* free statement handle */
   SQLFreeHandle(SQL_HANDLE_STMT, hstmt);

   /* disconnect from database */
   SQLDisconnect(hdbc);

   /* free connection handle */
   SQLFreeHandle(SQL_HANDLE_DBC, hdbc);

   /* free environment handle */
   SQLFreeHandle(SQL_HANDLE_ENV, henv);

   return(0);
}
/************************************************************
The following functions are given for completeness, but are
not relevant for understanding the database processing
nature of CLI
************************************************************/
#define MAX_NUM_PRECISION 15
/*#define max length of char string representation of no. as:
= max(precision) + leading sign +E +expsign + max exp length
= 15 +1 +1 +1 +2
```

LISTING 21.2 CONTINUED

```
= 15 +5
*/
#define MAX_NUM_STRING_SIZE (MAX_NUM_PRECISION + 5)
SQLINTEGER display_length(SQLSMALLINT coltype, SQLINTEGER collen,
   SQLCHAR *colname)
{
   switch (coltype) {
     case SQL_VARCHAR:
     case SQL_CHAR:
     case SQL_BLOB:
     case SQL_CLOB:
     case SQL_BIT:
     case SQL_REF:
     case SQL_BIT_VARYING:
        return(max(collen,(SQLINTEGER)strlen((char *)colname)));
     case SQL_FLOAT:
     case SQL_DOUBLE:
     case SQL_NUMERIC:
     case SQL_REAL:
     case SQL_DECIMAL:
        return(max(MAX_NUM_STRING_SIZE,strlen((char *)colname)));
     case SQL_TYPE_DATE:
     case SQL_TYPE_TIME:
     case SQL_TYPE_TIME_WITH_TIMEZONE:
     case SQL_TYPE_TIMESTAMP:
     case SQL_TYPE_TIMESTAMP_WITH_TIMEZONE:
     case SQL_INTERVAL_YEAR:
     case SQL_INTERVAL_MONTH:
     case SQL_INTERVAL_DAY:
     case SQL_INTERVAL_HOUR:
     case SQL_INTERVAL_MINUTE:
     case SQL_INTERVAL_SECOND:
     case SQL_INTERVAL_YEAR_TO_MONTH:
     case SQL_INTERVAL_DAY_TO_HOUR:
     case SQL_INTERVAL_DAY_TO_MINUTE:
     case SQL_INTERVAL_DAY_TO_SECOND:
     case SQL_INTERVAL_HOUR_TO_MINUTE:
     case SQL_INTERVAL_HOUR_TO_SECOND:
     case SQL_INTERVAL_MINUTE_TO_SECOND:
        return(max(collen,(SQLINTEGER)strlen((char *)colname)));
     case SQL_INTEGER:
     case SQL_BLOB_LOCATOR:
```

LISTING 21.2 CONTINUED

```
        case SQL_CLOB_LOCATOR:
        case SQL_UDT_LOCATOR:
        case SQL_ARRAY_LOCATOR:
           return(max(10,strlen((char *)colname)));
        case SQL_SMALLINT:
           return(max(5,strlen((char *)colname)));
        default:
           (void)printf(''Unknown datatype, %d\n'', coltype);
           return(0);
     }
}

int build_indicator_message(SQLCHAR *errmsg, SQLPOINTER *data,
     SQLINTEGER collen, SQLINTEGER *outlen, SQLSMALLINT colnum)
{
     if (*outlen == SQL_NULL_DATA) {
        (void)strcpy((char *)data, ''NULL'');

        *outlen=4;
     }
     else {
        sprintf((char *)errmsg+strlen((char *)errmsg),
           ''%d chars truncated, col %d\n'', *outlen-collen+1,
           colnum);

        *outlen=255;
     }

     return(0);
```

Summary

In this chapter, you looked at the SQL application programming interface, called call level interface (CLI). CLI is a powerful tool that allows database access from your own programs, written in any of a group of languages, similarly to embedded SQL. With its numerous and rich routines that allow you to access the data, SQL/CLI gives you more flexibility in what you can do. You saw how inserts, updates, and deletes can be conducted with SQL/CLI, looked at querying data and processing the query results, and learned how cursors can be used in updates, deletes, and transactions.

CHAPTER 22

Persistent Stored Modules (PSM)

In This Chapter

Persistent stored modules (PSM) are extensions that were added to the SQL-92 standard in 1996 and became part of the SQL-3 standard later on. With these extensions, new programming language procedural control flow features were added to the SQL language, such as assignment, variables, looping, branching, procedure block structure, procedure and function calls, and exception handling. These extensions provide a powerful facility for stored procedures—that is, SQL procedures stored and optimized at the server that can be invoked from a client with a single call. This is a fairly important requirement for better efficiency and performance in client/server environments.

An advantage of the PSM specification is that non-SQL data repositories can now present themselves to a SQL environment as conforming to a minimal level of SQL data manipulation, while offering their value-added features as SQL-callable functions and procedures.

The topics covered in this chapter include the following:

- Overview of PSM
- Modules, routines, and SQL schemas
- PSM SQL statements
- Exception handling
- Vendor implementations

Overview of PSM

The SQL persistent stored modules (SQL/PSM) specification was adopted as an addendum to the SQL-92 standard in 1996 and became part of the SQL-3 standard afterward. Many database management systems adopted some sort of this specification, even before it was published. Examples of these implementations are the Oracle PL/SQL, which stands for *procedural language/SQL*, and Microsoft Transact-SQL used with Microsoft SQL Server. SQL/PSM expands SQL by adding new elements that increase its power and flexibility:

- Procedural language extensions, such as control flow features: conditional statements, looping structures, declaring variables, and so forth.
- Multi-statement and stored procedures, enabling statement compilation and execution by creating procedures and storing them at the RDBMS.
- External function and procedure calls allow SQL code to tap into the wealth of external functions and procedures that only increase its power more.

In addition to being a valuable application development tool, SQL/PSM also gives the foundation support for the object-oriented capabilities in SQL-3. The following is a more focused discussion of the SQL/PSM features mentioned here.

Multi-Statement and Stored Procedures

Multi-statement and stored procedures allow the database developer to write multiple statements that access the database and perform some work at its level. These statements can run interactively as a batch or as a stored procedure. If the statements are formatted as a stored procedure, the procedure is compiled and stored in the database for use by applications accessing the database at any time, or even for interactive use by users having direct access to the DBMS.

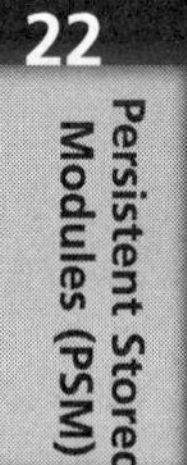
22
Persistent Stored
Modules (PSM)

Multi-statement and stored procedures offer a variety of advantages in a client/server environment:

- **Performance:** Because a stored procedure can perform multiple SQL statements before it returns the results to the calling client application, network interactions with the client are significantly reduced.
- **Security:** Users can be given the right to call a stored procedure that updates a table or set of tables, but denied the right to update the tables directly. This feature allows the database developer to restrict certain users from updating the table or to allow them to update only certain fields.
- **Shared Code:** The code in a stored procedure is written, tested, and stored in the database. This code does not have to be rewritten and retested for each client tool that accesses the database.
- **Control:** Provides a single point of definition and control for application logic. PSM also provides a place where business logic can be incorporated into client/server applications. For instance, you can enforce business rules through these procedures. If violations of the rules occur, you can have the procedure raise an exception to the calling program that gives detailed information about the error.

Procedural Language Extensions

Procedural language adds the power of a traditional programming language to SQL through flow control statements and a variety of other programming constructs, such as the following:

- Flow control statements
- `If...Then...Else` constructs

- Looping constructs, such as `Do ... Loop` and `FOR ... NEXT`
- Exception handling, including raising custom error codes to the calling functions and procedures, which makes debugging these procedures easier
- Case statements that allow selection of a case from many possible conditions
- `Begin...End` blocks that encompass code that runs as one unit

The procedural language extensions include other useful constructs, usually seen in regular programming languages, such as:

- Variable declarations. These variables have scope and values that can be controlled by the procedure or can even be passed from one procedure to another.
- Statements for value assignment.
- Diagnostics for debugging, process, and status information.

With these extensions, multi-statement procedures include a mix of the constructs mentioned here, in addition to the multiple SQL statements embedded within. These features contribute to making this combination a powerful tool in the hands of database developers and administrators.

External Procedure and Function Calls

Some SQL implementations, such as Microsoft's Transact-SQL and Oracle's PL/SQL, already allow calling external functions and procedures written by users in different programming languages and compiled as dynamic or static code libraries. The SQL/PSM specification makes this the rule, augmenting built-in features with calls to user-written procedures that are external to the database software. Needless to say, this feature lends a lot of power to SQL/PSM code. Database developers can write much of the business logic in the language they prefer and are most proficient in, and can call these functions and procedures from within their SQL/PSM code. In short, this feature has the following benefits:

- A particular site or application can add its own database functions specific to its way of conducting business, without affecting other sites by changing the stored modules.
- User functions can also be used throughout database applications, not just called from the SQL/PSM code.
- The greatest benefit of this capability is that it gives database developers and their applications access to a rich set of procedures and functions that can add many benefits to these applications.

With this overview of SQL/PSM, you have a basic idea of what this specification is all about, so let's dive into more details about the different parts of this specification.

Modules, Routines, and SQL Schemas

As you have seen in previous chapters, SQL database architecture includes a hierarchy of objects, illustrated in Figure 22.1. The highest level of the SQL database architecture is the SQL environment, or a database site (usually referred to as the *database server*). This is the object that database instances are created in. The next object in the hierarchy is the SQL catalog, or named logical database. A catalog can contain several SQL schemas that are attached directly to the users who created them. SQL schemas, in turn, contain several schema objects, such as user tables and triggers.

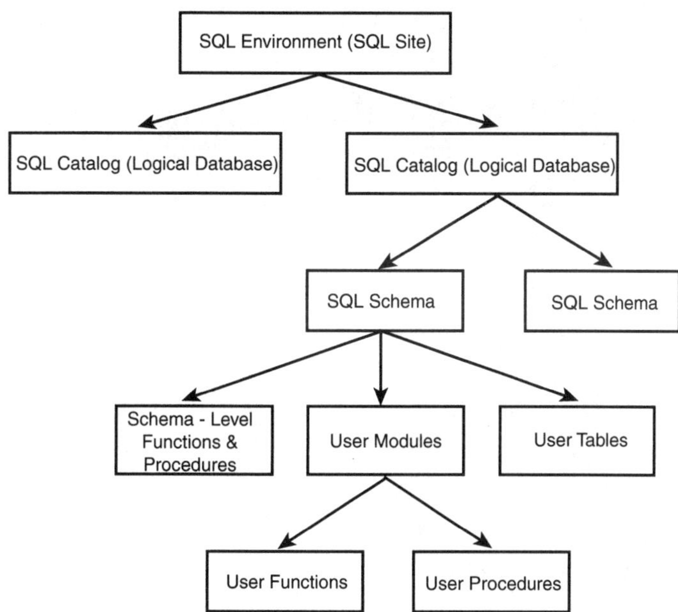

FIGURE 22.1
A simple diagram of the SQL database architecture.

One of the schema objects, as shown in Figure 22.1, is the user module. A *module* is a collection of user functions and procedures. A schema can also include functions and procedures that are not part of a module. These functions and procedures are referred to as *schema-level functions and procedures*.

Now that you have had a look at the big picture and where SQL modules, functions, and procedures fit in, let's take a closer look at these objects.

Modules

As mentioned, a user module is saved and persisted in the database. The user module includes an interface and a collection of functions and procedures that implement the interface. A module can also be a server-level module or a client module.

Client Modules

As the name implies, client modules are defined and persisted on a client to the database server, outside any schema on the server. These modules support a SQL agent module on a different server, or on the same server, but in a different SQL space.

Client modules are defined with the module definition statement and dropped with the `DROP MODULE` statement. The module declaration includes many items, some of which are optional. The declaration, or definition, is shown as follows according to the PSM specification:

```
<SQL-client module definition> ::=
  <module specification>
```

The module specification is defined as

```
<module specification> ::=
  <module header>
  <module contents>..
```

The module header is defined as

```
<module header> ::=
  <module name clause>
  <language clause>
  <module authorization clause>
  <[<module path specification>]
```

The module name clause is defined as

```
<module name clause> ::=
  MODULE [<module name>]
  [<module character set specification>]
```

The module name is defined as

```
<module name> ::=
  <SQL-client module name>
```

The SQL-client module name is defined as

```
<SQL-client module name> ::= <identifier>
```

The module character set specification is defined as

```
< module character set specification> ::=
  NAMES ARE <character set specification>
```

The language clause, which is part of the module header specification, is defined as

```
<language clause> ::=
  LANGUAGE <language name>
```

And the language name is defined as

```
<language name> ::=
  SQL¦ C ¦ FORTRAN ¦ PASCAL ¦ ADA ¦ PLI ¦ COBOL ¦ MUMPS
```


The module authorization clause, which is part of the header clause, is defined as

```
<module language authorization clause> ::=
  SCHEMA <schema name>
  ¦AUTHORIZATION <module authorization identifier>
  ¦SCHEMA <schema name> AUTHORIZATION <module authorization identifier>
```

The module authorization identifier is defined as

```
<module authorization identifier> ::=
  <authorization identifier>
```

In this module, the authorization identifier is defined as

```
<authorization identifier> ::= <identifier>
```

The optional module path specification found in the header clause is defined as

```
<module path specification> ::=
  <path specification>
```

where

```
<path specification> ::=
  PATH <schema name list>
```

and

```
<schema name list> ::=
  <schema name> [, <schema name> [, <schema name>..>
```

This code might be cryptic, so I'll explain it. The module definition starts with a module specification, which includes a module header and module contents. The module header defines items such as module name clause, the language clause, the module authorization clause, and, optionally, the module path information clause.

The module name clause, as the name implies, includes the module name specification. The name has to comply with the standard's naming conventions. The language clause allows you to specify the language used to write the module. You have a wide array of languages to choose from: SQL, C, FORTRAN, PLI, MUMPS, ADA, COBOL, and Pascal.

The module authorization clause defines who has access privileges to use the module and what those privileges are. With this information, you can generally specify either the schema under which the module will run or which user has the authority to use it.

The path specification allows you to define where the module exists. You can generally have the module in several schemas. The list of these schemas is defined in this clause.

Take a look at an example that defines a module named `cust_module`. The module is located in three schemas: `usc1`, `usc2`, and `usc3`. The user `cust_user` has unlimited access privileges to the module. Finally, the module is written in C. Listing 22.1 shows what the module header specification looks like.

LISTING 22.1 Example of Specifying a Module Header

```
MODULE cust_module
  LANGUAGE C
  AUTHORIZATION cust_user
  PATH usc1, usc2, usc3
```

Let's look at the module contents specification. These contents can include several elements, which are usually cursor declaration, global declaration, and a collection of procedures that can be called from a host language. The procedures are the major contents of the SQL module.

```
<module contents> ::=
  <declare cursor>
  ¦<externally invoked procedure>;
  ¦<SQL-invoked routine>;
  ¦<global declaration>
```

In this example, the SQL-invoked routine is defined as a schema function or procedure:

```
<SQL-invoked routine> ::=
  <schema routine>
```

The global declaration is defined as a temporary table declaration in SQL:

```
<global declaration> ::=
  <temporary table declaration>
```

An external client module procedure, which is an optional part of the module contents, is defined as follows:

```
<externally-invoked procedure> ::=
  PROCEDURE <procedure name>
    <host parameter declaration setup>;
   <SQL procedure statement>;
   <SQL procedure statement>;
   ...
```

In this definition, the procedure name is defined as

```
<procedure name> ::= <identifier>
```

In the externally invoked procedure definition shown here, the keyword `PROCEDURE` indicates the beginning of the named external procedure embedded in the module.

Note

A SQL status parameter must be included as part of the procedure declaration. This parameter indicates to the calling routine the status of the procedure's execution. Two SQL status indicators can be used for this purpose: `SQLCODE` and `SQLSTATE`. Although `SQLCODE` is the old implementation, most SQL implementations still accept it. This indicator can have a zero or negative value. A zero indicates success, and a negative value means failure. A special value of `100` indicates no data found.

`SQLSTATE`, introduced in SQL-92, is a five-digit code; the two left digits indicate an error class, and the remaining three digits indicate the error subclass or error itself. For more details on `SQLCODE` and `SQLSTATE`, please refer to Chapter 17, "Embedded SQL."

Let's extend the module declaration in Listing 22.1 to include some procedures. The expanded example is shown in Listing 22.2.

LISTING 22.2 Example of a Module Content Specification

```
MODULE cust_module
  LANGUAGE C
  AUTHORIZATION cust_user
  PATH usc1, usc2, usc3

/*declare the first procedure*/
PROCEDURE cust_insert(SQLCODE,
           :cust_name CHARACTER(30),
           :cust_address CHARACTER(80),
           :cust_city CHARACTER(30),
           :cust_state CHARACTER(2),
           :cust_zip CHARACTER(10));

    /*SQL statements follow:*/
    INSERT INTO customer
      (name, address, city, state, zip)
    VALUES(:cust_name,
       :cust_address,
       :cust_city,
       :cust_state,
       :cust_zip);

/*declare the second procedure*/
PROCEDURE cust_change(SQLCODE,
           :cust_id NUMBER
           :cust_name CHARACTER(30),
           :cust_address CHARACTER(80),
           :cust_city CHARACTER(30),
           :cust_state CHARACTER(2),
           :cust_zip CHARACTER(10));

    /*SQL statements follow:*/
    UPDATE customer SET
       name = :cust_name,
       address = :cust_address,
       city = :cust_city,
       state = :cust_state,
       zip = :cust_zip)
    WHERE customer_id = :cust_id;

/*declare the third procedure*/
PROCEDURE cust_get(SQLCODE,
```

LISTING 22.2 CONTINUED

```
          :cust_name CHARACTER(30),
          :cust_id NUMBER);

    /*SQL statements follow:*/
    SELECT name
    INTO :cust_name
    FROM customer
    WHERE cust_id = :cust_id

/*More procedure declaration can follow here*/
```


In these procedures, notice that parameters were identified. They are specified in parentheses after the procedure name. These parameters can also have indicators to check for NULL values. To learn more about indicators, refer to Chapter 17. Parameters are declared as follows:

```
<host parameter declaration setup> ::=
  <host parameter declaration list>
  ¦<host parameter declaration>...
```

The host parameter declaration list is defined by

```
<host parameter declaration list> ::=
  (<host parameter declaration [, host parameter declaration..])
```

And the host parameter declaration is defined by

```
<host parameter declaration> ::=
  <host parameter name> <data type>
  ¦<status parameter>
```

The status parameter is defined by

```
<status parameter> ::=
  SQLSTATE
```

The declaration section can include declarations of one or more parameters for the procedure. These parameters are identified by a valid name and a data type.

The body of the procedure includes a number of valid SQL statements with other statements listed in the procedure body declaration, as shown:

```
<SQL procedure statement> ::=
  <SQL executable statement>
```

The SQL executable statement is defined by

```
<SQL executable statement> ::=
  <SQL schema statement>
  ¦<SQL data statement>
  ¦<SQL control statement>
  ¦<SQL transaction statement>
  ¦<SQL connection statement>
  ¦<SQL session statement>
  ¦<SQL diagnostics statement>
```

In Listing 22.2, SQL data statements were used. These statements included the `SELECT`, `INSERT`, and `UPDATE` keywords.

After the SQL client module has been built and stored, it can be accessed by any program or applications as long as the user has access authorization to the module. The call to the procedures and functions in the module are similar to any other calls by programming language. Listing 22.3 shows how the procedures in Listing 22.2's module can be called from within a C program.

LISTING 22.3 Example Showing How Client Module Procedures Can Be Called

```
int main()
  {
  /*Variable declarations*/
  long  SQLCODE;
  long  cust_id = 123
  char  *ret_cust_name; //returned customer name
  char  *cust_name = ''John Doe''; //inserted customer name
  char  *cust_address = ''123 Main St.'';  //customer address
  char  *cust_city = ''anytown'';    //customer city
  char  *cust_state = ''MI''; //customer state
  char  *cust_zip = ''48484-4023''; //customer zip code

  /*program code goes here*/
  ...
  ...
  /*get the customer
  cust_get(&sqlcode, cust_id, &ret_cust_name)
  ...
  ...
  /*insert a new customer*/
  cust_insert(&sqlcode,
        :cust_name,
        :cust_address,
        :cust_city,
```

LISTING 22.3 CONTINUED

```
        :cust_state,
        :cust_zip);
  ...
  ...
  return 0;
  }
```

> **Note**
>
> In Listing 22.3's code, the ampersand (&) is used as a prefix for the output variables to distinguish them from input variables. Other programming languages might differ in the way they express output and input parameters.

Server Modules

The server module is another type of module that exists on the database server and is considered a schema object. This module is usually in the same domain as the database and runs in that domain, unlike the client module, which is located on a client to the database server.

Declaring the server module is similar to declaring the client module. It also contains functions and procedures that can be accessed within the database domain. Server modules can be dropped with the `DROP MODULE` or `DROP SCHEMA` statement. These modules can also be altered, which gives users more flexibility.

Procedures and functions can also exist in the database without being attached to a module. In this case, these function and procedures exist in the main database (above the schema level). These functions and procedures are sometimes grouped into packages. Packages and freely floating procedures and functions are referred to as *persistent stored modules*, discussed in the following section.

Persistent Modules

Persistent stored modules refer to procedures and functions in the main database, not in any of its schemas. These routines include appropriate declarations of cursors, variables, types, and so forth. These routines are also written in the SQL language, not in any other host language.

Persistent module routines do not require status parameters because they operate within the database; if accessed from outside the database, the database engine returns the error code. These routines also don't require indicator variables to help with NULL values for the same reason mentioned previously.

As an example of using these routines, Listing 22.4 shows the same example as Listing 22.2, but with persistent stored procedures and modules. Notice the differences in syntax, especially variable declaration and use. Also, notice that a schema was defined for this example and that the language specification chooses SQL as the module's language.

LISTING 22.4 Example of Persistent Stored Modules

```
MODULE cust_module
  LANGUAGE SQL
  AUTHORIZATION cust_user
  SCHEMA usc1

/* module declaration section */
DECLARE ...
/*you can declare any cursors, variables, UDT, etc. here*/
...
...

/*declare the first procedure*/
PROCEDURE cust_insert(SQLCODE,
           cust_name CHAR (30),
           cust_address CHAR (80),
           cust_city CHAR (30),
           cust_state CHAR (2),
           cust_zip CHAR (10));

    /*SQL statements follow:*/
    INSERT INTO customer
      (name, address, city, state, zip)
    VALUES(cust_name,
        cust_address,
        cust_city,
        cust_state,
        cust_zip);

/*declare the second procedure*/
PROCEDURE cust_change(SQLCODE,
           cust_id NUMBER
```

LISTING 22.4 CONTINUED

```
          cust_name CHAR (30),
          cust_address CHAR (80),
          cust_city CHAR (30),
          cust_state CHAR (2),
          cust_zip CHAR (10));

    /*SQL statements follow:*/
    UPDATE customer SET
       name = cust_name,
       address = cust_address,
       city = cust_city,
       state = cust_state,
       zip = cust_zip)
    WHERE customer_id = cust_id;

/*declare the third procedure*/
PROCEDURE cust_get(SQLCODE,
         :cust_name CHARACTER(30),
         :cust_id NUMBER);

    /*SQL statements follow:*/
    SELECT name
    INTO :cust_name
    FROM customer
    WHERE cust_id = :cust_id

/*More procedure declaration can follow here*/
```


SQL Routines (Functions and Procedures)

As you saw in the previous section, routines in SQL-3 are in the database server modules, which makes them accessible directly through the schema that contains them. A SQL routine can be a function, which returns a value, or a procedure, which does not return a value.

Functions and procedures are created with the `CREATE FUNCTION` and `CREATE PROCEDURE` statements and stored in the database. Once saved, the user can see them as any other schema object, such as tables or triggers. Their properties can also be queried from the system catalogs, just like other schema objects.

To create a function that returns the number of employees whose salaries exceed $50,000, you can use the function in Listing 22.5.

LISTING 22.5 Example of a SQL Function

```
CREATE FUNCTION high_paid
    (name  CHAR(30),
    (max sal DECIMAL))
RETURNS INTEGER;

BEGIN
  DECLARE iCount INTEGER;
  SELECT COUNT(*)
  INTO iCount
  FROM employee
  WHERE salary > 50000;
/*set return value*/
RETURN iCount;
End;
```

Notice the structure of the function in Listing 22.5; it's illustrated in Figure 22.2.

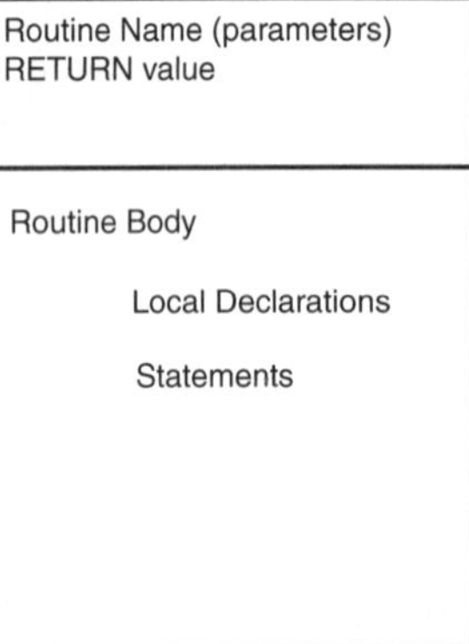

FIGURE 22.2
Structure of the SQL routine.

Figure 22.2 shows clearly that the SQL routine has two parts: the routine declaration part, which includes its name and parameters and the return value, and the routine body, which includes local declarations and SQL and other statements.

External Routines

External routines, located outside the database domain, are usually written in languages other than SQL. Supported languages include C, PLI, Pascal, COBOL, MUMPS, FORTRAN, and ADA. These routines can have embedded SQL in the form of static SQL, dynamic SQL, or Call Level Interface (CLI).

External routines must have a status parameter as one of their arguments. This parameter indicates the status of the routine's execution. Its value is usually SQLCODE or SQLSTATE, depending on the SQL implementation and the host language for the external routine. External routine parameters can be IN, OUT, or IN/OUT parameters, and can have indicator variables that determine whether a NULL value is passed or returned. The return value of an external function *must* have an indicator variable.

The issue of data types is a big one in external routines. Parameter data types should map to SQL-supported data types, such as CHAR, VARCHAR, NUMERIC, DECIMAL, and DATE. Sometimes, you even need to cast a data type from the host language to SQL, using the CAST FROM clause for return values.

External routines open the door for database developers to use code libraries written in languages other than SQL to do a variety of tasks that cannot be done from within SQL. However, be careful when using external routines because of the data type issues and the loss of database engine checking after the execution gets out of the database domain.

Schema Routines

Schema routines refer to functions and procedures stored in the database server and known to the database. If these routines are written in SQL, they are called *SQL routines* (see previous section). If the language used to write these routines is not SQL, they are referred to as *external routines*.

Schema routines are invoked from within SQL by using the CALL statement. They can also be invoked by external sources, as in conventional programming languages.

Schema routines can be overloaded, allowing their names to be reused. The same name can be used for multiple routines in the schema as long as the list of parameters is not the same among these routines. This characteristic of object-oriented programming is introduced for the first time in the SQL standard.

Functions have return values, but their parameters can only be IN parameters. Procedures, on the other hand, can have IN, OUT, and IN/OUT parameters. They don't have a return value. IN parameters specify that the parameter is an input to the routine. OUT parameters are used by the routine to convey variable values to the calling program. IN/OUT parameters are two-way parameters; they introduce values to be used by the routine, and when the routine is done executing, it assigns values to them to be carried back to the calling program.

Parameters to these routines can have any SQL-supported data types, and their number is limited only by what the SQL implementation specifies. These parameters don't have to include a SQL status parameter nor do they have to have indicator variables.

PSM SQL Elements

Now that you have learned about modules and routines and their relationship to schemas, you can learn about the language elements used in SQL routines. These elements make SQL procedural after being strictly declarative in the past. Thanks to the procedural features of post-SQL-92 SQL (specifically with the introduction of PSM), you can use the language to write complete programs and libraries that perform certain tasks in the database and reuse these libraries. What are the elements that add this benefit to an already great language? To find out, sit back, relax, and read the rest of the chapter.

Compound Statements

With compound statements, several SQL statements can be grouped in one group or structure. The keywords `BEGIN` and `END` are used to indicate the beginning and end of the compound statement's structure. The general syntax of compound statements is as follows:

```
<compound statement> ::=
  [<begin label>:]
  BEGIN <NOT] ATOMIC]
    [<local declaration list>]
    [<local handler declaration list>]
    [<SQL statement list>]
  END
  [<end label>]
```

As you can see, the keywords `BEGIN` and `END` are the only required elements in this structure. An optional label can be used before the `BEGIN` keyword or after the `END` keyword. The keyword `ATOMIC`determines whether the statements should be run as one unit or each statement should run alone. With the `ATOMIC` option, any failure in a statement within the compound statement results in failure of the entire compound statement and all individual statements within it. With the default (non-`ATOMIC`) option, a failure in one statement in the compound statement does not cause the failure of other statements in the block.

> **Note**
>
> When compound statements are declared `ATOMIC`, you cannot use `ROLL BACK` or `COMMIT` statements within the compound statement. However, when the `NOT ATOMIC` option is used, you can use such statements as appropriate.

Cursors and variables can be declared locally within a compound statement. When this happens, these elements have a local scope only, meaning they are recognized only inside the compound statement and exist only while the statement is running. After the statement finishes, these elements are destroyed.

Note

Variables declared locally in a compound statement (or *block*) should follow variable declaration and naming conventions. For instance, their name must be unique within the compound statement. If a local variable name happens to be the same as a variable used outside the compound statement, the local variable prevails, but only within the compound statement.

Listing 22.6 is an example of a compound statement that includes a SELECT and UPDATE on the employee table.

LISTING 22.6 Compound Statement Example

```
BEGIN
  /*SELECT statement*/
  SELECT emp_Name, manager_id
  FROM employee
  WHERE emp_id = 123;
  /*UPDATE statement*/
  UPDATE employee SET
  Manager_id = 23
  WHERE emp_id = 123;
END;
```

Compound statements can be executed interactively against the database by using an appropriate client tool. For instance, for Oracle, you can type the preceding statement in SQL*PLUS, a client tool that ships with the Oracle database server and client software, to execute it as one unit. In SQL Server 7.0, you can use the Query Analyzer to run this compound statement with a slight syntax modification.

Compound statements can also be embedded in host language programs, just like any embedded SQL statement. As an example, Listing 22.7 shows a C program that runs the compound statement presented earlier. You need a SQL preprocessor to transform the code listing into code that a C compiler will accept.

LISTING 22.7 Embedding Compound Statements in Host Language Programs

```
int main(){
  EXEC SQL
    BEGIN
      /*SELECT statement*/
      SELECT emp_Name, manager_id
      FROM employee
      WHERE emp_id = 123;
      /*UPDATE statement*/
      UPDATE employee SET
      Manager_id = 23
      WHERE emp_id = 123;
    END;

  return 0;
}
```

Compound statements can include any of the PSM elements, not just SQL statements. You will see examples of this type of use in the following sections.

Variables

SQL routines can have local or global variables. This is the syntax for variable declarations:

```
<SQL variable declaration> ::=
  DECLARE
  <SQL variable name list>
  { <data type> ¦ <domain name>}
  [default clause]
```

The `DECLARE` keyword is used to indicate a variable declaration to the compiler. `DECLARE` is followed by the variable name and optional data type. A default value can also be assigned to the variable at the time of the declaration.

The following are examples of data variable declarations:

```
DECLARE cust_name VARCHAR(30);

DECLARE area_code INTEGER DEFAULT 248;
```

In the first statement, the variable `cust_name` is declared of the type `VARCHAR`with a maximum length of 30 characters. In the second example, the variable `area_code` is declared as `INTEGER`, with a default (initial) value of `248`.

To assign the result of an expression to a variable, you can use the assignment statement with the SET keyword:

```
SET var_name = expression;
```

As an example, to assign the name John Doe to the cust_name variable declared previously, you write

```
DECLARE cust_name VARCHAR(30);
SET cust_name = 'John Doe';
```


You can also assign the value of a variable to another variable. To expand the previous example, you can write the following:

```
DECLARE cust_name VARCHAR(30);
DECLARE cust_name_ind INTEGER; //Indicator variable
DECLARE another_name VARCHAR(20);
SET cust_name = 'John Doe';
SET another_name = :cust_name INDICATOR cust_name_ind;
```

This code assigns the value John Doe to the variable cust_name, and then assigns the value of that variable to the variable another_name.

Note

Notice the use of the indicator variables in these examples. The indicator variable cust_name_ind indicates whether cust_name is NULL. The indicator variable has another use; if the length of cust_name exceeds the declared length of another_name, a number of characters corresponding to the length of another_name (20, in this case) is returned. The actual length of cust_name is stored in the indicator variable.

Conditions

Condition handling has always been an important part of any programming language. Conditions are synonymous to logic. With no conditions, logic becomes difficult to implement. PSM introduced the use of conditions in SQL in two major ways: the IF statement and the CASE statement. This section discusses the use of these two statements in SQL.

IF Statement

The IF statement was missing in the SQL-92 standard. This statement was added when PSM became available in 1996, and was officially added to the new SQL-3 standard (see Chapter 23, "The Next Standard: SQL-99." This is the general syntax for this statement:

```
If condition true
  THEN SQL statements
  ELSEIF condition true
  THEN SQL statements
  ...
  ...
  ...
  ELSE SQL statements
END IF
```

As an example, you have a department table with a field called `total_employees`. This field holds the total number of employees in the corresponding department (notice that such a field might denormalize the database). A new employee was just added, so you need to update the number in the `total_employees` field of the `department` table, according to what department the new employee belongs to. Let's assume that the `emp_id` value for the new employee is `123`. Listing 22.8 shows how the required field can be updated according to the new employee's department.

LISTING 22.8 Example of the IF statement

```
IF (SELECT dept_id
  FROM employee
  WHERE emp_id = 123) = 1 //Sales department
THEN
  BEGIN
    DECLARE current_total INTEGER;
    current_total = (SELECT total_employees
              FROM department
              WHERE dept_id = 1);
    UPDATE department
    SET total_employees = :current_total
    WHERE dept_id = 1;
  END;
ELSEIF (SELECT dept_id
    FROM employee
    WHERE emp_id = 123) = 2 //HR department
THEN
```

LISTING 22.8 CONTINUED

```
  BEGIN
    DECLARE current_total INTEGER;
    current_total = (SELECT total_employees
              FROM department
              WHERE dept_id = 2);
    UPDATE department
    SET total_employees = :current_total + 1
    WHERE dept_id = 2;
  END;
ELSEIF (SELECT dept_id
    FROM employee
    WHERE emp_id = 123) = 3 //Engineering department
THEN
  BEGIN
    DECLARE current_total INTEGER;
    current_total = (SELECT total_employees
              FROM department
              WHERE dept_id = 3);
    UPDATE department
    SET total_employees = :current_total + 1
    WHERE dept_id = 3;
  END;
ELSE
  BEGIN
    DECLARE current_total INTEGER;
    current_total = (SELECT total_employees
              FROM department
              WHERE dept_id > 3);
    UPDATE department
    SET total_employees = :current_total + 1
    WHERE dept_id = > 3;
  END;
END IF;
```

This listing demonstrates how to use regular non-SQL statements in compound statements, shows that you can have multiple `ELSEIF` clauses in your `IF` statement, and illustrates how internal variables are used within the compound statements.

`CASE` Statement

The `CASE` statement, like similar statements in other programming languages, enumerates a list of possible conditions in one structure. In this statement, an expression is evaluated;

based on the result of the evaluation, the execution takes a certain path or follows a different plan. This is the syntax for this statement:

```
<simple case> ::=
  CASE <case operand>
    <simple when clause>...
    [ <else clause> ]
  END
```

The case operand is defined as

```
<case operand> ::=
  <value expression>
```

and

```
<simple when clause> ::=
  WHEN <when operand>
  THEN <result>
```

and

```
<when operand> ::= <value expression>
<result> ::= <value expression>¦NULL
<else clause> ::= ELSE <result>
```

In this structure, the value expression could be any valid expression, such as an SQL statement, numerical expression, or logical comparison.

Listing 22.9 shows the same example you saw in the `IF` statement section, but uses the `CASE` statement.

LISTING 22.9 Example of CASE Statement Use

```
DECLARE current_total INTEGER;
CASE (SELECT dept_id
   FROM employee
   WHERE emp_id = 123)
WHEN 1 THEN   //Sales department
  BEGIN
    current_total = (SELECT total_employees
             FROM department
             WHERE dept_id = 1);
    UPDATE department
    SET total_employees = :current_total + 1
    WHERE dept_id = 1;
  END;
```

LISTING 22.9 CONTINUED

```
WHEN 2 THEN   //HR department
  BEGIN
    current_total = (SELECT total_employees
              FROM department
              WHERE dept_id = 2);
    UPDATE department
    SET total_employees = :current_total
    WHERE dept_id = 2;
  END;
WHEN 3 THEN   //Engineering department
  BEGIN
    current_total = (SELECT total_employees
              FROM department
              WHERE dept_id = 3);
    UPDATE department
    SET total_employees = :current_total
    WHERE dept_id = 3;
  END;
ELSE
  BEGIN
    current_total = (SELECT total_employees
              FROM department
              WHERE dept_id > 3);
    UPDATE department
    SET total_employees = :current_total
    WHERE dept_id = > 3;
  END;
END;
```


Loops

Loop structures are another essential element in any programming language. These structures enable you to perform repetitive tasks and greatly reduce the amount of code you write. Several loop statements are supplied in the post-SQL-92 standard and incorporated into the SQL-3 standard. This section covers these statements.

FOR Statement

The FOR statement in SQL routines and in the SQL-3 standard is different from similar statements in other programming languages. The FOR statement is an iterative statement in SQL routines. It iterates over elements of a result table for all rows within the table. The

LEAVE clause can be used to end the loop early when a certain condition is met. This is the syntax for the FOR statement:

```
Label: FOR <variable_name>
  AS <cursor_specification>
  DO <SQL statements>
END FOR;
```

As an example of the FOR statement, Listing 22.10 iterates through the employee table for those whose hire date was before January 1999. If the employee makes more than $50,000, you need to add a record in another table called high_paid that lists the employee's name and salary. This is done by modifying the salary field.

LISTING 22.10 Example of the FOR Statement

```
/*create the high_paid table, in case it does not exist*/
CREATE TABLE high_paid(
  emp_name   VARCHAR(30),
  salary    DECIMAL(8,2));

/*Now populate the new table*/
emp_for_loop: FOR emp AS
     SELECT * FROM employee
     WHERE hire_date < '01-Jan-99'
DO
  INSERT INTO high_paid
    VALUES(emp.emp_name, emp.salary);
END FOR;
END;
END FOR;
```

LOOP Statement

The LOOP statement allows a programmer to perform repeated statements infinitely. The LEAVE keyword is used to exit the LOOP structure. The syntax for this statement is as follows:

```
Label: LOOP
  SQL statements
END LOOP ;
```

As an example, Listing 22.11 performs the same operation as in Listing 22.10, but uses the LOOP structure.

LISTING 22.11 Example of the `LOOP` Statement

```
/*create the high_paid table, in case it does not exist*/
CREATE TABLE high_paid(
  emp_name    VARCHAR(30),
  salary     DECIMAL(8,2));

/*Now populate the new table using the LOOP structure*/
BEGIN
DECLARE emp_name  VARCHAR(30);
DECLARE emp_salary DECIMAL(8,2);

/*Start the loop*/
emp_ loop: LOOP
IF (SELECT emp_id FROM employee
    WHERE hire_date < '01-Jan-99'
    ORDER BY emp_id) > 200 THEN
      LEAVE emp_loop;
  ELSE
    SELECT emp_name, salary
    INTO :emp_name, :emp_salary
    FROM employee
    WHERE hire_date < '01-Jan-99';
    INSERT INTO high_paid
      VALUES(:emp_name, :emp_salary);
END IF;
END LOOP;
END;
```

In Listing 22.11, after you make sure the table exists, you assign the employee name and salary to the two block variables: `emp_name` and `emp_salary`. You then use these two variables to insert the new record in the `high_paid` table. Note that you exit the `LOOP` structure when you encounter an employee ID value greater than `200`.

`REPEAT` Statement

This statement differs from the `LOOP` statement in that it requires an explicit ending condition in a certain location of the statement, usually at the end of the statement's structure. This is the syntax for the `REPEAT` statement:

```
Label: REPEAT
    SQL statements
    ...
  UNTIL <condition>
```

```
END REPEAT;
```

As an example, Listing 22.12 shows how the REPEAT statement can be used instead of the LOOP structure shown in the previous example.

LISTING 22.12 Example of the REPEAT Statement

```
/*create the high_paid table, in case it does not exist*/
CREATE TABLE high_paid(
  emp_name   VARCHAR(30),
  salary    DECIMAL(8,2));

/*Now populate the new table using the REPEAT structure*/
BEGIN
DECLARE emp_name  VARCHAR(30);
DECLARE emp_salary DECIMAL(8,2);

/*Start the loop*/
emp_ repeat: REPEAT

    SELECT emp_name, salary
    INTO :emp_name, :emp_salary
    FROM employee
    WHERE hire_date < '01-Jan-99';

    INSERT INTO high_paid
      VALUES(:emp_name, :emp_salary);

  UNTIL (SELECT emp_id FROM employee
      WHERE hire_date < '01-Jan-99'
      ORDER BY emp_id) > 200

END REPEAT;
END;
```

WHILE Statement

This is another statement that allows repeating a group of SQL and other statements as long as a tested condition is TRUE. The condition is tested at the beginning of the statement, in this case. The syntax for this statement is as follows:

```
Label: WHILE <condition>
   DO
    SQL Statements
```

```
  ...
END WHILE;
```

Listing 22.13 illustrates the use of the WHILE statement to do the same task as you did with the REPEAT statement.

LISTING 22.13 Example of the WHILE Statement

```
/*create the high_paid table, in case it does not exist*/
CREATE TABLE high_paid(
  emp_name    VARCHAR(30),
  salary     DECIMAL(8,2));

/*Now populate the new table using the WHILE structure*/
BEGIN
DECLARE emp_name  VARCHAR(30);
DECLARE emp_salary DECIMAL(8,2);

/*Start the loop*/
emp_ repeat: WHILE

        (SELECT emp_id FROM employee
         WHERE hire_date < '01-Jan-99'
         ORDER BY emp_id) > 200

    DO
      SELECT emp_name, salary
      INTO :emp_name, :emp_salary
      FROM employee
      WHERE hire_date < '01-Jan-99';

      INSERT INTO high_paid
        VALUES(:emp_name, :emp_salary);

    END WHILE;
END;
```

Exception Handling

Sources of errors are numerous. An error could be a result of a logical operation that produced an illegal result, a syntax error in the code, or a business error resulting in a situation that needs to be handled according to specific business rules. As a programmer, you need to handle these errors no matter what their sources are.

PSM introduced an EXCEPTION block that can be used for error handling. The structure of a PSM routine with the EXCEPTION block is shown here:

```
DECLARE
  Variable and other declarations
  ...
BEGIN
  SQL Statemnts
  ...
  ...
EXCEPTION
  WHEN exception_name OR exception_name
  THEN
    Error handler code
END;
```

You can test for standard exceptions, such as NO_DATA_FOUND, or you can raise exceptions when you need to by following these steps:

- Declare and name the exception in the declaration section.
- Test for a condition when the exception might occur.
- If the condition is TRUE, use the SIGNAL statement (see the next section) to raise it.
- Finally, add error handling code in the exception handling section of your procedure. All these steps are explained and illustrated in more detail in the following section.

Note

Standard exceptions are passed back from the database engine as the SQLCODE, SQLERROR, or SQLSTATE variables. These exceptions are limited in the SQL standard, but are numerous in different SQL implementations.

SIGNAL Statement

As mentioned, the `SIGNAL` statement can be used to raise an error that had been declared. After the exception is raised, execution moves to the `EXCEPTION` section, where the code corresponding to the raised exception runs.

The following sample code illustrates how this can be done:

```
DECLARE
  xyz_exception EXCEPTION;
  Other declarations
  ...
BEGIN
  SQL Statemnts
  ...
  IF <condition> THEN
    SIGNAL xyz_exception
  END IF;
  ...
EXCEPTION
  WHEN exception_name OR exception_name
  THEN
    Error handler code
END;
```

The `RESIGNAL` statement can be used to raise an exception that had already been raised. Condition handlers are declared for individual compound statements or blocks. The scope of the condition handling is that of the block's local or contained statements.

Condition handlers are found in the scope of the compound statements, not just in the procedure scope. The syntax for these handlers is shown here:

```
<handler declaration> ::=
  DECLARE <handler type> HANDLER
    FOR <condition value list>
      <handler action>

<handler type> ::=
  CONTINUE¦
  EXIT¦
  UNDO
```

and

```
<handler action> ::=
  <SQL procedure statements>
```

```
<condition value list> ::=
  <condition value>[, <condition value...]
```

and

```
<condition value> ::=
  <SQLSTATE value>¦
  <condition name>¦
  <SQLEXCEPTION>¦
  <SQLWARNING>¦
  <NOT FOUND>
```

In this syntax, the handler type can be CONTINUE, UNDO, or EXIT. The CONTINUE handler performs a designated handler operation. The EXIT handler exits the compound statement, returning control to the statement following the statement that led to the compound statement in which the handler is located. The UNDO handler rolls back any changes made in the compound statement, including canceling any triggers that might have been activated as a result of actions taken in the compound statement. The UNDO handler then returns control to the statement following the one that led to the compound statement in which it existed.

Vendor Implementations

Many vendors have already implemented some sort of the PSM standard. Because these implementations started before the standard was released, there are many variations among them and differences from the PSM standard. One implementation that is closest to the PSM standard is the Oracle implementation in its PL/SQL extensions. PL/SQL has many of the structures presented in this chapter, as well as other useful extensions. Microsoft SQL Server's Transact-SQL is another implementation that is close to the PSM standard. It has more differences from the standard than Oracle's PL/SQL, however. I am not going to discuss these implementations here, especially because PL/SQL and T-SQL are discussed in more detail in Chapter 25, "Oracle PL/SQL," and Chapter 26, "Microsoft Transact-SQL." Please review these two chapters and try to compare the concepts you learned here to the characteristics of those two languages.

Summary

In this chapter, you have looked at the powerful persistent stored modules introduced as an extension to the SQL-92 standard in 1996, and added to the SQL-3 standard as one of its essential eight parts. With PSM, new possibilities for using SQL are open to database developers and administrators. PSM allows them to create and store libraries of procedures and functions that they use over and over, saving them a great deal of effort and time.

This chapter has presented an overview of the PSM standard, describing the routines and modules and the different new elements introduced to the SQL language.

CHAPTER 23

The Next Standard: SQL-99

In This Chapter

Now that you have read and learned about the ins and outs of the SQL-92 standard and the other parts of the SQL standard that reference SQL-92, SQL call level interface (SQL/CLI), and persistent stored modules (SQL/PSM), it is time for an overview. The new SQL standard is SQL3, the project alias used by both the ANSI and the ISO SQL Standards committees. Some references call this standard SQL-99 or SQL:1999, the Y2K reference, because it was released in 1999 as the International Standard and will later become the ANSI Standards for the SQL Database Language in the United States. This chapter presents a quick overview of why this standard was needed, who is already implementing parts of it, what is to be expected of the SQL-99 standard, and how different it is from the SQL-92 standard. Keep in mind that many RDBMSs have not implemented this standard yet. This chapter is meant to show you what is coming in the months ahead. The topics that I cover in this chapter include the following:

- Overview of SQL-99
- Impact of the SQL-99 standard
- SQL-99 features and elements
- Abstract data types (ADTs)

Overview of SQL-99

In 1992, the American National Standards Institute, along with other standards organizations, started to aggressively work on developing a new criterion for the SQL database language. The ANSI X3H2 committee was leading the way, developing dramatic SQL-92 standard extensions. The most dramatic SQL-92 change does not strictly adhere to the 1970 relational data model, as published by Dr. E. F. Codd. Another major change is that the SQL-99 language specification now consists of individual parts that compose a core language and extensions to that core, as well as a series of packages.

The SQL3 projects were really a group of projects that were progressed to standard status, either in groups or separately. Here is a list of the projects that make up the SQL3 Project:

Part 1: Framework

Part 2: Foundation

Part 3: Call Level Interface (CLI)

Part 4: Persistent Stored Modules (PSM)

Part 5: Language Bindings

Part 6: XA Specification

Part 7: Temporal

Part 8: Object

Part 9: Management of External Data (MED)

Part 10: Object Language Bindings

Again, not all of these projects have progressed to standard status at this time. In fact, what is being referred to here as SQL-99 is actually: Part 1, Part 2, Part 3, Part 4, and Part 5. All but Part 3, SQL/CLI, has completed the ISO/IEC Standards Process. SQL/CLI will complete the process in October of 1999.

The formal titles of the new standard are

ISO/IEC 9075-1:1999, Information technology --- Database languages --- SQL --- Part 1: Framework (SQL/Framework)

ISO/IEC 9075-2:1999, Information technology --- Database languages --- SQL --- Part 2: Foundation (SQL/Foundation)

ISO/IEC 9075-3:1999, Information technology --- Database languages --- SQL --- Part 3: Call-Level Interface (SQL/CLI)

ISO/IEC 9075-4:1999, Information technology --- Database languages --- SQL --- Part 4: Persistent Stored Modules (SQL/PSM)

ISO/IEC 9075-5:1999, Information technology --- Database languages --- SQL --- Part 5: Host Language Bindings (SQL/Bindings)

while the formal numbers of the new standards are

ISO/IEC 9075-1:1999

ISO/IEC 9075-2:1999

ISO/IEC 9075-3:1999

ISO/IEC 9075-4:1999

ISO/IEC 9075-5:1999

So is it SQL3, SQL-99 or SQL:1999? Well, for now it is SQL-99. The SQL Standard's editor, Jim Melton, is promoting SQL:1999 because of the Y2K issues. However, I know SQL-99 is better than what we had in 1989 and I sure hope we have something much better by the time we reach 2099, so I'll stick with its current alias, SQL-99.

Let's run through a status of the projects as they stand today:

Part 1: Framework

This progressed as part of the SQL-99 standard. It is a project for the development of SQL-200x, the next version of the SQL standard, which is tentatively scheduled for release in 2003. If you download this document from the ANSI/ISO committee archive site's ftp server, you will be getting a work-in-progress document that has nothing to do with SQL-99. You must order the SQL-99 documents from either ISO/IEC or ANSI, once it becomes an ANSI standard early next year.

Part 2: Foundation

Part 2 has the same status as Part 1.

Part 3: Call Level Interface (CLI)

Part 2 has the same status as Part 1.

Part 4: Persistent Stored Modules (PSM)

Part 2 has the same status as Part 1.

Part 5: Language Bindings

This project has been dropped for maintenance reasons, and the work has been combined in Part 2 for the next SQL-200x . It was too time-consuming to update two documents and the necessary changes could potentially introduce a major bug infestation into the standard. At the May 1999 ISO WG3 meeting in Matue, Japan, it was agreed that Part 5 and Part 2 would be consolidated. Part 5 will not be reassigned to a new project; it will just be left out of future standards references.

Part 6: XA Specification

This part of the standard was dropped due to the committee members' lack of interest. This is not to say that XA has not found its way into today's database products. XA implementations are based upon the original XA specification from the X/Open Group.

Part 7: Temporal

Temporal has been on hold for some time now, due to a poor assessment of the problematic issues temporal data bring to the database. Oracle has shown an interest in reviving work on this part of the standard, once the MED and OLAP projects are completed.

Part 8: Object

Again this project was dropped, and the material was combined in the other parts that make up the SQL-99 Standard.

Part 9: Management of External Data (MED)

MED is currently being constructed by IBM, Informix, Oracle, and Compaq. It is going through the editing process at the ISO/IEC level and will continue progress. The WG3 meeting in Amsterdam in October of 1999 and the WG3 meeting in New Mexico in January 2000 will be solidifying MED. It should become part of the SQL Standard in 2000 or 2001 and will reference and be aligned with SQL-99.

Part 10: Object Language Bindings

SQL/OLB is currently an ANSI-only standard and is aligned to SQL-92 and JDBC 1.1. It is the Java Bindings of SQL. It was originally part of the SQLJ group of standards—SQLJ part 0 to be exact. It was developed by a group of companies: Cloudscape (now part of Informix), Compaq, IBM, Informix, Oracle, Sybase and Sun Microsystems. Currently, work is ongoing to align this part of the standard to SQL-99, JDBC and Java 1.2, before it becomes an ISO/IEC standard. Once it becomes an ISO standard it will replace the current ANSI-only version. The other two parts of SQLJ will become ANSI-only standards later this year. They will not become part of the SQL standard, but will remain standalone. They will; however, be maintained by the ANSI X3H2 and ISO/JTC1/SC32/WG3 Database Language Committees.

Amendment to SQL-99: OLAP Functions

Currently, there is a lot of work going on to extend the OLAP functionality of SQL-99. Oracle, IBM, and Informix are leading the efforts. It is not desirable to have OLAP become a separate part of the standard. That is why it has amendment status. It will be combined with SQL-99 as soon as SQL-99 is republished. However, once it goes through the standards process it will be part of SQL-99. It is expected to become a standard at the same time MED is standardized. It should become part of the SQL standard in 2000 or 2001 and it will reference and be aligned with SQL-99.

Over time, other projects may begin and they too may become part of the future SQL standard. Having a project and a finished standard are two very different things.

Here is a list of the SQL Committee projects and the standards that they produced:

SQL0 Produced SQL-86

SQL1 Produced SQL-89

SQL2 Produced SQL-92

SQL3 produced SQL-99. The new project name has gone the way of the millennium with SQL-200x. If you really want to cite the standard, use ISO/IEC or the number and title. You will not go wrong and people will not be led astray.

SQL-99 is designed to be backward-compatible with older applications written according to the SQL-92 standard, so that no confusion results from adopting the new standard. Even though it is drastically different, the data model for the SQL3 standard supports applications written according to the SQL-92 standard without changing them. However, there are a number of features that are incompatible and can be found in Part 2: Foundation (SQL/Foundation), Annex E (informative), Incompatibilities with ISO/IEC 9075:1992 and ISO/IEC 9075-4:1996. This covers the base SQL-92 Standard and the SQL/PSM-96 Standard that has some small incompatibilities.

SQL-99 enhances the basic SQL-92 relational data model by including objects, row types, collections, and abstract data types, in addition to the basic data types supported by the relational model.

New data types introduced in the SQL-99 standard include Boolean, enumeration, extensions to character sets (character large objects—text), national character large objects—translations, binary large objects, row types, set and multi-set types, list, and abstract data types. These data types can be diversely combined in tables, routine parameters, joins, ADTs, objects, domain variables, and so forth.

SQL-99 relations need not be normalized. This breaks the long-lived normalization rules that guard against data redundancy. The redundancy can be presented as repeated groups of data and non-singular data types, such as embedded rows, embedded objects, or ADTs.

SQL-99 Framework

The SQL framework is a map that guides you to the various parts of the SQL-99 standard. The framework provides a repository of information and specifications shared by all parts of the standard, such as conventions and definitions. The SQL framework defines two major areas of the new standard—the SQL foundation and a series of independently specified packages—which are highlighted in the following sections. The framework also contains a section that deals with conformance, one of the most important sections of the new SQL-99 standard. Conformance is what a product must contain to claim confluence with the new standard. The minimum conformance must include the following:

- An SQL implementation should support Core SQL and at least one of the following:
    - The SQL-client module binding, as specified in ISO/IEC 9075-2, for at least one host language.
    - Embedded SQL, as specified in ISO/IEC 9075-2, for at least one host language.

This is taken directly from the standard.

Core SQL has taken the place of entry-level conformance in SQL-92. We will have to watch the vendors and see who will be first in Core SQL compliance. There is more than mere entry-level features in Core, and at the present time no vendor can claim Core compliance. It has been estimated that it will take two product cycles to add all the features needed for Core.

Without Core SQL conformance, no other part of SQL-99 can be implemented, and conformance claims can't be made. Core is the starting point for all SQL-99 implementations. The list of Core features can be found at the end of Part 2: Foundation (SQL/Foundation), Annex F (informative), SQL features, and Package Taxonomy, Table 31—SQL/Foundation feature taxonomy and definition for Core SQL.

The SQL-99 Foundation

This is the foundation of the new standard and includes changes to the SQL-92 relational model. The foundation includes descriptions of the new variable types, stored functions and stored procedures, triggers, user-defined tables, and new schema objects, among other elements discussed in the following sections.

- For the first time, triggers became part of the SQL standard. Many SQL database vendors have used these schema objects for quite some time now. They enhance the database's ability to respond to actions and events that affect the data stored in its tables.
- SQL now supports abstract data types, which are user-defined data types that exhibit some behavior and encapsulate internal structures. ADTs have public, private, and protected access characteristics.
- Arrays are now supported in SQL, unlike the SQL-92 standard that required you to use a "hack" to represent arrays.
- Row types are introduced in SQL-99, which allows you to specify fields within a table that are actually a collection of fields.

- More predicates were added to the SQL language, such as FOR ALL, FOR SOME, and SIMILAR TO.
- Views can now be updated in SQL-99, which was possible only after playing many tricks with the SQL-92 standard.
- The SQL foundation also included many enhancements to database security by introducing roles.
- Savepoints have become part of the standard, which makes writing SQL code to perform transactions much easier and more flexible.
- Recursion, a powerful feature of modern programming languages, has been added to the SQL language with the SQL3 standard.

These points are explained in more detail later in the chapter. But for now, let's discuss the other parts of the SQL framework, the module extensions.

Call Level Interface (CLI)

SQL Call Level Interface (SQL/CLI) is the set of language specifications used by DBMS vendors to enable direct SQL engine access through completely specified call routines. Microsoft, for example, has implemented SQL/CLI and calls it ODBC. For a detailed discussion of CLI, please read Chapter 21, "Call Level Interface."

SQL Persistent Stored Module (PSM)

The SQL persistent stored module is a collection of user-defined procedures and functions that can be called from within the SQL code or from other programming languages. These routines are grouped in modules that can exist inside or outside the database domain. The ones that exist inside the database domain are written in SQL; those that exist outside are written in many programming languages, including SQL, C, FORTRAN, PLI, Pascal, and COBOL.

For a detailed discussion of PSM, read Chapter 22, "Persistent Stored Modules."

SQL Bindings

SQL bindings allow a connection between SQL and other programming languages. With SQL bindings, programmers can embed SQL statements in code written in the programming languages of their choice. The SQL binding statement EXEC SQL is used to initiate the connection between the programming language and the database engine. With this statement, the programming language compiler knows to compile the statement that follows this keyword separately from the rest of the code because it is intended for use by the database engine.

With the `EXEC SQL` statement, developers can embed SQL statements in their code that change the data definition, such as creating new tables or altering existing ones. The statements can also manipulate the data in the tables by inserting new records and updating or deleting existing ones. SQL bindings also enable developers to execute SQL exceptions and warnings and define rights and privileges to database objects.

For detailed information on embedded SQL, read Chapter 17, "Embedded SQL."

SQL Temporal

SQL Temporal is a specification that extends the SQL temporal data types. These are the main data type extensions, according to this specification: As I mentioned earlier, this part of the SQL standard is still under development and may change considerably before it is published.

- `DATATIME` An extension of the `TIMESTAMP` standard data type.
- `INTERVAL` Expresses the duration of an event or action, such as the age of a person or the duration of a soccer game.
- `PERIOD` Includes two dates saved together, a start date and an end date. For example, writing this book started on May 15, 1999, and ended on July 15, 1999. The two dates are saved together as a `PERIOD` type.

These data types interact with each other. Their interactions led to the introduction of several new predicates. Assuming you have two temporal variables, `X` and `Y`, some of the predicates include the following:

- `X = Y` The two variables are equal. If they are `DATETIME`, they express equal data and time values. If they are `PERIOD`s, they express equal periods.
- `X MEETS Y` The end of the `X` variable is at the start of variable `Y`. For instance, the `PERIOD` value `May 15, 1999` to `July 15, 1999` meets the period of `July 15, 1999` to `August 1, 1999`.
- `X OVERLAPS Y` As the name of the predicate indicates, part of the two variables overlap. In the previous example, if `Y` were a period between July 1, 1999 and August 1, 1999, then `X` and `Y` overlap the period from July 1, 1999 to July 15, 1999.

- `X CONTAINS Y` In this special case of the `OVERLAP` predicate, `Y` is included completely within `X`. In the example, this happens if `Y` is a period such as June 1, 1999 to June 15, 1999.
- `X PRECEDES Y` As the name of the predicate implies, `X` finished before `Y` started.

Logical operations and date/time arithmetic are also specified by the SQL Temporal extensions.

SQL Object

The addition of new abstract data types makes it easier to model more complex objects and to increase the database's ability to meet expanded application data requirements. The SQL object component defines new data types that make it possible to treat data as objects, with full implementation of the object-oriented programming features of inheritance, encapsulation, and so forth. The SQL object component of the SQL-99 standard supports the following:

- Generalization and specialization hierarchies
- Single inheritance
- User-defined data types (UDTs)
- Specification of abstract data types
- Object identifiers, methods, inheritance, polymorphism, and encapsulation

These types of support make it possible for DBMSs to understand application-specific data types, increasing the database's ability to model complex objects and meet more of the application requirements.

The main change from the SQL-92 standard is the addition of the row object data type. A row object has a row identifier and can reference other row objects or be referenced by other row objects.

A more detailed discussion of the object-oriented features of SQL-99 follows later in this chapter.

SQL/Multimedia (MM) Components

SQL/MM is another set of standards that are not part of the SQL-99 standard, with full specifications for a discrete set of data management features to address the data processing needs of full-text, spatial, general-purpose, and still-image specifications and routines completely within the SQL language.

SQL/MM is a collection of modules and routines that became possible with the unique features that are aligned with the SQL-99 standard. Because UDT (or ADT) has been introduced to SQL, users can use the CLI specification to embed SQL code in their routines. The introduction of BLOB and CLOB data types and other features of SQL made it possible to develop these libraries that can be used by DBMS vendors who want to support multimedia in their database engine.

SQL/MM is not expected to be released with the SQL-99 standard; rather, it will follow it. The committees, JTC1/SC32/WG4 at the ISO/IEC level and the ANSI X3H2, responsible for developing SQL/MM, are working on developing libraries of abstract data types and their operations and functions that would suit multimedia purposes.

Effects of the SQL-99 Standard

The SQL-99 standard comes with many new features to enrich the SQL programming language. The new standard makes SQL a true programming language that can be used to build programs or libraries used by other programs written in different languages. SQL-99 took a different look at database models, particularly the relational model, and combined their strengths to come up with a uniquely powerful model. The object-oriented nature of the SQL-99 standard will influence the way applications are written.

Impact of SQL-99 on Database Models

SQL is no longer a simple language for defining, accessing, and managing tables consisting only of single-value columns of data. For the basic data model capabilities, the SQL-99 language more closely supports the independent logical file data model from the 1960s.

However, SQL-99 has gone beyond the capabilities of the independent logical file data model by incorporating features such as user-defined types, embedded programming language, and libraries of SQL-99-defined routines for areas such as full-text management and spatial data. The differences between these SQL-99 extensions and the relational data model are huge. In fact, the SQL-99 standard and its extensions completely deviate from the relational model.

The impact of SQL-99 on network and hierarchical data model DBMSs is significant. Network data model DBMSs have traditionally allowed complex data record structures with arrays, groups, repeating groups, and nested repeating groups. A unique characteristic of the SQL3 data model is that it now allows arrays. In addition, the elements of the array can be outward references to other data. Because the order of the elements in an SQL-99 array is maintained by the SQL-99 DBMS, the array, with its outward references, is essentially a *CODASYL* set (stands for *COnference on DAta SYstems Languages*). This is a dramatic departure from the relational data model.

Two of the only remaining and viable network DBMSs are IDMS by Computer Associates and Oracle DBMS (formerly the VAX DBMS from DEC). Both have had a SQL language interface for about 10 years. How Computer Associates plans to take advantage of the existing IDMS facilities with SQL-99 is not known; however, Computer Associates is a very active member of the X3H2 Committee. An important customer of Oracle's DBMS is Intel, who uses a C manufacturing package, formally from the recently sold Consilium, to manage computer chip manufacturing. It isn't known how the Oracle Corporation plans to take advantage of the existing facilities with SQL-99.

Of the few hierarchical DBMSs, System 2000 and IBM's IMS will likely not be affected at all. System 2000 is no longer being advanced by SAS, and IBM has a full implementation of DB2 on many different operating systems. The SQL/MED part of the standard, when it is released, will address the management of external data in the older type data stores.

SQL-99's impact on independent logical file DBMSs, such as Adabas, Focus, and Datacom/DB, is significant. These DBMSs already support many of the SQL-99 data model features. However, there are many SQL Core features that would be needed before they could claim conformance. This is very unlikely.

Simply stated, the SQL-99 language defines a unique data model. It contains the following:

- The ability to model CODASYL sets
- Many of the natural data-clustering features of the hierarchical data model
- Explicit many-to-many and inferential relationships, such as the independent logical file data model
- The unique ability to directly model recursive relationships

Therefore, it can only be said that the SQL-99 data model is unique. Clearly, it is not the relational data model, CODASYL network, hierarchical, or independent logical file data models. Simply, SQL-99 is a combination of data models.

Impact of SQL-99 on Database Applications

For the past 20 years, database designers and vendors have struggled with highly normalized databases that perform poorly. The only solution is to denormalize by collapsing hierarchies of non-redundant tables into a single flat table with replicated data. Although these highly redundant collapsed tables speed data reporting, they slow updating and become a significant risk for data integrity. That is because the data is highly disbursed and duplicated across these report-tuned denormalized database structures commonly known as *data warehouses*. For all these reasons, most organizations allow reporting only through online analytical processing (OLAP) systems, that is, from data warehouse databases. As mentioned earlier, much work is taking place to enrich the OLAP features of SQL-99.

As DBMS vendors implement SQL-99, the database design process will transform itself from designing third normal table designs and then denormalizing these tables for cost-effective reports to a set of database design activities similar to the ones commonly performed before the advent of the SQL standards. There will have to be a greater knowledge of the application's processing to take advantage of the natural data structure hierarchies now possible within SQL-99 tables.

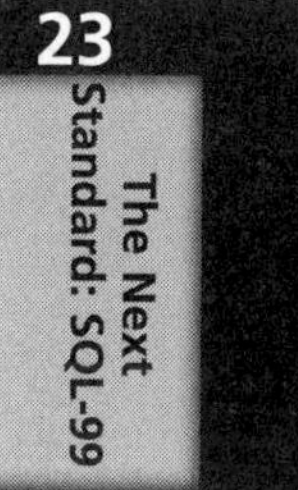

Although processing speeds will noticeably improve with SQL-99 conforming DBMSs, the effort and processing time required to accomplish database redesigns and reorganizations will dramatically increase.

In short, we are returning to the past—that is, adopting the data structures of the network and independent logical file DBMSs. We will see increased performance for well-designed and highly tuned databases, but we will also see the return of increased designer and analyst time for database design and redesign.

SQL-99 Features and Elements

After the previous overview of the SQL-99 standard, let's take a closer look at the SQL-99 foundation and discuss some of its features and elements.

Database Structure

The table (relation) is still the central unit in the database system, according to the SQL-99 standard. The big difference from the SQL-92 standard when it comes to tables is that tables don't have to follow the strict normal form rules in the new standard. A table still consists of a number of rows and columns. After a table is created and stored in the database, its name cannot be changed or duplicated.

Table columns are the attributes of the entity the table is representing. The column names should be unique within a table and cannot be changed or duplicated. Column names can, however, be duplicated among tables. In other words, two tables, `employee` and `customer`, can have the same column names (such as `fname` and `lname`) for first name and last name. However, the table name has to be used when referring to them with dot notation (`employee.fname` and `customer.fname`, for example). The column's data type determines a range or domain of possible values for it.

The principles of primary key, candidate key, and foreign key attributes still apply in SQL-99. A primary key can also be a composite made up of more than one column.

To create a table, you still need to use the `CREATE TABLE` statement. Listing 23.1 shows an example of creating the `employee` table.

LISTING 23.1 Creating the **`employee`** Table

```
CREATE TABLE employee
  (emp_no  INTEGER
     CONSTRAINT employee_emp_no_pf PRIMARY KEY,
   fname  VARCHAR(20)
     CONSTRAINT employee_fname_notnull NOT NULL,
   lname  VARCHAR(30)
     CONSTRAINT employee_lname_notnull NOT NULL,
    Address  VARCHAR(50),
    City     VARCHAR(30),
    State    VARCHAR(2),
    Zip     VARCHAR(10),
   dept_id  INTEGER,
   phone_no  CHAR(10),
   hire_date  DATETIME,
   emp-title  VARCHAR(50));
```

A table can still be submitted to a number of relational operations that allow retrieving records from it, inserting new records in it, and updating or deleting some of its existing records.

New Data Types

Several new data types have been introduced in SQL-99 that make SQL integration with other programming languages easier and more effective. The following sections list the new types supported by the SQL3 standard.

BOOLEAN

The BOOLEAN data type in SQL-99 is not the same as the logical operators in SQL-92. This type is a true Boolean and can have only two values: TRUE or FALSE.

As an example of a BOOLEAN type, let's re-create the employee table from Listing 23.1 to include a field that specifies whether the employee is a summer intern (see Listing 23.2).

LISTING 23.2 Using the BOOLEAN Data Type in the employee Table

```
CREATE TABLE employee
  (emp_no  INTEGER
     CONSTRAINT employee_emp_no_pf PRIMARY KEY,
   fname  VARCHAR(20)
     CONSTRAINT employee_fname_notnull NOT NULL,
   lname  VARCHAR(30)
     CONSTRAINT employee_lname_notnull NOT NULL,
    Address  VARCHAR(50),
    City    VARCHAR(30),
    State   VARCHAR(2),
    Zip    VARCHAR(10),
dept_id  INTEGER,
   phone_no  CHAR(10),
   hire_date  DATETIME,

   summer_intern BOOLEAN,
   emp-title  VARCHAR(50));
```

Using the new column in SQL statements is the same as in SQL-92. Listing 23.3 shows the BOOLEAN field being used in the WHERE clause in a SELECT statement.

LISTING 23.3 Using the BOOLEAN Field in a SELECT Statement

```
SELECT emp_id,
    fname,
    lname,
    address,
    city,
    state,
    phonr_no
FROM  employee
WERE  summer_intern = TRUE;
```

Binary Large Objects (BLOBS)

Binary large data objects hold binary data, such as pictures and multimedia signatures. In Listing 23.4, let's add a BLOB field to the employee table that will store the employee's photo.

LISTING 23.4 Using the BLOB Data Type in the employee Table

```
CREATE TABLE employee
  (emp_no  INTEGER
     CONSTRAINT employee_emp_no_pf PRIMARY KEY,
   fname  VARCHAR(20)
     CONSTRAINT employee_fname_notnull NOT NULL,
   lname  VARCHAR(30)
     CONSTRAINT employee_lname_notnull NOT NULL,
    Address  VARCHAR(50),
    City     VARCHAR(30),
    State    VARCHAR(2),
    Zip     VARCHAR(10),
   dept_id  INTEGER,
   phone_no  CHAR(10),
   hire_date  DATETIME,
   summer_intern BOOLEAN,

   emp_photo BLOB(2M),
   emp-title  VARCHAR(50));
```

In this listing, a field called emp_photo was added. The field's maximum length is 2MB.

With BLOB fields, you can do almost all the usual operations you perform on non-BLOB fields. You can, for example, concatenate BLOBs, get their length, and equate them with = and <> operators. However, you cannot do logical comparisons, such as greater than or less than, on them.

Character Large Objects (CLOBS)

This data type also holds large amounts of data that do not conform to the database structure. It can be used for a written report to be saved in the database—or an employee résumé. Listing 23.5 shows how a resume field with a maximum length of 200KB can be added to the employee table.

LISTING 23.5 Using the `CLOB` Data Type to Store Employee Résumés

```
CREATE TABLE employee
  (emp_no  INTEGER
     CONSTRAINT employee_emp_no_pf PRIMARY KEY,
   fname  VARCHAR(20)
     CONSTRAINT employee_fname_notnull NOT NULL,
   lname  VARCHAR(30)
     CONSTRAINT employee_lname_notnull NOT NULL,
    Address  VARCHAR(50),
    City    VARCHAR(30),
    State   VARCHAR(2),
    Zip    VARCHAR(10),
   dept_id  INTEGER,
   phone_no  CHAR(10),
   hire_date  DATETIME,
    summer_intern BOOLEAN,
    emp_photo BLOB(2M),
    emp_resume CLOB(200K),

   emp-title  VARCHAR(50));
```

The same rules that apply to `BLOB` apply to `CLOB` data types.

ROW Types

The `ROW` type identifies a structure within the database table definition. It is actually a table that acts as a nested table within the original table. This is the general syntax for creating a `ROW` type:

```
<row type> ::=
  ROW <row type body>
```

If you have the following

```
<row type body> ::=
  (<field definition> [{, field definition}...])
```

and

```
<field definition> ::=
  <field name> {<data type> ¦ <domain name>}
  [collate clause]
```

then this is the field name:

```
<field name> ::= <identifier>
```

```
<domain name> ::= <schema qualified name>
```

Listing 23.5 uses the `employee` table again and converts the address information into a `ROW` type.

LISTING 23.5 Using the **ROW** Type to Store Employee Address Information

```
CREATE TABLE employee
  (emp_no  INTEGER
     CONSTRAINT employee_emp_no_pf PRIMARY KEY,
   fname  VARCHAR(20)
     CONSTRAINT employee_fname_notnull NOT NULL,
   lname  VARCHAR(30)
     CONSTRAINT employee_lname_notnull NOT NULL,
    address  ROW(,
            address  VARCHAR(30),
            City    VARCHAR(30),
            State   VARCHAR(2),
            Zip    VARCHAR(10)
           ),
   dept_id  INTEGER,
   phone_no  CHAR(10),
   hire_date  DATETIME,
    summer_intern BOOLEAN,
    emp_photo BLOB(2M),
    emp_resume CLOB(200K),
   emp-title  VARCHAR(50));
```

`ROW` types can also be used in views in much the same way you use them in tables.

You can define a `ROW` type separately, give it a name, and use it later in the table creation statement. Listing 23.6 shows an example of this method.

LISTING 23.6 Creating a Named **ROW** Type and Then Using It to Create the **employee** Table

```
CREATE ROW TYPE address_type (
            address  VARCHAR(30),
            City    VARCHAR(30),
            State   VARCHAR(2),
            Zip    VARCHAR(10)
           );
/*use the ROW type just created in the table definition. */
CREATE TABLE employee
  (emp_no  INTEGER
```

LISTING 23.6 CONTINUED

```
    CONSTRAINT employee_emp_no_pf PRIMARY KEY,
  fname  VARCHAR(20)
    CONSTRAINT employee_fname_notnull NOT NULL,
  lname  VARCHAR(30)
    CONSTRAINT employee_lname_notnull NOT NULL,
   address  address_type,
  dept_id  INTEGER,
  phone_no  CHAR(10),
  hire_date  DATETIME,
   summer_intern BOOLEAN,
   emp_photo BLOB(2M),
   emp_resume CLOB(200K),
  emp-title  VARCHAR(50));
```

Array Types

Arrays are supported and specified as collection types in SQL-99. They define a collection of columns within an ARRAY field. The data types of these columns can be any SQL3-supported data type, including ROW types. For example, an employee might have more than one phone number or more than one email address. Listing 23.7 shows how you can use up to three phone numbers and three email addresses. To do this, you just need to add the keyword ARRAY with the number of elements it will have.

LISTING 23.7 Using Arrays to Hold Multiple Phone Numbers

```
CREATE TABLE employee
 (emp_no  INTEGER
    CONSTRAINT employee_emp_no_pf PRIMARY KEY,
  fname  VARCHAR(20)
    CONSTRAINT employee_fname_notnull NOT NULL,
  lname  VARCHAR(30)
    CONSTRAINT employee_lname_notnull NOT NULL,
   address  address_type,
  dept_id  INTEGER,
  phone_no  CHAR(10) ARRAY(3),
   email   VARCHAR(30) ARRAY(3),
  hire_date  DATETIME,
   summer_intern BOOLEAN,
   emp_photo BLOB(2M),
   emp_resume CLOB(200K),
  emp-title  VARCHAR(50));
```

Arrays indicate repeating groups of data in the table or data structure they are used in. This is contradictory to the normalization rules, which call for eliminating such repeating groups of data.

Abstract Data Types (ADTs)

ADTs are one of the most significant changes to the SQL standard. They are the same as user-defined data types. As the name implies, these types are complex structures defined by users to satisfy some storage needs they have. Listing 23.8 is an example of creating a type that holds some customer representative information.

LISTING 23.8 Example of Creating a User-Defined Type

```
CREATE TYPE customer_representative(
      rep_name    VARCHAR(30),
      rep_title   VARCHAR(30),
      rep_address address_type,
      rep_phone   VARCHAR(15) ARRAY(3),
      rep_photo   BLOB);
```

Notice from Listing 23.8 how flexible a UDT can be. It can have almost any type supported by SQL, in addition to other UDTs as part of its definition. Arrays can also be used with the UDT definition to indicate repeating groups of columns.

ADTs are completely encapsulated, but exhibit an interface through ADT functions. You can access ADTs only through this interface. The attributes (fields) in the ADT have similar characteristics to those of tables. They have to be uniquely named within the ADT, so they cannot be repeated.

Because of the importance of these structures, ADT is discussed in more detail later in this chapter in "Abstract Data Types in SQL-99."

Distinct Types

Distinct types are a specialization of the basic data types and represent the most basic form of a user-defined data type. This is the syntax for these structures:

```
<distinct type definition> ::=
  CREATE DISTINCT TYPE <distinct type name>
    AS <data type>
    [<case to distinct>] [<case to source>]
```

For example, you can declare the following two data types representing U.S. dollars and Canadian dollars and use them in creating two different sales tables. Listing 23.9 shows how to do this.

LISTING 23.9 Example of Using Distinct Types

```
/* The first type */
CREATE DISTINCT TYPE US_dollar AS
    DECIMAL(8,2);

/* the second type */
CREATE DISTINCT TYPE CA_dollar AS
    DECIMAL(8,2);

/* Create the U.S. sales table */
CREATE TABLE US_sales(
    cust_id   INTEGER,
    emp_id    INTEGER,
    order_num INTEGER,
    amount    US_dollar
);

/* Create the Canadian sales table */
CREATE TABLE CA_sales(
    cust_id   INTEGER,
    emp_id    INTEGER,
    order_num INTEGER,
    amount    CA_dollar
);
```


In this example, you have two data types that represent the same basic type (currency or decimal). This is a case of renaming a basic data type in two different ways. These two distinct types are used in creating two different sales tables and will never be equivalent.

SET Data Type

This data type groups the instances of related data types in a data structure called SET. For instance, you could use a SET type to group the phone numbers of an employee or a customer in one single unit.

LIST Data Type

This is similar to the SET data type, except that the items in the list are ordered according to a particular field. For example, a list of employees in a department can be created and ordered by employee name.

`MULTILIST` Data Type

This is another collection data type. It groups a set of records regardless of whether some duplicates exist in the set.

Subtables and Supertables

Subtables and supertables are data structures used in SQL3 to represent collection hierarchies. The following rules apply when dealing with such structures:

- The supertable is the top-most level of the hierarchy.
- A subtable should inherit the same attributes (fields) from the supertable.
- If the names of the fields in the subtable are different, they should be renamed.
- A subtable's rows correspond to only one record of the supertable.
- A row in the subtable must have elements from the supertable, but not the other way around.
- Deletes and updates are cascaded from the supertable to the subtable(s) underneath it. If a record is deleted in a supertable, the corresponding records in the subtable are also deleted to maintain database consistency and correctness.

As an example, Listing 23.10 defines a table called `continents` that holds information about the world's continents and serves as a supertable for tables called `America`, `Asia`, `Europe`, `Africa`, and so forth.

LISTING 23.10 Creating the `continent` Table

```
CREATE TABLE continent(
  Name       VARCHAR(15),
  Surface_Area  INTEGER,
  Population INTEGER);
```

Listing 23.11 then creates subtables composed from the elements in the supertable.

LISTING 23.11 Creating the Subtables

```
CREATE TABLE America UNDER continent (
    Countries  varchar(30)  ARRAY(40));

CREATE TABLE Europe UNDER continent(
    Countries  varchar(30)  ARRAY(50));

CREATE TABLE Asia UNDER continent(
```

LISTING 23.11 CONTINUED

```
    Countries  varchar(30)  ARRAY(80));

CREATE TABLE Africa UNDER continent(
    Countries  varchar(30)  ARRAY(50));
```

The keyword `UNDER` specifies that the created table is composed of the supertable with some additional information. Also, you can add attributes to the subtable; as shown in the listing, the `countries` field was added as an array of `VARCHAR` type.

Abstract Data Types in SQL-99

As defined previously, ADTs are flexible data structures that allow the database developer to map many attributes of an entity to one single structure that encapsulates information about the entity. The abstract data type defines the contents of the entities and can be accessed only through the ADT functions.

The SQL-99 standard indicates that ADTs have the same syntax as user-defined data types. The syntax of the UDT is as follows:

```
<type predicate item> ::=
  <expression type>
  ¦TYPE <data type>

<expression type> ::=
  TYPE(<value expression>)

<data type> ::=
  <predefined type>
  ¦<row type>
  ¦<user-defined data type>
  ¦<collection type>

<user-defined data type> ::=
  <abstract data type>
  ¦<distinct type name>

<abstract data type> ::=
  <abstract data type name>

<abstract data type name> ::=
  <local or schema-qualified name>
```

To create a data type, you can issue a statement like this one:

```
CREATE TYPE type_name
  <ADT type_name body>
```

The body of the ADT specifies the stored information, routines providing the desired behavior, operators, ordering, and so on.

The ADT supplies an interface to the outside world, allowing access to its stored information only through this interface. The interface is a collection of functions and procedures that restricts access according to how the ADT's designer sets it up.

Attributes inside the ADT are declared public, private, or protected by using the keywords `PUBLIC`, `PRIVATE`, or `PROTECTED`. Public attributes can be seen and accessed by those who have access rights to the ADT. Private attributes can be accessed only from within the ADT, not from the outside. Protected attributes can be seen and accessed within the ADT and its subtypes.

Listing 23.12 creates an ADT called `address` and shows that every attribute will have two functions by default: `observer` and `mutator`.

LISTING 23.12 Creating the `address` ADT

```
CREATE ROW TYPE address_type (
    Street   VARCHAR(30),
    City     VARCHAR(30),
    State    VARCHAR(2),
    Zip     VARCHAR(10)
    );

FUNCTION street (address) RETURNS VARCHAR(30)
FUNCTION street (address, VARCHAR(30)) RETURNS address

FUNCTION city (address) RETURNS VARCHAR(30)
FUNCTION city (address, VARCHAR(30)) RETURNS city

FUNCTION street (state) RETURNS VARCHAR(2)
FUNCTION street (state, VARCHAR(2)) RETURNS state

FUNCTION street (zip) RETURNS VARCHAR(10)
FUNCTION street (zip, VARCHAR(10)) RETURNS zip
```

The `observer`function returns the value of the attribute in the ADT, and the mutatorfunction allows you to change this value.

For example, if the address is `123 main st.` , the `observer` function returns this value:

```
x = street(address)
```

The `mutator` function allows you change it as follows:

```
Y = street(address, '345 division ave.')
```

ADT Attributes

ADT attributes have a name and data type. The name has to be a valid name, not a reserved keyword, such as `INSERT` or `SELECT`. Also, the data type for the attribute can be any valid basic SQL data type or extended data type, such as another ADT. As an example, a data type called `person` can use the `address` ADT created previously as the data type for its `p_address` attribute, as shown in Listing 23.13.

LISTING 23.13 Creating the `person` ADT

```
/*Make sure the address ADT is created first*/
CREATE ROW TYPE address_type (
    Street   VARCHAR(30),
    City    VARCHAR(30),
    State   VARCHAR(2),
    Zip    VARCHAR(10)
    );

/*Create the person ADT*/
CREATE TYPE person (
      P_name    VARCHAR(30),
      p_title  VARCHAR(30),
      p_address address_type,
      p_phone  VARCHAR(15) ARRAY(3),
      p_sex   Char(1),
      p_birth_date date,
      p_photo  BLOB);
```

ADT attributes can be either stored or virtual attributes, depending on how the value of the attribute is represented and determined. Stored attributes are represented by the data stored within the attribute associated with the ADT instance. Each ADT instance is associated with a possible value from the possible collection of values. Virtual attributes, on the other hand, derive their values from the execution of a user-defined function, not from data stored in the ADT. As an example, consider the ADT called `rental` in Listing 23.14.

LISTING 23.14 Creating the `rental` ADT

```
CREATE TYPE rental (
  rental_id      INTEGER,
  rental_type     VARCHAR(20),
  start_date     DATE,
  end_date     DATE,
  rental_duration  INTEGER,
  rental_person   person,
);
```

In this example, the `rental_duration` attribute is likely to be a calculated field. A user-defined function can be used to find its value based on the `start_date` and `end_date` values. The function might look like Listing 23.15.

LISTING 23.15 Example of Using a Virtual Attribute

```
PUBLIC FUNCTION rental_duration(x rental) RETURNS INTEGER
  BEGIN
    DECLARE :x rental;
    DECLARE :r INTEGER;
      SET :r = end_date(x) - start_date(x);
RETURN r;
  END;
END FUNCTION
```

Therefore, the `rental_duration` attribute is a virtual attribute, but other attributes, such as `start_date` and `end_date`, are stored attributes.

ADT Creation and Initialization

You have already seen many examples of creating ADTs. Now you'll see how these ADTs can be initialized so they can do their job.

Initializing an ADT requires specifying a constructor function for the ADT type. This constructor has the following syntax:

```
CONSTRUCTOR FUNCTION <adt name>(optional parameter list) RETURNS <adt type>
  <function declarations>
  <body of constructor>
```

In the `address` ADT, for example, the constructor function used to initialize the ADT has the form shown in Listing 23.16.

LISTING 23.16 Constructor Function to Initialize an Empty Instance of the `address` ADT

```
CONSTRUCTOR FUNCTION address() RETURNS address
  DECLARE :a adress
  BEGIN
    NEW :a;
    SET :a.street = NULL;
    SET :a.city = NULL;
    SET :a.state = NULL;
    SET :a.zip = NULL;
    RETURN :a;
  END;
END FUNCTION
```

If you want to assign values to the ADT attributes, you might want to consider writing the constructor function as shown in Listing 23.17.

LISTING 23.17 A Constructor That Can Be Used to Set Values of the `address` ADT's Attributes

```
CONSTRUCTOR FUNCTION address
  (s VARCHAR(30),
   c VARCHAR(30),
   st VARCHAR(2),
   z VARCHAR(10)) RETURNS address
  DECLARE :a adress
  BEGIN
    NEW :a;
    SET :a.street = s;
    SET :a.city = c;
    SET :a.state = st;
    SET :a.zip = z;
    RETURN :a;
  END;
END FUNCTION
```


This example shows how you can parameterize the constructor function to assign values to the ADT attributes through the function's parameters. If you don't pass value for these parameters, the SQL defaults for the appropriate data type are used.

To remove an instance of an ADT from the database, you can use destructor functions. The general syntax for these functions is as follows:

```
DESTRUCTOR FUNCTION <adt name> (:p parameter) RETURNS <adt name>
```

```
  BEGIN
    garbage collection work
    DESTROY :p;
    RETURN :p;
  END;
END FUNCTION
```

For the address ADT example, the destructor function looks like the code in Listing 23.18.

LISTING 23.18 A Destructor Removes an **address** ADT Instance from the Database

```
DESTRUCTOR FUNCTION clear_address (:a address) RETURNS address
  BEGIN
    DESTROY :a;
    RETURN :a;
  END;
END FUNCTION
```

Accessing ADT Attributes

You have already seen that you can use observer and mutator functions to access an ADT's attributes. You can also use dot notation, which is actually a way to invoke the observer and mutator functions without explicitly calling them, by syntactically referring to the desired attributes. For example, the code in Listing 23.19 invokes the observer function of the address ADT.

LISTING 23.19 Using Dot Notation to Access ADT Attributes

```
/*Make sure the address ADT is created first*/
CREATE ROW TYPE address_type (
    Street   VARCHAR(30),
    City    VARCHAR(30),
    State   VARCHAR(2),
    Zip    VARCHAR(10)
    );

/*Use dot notation to get the value of the street attribute*/
BEGIN
 DECLARE a address;
   DECLARE s VARCHAR(30);
   SET s = a..street;
END;
```

ADT Manipulation

Now that you have learned about ADTs and how to incorporate them into your database table design, you need to find out how to manipulate them while they are stored in the database. Mainly, you need to know how to treat these ADTs in `SELECT`, `INSERT`, `UPDATE`, and `DELETE` operations. This section sheds some light on how to do this.

SELECT Statement

This is the general syntax for the `SELECT` statement:

```
SELECT (columns, attributes, ADTs, etc.)
FROM table(s)
WHERE condition statement
```

For example, in the `employee` ADT, you can issue the `SELECT` statement shown in Listing 23.20 to select from the `employee` table.

LISTING 23.20 Selecting from a Table with ADT Attributes

```
/*Let's create the employee table in case it does not exist*/
CREATE TABLE employee
  (emp_no  INTEGER
     CONSTRAINT employee_emp_no_pf PRIMARY KEY,
   fname  VARCHAR(20)
     CONSTRAINT employee_fname_notnull NOT NULL,
   lname  VARCHAR(30)
     CONSTRAINT employee_lname_notnull NOT NULL,
    address  address,
   dept_id  INTEGER,
   phone_no  CHAR(10) ARRAY(3),
    email   VARCHAR(30) ARRAY(3),
   hire_date  DATETIME,
    emp_salary  DECIMAL(8,2),
    summer_intern BOOLEAN,
    emp_photo BLOB(2M),
    emp_resume CLOB(200K),
   emp-title  VARCHAR(50)
);

/* issue the SELECT statement:
SELECT *
FROM  employee
WHERE employee..emp_salary > 99999;
```

The table fields returned as a result include emp_no, fname, lname, address, and so forth. The address field is returned as one unit—for instance, 123 Main St. Anytown, MI 48084 .

To return individual components of the address ADT, you need to write:

```
SELECT address..street,
    address..city,
    address..state,
    address..zip,
FROM employee
WHERE employee..salary > 99999;
```

You can also order by the zip code, for instance, by adding the clause ORDER BY address..zip; .

UPDATE Operator

A syntax similar to that used with the SELECT statement allows you to update attributes within the ADT. For example, assuming an employee moved to a different city in the same state, you need to update the street and city attributes for that employee's address ADT field. Listing 23.21 shows how you can do so.

LISTING 23.21 Updating Attributes Within the address ADT

```
UPDATE employee
SET address..street = street('242 Washigton Blvd.');

UPDATE employee
SET address..city = city('Royal Oak');

UPDATE employee
SET address..zip = city('48237');
```

INSERT Operator

The INSERT statement has been improved to support the added data types in the SQL3 standard, especially ADTs. With ADT types, the INSERT statement needs to use the constructor functions to create an instance of the ADT before the record can be inserted. The example in Listing 23.22 illustrates how this is done.

LISTING 23.22 Inserting Records with ADT Types

```
INSERT INTO employee
VALUES(emp_no(100),
    fname('John'),
```

LISTING 23.22 CONTINUED

```
    lname('Doe'),
    address(street('123 Main St.'),
        city('Oak Ridge'),
        state('MI'),
        zip('48023')),
    dept_id(12),
    phone_no('313-313-3323'),
    email('jdoe@email.com'),
    hire_date('Jun-01-98'),
    summer_intern(FALSE),
    emp_photo(NULL),
    emp_resume(NULL),
    emp_title('Project Manager')
);
```

Query Expressions and Joins

When a SELECTstatement has to span multiple tables over joins, you can still follow the general rules you learned in the SQL-92 standard. For example, if you want to find out the employee name, address, and department name, you can write the code shown in Listing 23.23, assuming you have a department table created.

LISTING 23.23 Selecting from Multiple Tables with ADT

```
SELECT emp_fname || ' ' || emp_lname AS name,
    address,
    department_name
FROM  employee,
    Department
WHERE department.department_id = employee.dept_id
ORDER BY department_name;
```

Summary

This chapter has barely scratched the surface when it comes to representing the ins and outs of the new SQL-99 standard. The chapter started with an overview of the standard, discussing its foundation and other parts of the standard. Next, I covered the foreseeable impact the new standard will have on existing database system models and database applications. You also learned about the new features in the SQL-99 foundation and Core SQL, including data types and table structures, among other things. Finally, you explored the important abstract data types (ADTs) in more detail.

CHAPTER 24

Oracle SQL

In This Chapter

The Oracle Database Server is the most popular piece of database software in the business world today. Oracle implemented the SQL-92 specification into its database engine and has extended the command set to add much more functionality than the specification offers. This chapter looks at those enhancements as well as Oracle's command-line SQL interface: SQL*Plus.

Extended Data Types, Operators, and Functions

Let's start off with a look at what has been done in the area of data types, operators, and database function calls. Oracle has implemented quite a few of each to add functionality to the database and to support object-oriented structures, which are new for Oracle version 8.

Extended Data Types

This section covers the data types Oracle has added to the standard SQL-92 data types.

DATE

The `DATE` data type stores exactly what its name implies: date information. The `DATE` data type contains values for `Century`, `Year`, `Month`, `Day`, `Hour`, `Minute`, and `Second`.

Although you can store date information as `CHAR` and `NUMBER` typed values, you need to convert that information to a `DATE` type before the date can be used with the Oracle date functions. To do this, you use the `TO_DATE` function, explained in the "Extended Functions" section later in this chapter.

The format of the date itself within the `DATE` data type is governed by the `init.ora` parameter `NLS_DATE_FORMAT`. The default format is `'DD-MON-YY'`, which includes a two-digit day of month (`DD`), a three-letter abbreviation for the name of the month (`MON`), and a two-digit year (`YY`).

> **Tip**
>
> When using date values, try to make it a habit to use the full date and time. If you don't, keep in mind that if you specify a `DATE` value that contains the date information but no time of day information, then Oracle fills in the void with the time 12:00 midnight. If you specify a time without a date, then Oracle fills in the date as the first day of the current month (not the current day, as you would expect).

NUMBER

The NUMBER data type is used to store numeric values. It can handle various types of numeric values, including positive and negative integers, floating-point numbers, fixed-point numbers, and, of course, zero. For those readers who are developers and were expecting to see numeric types such as `int`, `float`, and `long`, the NUMBER data type handles all those kinds of numeric values.

Because all numeric values are read in as floating point, the definition of the NUMBER determines how the numeric information is stored. For example, to store an integer value, define your numeric value like this:

```
NUMBER(p)
```

In this definition, p is the number of digits (precision) that the NUMBER can store.

To store monetary values, specify both the precision and scale. Scale is defined as the number of digits to the right of the decimal sign, as shown here:

```
NUMBER(p,2)
```

Finally, if you define a NUMBER with neither the precision nor scale, the default is to store it as a floating-point number with a precision of 38 (the highest it can go).

If you make a mistake and your input data is larger than you allowed for, one of two things happen. If the extra data is to the right of the decimal point, it is truncated and rounded off. If the integer portion of the value is too big, Oracle returns an error.

VARCHAR2

VARCHAR2 is basically an extension of the standard character string data type CHAR. This new and improved version differs from CHAR in the following ways:

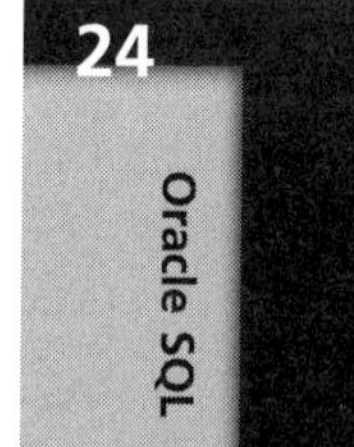

- VARCHAR2 data values are not blank-padded.
- VARCHAR2 has a maximum length of 4,000 characters; CHAR has a maximum length of 2,000 characters.

Using VARCHAR2 instead of CHAR has advantages, other than the obvious larger storage capacity. Because VARCHAR2 is not blank-padded for the string values that are not at the maximum length, you have more space savings in your data blocks, so you require less disk space to hold the same data.

Note

The definition and behavior of the VARCHAR2 data type is exactly the same as the current ANSI standard data type VARCHAR. Oracle recommends that you use VARCHAR2 for variable-length character data as a protection against a potential change in the ANSI standard for VARCHAR.

LONG

The LONG data type is a close relative to VARCHAR2. LONG columns store variable-length character strings, not long integers as you might think, but they do not have the 4,000-character limitation that VARCHAR2 has.

LONG data can be up to 2GB in length. This data, like VARCHAR2, is not blank-padded on the right. Oracle has placed the following restrictions on the use of the LONG data type:

No more than one LONG column in any given database table.

You cannot place an index on a LONG column or specify a LONG column in any integrity constraints.

Stored functions cannot return a LONG value.

In SQL SELECT statements, you cannot specify LONG columns in WHERE, GROUP BY, ORDER BY, or CONNECT BY clauses or by using the DISTINCT operator.

RAW and LONGRAW

The RAW data type is used to store information in a binary format, such as multimedia data (video or audio), documents processed with an optical scanner, or any other data that is neither character nor number based.

RAW data differs from character data in that RAW data is not converted by the IMPORT utility when you move the RAW data between systems that use different NLS_LANGUAGE values. That's because the data is binary and the Oracle database has no knowledge of what the data actually is.

RAW data columns can be up to 2,000 characters in length.

LONGRAW is the big brother of the RAW data type. It has all the same features of RAW, but LONGRAW data can be up to 2GB in length.

Both RAW and LONGRAW data are stored in the database as binary (hexadecimal) data; however, you cannot place an index on a column defined as LONGRAW.

ROWID

A ROWID is a unique address that points to a particular row in a database table. In Oracle 7, you can get the ROWID for table data by accessing the column of the table named ROWID. The data in the ROWID column is of type ROWID.

In Oracle 8, the ROWID column has been enhanced to support Oracle's partitioning option. In Oracle8, extended ROWID information can be accessed by calling the stored functions in the DBMS_ROWID package supplied with the database.

LOBS

LOBs (Large Objects), new in Oracle version 8, are intended to be used for storing binary and character data. Previously, the RAW and LONGRAW data types were used. The LOB types have advantages over their RAW counterparts, and I will discuss these as I describe each LOB data type.

All LOB data types share the following major characteristics that differentiate them from RAW:

- LOBs can be attributes in an Oracle 8 object.
- When you access a LOB, a locator is returned, not the actual data.
- In most cases, LOBs can be up to 4GB.
- You can declare more than one LOB column in a single table.
- You can use the SELECT command on LOG objects and attributes.

Let's take a quick look at the individual LOB types.

BLOB stands for Binary Large Object. BLOB data has the same characteristics as RAW data. Multimedia data, scanned images, and such that Oracle does not know the layout of can be stored in the database by using BLOBs. BLOBs have advantages over the RAW and LONGRAW types in that BLOBs can be up to 4GB, but LONGRAW can extend only to 2GB. As mentioned, BLOB data can be accessed via SQL, the DBMS_LOB database package, or the OCI interface used by software developers.

CLOB stands for Character Large Object. You store large objects of single-byte character data in a CLOB. This does not include the multi-byte national character sets.

For multi-byte national character sets, you use NCLOB. They must be fixed; with multi-byte character sets, variable-length character sets are not supported.

The last LOB data type covered here is BFILE. The BFILE data type is an *external* LOB data type. In the Oracle database, the BFILE actually points to an external file, residing on a disk. A pointer to the file is stored within the database. You cannot modify the data in a BFILE, but you can have read-only access through the OCI interface and the DBMS_LOB package.

Extended Operators

Next on the list are operators. Oracle added six additional operators to the ones in SQL-92. Oracle also extended some already existing operators.

Character Concatenation Operator

To concatenate character data, use the concatenation operator, represented by two vertical bars (¦¦). The following sample query shows that the text, `Employee #`, is prepended to the value `EMPNO`, and the text, `Name`, is prepended to the value for `ENAME`:

```
SQL> select 'Employee # ' ¦¦ EMPNO ¦¦ '  Name : ' ¦¦ ENAME
 2 ''Attendance List'' FROM EMP;
```

Take a look at the output of the sample query:

```
Attendance List
----------------------------------------------------------------------
Employee # 7369  Name : SMITH
Employee # 7499  Name : ALLEN
Employee # 7521  Name : WARD
Employee # 7566  Name : JONES
Employee # 7654  Name : MARTIN
Employee # 7698  Name : BLAKE
Employee # 7782  Name : CLARK
Employee # 7788  Name : SCOTT
Employee # 7839  Name : KING
Employee # 7844  Name : TURNER
Employee # 7876  Name : ADAMS
```

The maximum length of the concatenated data follows with the data type of the information. Because `ENAME` is of type `VARCHAR2`, the maximum length for this concatenated string is 4,000 characters.

Comparison Operators

There are three comparison operators (all for inequality) available in Oracle that are extensions of SQL-92:

```
!=  ^=  ¬=
```

These operators are available for platforms that do not support the standard SQL-92 inequality operator. The following four SQL queries all produce the same result:

```
SQL> SELECT ENAME, SAL FROM EMP WHERE SAL <> 1300;
SQL> SELECT ENAME, SAL FROM EMP WHERE SAL != 1300;
```

```
SQL> SELECT ENAME, SAL FROM EMP WHERE SAL ^= 1300;
SQL> SELECT ENAME, SAL FROM EMP WHERE SAL ¬ = 1300;
```

MINUS Set Operator

The MINUS operator is placed between two queries, with the result being that the rows are returned by the first query but not by both queries.

As an example, take a look at this sample statement:

```
SQL> SELECT ENAME, SAL, JOB FROM EMP
 2 WHERE SAL > 2000
 3 MINUS
 4 SELECT ENAME, SAL, JOB FROM EMP
 5 WHERE JOB = 'MANAGER';
ENAME      SAL        JOB
---------- ---------- ---------
FORD       3000       ANALYST
KING       5000       PRESIDENT
SCOTT      3000       ANALYST
```

This query returns all employees with a salary higher than $2,000 who are not managers. The MINUS operator is best used with two separate tables that have the same type data. This way you can get the rows that are in one table but not both.

INTERSECT Set Operator

The INTERSECT operator is sort of an inverse of the MINUS operator. You use it to return the rows that appear in both queries. Let's use the same example as before, but change the MINUS operator to INTERSECT:

```
SQL>  SELECT ENAME, SAL, JOB FROM EMP
 2 WHERE SAL > 2000
 3 INTERSECT
 4 SELECT ENAME, SAL, JOB FROM EMP
 5 WHERE JOB = 'MANAGER'

ENAME      SAL        JOB
---------- ---------- ---------
BLAKE      2850       MANAGER
CLARK      2450       MANAGER
JONES      2975       MANAGER
```

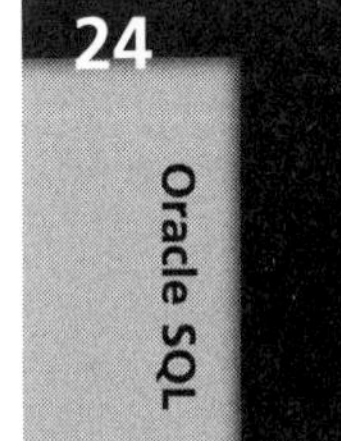

This query returns all the managers with a salary higher than $2,000.

Outer Join Operator

The outer join operator is represented by the plus sign (+). Using an outer join extends the results of a query by including rows in which no data was found in a column being selected. This operation is useful in returning rows where the rows being read in have `NULL` columns.

These rows normally are never returned by the query because the null field never meets the query's criteria. Take a look at the following example using the `EMP` and `DEPT` tables:

```
SQL> SELECT ENAME, JOB, DNAME
     FROM EMP, DEPT
     WHERE EMP.DEPTNO (+) = DEPT.DEPTNO
       AND JOB (+) = 'PRESIDENT';
```

This example causes the query to return all the department names, even though there are no employees working in those departments with the job title President. The output of this query confirms that:

```
ENAME      JOB       DNAME
---------- --------- --------------
KING       PRESIDENT ACCOUNTING
           RESEARCH
           SALES
           OPERATIONS
```

`PRIOR` Operator

The `PRIOR` operator is used when creating tree-structured queries. You use the `PRIOR` operator in the `CONNECT BY` clause to define the relationship between the parent and child rows. In the following example, the `PRIOR` operator is used to define this relationship:

```
CONNECT BY PRIOR EMP = MGR
```

Extended Functions

The SQL-92 standard provides for only about a half-dozen functions. Oracle had added many others, such as number functions, character functions, and date functions. The next few sections of this chapter describe them.

Number Functions

The *number* functions are the SQL functions that process numeric input and return numeric values. They are the typical math functions you find on a calculator or in a compiled programming language. All functions return a numeric result. Table 24.1 lists these functions.

TABLE 24.1 Oracle SQL Number Functions

Function Name	*Input Values*	*Description*
ABS	1	Returns the *absolute value* of the input value.
ACOS	1	Returns the *arc cosine* of the input value, in radians.
ASIN	1	Returns the *arc sine* of the input value, in radians.
ATAN	1	Returns the *arc tangent* of the input value, in radians.
ATAN2	2	Returns the *arc tangent* of the two values, in radians.
CEIL	1	Returns the *smallest integer* that is greater than or equal to the input.
COS	1	Returns the *cosine* of the input value, in radians.
COSH	1	Returns the *hyperbolic cosine* of the input value.
EXP	1	Returns *e* raised to the power specified by the input value.
FLOOR	1	Returns the *largest integer* that is less than or equal to the input value.
LN	1	Returns the *natural logarithm* of the input value
LOG	2	Returns the *logarithm* where the first value is the base, the second is *n*.
MOD	2	Returns the *remainder* of the first value divided by the second.
POWER	2	Returns the first value *raised to the power* specified in the second.
ROUND	1 or 2	Returns the first value *rounded* to the nearest integer, or to the number of decimal places specified in the second value.
SIGN	1	Returns 1 if the input value is positive, -1 if negative, and 0 if it is zero.
SIN	1	Returns the *sine* of the input value, in radians.
SINH	1	Returns the *hyperbolic sine* of the input value.
SQRT	1	Returns the *square root* of the input value.
TAN	1	Returns the *tangent* of the input value, in radians.
TRUNC	2	Returns the first value *truncated* by the number of digits in the second value.

Let's use the DUAL pseudotable to show a couple of examples of how these functions work:

Absolute Value:

```
SQL> SELECT ABS(-12.5) ''ABS()'' FROM DUAL;
```

```
   ABS()
----------
      12.5
```

Ceiling:

```
SQL> SELECT CEIL(12.5) ''CEIL'' FROM DUAL;

   CEIL
----------
        13
```

Cosine:

```
SQL> SELECT COS(45) ''COS()'' FROM DUAL;

   COS()
----------
.525321989
```

Power:

```
SQL> SELECT POWER(20,3) ''POWER'' FROM DUAL;

   POWER
----------
      8000
```

Rounding:

```
SQL> SELECT ROUND(123.4567,2) ''ROUND'' FROM DUAL;

   ROUND
----------
    123.46
```

Sign:

```
SQL> SELECT SIGN(100) FROM DUAL;

 SIGN(100)
----------
         1
```

Character Functions

Oracle has a vast range of functions that process character input and character strings. There are functions to change case, trim or pad strings, concatenate, and return specific parts of the input string. Table 24.2 lists the Oracle functions that process character input.

TABLE 24.2 Oracle SQL Character Functions

Name	Input Values	Return Type	Description
ASCII	1	NUMBER	Returns the *ASCII value* of the passed in character.
CHR	1	CHAR	Returns the *character* given the character's numeric code.
CONCAT	2	CHAR	Returns the two input strings *concatenated* together.
INITCAP	1	CHAR	Returns the input string with the first character of each word *capitalized.*
INSTR	2, 3 or, 4	NUMBER	Returns the position of a specific *occurrence* of a specific character in the input string.
INSTRB	2, 3 or, 4	NUMBER	Same as INSTR, used with multiple-byte character sets.
LENGTH	1	NUMBER	Returns the *length* of the passed-in character string.
LENGTHB	1	NUMBER	Same as LENGTH, used with multiple-byte character sets.
LOWER	1	CHAR	Returns the input string with all characters *lowercase.*
LPAD	3	CHAR	Returns the first value *left-padded* with the third value to a length specified by the second value.
LTRIM	2	CHAR	Returns the first value *trimmed from the left* the number of characters in the second value.
NLS_INITCAP	2	CHAR	Returns the first value, all words *capitalized.* The second value is for the NLS sort sequence, which is used to handle special upper-/lowercase conversions.
NLS_LOWER	2	CHAR	Returns the first value, all characters *lower-case.* The second value is for the NLS sort sequence, which is used to handle special upper-/lowercase conversions.
NLSSORT	1 or 2	CHAR	Returns a *sorted string* of the first value. The second value is used for a NLS sort sequence.

TABLE 24.2 Oracle SQL Character Functions

Name	*Input Values*	*Return Type*	*Description*
NLS_UPPER	2	CHAR	Returns the first value, all characters *uppercase*. The second value is for the NLS sort sequence, which is used to handle special upper-/lowercase conversions.
REPLACE	2 or 3	CHAR	Returns the first value after having *replaced* all occurrences of the second value with the characters in the third value. If the third value is not used, the replacement string is NULL.
RPAD	2 or 3	CHAR	Returns the first value *right-padded* with the third value to a length specified by the second value. If the third value is not used, the default padding character is a blank.
RTRIM	1 or 2	CHAR	Returns the first value *trimmed from the right* the number of characters in the second value. If the second value is not used, it defaults to a blank.
SOUNDEX	1	CHAR	Returns the *phonetic representation* of the passed-in value.
SUBSTR	2 or 3	CHAR	Returns a *substring* of the first value, starting at the position specified by the second value for a length specified by the third value.
SUBSTRB	2 or 3	CHAR	Same as SUBSTR, unless used with multiple-byte characters. In that case, the second and third values are interpreted as bytes rather than as character positions.
TRANSLATE	3	CHAR	Returns a character string *translated* by the second value (from values) and the third value (to values).
UPPER	1	CHAR	Returns the passed-in value, all characters *uppercase*.

Let's take a look at some sample uses of these functions in:

ASCII:

```
'SQL> SELECT ASCII('J') ''ASCII Value'' FROM DUAL;

ASCII Value
-----------
         74
```

Note that if you pass in more than one character—for example, 'JOE'—the function returns the ASCII value of the first character in the string.

INITCAP:

```
SQL> SELECT INITCAP('joe duer') ''Name'' FROM DUAL;
Name
--------
Joe Duer
```

INITCAP raises the case of the first character of each word in the string.

LPAD:

```
SQL> SELECT LPAD(1234.45, 10,'0') ''Paycheck'' FROM DUAL;

Paycheck
----------
0001234.45
```

Because the length of the first value (1234.56) is 7, LPAD places three leading zeros into the string, for a total length of 10.

SOUNDEX:

```
SQL> SELECT SOUNDEX('Joe Duer') FROM DUAL;

SOUN
----
J360
```

SOUNDEX uses a specific pattern to generate the phonetic code. This function can be used to compare words that sound alike but are spelled differently.

TRANSLATE:

```
SQL> SELECT TRANSLATE ('RMWAXGWJ',

 2 '0123456789ABCDEFGHIJKLMNOPQRSTUVWXYZ ',
 3 '0000000000 ZYXWVUTSRQPONMLKJIHGFEDCBA') ''Translation'' FROM DUAL;
Translate
--------
JOE DUER
```

TRANSLATE locates each character of the source string in the 'From' list (the second value passed in) and translates it to the corresponding character in the 'To' list (the last value passed in). It works both ways. If you passed in ' JOE DUER ' as the first value, your output would have been RMWAXGWJ.

UPPER:

```
SQL> SELECT

 2 UPPER('This is a really long string with numbers 123 in it.')
 3 ''Uppercase String'' FROM DUAL;

Uppercase String
----------------------------------------------------
THIS IS A REALLY LONG STRING WITH NUMBERS 123 IN IT.
```

UPPER doesn't have a problem if there are non-alpha characters in the input string.

Date Functions

Next on the list are the extensions to the date functions, shown in Table 24.3.

TABLE 24.3 Oracle SQL Date Functions

Name	*Input Values*	*Return Type*	*Description*
ADD_MONTHS	2	DATE	Returns the date passed in as the first value added to the *number of months* specified by the second value.
LAST_DAY	1	DATE	Returns the date of the *last day of the month* passed in with the first value.
MONTHS_BETWEEN	2	NUMBER	Returns the *number of months* (a floating-point result) between the two dates passed in.
NEW_TIME	3	DATE	Converts dates between *time zones*.
NEXT_DAY	2	DATE	Returns the next *weekday* specified by the second value that occurs after the date passed in the first value.
ROUND	1 or 2	DATE	*Rounds* the date passed in to the nearest month, year, and so on.
SYSDATE	0	DATE	Returns the *current* date and time.
TRUNC	1 or 2	DATE	Returns only the portion of the date requested, *truncating* the rest.

Let's take a quick look at some sample uses of the date functions.

ADD_MONTHS:

```
SQL> SELECT ADD_MONTHS('23-MAY-1965',480) ''She turns 40'' FROM DUAL;
```

```
She turns
---------
23-MAY-05
```

Passing in a negative number as the second value causes ADD_MONTHS to subtract that number of months from the date passed in.

MONTHS_BETWEEN:

```
SQL> SELECT MONTHS_BETWEEN('01-SEP-1999','29-JAN-1961')
 2 ''Months old'' FROM DUAL;

Months old
----------
463.096774
```

If you switch the two dates passed in, you get the same result, but as a negative value.

NEXT_DAY:

```
SQL> SELECT NEXT_DAY('30-SEP-1999','MONDAY')
 2 ''First Monday in October'' FROM DUAL;

First Mon
---------
04-OCT-99
```

Note that for a query like this one you should use the last day of the previous month for your input. If you had used '01-OCT-1999' and it had been a Monday, the function would have returned '08-OCT-99', which would have been the second Monday.

ROUND:

```
SQL> SELECT ROUND(TO_DATE('16-SEP-1999'),'MONTH')
 2 ''Rounded Month'' FROM DUAL;

Rounded M
---------
01-OCT-99
```

The ROUND function rounds up to the next month on the 16th or later. It rounds down to the current month if it's the 15th or earlier.

SYSDATE:

```
SQL> SELECT SYSDATE ''Date'' FROM DUAL;
Date
```

```
---------
18-JUN-99
```

The SYSDATE function takes no parameters and is generally used to generate input for other functions that require the current date and time.

Conversion Functions

Table 24.4 lists the functions that do data conversions between data types.

TABLE 24.4 Oracle SQL Conversion Functions

Name	*Input Values*	*Return Type*	*Description*
CHARTOROWID	1	ROWID	Converts a character input to a ROWID value.
CONVERT	2 or 3	CHAR	Converts a string from one character set to another.
HEXTORAW	1	RAW	Converts a character string of hexadecimal digits to a raw value.
RAWTOHEX	1	CHAR	Converts a raw value to a character string of hexadecimal digits equal to that value.
ROWIDTOCHAR	1	VARCHAR2	Converts a ROWID value to VARCHAR2.
TO_CHAR(DATE)	1, 2, or 3	VARCHAR2	Converts a DATE value to VARCHAR2.
TO_CHAR (NUMBER)	1, 2, or 3	VARCHAR2	Converts a NUMBER value to VARCHAR2.
TO_DATE	1, 2, or 3	DATE	Converts a character string to a DATE value.
TO_MULTIBYTE	1	CHAR	Converts single byte characters to multi-byte.
TO_NUMBER	1, 2, or 3	NUMBER	Converts a character string of digits into a NUMBER.
TO_SINGLE_-BYTE	1	CHAR	Converts multi-byte characters to single byte.
TRANSLATE	1	CHAR	Converts between character sets.

Once again, let's create some examples that show how these functions work.

TO_CHAR:

```
SQL> SELECT TO_CHAR (1200+1500) ''CHAR'' FROM DUAL;

CHAR
----
2700
```

The function adds the two numbers, converts the result to CHAR, and then prints it.

TO_DATE:

```
SQL> SELECT ROUND (TO_DATE ('23-MAY-1999'),'YEAR')
 2 ''Rounded Year'' FROM DUAL;

Rounded Y
---------
01-JAN-99
```

This example combines the ROUND function with the TO_DATE function. What happens is the TO_DATE function executes first, converting the text string into a DATE data type. That value is passed to the ROUND function, which rounds it down to the first of the year.

Miscellaneous Functions

There are more functions to the Oracle SQL specification than I have discussed already. Here is a list of the major ones, shown in Table 24.5.

TABLE 24.5 Miscellaneous Oracle SQL Functions

Name	*Input Values*	*Return Type*	*Description*
DUMP	1, 2, 3, or 4	VARCHAR2	Returns the *internal representation* of the data passed in.
EMPTY_BLOB	0	LOB	Returns a pointer to an *empty BLOB* locator. Used to initialize a BLOB variable, column, or attribute.
EMPTY_CLOB	0	LOB	Same as EMPTY_BLOB, but used with *CLOB*s.
BFILENAME		BFILE	Returns a *BFILE* locator that points to a file on the operating system.
GREATEST	1 .. n	Based on input	Returns the *highest value* for a list of values. CHAR or VARCHAR2 input generates VARCHAR2 output.
LEAST	1 .. n	Based on input	Returns the *lowest value* for a list of values. CHAR or VARCHAR2 input generates VARCHAR2 output.
NVL	2	Based on input	If first value is not NULL, then the first value is returned. If it is NULL, then the second value is returned.
UID	0	NUMBER	Returns the *user ID* of the current user.
USER	0	VARCHAR2	Returns the *username* of the current user.

TABLE 24.5 Miscellaneous Oracle SQL Functions

Name	*Input Values*	*Return Type*	*Description*
USERENV	1	VARCHAR2	Returns *session environment* information.
VSIZE	1	NUMBER	Returns the *size* of the data passed in.
DEREF	1	REF	Returns the object *reference* for the input value.
REFTOHEX	1	CHAR	Converts the input value to a *hexadecimal* number.
MAKE_REF	2 .. n	REF	Creates a *REF* to a row of an Oracle object.

Here are some sample uses of these miscellaneous functions:

DUMP:

```
SQL> SELECT DUMP('JOE DUER',16) ''Name Dump'' FROM DUAL;

Name Dump
-------------------------------------
Typ=96 Len=8: 4a,4f,45,20,44,55,45,52
```

In this example, the second value in the `DUMP` function is the radix of how I want the data displayed. In this case, it was hexadecimal (Base 16). This affects only the display of the character data; the `Type` and `Length` fields are always printed in Base 10. You could include the third and fourth values as well. They are the start position and length, respectively.

BFILENAME:

```
SQL> INSERT INTO MYTABLE VALUES
(BFILENAME ('/ora22/oradata/jdbase/external','myfile.dat'));
```

In this example, the data in `'myfile.dat'` was not actually copied into the database; a *pointer* to the file was inserted into the table `MYTABLE`. The file does not have to exist at the point you insert it into the table. It must be there, though, when you use `SELECT` on it.

GREATEST:

```
SQL> SELECT GREATEST(22,55,33,66,88,3)
 2 ''Greatest'' FROM DUAL;

 Greatest
----------
        88
```

When using this function with character data, the GREATEST function returns the LAST value after it arranges the values in alphabetical order.

LEAST:

```
SQL> SELECT LEAST ('Linda','Bronwyn','Brian','Chen')
 2 ''Least'' FROM DUAL;

Least
-----
Brian
```

The LEAST function returns the lowest value of the list passed in. For alphanumeric data, the list is sorted alphabetically and the first value is returned. For numeric data, the lowest value is returned.

UID, **USER**, **USERENV**:

```
SQL> SELECT UID, USER ''Username'', USERENV('ISDBA')
 2 ''DBA'' FROM DUAL;
       UID Username                     DBA
---------- ---------------------------- ------
        20 JDUER                        TRUE
```

These three functions return user information. UID and USER take no input data, but USERENV does. USERENV accepts the values 'ISDBA', 'TERMINAL', SESSIONID', 'ENTRYID', 'LANG' or 'LANGUAGE', and 'INSTANCE'. You use them to get user information about your own session from within a script.

Oracle Extensions to the SQL-92 Command Set

Now that functions are out of the way, let's take a look at the extensions Oracle has added to the SQL command set. These commands were added to support all the additional functionality Oracle implemented into the database over and above the SQL-92 standard. This part of the chapter takes these commands one at a time and describes their most important and common features.

CREATE CONTROLFILE

The *control file* is the single most important file in an Oracle database. It contains all the information about the database's structure, including the name of the database and its creation date, the filenames and directory locations for all the tablespace data files, and redo log file information. The values for various database parameters are also included in the control file.

Oracle creates the initial two copies of the control file when the database is created. The size of the control file can change over time as the number of data files in the database increases and also after an Oracle Server software upgrade.

Oracle has gone through great pains to make the control file recoverable. If the control file gets corrupted or deleted, your database is essentially useless, unless you can restore from tape or rebuild the control file. Oracle must have assumed that users might destroy their database control file (and all copies) and have no backup. This is where the `CREATE CONTROLFILE` command comes into play.

The `CREATE CONTROLFILE` command allows you to re-create your corrupted or missing control file. You do this by specifying all the information that was in the control file when it was lost. This information includes the following:

- The database name
- Redo log filenames and sizes
- Data filenames and sizes
- Value for `MAXLOGMEMBERS`
- Value for `MAXLOGFILES`
- Value for `MAXDATAFILES`
- Value for `MAXINSTANCES`
- Archive log mode status

Here is a sample `CREATE CONTROLFILE` command:

```
SVRMGR> CREATE CONTROLFILE
   2> DATABASE JDBASE
   3> LOGFILE GROUP 1
   4> ('/ora22/oradata/jdbase/jdbaseredo1a.rdo') SIZE 100M,
   5> GROUP 2
   6> ('/ora23/oradata/jdbase/jdbaseredo2a.rdo') SIZE 100M
   7> NORESETLOGS
   8> DATAFILE '/ora05/jdbase/jdbasedata01.dbf' SIZE 5000M,
   9> '/ora06/jdbase/jdbaseindx01.dbf' SIZE 2000M
  10> MAXDATAFILES 50
  11> MAXLOGFILES 10
```

```
12> MAXINSTANCES 16
13> MAXLOGMEMBERS 3
14> ARCHIVELOG;
```

Warning

Be *extremely* careful if you decide to test the CREATE CONTROLFILE command. You could accidentally overwrite your databases control file with your test file. Make sure you have good backups of all database components (control files, data files, and so forth) if you're not 100% sure you know what you are doing.

In this example, line 2 specifies the name of the database: JDBASE. Lines 3 through 6 specify the redo log filenames and sizes. On line 7 is the qualifier NORESETLOGS. You use this if you have all your redo logs online. If you have lost the redo logs as well, use RESETLOGS.

Lines 8 and 9 show the names and sizes of the database data files. In reality, this list will most probably be much longer than the two files listed here. You must list *every* database data file here, or you will lose that data even with the data files online.

Lines 10–13 define the values for MAXLOGFILES, MAXDATAFILES, MAXLOGMEMBERS, and MAXINSTANCES.

Line 14 specifies that the database was in ARCHIVELOG mode.

Any information you leave out is filled in with default information.

With the new control file created, you can bring the database instance up and recover the database.

CREATE CLUSTER, ALTER CLUSTER, and DROP CLUSTER

A *cluster* is a database object that can come into play when you have multiple tables with one or more columns in common. When you create a cluster and add the common columns to it, you change the data so there is actually one copy if it is physically stored in the database. The common columns specified for the cluster are called the *cluster key*.

There are two types of clusters. An *indexed* cluster stores all rows with the same cluster key value together. Each cluster key value is stored only once, saving on disk space and improving performance. After creating an indexed cluster, you need to create an index on the cluster key before running any queries against it.

In addition to an indexed cluster, you can also create a *hash* cluster. It's similar to an indexed one, except that instead of storing rows by cluster key value, they are stored by hash value. When creating a hash cluster, you can specify the hash function in the `CREATE` statement, or use the one Oracle provides.

Here is an example of a creating a hash cluster:

```
SQL> CREATE CLUSTER VAXCLUSTER
 2 (NODENUMBER NUMBER(5))
 3 SIZE 5K
 4 TABLESPACE USERS
 5 HASHKEYS 100
 6 MAXTRANS 8
 7 CACHE;

Cluster created.
```

This command creates a cluster called `VAXCLUSTER`, which allocates 5KB from the `USERS` tablespace. The cluster is a hash cluster, and creates the hash keys by using the Oracle internal hash function (you can specify your own with the `HASH IS` command clause). The cluster can hold 100 keys and have a maximum of eight transactions using it at any given time. After the cluster is created, it's loaded into the database cache.

After the cluster is created, you add tables to it with the common columns listed in the `CLUSTER` clause.

You can modify most of the cluster characteristics with the `ALTER CLUSTER` command, as shown here:

```
SQL> ALTER CLUSTER VAXCLUSTER
 2 MAXTRANS 64;

Cluster altered.
```

This command changes the maximum number of concurrent transactions from 8 to 64. You can also change storage parameters and force allocation of extents.

To remove a cluster, simply use the `DROP CLUSTER` command:

```
SQL> DROP CLUSTER VAXCLUSTER;

Cluster dropped.
```

You might also want to drop the tables that you added into the cluster.

CREATE DATABASE and ALTER DATABASE

You use the CREATE DATABASE command to define the structure of a new database and to create the actual database instance and data files. You use ALTER DATABASE to change the database's structure or operation after it is created and running.

Although many people use the Oracle installer to create their databases, there are advantages to using the CREATE DATABASE statement over the installer.

By creating the database manually, you'll gain more experience with the software than if you used the installer. The installer uses many defaults when creating the database, such as the database block size (db_block_size). The installer also executes the catalog scripts to populate the data dictionary. Doing this yourself gives you a more thorough knowledge of how the database works and makes you a better database administrator.

Let's take a look at this sample CREATE DATABASE command:

```
$ svrmgrl
Oracle Server Manager Release 3.0.5.0.0 - Production

© Copyright 1997, Oracle Corporation. All Rights Reserved.

Oracle8 Enterprise Edition Release 8.0.5.0.0 - Production
With the Partitioning option
PL/SQL Release 8.0.5.0.0 - Production

SVRMGR> CONNECT INTERNAL
Connected.
SVRMGR> STARTUP NOMOUNT PFILE='$ORACLE_HOME/dbs/init.ora'
ORACLE instance started.
Total System Global Area            4554256 bytes
Fixed Size                     48656 bytes
Variable Size                   4227072 bytes
Database Buffers                  204800 bytes
Redo Buffers                    73728 bytes
SVRMGR> CREATE DATABASE testdb
   2> LOGFILE
   3> GROUP 1 ('/ora02/oradata/testdb/redo01a.rdo') SIZE 5M,
   4> GROUP 2 ('/ora03/oradata/testdb/redo02a.rdo') SIZE 5M
   5> MAXLOGFILES 4
   6> MAXDATAFILES 64
   7> MAXINSTANCES 2
```

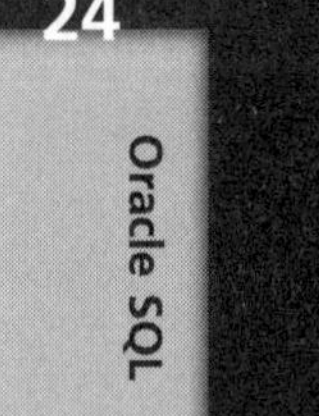

```
   8> DATAFILE '/ora04/oradata/testdb/system01.dbf' SIZE 100M;
Statement processed.
SVRMGR>
```

You use the CREATE DATABASE command from the Server Manager utility. First, use the CONNECT INTERNAL command so that you can start a new database instance. Next, the STARTUP NOMOUNT command creates the database instance, even though the database does not exist yet. Last, you see the CREATE DATABASE command, which creates the actual database structures.

Note

After the CREATE DATABASE command is finished, you need to run the catalog scripts that populate the data dictionary. Catalog.sql and catproc.sql are the most important and must be run first. There are other catalog scripts you might have to run based on the Oracle software options you have licensed. The catalog scripts are in the /rdbms subdirectory of ORACLE_HOME.

The ALTER DATABASE command changes the structure of the database after it has been created. Among the changes you can make are the following:

- Renaming data files
- Adding redo log file members
- Changing the archived log mode
- Mounting, opening, and closing the database
- Recovering the database

You cannot change some database characteristics, such as the database name.

This example starts the database not mounted, then mounts it, recovers it, and opens it for users.

```
$ svrmgrl

Oracle Server Manager Release 3.0.5.0.0 - Production

© Copyright 1997, Oracle Corporation. All Rights Reserved.

Oracle8 Enterprise Edition Release 8.0.5.0.0 - Production
With the Partitioning option
```

```
PL/SQL Release 8.0.5.0.0 - Production

SVRMGR> CONNECT INTERNAL
Connected.
SVRMGR> STARTUP NOMOUNT PFILE='$ORACLE_HOME/dbs/init.ora'
ORACLE instance started.
Total System Global Area          4554256 bytes
Fixed Size                   48656 bytes
Variable Size                 4227072 bytes
Database Buffers                204800 bytes
Redo Buffers                  73728 bytes
SVRMGR> ALTER DATABASE MOUNT;
Statement processed.
SVRMGR> ALTER DATABASE RECOVER;
Statement processed.
SVRMGR> ALTER DATABASE OPEN;
Statement processed.
```

CREATE DATABASE LINK and DROP DATABASE LINK

A *database link* is a logical connection between two databases. It allows you to perform SQL operations against a remote database object as though it were local. Database links can be created for public or private access and may be shared.

After the database link is created, you access it by simply adding *@dblinkname* to the table name you are querying. Because the database links two databases, you do not need to create a link for each table you need to access. By creating the link, you have access to all objects in the remote database, if you have the privileges to access them.

You create a database link with the CREATE DATABASE LINK command:

```
SQL> CREATE SHARED PUBLIC DATABASE LINK
 2> jdbase.carpathia.joeduer.com
 3> CONNECT TO JDUER IDENTIFIED BY BASEBALL
 4> AUTHENTICATED BY SECURITY IDENTIFIED BY T2987YR7847
 5> USING jdbase;
```

The previous example creates a shared public database link from the current database to the database jdbase on server system carpathia.joeduer.com. The CONNECT TO clause specifies that the link connect to the remote database with the user account JDUER. The path to the remote database is specified in the USING clause; jdbase is a Net8 service name.

As discussed before, simply append the dblinkname to the table name when accessing the remote data:

```
SQL> SELECT * FROM SAMPLE_DATA@jdbase.carpathia.joeduer.com;
```

To destroy a database link, simply use the DROP DATABASE LINK command:

```
SQL> DROP DATABASE LINK jdbase.carpathia.joeduer.com;
```

CREATE DIRECTORY and DROP DIRECTORY

In the Oracle database, a *directory* is actually a pointer to a file system directory that resides outside the database. Oracle directories are required so that the external file data type (BFILE) can be supported.

The creation of a directory alias is actually very simple; all you have to do is use the CREATE DIRECTORY command with the alias name and the physical directory name, as shown in this example:

```
SQL> CREATE DIRECTORY bfile_extern AS '/ora15/oradata/jdbase/extern';

Directory created.
```

So the alias bfile_extern now points to an O/S-level directory where the BLOBs (Binary Large Objects) are located. You use the alias when referring to BLOB objects in your PL/SQL procedures and compiled applications.

There is no corresponding ALTER command for directories, but if you wanted to change the physical directory specification without dropping and re-creating the alias, replace CREATE with CREATE OR REPLACE :

```
SQL> CREATE OR REPLACE DIRECTORY bfile_extern
 2> AS '/ora16/oradata/jdbase/extern';

Directory created.
```

If you want to completely dump the directory alias, you use the DROP DIRECTORY command:

```
SQL> DROP DIRECTORY bfile_extern;

Directory dropped.
```

This command does not delete any files in the external directory, just the pointer to it in the database.

CREATE FUNCTION, ALTER FUNCTION, and DROP FUNCTION

A *function* in the Oracle database is a group of PL/SQL statements that process data and return a typed result. Along with the many functions that come with Oracle discussed at the start of the chapter, you can also create your own functions that are stored in the database. You can write the function in PL/SQL, or you can *register* an external function, which essentially points the function to a compiled piece of code that resides in a library. I will focus on PL/SQL functions in this section.

Because PL/SQL is covered in so much depth in the next chapter, I will create only a simple function for my purposes here. Take a look at the sample `CREATE FUNCTION` command, which creates a function called `INCREMENTNUM`:

```
SQL> CREATE OR REPLACE FUNCTION
  INCREMENTNUM (inputval IN NUMBER)
RETURN NUMBER IS
BEGIN
  RETURN(inputval + 1);
END;
/

Function created.
```

You access this user-defined function the same way as the others:

```
SQL> SELECT INCREMENTNUM(22) ''++'' FROM DUAL;

    ++
----------
        23
```

The `ALTER FUNCTION` command is used essentially to recompile functions that might have somehow become invalidated by changes elsewhere in the database. To recompile a function, use this command:

```
SQL> ALTER FUNCTION JDUER.INCREMENTNUM COMPILE;

Function altered.
```

The schema name is included in the example; if the function is local to you, it is not necessary to include the schema name.

To delete an existing function, use the `DROP FUNCTION` command:

```
SQL> DROP FUNCTION INCREMENTNUM;
```

```
Function dropped.
```

CREATE INDEX, ALTER INDEX, and DROP INDEX

An *index* is an ordered list containing all the values for one or more columns of row data at any given time. Indexes are created to speed performance of database operations and, if done right, can be a real timesaver. If done wrong, you can make your system performance worse.

Oracle supports UNIQUE and BITMAP indexes as well as the standard indexes. UNIQUE indexes require that all the values in the columnar data be unique. BITMAP indexes specify that the index be created as a bitmap, instead of the B-Tree format.

You can bypass writing the index to the redo logs, thus speeding the index's creation. In many cases, the index is a re-creatable object and does not need to be recovered from the redo logs or from tape. If something happens to the index, all you have to do is re-create it. That's the reason for bypassing the logging of the index creation.

```
SQL> CREATE INDEX auto_index
 2> ON car_information (vin_no)
 3> NOLOGGING
 4> PARALLEL (DEGREE 4);
```

```
Index created
```

This sample command creates an index called auto_index on the car_information table, using the VIN number as the key. The keys are sorted in ascending order, and the index creation is not being logged to the redo logs. The PARALLEL clause specifies that the index be created in parallel—that is, using four servers concurrently to create the index.

The ALTER INDEX command is used to modify the attributes of an existing index. Among the changes you can make in an index are the following:

- LOGGING or NOLOGGING to the redo logs
- Requesting that the index be rebuilt
- Rebuilding partitions (Oracle Partitioning option)
- Changing default attributes (such as tablespace location)
- Renaming the index

Here's an example of using ALTER INDEX :

```
SQL> alter index auto_index rebuild;
```

```
Index altered.
```

To remove an index, you use the DROP INDEX command:

```
SQL> DROP INDEX AUTO_INDEX;

Index dropped.
```

CREATE LIBRARY and DROP LIBRARY

The CREATE LIBRARY command creates a library object in the Oracle database. A *library object* is a pointer to a system-shared library file residing on the operating system's file system. The library name is used by SQL and PL/SQL scripts to execute external functions written in compiled languages, such as C or C++.

Creating the library object is fairly simple, as shown in the following command:

```
SQL> CREATE LIBRARY EXTERNLIB
  2 AS '/ora02/oradata/jdbase/extern/sharefunc.so';

Library created.
```

Dropping the library is just as easy. Remember that dropping the library removes only the pointer in the database. The external shared library file is not deleted.

```
SQL> DROP LIBRARY EXTERNLIB;

Library dropped.
```

CREATE PACKAGE, ALTER PACKAGE, and DROP PACKAGE

A database *package* is a collection of compiled PL/SQL functions and procedures. You create packages and group related functions and procedures. There are two steps to creating a usable package.

First, you use the CREATE PACKAGE command to create the package specification in the database. The package specification is essentially the function and procedure prototypes.

After that, you use the CREATE PACKAGE BODY command to load in the code for the functions and procedures. CREATE PACKAGE BODY is covered in the next section.

When creating packages—or functions and procedures for that matter—you definitely want to store your source in SQL script files and execute them from within SQL*Plus. Just imagine typing in a 500-line function in SQL*Plus, finding an error, and not being able to change it.

Take a look at this sample script to create a package specification for a few simple math functions:

```
SQL> @create_spec.sql
SQL> CREATE OR REPLACE PACKAGE math_funcs AS
  FUNCTION INCREMENTNUM (inputval NUMBER)
  RETURN NUMBER;
  FUNCTION DECREMENTNUM (inputval NUMBER)
  RETURN NUMBER;
  FUNCTION DOUBLENUM (inputval NUMBER)
  RETURN NUMBER;
 END math_funcs;
 /

Package created.
```

This package specification contains three functions: `INCREMENTNUM`, `DECREMENTNUM`, and `DOUBLENUM`. All three functions have a return data type of `NUMBER`. The next section shows how to create the package body and execute these functions

You use the `ALTER PACKAGE` command to recompile the package specification, which could become invalid because of structural changes in the database that occur over time. It is a common occurrence to recompile invalid database objects.

```
SQL> ALTER PACKAGE math_funcs COMPILE;

Package altered.
```

To remove a package from the database, you use the `DROP PACKAGE` command:

```
SQL> DROP PACKAGE math_funcs;

Package dropped.
```

This command removes the package specification and all the functions and procedures in it.

CREATE PACKAGE BODY and ALTER PACKAGE COMPILE BODY

The `CREATE PACKAGE BODY` command is what you use to install the actual PL/SQL functional and procedural code into the database package.

Let's create the functions for the package specification that you created with `create_spec.sql`. The source is in Listing 24.1, and you will find this file on the CD-ROM included with the book.

LISTING 24.1 `CREATE_BODY.SQL`—Source SQL to Create `math_funcs` Package Body

```
CREATE OR REPLACE PACKAGE BODY math_funcs AS

FUNCTION INCREMENTNUM (inputval IN NUMBER)
RETURN NUMBER IS
BEGIN
    RETURN (INPUTVAL + 1);
END;
FUNCTION DECREMENTNUM (inputval IN NUMBER)
RETURN NUMBER IS
BEGIN
    RETURN (INPUTVAL - 1);
END;

FUNCTION DOUBLENUM (inputval IN NUMBER)
RETURN NUMBER IS
BEGIN
    RETURN (INPUTVAL * 2);
END;

END math_funcs;
```

Execute this procedure to create the package body:

```
SQL> @create_body
SQL> CREATE OR REPLACE PACKAGE BODY math_funcs AS

FUNCTION INCREMENTNUM (inputval IN NUMBER)
RETURN NUMBER IS
BEGIN
    RETURN (INPUTVAL + 1);
END;

FUNCTION DECREMENTNUM (inputval IN NUMBER)
RETURN NUMBER IS
BEGIN
    RETURN (INPUTVAL - 1);
END;

FUNCTION DOUBLENUM (inputval IN NUMBER)
RETURN NUMBER IS
BEGIN
    RETURN (INPUTVAL * 2);
```

```
END;

END math_funcs;
/
Package body created.
```

You can check the database for any invalid function or procedures by querying the USER_OBJECTS view:

```
SQL> SELECT OBJECT_TYPE, OBJECT_NAME FROM USER_OBJECTS
WHERE STATUS='INVALID';

no rows selected
```

If you need to recompile an object because it is invalid, you use the ALTER PACKAGE COMPILE BODY command, as shown here:

```
SQL> ALTER PACKAGE math_funcs COMPILE BODY;

Package body altered.
```

CREATE PROCEDURE, ALTER PROCEDURE, and DROP PROCEDURE

A *procedure*is much like a function, except it does not return a value. Generally, functions are single-purpose units that calculate a single value and return the result. On the other hand, procedures are more of an application-type object; the source is written much more in depth, and the scope of the procedure is much wider than that of a function.

Creating and maintaining procedures is similar to how functions are done. To create a procedure, you use the CREATE PROCEDURE command, as shown here:

```
SQL> CREATE OR REPLACE PROCEDURE COLA (PERCENT IN NUMBER) AS
BEGIN
 UPDATE EMP
 SET SAL = SAL + (SAL * (PERCENT/100));
END;
/

Procedure created.
```

This procedure reads in all the employee salaries from the EMP table and gives each employee a percentage cost-of-living raise. The actual percentage is passed in as an argument into the COLA procedure. First, list the current salaries:

```
SQL> SELECT ENAME, SAL FROM EMP;

ENAME             SAL
---------- ---------
SMITH             800
ALLEN            1600
WARD             1250
JONES            2975
MARTIN           1250
BLAKE            2850
CLARK            2450
SCOTT            3000
KING             5000
TURNER           1500
ADAMS            1100
JAMES             950
FORD             3000
MILLER           1300

14 rows selected.
```

Now execute the `COLA` procedure to update the salaries. A 10% raise should do it!

```
SQL> EXECUTE COLA(10);

PL/SQL procedure successfully completed.
```

Now look at the salaries. Each employee is being pay 10% more.

```
SQL> SELECT ENAME, SAL FROM EMP;

ENAME             SAL
---------- ---------
SMITH             880
ALLEN            1760
WARD             1375
JONES          3272.5
MARTIN           1375
BLAKE            3135
CLARK            2695
SCOTT            3300
KING             5500
TURNER           1650
ADAMS            1210
JAMES            1045
```

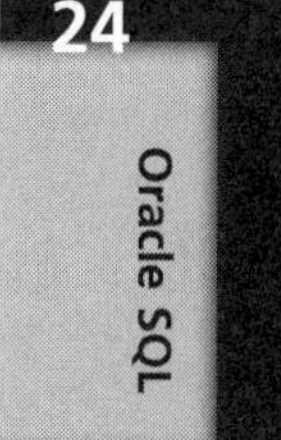

```
FORD             3300
MILLER           1430

14 rows selected.
```

This is the simplest way to execute the COLA stored procedure. You can call the COLA procedure from within another, larger procedure as part of your application. Running the procedure on its own, as in the previous example, is a good way to test a procedure without running the entire application.

Should a procedure become invalid, you can recompile it with the ALTER PROCEDURE COMPILE command:

```
SQL> ALTER PROCEDURE COLA COMPILE;

Procedure altered.
```

To delete a procedure, you use the DROP PROCEDURE command, as shown in the following example:

```
SQL> DROP PROCEDURE COLA;

Procedure dropped.
```

CREATE PROFILE, ALTER PROFILE, and DROP PROFILE

A *profile* is a set of parameters used to control the amount of database resources that can be used during a particular session. Profiles are a way for database administrators to restrict users so that the database has enough free resources to perform well for all users at all times. By default, new users are assigned to the DEFAULT profile, which has no resource restrictions enabled.

You create a profile using the CREATE PROFILE command. Table 24.6 lists the major items you can include in the CREATE PROFILE command.

TABLE 24.6 Oracle User Profile Settings

Name	*Description*
SESSIONS_PER_USER	The number of *concurrent sessions* the user can have connected.
CPU_PER_SESSION	The amount of CPU time that can be used during the *session*.
CPU_PER_CALL	The amount of CPU time that can be used for a *database call*.
CONNECT_TIME	The maximum amount of time that the session can be *connected*.
IDLE_TIME	The length of time Oracle will wait before disconnecting an *idle* user.
LOGICAL_READS_PER_SESSION	The maximum number of *data blocks* that can be read during the session.

TABLE 24.6 Oracle User Profile Settings

Name	Description
LOGICAL_READS_PER CALL	The maximum number of data blocks that can be read per *call*.
PRIVATE_SGA	The maximum amount of *SGA memory* that can be used privately.
FAILED_LOGIN_ATTEMPTS	The number of *login failures* before the user is locked out.

Let's create a profile using the CREATE_PROFILE command:

```
SQL> CREATE PROFILE USER_PROFILE LIMIT
 2 FAILED_LOGIN_ATTEMPTS 6
 3 IDLE_TIME 180
 4 SESSIONS_PER_USER 1
 5* CONNECT_TIME 600

Profile created.
```

This command creates a profile called USER_PROFILE that does the following:

- Allows six incorrect password tries before locking the account.
- Disconnects the user after three hours of inactivity.
- Does not allow the user multiple concurrent sessions.
- Puts a 10-hour connection time limit on the user.

You enable the profile for a particular user with the ALTER USER command:

```
SQL> ALTER USER JDUER PROFILE USER_PROFILE;

User altered.
```

The ALTER PROFILE command is used to change any of the preceding values after the profile is created:

```
SQL> SELECT RESOURCE_NAME, LIMIT
 2 FROM DBA_PROFILES
 3 WHERE PROFILE='USER_PROFILE' AND
 4* RESOURCE_NAME='IDLE_TIME'

RESOURCE_NAME                    LIMIT
-------------------------------- ----------------------------------------
IDLE_TIME                        60
```

You can completely get rid of a profile by using the DROP PROFILE command:

```
SQL> DROP PROFILE USER_PROFILE;

Profile dropped.
```

CREATE ROLLBACK SEGMENT, ALTER ROLLBACK SEGMENT, and DROP ROLLBACK SEGMENT

Rollback segments are where Oracle keeps track of transactions in progress. When a transaction is not committed or fails while being processed, Oracle looks into the rollback segment assigned to the user to put the data back to its original state.

Most Oracle databases have several rollback segments online. Some have large rollback segments available for long running queries. You use the SET TRANSACTION SQL command to specifically use that large rollback segment. Otherwise, Oracle assigns your query to any of the available online rollback segments.

You create a new rollback segment with the CREATE ROLLBACK SEGMENT command. You specify the new rollback segment's name, the tablespace that will hold the rollback segment, and the storage parameters:

```
SQL> CREATE ROLLBACK SEGMENT JDBASE_RBS_05
 2 TABLESPACE RBS
 3 STORAGE (INITIAL 100K NEXT 100K MINEXTENTS 20 MAXEXTENTS 240);

Rollback segment created.
```

This command creates rollback segment JDBASE_RBS_05 in the RBS tablespace. The storage parameters are set to an initial extent of 100KB bytes, a next extent of 100KB; 20 extents are allocated when the rollback segment comes online, and it can extend up to 240 extents.

Tip

The TABLESPACE clause of the CREATE ROLLBACK SEGMENT command is optional, but make sure you use it. If you omit it, the rollback segment is created, but in the SYSTEM tablespace! For performance reasons, that is the *last* place you want it. If for some reason you do create it in the SYSTEM tablespace, all you have to do is drop the rollback segment and re-create it in the correct tablespace.

You use the ALTER ROLLBACK SEGMENT command to change an existing rollback segment. The segment can be online and active.

```
SQL> ALTER ROLLBACK SEGMENT JDBASE_RBS_05
 2 STORAGE (MAXEXTENTS UNLIMITED);

Rollback segment altered.
```

In this example, the MAXEXTENTS value is essentially disabled. The rollback segment can extend indefinitely until the RBS tablespace runs out of free space.

To delete a rollback segment, you use the DROP ROLLBACK SEGMENT command:

```
SQL> DROP ROLLBACK SEGMENT JDBASE_RBS_05;

Rollback segment dropped.
```

Keep in mind that you cannot drop a rollback segment while it is online. Use the ALTER ROLLBACK SEGMENT command to take if offline before dropping it.

CREATE ROLE, ALTER ROLE, and DROP ROLE

Roles are used to manage database access privileges. You grant combinations of database privileges to a newly created role, and then grant that role to a user. This method gives the user the access you specifically granted to the role. Roles can be granted to other roles as well. You use the CREATE ROLE command to create a new role with no privileges granted to it:

```
SQL> CREATE ROLE ACCESS_ROLE NOT IDENTIFIED;

Role created.
```

This example creates a role with no password associated with it. You have the option of using the IDENTIFIED BY clause to add a password to the role. Users who want to enable this role have to supply this password. The other options are to have the role not identified (O/S authentication) or use the keyword GLOBALLY to have it authenticated by Oracle Security Server.

The ALTER ROLE command changes the role's authentication method:

```
SQL> ALTER ROLE ACCESS_ROLE IDENTIFIED BY NEWPASSWORD;

Role altered.
```

Last, you use the DROP ROLE command to remove the role from the database.

```
SQL> DROP ROLE ACCESS_ROLE;

Role dropped.
```

When you drop the role, Oracle automatically revokes it from all the users and roles it was granted to.

CREATE SEQUENCE, ALTER SEQUENCE, and DROP SEQUENCE

A *sequence* is simply a unique sequence number generator. Each time the sequence is referenced by a user, the number is incremented. This ensures that no matter how many users request a sequence number, the same number is never returned twice, causing a duplicate.

The `CREATE SEQUENCE` command starts up the sequence counter. If you use no qualifiers at all, your sequence number starts at 1 and is incremented by 1 each time it is accessed until the number reaches 10^27. You have the option to do the following:

- Increment the counter by more than 1 at a time.
- Start with any number.
- Define a maximum value for the sequence and optionally have the sequence restart at 1 when that number is reached.
- Cache a set of sequence numbers in memory for faster access.

Here is a sample command to create a sequence:

```
SQL> CREATE SEQUENCE EVEN_NUMBERS
 2 START WITH 2
 3 INCREMENT BY 2
 4 MINVALUE 2
 5 MAXVALUE 65536
 6 CYCLE
 7* CACHE 10

Sequence created.
```

This sequence generates all the even numbers, starting with 2 and up through 65,536, and then restarts from 2 again. Ten sequence numbers are cached for quick access.

You access the sequence number by selecting on the `NEXTVAL` pseudocolumn, as shown in the following example:

```
SQL> select even_numbers.nextval from dual;

  NEXTVAL
----------
         2
```

```
SQL> select even_numbers.nextval from dual

  NEXTVAL
----------
         4

SQL> select even_numbers.nextval from dual

  NEXTVAL
----------
         6
```

You use the ALTER SEQUENCE command to change the characteristics of the sequence:

```
SQL> ALTER SEQUENCE EVEN_NUMBERS
 2 MAXVALUE 100000;

Sequence altered.
```

You can remove the sequence from the database by using the DROP SEQUENCE command:

```
SQL> DROP SEQUENCE EVEN_NUMBERS;

Sequence dropped.
```

CREATE SYNONYM and DROP SYNONYM

A *synonym* is exactly what the name implies—a name that points to a database object. To access the object, you can spell out the full path of the object or use the synonym.

Synonyms can be public (global) or private (schema only). They are generally used to give quick access to an object in another user's schema without having to spell out the full path to the object. Also, by using synonyms, the object can be moved within the database; as long as the synonym is updated with the new location, the change is transparent to the users of the object.

You create a synonym by using the CREATE SYNONYM command:

```
SQL> CREATE PUBLIC SYNONYM EMP FOR JDUER.EMP;

Synonym created.
```

Now I can select on the EMP table from any schema in the database without having to use JDUER.EMP.

```
SQL> CONNECT JSMITH/FOOTBALL
```

```
Connected.
SQL> DESCRIBE EMP;
 Name                              Null?    Type
 -------------------------------- -------- ----
 EMPNO                             NOT NULL NUMBER(4)
 ENAME                                      VARCHAR2(10)
 JOB                                        VARCHAR2(9)
 MGR                                        NUMBER(4)
 HIREDATE                                   DATE
 SAL                                        NUMBER(7,2)
 COMM                                       NUMBER(7,2)
 DEPTNO                                     NUMBER(2)
```

You use the `DROP SYNONYM` to remove the synonym from the database. You would normally do that if the table has been dropped.

```
SQL> DROP PUBLIC SYNONYM EMP;

Synonym dropped.
```

CREATE TABLESPACE, ALTER TABLESPACE, and DROP TABLESPACE

A *tablespace* is a storage area in the database for database objects. Tables, indexes, the data dictionary, and even the rollback segments are assigned to one or more tablespaces.

In reality, a tablespace is one or more data files that reside on disk. First, you create an empty tablespace by specifying the file location, size, and default storage parameters, and then you can create objects within the tablespace.

You create a tablespace with the `CREATE TABLESPACE` command:

```
SQL> CREATE TABLESPACE NEW_DATA
 2 DATAFILE '/ora03/oradata/jdbase/newdata01.dbf' SIZE 1000M
 3 AUTOEXTEND OFF
 4 DEFAULT STORAGE(INITIAL 10M NEXT 5M MINEXTENTS 1 MAXEXTENTS 240)
 5 ONLINE;

Tablespace created.
```

This example creates the `NEW_DATA` tablespace, with one 1GB data file. The default storage parameters are set, and `AUTOEXTEND` on the data file is turned off. Because the `ONLINE` clause was specified, the new tablespace becomes available to users immediately.

The ALTER TABLESPACE command changes the attributes of the existing tablespace. For example, you could change the default storage parameters, add another data file, coalesce the data within the tablespace, or take the tablespace offline.

On a system management note, it is the ALTER TABLESPACE BEGIN BACKUP and ALTER TABLESPACE END BACKUP commands that switch a tablespace in and out of hot backup mode.

```
SQL> ALTER TABLESPACE NEW_DATA
 2 ADD DATAFILE '/ora04/oradata/jdbase/newdata02.dbf' SIZE 1000M
 3 AUTOEXTEND ON NEXT 500M MAXSIZE 10000M;

Tablespace altered.
```

This example adds a data file to the NEW_DATA tablespace. This time AUTOEXTEND is enabled. When the file becomes full, it automatically extends by allocating more disk space, 500MB at a time. It keeps doing that until the file reaches its maximum size of 10GB.

When you want to get rid of a tablespace, use the DROP TABLESPACE command:

```
SQL> DROP TABLESPACE NEW_DATA
 2 INCLUDING CONTENTS
 3 CASCADE CONSTRAINTS;

Tablespace dropped.
```

This command drops the tablespace as well as all the objects inside it and any constraints that were enabled.

CREATE TRIGGER, ALTER TRIGGER, and DROP TRIGGER

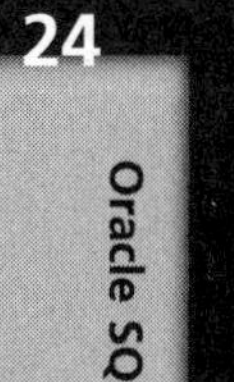

A *trigger* is a database object that is executed when a specific database event occurs. For example, suppose for auditing purposes that you wanted to log each time a record was inserted into a table and by whom. You could create a database trigger on that table that fires each time an insert is performed on the table.

The trigger itself is actually a PL/SQL block of code that is called when the event occurs.

There are many possibilities for implementing triggers in an Oracle database. You can set the trigger to fire on delete or update operations, too. You can even specify whether the trigger fires before or after the row data is changed. You can use the BEFORE clause to intercept the insert and actually prevent it from occurring if it violates some parameter you specify. Let's take a look at a simple trigger that writes a record to an auditing table each time there's an insert to the EMP table:

```
SQL> CREATE OR REPLACE TRIGGER EMP_INSERT
 AFTER INSERT ON EMP FOR EACH ROW
 BEGIN
  INSERT INTO EMP_AUDIT
   VALUES('INSERT by ' || USER ||
        'Key val : ' || :new.key);
 END;
Trigger created.
```

Because the trigger is a PL/SQL block, there are almost an infinite number of possibilities for implementation.

The `ALTER TRIGGER` command enables and disables existing triggers. Also, you use the `ALTER TRIGGER` command to recompile and generating debugging information. The debug information is used by the PL/SQL debugger.

```
SQL> ALTER TRIGGER EMP_INSERT DISABLE;

Trigger altered.
```

The `DROP TRIGGER` command is used to remove an existing trigger from the database. You do not have to disable it before removing it.

```
SQL> DROP TRIGGER EMP_INSERT;

Trigger dropped.
```

CREATE TYPE, ALTER TYPE, and DROP TYPE

The `CREATE TYPE` command creates an Oracle data type for use in object-oriented programming. You can create four different data types:

- Object type
- Named varying array (`VARRAY`) type
- Nested table type
- Incomplete object type

> **Note**
>
> These commands do not work unless you have the Oracle `Objects` option licensed and installed.

Let's take a look at the object type:

```
SQL> CREATE OR REPLACE TYPE new_employee_type AS OBJECT
 2> (ENAME CHAR(20),
 3> SALARY NUMBER(9),
 4> EMP_FILE CLOB,
 5> ID_BADGE_PIC BLOB);

Type created.
```

The AS clause determines the type of TYPE to be created. You use AS TABLE OF to create a nested table of some data type, and use the AS VARRAY clause to create an array object. Leaving out the AS clause creates an incomplete object type.

You use the CREATE TYPE BODY (see the next section) to load in the object procedures and functions.

The ALTER TYPE command recompiles the type specification or the type body:

```
SQL> ALTER TYPE new_employee_type COMPILE SPECIFICATION;

Type altered.

SQL> ALTER TYPE new_employee_type COMPILE BODY;

Type altered.
```

You can also use the REPLACE AS OBJECT clause to insert new methods into existing object types.

You use the DROP TYPE command to remove a defined object type from the database:

```
SQL> DROP TYPE new_employee_type;

Type dropped.
```


CREATE TYPE BODY and DROP TYPE BODY

The CREATE TYPE BODY command is similar to the CREATE PACKAGE BODY command, which loads the actual code for all the procedures and functions in the package. The CREATE TYPE BODY command does the same thing, loading all the object type methods into the object type. Take a look at the following example, which creates the type body for the new_employee_type object type.

```
SQL> CREATE TYPE BODY new_employee_type IS
BEGIN
```

```
/* METHOD CODE */
...
END;

Type body created.
```

There is no ALTER TYPE BODY command. To recompile the type methods, use the ALTER TYPE command.

To drop an object type body, use the DROP OBJECT TYPE command, as shown here:

```
SQL> DROP TYPE BODY new_employee_type;

Type body dropped.
```

CREATE USER, ALTER USER, and DROP USER

The CREATE USER command creates user accounts in the Oracle database. User information can be viewed from the DBA_USERS database view. Take a look at the following bulleted list, which shows what type of information can be defined when creating a new database account:

- The username for the new user
- The default and temporary tablespace for the user
- Tablespace quotas
- Default roles
- Password information and retention
- Account lock/unlock status

Take a look at this sample CREATE USER command:

```
SQL> CREATE USER JSMITH
 2 IDENTIFIED EXTERNALLY
 3 DEFAULT TABLESPACE USERS
 4 TEMPORARY TABLESPACE TEMP
 5 QUOTA 50M ON USERS
 6 QUOTA 1000M ON TEMP
 7 PROFILE INTERACTIVE_USER;

User created.
```

This example creates user JSMITH with no password (Oracle trusts the operating system to authenticate him). You specified the user's default and temporary tablespaces and added quota restrictions to both of them. Also, the user was assigned to the INTERACTIVE_USER profile, which has system resource quotas enabled.

To change any of this information, you use the ALTER USER command. This command is usually for users who have forgotten their passwords. For this example, raise the quota on the USERS tablespace for the new user:

```
SQL> ALTER USER JSMITH
 2> QUOTA 100M ON USERS;

User altered.
```

To remove a user account, use the DROP USER command. Be sure to use the CASCADE clause to drop all the user's schema objects.

```
SQL> DROP USER JSMITH CASCADE;
User dropped.
```

CREATE VIEW, ALTER VIEW, and DROP VIEW

A *view* is best described as a logical table. No data actually exists in the view, but the view reads data in other physical tables and presents the data as its own. Views add security to the physical tables by restricting access to only those rows that exist in the view. Views simplify certain queries; because views can be composed of columns from different tables, having the data all in one view makes it easier to query and update.

Views can be created from local data or with data accessed through a database link. If you have the Oracle Objects option, you can create a view of a typed object. Views can be created read-only as well.

The data populated in the view is created from a SELECT statement in the CREATE VIEW command. Let's create a view called EMP_STAFF, which contains all the employees below manager level:

```
SQL> CREATE OR REPLACE VIEW EMP_STAFF
 2 AS
 3 SELECT * FROM EMP
 4 WHERE JOB NOT IN ('MANAGER','PRESIDENT');

View created.
```

Now query the view to make sure the employees with the title MANAGER or PRESIDENT are not there:

```
SQL> SELECT ENAME, JOB FROM EMP_STAFF;
```

```
ENAME      JOB
---------- ---------
SMITH      CLERK
ALLEN      SALESMAN
WARD       SALESMAN
MARTIN     SALESMAN
SCOTT      ANALYST
TURNER     SALESMAN
ADAMS      CLERK
JAMES      CLERK
FORD       ANALYST
MILLER     CLERK

10 rows selected.
```

Use the `ALTER VIEW` command to rebuild the view. You need to do this if the view becomes invalid.

```
SQL> ALTER VIEW EMP_STAFF COMPILE;

View altered.
```

To drop the view, you use the `DROP VIEW` statement:

```
SQL> DROP VIEW EMP_STAFF;

View dropped.
```

The view is removed, but the actual data remains untouched.

Other Oracle SQL Commands

This section looks at some other SQL commands that are part of the Oracle SQL command set. These commands are generally used to manage the data in the database, not necessarily to maintain it.

ANALYZE

You use the `ANALYZE` command to generate statistics about a particular database object. You also use `ANALYZE` to locate migrated or chained rows in a table, and it can be used to read and look for corruption in the table. In Oracle 8, with the `Object` option installed, the `ANALYZE` command generates statistics on scalar objects and validates object references.

The statistics can be `COMPUTEd` (all rows read) or `ESTIMATEd` (a sampling of rows read).

AUDIT and NOAUDIT

The AUDIT command enables database monitoring of database changes. A wide-ranging list of events can be audited, from making row inserts to granting roles. There are also different ways to implement the auditing: by user, by session, or by access.

The NOAUDIT command is used to disable the auditing.

COMMENT

COMMENT is used to add a remark about a specific database object to the data dictionary. *This is not for adding comments to your PL/SQL scripts*. These comments are stored in the database. For commenting in your PL/SQL scripts, use REM.

EXPLAIN PLAN

The EXPLAIN PLAN command creates an explain plan of a particular database query. An *explain plan* is the path Oracle uses in processing the statement. It is used primarily for tuning purposes and to help decide on implementing indexes.

RENAME

RENAME changes the name of database objects you have created. It is a simple command that works in much the same way as the operating system RENAME command.

REVOKE

The REVOKE command pulls back a privilege granted to a user or another role. You use the GRANT command to add the privilege to the role or user.

SAVEPOINT

A *savepoint* is a defined point within processing to which a transaction rollback can be executed. Savepoints are useful in running applications with a long series of steps. They can be used to roll back to a certain point, instead of having to start all over if there's an error.

SET CONSTRAINT

The SET CONSTRAINT command determines whether a deferrable constraint is checked following each SQL statement or whether the transaction is committed.

SET TRANSACTION

The SET TRANSACTION command sets the characteristics of the current transaction. You can specify that the transaction be read only or read/write. You can specify which specific rollback segment is assigned to the transaction. You can also specify the transaction's isolation level, to either `SERIALIZABLE` (the SQL-92 definition) or `READ COMMITED`, which is the default Oracle behavior.

TRUNCATE

The `TRUNCATE` command deletes all the rows for a particular table or cluster but leaves the table structure in place. You can specify that the tablespace storage allocated to the table be freed or saved so that it's reused when new rows are added into the table. `TRUNCATE` is much more efficient than `DELETE` when you are deleting all the rows of a table.

Generating SQL with SQL

One of the great things Oracle can do is generate a SQL script from within another SQL script. That is, as a SQL script runs, its output is another SQL script.

Let's talk about an easy script you can create that will help any DBA who uses databases in `ARCHIVELOG` mode (that's *all* DBAs, I hope) and does not use Recovery Manager for backups.

When you do your nightly backup, you need to put each of the tablespaces into *hot backup* mode before you write the database files to tape. Many people write a script to do that, and call that script from within the backup procedure.

The problem comes when you add a new tablespace to the database. If you don't remember to update that script, you will have a lot of trouble if you have to recover your database from tape. That is definitely not the time to find out you have a problem!

The answer to this dilemma is to create a script that reads all the tablespace names from `DBA_TABLESPACES` and creates a script that puts each of the tablespaces into hot backup mode. Spool your output to another file with a `.sql` extension, and use this SQL statement:

```
SQL> SELECT 'ALTER TABLESPACE ' ||
 2 TABLESPACE_NAME ||
 3 ' BEGIN BACKUP;' FROM
 4 DBA_TABLESPACES WHERE
 5 STATUS = 'ONLINE';
```

This statement generates the following text:

```
ALTER TABLESPACE SYSTEM BEGIN BACKUP;
ALTER TABLESPACE RBS BEGIN BACKUP;
ALTER TABLESPACE TEMP BEGIN BACKUP;
ALTER TABLESPACE TOOLS BEGIN BACKUP;
ALTER TABLESPACE USERS BEGIN BACKUP;
```

```
ALTER TABLESPACE DESIGNER BEGIN BACKUP;
ALTER TABLESPACE DESIGNER_I BEGIN BACKUP;
```

All you have to do is spool that off to another file, and then the backup procedure can call it. In this way, all your online tablespaces are placed into backup mode for each backup operation, without anyone having to remember to maintain the backup script. Don't forget to write the script to take the tablespaces *out* of hot backup mode when the tape backup is finished.

SQL*Plus

SQL*Plus is the command-line SQL interface that Oracle supplies with its client and server software. With the exception of the database management commands (`STARTUP`, `SHUTDOWN`, and so forth), all SQL commands can be executed in SQL*Plus.

In addition to SQL, SQL*Plus includes formatting commands so that you can generate reports with SQL*Plus and have good control of what the SQL output looks like.

Now take a look at how you start SQL*Plus, connect to the database, and format a sample query.

Starting SQL*Plus

The command to start the command-line version of SQL*Plus is `sqlplus` (Windows users can start the GUI version from the Start menu):

```
sqlplus

SQL*Plus: Release 8.0.5.0.0 - Production on Sun Jun 20 14:53:33 1999

© Copyright 1998 Oracle Corporation. All rights reserved.

Enter user-name:
```

You are then prompted for your username and password and connected to the database named in the environment variable `ORA_SID` or `ORACLE_SID`, depending on your operating system. You have the option of including your username and password right on the command line, as shown here:

```
sqlplus jduer/baseball

SQL*Plus: Release 8.0.5.0.0 - Production on Sun Jun 20 14:54:55 1999

© Copyright 1998 Oracle Corporation. All rights reserved.
```

```
Connected to:
Oracle8 Enterprise Edition Release 8.0.5.0.0 - Production
With the Partitioning option
PL/SQL Release 8.0.5.0.0 - Production

SQL>
```

This method works fine for local databases, but what if you want to connect to a remote database? Then you specify a Net8 service name on the command line after your password. You prepend an @ to the service name so that Oracle knows it is not part of your password:

```
sqlplus jduer/mustang@serversys

SQL*Plus: Release 8.0.5.0.0 - Production on Sun Jun 20 15:32:05 1999

# Copyright 1998 Oracle Corporation. All rights reserved.

Connected to:
Oracle8 Enterprise Edition Release 8.0.5.0.0 - Production
With the Partitioning option
PL/SQL Release 8.0.5.0.0 - Production

SQL>
```

This sample command looks up the service name in the TNSNAMES.ORA file and then connects to the remote database using the network information included in TNSNAMES. If you get an error connecting in this way, usually the problem can be tracked down to the TNSNAMES.ORA file.

Formatting Output

SQL*Plus has a set of formatting commands that allow you to customize the output from your SQL statements. In this example, you will take a look at the COLUMN and TTITLE commands, which are the most commonly used when formatting output. First, format a query of the DBA_USERS table so that each row prints on one line:

```
TTITLE CENTER 'User account listing for database JDBASE' -
 RIGHT 'Page No. ' FORMAT 9999 SQL.PNO SKIP 2
COLUMN USER_ID HEADING ''User ID'' FORMAT 9999999
COLUMN USERNAME HEADING ''Username'' FORMAT A15
COLUMN PASSWORD HEADING ''Password'' FORMAT A16
COLUMN CREATED HEADING ''Creation Date'' FORMAT A9
COLUMN ACCOUNT_STATUS HEADING ''Status'' FORMAT A10
```

```
COLUMN PROFILE HEADING ''Profile'' FORMAT A15
SELECT USER_ID, USERNAME, PASSWORD, CREATED,
 ACCOUNT_STATUS, PROFILE
 FROM DBA_USERS;
```

Let's take a look at TTITLE first. The TTITLE command writes a title at the top of each page of the report. You can left- or right-justify it or center it as was done in the example. It also added a page number, which Oracle maintains on the variable SQL.PNO. Last, a SKIP clause is included at the end of the TTITLE command to create a blank line between the report's title and column headers.

The COLUMN commands are used to format the output of the individual rows. You can justify them as well, but the example doesn't specify that, which means all columns are left-justified. The HEADING clause customizes how the column heading prints in the report. Even if you use the same name as the column, using mixed-case characters looks much better than the all-uppercase default. After the HEADING clause is the FORMAT clause, which tells SQL*Plus how many characters to use for each column and the data type of the data to be printed.

Last is the query from DBA_USERS, which selects six columns of all the rows in the table. Take a look at the report's output:

```
User account listing for database JDBASE   Page No.   1

 User ID Username         Password         Creation  Status     Profile
-------- ---------------- ---------------- --------- ---------- ------------
       0 SYS              623EBC96416518E2 14-NOV-98 OPEN       DEFAULT
       5 SYSTEM           F2A1BC56BBB975B8 14-NOV-98 OPEN       DEFAULT
      17 DBSNMP           E066D214D5421CCC 14-NOV-98 OPEN       DEFAULT
      19 TRACESVR         F9DA8977092B7B81 14-NOV-98 OPEN       DEFAULT
      20 JDUER            FABE0FAF742A851F 14-FEB-99 OPEN       DEFAULT
      24 JDUEROEM         FA45B590C9D80090 22-MAR-99 OPEN       DEFAULT
      22 WWW_DBA          C34EC4DC32F4BCA0 22-FEB-99 OPEN       DEFAULT
      23 WWW_USER         0E9A5099A313ED57 22-FEB-99 OPEN       DEFAULT

8 rows selected.
```

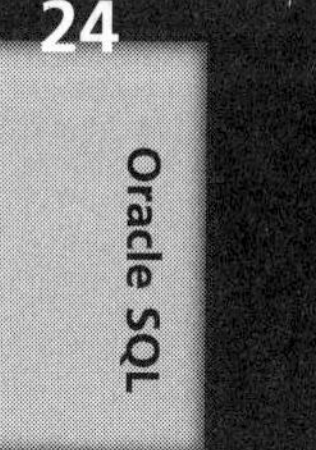

If you wanted to get rid of that last line, 8 rows selected, just add a SET FEEDBACK OFF command to your report script.

Summary

In this chapter, you have learned about the Oracle database extensions to the SQL-92 specification. As you have seen, the extensions are, for lack of a better word, extensive.

There is no way I could have covered every possible combination of commands and clauses in a single chapter, but all the most important and common topics are here for you to refer to.

If you need more information than what's provided here, there is always the Oracle documentation set. All the SQL commands and clauses are listed in the book, *SQL Reference*.

For more information about SQL*Plus, take a look at the *SQL*Plus User's Guide and Reference*, which has all the formatting commands and clauses.

CHAPTER

Oracle PL/SQL

In This Chapter

PL/SQL stands for *Procedural Language/SQL*. Originally sold by Oracle as an add-on to the Oracle Server, PL/SQL is now an integrated component of the Oracle software.

Because SQL is limited in its support of advanced programming topics, PL/SQL was created to fill in the gap. With PL/SQL, you can modularize your SQL code into functions, procedures, and packages. You can traverse selected data through the use of cursors, and with PL/SQL, you now have access to control functionality such as `IF...THEN` statements, `FOR` loops, and exception handling.

Given all that, you will be able to see that PL/SQL extends SQL so that it is a contender with the compiled programming languages in functionality and ease of use. There are also performance advantages to PL/SQL, which are discussed in this chapter, too.

Let's begin by taking a quick look at PL/SQL's overall features from the mile-high view. Then you will dig a little deeper into the types of PL/SQL programs that can be created and the details of what goes into making a PL/SQL program.

Features and Advantages of PL/SQL

The basic unit of a PL/SQL application is called a *block*, which is a collection of PL/SQL statements grouped as a logical unit. You can create five different types of program units with PL/SQL blocks:

Anonymous blocks

Stored functions

Stored procedures

Packages

Triggers

Anonymous Blocks

An *anonymous block* is the most basic PL/SQL block you can create. It is called "anonymous" because it is unnamed and is not stored in the Oracle database as a callable object. Anonymous blocks can be executed from SQL*Plus, either by typing them in at the `SQL>` prompt or by executing them from a SQL script file stored in disk. They can be executed from other tools as well, such as Server Manager, but in all cases, the anonymous block must be loaded from an external source; it cannot be called from within the database.

A good analogy for an anonymous block is entering a quick one-line program in a BASIC interpreter. Because it has not been saved with a name, it exists only as long as you stay in the interpreter. After you exit, it is gone forever.

Stored Functions

A *stored function* is a named, user-created function stored in the Oracle database. Many functions come with the Oracle Server—math, character, and date functions, among others. The functions you write yourself and store in the database for use by other functions and procedures are called stored functions.

Stored functions are written to perform a single task, usually to calculate a single value. That calculated value is the return value for the function.

Stored functions are created with the SQL command `CREATE FUNCTION`.

Stored Procedures

Stored functions must return a typed value to the caller, but stored procedures do not have that requirement.

A *stored procedure* is a named PL/SQL block where the meat of the application code is written. Within the stored procedure, you set up cursors, process the rows returned in the cursor, execute any exception logic, and write your output.

> **Note**
>
> What is a cursor? A cursor is best described as a pointer to the resulting rows of a database query. A pointer to a single-row result is called an *implicit* cursor. Implicit cursors do not have to be defined in the PL/SQL script. A cursor that points to a multiple-row result is called an *explicit* cursor. You use cursors to traverse one at a time through a group of returned rows (called a *resultset*).

Almost all the sample scripts in this chapter involve creating stored procedures with the `CREATE PROCEDURE` command.

Packages

A *package* is a group of related stored procedures and functions. Packages are created to help you organize your user-written code. Oracle packages many of its procedures into several packages that can be called from your SQL scripts and procedures.

There are two components to an Oracle package: the package *specification*, which contains the prototypes for all the functions and procedures in the package, and the package *body*, the actual PL/SQL code to compile and store in the package.

The package specification is created by using the command `CREATE PACKAGE`. The package body is created with the command `CREATE PACKAGE BODY`.

Triggers

A database *trigger* is a PL/SQL block executed when a certain database event occurs, such as an insert, update, or delete of a row in a table. You can set the trigger to execute just before or just after the event occurs.

The trigger can be set to *fire* after each row processed by the SQL statement or once for the execution of the entire statement.

Generally, triggers are used to implement auditing and enforcing security policies.

Oracle database triggers are created with the SQL command `CREATE TRIGGER`.

Advantages of PL/SQL over SQL

Other than the programmability features already discussed, PL/SQL has other advantages over using straight SQL scripts.

First, PL/SQL has an advantage when it comes to network bandwidth use. Because PL/SQL blocks are sent to the server as a whole, there is less network chatter between client and server, increasing the speed of execution.

Next, PL/SQL lends itself well to modular program development through the use of procedures and functions. SQL scripting is strictly a top-down programming environment.

PL/SQL also supports error exceptions, which SQL does not do. In PL/SQL you can define specific actions to be taken for a specific error and determine a default error behavior.

Anatomy of a PL/SQL Block

This section describes the three components of the PL/SQL block: the declaration section, the execution section, and the exception section. I will start off by doing a little setup on your database at home so that the samples included here will give you the same results you see in the book.

After that is done, you will look at the three sections individually.

Setting Up for the Examples

There are only three things you need to do to get the sample scripts in this section to work. First, you need to verify that you have access to the Oracle sample EMP table. Then you need to create the three tables used by the sample scripts (called EXCEPTION_TABLE, STAFFERS, and AUDIT_TABLE) and last, you need to run the sample scripts themselves.

Finding the EMP Table

The easiest way to find out if you have access to the EMP table is to describe it with the following command:

```
SQL> DESCRIBE EMP;
```

One of two things happen. If you see the following for output, then you are all set and ready to proceed to creating the tables:

```
Name                            Null?    Type
 ------------------------------ -------- ----
 EMPNO                          NOT NULL NUMBER(4)
 ENAME                                   VARCHAR2(10)
 JOB                                     VARCHAR2(9)
 MGR                                     NUMBER(4)
 HIREDATE                                DATE
 SAL                                     NUMBER(7,2)
 COMM                                    NUMBER(7,2)
 DEPTNO                                  NUMBER(2)
```

But if you see this, that means you need to create the tables before you can use them:

```
SQL> DESCRIBE EMP
ERROR:
ORA-04043: object EMP does not exist
```

All you need to do is run the demobld procedure in the sqlplus/demo subdirectory of ORACLE_HOME. You execute it with this command:

```
SQL> @$ORACLE_HOME/sqlplus/demo/demobld
```

If you are running SQL*Plus from a MS Windows system, use %ORACLE_HOME% instead of $ORACLE_HOME.

If you have trouble running that, you might have a tablespace quota issue or some other problem, so talk to your DBA or system manager for more help.

Create the Additional Tables

With EMP accessible, you need to create the tables that will receive the output of your sample PL/SQL block. The STAFFERS table will hold all the staff-level employees selected by the script, and EXCEPTION_TABLE will hold all the errors logged. Use the code in Listing 25.1 to create the tables.

LISTING 25.1 CREATETABLE.SQL—SQL Script to Create Sample Tables

```
CREATE TABLE EXCEPTION_TABLE
 (ERROR_DATE DATE, ERROR_MSG VARCHAR2(64))
 TABLESPACE USERS
 STORAGE (INITIAL 1K NEXT 1K);

CREATE TABLE STAFFERS
 ( EMPNO NUMBER(4),
  ENAME VARCHAR2(10),
  JOB   VARCHAR2(9),
  SAL   NUMBER(7,2),
  HIREDATE DATE)
 TABLESPACE USERS
 STORAGE (INITIAL 1K NEXT 1K);

CREATE TABLE AUDIT_TABLE
 ( USERNAME    VARCHAR(15),
  REASON      VARCHAR2(10),
  DESCRIPTION   VARCHAR2(64))
TABLESPACE USERS
 STORAGE (INITIAL 1K NEXT 1K);
```

The TABLESPACE clause is optional; if you don't include it, the table is created in your default tablespace. It was put in there so the table would have no chance of being created in Oracle's SYSTEM tablespace, thus slowing down system performance. It is cheap insurance.

You should see this message after entering those commands:

```
Table created.
```

If you get an error creating the table, it is most probably a tablespace naming or quota issue. Talk to your sysadmins or DBAs for help.

Running the Script

As discussed before, anonymous PL/SQL blocks cannot be stored in the database. To execute the sample block, then, you have to type in the block every time you want to execute it or type it into a `.sql` file with an editor and save it to disk. Better yet, you can pull the script (`staffers.sql`) from the CD-ROM in the back of the book and not have to type it at all! `Staffers.sql` is shown in Listing 25.2.

LISTING 25.2 `STAFFERS.SQL`—Sample Script for Executing an Anonymous PL/SQL Block

```
-- staffers.sql
--
-- 06/25/1999 by Joe Duer
-- This sample PL/SQL anonymous block uses the Oracle provided
-- sample EMP table to demonstrate how to create an anonymous
-- block and execute.
--
-- This block created a cursor that selects all the staff-level
-- employees from the EMP table and writes five columns of data to a
-- new table called STAFFERS.

         -- Declaration section
DECLARE
                -- Create the cursor
  CURSOR cursor1 is
   SELECT empno, ename, job, hiredate, sal FROM emp
    WHERE JOB NOT IN ('PRESIDENT','MANAGER')
     ORDER BY sal ASC;  -- start with lowest paid employee

                -- Declare identifiers
  cur_empno  NUMBER(4);
  cur_ename  VARCHAR2(10);
  cur_job   VARCHAR2(9);
  cur_hiredate DATE;
  cur_sal   NUMBER(7,2);

                -- Execution section
BEGIN
  OPEN cursor1;            /* Open up the cursor */
  FOR COUNTER IN 1..999 LOOP      /* Start loop counter */

                    /* Get first record, next */
   FETCH cursor1 INTO cur_empno,
        cur_ename, cur_job, cur_hiredate, cur_sal;
```

LISTING 25.2 CONTINUED

```
   EXIT WHEN cursor1%NOTFOUND;     /* When no more records    */
                     /* Write record to staffers */
   INSERT INTO staffers VALUES
(cur_empno, cur_ename, cur_job, cur_sal, cur_hiredate);
                     /* Write record to staffers */
   COMMIT;                /* COMMIT the transaction  */
  END LOOP;
  CLOSE cursor1;             /* close the cursor when done */
                -- Exception section
EXCEPTION
                     /* When select returns 0 rows */
  WHEN NO_DATA_FOUND THEN
   INSERT INTO EXCEPTION_TABLE
   VALUES (SYSDATE,'No data found.');
                     /* Any other error      */
  WHEN OTHERS THEN
   ROLLBACK;
   INSERT INTO EXCEPTION_TABLE
   VALUES (SYSDATE,'An error occurred.');
END;
/
```

You execute the sample script from SQL*Plus with the following command:

```
SQL> @staffers.sql
```

When it executes without errors, you see this message:

```
PL/SQL procedure successfully completed.
```

Double-check that the script actually worked by selecting from the STAFFERS table to see if it was populated:

```
SQL> SELECT * FROM STAFFERS;
   EMPNO  ENAME      JOB        SAL        HIREDATE
---------- ---------- --------- ---------- ---------
   7369   SMITH      CLERK      880        17-DEC-80
   7900   JAMES      CLERK      1045       03-DEC-81
   7876   ADAMS      CLERK      1210       12-JAN-83
   7521   WARD       SALESMAN   1375       22-FEB-81
   7654   MARTIN     SALESMAN   1375       28-SEP-81
   7934   MILLER     CLERK      1430       23-JAN-82
   7844   TURNER     SALESMAN   1650       08-SEP-81
```

```
    7499     ALLEN       SALESMAN  1760         20-FEB-81
    7788     SCOTT       ANALYST   3300         09-DEC-82
    7902     FORD        ANALYST   3300         03-DEC-81

10 rows selected.
```

When you successfully run the procedure, proceed to the next section.

Dissecting the Anonymous PL/SQL Block

Now that all the setup work is done, let's take a look at the sample block and how it works. As mentioned, there are three components to a PL/SQL block: The declaration section, the execution section, and the exception section. This code snippet from the sample script is the declaration section:

```
         -- Declaration section
DECLARE
                -- Create the cursor
  CURSOR cursor1 is
   SELECT empno, ename, job, hiredate, sal FROM emp
    WHERE JOB NOT IN ('PRESIDENT','MANAGER')
     ORDER BY sal ASC;  -- start with lowest paid employee

                -- Declare identifiers
  cur_empno  NUMBER(4);
  cur_ename  VARCHAR2(10);
  cur_job   VARCHAR2(9);
  cur_hiredate DATE;
  cur_sal   NUMBER(7,2);
```

The purpose of the *declaration section* is to define all the structures used in the block. All identifiers (variables), cursors, constants, and user-defined exceptions are defined in the declaration section. The declaration section is optional; you don't have to include it if you have a simple block with no objects to declare.

If you take a look at the code, you see that the first thing declared is the cursor, named `cursor1`. Notice that the `SELECT` statement defining the cursor is put in at the time it is declared, not when the cursor is opened.

Under the definition of the cursor is the declaration of the identifiers you're using in this block. There are five identifiers, one for each of the columns the cursor is reading from the `EMP` table. The values from the `EMP` table are written into these identifiers, which are used for the insert into the `STAFFERS` table.

The next section in the block is called the *execution section*, where all the work gets done. The following code snippet shows the execution section:

```
-- Execution Section
BEGIN
  OPEN cursor1;              /* Open up the cursor */
  FOR COUNTER IN 1..999 LOOP       /* Start loop counter */

                    /* Get first record, next */
   FETCH cursor1 INTO cur_empno,
        cur_ename, cur_job, cur_hiredate, cur_sal;

   EXIT WHEN cursor1%NOTFOUND;     /* When no more records   */
                    /* Write record to staffers */
   INSERT INTO staffers VALUES
(cur_empno, cur_ename, cur_job, cur_sal, cur_hiredate);

                    /* Write record to staffers */
   COMMIT;              /* COMMIT the transaction  */
  END LOOP;
  CLOSE cursor1;             /* close the cursor when done */
```

First, the cursor is opened. The query is executed and the resulting rows are put into an object called a *resultset.*

Next, a `LOOP` counter is started. The counter starts at 1 and stops looping at the latest 999 times.

The `FETCH` statement on the next line retrieves the first (or next) row of the resultset. The five fields of that row are written into the five identifiers listed in the `FETCH` command.

The next statement is an `EXIT` statement; in this case, the loop exits when a `not found` condition is returned from the `FETCH` command. That essentially means the loop exits when all records have been read.

After the `EXIT` statement is the `INSERT` statement, which adds a row to the `STAFFERS` table, using as its input values the data in the five identifiers. After the `INSERT` is a `COMMIT` command, which commits the change to the database.

The purpose of the `END LOOP` statement is obvious. At this line, execution moves back to the top of the loop and continues through another pass.

The first (and only) statement executed after the loop exits is the `CLOSE cursor1` statement. The `CLOSE` command closes the cursor and releases any resources associated with it. After it is closed, you cannot reopen it and continue on.

The last section of the block is the *exception section*, where the error logic is included. Here is the code from the exception section:

```
-- Exception section
EXCEPTION
                    /* When select returns 0 rows */
  WHEN NO_DATA_FOUND THEN
   INSERT INTO EXCEPTION_TABLE
   VALUES (SYSDATE,'No data found.');

                    /* Any other error      */
  WHEN OTHERS THEN
   ROLLBACK;
   INSERT INTO EXCEPTION_TABLE
   VALUES (SYSDATE,'An error occurred.');

END;
```

In this code, two `WHEN` error conditions are defined. First, when a "No data found" error occurs, the script writes a row to the `EXCEPTION_TABLE` table with the current date and the message "No data found." This condition is hit when the cursor is opened and no rows match the criteria of the `SELECT` statement.

The other `WHEN` condition is a catchall. The keyword `OTHER` means that if *any other* error occurs, then execute this logic. The preceding example, executes a `ROLLBACK` command to undo any changes made so far, and then you write a generic error message to the `EXCEPTION_TABLE` table, logging that an error had occurred.

Creating Stored Functions and Procedures

In this section of the chapter, you learn how stored procedures and stored functions work. *Stored* functions and procedures means they are named objects stored in the database, ready to use. You use the `CREATE FUNCTION` and `CREATE PROCEDURE` commands to create them. You need to create them only once, and then they are online in the database until you remove them with a `DROP` command.

Stored Functions

Now that the basic PL/SQL block has been explained, let's extend that knowledge and create your first named object—a stored function.

A stored function is a typed object that can take input data in the form of parameters, execute a function on the data, and return a single value of a specific type. Let's create a function that reads all the salaries from the STAFFERS table and returns their median. The *median* salary is the average of the lowest and highest salaries stored in the table. Because you're creating a named function in the database, use the CREATE OR REPLACE FUNCTION command. This command loads the function into the database if it compiles correctly. That way, you don't have to re-create it each time you want to use it as with the anonymous PL/SQL block. The code for creating the function is shown in Listing 25.3.

LISTING 25.3 MED_STAFFER_SAL.SQL—Source Code for Function to Calculate the Median Staffer Salary

```
-- This function calculates the median salary of the
-- employees in the STAFFERS table. The median is
-- calculated by averaging the highest and lowest
-- value in a list of values. In this case, the
-- highest and lowest salaries will be averaged.

CREATE OR REPLACE FUNCTION med_staffer_sal
RETURN NUMBER IS

  minimum_sal    NUMBER(7,2);
  maximum_sal     NUMBER(7,2);
  average_sal     NUMBER(7,2);

BEGIN

  SELECT MIN(SAL) INTO minimum_sal from STAFFERS;
  SELECT MAX(SAL) INTO maximum_sal from STAFFERS;

  average_sal := (minimum_sal + maximum_sal) / 2;

RETURN(average_sal);

END med_staffer_sal;
/
```

Execute the script and you will see the following message:

```
Function created.
```

> **Note**
>
> You need the CREATE PROCEDURE database privilege to run this script and create the sample procedures in this chapter. If you get an error executing Listing 25.3, this is most likely the problem. Talk with your DBA to be granted this privilege.

Now, to test the function standalone, simply call the function while querying the pseudotable DUAL, as shown in the following example:

```
SQL> SELECT MED_STAFFER_SAL FROM DUAL;

MED_STAFFER_SAL
---------------
           1900
```

Stored Procedures

With stored functions out of the way, let's get a little deeper into PL/SQL by creating a stored procedure. Stored procedures accept parameters for input in the same way functions do, but the mandatory typed return value that functions must supply is not provided by a stored procedure. Stored procedures are created with the CREATE OR REPLACE PROCEDURE SQL command.

For our sample procedure, you will create one called COLA that grants a cost-of-living increase to all employees in the STAFFERS table. In Chapter 24, "Oracle SQL," you created a simple COLA procedure that changed all the salaries at once with an UPDATE statement. For this example, you will create a cursor and update each salary individually so that you can add the function of writing each change you make to an audit table. The source for this new procedure is shown in Listing 25.4.

LISTING 25.4 COLA.SQL—New Stored Procedure Example

```
-- This procedure grants a COLA (cost of living) salary
-- increase to all members of the STAFFERS table. The
-- one parameter passed in is the percentage increase, which
-- is passed in as an integer -- that is, a 10% raise is passed
-- in as a value of 10.
-- 06/25/1999 - Joe Duer

CREATE OR REPLACE PROCEDURE COLA
  (percentage IN INTEGER) IS
```

LISTING 25.4 CONTINUED

```
        -- Declare identifiers
  cur_empno     NUMBER;
  cur_ename     VARCHAR2(10);
  cur_old_sal    NUMBER(7,2);
  new_sal    NUMBER(7,2);
  username    VARCHAR2(15);
  emp_count    NUMBER;

        -- Create the cursor
  CURSOR cursor1 is
   SELECT empno, ename, sal FROM staffers;

        -- Execution section
BEGIN

  OPEN cursor1;     /* Open the cursor */

        /* Get values before loop */
  SELECT USER INTO username FROM DUAL;
  SELECT COUNT(*) INTO emp_count FROM staffers;

  FOR COUNTER IN 1..emp_count LOOP
        /* Get the next record */
FETCH cursor1 INTO cur_empno, cur_ename, cur_old_sal;

   EXIT WHEN cursor1%NOTFOUND; /* WHEN DONE */

        /* calculate new salary */
   new_sal := cur_old_sal * (1 + (percentage / 100));

        /* change salary in database */
   UPDATE STAFFERS
    SET SAL = new_sal
    WHERE EMPNO = cur_empno;
        /* Insert record in AUDIT_TABLE */
   INSERT INTO AUDIT_TABLE
    VALUES(username,
    'COLA',
    cur_ename ¦¦ ' salary changed from '¦¦ cur_old_sal ¦¦
    ' to '¦¦ new_sal);

  COMMIT;      /* Commit the changes to the database. */
```

LISTING 25.4 CONTINUED

```
  END LOOP;      /* Go back for more */

  CLOSE cursor1;
        -- Exception section
EXCEPTION
  WHEN NO_DATA_FOUND THEN
   INSERT INTO EXCEPTION_TABLE
   VALUES (SYSDATE,'No data found.');

  WHEN OTHERS THEN
   INSERT INTO EXCEPTION_TABLE
   VALUES (SYSDATE,'An error occurred.');

END;        /* That's all folks! */

/
```

This procedure is similar to the sample anonymous PL/SQL block you saw earlier in the chapter, with the exception of a few enhancements.

The first thing you will notice in the procedure definition is a parameter *percentage* that is passed in. Also, notice that you do a select of `USER` from `DUAL` to get the username of the person executing the procedure.

Next, notice the change in the loop counter. Instead of a `FOR` loop of `1...999`, you now select the count of rows from the `STAFFERS` table and place that count in the identifier `EMP_COUNT`. This is much classier than the earlier example, which was meant to be as simple as possible.

First, to get the procedure into the database, either type in Listing 25.4 and execute it or run the script `cola.sql` found on the CD-ROM.

```
SQL> @cola

Procedure created.
```

Now take a look at the `STAFFERS` table, in particular the values of the `SAL` column before you give them a `COLA` increase.

```
SQL> SELECT * FROM STAFFERS;
```

```
   EMPNO    ENAME       JOB         SAL         HIREDATE
---------- ---------- --------- ----------- ---------
   7369     SMITH       CLERK       800         17-DEC-80
   7900     JAMES       CLERK       950         03-DEC-81
   7876     ADAMS       CLERK       1100        12-JAN-83
   7521     WARD        SALESMAN    1250        22-FEB-81
   7654     MARTIN      SALESMAN    1250        28-SEP-81
   7934     MILLER      CLERK       1300        23-JAN-82
   7844     TURNER      SALESMAN    1500        08-SEP-81
   7499     ALLEN       SALESMAN    1600        20-FEB-81
   7788     SCOTT       ANALYST     3000        09-DEC-82
   7902     FORD        ANALYST     3000        03-DEC-81

10 rows selected.
```

Now execute the stored procedure `COLA`, and pass in the value of `10` for a 10% salary increase:

```
SQL> EXEC COLA(10);

PL/SQL procedure successfully completed.
```

You should see a message that the procedure completed successfully. After it has run successfully, query the `STAFFERS` table again to see the salary increase:

```
SQL> SELECT * FROM STAFFERS;

   EMPNO    ENAME       JOB         SAL         HIREDATE
---------- ---------- --------- ----------- ---------
   7369     SMITH       CLERK       880         17-DEC-80
   7900     JAMES       CLERK       1045        03-DEC-81
   7876     ADAMS       CLERK       1210        12-JAN-83
   7521     WARD        SALESMAN    1375        22-FEB-81
   7654     MARTIN      SALESMAN    1375        28-SEP-81
   7934     MILLER      CLERK       1430        23-JAN-82
   7844     TURNER      SALESMAN    1650        08-SEP-81
   7499     ALLEN       SALESMAN    1760        20-FEB-81
   7788     SCOTT       ANALYST     3300        09-DEC-82
   7902     FORD        ANALYST     3300        03-DEC-81

10 rows selected.
```

This looks great. Now you should check the `AUDIT_TABLE` table to see if the procedure logged all the salary changes:

```
SQL> COLUMN DESCRIPTION FORMAT A40;
SQL> SELECT * FROM AUDIT_TABLE;
USERNAME        REASON     DESCRIPTION
--------------- ---------- ----------------------------------------
JDUER           COLA       SMITH salary changed from 800 to 880
JDUER           COLA       JAMES salary changed from 950 to 1045
JDUER           COLA       ADAMS salary changed from 1100 to 1210
JDUER           COLA       WARD salary changed from 1250 to 1375
JDUER           COLA       MARTIN salary changed from 1250 to 1375
JDUER           COLA       MILLER salary changed from 1300 to 1430
JDUER           COLA       TURNER salary changed from 1500 to 1650
JDUER           COLA       ALLEN salary changed from 1600 to 1760
JDUER           COLA       SCOTT salary changed from 3000 to 3300
JDUER           COLA       FORD salary changed from 3000 to 3300

10 rows selected.
```

Digging Deeper into PL/SQL

In the previous section, you learned how to create PL/SQL stored functions and procedures. At this point, you know enough about PL/SQL to be able to handle a deeper, more technical discussion about its features.

In this section, you will take a more referential look at the PL/SQL statements and features you have seen so far, such as data types and literals, and then learn about more PL/SQL components—`LOCK TABLE`, `SAVEPOINT`, and `GOTO`, for example—that you have not seen before.

The next section of the chapter discusses the creation of packages and triggers and incorporates what you have learned in this chapter into the sample code so that you can use much more complicated sample scripts.

PL/SQL Literals, Data Types, and Operators

Let's start with the simple stuff—the real PL/SQL basics. You probably know most of this information already because it is common to all programming languages. With that in mind, I will summarize this information and present it to you in the form of a few tables.

The simple symbols are characters used in PL/SQL as delimiters and operators. Table 25.1 summarizes them.

TABLE 25.1 PL/SQL Simple Symbols

Symbol	*Character*	*Description*
+	plus sign	Addition operator
%	percent sign	Attribute indicator
'	single quote	Character string delimiter (open or closed)
.	period	Component selector
/	forward slash	Division operator
(	open parenthesis	Expression or list open delimiter
)	close parenthesis	Expression or list close delimiter
:	colon	Host variable indicator
,	comma	Item separator
*	star	Multiplication operator
"	double quote	Quoted identifier delimiter
=	equal sign	Relational operator
<	less than sign	Relational operator
>	greater than sign	Relational operator
@	at sign	Remote access indicator
;	semicolon	Statement terminator
-	minus sign	Subtraction/negation operator

Table 25.2 lists the PL/SQL compound symbols.

TABLE 25.2 PL/SQL Compound Symbols

Symbol	*Description*
**	Exponentiation operator
<>	Relational operator
!=	Relational operator
~=	Relational operator
<=	Relational operator
>=	Relational operator
:=	Assignment operator
..	Range operator
||	Concatenation operator
<<	Label delimiter—prepended
>>	Label delimiter—appended
--	One-line comment indicator
/*	Open comment
*/	Close comment

Now take a look at literals. A *literal* is a face-value piece of information. That is, no part of the literal's value is hidden in an identifier or needs to be calculated. Table 25.3 shows some sample literals and their type.

TABLE 25.3 Literals

Type	*Examples*
Integer	0, 12, -99, 12000 -1
Real	2.8, -9.287, +12.3, .987
Exponential	12e10, -3.2e4, 3e-3
Character	'q', 'Q', '&', '3', ' '
String	'Hi there!', 'TODAY', 'My name is Joe'
Boolean	TRUE, FALSE, NULL

Okay, with literals out of the way, let's move on to data types. Table 25.4 lists all data types available for use with PL/SQL.

TABLE 25.4 PL/SQL Data Types

Type	*Data Type Name*
SCALAR	BINARY_INTEGER
SCALAR	DEC
SCALAR	DECIMAL
SCALAR	DOUBLE PRECISION
SCALAR	FLOAT
SCALAR	INT
SCALAR	INTEGER
SCALAR	NATURAL
SCALAR	NATURALN
SCALAR	NUMBER
SCALAR	NUMERIC
SCALAR	PLS_INTEGER
SCALAR	POSITIVE
SCALAR	POSITIVEN
SCALAR	REAL
SCALAR	SIGNTYPE
SCALAR	SMALLINT
SCALAR	CHAR
SCALAR	CHARACTER
SCALAR	LONG
SCALAR	LONG RAW
SCALAR	NCHAR
SCALAR	NVARCHAR2
SCALAR	RAW
SCALAR	ROWID
SCALAR	STRING
SCALAR	VARCHAR
SCALAR	VARCHAR2
SCALAR	BOOLEAN

Table 25.4 PL/SQL Data Types

Type	*Data Type Name*
SCALAR	DATE
COMPOSITE	RECORD
COMPOSITE	TABLE
COMPOSITE	VARRAY
REFERENCE	REF CURSOR
REFERENCE	REF 'object type'
LARGE OBJECT	BFILE
LARGE OBJECT	BLOB
LARGE OBJECT	CLOB
LARGE OBJECT	NCLOB

Now that you have seen all the data types, take a look at the different ways of defining them in a function or procedure. First, to declare a variable in a PL/SQL script, you can simply declare the variable name and data type and the optional initialization value, as shown in these examples:

```
Counter   INTEGER;
StringVar   VARCHAR2(50);
RetireAge   SMALLINT := 70;
Code     CHAR 'X';
```

Next, you can use the `%TYPE` attribute to create the variable with the same data type as another variable, as shown here:

```
Counter2  Counter%TYPE
Full_Name  StringVar%TYPE
Age    RetireAge%TYPE := 22;
```

The last way to declare a variable is with the `DEFAULT` keyword, which comes into play when using parameters with stored procedures and functions. It allows you to specify a default value when a function or procedure is called and the values are not supplied. Take a look at the rewritten procedure specification for the `COLA` procedure written earlier:

```
CREATE OR REPLACE PROCEDURE COLA
  (percentage IN INTEGER DEFAULT 5) IS
```

This means that if the `COLA` procedure is called and no input parameters are passed in, the default value of `5` is inserted in its place and all the staffers get a 5% COLA increase.

More PL/SQL Statements

Let's move ahead with more of the basic PL/SQL statements. Some you have seen before, and some you have not.

COMMIT

The COMMIT statement makes any database changes permanent and usable by other users. Before the COMMIT statement is executed, only the person making the changes sees them. The COMMIT statement also releases all table- and row-level locks and erases any SAVEPOINT information added since the last COMMIT or ROLLBACK. ROLLBACK is the opposite of COMMIT in that it specifically undoes all changes that were not committed.

COMMIT has two optional parameters. The first parameter is the keyword WORK. It has no effect on the COMMIT; it is used only for readability.

The other parameter is the keyword COMMENT. You can use it along with a text string to associate the comment with the committed transaction. The maximum length of the comment is 50 characters. Here are some examples of using the COMMIT statement with these parameters:

Examples:

```
COMMIT;
COMMIT WORK;
COMMIT WORK COMMENT 'COLA adjustment committed';
```

DELETE

The PL/SQL DELETE statement is the SQL DELETE statement. You use DELETE to remove rows from a table. When deleting from a table, you qualify what is to be deleted by using the WHERE clause, which can be a conditional statement, such as WHERE (SAL < 1000), or can specify deleting the record at the current cursor position if you have one open and pointing to a row. You can also use the RETURNING and INTO clauses to copy a value from the row being deleted into a host array.

Here are some examples of using the DELETE statement, but see Chapter 7, "Inserts, Updates, and Deletes," for more detailed information.

```
DELETE FROM STAFFERS WHERE (SAL < 1000);
DELETE FROM STAFFERS WHERE (SAL < 1000)
  RETURNING SAL INTO :STAFF_SALS;
```

EXIT

The EXIT statement is used to exit from a loop condition. It takes two parameters: the label name of the loop you want to exit, and a WHEN clause. The WHEN clause creates a conditional exit; the loop is exited only when the condition in the WHEN clause is met.

You do not have to exit the loops in the reverse order of how they were entered. The EXIT command allows you to exit any of the outer loops as well as the current loop. Here are some examples:

```
EXIT;
EXIT inner_loop;
EXIT outer_loop WHEN cursor1%NOTFOUND;
```

GOTO

The GOTO statement performs an unconditional program branch to another statement in a PL/SQL program. The "branch to" destination is defined by the one parameter that the GOTO statement takes—a label.

The label can be a statement label or a block-level label. Labels are represented in PL/SQL as <<*label name*>>, as shown in these examples:

```
GOTO label;
IF condition THEN GOTO label;
```

IF

The IF statement in PL/SQL works much the same as the IF statement in compiled programming languages like C. The PL/SQL IF statement is composed of the following keywords:

- IF
- THEN
- ELSE
- ELSIF (ELSE IF)
- END IF

You can combine these keywords in three ways: IF-THEN, IF-THEN-ELSE, and IF-THEN-ELSIF....

You can have multiple ELSIF clauses in your IF statement, and each IF and ELSIF must be followed by a conditional statement that is evaluated.

The IF statement evaluates the conditional statement and then branches based on the result. If the result is a Boolean TRUE, then the logic after the IF statement is executed. If the result is a Boolean FALSE, then the logic after the ELSE or ELSIF keyword is executed. If there are no ELSE or ELSIF keywords after the IF statement, then nothing is done and the next statement in the block is executed. The following statements are examples of the IF statement:

```
IF sal > 5000 THEN sal := sal * 0.9
ENDIF
IF sal > 5000 THEN sal := sal * 0.9 ELSE sal := sal * 1.1;
ENDIF
IF sal > 5000 THEN sal := sal *0.8;
ELSIF sal < 2000 THEN
  sal := sal * 1.5;
  ELSE sal := sal *1.1
ENDIF;
```

INSERT

The INSERT statement is the SQL INSERT statement. You use the INSERT statement to add rows to a table. You can specify the values you want added with the VALUES keyword, or you can do the insert by using the returned rows of another SELECT statement (called a subquery). Also, the RETURNING keyword allows you to put the inserted values into a host array so that your script has them available and you won't have to select them again after the insert has been completed.

Here are some examples of the INSERT statement; see Chapter 7 for more detailed information.

```
INSERT INTO STAFFERS
 (EMPNO, ENAME, JOB, SAL, HIREDATE)
 VALUES (1234, 'JOHNSON', 'ANALYST', 4356, '01-JAN-99');

INSERT INTO STAFFERS
 (EMPNO, ENAME, JOB, SAL, HIREDATE)
 VALUES (cur_empno, cur_ename, cur_job, cur_sal, SYSDATE);
```

LOCK TABLE

The LOCK TABLE statement places a table-level lock on a specific table. It's used to lock a table so that you can share or deny access to that particular table while maintaining its integrity.

When locking the table, you specify the *lock mode*. Six lock modes are available:

ROW SHARE

ROW EXCLUSIVE

SHARE UPDATE

```
SHARE
SHARE ROW EXCLUSIVE
EXCLUSIVE
```

The last parameter you can pass to `LOCK TABLE` is the `NOWAIT` keyword. By default, if another user has a higher level lock than the one you are requesting, the `LOCK TABLE` command waits until the table is free, and then applies the lock. By specifying `NOWAIT`, the `LOCK TABLE` command exits immediately, and execution continues at the next line of your PL/SQL script. The following statement shows an example of using the `NOWAIT` keyword:

```
LOCK TABLE STAFFERS IN EXCLUSIVE MODE NOWAIT;
```

Looping Statements

There are a few ways to implement looping logic in your PL/SQL programs:

- `LOOP`
- `FOR LOOP`
- `WHILE LOOP`

The way these statements work parallels well with the `FOR` loop and `WHILE` loop in the compiled programming languages. Each of the looping statements uses an `END LOOP` statement to designate the *bottom* of the loop. Let's take a quick look at each.

The `LOOP` statement creates an unconditional loop—one that never exits unless you specifically code for it inside the loop. Here is an example:

```
LOOP
  sql statement;
  sql statement;
  sql statement;
  EXIT WHEN cur1%NOTFOUND;
  sql statement;
  sql statement;
END LOOP;
```

This loop will run indefinitely until it hits the error condition in the `EXIT` statement. If you took out the `EXIT` statement, the `LOOP` would never exit (barring a fatal error).

A `FOR LOOP` is exactly the same as in other computer languages. The loop initializes a counter and increments it each time the loop is completed. When the counter reaches its goal, the loop exits. Take a look at this example:

```
FOR counter IN 1.. 999 LOOP
 sql statement;
```

```
 sql statement;
 sql statement;
 sql statement;
 sql statement;
END LOOP;
```

This loop will execute 999 times, and then continue on to the next section of code.

A WHILE loop checks a Boolean condition before each execution of the loop. The loop exits when the condition returns a FALSE or NULL. If the condition is not TRUE the first time the loop is encountered, then the loop is not executed at all.

Here is an example of a WHILE loop:

```
WHILE test condition LOOP
 sql statement;
 sql statement;
 sql statement;
 sql statement;
 sql statement;
END LOOP;
```

The loop continues to run until the condition specified in the WHILE statement is met.

NULL

The NULL statement does not do anything; it simply passes control to the next statement. It's equivalent to the NOP (No Operation) assembler instruction. The NULL statement is generally used as a placeholder in IF-THEN-ELSE statements, when the original logic is removed or commented out and you just need a single statement added so that the block compiles correctly. Here's an example of using the NULL statement:

```
IF sal < 5000 THEN
  sal := sal * 1.1;
ELSE
-- sal := sal * 0.8 <== Commented out
  NULL;    /* NULL added in so syntax checker won't find error */
ENDIF;
```

RETURN

The RETURN statement exits the current subprogram and returns program control to the caller. Program execution then resumes at the statement after the call to the subprogram.

RETURN can return an exit status back to the caller or an identifier value. Functions use RETURN to pass their typed value back to the caller of the function, as shown in these examples:

```
RETURN(100);
RETURN(ename);
```

ROLLBACK

The ROLLBACK statement undoes database changes that have not been committed to the database yet. You can undo all the changes, or you can roll back to a specific savepoint and then commit. Savepoints are created by the SAVEPOINT command. For a full rollback, you can specify the statement ROLLBACK or ROLLBACK WORK (the WORK keyword has no effect other than to increase readability). To roll back to a specific savepoint, you use ROLLBACK TO SAVEPOINT *savepoint name*. Here are some examples of using ROLLBACK:

```
ROLLBACK;
ROLLBACK WORK;
ROLLBACK WORK TO SAVEPOINT save_1;
```

SAVEPOINT

The SAVEPOINT statement creates a savepoint at the current location. You can create as many savepoints as you need during the course of processing a transaction. Each savepoint is assigned a unique identifier.

Savepoints are used by the ROLLBACK statement to roll back a specific portion of a transaction. Then the remaining processing can be committed to the database. This eliminates the need to reprocess everything.

All savepoints are erased after a full roll back or a commit. Here's an example of the SAVEPOINT statement:

```
SAVEPOINT save1;
```

UPDATE

The UPDATE statement updates one or more columns of the selected rows in a table. The WHERE clause is used to specify the condition that causes a partilular row to be updated. The SET keyword indicates the new value for the column. You can update several columns in the same SET clause. You can specify the update value or include a query with the SET clause that reads in the value to be put in the updated record.

For more detailed information on the UPDATE command, see Chapter 7; here are some examples:

```
UPDATE STAFFERS SET SAL = SAL * 0.8;
UPDATE STAFFERS SET SAL = SAL * 0.8
  WHERE SAL < 4000;
```

Collections

A *collection* is, roughly speaking, Oracle's implementation of an array. Essentially you create the collection with a single identifier, and then load the values into the connection. Each value in the collection shares the same identifier name, but they are made unique by their subscript numbers (just like arrays). There are two types of collections: nested table collections and varray collections.

A *nested table* collection is a group of values linked together. A nested table is different from an array because it has no upper boundary. Also, when you delete an element from an array, an empty position remains in the array. Nested tables do not have that characteristic. When you remove an element from a nested table, the two adjacent values in the nested table are linked, closing the gap. If you like, you can think of a nested table as a linked list. Keep in mind, though, that the subscript numbers do not change. If you delete element subscript 8, then the nested table will contain elements 1 through 7, 9, 10, and so forth.

A *varray* collection is more like an array than a nested table. Varrays do have an upper limit to the number of values they can hold. Also, when you remove an element from a varray, the empty position remains.

For this example, create a SALARY_HISTORY collection to add to the STAFFERS table. The SALARY_HISTORY column will be a nested table of NUMBER(7,2), which is the same as the SAL column. The SALARY_HISTORY column will contain all salary rate changes for the employee.

Because you don't know how long the employee will stay at the company and how many salary changes will occur, it is best to use a nested table rather than a varray. Take a look at the SQL statement to create the collection SALARY_HISTORY:

```
CREATE TYPE SALARY_HISTORY AS TABLE OF NUMBER(7,2);
```

Note

You need to have the Objects option of Oracle Server licensed and installed to use the CREATE TYPE command.

```
ALTER TABLE STAFFERS
  ADD (HISTORY SALARY_HISTORY);
```

Cursors

Now it is time to take a look at cursors and the PL/SQL statements that go along with them. This section covers the following statements:

- OPEN
- FETCH
- CLOSE

You got a taste of how cursors work early in the chapter when you learned how to make a stored procedure. In this section, I will go over those commands in detail to give you a better understanding of how cursors work.

Initializing the Cursor

There are two types of cursors in the Oracle Server. *Implicit* cursors are not defined by the user; they are created when needed for queries that return only a single row. If you make a query that returns more than one row and don't have a cursor defined, you get an error. You cannot use the OPEN, FETCH, and CLOSE commands on an implicit cursor.

Explicit cursors are defined in the PL/SQL block with a statement of the following form:

```
CURSOR curname ( param1 TYPE, ...) IS
  SELECT ... FROM ...;
```

It is at this point that the query is executed and the returned rows are placed in what is called a resultset. The next thing you have to do before you can use the data in the resultset is to use the OPEN command to open the cursor.

OPEN

The OPEN command is used to open a predefined explicit cursor. If you want the cursor to point to the first record in the resultset, use the OPEN command with no parameters added:

```
OPEN cur_1;
```

You do have the option of passing parameters to the OPEN statement. You define them in the CURSOR statement and then pass them in with the OPEN statement, as shown here:

```
CURSOR cur_1 (cur_ename VARCHAR2(10)) IS
  SELECT EMPNO, ENAME, SAL FROM STAFFERS;
OPEN cur_1('SMITH');
```

FETCH

The FETCH statement reads the rows from the resultset into identifiers readable by the PL/SQL program. You must create identifiers for each of the cursor columns, and they must match data types. Also, in the FETCH statement, you must read the columns in the same order as when the cursor was created. For example, the code snippet in the previous section would be expanded to look like this:

```
Cur_empno staffers.empno%TYPE;
Cur_ename staffers.ename%TYPE;
Cur_sal staffers.sal%TYPE;

CURSOR cur_1 (cur_ename VARCHAR2(10)) IS
  SELECT EMPNO, ENAME, SAL FROM STAFFERS;

OPEN cur_1('SMITH');

FETCH cur_1 into cur_empno, cur_ename, cur_sal;
```

All you have to do now is add your processing logic and a LOOP statement, and you have a working procedure.

CLOSE

The CLOSE statement closes a currently open cursor. When you close it, the resultset becomes undefined. You can reopen the cursor if you want, without having to redefine it. If you try to FETCH on a closed cursor, an error is generated. The syntax of the CLOSE command is simple, as shown in the following example:

```
CLOSE cur_1;
```

Creating and Using Packages

A *package* is a set of related stored functions and procedures grouped into a logical unit. Oracle has some packages for the PL/SQL developer to use while writing code. You create your own packages by creating a package specification and package body. You use the CREATE PACKAGE and CREATE PACKAGE BODY to load the prototypes and compile the source into the database. In this section you will create a package called STAFFERMNT that includes many of the sample functions and procedures. I will also add some more so you can get a good look at what packages look like and how you can use them.

First you need to define what functions and procedures will be in the package. Then you create the package specification and load it into the database with the CREATE PACKAGE command. Next, you'll look at the individual functions and procedures and what they do.

Last, you compile and load the package body into the database with the CREATE PACKAGE BODY command.

Creating the Package Specification

Before you create the package specification you need to define what functions go into the package. Table 25.5 shows the individual elements of the STAFFERMNT package.

TABLE 25.5 STAFFERMNT Package Functions and Procedures

Return Value	*Type*	*Name*	*Description*
NUMBER	FUNCTION	GET_SALARY	Returns the current salary of employee
NUMBER	FUNCTION	GET_MED_SAL	Returns median salary
	PROCEDURE	HIRE_EMPLOYEE	Adds a row to STAFFERS
	PROCEDURE	FIRE_EMPLOYEE	Removes a row from STAFFERS
	PROCEDURE	COLA	Grants a cost-of-living salary increase
	PROCEDURE	SET_SALARY	Changes an individual salary rate
	PROCEDURE	SET_EMPLOYEE_ INFO	Updates employee info, minus salary
	PROCEDURE	CLOSE_ DIVISION	Fires all the employees

Next, take a look at Listing 25.5. This listing contains all the function prototypes for the package. All you have to do to create the package specification is execute this file.

LISTING 25.5 STAFFERMNTSPEC.SQL—STAFFERMNT Package Specification Creation Script

```
-- STAFFERMNTSPEC.SQL
-- This script creates the package specification for
-- the new STAFFERMNT package.
--
-- 06/25/1999 by Joe Duer
--

CREATE OR REPLACE PACKAGE STAFFERMNT AS

-- GET_SALARY - This function takes the unique employee
-- number as input and returns that employee's current
-- salary.
 FUNCTION GET_SALARY (employee_num NUMBER)
    RETURN NUMBER;

-- GET_MED_SAL - This function does not take an input
-- parameter; it gets the lowest and highest salary
```

LISTING 25.5 CONTINUED

```
-- in the STAFFERS table and returns the average of
-- the two (the median salary).
 FUNCTION GET_MED_SAL
    RETURN NUMBER;

-- HIRE_EMPLOYEE - This procedure takes five input
-- parameters: Employee #, Name, Title, Salary, and
-- Start date. A record is added to the STAFFERS table.
 PROCEDURE HIRE_EMPLOYEE (employee_num NUMBER,
              employee_name VARCHAR2,
              title     VARCHAR2,
              salary    NUMBER,
              start_date  DATE);

-- FIRE_EMPLOYEE - This procedure will remove the
-- specified employee from the STAFFERS table. Both
-- the employee number and name are required to make
-- sure a typo does not terminate the wrong person.
 PROCEDURE FIRE_EMPLOYEE (employee_num NUMBER,
              employee_name VARCHAR2);

-- COLA - This procedure grants a cost-of-living increase
-- to all employees in the STAFFERS table. The one
-- parameter you pass in is the increase perentage,
-- expressed as an integer.
 PROCEDURE COLA (percentage INTEGER);

-- SET_SALARY - This procedure changes an individual
-- employee's salary rate. The two parameters passed in
-- are the employee's number and the new salary rate.
 PROCEDURE SET_SALARY (employee_num NUMBER,
            new_salary  NUMBER);

-- SET_EMPLOYEE_INFO - This procedure is used to update
-- any information that may be incorrect in the STAFFERS
-- table. All information except salary is passed in. The
-- procedure finds the record based on the employee_number
-- and then updates that one record with the rest of the
-- input parameters.
 PROCEDURE SET_EMPLOYEE_INFO (employee_num   NUMBER,
               employee_name  VARCHAR2,
               title      VARCHAR2,
```

LISTING 25.5 CONTINUED

```
                start_date    DATE);

-- CLOSE DIVISION - This is a nasty procedure that fires
-- all the employees in the STAFFERS table. This procedure
-- reads each employee from the table and calls FIRE_EMPLOYEE
-- to update the table. This procedure takes no input
-- parameters.
 PROCEDURE CLOSE_DIVISION;

END STAFFERMNT;
/
```

When you execute this procedure, you see the following message:

```
Package created.
```

Creating the Package Body

Now take a look at the individual functions and procedures to be created in the package body. You don't have to type in any of the code for the package body as you are reading through this section of the chapter. In the last part of this section, you are pointed to a SQL script file on the CD-ROM that you can execute to create the package body.

GET_SALARY

This function simply looks up the salary of the employee that was passed in to the function. Take a look at the source code:

```
-- This function returns the current salary of the
-- employee specified by the input parameter. The
-- single input parameter this function takes is
-- the employee number of the employee to be looked up.
--
-- 06/25/1999 - Joe Duer

FUNCTION GET_SALARY
    (employee_num NUMBER)
RETURN NUMBER IS

            /* Declaration section */
employee_sal      NUMBER(7,2);

            /* Execution section  */
```

```
BEGIN

  SELECT SAL INTO employee_sal from STAFFERS
WHERE EMPNO = EMPLOYEE_NUM;
RETURN(employee_sal);

            /* Exception section  */
EXCEPTION
  WHEN NO_DATA_FOUND THEN
   INSERT INTO EXCEPTION_TABLE
   VALUES (SYSDATE,'get_salary: No data found.');

  WHEN OTHERS THEN
   INSERT INTO EXCEPTION_TABLE
   VALUES (SYSDATE,'get_salary: An error occurred.');
END get_salary;
```

There is no entry into the AUDIT_TABLE table, essentially because this is a READ-ONLY transaction. In a real-world situation, however, maybe salary lookups should be logged.

GET_MED_SAL

The GET_MED_SAL function simply returns the *median* salary for the STAFFERS table. There are no input parameters. This type of function would probably be used in some kind of report. Take a look at the source code, shown here:

```
-- This function calculates the median salary of the
-- employees in the STAFFERS table. The median is
-- calculated by averaging the highest and lowest
-- value in a list of values. In this case, the
-- highest and lowest salaries are averaged.

FUNCTION get_med_sal
RETURN NUMBER IS

            /* Declaration section */
  minimum_sal NUMBER(7,2);
  maximum_sal     NUMBER(7,2);
  average_sal     NUMBER(7,2);

            /* Execution section  */
BEGIN

  SELECT MIN(SAL) INTO minimum_sal from STAFFERS;
```

```
  SELECT MAX(SAL) INTO maximum_sal from STAFFERS;

  average_sal := (minimum_sal + maximum_sal) / 2;

RETURN(average_sal);

            /* Exception section  */
EXCEPTION
  WHEN NO_DATA_FOUND THEN
   INSERT INTO EXCEPTION_TABLE
   VALUES (SYSDATE,'get_med_sal: No data found.');

  WHEN OTHERS THEN
   INSERT INTO EXCEPTION_TABLE
   VALUES (SYSDATE,'get_med_sal: An error occurred.');

END get_med_sal;
```

This is essentially the same function you saw earlier, except for the addition of EXCEPTION logic. This function also uses implicit cursors to read from the STAFFERS table. Also, there is no entry into the AUDIT_TABLE table for executions of this function because it is READ-ONLY, and the information returned is not all that important.

HIRE_EMPLOYEE

In this procedure, you allow the user to add a new employee. It requires five input parameters: the employee's employee number, name, title, salary, and hire date.

The procedure inserts the employee into the STAFFERS table and then logs an entry in the AUDIT_TABLE table. Any errors during the procedure are written to the EXCEPTION_TABLE table.

```
-- This procedure processes a new employee hiring. You need
-- to pass in the following parameters when calling this
-- procedure: employee number, employee_name, title, salary,
-- and hire date. All successful calls to this procedure are
-- logged. Errors are written to EXCEPTION_TABLE.
--
-- 06/25/1999 - Joe Duer

CREATE OR REPLACE PROCEDURE HIRE_EMPLOYEE
           (employee_num  NUMBER,
        employee_name    VARCHAR2,
        title      VARCHAR2,
```

```
        salary      NUMBER,
        start_date     DATE) IS

        -- Declare identifiers
username    VARCHAR2(15);

        -- Execution section
BEGIN

  SELECT USER INTO username FROM DUAL;

  INSERT INTO STAFFERS
  VALUES(employee_num, employee_name,
    title, salary, start_date);

        /* Insert record in AUDIT_TABLE */
  INSERT INTO AUDIT_TABLE
    VALUES(username,
    'NEWHIRE',
    employee_name || ' hired, employee # is '|| employee_num);

  COMMIT;      /* Commit the changed to the db. */

        -- Exception section
EXCEPTION

WHEN OTHERS THEN
   ROLLBACK;
   INSERT INTO EXCEPTION_TABLE
   VALUES (SYSDATE,'hire_employee: An error occurred.');

END;        /* That's all folks! */
```

A ROLLBACK statement is included in the exception section because this procedure writes to two different tables. There is only one COMMIT statement, so if the writing of the audit record fails, the whole transaction fails and the insert to the STAFFERS table is rolled back.

A lot of checking could go into this procedure, such as duplicate employee numbers and a sanity check on the salary, but for your purposes here, the code is fine. All transactions are logged and errors written to the audit table.

FIRE_EMPLOYEE

The FIRE_EMPLOYEE procedure removes the specified record from the STAFFERS table. Two input parameters are passed in: the employee's name and employee number. Both parameters are required as a small bit of insurance against a typographical error. No cursors are defined in this procedure because the one SELECT statement uses an implicit cursor. All successful executions are logged to the audit table for security purposes. All errors are logged to the exception table.

```
-- This procedure terminates an employee by removing him
-- from the STAFFERS table. Once again, the transaction is
-- logged. There are two parameters required by this
-- procedure: employee_num and employee_name. Using both
-- help ensure that the correct person is canned. If the
-- input parameters don't point to the same row, then the
-- transaction fails.
--
-- 06/25/1999 - Joe Duer

CREATE OR REPLACE PROCEDURE FIRE_EMPLOYEE
(employee_num NUMBER,
     employee_name VARCHAR2) IS

        -- Declare identifiers
  username    VARCHAR2(15);

        -- Execution section
BEGIN

        /* get the name of user */
SELECT USER INTO username FROM DUAL;

        /* drop the employee from the table */
   DELETE FROM STAFFERS
WHERE EMPNO = employee_num
AND ename = employee_name;
        /* Insert record in AUDIT_TABLE */
   INSERT INTO AUDIT_TABLE
    VALUES(username,
    'FIREEMP',
    employee_name || ' TERMINATED employee # '|| employee_num);

  COMMIT;      /* Commit the changes to the db. */
```

```
        -- Exception section
EXCEPTION
  WHEN NO_DATA_FOUND THEN
   INSERT INTO EXCEPTION_TABLE
   VALUES (SYSDATE,'FireEmp: No data found.');

  WHEN OTHERS THEN
   INSERT INTO EXCEPTION_TABLE
   VALUES (SYSDATE,'FireEmp: An error occurred.');

END;        /* That's all, folks! */
```

COLA

This procedure grants a cost-of-living salary increase to all the members of the STAFFERS table. It is a procedure you have seen before, so I won't spend much time explaining it.

```
-- This procedure grants a COLA (cost of living) salary
-- increase to all members of the STAFFERS table. The
-- one parameter passed in is the percentage increase, which
-- is passed in as an integer -- ie: A 10% raise is passed
-- in as a value of 10.
-- 06/25/1999 - Joe Duer

CREATE OR REPLACE PROCEDURE COLA
  (percentage IN INTEGER) IS

        -- Declare identifiers
  cur_empno     NUMBER;
  cur_ename     VARCHAR2(10);
  cur_old_sal   NUMBER(7,2);
  new_sal    NUMBER(7,2);
  username    VARCHAR2(15);
  emp_count    NUMBER;

        -- Create the cursor
  CURSOR cursor1 is
   SELECT empno, ename, sal FROM staffers;

        -- Execution section
BEGIN

  OPEN cursor1;    /* Open the cursor */
```

```
        /* Get values before loop */
  SELECT USER INTO username FROM DUAL;
  SELECT COUNT(*) INTO emp_count FROM staffers;

  FOR COUNTER IN 1..emp_count LOOP
        /* Get the next record */
   FETCH cursor1 INTO cur_empno, cur_ename, cur_old_sal;

   EXIT WHEN cursor1%NOTFOUND; /* WHEN DONE */

        /* Calculate new salary */
   new_sal := cur_old_sal * (1 + (percentage / 100));

        /* Change salary in database */
   UPDATE STAFFERS
    SET SAL = new_sal
    WHERE EMPNO = cur_empno;
        /* Insert record in AUDIT_TABLE */
   INSERT INTO AUDIT_TABLE
    VALUES(username,
    'COLA',
    cur_ename ¦¦ ' salary changed from '¦¦ cur_old_sal ¦¦
    ' to '¦¦ new_sal);

  COMMIT;      /* Commit the changes to the db. */

  END LOOP;      /* Go back for more */

  CLOSE cursor1;
        -- Exception section
EXCEPTION
  WHEN NO_DATA_FOUND THEN
   INSERT INTO EXCEPTION_TABLE
   VALUES (SYSDATE,'Cola: No data found.');

  WHEN OTHERS THEN
   INSERT INTO EXCEPTION_TABLE
   VALUES (SYSDATE,'Cola: An error occurred.');

END;        /* That's all folks! */
```

The only change from the original version is the text added to the insertion into EXCEPTION_TABLE. Now the procedure name precedes the error text.

SET_SALARY

The SET_SALARY procedure is used to change the salary of a single employee. All you need to use this procedure are the employee number and the new salary.

```
-- SET_SALARY - This procedure changes an individual
-- employee's salary rate. The two parameters passed in
-- are the employee's number and the new salary rate.
-- 06/25/1999 - Joe Duer

CREATE OR REPLACE PROCEDURE SET_SALARY
(employee_num NUMBER,
      new_salary  NUMBER) IS

        -- Declare identifiers
  employee_name  VARCHAR2(10);
  old_sal     NUMBER(7,2);
  username    VARCHAR2(15);

        -- Execution section
BEGIN
        /* get values from STAFFERS */
  SELECT USER INTO username FROM DUAL;
  SELECT sal, ename INTO old_sal, employee_name FROM STAFFERS
  WHERE empno = employee_num;

        /* Adjust employee salary */
  UPDATE STAFFERS
    SET SAL = new_salary
    WHERE EMPNO = employee_num;

        /* Insert record in AUDIT_TABLE */
   INSERT INTO AUDIT_TABLE
    VALUES(username,
    'SETSAL',
    employee_name ¦¦ ' salary changed from '¦¦ old_sal ¦¦
    ' to '¦¦ new_salary);
  COMMIT;      /* Commit the changes to the db. */

        -- Exception section
EXCEPTION
```

```
  WHEN NO_DATA_FOUND THEN
   INSERT INTO EXCEPTION_TABLE
   VALUES (SYSDATE,'SetSal: No data found.');

  WHEN OTHERS THEN
   INSERT INTO EXCEPTION_TABLE
   VALUES (SYSDATE,'SetSal: An error occurred.');

END;        /* That's all, folks! */
```

This is a fairly simple procedure that changes the salary of a specific employee. This procedure is used in place of `SET_EMPLOYEE_INFO`, which does not allow the user to change the `salary` field.

SET_EMPLOYEE_INFO

The `SET_EMPLOYEE_INFO` procedure is used to update employee information in the `STAFFERS` table. There is no access to the employee salary from this procedure. This is a maintenance function for the employee's name, title, and start date. Changes to salary must go through the `SET_SALARY` procedure.

```
-- SET_EMPLOYEE_INFO - This procedure is used to update
-- any information that may be incorrect in the STAFFERS
-- table. All information except salary is passed in. The
-- procedure finds the record based on the employee_number
-- and then updates that one record with the rest of the
-- input parameters.
-- 06/25/1999 - Joe Duer

CREATE OR REPLACE PROCEDURE SET_EMPLOYEE_INFO
(employee_num  NUMBER,
          employee_name   VARCHAR2,
          title     VARCHAR2,
          start_date  DATE) IS

        -- Declare identifiers
username    VARCHAR2(15);

        -- Execution section
BEGIN

        /* Get value for audit table */
  SELECT USER INTO username FROM DUAL;
```

```
        /* Change info in database */
   UPDATE STAFFERS
    SET ename = employee_name,
     job = title,
     hiredate=start_date

    WHERE EMPNO = employee_num;

        /* Insert record in AUDIT_TABLE */
   INSERT INTO AUDIT_TABLE
    VALUES(username,
    'SETINFO',
    employee_name || ' employee informaion updated ');

  COMMIT;      /* Commit the changes to the db. */

        -- Exception section
EXCEPTION
  WHEN NO_DATA_FOUND THEN
   INSERT INTO EXCEPTION_TABLE
   VALUES (SYSDATE,'SetEmp: No data found.');

  WHEN OTHERS THEN
   INSERT INTO EXCEPTION_TABLE
   VALUES (SYSDATE,'SetEmp: An error occurred.');

END;        /* That's all, folks! */
```

CLOSE_DIVISION

The CLOSE_DIVISION procedure eliminates all the employees from the STAFFERS table. It is true that a single TRUNCATE TABLE command could do the job, but in this example you create a cursor and traverse through the table, canning employees one at a time. You write all actions to the AUDIT_TABLE table, so there is a log of what happened. If you used the TRUNCATE TABLE command, you wouldn't have that log.

```
-- CLOSE DIVISION - This is a nasty procedure that fires
-- all the employees in the STAFFERS table. This procedure
-- reads each employee from the table and deletes them from
-- the table. This procedure takes no input parameters.
-- 06/25/1999 - Joe Duer

CREATE OR REPLACE PROCEDURE CLOSE_DIVISION IS
```

```
        -- Declare identifiers
  cur_empno    NUMBER;
  cur_ename    VARCHAR2(10);
  username    VARCHAR2(15);
  emp_count    NUMBER;

        -- Create the cursor
  CURSOR cursor1 is
   SELECT empno, ename FROM staffers;

        -- Execution section
BEGIN

  OPEN cursor1;    /* Open the cursor */

        /* Get values before loop */
  SELECT USER INTO username FROM DUAL;
  SELECT COUNT(*) INTO emp_count FROM staffers;

  FOR COUNTER IN 1..emp_count LOOP
        /* Get the next record */
   FETCH cursor1 INTO cur_empno, cur_ename;

   EXIT WHEN cursor1%NOTFOUND; /* WHEN DONE */

        /* REMOVE EMPLOYEE from database */
   DELETE FROM STAFFERS
WHERE empno = cur_empno
  AND ename = cur_ename;

        /* Insert record in AUDIT_TABLE */
   INSERT INTO AUDIT_TABLE
    VALUES(username,
    'FIRE',
    cur_ename || ' has been terminated.');

  COMMIT;      /* Commit the changes to the db. */

  END LOOP;      /* Go back for more */

  CLOSE cursor1;
        -- Exception section
EXCEPTION
```

```
  WHEN NO_DATA_FOUND THEN
   INSERT INTO EXCEPTION_TABLE
   VALUES (SYSDATE,'Fire: No data found.');

  WHEN OTHERS THEN
   INSERT INTO EXCEPTION_TABLE
   VALUES (SYSDATE,'Fire: An error occurred.');

END;        /* That's all, folks! */
```

Using the CREATE PACKAGE BODY Command

Now that you have seen all the functions and procedures that make up the package body, it is time to use the CREATE PACKAGE BODY command to create the STAFFERMNT package body.

In a nutshell, you need to create a script that has as its first line:

```
CREATE PACKAGE BODY STAFFERMNT AS
```

Then insert all the function and procedure code you saw earlier (remember to remove the text CREATE OR REPLACE from each function and procedure).

You end the script with an END statement, along with the package body name as shown here:

```
END staffermnt;
```

Don't forget to terminate the script with the forward slash character (/). This character begins compiling the package body into the database.

The script will be rather large when you create it, about five pages, so I will not print it here in the chapter. If you have any trouble creating the script or you don't want to create the script, however, the script file STAFFERSMNTBODY.SQL is included on the CD-ROM that comes with this book.

When you run the script (either your own or the one on the CD-ROM), you will see this message:

```
Package body created.
```

When you see that message, you are done installing the STAFFERMNT package.

Oracle-Provided Packages

Oracle provides several packages with PL/SQL for your user-written functions and procedures.

`STANDARD`: The `STANDARD` package contains all the functions, data types, predefined exceptions, and so forth that form the PL/SQL environment.

`DBMS_STANDARD`: The `DBMS_STANDARD` package adds functions and procedures to PL/SQL that help application developers interact with the database server more effectively.

`DBMS_OUTPUT`: This package contains procedures that allow you to write output to the screen during script execution. This is a particularly good debugging tool.

`DBMS_PIPE`: The `DBMS_PIPE` package allows application developers to create named pipes that can be used for communication between database sessions. You use the `send_message` and `receive_message` procedures to send the messages through the pipe from one session to the other.

`UTIL_FILE`: The `UTIL_FILE` package allows you to open and write to files residing on the O/S file system.

`UTL_HTTP`: This package gives you the ability to make HTTP call-outs. You pass in a URL and then get the HTML data from the source.

`DBMS_ALERT`: This package allows you to set off database triggers whenever certain database events occur. You set the trigger to go off when a certain value changes.

Summary

This chapter has introduced Oracle's procedural language called PL/SQL. You have learned about the basic language syntax, how to create stored procedures and functions, cursors, exception handling, and creating a database package.

Although I covered all the major topics, I did not cover every option of every PL/SQL command. That would require a book of its own. If you get familiar with the fundamentals in this chapter, you will be ready to look a little further into the Oracle documentation and be able to understand all the additional features that the PL/SQL language offers.

CHAPTER

Microsoft Transact-SQL

In This Chapter

What Is Transact-SQL?

Microsoft SQL Server 7.0 provides Transact-SQL as the programming language for writing logic that executes on the server. Transact-SQL has extensions to the standard SQL commands that allow programmers to implement complex business logic on the server. This feature improves performance and reduces round-trip messages between the client and the server. Transact-SQL also allows the programmer to create compiled and stored procedures on the server. These stored procedures improve performance, ensure security, and help enforce business rules. Transact-SQL also has SQL statements that can be used to configure and administer Microsoft SQL Server. The commands are sent to SQL Server as Transact-SQL statements. The following elements are used in Transact-SQL:

- Identifiers: Names of objects in the database, such as tables, views, stored procedures, and triggers
- Data types: Used to define the data in a table column or a local variable in a stored procedure
- Functions: System-defined functions that take one or more parameters and return a value or a set of values
- Expressions: Units of syntax that can be resolved to a single value
- Operators: Used to perform operations on single expressions
- Comments: Non-executable statements in a script used for documentation purposes
- Reserved keywords: Words used by Microsoft SQL Server

Identifiers are the names of database objects. They are optional for certain objects, such as constraints and defaults. Identifiers, which can be 1 to 128 characters long, are created when objects are defined in the database. For local temporary tables or stored procedures, they cannot be more than 116 characters. For example, the following `CREATE TABLE` statement is used to create a table:

```
CREATE TABLE Salesperson (ID int not null PRIMARY KEY,
       Last_Name varchar(30) not null, First_Name varchar(30) null))
```

The identifier `Salesperson` is used to refer to the table object. The columns are referred as `ID`, `Last_Name`, and `First_Name`. The `PRIMARY KEY` constraint on the table is unnamed. In this case, SQL Server generates a unique name internally to represent the constraint. These are the rules for defining identifiers:

- The first character must be a letter as defined by the Unicode Standard 2.0 or the _ (underscore), @ (at sign), or # (number sign) symbol.
- The characters after that can be letters defined in the Unicode Standard 2.0 or decimal numbers from either Basic Latin or other national scripts or the @, $, #, or _ symbols.
- The identifier must not be a Transact-SQL reserved word. Both the uppercase and lowercase versions of reserved words are for internal use.
- Special characters or embedded spaces are not allowed in the identifier name.

Certain symbols like @ or $ at the beginning of an identifier have a special meaning in SQL Server. All local variable names or parameters to stored procedures begin with the @ character. An identifier that begins with a # character denotes a temporary table or stored procedure. The double ## character denotes a global temporary object, and the double @@ character means global variables. Global variables cannot be defined in Transact-SQL programmatically; they are only system supplied.

An object name in Microsoft SQL Server consists of four identifiers: server name, database name, owner name, and object name. The complete format for the object name is as follows:

```
<server name>.<database name>.<owner name>.<object name>
```

The server, database, and owner names are optional for referring to an object; they are called as *qualifiers*. The qualifiers can be omitted by just using the period, as shown in the following examples of object names:

```
sqlsvr01.pubs.dbo.authors
sqlsvr01...authors
pubs.dbo.authors
pubs..authors
dbo.authors
authors
```

All the object names refer to the `authors` table in the `pubs` database. The `authors` identifier name by itself refers to the `authors` table in the current database. If the user is connected to the `pubs` database, it refers to the `authors` table in that database. An object name with all four parts is referred to as a *fully qualified* name. Each object created must have a unique fully qualified name. For example, there can be two `authors` tables in the `pubs` database as long as their owner names are different. Column names are unique within a table or view. All objects in the local server are usually referred to by their three-part name.

When you're referring to an object, the following defaults are used for the identifier parts that are not supplied:

- <server name> defaults to the local server.
- <database name> defaults to the current database.
- <owner name> defaults to the user logged in to the server and his or her name in the database. If the user does not own an object with the specified name, then SQL Server looks for the object with the same name owned by the database owner, or dbo.

Objects in remote servers are referred to by their four-part names, such as remote stored procedures or tables used in distributed queries. This is the format of a four-part name for an object on a remote server:

```
<linked server>.<catalog>.<schema>.<object name>
```

In this format, <linked server> is the name of the linked server containing the object being referred to, <catalog> refers to the catalog or database that contains the object, <schema> is the owner of the object or the schema that contains the object, and <object name> is the name of the table or object. The linked server is an OLE DB data source that can return a result that Microsoft SQL Server can use as part of a Transact-SQL statement. For more information about four-part names and distributed queries, see the "Distributed Queries" topic in the Microsoft SQL Server Books Online.

Any identifier that conforms to all the rules for the format of identifiers can be specified as is. If an identifier uses a name that does not follow any of the rules for identifiers, then delimited identifiers have to be used. Delimited identifiers are used when the object name or portions of it are a reserved word or contain special characters. Microsoft SQL Server uses the double quotation mark (") or square brackets ([]) for delimiting identifiers.

```
[Empty Table]
"Credit & Debit Table''
```

Quoted identifiers can be used only when the QUOTED_IDENTIFIER setting is ON. This option can be set with the SET QUOTED_IDENTIFIER ON Transact-SQL statement, the "quoted identifier" option of the sp_dboption stored procedure, or the "user options" option of the sp_configure stored procedure. Microsoft SQL Server follows the SQL-92 rules when the QUOTED_IDENTIFIER setting is ON. Double quotation marks are used to delimit identifiers, and single quotation marks are used to enclose character strings. Bracketed identifiers can be used with or without the QUOTED_IDENTIFIER setting. Some examples that use delimited identifiers are shown in Listing 26.1.

LISTING 26.1 LST26_3.TXT—Examples of Quoted and Bracketed Identifiers

```
SET QUOTED_IDENTIFIER OFF
GO
CREATE TABLE [Credit & Debit Table]
```

LISTING 26.1 CONTINUED

```
(
[Account Number] int NOT NULL,
[Transaction Type] char(1) NOT NULL,
[Credit Or Debit Amount] money NOT NULL,
Balance money NOT NULL
)
GO
SET QUOTED_IDENTIFIER ON
GO
Insert Into ''Credit & Debit Table'' Values(1243, 'C', $1000, $5500)
Insert Into [Credit & Debit Table] Values(2443, 'D', $200, $2300)
go
SET QUOTED_IDENTIFIER OFF
GO
Update [Credit & Debit Table]
Set [Credit Or Debit Amount] = [Credit Or Debit Amount] - $400,
  Balance = Balance + $400
Where [Account Number] = 1243 And [Transaction Type] = 'C'
GO
```

You can see that the bracketed identifiers work with the `QUOTED_IDENTIFIER` setting `ON` or `OFF`.

Data Types

Microsoft SQL Server has data types that can be used to define columns in tables and variables in Transact-SQL scripts. The system-supplied data types can be broadly classified into eight categories: integer, numeric, non-Unicode character, Unicode character, binary, datetime, money, and special data types.

Integer

- `tinyint` Integer data from 0 through 255. Storage size is 1 byte.
- `smallint` Integer data from -32,768 (2^15) through 32,767 (2^15 - 1). Storage size is 2 bytes.
- `int` Integer data from -2,147,483,648 (-2^31) through 2,147,483,647 (2^31 - 1). Storage size is 4 bytes.

Numeric

- `float` Approximate numeric data with floating precision from -1.79E + 308 through 1.79E + 308. Storage size is up to 8 bytes, depending on the precision.
- `real` Approximate numeric data with floating precision from -3.40E + 38 through 3.40E + 38. Storage size is 4 bytes. Real data type is internally represented as `float(24)`.
- `decimal` Fixed precision and scale numeric data from -10^38 -1 through 10^38 -1. Storage size is up to 17 bytes, depending on the precision.

The `float` data type is declared as `float(n)`; *n* is the number of bits used to store the mantissa of the value in scientific notation. Microsoft SQL Server uses the round-up method of the IEEE 754 specification to represent floating-point values. The values of `n` range from `1` through `53`. The storage size for the `float` data type is shown in Table 26.1.

TABLE 26.1 Storage Size for the `float` Data Type

n	*Storage Size*
1-24	4
25-53	8

The `decimal` data type is declared as `decimal(p, s)` ; `p` is the precision and `s` is the scale. Both precision and scale are optional. Precision (`p`) is the maximum number of decimal digits that can be stored, both to the left and the right of the decimal point. The maximum precision is 38 digits. Scale (`s`) is the maximum number of decimal digits that can be stored to the right of the decimal point. Scale must be from `0` through `p`. The default scale is `0`. The storage size of the `decimal` data type is shown in Table 26.2. The data values are stored exactly as specified.

TABLE 26.2 Storage Size for the `numeric` Data Type

Precision	*Storage Size*
10-19	9
20-28	13
29-38	17

Each `decimal` data type with a specific combination of precision and scale is a different data type. For example, `decimal(10,2)` and `decimal(15,5)` are considered different data types. The global variable `@@MAX_PRECISION` returns the maximum level of precision that is configured in the SQL Server.

Non-Unicode Character

- `char` Fixed-length character data with a maximum length of 8,000 characters. Storage size is `n` bytes; `n` is the number of characters specified.
- `varchar` Variable-length character data with a maximum length of 8,000 characters. Storage size is the actual length of the data specified up to a maximum of `n` bytes.
- `text` Variable-length character data with a maximum length of 2,147,483,647 (2^31 - 1) characters.

The fixed-length character data type is specified as `char(n)`. The variable-length character data type is specified as `varchar(n)`. In both data types, `n` is the number of characters. When `n` is not determined, the default length is `1`. The `character` data types store data composed of uppercase or lowercase characters, numerals, and special characters.

Unicode Character

- `nchar` Fixed-length character data with a maximum length of 4,000 characters. Storage size is `2*n` bytes; `n` is the number of characters used.
- `nvarchar` Variable-length character data with a maximum length of 4000 characters. Storage size is 2 multiplied by the actual number of characters, up to a maximum of `2*n` bytes.
- `ntext` Variable-length character data with a maximum length of 1,073,741,823 (2^30 - 1) characters.

The fixed-length Unicode character data type is specified as `nchar(n)`. The variable-length Unicode character data type is specified as `nvarchar(n)`. In both data types, `n` is the number of characters. When `n` is not determined, the default length is `1`. Unicode data uses the UCS-2 character set. The Unicode specification defines a single encoding scheme to represent all characters. The encoding scheme uses 2 bytes to encode each character, so there are enough patterns to represent 65,536 characters. Unicode supports a wider range of characters. However, more space is needed to store Unicode characters. The Unicode data types are based on the National Character data types in the SQL-92 standard. Unicode constants are indicated with a leading `N` in Microsoft SQL Server like `N'Unicode'`.

Binary

- `binary` Fixed-length binary data with a maximum length of 8,000 bytes. Storage size is `n + 4` bytes; `n` is the length of the binary data.

- `varbinary` Variable-length binary data with a maximum length of 4,000 bytes. Storage size is `n + 4` bytes; `n` is the length of the binary data.
- `image` Variable-length binary data with a maximum length of 2,147,483,647 (2^31 - 1) bytes.

The fixed-length binary data type is specified as `binary(n)`, and `varbinary(n)` indicates the variable-length binary data type. In both, `n` is the number of bytes. When `n` is not specified, the default length is `1`.

Datetime

- `Smalldatetime` Date and time values from January 1, 1900 through June 6, 2079, with an accuracy of one minute. Storage size is 4 bytes.
- `datetime` Date and time values from January 1, 1753 through December 31, 9999, with an accuracy of three-hundredths of a second. Storage size is 8 bytes.

The `datetime` and `smalldatetime` data types store date and time values. There is no separate data type to store time and date values alone. If only a time is specified, the date defaults to January 1, 1900. If only a date is specified, the time defaults to 12:00 a.m. Date and time values are enclosed in single quotes; you can use alphabetic (`'January 10, 1999'`), numeric (`'01/10/1999'`), or unseparated string (`'1999-01-10'`) formats. The `datetime` data type is stored internally as two 4-byte integers. The first 4 bytes store the number of days before or after the system reference date of January 1, 1900. The second 4 bytes store the number of milliseconds after midnight. The `smalldatetime` data type is stored internally as two 2-byte integers. The first 2 bytes store the number of days after January 1, 1900. The second two bytes store the number of minutes after midnight.

Money

- `money` Monetary values from -922,337,203,685,477.5808 (-2^63) through 922,337,203,685,477.5807 (2^63 -1), with an accuracy of ten-thousandth of a monetary unit. Storage size is 8 bytes.
- `smallmoney` Monetary values from -214,748.3648 (-2^31) through 214,748.3647 (2^31 -1), with an accuracy of ten-thousandth of a monetary unit. Storage size is 4 bytes.

Monetary data stores positive and negative amounts of money with an accuracy of four decimal places and uses the currency symbol. For a list of currency symbols supported in Microsoft SQL Server, refer to the "Using Monetary Data" topic in Microsoft SQL Server Books Online.

Special

- `bit` Stores an integer value of `1`, `0`, or `NULL`. Uses 1 byte to store eight or fewer numbers of bit values. Uses 2 bytes to store nine to sixteen bit values and so on.
- `cursor` Stores a reference to a server-side cursor. The `cursor` data type cannot be used for a table column. Variables declared with the `cursor` data type are always nullable.
- `timestamp` Unique number within a database. Storage size is 8 bytes.
- `uniqueidentifier` A globally unique identifier, or GUID. Storage size is 16 bytes.

The `timestamp` data type is a database-wide unique number. Only one timestamp column can be defined in a table. The value in the timestamp column is updated when a row is inserted or updated. The global variable `@@DBTS` returns the last used timestamp value for the current database. A new timestamp value is generated when a row with a timestamp column is inserted or updated.

The `uniqueidentifier` data type can be initialized using the `NEWID()` function or a string constant of the form `xxxxxxxx-xxxx-xxxx-xxxx-xxxxxxxxxxxx`; `x` is a hexadecimal digit. The only operations allowed on the `uniqueidentifier` data type are the equality operators (= and <>) and the `IS NULL` and `IS NOT NULL` operators.

Microsoft SQL Server provides synonyms for SQL-92 compatibility. Table 26.3 lists the SQL-92 synonyms and the data type it is mapped to in SQL Server.

TABLE 26.3 SQL-92 Synonyms for Data Types

Synonym	*Mapped Data Type*
Integer	int
float(n) n = 1-7	real
float(n) n = 8-15	float
double precision	float
dec	decimal
numeric	decimal
character	char
character(n) n = 1-8000	char(n)
char varying or character varying	varchar
character varying(n) n = 1-8000	varchar(n)
national char(n) n = 1-4000	nchar(n)
national character(n) n = 1-4000	nchar(n)
national char varying(n) or national character varying(n) n = 1-4000	nvarchar(n)
national text	ntext
binary varying	varbinary

Microsoft SQL Server supports user-defined data types, based on the system data types, that allow the same data type to be shared across different tables. For example, a user-defined data type called SSN can be created based on the char data type. To create a user-defined data type, use the system stored procedure sp_addtype, which has the following syntax:

```
sp_addtype @typename = <name>,
@phystape = <system data type>, @nulltype = <nullability>
```

In this procedure, <name> is the name of the user-defined data type that is unique within a database. The name should follow the rules for identifiers. The <system data type> parameter is the data type on which the user-defined data type is based; <nullability> indicates how the user-defined data type handles null values. The valid values for <nullability> are NOT NULL, NULL, and NONULL. If <nullability> is not explicitly defined, then the systemwide default is used. To see an example of how to create a user-defined data type, take a look at the Transact-SQL code in Listing 26.2. It creates a user-defined data type for SSN, binds a rule to the data type, and demonstrates how to use the data type in a table.

LISTING 26.2 LST26_2.TXT—User-Defined Data Type for SSN

```
CREATE RULE SSN_Rule AS
@SSN LIKE REPLICATE('[0-9]', 3) + '-' + REPLICATE('[0-9]', 2) +
     '-' + REPLICATE('[0-9]', 4)
go
exec sp_addtype 'SSN', 'varchar(11)', 'NOT NULL'
exec sp_bindrule 'SSN_Rule', 'SSN'
go
CREATE TABLE People ( First_Name varchar(20) NULL,
           Last_Name varchar(20) NOT NULL, SSN SSN)
go
Insert Into People Values('John', 'Smith', '123-44-5632')
go
Print 'Trying to insert row with invalid SSN format...'
Insert Into People Values('Meander', 'Smith', '123u8488844')
go
/*
Server: Msg 513, Level 16, State 1, Line 1
A column insert or update conflicts with a rule imposed by a previous
CREATE RULE statement. The statement was terminated. The conflict occurred
in database 'pubs', table 'People', column 'SSN'.
The statement has been terminated.
```

LISTING 26.2 CONTINUED

```
*/
Print ''
Print 'Trying to insert row with NULL value for SSN...'
Insert Into People Values('Meander', 'Smith', NULL)
go
/*
Server: Msg 515, Level 16, State 2, Line 1
Cannot insert the value NULL into column 'SSN', table 'pubs.dbo.People';
column does not allow nulls. INSERT fails.
The statement has been terminated.
*/
```

Listing 26.2 uses several statements provided by Transact-SQL. The `CREATE RULE` statement creates user-defined rules in the database that can be shared by several tables—that is, they can be bound to columns in different tables. The rules created by the `CREATE RULE` statement can be bound to a column or user-defined data type. This statement's syntax is as follows:

```
CREATE RULE <rule name> AS <condition expression>
```

In this statement, `<rule name>` is the name of the rule, and should conform to the rules for identifiers. The `<condition expression>` parameter is the conditions the rule should evaluate. The expression can consist of arithmetic operators, relational operators, predicates, and built-in functions that do not refer to any database objects. It includes a local variable that refers to the value supplied with the `INSERT` or `UPDATE` statement. When a rule is bound to a column in a table, it does not apply to any existing data in the table. A rule can be created only in the current database. After a rule is created, the `sp_bindrule` system stored procedure binds the rule to a column or user-defined data type. In the example, the `CREATE RULE` statement creates a rule called `SSN_Rule` that ensures the `SSN` value entered is in the correct format and validates the characters entered. The statement uses the `LIKE`predicate to check that the `SSN` format is `xxx-xx-xxxx` with only numerals in each position. To do this, you must form a pattern that `LIKE` can use:

```
'[0-9][0-9][0-9]-[0-9][0-9]-[0-9][0-9][0-9][0-9]'
```

This expression instructs `LIKE` to check that each digit is only numerals, which are separated by dashes. The `REPLICATE` function generates duplicates of a string. The `sp_addtype` stored procedure creates the user-defined data type called `SSN` using the `varchar` base data type. The `SSN` data type is also specified as `NOT NULL` able. The `sp_bindrule` stored procedure binds the rule to the user-defined data type and to any columns defined as the `SSN` data type. This procedure has a parameter called `@futureonly` that prevents the rule from being binded to existing columns. The `CREATE TABLE` statement creates a simple table that contains people's names and SSNs. The insert statements demonstrate how the rule is applied to the values of `SSN`. The first insert statement is processed successfully because the `SSN` value is in the correct format. The second and third insert statements fail because the value isn't in the correct format. The messages shown in comments in Listing 26.2 indicate that the value entered violated with the condition in the rule and the user-defined data type.

Objects containing data are associated with a data type that defines what type of data the object can contain. In Microsoft SQL Server, the following objects are specified with data types:

- Columns in tables or views
- Variables used in Transact-SQL code
- Parameters of stored procedures
- Functions that return any value or set of values

Associating an object with a data type defines the kind of data that can be stored in the object, the length of the data, and the precision and scale for `numeric` data types. The values for data types are specified as constants. The format of a constant depends on the data type; here are some examples:

- `integer` constants: `1243` or `-9498`
- `decimal` constants: `2423.987`, `-9438.48`, or `14.0`
- `float` constants: `24.698E2`, `5.9E-12`, or `-0.1E2`
- `character` constants: `'Smith'` or `'D''Isaster'`
- `Unicode` constants: `N'Bourée'`
- `binary` constants: `0xabcd` or `0x1E94`
- `datetime` constants: `'1999-04-10'`, `'January 10, 1990'` , `'20:20:04'`, or `'10:20 PM'`
- `money` constants: `$1340`, , `$29.95`, or `-$566`
- `bit` constants: `1` or `0`
- `uniqueidentifier` constants: `0x12eb94cd094aa83bc830c8356edff447` or `'3DC6-AB8D-9E45-0BA8-DEF7-103C-67D8-3DAB'`

Data Type Conversions

In Transact-SQL, data type conversion occurs when any operation is performed on two objects with different data types. The conversions happen either implicitly or explicitly. *Implicit conversions* are performed automatically by the server; no user intervention is required. In this case, if an object of a data type is combined with another object of a data type, then the data type of one object is converted to the other compatible format. For example, if an addition operation is performed between two variables, one of `smallint` data type and the other of `int` data type, then the `smallint` value is first converted into `int` data type and the operation is performed. *Explicit conversions* are done programmatically with the `CAST` or `CONVERT` functions, which are used to convert a value from one data type to another. The value can be a local variable, a column, or an expression. The `CAST` function is based on the SQL-92 standard. When converting from one data type to another, certain conversions are not supported.

The data type precedence rules determine which data type is converted to the other when two expressions of different data types are combined by an operator. The data type with the lower precedence is converted to the data type with the higher precedence. If the conversion is not a supported implicit conversion, an error is returned. When both operand expressions have the same data type, the result of the operation has that data type.

The precedence order for Microsoft SQL Server data types is shown in the following list:

`datetime` (highest)

`smalldatetime`

`float`

`real`

`decimal`

`money`

`smallmoney`

`int`

`smallint`

`tinyint`

`bit`

`ntext`

`text`

`image`

`timestamp`

`nvarchar`

```
nchar
varchar
char
varbinary
binary
uniqueidentifier
```
(lowest)

The data type precedence rules are modified by the comparison operators because they always return a true or false value. When a comparison operator is applied to expressions of two different data types, one expression is converted to the data type of the other before the comparison is made. The data type precedence rules are applied for this internal conversion, with the following exceptions:

- If one of the expressions is an aggregate function that is not in a subquery, and the other expression is not an aggregate, then the data type of the aggregate function is used regardless of the precedence rules.
- If one of the expressions is a column, and the other is not a column or aggregate function, the data type of the column is used regardless of the precedence rules.

From: \ To:	binary	varbinary	char	varchar	nchar	nvarchar	datetime	smalldatetime	decimal	numeric	float	real	int(INT4)	smallint(INT2)	tinyint(INT1)	money	smallmoney	bit	timestamp	uniqueidentifier	image	ntext	text
binary		◉	◉	◉	◉	◉	◉	◉	◉	◉	○	○	◉	◉	◉	◉	◉	◉	◉	◉	◉	○	○
varbinary	◉		◉	◉	◉	◉	◉	◉	◉	◉	○	○	◉	◉	◉	◉	◉	◉	◉	◉	◉	○	○
char	●	●		◉	◉	◉	◉	◉	◉	◉	◉	◉	◉	◉	◉	●	●	◉	●	◉	◉	◉	◉
varchar	●	●	◉		◉	◉	◉	◉	◉	◉	◉	◉	◉	◉	◉	●	●	◉	●	◉	◉	◉	◉
nchar	●	●	◉	◉		◉	◉	◉	◉	◉	◉	◉	◉	◉	◉	●	●	◉	●	◉	○	◉	◉
nvarchar	●	●	◉	◉	◉		◉	◉	◉	◉	◉	◉	◉	◉	◉	●	●	◉	●	◉	○	◉	◉
datetime	●	●	◉	◉	◉	◉		◉	●	●	●	●	●	●	●	●	●	●	●	○	○	○	○
smalldatetime	●	●	◉	◉	◉	◉	◉		●	●	●	●	●	●	●	●	●	●	●	○	○	○	○
decimal	◉	◉	◉	◉	◉	◉	◉	◉	★	★	◉	◉	◉	◉	◉	◉	◉	◉	◉	○	○	○	○
numeric	◉	◉	◉	◉	◉	◉	◉	◉	★	★	◉	◉	◉	◉	◉	◉	◉	◉	◉	○	○	○	○
float	◉	◉	◉	◉	◉	◉	◉	◉	◉	◉		◉	◉	◉	◉	◉	◉	◉	○	○	○	○	○
real	◉	◉	◉	◉	◉	◉	◉	◉	◉	◉	◉		◉	◉	◉	◉	◉	◉	○	○	○	○	○
int(INT4)	◉	◉	◉	◉	◉	◉	◉	◉	◉	◉	◉	◉		◉	◉	◉	◉	◉	◉	○	○	○	○
smallint(INT2)	◉	◉	◉	◉	◉	◉	◉	◉	◉	◉	◉	◉	◉		◉	◉	◉	◉	◉	○	○	○	○
tinyint(INT1)	◉	◉	◉	◉	◉	◉	◉	◉	◉	◉	◉	◉	◉	◉		◉	◉	◉	◉	○	○	○	○
money	◉	◉	●	●	●	●	◉	◉	◉	◉	◉	◉	◉	◉	◉		◉	◉	◉	○	○	○	○
smallmoney	◉	◉	●	●	●	●	◉	◉	◉	◉	◉	◉	◉	◉	◉	◉		◉	◉	○	○	○	○
bit	◉	◉	◉	◉	◉	◉	◉	◉	◉	◉	◉	◉	◉	◉	◉	◉	◉		◉	○	○	○	○
timestamp	◉	◉	◉	◉	○	○	◉	◉	◉	◉	○	○	◉	◉	◉	◉	◉	◉		○	◉	○	○
uniqueidentifier	◉	◉	◉	◉	◉	◉	○	○	○	○	○	○	○	○	○	○	○	○	○		○	○	○
image	◉	◉	○	○	○	○	○	○	○	○	○	○	○	○	○	○	○	○	◉	○		○	○
ntext	○	○	●	●	◉	◉	○	○	○	○	○	○	○	○	○	○	○	○	○	○	○		○
text	○	○	◉	◉	●	●	○	○	○	○	○	○	○	○	○	○	○	○	○	○	○	○	

● Explicit conversion
◉ Implicit conversion
○ Conversion not allowed
★ Requires CONVERT when loss of precision or scale will occur

FIGURE 26.1
Figure 26.1 is a chart listing all explicit and implicit data type conversions supported by Microsoft SQL Server.

This is the syntax of the `CAST` and `CONVERT` functions:

```
CAST(<expression> AS <data type>)
```

```
CONVERT(<data type>, <expression>, <style>)
```

In these functions, `<expression>` is a constant, variable, or column. The `<data type>` parameter is the system-supplied data type the `<expression>` has to be converted to. The `<style>` parameter is the date format used to convert `datetime` data types to character strings. Table 26.4 lists the styles available for `datetime` conversions.

TABLE 26.4 Styles for `datetime` Conversions

Without Century	*With Century*	*Format Type*	*Input/Output*
0	100	Default	mon dd yyyy hh:miAM (or PM)
1	101	USA	mm/dd/yy
2	102	ANSI	yy.mm.dd
3	103	British or French	dd/mm/yy
4	104	German	dd.mm.yy
5	105	Italian	dd-mm-yy
6	106	-	dd mon yy
7	107	-	mon dd, yy
8	108	-	hh:mm:ss
9	109	Default + milliseconds	mon dd yyyy hh:mi:ss: mmmAM (or PM)
10	110	USA	mm-dd-yy
11	111	Japan	yy/mm/dd
12	112	ISO	Yymmdd
13	113	Europe Default + milliseconds hh:mm:ss: mmm(24h)	dd mon yyyy
14	114	-	hh:mi:ss:mmm(24h)
20	120	ODBC Canonical	yyyy-mm-dd hh:mi:ss(24h)
21	121	ODBC Canonical + milliseconds	yyyy-mm-dd hh:mi:ss.mmm(24h)

Microsoft SQL Server interprets two-digit years based on a cutoff year of 2049. That is, the two-digit year 49 is interpreted as 2049 and the two-digit year 50 is interpreted as 1950. This configuration option can be used to change the cutoff year used by SQL Server. When you convert `smalldatetime` values to styles that include seconds or milliseconds, the seconds or milliseconds positions show zero.

Table 26.5 lists the style values for converting floating-point values to character data.

TABLE 26.5 Styles for Floating-Point Conversions

Value	*Output*
0	Maximum of six digits of the value is converted
1	Maximum of eight digits with scientific notation
2	Maximum of 16 digits with scientific notation

Table 26.6 lists the style values for converting monetary data to character data.

TABLE 26.6 Styles for `money` Conversions

Value	*Output*
0	No commas every three digits to the left of the decimal point, and two digits to the right of the decimal point in the character data
1	Commas every three digits to the left of the decimal point, and two digits to the right of the decimal point in the character data
2	No commas every three digits to the left of the decimal point, and four digits to the right of the decimal point in the character data

The text and image data types are not implicitly converted. These data types have to be explicitly converted. The text data can be converted to character data with a maximum length of 8,000 characters. The image data can be converted to binary data with a maximum of 8,000 bytes. When converting character or binary expressions (`char`, `nchar`, `nvarchar`, `varchar`, `binary`, or `varbinary`) to an expression of a different data type, data can be truncated or only partially displayed, or an error is returned because the result is too short to display.

When performing conversions that convert a value from its original data type and back again, Microsoft SQL Server guarantees that the same value is returned. For example, the code Listing in 26.3 converts a decimal value to `varbinary` and back to decimal again. The original value is retained after the conversions.

LISTING 26.3 LST26_3.TXT—Round-Trip Conversions of Decimal Data Types

```
DECLARE @dec decimal (3, 2)
SET @dec = 4.87
SELECT CONVERT(decimal(3,2), CAST(@dec AS varbinary(20))) AS Value1,
    CONVERT(decimal(3,2), CONVERT(varbinary(20), @dec)) AS Value2,
    CAST(CAST(@dec AS varbinary(20)) AS decimal(3,2)) AS Value3
```

Microsoft SQL Server does not, however, guarantee that the conversion of a decimal or numeric value to binary, or vice versa, will be the same across releases. When data types are converted with a different number of decimal places, the value is truncated to the most precise digit. When the target data type has fewer decimal places than the source data type, the value is rounded. The Transact-SQL code in Listing 26.4 shows the conversion truncation and rounding scenarios.

LISTING 26.4 LST26_4.TXT—Truncated and Rounded-Off Scenarios for Decimal Data Types

```
DECLARE @dec decimal (3, 2)
SET @dec = 4.87
/* The value is truncated to the most precise digit. */
SELECT CAST(@dec AS tinyint) AS Truncated_Value
/* The value is rounded off to the nearest decimal digit. */
SELECT CAST(@dec AS dec(3,1)) AS Rounded_Value
```

The conversion of character or Unicode character data types to integer, numeric, or floating-point data types returns an error message. The conversion of empty strings to integer or numeric data types returns an error message. When binary data is converted to character data and an odd number of values is specified following the `x`, the value is padded with zeroes to make it even. For binary data, every two characters count as one. For example, a length of `6` means that six two-character values will be specified. Listing 26.5 shows some examples of using the `CAST` and `CONVERT` functions.

LISTING 26.5 LST26_5.TXT—Examples of the CAST and CONVERT Functions

```
Declare @Str varchar(10)
Set @Str = '10'
SELECT CAST(@Str AS int) AS Int_Value
GO
Declare @Datetime datetime, @SmallDatetime smalldatetime
Set @Datetime = '1999-01-11 10:20:04.209'
Set @SmallDatetime = '1999-01-11 10:20'
SELECT CONVERT(varchar(10), @Datetime, 101) AS USA_Format,
    CONVERT(varchar(19), @SmallDatetime) AS Default_Format,
    CONVERT(varchar(8), @Datetime, 8) AS Time_Format,
    CONVERT(datetime, @Smalldatetime) AS Datetime_Format
go
/* Using CAST in SELECT statement. */
SELECT CAST(job_id AS varchar) + '. ' + job_desc FROM pubs..jobs
```

SQL Server also handles data type conversions automatically in certain cases. For example, if a `smallint` and an `int` expression is being compared, the `smallint` value is converted to `int` automatically. Converting any non-zero integer value to `bit` results in a value of `1`.

Functions

Microsoft SQL Server provides built-in functions to perform operations efficiently. The functions can be categorized as follows:

- Aggregate functions: Perform aggregate operations on a set of values
- Configuration functions: Return information about the SQL Server configuration settings
- Cursor functions: Return information about cursors
- Datetime functions: Perform operations on `datetime` and `smalldatetime` values
- Mathematical functions: Perform trigonometric, geometric, and math operations
- Metadata functions: Return information on attributes of databases and their objects
- Rowset functions: Return resultset that can be used as part of a Transact-SQL statement
- Security functions: Return information about database users, database roles, and system roles
- String functions: Perform operations on character and Unicode character data
- System functions: Perform operations on system objects
- System statistical functions: Provide information about system level performance
- Text and image functions: Perform operations on text and image data types

The Transact-SQL functions can be used as part of a `SELECT` statement, `WHERE` clause of a `SELECT` or DML statement, expressions, `CHECK` and `DEFAULT` constraints, and rule definitions.

The aggregate functions perform calculations on a set of values and return a single value. All aggregate functions ignore `NULL` values except for `COUNT`. Aggregate functions are used with the `GROUP BY` clause of the `SELECT` statement. They can be used as expressions in the select list of a `SELECT` statement, a `HAVING` clause, or a `COMPUTE` or `COMPUTE BY` clause. Examples of aggregate functions are `AVG`, `SUM`, `COUNT`, `MIN`, and `MAX`.

The configuration functions—such as `@@CONNECTIONS`, `@@DATEFIRST`, `@@DBTS`, `@@LANGUAGE`, `@@OPTIONS`, `@@SPID`, and `@@SERVERNAME`—are scalar functions that return information about the current configuration options. Even though the name of the functions start with double @ characters like global variables, they are internally mapped to functions.

The cursor functions, such as @@FETCH_STATUS, @@CURSOR_ROWS, and CURSOR_STATUS, return the fetch status, number of rows in a cursor, and the open/closed state of a cursor.

The datetime scalar functions perform operations on datetime or smalldatetime values and return either a string, an integer, or a datetime value, depending on the operation. Examples are DATEADD, DATEDIFF, DAY, and GETDATE. The GETDATE() function, for example, returns the current date and time value on the server. The DAY() function returns an integer representing the day part of a datetime value.

The mathematical functions perform a calculation based on the numeric input value and return a numeric value as output. Examples are ABS, ACOS, POWER, RAND, ROUND, and SIGN. The ABS() function returns the positive absolute value of a numeric expression.

The metadata functions return information about the database and database objects, such as tables, views, and columns. Examples are COL_LENGTH, COL_NAME, COLUMN_PROPERTY, DATABASEPROPERTY, DB_ID, DB_NAME, OBJECT_ID, and TYPEPROPERTY. The DB_NAME() function returns the name of the current database. The DATABASEPROPERTY() function can be used to get information on settings such as ANSI NULL default, create statistics, and bulk copy of a database. The OBJECT_ID() function returns the numeric identifier of an object in a database.

The rowset functions return a resultset that can be used as an object in place of a table in a SELECT or DML statement. Examples are CONTAINSTABLE, FREETEXTTABLE, OPENQUERY, and OPENROWSET. The OPENQUERY function is used to execute a pass-through query on a linked server and return the resultset. The resultset can be referenced in the FROM clause of a SELECT, UPDATE, INSERT, or DELETE statement.

The security functions provide information about database users, roles, and logins in SQL Server. Examples are IS_MEMBER, IS_SRVROLEMEMBER, SUSER_SID, SUSER_SNAME, USER_ID, and USER. The SUSER_SID() function returns the security identification number of a SQL Server login. The IS_MEMBER() function is used to determine whether a user is a member of a Windows NT Group or SQL Server database role. The IS_SRVROLEMEMBER() function, on the other hand, can be used to determine the membership of a login in a role. The system-defined roles are sysadmin, dbcreator, diskadmin, processadmin, serveradmin, setupadmin, and securityadmin.

The string functions perform operations on string values and return a string or numeric value. Examples are ASCII, CHAR, CHARINDEX, DIFFERENCE, LEN, LEFT, LOWER, LTRIM, NCHAR, PATINDEX, QUOTENAME, REPLICATE, REVERSE, SOUNDEX, SUBSTRING, and UNICODE. The ASCII() function returns the ASCII value of the specified character. The CHAR()

function returns the character for the specified ASCII code. The CHARINDEX() function returns the starting position of a search expression in a string. The LEN() function returns the number of characters in a string, excluding the trailing blanks. The SUBSTRING() function returns part of a character, binary, text, or image expression.

The system functions return information about values and settings in SQL Server or perform operations on values. Examples are APP_NAME, CASE, CAST, CONVERT, COALESCE, CURRENT_TIMESTAMP, DATALENGTH, @@ERROR, GETANSINULL, HOST_NAME, @@IDENTITY, ISDATE, ISNULL, ISNUMERIC, NEWID, NULLIF, PARSENAME, PERMISSIONS, @@ROWCOUNT, SESSION_USER, @@TRANCOUNT, and USER_NAME. The APP_NAME() function returns the application name of the current connection to SQL Server. The CURRENT_TIMESTAMP is a special type of function called NILADIC that is SQL-92 compatible. It returns the current date and time value on the server. The @@ERROR function returns the error number of the last error that occurred in the executing connection. The ISNULL function checks whether a value is null or non-null. The @@ROWCOUNT function returns the number of rows affected by the last SELECT or DML statement.

The system statistical functions return performance data about the server. Examples are @@CPU_BUSY, @@IDLE, @@IO_BUSY, @@PACK_RECEIVED, @@PACK_SENT, @@PACKET_ERRORS, @@TIMETICKS, @@TOTAL_ERRORS, @@TOTAL_READ, and @@TOTAL_WRITE. The @@CPU_BUSY function returns the time value in milliseconds that SQL Server has spent doing work since the last startup. The @@IDLE function returns the time value in milliseconds that SQL Server has been idle since the last startup. The @@TOTAL_ERRORS function returns the number of disk input/output errors encountered since the last startup.

The text and image scalar functions perform an operation on a text or image value and return information about that value. Examples are PATINDEX, TEXTPTR, and TEXTVALID. The PATINDEX() function returns the starting position of the first occurrence of a pattern in the specified value. It returns zero if the pattern cannot be found in the value. The TEXTPTR() function returns the pointer value in binary format that corresponds to the text, image, or ntext column. The text pointer value can be used in READTEXT, WRITETEXT, or UPDATETEXT statements to perform operations on the column. The TEXTVALID() function checks the validity of a given text pointer value.

For a complete description of the functions available in Microsoft SQL Server, see the "Functions (T-SQL)" topic in the SQL Server Books Online.

Stored Procedures and Triggers

Transact-SQL has a way for commands to be cached on the server for later use. Any Transact-SQL batch can be stored as a procedure on the server by using the CREATE

PROCEDURE statement. Stored procedures in Microsoft SQL Server have the following attributes:

- Input and output parameters can be specified for stored procedures.
- Return a value about the execution status by using the RETURN statement, which has to be programmed by the user.
- Can be used to execute conditional logic and multiple statements on the server.

Microsoft Transact-SQL also has local and global temporary stored procedures. Procedure names with a # prefix indicate a local temporary stored procedure and those with two ## characters indicate a global temporary stored procedure. These stored procedures exist only as long as the SQL Server is running. With a local temporary stored procedure, only the connection that created it can execute it, and the procedure is automatically dropped when it goes out of scope or the user logs out. A global temporary stored procedure, on the other hand, exists until the connection that created it is closed and any currently executing copies of the stored procedure are completed.

The Transact-SQL EXECUTE statement executes a stored procedure, which doesn't return values as a function does. It cannot be used as part of an expression. The advantages of using a stored procedure are the following:

- Reusability: Business logic can be implemented in a stored procedure and reused
- Flexibility: Stored procedures can be modified independently of the client application
- Performance: Stored procedures result in faster execution and reduce network traffic
- Security: Ensure secure access to data by allowing users to modify data through stored procedures

Triggers are special kinds of stored procedures that run automatically after a data manipulation statement is executed. Triggers can be used to maintain data integrity that cannot be enforced with the declarative referential integrity methods or to perform other user-defined activities, such as auditing, summaries, or notifications.

Stored Procedures

The CREATE PROCEDURE statement is used to create stored procedures. The CREATE PROCEDURE statement must be the only statement in a Transact-SQL batch. The permission to create stored procedures defaults to the database owner and can be granted to other users. The names of stored procedures should follow the identifier rules. Microsoft SQL Server has a special kind of stored procedures called *system stored procedures* for performing administrative activities on the server. They are stored in the master database and the names start with *sp_ prefix*. System stored procedures can be executed from any database without qualifying the master database name. SQL Server first looks for stored procedures beginning with *sp_ prefix* in the master database, then looks for the procedure based on the qualifiers specified, and finally looks for a procedure with the dbo as owner. Stored procedures can be grouped logically by supplying identification numbers. Grouping procedures in this manner allows them all to be dropped at the same time. For example, stored procedures GetAuthors;1 and GetAuthors;2 can be grouped together logically. The CREATE PROCEDURE statement is used to create the stored procedure; its syntax is as follows:

```
CREATE PROCEDURE <procedure_name>;<number>
(
@parameter <data_type> [VARYING] [= <default>] [OUTPUT] ...n
)
WITH RECOMPILE ¦ ENCRYPTION ¦ RECOMPILE, ENCRYPTION
AS
<SQL statements>
GO
```

In this statement, <procedure name> is the name of the stored procedure, which should conform to all the identifier rules. The <number> parameter is optional and can be used to group stored procedures of the same name. The @parameter option is the parameter to the stored procedure, which can have a maximum of 1024 parameters. The value for each parameter has to be supplied when executing the stored procedure unless a default is bound to it. The parameters are local to the stored procedure. The <data type> parameter indicates the data type for the parameter. The cursor data type can be used only with OUTPUT type of parameters and the VARYING keyword must be used. The <default> parameter specifies a default value for the parameter. The default can only be a constant or NULL. The RECOMPILE option for the stored procedure means that SQL Server will not cache the plan for this stored procedure, so it's recompiled every time it is executed. The ENCRYPTION option indicates that SQL Server will encrypt the text that defines the stored procedure; it's used for security purposes when distributing the application code. The <sql statements> parameter determines the statements that constitute the stored procedure. The maximum size of a stored procedure is 128MB.

The settings of SET QUOTED_IDENTIFIER and SET ANSI_NULLS are saved when a stored procedure is created or altered. These settings are used at the time of the stored procedure's execution. The settings of these statements are used only at parse time. Hence, specifying the settings within the stored procedure doesn't affect the stored procedure's functionality. Other SET options, such as ARITH_ABORT and ARITH_IGNORE, are not stored with the procedure. Similarly, the ANSI_DFLT_ON and ANSI_DFLT_OFF options control how SQL Server handles columns that do not have the nullability attribute specified. So when creating tables from stored procedures, specifying NULL or NOT NULL attributes for columns ensures that the stored procedure execute correctly regardless of the settings in the session.

Any SET statement specified inside a stored procedure remains in effect only during the execution stage.

Microsoft SQL Server uses deferred name resolution and compilation when creating a stored procedure. When a stored procedure is created, the text is first parsed for syntactical errors. If a syntactical error is encountered, the stored procedure is not created and an error is returned. Otherwise, the text of the stored procedure is stored in the syscomments system table. When a stored procedure is executed for the first time, the query processor reads the text of the stored procedure and checks that the names of the objects used by the procedure are present. This process is called *deferred name resolution* because objects referenced by the stored procedure need not exist when the stored procedure is created, but only when it is executed. During the resolution stage, the use of the object is also validated. For example, if a table specifies a column data type as character and a binary value is being inserted from the stored procedure, it will raise an error. After the resolution stage is successfully passed, the query optimizer analyzes the text of the stored procedure and creates an execution plan. The execution plan provides the fastest method of executing the stored procedure, based on the following information:

- Amount of data in the tables
- Indexes defined on tables and the data distribution
- Search conditions used in the WHERE clause of the SELECT or DML statements
- Type of joins being performed
- Cursors being used in the stored procedure
- Temporary tables or stored procedures created in the stored procedure

The process of analyzing these factors and creating an execution plan is called *compilation*. The execution plan of a stored procedure remains in memory until SQL Server is restarted or when space is needed for other objects.

Now let's look at a simple stored procedure in Listing 26.6. It retrieves a list of orders for a specified city and for shipping dates later than a specified date. The stored procedure uses tables from the sample Northwind database installed with Microsoft SQL Server 7.0.

LISTING 26.6 LST26_6.TXT—Stored Procedure Example

```
Use Northwind
go
CREATE PROCEDURE GetOrdersForCityDate
(
@ShipDate datetime,
@ShipCity nvarchar(15) = 'Seattle'
```

LISTING 26.6 CONTINUED

```
)
AS
SELECT Customers.CompanyName, Customers.ContactName, Orders.OrderID
FROM Customers INNER JOIN Orders
   ON Customers.CustomerID = Orders.CustomerID
WHERE Orders.ShippedDate >= @ShipDate And Orders.ShipCity = @ShipCity
ORDER BY 1, 2
GO
Exec  GetOrdersForCityDate  @ShipDate  =  '1998-03-11  00:00',  @ShipCity  =
N'London'
go
Exec GetOrdersForCityDate '1998-02-11 00:00', @ShipCity = N'Mxico D.F.'
go
/* Use the default value for the city parameter. */
Exec GetOrdersForCityDate '1998-03-11 00:00', DEFAULT
go
Exec GetOrdersForCityDate '1998-04-11 00:00'
go
/* Modify stored procedure to change the default city to 'San Francisco'. */
ALTER PROCEDURE GetOrdersForCityDate
(
@ShipDate datetime,
@ShipCity nvarchar(15) = 'San Francisco'
)
AS
SELECT Customers.CompanyName, Customers.ContactName, Orders.OrderID
FROM Customers INNER JOIN Orders
   ON Customers.CustomerID = Orders.CustomerID
WHERE Orders.ShippedDate >= @ShipDate And Orders.ShipCity = @ShipCity
ORDER BY 1, 2
GO
Exec GetOrdersForCityDate '1998-02-04 00:00', DEFAULT
go
```

The `GetOrdersForCityDate` stored procedure shows the different features of a stored procedure. Values can be passed to stored procedures by explicitly naming the parameter and assigning the value or specifying the parameters in the defined order. The `DEFAULT` keyword is used in place of a parameter value to indicate that the default value supplied in the procedure should be used. The default value is also used if a parameter value is not provided. The code listing also demonstrates the use of the `ALTER PROCEDURE` statement to modify the contents of the stored procedure. It can be executed without changing permissions and without affecting any dependent objects. The syntax of the ALTER PROCEDURE statement is the same as the CREATE PROCEDURE statement.

The Transact-SQL code in Listing 26.7 contains a modified version of the GetOrdersForCityDate stored procedure that demonstrates using the OUTPUT parameter and RETURN statement.

LISTING 26.7 LST26_7.TXT—Stored Procedure with **OUTPUT** Parameter and **RETURN** Statement

```
Use Northwind
go
ALTER PROCEDURE GetOrdersForCityDate
(
@ShipDate datetime,
@ShipCity nvarchar(15),
@NumberOfOrders int = NULL OUTPUT
)
AS
SELECT Customers.CompanyName, Customers.ContactName, Orders.OrderID
FROM Customers INNER JOIN Orders
   ON Customers.CustomerID = Orders.CustomerID
WHERE Orders.ShippedDate >= @ShipDate And Orders.ShipCity = @ShipCity
ORDER BY 1, 2
SET @NumberOfOrders = @@ROWCOUNT
RETURN(CASE WHEN @NumberOfOrders > 0 THEN 1 ELSE 0 END)
GO
Declare @NumberOfOrders int, @ReturnCode int
Exec @ReturnCode = GetOrdersForCityDate '1998-03-11 00:00',
                   N'London', @NumberOfOrders OUTPUT
SELECT @NumberOfOrders AS [Number Of Orders], @ReturnCode AS [Return Code]
go
```

The @NumberOfOrdersOUTPUT parameter is used to return the number of orders that matched the search condition. You get the number of rows affected by the SELECT statement with the @@ROWCOUNT system function. The RETURN statement then checks the value of the number of orders and returns a 1 or 0 value. The CASE statement is used to perform the check. The OUTPUT keyword has to be specified for output type of parameters while executing the stored procedure.

Microsoft SQL Server supports marking stored procedures for automatic execution. Stored procedures marked thus are executed every time SQL Server starts. This feature can be used to perform certain tasks when the server starts or to run a background process. The sp_procoption system stored procedure can be used to set a stored procedure for automatic execution.

The sp_rename system stored procedure can be used to rename a stored procedure, and the sp_helptext system stored procedure can be used to view the text of the stored procedure. The DROP PROCEDURE statement can be used to drop a stored procedure.

Triggers

Triggers are special stored procedures automatically invoked whenever the data in a table is modified. The trigger and the DML statement that fired the trigger are treated as a single transaction that can be rolled back from within the trigger. If a fatal error is encountered, SQL Server automatically rolls back the transaction. Multiple triggers of the same type can be defined on a table, which allows business rules to be developed independently. You can also find the difference in the data before and after a DML operation from within a trigger. The CREATE TRIGGER statement is used to create a trigger on a table. It must be the first statement in the batch. The permission to create triggers defaults to the table owner, who cannot transfer it to others. A trigger cannot be created on a view, temporary table, or system table. Triggers are always fired after the entire DML statement is completed, regardless of how many rows it affects. The syntax of the CREATE TRIGGER statement is as follows:

```
CREATE TRIGGER <trigger_name> ON <table_name>
WITH ENCRYPTION
FOR {[DELETE] [,] [INSERT] [,] [UPDATE]}
AS
<sql_statements>
```

In this statement, <trigger_name> is the name of the trigger, which should follow all the identifier rules. The <table_name> parameter indicates the table on which the trigger is created. The DELETE, INSERT, and UDPATE options specify which DML statements activate the trigger. The <sql_statements> parameter comprises the Transact-SQL statements that form the logic of the trigger. Any Transact-SQL statement can be used in a trigger, except statements such as ALTER, DROP, CREATE, BACKUP/RESTORE, and TRUNCATE. Two special tables—inserted and deleted—can be used within triggers. These logical tables contain the old or new values of rows affected by the DML statement. The text, ntext, and image columns of a table cannot be referenced in the inserted and deleted tables. Two special functions, UPDATE() and COLUMNS_UPDATED(), can be used within an INSERT or UPDATE trigger to determine whether a column or columns were inserted or updated. The UPDATE() function takes a column name of the table as a parameter and returns true if an update was performed. The COLUMNS_UPDATED() function does not take any parameters and returns a varbinary pattern that indicates which columns in the table were inserted or updated.

Triggers can be encrypted by using the `WITH ENCRYPTION` clause to prevent other users from viewing the code. The code in Listing 26.8 shows a table with two update triggers.

LISTING 26.8 LST26_8.TXT—Table with Two Update Triggers

```
Use pubs
GO
CREATE TABLE Salesperson (Last_Name varchar(20) NOT NULL,
             First_Name varchar(20) NULL,
             ID int NOT NULL)
GO
CREATE TRIGGER Insert_Salesperson ON Salesperson FOR UPDATE
AS
IF UPDATE(Last_Name)
  PRINT 'Last name of the salesperson was modified.'
GO
CREATE TRIGGER Update_Salesperson ON Salesperson FOR UPDATE
AS
IF (COLUMNS_UPDATED() & 2 = 2)
  PRINT 'First name of the salesperson was modified.'
GO

INSERT Salesperson (Last_Name, ID) values('Smith', 1243)
UPDATE Salesperson SET First_Name = 'John' WHERE ID = 1243
UPDATE Salesperson SET Last_Name = 'Smith', First_Name = 'Brian'
WHERE ID = 1243
GO
/* Try to update a nonexistent salesperson. Triggers print the messages
  even if no rows are being updated. */
UPDATE Salesperson Set Last_Name = 'Smith', First_Name = 'Brian'
WHERE ID = 2334
GO
/* Modify trigger to check for @@ROWCOUNT */
ALTER TRIGGER Insert_Salesperson ON Salesperson FOR UPDATE
AS
IF UPDATE(Last_Name) And @@ROWCOUNT > 0
  PRINT 'Last name of the salesperson was modified.'
GO
CREATE TRIGGER Update_Salesperson ON Salesperson FOR UPDATE
AS
IF (COLUMNS_UPDATED() & 2 = 2) And @@ROWCOUNT > 0
  PRINT 'First name of the salesperson was modified.'
/* Now if the update statement did not affect any rows, no message is
```

LISTING 26.8 CONTINUED

```
  printed from the triggers. */
UPDATE Salesperson Set Last_Name = 'Smith', First_Name = 'Brian'
WHERE ID = 2324
GO
```

Both the triggers are fired after the update statement is performed. The triggers print a message after checking the column that was updated by the DML statement. The triggers without the row count check print the messages regardless of whether the UPDATE statement affected any rows. The @@ROWCOUNT check ensures that the DML statement did affect rows. When a trigger that issues a ROLLBACK TRANSACTION statement is executed in a batch, the entire batch is cancelled. If the trigger that issues a ROLLBACK TRANSACTION statement is executed from within a user transaction, the entire transaction is rolled back.

When a trigger performs an action that initiates another trigger, which can initiate another trigger, and so on, they are called as *nested triggers*. Triggers can be nested up to 32 levels, and the "nested triggers" server option controls this setting. If nested triggers are allowed and a trigger in the chain sets off an infinite loop, the nesting level is exceeded and the trigger terminates. A trigger can be made to call itself recursively by using the "recursive triggers" database option. The recursion can be direct or indirect. In *direct recursion*, the trigger on a table modifies the same table from within the trigger.
For example, an update trigger on table Table1 that updates the same table from within the trigger results in direct recursion. In *indirect recursion*, the trigger on a table that fires another trigger issues a DML statement that can fire the same trigger. For example, an update trigger on table Table1 is fired first. The update trigger then updates table Table2, which causes the update trigger on Table2 to fire. The trigger on Table2 in turn updates table Table1, which fires the update trigger on Table1 again.

The sp_helptrigger system stored procedure can be used to view the types of triggers defined on a table. The sp_helptext system stored procedure can be used to view the text of the trigger. The DROP TRIGGER statement can be used to drop a stored procedure. Triggers can also be disabled by using the ALTER TABLE statement.

Cursors in SQL Server 7.0

All operations in Microsoft SQL Server 7.0 are performed on a set of rows. The rows returned by a SELECT statement that satisfy the WHERE clause are known as the *resultset*. Interactive applications work on a subset of the resultset at a time. Cursors in SQL Server provide this ability for the applications. Cursors allow positioning in resultsets, retrieval of row or rows, data modifications to the positioned row, and a mechanism to manipulate data serially. Microsoft SQL Server supports three cursor implementations:

- Transact-SQL cursors that are declared and used in batches, stored procedures, or triggers
- Application programming interface (API) server cursors used by the OLE DB, ODBC, and DB-Library API functions to work with resultsets
- Client cursors implemented in the cursor library on the client machine

The SQL Server ODBC driver and the OLE DB provider for SQL Server implement default resultsets when no cursor attributes are supplied. The driver and provider open a server-side cursor only if any of the cursor attributes or properties are changed from their defaults. A cursor is implicitly opened for any resultset returned by a Transact-SQL statement. The cursor attributes can be set by the application before executing a Transact-SQL statement that returns a resultset. The API cursor functions are then used to fetch one row or batch of rows at a time from the resultset on the server. The illustration in Figure 26.2 from the SQL Server Books Online shows the type of cursor or resultset implemented based on the cursor settings. The value `''Do not combine cursor types''` indicates that both a server-side cursor and an API cursor are requested at the same time. This is not a recommended option and can result in unpredictable behavior.

FIGURE 26.2
API Cursor Settings

API Cursor Settings	Transact-SQL Statement Executed	
	DECLARE CURSOR	SELECT, Batch Procedure
OLE DB/ODBC/ADO Default cursor settings	Transact-SQL cursor	Default result set
OLE DB/ODBC/ADO Nondefault cursor settings no client cursor library	Do not combine cursor types	API server cursor Batches and procedures not supported
OLE DB/ODBC/ADO Nondefault cursor settings client cursor library loaded	Do not combine cursor types	Default result set cached into client cursor
DB-Library Core Functions	Transact-SQL cursor	Default result set
DB-Library Cursor Functions DBCLIENTCURSOR not set	Do not combine cursor types	API server cursor Batches and procedures not supported
DB-Library Cursor Functions DBCLIENTCURSOR set	Do not combine cursor types	Default result set cached into client cursor

The Transact-SQL cursors are SQL-92 compatible, and SQL Server cursor support goes beyond the specifications. For a more in-depth discussion about cursors in Microsoft SQL Server, refer to Chapter 18, "Implementing Cursors."

Error Handling

Errors raised in Microsoft SQL Server can be errors caused by a statement execution or those explicitly raised by the user. All errors in SQL Server have the following properties:

- Error number: Each error condition has a unique number.
- Error message: Unique message that gives you details about the error condition.
- Severity level: Indicates the severity of the error message. Error messages with high severity levels indicate that action has to be taken immediately.
- State code: Error codes that can be raised from the source code for SQL Server. These fatal errors usually occur because of some unhandled exceptions.
- Object name: Gives the name of the stored procedure if an error occurred within it.
- Line number: Gives the line number of the statement that caused the error condition.

All the error messages in SQL Server are stored in the `sysmessages` system table in the master database. User-defined error messages can be stored in the `sysmessages` table by using the `sp_addmessage` system stored procedure. Errors raised by SQL Server or the `RAISERROR` statement are not part of any resultset. The error messages are returned to the application by a special error-handling mechanism. Each API has its own functions to provide the error messages. SQL Server has two ways of returning error information:

- Errors: Messages with severity level of 11 or higher
- Messages: Messages with severity level of 10 or lower and output of `PRINT` and DBCC statements

The API functions give you a way to distinguish between error and messages. For example, ODBC returns a `SQL_SUCCESS_WITH_INFO` value for messages and a `SQL_ERROR` value for errors. Two type of errors can occur in SQL Server:

- Syntax errors: Can occur in Transact-SQL batches, stored procedures, or triggers. They are detected when parsing the text of the batch or stored procedure.
- Execution-time errors: Fatal or non-fatal error conditions, such as constraint violations, duplicate key inserts, and dropped tables, that can happen during the execution of a Transact-SQL batch or stored procedure.

The `@@ERROR` system function returns the error number of the error that occurred in the last statement executed in a batch. This function can be used to test for the success or failure of a statement. It returns `0` if the last Transact-SQL statement executed successfully. If the statement returns an error, then `@@ERROR` returns the error number. The value of `@@ERROR` changes on the completion of each Transact-SQL statement, so processing error information has to be handled after every execution of every statement. The value of `@@ERROR` can be saved to a local variable and used later in the code. Only the error number is supplied by SQL Server within a Transact-SQL batch. The error message, severity, and state are returned to the calling application. The Transact-SQL batch in Listing 26.9 shows how error handling is performed.

LISTING 26.9 LST26_9.TXT—Transact-SQL Batch with @@ERROR Checks

```
DECLARE @Description nchar(50)
SELECT @Description = TerritoryDescription
FROM Northwind..Territories
WHERE TerritoryID = '02116'
IF @@ERROR <> 0 PRINT 'Unable to get description for territory.'
GO
INSERT NorthWind..Territories VALUES('48795', 'Orlando', 'A')
IF @@ERROR <> 0 PRINT 'Unable to insert row into table.'
GO
```

In the code, the `INSERT` statement tried to supply an invalid value for the `ID` field, which resulted in the error message `Syntax error converting the varchar value 'A' to a column of data type int` , but the `PRINT` message after the `INSERT` statement was not executed. That's because the implicit conversion of the value `'A'` to the `int` data type occurs before the batch is executed. Now let's look at another Transact-SQL batch in Listing 26.10 that specifically traps the check constraint violation error.

LISTING 26.10 LST26_10.TXT—Trapping the Check Constraint Violation Error

```
UPDATE Northwind..[Order Details]
SET Discount = -100
WHERE OrderID = 10248
IF @@ERROR = 547
 PRINT 'The CHECK constraint on the discount column was violated.'
GO
SET XACT_ABORT ON
GO
UPDATE Northwind..[Order Details]
SET Discount = -200
WHERE OrderID = 10248
IF @@ERROR = 547
 PRINT 'The CHECK constraint on the discount column was violated.'
GO
```

In the Transact-SQL batch, the `@@ERROR` check traps the constraint violation error and the print message is printed after the error message. The execution of a batch continues with the next statement, even if an error condition occurs in this typical scenario. The behavior of the batch can be changed by issuing the `SET XACT_ABORT ON` statement. This setting aborts the entire batch if an error is raised within the batch. So in the second UPDATE statement shown in Listing 26.10, the PRINT statement is not executed.

Transact-SQL has the RAISERROR statement to send messages back to the application or an error message. It can be used to return any messages defined in the sysmessages system table or a user-specified string. RAISERROR is also used to set a flag indicating that an error has occurred. This is its syntax:

```
RAISERROR(<message number> ¦ <message string,
<severity level>, <sql state>, <argument list>)
WITH LOG ¦ NOWAIT ¦ SETERROR
```

The <message number> parameter refers to any valid error message stored in the sysmessages table. User-defined error numbers should be greater than 50,000. The <message string> parameter specifies the message that needs to be formatted, like the PRINTF function style in C. The length of the error message cannot exceed 8,000 characters. The format for <message string> is %<flag][width][precision][{h¦l}> type . The flag option is a code that determines the spacing and justification of the message. The valid values are shown in Table 26.7.

TABLE 26.7 Values for Flag Option

Code	*Prefix or Justification*	*Description*
- (minus)	Left	Result is left-justified based on the specified width
+ (plus)	+ (plus) or - (minus) prefix	The output value is prefixed by the sign of the value
0 (zero)	Padded with zeroes	If width is prefaced with 0, zeros are added until the minimum width is reached
# (number)	0x or 0X prefix for hex numbers	When used with the o, x, or X format, the # flag prefaces any nonzero value with 0, 0x, or 0X, respectively
" (blank)	Padded with spaces	Preface the output value with blank spaces if the value is signed and positive

The [width] parameter is the minimum width of the output value. The [precision] parameter is the maximum number of characters printed or the number of digits printed for numeric values. The [type] parameter specifies the data type of the value, with h denoting short int values and l denoting long int values. The <severity> parameter is the severity level of the error message. Severity levels from 0 through 18 can be used by any user. Severity levels from 19 through 25 can be used only by system administrators and only with the WITH LOG option. The <sql state> parameter is an arbitrary number from 1 through 127. The <argument list> parameter supplies the values for any parameters in the error message. The LOG option writes error messages to the SQL Server error log and the

Windows NT application log. The `NOWAIT` option sends the message immediately to the client application. The `SETERROR` option sets the `@@ERROR` value to the message number or 50,000. The Transact-SQL code in Listing 26.11 shows some examples of the `RAISERROR` statement.

LISTING 26.11 `LST26_11.TXT`—`RAISERROR` examples

```
UPDATE Northwind..[Order Details]
SET Discount = -200
WHERE OrderID = 10248
IF @@ERROR = 547
BEGIN
 RAISERROR('The value of discount should be between %d and %d.', 16, 1, 0, 1)
 RAISERROR('Update operation was not completed successfully.', 1, 2)
  WITH SETERROR
END
GO
```

The `FORMATMESSAGE` system function can be used to format a message from the `sysmessage` system table. If the defined error message requires any parameters, they can be supplied as arguments to the `FORMATMESSAGE` function, which has the following syntax:

```
FORMATMESSAGE(<message number>, <argument list>)
```

In this function, `<message number>` is the number of an existing error message, and `<argument list>` is the value of the parameters for the error message. `FORMATMESSAGE` retrieves the error message based on the user's current language settings. If there is no localized version of the error message, the U.S. English version of the error message is returned.

The `sp_addmessage` system stored procedure adds a user-defined error message to the `sysmessages` table. Its syntax is as follows:

```
sp_addmessage @msgnum = <message number>,
 @severity = <severity level>, @msgtext = <error message>,
 @lang = <language>, @with_log = <with log>,
 @replace = <replace>
```

In this procedure, `<message number>` is the error message's number, which should be unique for the language and be greater than 50,001. The `<severity level>` parameter indicates the severity level of the error message. Valid values are 1 through 25; 19 through 25 can be used only by system administrators. The `<error message>` parameter is the string that forms the error message. The `<language>` parameter specifies the language of the error message and defaults U.S. English. The `<with log>` parameter can take the values `true` or false, which indicate whether the error message is written to the Windows NT event log. The <replace> parameter is specified as the string 'REPLACE' and can be used to replace the text and severity of an existing message. The Transact-SQL code in Listing 26.12 shows how to add user-defined error messages and use them in batches.

LISTING 26.12 LST26_12.TXT—User-Defined Error Messages

```
Exec sp_addmessage 60006, 16,
 N'Discount values should be between 0 and 1.
 Please enter an appropriate value'
GO
/* Display the error message using formatmessage. */
PRINT FORMATMESSAGE(60006)
PRINT ''
GO
UPDATE Northwind..[Order Details]
SET Discount = -200
WHERE OrderID = 10248
IF @@ERROR = 547 RAISERROR(60006, 16, 1)
GO
/* Drop the user-defined error message. */
Exec sp_dropmessage 60006
GO
```

The Transact-SQL batch shown in Listing 26.15 also shows how to use the FORMATMESSAGE function to format an error message. The sp_dropmessage system stored procedure is used to drop the user-defined error message that was added to the sysmessages table. The sp_altermessage system stored procedure alters the WITH_LOG option of an existing error message.

The severity level of an error message gives you valuable information about the type of problem Microsoft SQL Server has encountered. As discussed, severity levels 1 through 10 are informational messages, severity levels 11 through 16 are user generated, and severity levels 17 through 25 indicate software or hardware problems on the server. Table 26.8 lists the severity levels and the information they supply.

TABLE 26.8 Values for Flag Options

Severity Level	*Information*
0-10	Status and informational messages
11-16	User-defined errors
17	Insufficient resources
18	Non-fatal internal error
19	Error in resource

TABLE 26.8 Values for Flag Options

Severity Level	Information
20	Fatal error in the current process
21	Fatal error in the database process
22	Fatal error in table integrity
23	Fatal error in database integrity
24-25	Hardware error

All error conditions in SQL Server can be monitored by using the built-in alert notification mechanism. Now let's take a brief look at how error handling is done in the APIs that can be used to access SQL Server.

Error Handling in ODBC

The ODBC API returns a return code and diagnostic information after every function call. The return code indicates the success or failure of the function call. The diagnostic information supplies status information about the execution of the function call. The diagnostic information can be used to determine syntax errors and exceptions in the code. It also gives you information about runtime errors such as constraint violations or insufficient log space. An error message in ODBC has three attributes:

- `SQLSTATE`: A five-character code defined in the ODBC specification. `SQLSTATE` provides a way for applications to code error handling that works the same across different data sources.
- Native error number: Error number of the error that occurred in SQL Server.
- Error message: Error message returned by SQL Server.

If an ODBC function call returns a code other than `SQL_SUCCESS`, the `SQLGetDiagRec` function is called to return the error information. For example, if a Transact-SQL statement that references an invalid database object is executed, SQL Server returns the message `Invalid object name '%s'` ; `%s` refers to the name of the missing or invalid object. The `SQLGetDiagRec` function is this case returns the following information:

- `SQLSTATE`: 42000
- Native error number: 208
- Error message: `Invalid object name 'Empmgr'`

The `SQLGetDiagField` function also allows ODBC drivers to specify driver-specific diagnostic fields in the diagnostic records returned by the driver. The SQL Server ODBC driver specifies driver-specific fields to hold SQL Server error information, such as the SQL Server severity and state codes.

Error Handling in ADO

The Errors collection and Error object provide the data source-specific error messages returned from the server. The error information in ADO has the same attributes as ODBC error messages: SQLSTATE, native error number, and error message. All error messages returned from the server are stored in the Errors collection. Warning messages are stored in the Errors collection, too, with a positive error number value. These are the properties associated with the Error object:

- Description: Text of the error message
- Number: Indicates the long integer value of the error
- Source: Indicates the object that raised the error
- SQLState: Information about the SQL Server error message
- NativeError: Error number returned from SQL Server
- HelpFile: Name of the help file that contains information about this error
- HelpContext: Name of the topic in the help file

The sample Visual Basic code in Listing 26.13 demonstrates how to read error information from the Errors collection.

LISTING 26.13 LST26_13.TXT—Visual Basic Sample for Reading Error Information

```
Dim SQLConnection AS New ADODB.Connection
Dim SQLError As ADODB.Error
Dim ResultSet AS ADODB.Recordset
On Error Goto ErrorHandler

SQLConnection.Open ''pubs'', ''sa''
Set ResultSet = SQLConnection.Execute(''SELECT * FROM DummyTable'')

EndOfSub:
SQLConnection.Close
Set SQLConnection = Nothing
Exit Sub

ErrorHandler:
For Each SQLError In SQLConnection.Errors
 Debug.Print SQLError.SQLState
 Debug.Print SQLError.Source
 Debug.Print SQLError.NativeError
```

LISTING 26.13 CONTINUED

```
 Debug.Print SQLError.Description
Next
Goto EndOfSub
```

The error handling in ADO for data provider errors is different from the ADO errors.

Error Handling in DB-Library

DB-Library uses a separate mechanism for handling error messages and returning them to the calling application. Any application that uses the DB-Library API has to define two callback functions: one for handling errors and another for handling messages. DB-Library returns `PRINT` messages, low-severity error messages, and `RAISERROR` messages from batches to the message handler. High-severity error messages and `RAISERROR` messages are returned to the error handler. The `dbmsghandle` function installs the message handler, and the `dberrhandle` function installs the error handler.

Summary

This chapter has introduced some of the basic capabilities of SQL Server. For more information on what's available in SQL Server and the programming features, refer to the Books Online documentation.

APPENDIX A

An Introduction to SQL

IN THIS APPENDIX

This appendix gives you a brief introduction and history of SQL and then discusses the importance of the SQL language and the role it plays today. Next, the standards organizations that have promoted SQL, including ANSI, are covered. The SQL syntax structure is described, and then you learn about the SELECT statement in detail. I'll also introduce some of the more complex options to the SELECT statement, including table joins and subqueries.

A Brief Introduction and History of SQL

SQL, officially pronounced "ess-que-el" but sometimes pronounced "sequel," stands for Structured Query Language. Regardless of how you decide to pronounce it, SQL is the universal standard language for relational database management systems (RDBMS). It is a nonprocedural language used to communicate with a database to perform tasks such as managing database objects and retrieving and manipulating data within a database. When SQL is called *nonprocedural*, that basically means you say *what* to do rather than *how* to do it, as you would in a 3GL such as Pascal, COBOL, or C. It was originally developed by IBM in the 1970s for a prototype RDBMS named System R. At that time, the language was called SEQUEL, which stood for "Structured English Query Language." However, because of legal trademark reasons, the language was renamed SQL, for "Structured Query Language." Although IBM began developing SQL, a different company, Relational Software, Inc. (later to be known as Oracle), actually beat them to market in 1979 with the first commercially available SQL implementation. It didn't become an official ANSI standard, however, until 1986. Since then, it has evolved tremendously and has become both the national and international standard language for relational database management systems.

Importance of the SQL Language

You don't have to be a database administrator to realize the importance of the SQL language. It doesn't matter whether you're a programmer, UNIX systems administrator, Web developer, systems analyst, or someone just entering a technology-related field—chances are you work with relational databases systems in one way or another. SQL is the standard universal database language worldwide. Because every major successful database product on the market uses or supports SQL, you can transfer the majority of the SQL skills you learn from one database system to another. To date, there are literally hundreds of database systems, application products, and development tools that support or use SQL, including Oracle, Sybase, Microsoft SQL Server, Microsoft Access, Informix, Ingres, mySQL, Ocelot, Borland's Delphi, Powersoft's PowerBuilder, ODBC, Elemental Software's Drumbeat 2000, and Allaire's Cold Fusion.

According to ANSI (American National Standards Institute), SQL is the standard language for relational database management systems. ANSI, which is in charge of facilitating and coordinating the United States' private sector voluntary standardization system, will provide anyone with the currently defined ANSI SQL standard, ANSI X3.135-1992 (R1998), for a fee of $220 (as of this writing). This 626-page document can be ordered electronically or printed from ANSI's Web site: `www.ansi.org`. The current standard, recently revised in 1998, is commonly known as SQL-92 or SQL2. Unless you're a software company writing a new database system, you probably won't need this document. It isn't exactly the easiest reading material on SQL. In fact, it is dry and difficult to follow. Luckily, books like this one can give you everything that you need to know about standard ANSI SQL in a much more enjoyable and comprehensible reading format.

This book covers the current ANSI SQL2 standard. The official standard is divided into three different levels: entry, intermediate, and full. When a particular vendor claims its implementation is ANSI SQL2 compliant, it is important to find out at which level it's compliant. However, most database products and implementations of SQL are entry-level compliant.

Not only is SQL an official ANSI standard, but it is also a U.S. Federal Government standard, meaning SQL is an important requirement for large government database projects. The FIPS (Federal Information Processing Standards) publication that establishes ANSI X3.135-1992 as the federal government standard is FIPS Publication 127-2.

In addition, IBM, which originally developed SEQUEL in the early 1970s, has been a major player in SQL's development and support. Of course, it still uses SQL in its DB2 database system. DB2 was introduced in 1983 and is still heavily used today on IBM platforms. IBM also provides support for SQL on all its computer systems, from the low-end PCs to the high-end mainframes.

There is also a group of vendors, called the X/Open SQL Access Group, whose purpose is to define the set of methods and standards that support database portability and interoperability between different vendors' SQL implementations. Some of the members of this group include AT&T, Borland International, Computer Associates, IBM, Informix Software, Microsoft, Oracle, Sybase, and several others. One of the SQL Access Group's contributions to the current ANSI SQL-92 standard is a feature called *Call-Level Interface*, also referred to as *SQL/CLI*. Microsoft, which helped create the CLI, was the first company to offer a commercial product, called ODBC (Open Database Connectivity), based on the

CLI. Other major software companies, such as Oracle, Informix, Borland, Sybase, IBM, and Computer Associates, also offer ODBC support. With companies like these supporting and promoting database portability and interoperability, it is easy to see how important a role SQL plays in the industry.

Knowing SQL can also help you get more out of products such as Microsoft Access that generate the SQL code for you by using GUI tools. Although the SQL statements are generated automatically with the GUI tools, you have much more control and flexibility if you can create your own statements or change the dynamically generated statements into what you really want. Manually created SQL statements are typically easier to read and usually more optimized than dynamically generated ones. Programs such as Access normally give you a way to create your own SQL statements or modify the dynamically generated ones.

Although the majority of database systems, such as Oracle and Microsoft SQL Server, are only entry-level ANSI SQL compliant, few, if any, are fully or intermediate-level compliant. Most database systems also have their own unique proprietary extensions that work only on their databases. However, most standard SQL commands usually work on most SQL implementations with few modifications. However, when in doubt, check your database-specific documentation.

SQL Syntax

SQL statements are used to perform a wide variety of functions in SQL databases, including:

- Data definition
- Information retrieval
- Data manipulation
- Data control

SQL statements always begin with a command (verb) and are followed by a combination of one or more clauses, expressions, operators, or parameters. Some of the SQL commands include `SELECT`, `INSERT`, `UPDATE`, `DELETE`, `CREATE TABLE`, `DROP TABLE`, `ALTER TABLE`, `GRANT`, `REVOKE`, `COMMIT`, and `ROLLBACK`. Many other commands are available in SQL, and they are covered throughout this book.

You should not name any of your database objects, such as tables and columns, after any reserved SQL keywords. Here is a list of the ANSI SQL2 reserved keywords:

ABSOLUTE
ACTION
ADD
ALL
ALLOCATE
ALTER
AND
ANY
ARE
AS
ASC
ASSERTION
AT
AUTHORIZATION
AVG
BEGIN
BETWEEN
BIT
BIT_LENGTH
BOTH
BY
CASCADE
CASCADED
CASE
CAST
CATALOG
CHAR
CHARACTER
CHAR_LENGTH
CHARACTER_LENGTH
CHECK
CLOSE
COALESCE
COLLATE
EXCEPT
EXCEPTION
EXEC
EXECUTE
EXISTS
EXTERNAL
EXTRACT
FALSE
FETCH
FIRST
FLOAT
FOR
FOREIGN
FOUND
FROM
FULL
GET
GLOBAL
GO
GOTO
GRANT
GROU
HAVING
HOUR
IDENTITY
IMMEDIATE
IN
INDICATOR
INITIALLY
INNER
INPUT
INSENSITIVE
INSERT
INT
OVERLAPS
PAD
PARTIAL
POSITION
PRECISION
PREPARE
PRESERVE
PRIMARY
PRIOR
PRIVILEGES
PROCEDURE
PUBLIC
READ
REAL
REFERENCES
RELATIVE
RESTRICT
REVOKE
RIGHT
ROLLBACK
ROWS
SCHEMA
SCROLL
SECOND
SECTION
SELECT
SESSION
SESSION_USER
SET
SIZE
SMALLINT
SOME
SPACE
SQL

COLLATION
COLUMN
COMMIT
CONNECT
CONNECTION
CONSTRAINT
CONSTRAINTS
CONTINUE
CONVERT
CORRESPONDING
COUNT
CREATE
CROSS
CURRENT
CURRENT_DATE
CURRENT_TIME
CURRENT_TIMESTAMP
CURRENT_USER
CURSOR
DATE
DAY
DEALLOCATE
DEC
DECIMAL
DECLARE
DEFAULT
DEFERRABLE
DEFERRED
DELETE
DESC
DESCRIBE
DESCRIPTOR
DIAGNOSTICS
DISCONNECT
INTEGER
INTERSECT
INTERVAL
INTO
IS
ISOLATION
JOIN
KEY
LANGUAGE
LAST
LEADING
LEFT
LEVEL
LIKE
LOCAL
LOWER
MATCH
MAX
MIN
MINUTE
MODULE
MONTH
NAMES
NATIONAL
NATURAL
NCHAR
NEXT
NO
NOT
NULL
NULLIF
NUMERIC
OCTER_LENGTH
OF
SQLCODE
SQLERROR
SQLSTATE
SUBSTRING
SUM
SYSTEM_USER
TABLE
TEMPORARY
THEN
TIME
TIMESTAMP
TIMEZONE_HOUR
TIMEZONE_MINUTE
TO
TRAILING
TRANSACTION
TRANSLATE
TRANSLATION
TRIM
TRUE
UNION
UNIQUE
UNKNOWN
UPDATE
UPPER
USAGE
USER
USING
VALUE
VALUES
VARCHAR
VARYING
VIEW
WHEN

```
DISTINCT        ON          WHENEVER
DOMAIN          ONLY        WHERE
DOUBLE          OPEN        WITH
DROP            OPTION      WORK
ELSE            OR          WRITE
END             ORDER       YEAR
END-EXEC        OUTER       ZONE
ESCAPE          OUTPUT
```


One of the beauties of SQL is that the statements are "English-like" and fairly easy to follow after you break them down. Simply put, a SQL statement starts with a command (verb) and is followed by a noun, which is an object such as a table name or column name. The rest of the statement is composed of a combination of keywords, clauses, expressions, parameters, and operators that describe what to do in an "English-like" format.

Here is an example of a SQL statement:

```
SELECT firstname, lastname
FROM employee
WHERE lastname = 'Jones';
```

This statement selects the values in the `firstname` and `lastname` columns for any rows in the `employee` table where the `lastname` is equal to `Jones`.

Although the official SQL keywords—`SELECT`, `FROM`, and `WHERE`—are capitalized, you don't have to follow that format. SQL statements aren't case sensitive, but any references to data from the database are case sensitive. The following command does not retrieve the same information as the previous command because `JONES` is capitalized:

```
SELECT firstname, lastname
FROM employee
WHERE lastname = 'JONES';
```

It is important to determine whether the SQL implementation you are using requires a semicolon after each SQL statement. The semicolon tells the interpreter that the statement is complete. Most RDBMSs, such as Oracle, require the semicolon after each statement.

Keep in mind, too, that spacing is flexible. The following statement returns the same results as the first example:

```
SELECT firstname, lastname FROM employee WHERE lastname = 'Jones';
```

Breaking up the clauses into separate lines is an easier way to read the statements.

SELECT Statement

The SELECT statement retrieves the information you want from the database, which is basically a collection of one or more tables. The data you're retrieving is stored in these table objects.

Note: Because querying the database is the most fundamental task performed on a SQL database, some consider the SELECT statement to be the core of SQL. Considering that the data in the database isn't very useful if it can't be retrieved in exactly the way you want it, I have to agree with them. You will be submitting SELECT statements more than any other SQL command.

The SELECT statement queries the database by describing what it is you want to retrieve. Here is the syntax description for the SELECT statement:

```
SELECT [ ALL ¦ DISTINCT ] list-of-columns
FROM list-of-tables
[ WHERE search-condition ]
[ ORDER BY ordering-columns [ ASC ¦ DESC ] ]
[ GROUP BY grouping-column-list ]
[ HAVING search-condition ]
```

Note

The [and] characters mean the clause or keyword is optional.

If you're new to SQL, this complete syntax description can be a little intimidating. Although the SELECT statement offers all these features, you can still run useful queries with just the basics. There are many features and options for the SELECT statement, but start with the basics, and then work your way up to the more complex features and options, including joins and subqueries.

Clauses, Expressions, and Operators

Using SELECT with the FROM Clauses

A simple query can be performed with only two required components: the SELECT command and the FROM clause. The other key clauses are WHERE, ORDER BY, GROUP BY, and HAVING.

Immediately after the SELECT command, you list the column names or attributes whose values are returned in the query's results.

The SELECT statement does not work by itself, so the FROM clause must follow the SELECT command. The FROM clause lists the table names that contain the data to be scanned or queried. Here is the basic format using only these two required components:

```
SELECT [ ALL ¦ DISTINCT ] list-of-columns
FROM list-of-tables
```

You will be using the following customer table throughout this appendix to understand the use of the SELECT statement. Please note that Table A.1 is for demonstration purposes only; a real customer table would likely contain much more information, such as addresses.

TABLE A.1 The customer Table

ID	First	Last	City	State	Credit_Limit
1001	Leroy	Smith	San Diego	CA	$500.00
1002	Wendell	Cunningham	Hershey	PA	$450.00
1003	Karen	Lopez	Flagstaff	AZ	$800.00
1004	Joanie	Stewart	Los Angeles	CA	$1,000.00
1005	Mike	Rhodes	Seattle	WA	$900.00
1006	Lori	Evans	New York	NY	$350.00
1007	Kelly	Weber	Austin	TX	$1,100.00
1008	Joe	Gomez	Phoenix	AZ	$650.00
1009	Jane	Clark	Scottsdale	AZ	$450.00
1010	Amanda	Smith	Los Angeles	CA	$800.00
1011	Peter	Jones	Dallas	TX	$1,000.00

The following SELECT statement selects all values in the First, Last, and City columns from the customer table.

```
SELECT first, last, city
FROM customer;
```

This is the result of the query:

First	Last	City
Leroy	Smith	San Diego
Wendell	Cunningham	Hershey
Karen	Lopez	Flagstaff
Joanie	Stewart	Los Angeles
Mike	Rhodes	Seattle
Lori	Evans	New York
Kelly	Weber	Austin
Joe	Gomez	Phoenix
Jane	Clark	Scottsdale
Amanda	Smith	Los Angeles
Peter	Jones	Dallas

If you want to display all columns in the table, you can use the `*` wildcard instead of listing all the column names individually. This feature is convenient if you don't know all the column names or don't feel like typing them in.

The following statement selects all rows or values for all columns from the `customer` table:

```
SELECT * FROM customer;
```

The query produces the following results:

ID	First	Last	City	State	Credit_Limit
1001	Leroy	Smith	San Diego	CA	$500.00
1002	Wendell	Cunningham	Hershey	PA	$450.00
1003	Karen	Lopez	Flagstaff	AZ	$800.00
1004	Joanie	Stewart	Los Angeles	CA	$1,000.00
1005	Mike	Rhodes	Seattle	WA	$900.00
1006	Lori	Evans	New York	NY	$350.00
1007	Kelly	Weber	Austin	TX	$1,100.00
1008	Joe	Gomez	Phoenix	AZ	$650.00
1009	Jane	Clark	Scottsdale	AZ	$450.00
1010	Amanda	Smith	Los Angeles	CA	$800.00
1011	Peter	Jones	Dallas	TX	$1,000.00

Using SELECT with the DISTINCT Keyword

When the `DISTINCT` keyword is used with the `SELECT` statement, it displays only the rows that have unique data in the specified columns. For example, if you want to display a non-duplicate list of all the states in the `customer` table, enter the following:

```
SELECT DISTINCT state
FROM customer;
```

This statement results in the following:

State
AZ
CA
NY
PA
TX
WA

Note

`ALL` is the default if neither `ALL` nor `DISTINCT` are specified.

Using the WHERE Clause

A more targeted `SELECT` statement usually includes the `WHERE` clause. If you don't want all records retrieved, the `WHERE` clause allows you describe the exact conditions that cause one or more rows to be retrieved in your query. With the `WHERE` clause, you can be more selective in what you want to retrieve. Without it, all rows in the selected tables are retrieved.

Here is the format for a simple `SELECT` statement that includes the `WHERE` clause:

```
SELECT [ ALL ¦ DISTINCT ] list-of-columns
FROM list-of-tables
[ WHERE search-condition ]
```

The following `SELECT` statement returns the values in the `First`, `Last`, and `City` columns from the `customer` table for any rows that have the value `Smith` in the `Last` column:

```
SELECT first, last, city
FROM customer
```

```
WHERE last = 'Smith'
```

This is the output:

First	Last	City
Leroy	Smith	San Diego
Amanda	Smith	Los Angeles

The `WHERE` clause determines which data values or rows are returned based on the search conditions described after the keyword `WHERE`. SQL has a comprehensive set of search condition operators and keywords that allow you to perform a myriad of different queries. They are covered throughout this appendix.

Using the ORDER BY Clause

The `ORDER BY` clause is a useful feature that allows you to sort the results of a query in either ascending or descending order based on the column names you supply. If you leave off the `ORDER BY` clause, the results of the query display everything, based on the order in which it was retrieved from the database.

Here is the format for using `ORDER BY` :

```
SELECT [ ALL ¦ DISTINCT ] list-of-columns
FROM list-of-tables
[ ORDER BY ordering-columns [ ASC ¦ DESC ] ]

ASC = ascending order
DESC = descending order
```

The following statement returns all values in the `First`, `Last`, `City`, and `State` columns from the `customer` table and displays them in ascending order by the values in the `Last` column:

```
SELECT first, last, city, state
FROM customer
ORDER BY last;
```

The query produces these results:

First	Last	City	State
Jane	Clark	Scottsdale	AZ
Wendell	Cunningham	Hershey	PA
Lori	Evans	New York	NY
Joe	Gomez	Phoenix	AZ

Peter	Jones	Dallas	TX
Karen	Lopez	Flagstaff	AZ
Mike	Rhodes	Seattle	WA
Leroy	Smith	San Diego	CA
Amanda	Smith	Los Angeles	CA
Joanie	Stewart	Los Angeles	CA
Kelly	Weber	Austin	TX

Ascending order is the default, so the `ASC` keyword wasn't required; however, if you want the results displayed in descending order, you must specify the `DESC` keyword, as shown here:

```
SELECT first, last, city, state
FROM customer
ORDER BY last DESC;
```

Now the results look like this:

First	*Last*	*City*	*State*
Kelly	Weber	Austin	TX
Joanie	Stewart	Los Angeles	CA
Leroy	Smith	San Diego	CA
Amanda	Smith	Los Angeles	CA
Mike	Rhodes	Seattle	WA
Karen	Lopez	Flagstaff	AZ
Peter	Jones	Dallas	TX
Joe	Gomez	Phoenix	AZ
Lori	Evans	New York	NY
Wendell	Cunningham	Hershey	PA
Jane	Clark	Scottsdale	AZ

Aggregate Functions

Aggregate functions are covered here because they are required in `SELECT` statements that include the `GROUP BY` clause; however, these functions can be used in the `SELECT` statement without the `GROUP BY` clause.

SQL gives you six useful aggregate functions:

`AVG()` Computes the average of all the non-null values in a given column. `AVG` works with numeric values only.

`MIN()`	Determines the smallest non-null value in a given column.
`MAX()`	Determines the largest non-null value in a given column.
`SUM()`	Computes the sum of all numeric values in a column.
`COUNT()`	Computes the number of values in a column.
`COUNT(*)`	Computes the number of rows in the table.

These functions can be quite useful because they allow you to compute functions on an entire column of data. When one of them is applied to a column, a single summarized value is returned instead of each individual row being listed.

For example, if you want to know the average credit limit for all customers, you could use the `AVG` function. The following statement computes the average of all the values in the `Credit_Limit` column:

```
SELECT AVG(credit_limit)
FROM customer;
```

This is the result:

AVG(Credit_Limit)
727.27273

If you want to know the maximum credit limit in the `Credit_Limit` column, you could enter the following statement:

```
SELECT MAX(credit_limit)
FROM customer;
```

You get the following result:

MAX(Credit_Limit)
1100

Using the GROUP BY Clause

This is the format of the optional `GROUP BY` clause:

```
[ ] = optional

SELECT [ ALL ¦ DISTINCT ] list-of-commands
FROM list-of-tables
[ GROUP BY grouping-column-list]
```

The `GROUP BY` clause basically divides the columns specified after the keywords `GROUP BY` into groups. The elements or rows of each group are determined by the identical values in the field specified after the keywords `GROUP BY`. The purpose of dividing them up into groups is so that an aggregate function can be applied to each group. This particular clause can best be explained by example. Suppose you want to calculate the customers' average credit limit in each state:

```
SELECT state, AVG(credit_limit)
FROM customer
GROUP BY state;
```

This is the result:

State	*AVG(Credit_Limit)*
AZ	633.33333
CA	766.66667
NY	350
PA	450
TX	1,050
WA	900

This statement selected all the values of the `State` column from the `customer` table, divided them into different groups based on identical values in the `State` column (all the same states ended up in the same group), and then the `AVG` function was applied to the values of the `Credit_Limit` column for each group. The end result is the average credit limit for everyone in each state.

If you leave off the `State` column after the `SELECT` keyword, the query results still calculate and display the average credit limit for each state, but the associated state name is left off. Here's what the query would look like:

```
SELECT AVG(credit_limit)
FROM customer
GROUP BY state;
```

However, this method could make the results difficult to interpret, as shown in the following results. It is important to select all the necessary columns to make your queries meaningful.

AVG(Credit_Limit)
633.33333
766.66667
350
450

1,050

900

Using the HAVING Clause

The HAVING clause, which almost always follows a GROUP BY clause, indicates which row groups should be selected. If a GROUP BY clause isn't specified, then the group evaluated will be the group returned from the FROM and WHERE clauses. This group is implicitly defined in the absence of a GROUP BY clause.

Say you want to perform a query similar to the example in the preceding section, but you don't want the results displayed if the average credit limit is less than $500. Your query would be set up like this:

```
SELECT state, AVG(credit_limit)
FROM customer
GROUP BY state
HAVING AVG(credit_limit) >= 500
```

This query produces the following results:

State	*AVG(Credit_Limit)*
AZ	633.33333
CA	766.66667
TX	1,050
WA	900

Notice how the credit limit averages for NY and PA disappeared.

SQL Expressions and Operators

An *expression* is a combination of values and operators that are calculated for a result. Expressions follow clauses, such as the WHERE clause in a SELECT statement. An expression is evaluated, and the results are then used to determine the query's final output. Expressions, which can be in parentheses, can include one or more SQL operators, such as the comparison operators covered next. Here is an example of two SQL expressions within a WHERE clause, separated by the OR operator.

```
SELECT * FROM employee
WHERE (credit_limit > 1000 OR credit_limit <= 1100);
```

Test Comparison Operators

SQL has a wide variety of different test comparison operators and keywords that can be used in the search conditions of the optional `WHERE` clause.

The most common are the following comparison operators:

=	Equals
<	Less than
>	Greater than
<=	Less than or equal to
>=	Greater than or equal to
<>	Not equal to

The following statement selects the first name and credit limit of all customers in the `customer` table who have a value of larger than `500` in the `Credit_Limit` column:

```
SELECT first, credit_limit
FROM customer
WHERE credit_limit > 500;
```

This query produces the following results:

First	*Credit_Limit*
Karen	$800.00
Joanie	$1,000.00
Mike	$900.00
Kelly	$1,100.00
Joe	$650.00
Amanda	$800.00
Peter	$1,000.00

Boolean Operators

The following Boolean operators are available to use in search conditions: `AND`, `OR`, and `NOT`. These operators allow you to create more complex search conditions.

AND Operator

The following statement selects the first name and credit limit of all customers in the `customer` table who have a value higher than `500` and lower than `1,000` in the `Credit_Limit` column. Both sides of the `AND` operator must be true for the whole expression to be true.

```
SELECT first, credit_limit
FROM customer
WHERE credit_limit > 500 AND credit_limit < 1000
```

This is the result:

First	*Credit_Limit*
Karen	$800.00
Mike	$900.00
Joe	$650.00
Amanda	$800.00

OR Operator

If you want to display the customers with a credit limit of less than `500` or greater than `1,000`, you could use the `OR` operator as follows:

```
SELECT first, credit_limit
FROM customer
WHERE credit_limit < 500 OR credit_limit > 1000
```

You get the following results:

First	*Credit_Limit*
Wendell	$450.00
Lori	$350.00
Kelly	$1,100.00
Jane	$450.00

Notice that the credit limits of $500 and $1,000 were excluded from the results because you left off the = in the comparison test operators <= and >=.

NOT Operator

The `NOT` operator precedes a test condition and negates whatever the condition evaluates to. If a condition evaluates to `TRUE`, then `NOT` negates it and makes it `FALSE`. If a condition evaluates to `FALSE`, then it becomes `TRUE`. Here is an example that demonstrates two uses of the `NOT` operator. This SQL statement selects all values in all columns of the `customer` table in which the value in the `State` column is not `AZ`, `CA`, or `WA` and the value in the `First` column doesn't begin with a `J`:

```
SELECT * FROM customer
WHERE state NOT IN ('AZ', 'CA', 'WA')
AND first NOT LIKE 'J%';
```

Here are the results:

ID	First	Last	City	State	Credit_Limit
1002	Wendell	Cunningham	Hershey	PA	$450.00
1006	Lori	Evans	New York	NY	$350.00
1007	Kelly	Weber	Austin	TX	$1,100.00
1011	Peter	Jones	Dallas	TX	$1,000.00

Arithmetic Operators

SQL also allows you to use the following arithmetic operators within an expression: plus (+), minus (-), multiply (*), and divide (/).

For example, to submit a query that displays a listing of all customers and their credit limit if it's raised by 25%, enter the following:

```
SELECT first, last, credit_limit * 1.25
FROM customer;
```

These are the results:

First	Last	Credit_Limit*1.25
Leroy	Smith	$625.00
Wendell	Cunningham	$562.50
Karen	Lopez	$1,000.00
Joanie	Stewart	$1,250.00
Mike	Rhodes	$1,125.00
Lori	Evans	$437.50
Kelly	Weber	$1,375.00
Joe	Gomez	$812.50
Jane	Clark	$562.50
Amanda	Smith	$1,000.00
Peter	Jones	$1,250.00

Notice how the column name changed to the expression. You can avoid that by renaming the column output in the query results with a new column name after the expression:

```
SELECT first, last, credit_limit * 1.25 new_credit_limit
FROM customer;
```

Here are the results:

First	Last	New_Credit_Limit
Leroy	Smith	$625.00
Wendell	Cunningham	$562.50
Karen	Lopez	$1,000.00
Joanie	Stewart	$1,250.00
Mike	Rhodes	$1,125.00
Lori	Evans	$437.50
Kelly	Weber	$1,375.00
Joe	Gomez	$812.50
Jane	Clark	$562.50
Amanda	Smith	$1000.00
Peter	Jones	$1,250.00

Standard ANSI SQL-92 doesn't support the modulus (%) operator. If your SQL implementation supports it, this operator is used to compute the remainder of a division of two numbers, as shown here:

```
6 % 2 = 0
7 % 2 = 1
```

If you're using this operator, it is important not confuse the modulus operator with the wildcard (%) character used with the string comparison test operator LIKE.

LIKE Pattern-Matching Operator

One of the most powerful and commonly used operators in a conditional expression is the LIKE pattern-matching operator. LIKE allows you to select only rows that are "like" what you specify. That is, if they don't match exactly, you can't use the = operator. Instead, you must give it a sequence of characters to look for. The percent sign (%) can be used as a wildcard to match any possible character(s) that might appear before or after the characters specified, as shown in this example:

```
SELECT first, last, city FROM customer
WHERE first LIKE 'Kar%'
```

Here are the results:

First	Last	City
Karen	Lopez	Flagstaff

This SQL statement matched and returned the values in the `First`, `Last`, and `City` columns for all first names that started with `'Kar'`. Please note that the strings specified must be enclosed by single quotes.

`IN` Operator

The `IN` operator tests for set membership. It can be useful if you want to select certain rows from a table that exist within the set generated by the `SELECT` clause (based on the values specified after the keyword `IN`). Suppose you would like to display all rows from the `customer` table in which the `State` is either `CA` or `AZ`. You could enter this:

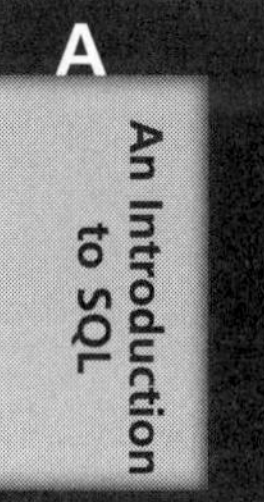


```
SELECT * FROM customer
WHERE state IN ('AZ', 'CA');
```

It gives you these results:

ID	*First*	*Last*	*City*	*State*	*Credit_Limit*
1001	Leroy	Smith	San Diego	CA	$500.00
1003	Karen	Lopez	Flagstaff	AZ	$800.00
1004	Joanie	Stewart	Los Angeles	CA	$1,000.00
1008	Joe	Gomez	Phoenix	AZ	$650.00
1009	Jane	Clark	Scottsdale	AZ	$450.00
1010	Amanda	Smith	Los Angeles	CA	$800.00

You can also get this result without the `IN` operator by using the `=` comparison test operator in a compound search condition. The following statement produces the same results:

```
SELECT * FROM customer
WHERE state = 'AZ' OR state = 'CA';
```

Here are the results:

ID	*First*	*Last*	*City*	*State*	*Credit_Limit*
1001	Leroy	Smith	San Diego	CA	$500.00
1003	Karen	Lopez	Flagstaff	AZ	$800.00
1004	Joanie	Stewart	Los Angeles	CA	$1000.00
1008	Joe	Gomez	Phoenix	AZ	$650.00
1009	Jane	Clark	Scottsdale	AZ	$450.00
1010	Amanda	Smith	Los Angeles	CA	$800.00

You might be wondering how useful `IN` is because you can get the same results with other test operators. Just imagine how convenient the syntax is with `IN` if you have a set with several dozen elements to look for. What if you had 30 states to check for? In this case, `IN` is a much more practical option.

The `NOT IN` set membership test retrieves all rows that are not in the set generated by the `SELECT` clause (based on the values specified after the keyword `IN`). Here's an example:

```
SELECT * FROM customer
WHERE state NOT IN ('AZ', 'CA');
```

It produces these results:

ID	*First*	*Last*	*City*	*State*	*Credit_Limit*
1002	Wendell	Cunningham	Hershey	PA	$450.00
1005	Mike	Rhodes	Seattle	WA	$900.00
1006	Lori	Evans	New York	NY	$350.00
1007	Kelly	Weber	Austin	TX	$1,100.00
1011	Peter	Jones	Dallas	TX	$1,000.00

BETWEEN Operator

Use the `BETWEEN` operator when you want to select records that exist between a range of values you supply. For example, if you want to display the values in the `First`, `Last`, and `Credit_Limit` columns of the `customer` table for everyone who has a credit limit between $500 and $800, enter the following:

```
SELECT first, last, credit_limit
FROM customer
WHERE credit_limit BETWEEN 500 AND 800;
```

It produces these results:

First	*Last*	*Credit_Limit*
Leroy	Smith	$500.00
Karen	Lopez	$800.00
Joe	Gomez	$650.00
Amanda	Smith	$800.00

It is important to note that the values specified after the `BETWEEN` operator are inclusive. Selecting records "between" $500.00 and $800.00 includes $500.00 and $800.00, too, if any exist.

You could also get these results without the `BETWEEN` operator by using comparison test operators in a compound conditional expression:

```
SELECT first, last, credit_limit
FROM customer
WHERE credit_limit >= 500.00 AND credit_limit <= 800.00
```

Here are the results:

First	Last	Credit_Limit
Leroy	Smith	$500.00
Karen	Lopez	$800.00
Joe	Gomez	$650.00
Amanda	Smith	$800.00

MATCH and UNIQUE Operators

MATCH and UNIQUE are two more conditional expression test operators. Although they are defined in the current ANSI SQL standard specification, they aren't commonly used or supported by most database systems, including Oracle. However, because they are defined in the SQL standard, I'll briefly cover them here.

The UNIQUE operator checks for the absence of duplicate rows. In other words, it tests to make sure every row of the specified table is unique. If all the rows are unique, then the expression evaluates to TRUE; however, if there is even one duplicate row, the expression evaluates to FALSE. The UNIQUE operator is specified before a table subquery (covered later):

```
UNIQUE ( table-subquery )
```

The MATCH operator tests for complex pattern-matching conditions. MATCH follows the SELECT statement that retrieves the row and appears before the table expression (subquery):

```
SELECT ... MATCH [UNIQUE] (table-expression)
```

A statement that includes the MATCH operator basically works by generating the row described in the SELECT statement to the left of MATCH and also generating the table in the table-expression or subquery to the right of the MATCH operator. The query evaluates to TRUE if the resulting subquery contains at least one row—that is, if the UNIQUE keyword isn't stated. If UNIQUE is used, the subquery must contain exactly one row.

UNION, MINUS, and INTERSECT Operators

SQL has the following operators for set operations: UNION, MINUS, and INTERSECT.

Tables A.2 and A.3 are used to demonstrate how these operations work.

TABLE A.2 The `unix101` Table

First	Last	Grade
William	Brown	C
Lisa	Edwards	A
Maria	Gomez	A
Jay	Jackson	C
Leroy	Jones	A
Joe	Stewart	C

TABLE A.3 The `java101` Table

First	Last	Grade
Chris	Copeland	A
Jose	Gonzales	A
Leroy	Jones	B
Mark	Matthews	C
Cindy	Sanders	B

`UNION` Operator

Suppose you want to display a listing of students who have taken both the `java101` class and the `unix101` class. You could use the `UNION` operator:

```
SELECT * FROM unix101
UNION SELECT * FROM java101;
```

You would have the following output:

First	*Last*	*Grade*
Chris	Copeland	A
Cindy	Sanders	B
Jay	Jackson	C
Joe	Stewart	C
Jose	Gonzales	A
Leroy	Jones	A
Leroy	Jones	B
Lisa	Edwards	A
Maria	Gomez	A
Mark	Matthews	C
William	Brown	C

The UNION operation combines the results of the two queries and eliminates any duplicate rows. Although you wanted a listing of all the students who have taken both classes, an extra row was retrieved because you selected *.

Because Leroy Jones got two different grades, his row was retrieved once for each class. The following is a more accurate query that selects the first and last names for everyone who has taken the unix101 and java101 classes:

```
SELECT first, last FROM java101
UNION SELECT first, last FROM unix101;
```

Here are the results:

First	Last
Chris	Copeland
Cindy	Sanders
Jay	Jackson
Joe	Stewart
Jose	Gonzales
Leroy	Jones
Lisa	Edwards
Maria	Gomez
Mark	Matthews
William	Brown

Notice how this time only 10 rows are retrieved. However, since eliminating duplicate rows is a default feature of the UNION operation, you can override it by using UNION ALL to retain any multiple rows. Note that the following SELECT statement retrieved 11 rows.

```
SELECT first, last FROM unix101 UNION ALL
SELECT first, last FROM java101;
```

You get the following results:

First	Last
William	Brown
Lisa	Edwards
Maria	Gomez
Jay	Jackson
Joe	Stewart
Leroy	Jones

Cindy	Sanders
Mark	Matthews
Chris	Copeland
Jose	Gonzales
Leroy	Jones

INTERSECT Operator

The INTERSECT operator retrieves the rows found in both queries, as shown here:

```
SELECT first, last FROM unix101 INTERSECT
SELECT first, last FROM java101;
```

Here are the results:

First	*Last*
Leroy	Jones

If you issue a SELECT statement with a * but don't specify the columns you want, the query doesn't select any rows because the grades make each entry different.

MINUS Operator

The MINUS operator retrieves all the rows that exist in the first query, but not the second query. The following SELECT statement selects the values in the First and Last columns from the unix101 table. If any of those rows or values exist in the java101 table, the statement doesn't display them, as shown in this example:

```
SELECT first, last FROM unix101
MINUS SELECT first, last FROM java101;
```

First	*Last*
Jay	Jackson
Joe	Stewart
Lisa	Edwards
Maria	Gomez
William	Brown

Since Leroy Jones is in the java101 table, his name was eliminated from the query results.

Although the INTERSECT and MINUS operators are supported by most RDBMSs, they aren't included in the current ANSI SQL standard specifications. You'll need to check your RDBMS documentation to see if they're available—or just try them out.

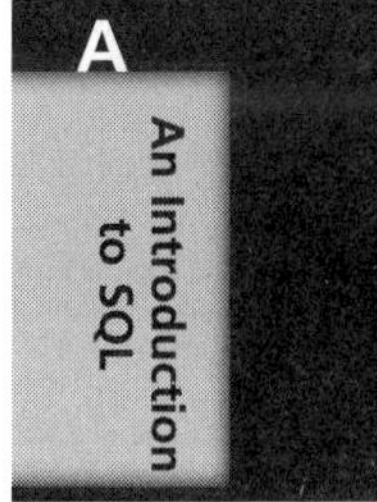

Combining Clauses

Now that I've covered the main clauses, expressions, operators, and functions, it's time to demonstrate the power of basic `SELECT` statements by combining them.

Suppose you want to submit a query that returns a unique listing of all students in the `unix101` and `java101` tables, ordered by their last names. The following `SELECT` statement accomplishes this:

```
SELECT first, last FROM unix101 UNION
SELECT first, last FROM java101
ORDER by last;
```

You get the following results:

First	*Last*
William	Brown
Chris	Copeland
Lisa	Edwards
Maria	Gomez
Jose	Gonzales
Jay	Jackson
Leroy	Jones
Mark	Matthews
Cindy	Sanders
Joe	Stewart

This next example uses the `customer` table defined at the beginning of this appendix:

```
SELECT * FROM customer;
```

Here are the results:

ID	*First*	*Last*	*City*	*State*	*Credit_Limit*
1001	Leroy	Smith	San Diego	CA	$500.00
1002	Wendell	Cunningham	Hershey	PA	$450.00
1003	Karen	Lopez	Flagstaff	AZ	$800.00
1004	Joanie	Stewart	Los Angeles	CA	$1,000.00
1005	Mike	Rhodes	Seattle	WA	$900.00
1006	Lori	Evans	New York	NY	$350.00
1007	Kelly	Weber	Austin	TX	$1,100.00

1008	Joe	Gomez	Phoenix	AZ	$650.00
1009	Jane	Clark	Scottsdale	AZ	$450.00
1010	Amanda	Smith	Los Angeles	CA	$800.00
1011	Peter	Jones	Dallas	TX	$1,000.00

Suppose you want to submit a query to display each state and the minimum credit limit for someone in that state. However, if the person's first name is `'Lori'` and their last name is `'Evans'`, you want to skip that record. You want the output displayed alphabetically in descending order. The following `SELECT` statement accomplishes all that:

```
SELECT state, MIN(credit_limit)
FROM customer
WHERE (last <> 'Evans' AND first <> 'Lori')
GROUP BY state
ORDER BY state DESC;
```

The results are as follows:

State	*MIN(Credit_Limit)*
WA	900
TX	1,000
PA	450
CA	500
AZ	450

This statement says to select the values in the `State` column and apply the `MIN` aggregate function to the values in the `Credit_Limit` column from the `customer` table where the last name isn't equal to `'Evans'` and the first name isn't equal to `'Lori'`, divide into groups by state (which the aggregate `MIN` function has been applied to), and then display the results in alphabetical descending order by state.

Table Joins and Subqueries

Now take a look at table joins and subqueries. Table joins are used when you need to place more than one table name in a `FROM` clause. Subqueries allow you to put `SELECT` statements within other `SELECT` statements.

Table Joins

A standard relational database usually contains more than one table, so it is important to be able to retrieve data from multiple tables in a single statement. SQL has the "join" mechanism, or operator, which is used in the `SELECT` statement to accomplish this task. The exact syntax of table joins vary depending on which RDBMS you're using and the SQL implementation supported. I will include the specifications from standard ANSI SQL as well as show what "should" work with some of the major RDBMSs in use today.

Inner Join

A *join* can be thought of as a multitable query. This mechanism of joining data from multiple tables is one of SQL's most important features. The most common type of join is the *inner join* , also commonly called an *equi-join*. The other type of join is called an *outer join*, which is covered later. The best way to explain an inner join is by an example. Say you have an additional table in your database that contains two columns:

`ID` Unique ID of the customer (this ID should also be in the `customer` table)

`Item` Identification number of the item that the customer has purchased

This table is called `items_purchased`.

Here is a copy of the original `customer` table:

ID	*First*	*Last*	*City*	*State*	*Credit_Limit*
1001	Leroy	Smith	San Diego	CA	$500.00
1002	Wendell	Cunningham	Hershey	PA	$450.00
1003	Karen	Lopez	Flagstaff	AZ	$800.00
1004	Joanie	Stewart	Los Angeles	CA	$1000.00
1005	Mike	Rhodes	Seattle	WA	$900.00
1006	Lori	Evans	New York	NY	$350.00
1007	Kelly	Weber	Austin	TX	$1100.00
1008	Joe	Gomez	Phoenix	AZ	$650.00
1009	Jane	Clark	Scottsdale	AZ	$450.00
1010	Amanda	Smith	Los Angeles	CA	$800.00
1011	Peter	Jones	Dallas	TX	$1000.00

Table A.4 is the `items_purchased` table.

TABLE A.4 The `items_purchased` Table

ID	Item
1003	20080
1001	20081
1008	20099
1004	20101
1004	20102
1011	20111

TABLE A.4 The `items_purchased` Table

ID	Item
1004	20102
1001	20050
1010	20081
1006	20049
1009	20049
1003	20099
1002	20080
1004	20111
1008	20079

If you want to know which item numbers are checked out to which customers, enter the following `SELECT` statement:

```
SELECT customer.first, customer.last, customer.id, items_purchased.item
FROM customer, items_purchased
WHERE customer.id = items_purchased.id
```

This statement works with most RDBMSs.

Here is the equivalent ANSI SQL-92 syntax specifications for the preceding `SELECT` statement:

```
SELECT customer.first, customer.last, customer.id, items_purchased.item
FROM customer INNER JOIN items_purchased
ON customer.id = items_purchased.id
```

Depending on the level of compliance with the SQL-92 specification, this statement may or may not work with the RDBMS that you're using. Check your RDBMS specific documentation to make sure.

Here are the results for the preceding `SELECT` statement:

First	*Last*	*ID*	*Item*
Leroy	Smith	1001	20081
Leroy	Smith	1001	20050
Wendell	Cunningham	1002	20080
Karen	Lopez	1003	20080
Karen	Lopez	1003	20099
Joanie	Stewart	1004	20101
Joanie	Stewart	1004	20102
Joanie	Stewart	1004	20102
Joanie	Stewart	1004	20111

Lori	Evans	1006	20049
Joe	Gomez	1008	20099
Joe	Gomez	1008	20079
Jane	Clark	1009	20049
Amanda	Smith	1010	20081
Peter	Jones	1011	20111

Note

Up to this point, I haven't qualified the column names with their associated table names. That is, I've used only the column name in the SELECT statements, not the `table_name.column_name`. This method was okay because you're dealing with just one table. However, for more than one table, it is important to prequalify the column names with the table names to avoid any confusion or erroneous results with this format: `table_name.column_name`. Although it isn't required to prequalify column names when they don't exist in all the tables in the SELECT statement, I recommend doing so to avoid any confusion or erroneous results.

The previous `SELECT` statement selects the values in the `ID` column from the `customer` table and the `Item` number from the `items_purchased` table when there is a matching `ID` number from each table. Although you used the `items_purchased` column from each table to join the two, you didn't have to retrieve or select that column to display in the results:

```
SELECT customer.first, customer.last, customer.id
FROM customer, items_purchased
WHERE customer.id = items_purchased.id
```

To perform an inner join, there must be a common link between the two tables—that is, each table must have a column that can be linked to a column in the other table. Records are joined when there are matching values in the specified field common to both tables. In the preceding example, the `ID` column was used to link the two tables.

Outer Join

In the previous example, the query results returned only rows that had a match between the two columns. Customer ID numbers `1005` and `1007` were not returned because there weren't matching entries in the `ID` columns of the `items_purchased` table. The outer join retrieves the unmatched rows as well as the matched rows from the tables. There are three outer join types:

- Left outer join—Select and display all rows from the first table (left) and only those with matching specified fields from the right table.
- Right outer join—Select and display all rows from the second table (right) and only those with matching specified fields from the left table.
- Full outer join—Select and display all rows from both the first (left) and second (right) tables, whether or not they have the matching fields.

Here is the ANSI SQL syntax description for outer joins. Please note that the keyword `OUTER` is optional; because it doesn't affect anything, I recommend you omit it.

```
SELECT list-of-columns
FROM list-of-tables
outer-join-type JOIN
ON conditional-expression
```

The syntax for joins varies among RDBMSs, especially for outer joins. For example, if you're using Oracle, the outer join keywords aren't used. Instead, it uses the `(+)` as the outer join operator, as shown here:

```
SELECT list-of-columns
FROM list-of-tables
WHERE first-table.column = second-table.column (+)
```

Here is another example of a join's syntax:

```
SELECT list-of-columns
FROM list-of-tables
WHERE first_table.column (+) = second_table.column
```

Subqueries

A *subquery* is a `SELECT` statement nested within another SQL statement. The results from this nested `SELECT` statement are used as the argument for the parent query. The nested `SELECT` statement can exist within a `SELECT`, `INSERT`, `UPDATE`, or `DELETE` statement or even another subquery. The nested `SELECT` statement usually follows a `WHERE`, `HAVING`, `EXISTS`, or `IN` clause. The resulting rows from the subquery are used in the `WHERE`, `HAVING`, `EXISTS`, or `IN` clause. In other words, the results of the nested `SELECT` statement are evaluated by the parent query.

There are basically two types of subqueries: correlated and noncorrelated. The way the subquery is written determines which one it is. If it's executed once for each row of the parent query, then it's called a *correlated subquery*. If it's executed once for the parent query, then it's a *noncorrelated subquery*.

It's time to demonstrate the use of a simple query with the tables shown in Tables A.5 and A.6.

TABLE A.5 The `employee` Table

FIRSTNAME	LASTNAME	TITLE
Mary Ann	Andrews	Secretary
Leroy	Brown	Programmer I
Pat	Gonzalez	Web Manager
Maria	Jackson	Programmer II
Bill	May	Owner
Peter	Smith	Accountant
Theresa	Thompson	Programmer IV

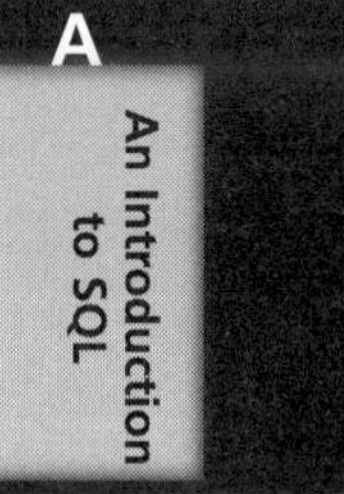

TABLE A.6 The `salary_schedule` Table

TITLE	SALARY
Custodian	$24,000.00
Secretary	$32,000.00
Programmer I	$39,500.00
Accountant	$41,500.00
Programmer II	$48,000.00
Web Manager	$52,000.00
Programmer IV	$64,000.00
Owner	$128,000.00

Suppose you want to submit a query that displays the `FIRSTNAME`, `LASTNAME`, and `TITLE` for employees who are making more than $40,000. Here's how you do that, using a subquery:

```
SELECT employee.firstname, employee.lastname, employee.title
FROM employee
WHERE employee.title IN
(SELECT salary_schedule.title FROM salary_schedule
WHERE salary_schedule.salary > 40000)
```

This query gives you the following results:

FIRSTNAME	*LASTNAME*	*TITLE*
Peter	Smith	Accountant
Bill	May	Owner
Maria	Jackson	Programmer II
Theresa	Thompson	Programmer IV
Pat	Gonzalez	Web Manager

This SELECT statement selects the TITLE from the salary_schedule table when the salary is higher than $40,000. The parent query then displays the FIRSTNAME, LASTNAME, and TITLE from the employee table if the TITLE is in the results from the subquery. You can often use joins to get the results from subqueries. For example, the following SELECT statement uses a join instead of a subquery and produces the same results as the previous subquery:

```
SELECT employee.firstname, employee.lastname, employee.title
FROM employee, salary_schedule
WHERE employee.title = salary_schedule.title AND salary_schedule.salary >
40000
```

Here are the results:

FIRSTNAME	LASTNAME	TITLE
Peter	Smith	Accountant
Bill	May	Owner
Maria	Jackson	Programmer II
Theresa	Thompson	Programmer IV
Pat	Gonzalez	Web Manager

Although subqueries generally tend to be more difficult to read and follow, they are sometimes the only alternative. Subqueries are covered in more detail in Chapter 13, "Subqueries."

Summary

After briefly introducing SQL's history, this appendix discussed the importance of SQL and how it has become the official standard language for relational database management systems throughout the world. You then learned the SQL syntax structure and covered the most important SQL command—SELECT—in great detail. You learned about different SELECT statement clauses, expressions, and operators, and got an introduction to two advanced SELECT statements: subqueries and table joins.

INDEX

Symbols

A

D

E

F

G

H

I

J

K

L

M

N

O

P

Q

R

T

U

V

W

X

Y

FROM KNOWLEDGE TO MASTERY

Unleashed *takes you beyond the average technology discussions. It's the best resource for practical advice from experts and the most in-depth coverage of the latest information.* **Unleashed**—*the necessary tool for serious users.*

Other Unleashed Titles

PowerBuilder 7.0 Unleashed
Simon Gallagher, Simon Herbert, Joe Quick, and Ken Reppart
0-672-31782-6
$49.99 US / $74.95 CAN

Microsoft Access 2000 Development Unleashed
Stephen Forte, Thomas Howe and James Ralston
0-672-31291-3
$49.99 US / $59.95 CAN

Oracle Development Unleashed, Third Edition Advanced Information Systems, Inc.
0-672-31575-0
$49.99 US / $74.95 CAN

Windows NT Server 4 Unleashed, Second Edition
Jason Garms
0-672-31249-2
$49.99 US / $70.95 CAN

Windows NT Workstation 4 Unleashed
Paul Cassel
0-672-31081-3
$49.99 US / $70.95 CAN

Red Hat Linux 6 Unleashed
David Pitts; Billy Ball
0-672-31689-7
$39.99 US / $59.95 CAN

Visual Basic 6 Unleashed, Professional Reference
Rob Thayer, et al.
0-672-31508-4
$49.99 US / $74.95 CAN

www.samspublishing.com

Microsoft SQL Server 7.0 Unleashed
Simon Gallagher, Sharon Bjeletich, Vipul Manocha, et al.
0-672-31227-1
$49.99 US / $74.95 CAN

Microsoft SQL Server 7.0 Programming Unleashed
Matt Shepker and John Papa
0-672-31293-X
$49.99 US / $74.95 CAN

Microsoft OLAP Unleashed
Tim Peterson and Jim Pinkelman
0-672-31671-4
$49.99 US / $74.95 CAN

All prices are subject to change.

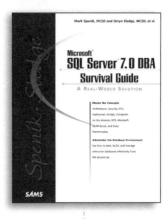

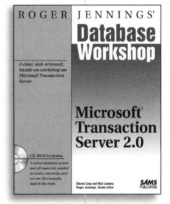

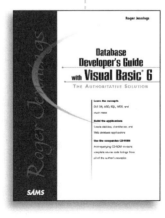

GNU GENERAL PUBLIC LICENSE

Version 2, June 1991

Preamble

The licenses for most software are designed to take away your freedom to share and change it. By contrast, the GNU General Public License is intended to guarantee your freedom to share and change free software—to make sure the software is free for all its users. This General Public License applies to most of the Free Software Foundation's software and to any other program whose authors commit to using it. (Some other Free Software Foundation software is covered by the GNU Library General Public License instead.) You can apply it to your programs, too.

When we speak of free software, we are referring to freedom, not price. Our General Public Licenses are designed to make sure that you have the freedom to distribute copies of free software (and charge for this service if you wish), that you receive source code or can get it if you want it, that you can change the software or use pieces of it in new free programs; and that you know you can do these things.

To protect your rights, we need to make restrictions that forbid anyone to deny you these rights or to ask you to surrender the rights. These restrictions translate to certain responsibilities for you if you distribute copies of the software, or if you modify it.

For example, if you distribute copies of such a program, whether gratis or for a fee, you must give the recipients all the rights that you have. You must make sure that they, too, receive or can get the source code. And you must show them these terms so they know their rights.

We protect your rights with two steps: (1) copyright the software, and (2) offer you this license which gives you legal permission to copy, distribute and/or modify the software.

Also, for each author's protection and ours, we want to make certain that everyone understands that there is no warranty for this free software. If the software is modified by someone else and passed on, we want its recipients to know that what they have is not the original, so that any problems introduced by others will not reflect on the original authors' reputations.

Finally, any free program is threatened constantly by software patents. We wish to avoid the danger that redistributors of a free program will individually obtain patent licenses, in effect making the program proprietary. To prevent this, we have made it clear that any patent must be licensed for everyone's free use or not licensed at all.

The precise terms and conditions for copying, distribution and modification follow.

GNU GENERAL PUBLIC LICENSE TERMS AND CONDITIONS FOR COPYING, DISTRIBUTION AND MODIFICATION

0. This License applies to any program or other work which contains a notice placed by the copyright holder saying it may be distributed under the terms of this General Public License. The "Program", below, refers to any such program or work, and a "work based on the Program" means either the Program or any derivative work under copyright law: that is to say, a work containing the Program or a portion of it, either verbatim or with modifications and/or translated into another language. (Hereinafter, translation is included without limitation in the term "modification".) Each licensee is addressed as "you".

Activities other than copying, distribution and modification are not covered by this License; they are outside its scope. The act of running the Program is not restricted, and the output from the Program is covered only if its contents constitute a work based on the Program (independent of having been made by running the Program). Whether that is true depends on what the Program does.

1. You may copy and distribute verbatim copies of the Program's source code as you receive it, in any medium, provided that you conspicuously and appropriately publish on each copy an appropriate copyright notice and disclaimer of warranty; keep intact all the notices that refer to this License and to the absence of any warranty; and give any other recipients of the Program a copy of this License along with the Program.

You may charge a fee for the physical act of transferring a copy, and you may at your option offer warranty protection in exchange for a fee.

2. You may modify your copy or copies of the Program or any portion of it, thus forming a work based on the Program, and copy and distribute such modifications or work under the terms of Section 1 above, provided that you also meet all of these conditions:

    (a) You must cause the modified files to carry prominent notices stating that you changed the files and the date of any change.

(b) You must cause any work that you distribute or publish, that in whole or in part contains or is derived from the Program or any part thereof, to be licensed as a whole at no charge to all third parties under the terms of this License.

(c) If the modified program normally reads commands interactively when run, you must cause it, when started running for such interactive use in the most ordinary way, to print or display an announcement including an appropriate copyright notice and a notice that there is no warranty (or else, saying that you provide a warranty) and that users may redistribute the program under these conditions, and telling the user how to view a copy of this License. (Exception: if the Program itself is interactive but does not normally print such an announcement, your work based on the Program is not required to print an announcement.)

These requirements apply to the modified work as a whole. If identifiable sections of that work are not derived from the Program, and can be reasonably considered independent and separate works in themselves, then this License, and its terms, do not apply to those sections when you distribute them as separate works. But when you distribute the same sections as part of a whole which is a work based on the Program, the distribution of the whole must be on the terms of this License, whose permissions for other licensees extend to the entire whole, and thus to each and every part regardless of who wrote it.

Thus, it is not the intent of this section to claim rights or contest your rights to work written entirely by you; rather, the intent is to exercise the right to control the distribution of derivative or collective works based on the Program.

In addition, mere aggregation of another work not based on the Program with the Program (or with a work based on the Program) on a volume of a storage or distribution medium does not bring the other work under the scope of this License.

3. You may copy and distribute the Program (or a work based on it, under Section 2) in object code or executable form under the terms of Sections 1 and 2 above provided that you also do one of the following:

   (a) Accompany it with the complete corresponding machine-readable source code, which must be distributed under the terms of Sections 1 and 2 above on a medium customarily used for software interchange; or,

   (b) Accompany it with a written offer, valid for at least three years, to give any third party, for a charge no more than your cost of physically performing source distribution, a complete machine-readable copy of the corresponding source code, to be distributed under the terms of Sections 1 and 2 above on a medium customarily used for software interchange; or,

(c) Accompany it with the information you received as to the offer to distribute corresponding source code. (This alternative is allowed only for noncommercial distribution and only if you received the program in object code or executable form with such an offer, in accord with Subsection b above.)

The source code for a work means the preferred form of the work for making modifications to it. For an executable work, complete source code means all the source code for all modules it contains, plus any associated interface definition files, plus the scripts used to control compilation and installation of the executable. However, as a special exception, the source code distributed need not include anything that is normally distributed (in either source or binary form) with the major components (compiler, kernel, and so on) of the operating system on which the executable runs, unless that component itself accompanies the executable.

If distribution of executable or object code is made by offering access to copy from a designated place, then offering equivalent access to copy the source code from the same place counts as distribution of the source code, even though third parties are not compelled to copy the source along with the object code.

4. You may not copy, modify, sublicense, or distribute the Program except as expressly provided under this License. Any attempt otherwise to copy, modify, sublicense or distribute the Program is void, and will automatically terminate your rights under this License. However, parties who have received copies, or rights, from you under this License will not have their licenses terminated so long as such parties remain in full compliance.
5. You are not required to accept this License, since you have not signed it. However, nothing else grants you permission to modify or distribute the Program or its derivative works. These actions are prohibited by law if you do not accept this License. Therefore, by modifying or distributing the Program (or any work based on the Program), you indicate your acceptance of this License to do so, and all its terms and conditions for copying, distributing or modifying the Program or works based on it.
6. Each time you redistribute the Program (or any work based on the Program), the recipient automatically receives a license from the original licensor to copy, distribute or modify the Program subject to these terms and conditions. You may not impose any further restrictions on the recipients' exercise of the rights granted herein. You are not responsible for enforcing compliance by third parties to this License.

7. If, as a consequence of a court judgment or allegation of patent infringement or for any other reason (not limited to patent issues), conditions are imposed on you (whether by court order, agreement or otherwise) that contradict the conditions of this License, they do not excuse you from the conditions of this License. If you cannot distribute so as to satisfy simultaneously your obligations under this License and any other pertinent obligations, then as a consequence you may not distribute the Program at all. For example, if a patent license would not permit royalty-free redistribution of the Program by all those who receive copies directly or indirectly through you, then the only way you could satisfy both it and this License would be to refrain entirely from distribution of the Program.

If any portion of this section is held invalid or unenforceable under any particular circumstance, the balance of the section is intended to apply and the section as a whole is intended to apply in other circumstances.

It is not the purpose of this section to induce you to infringe any patents or other property right claims or to contest validity of any such claims; this section has the sole purpose of protecting the integrity of the free software distribution system, which is implemented by public license practices. Many people have made generous contributions to the wide range of software distributed through that system in reliance on consistent application of that system; it is up to the author/donor to decide if he or she is willing to distribute software through any other system and a licensee cannot impose that choice.

This section is intended to make thoroughly clear what is believed to be a consequence of the rest of this License.

8. If the distribution and/or use of the Program is restricted in certain countries either by patents or by copyrighted interfaces, the original copyright holder who places the Program under this License may add an explicit geographical distribution limitation excluding those countries, so that distribution is permitted only in or among countries not thus excluded. In such case, this License incorporates the limitation as if written in the body of this License.
9. The Free Software Foundation may publish revised and/or new versions of the General Public License from time to time. Such new versions will be similar in spirit to the present version, but may differ in detail to address new problems or concerns.

Each version is given a distinguishing version number. If the Program specifies a version number of this License which applies to it and "any later version", you have the option of following the terms and conditions either of that version or of any later version published by the Free Software Foundation. If the Program does not specify a version number of this License, you may choose any version ever published by the Free Software Foundation.

10. If you wish to incorporate parts of the Program into other free programs whose distribution conditions are different, write to the author to ask for permission. For software which is copyrighted by the Free Software Foundation, write to the Free Software Foundation; we sometimes make exceptions for this. Our decision will be guided by the two goals of preserving the free status of all derivatives of our free software and of promoting the sharing and reuse of software generally.

NO WARRANTY

11. BECAUSE THE PROGRAM IS LICENSED FREE OF CHARGE, THERE IS NO WARRANTY FOR THE PROGRAM, TO THE EXTENT PERMITTED BY APPLICABLE LAW. EXCEPT WHEN OTHERWISE STATED IN WRITING THE COPYRIGHT HOLDERS AND/OR OTHER PARTIES PROVIDE THE PROGRAM “AS IS” WITHOUT WARRANTY OF ANY KIND, EITHER EXPRESSED OR IMPLIED, INCLUDING, BUT NOT LIMITED TO, THE IMPLIED WARRANTIES OF MERCHANTABILITY AND FITNESS FOR A PARTICULAR PURPOSE. THE ENTIRE RISK AS TO THE QUALITY AND PERFORMANCE OF THE PROGRAM IS WITH YOU. SHOULD THE PROGRAM PROVE DEFECTIVE, YOU ASSUME THE COST OF ALL NECESSARY SERVICING, REPAIR OR CORRECTION.

12. IN NO EVENT UNLESS REQUIRED BY APPLICABLE LAW OR AGREED TO IN WRITING WILL ANY COPYRIGHT HOLDER, OR ANY OTHER PARTY WHO MAY MODIFY AND/OR REDISTRIBUTE THE PROGRAM AS PERMITTED ABOVE, BE LIABLE TO YOU FOR DAMAGES, INCLUDING ANY GENERAL, SPECIAL, INCIDENTAL OR CONSEQUENTIAL DAMAGES ARISING OUT OF THE USE OR INABILITY TO USE THE PROGRAM (INCLUDING BUT NOT LIMITED TO LOSS OF DATA OR DATA BEING RENDERED INACCURATE OR LOSSES SUSTAINED BY YOU OR THIRD PARTIES OR A FAILURE OF THE PROGRAM TO OPERATE WITH ANY OTHER PROGRAMS), EVEN IF SUCH HOLDER OR OTHER PARTY HAS BEEN ADVISED OF THE POSSIBILITY OF SUCH DAMAGES.

END OF TERMS AND CONDITIONS